INTRODUCTION TO OPERATIONS AND SUPPLY CHAIN MANAGEMENT

SECOND EDITION

Cecil C. Bozarth
North Carolina State University

Robert B. Handfield
North Carolina State University

Upper Saddle River, New Jersey 07458

Library of Congress Cataloging-in-Publication Data
Bozarth, Cecil C.
Introduction to operations and supply chain management / Cecil Bozarth, Robert Handfield.— 2nd ed.
p. cm.
Includes bibliographical references and index.
ISBN 0-13-179103-6
1. Management. 2. Production management. 3. Business logistics. I. Handfield, Robert B. II. Title.
HD31.B7197 2008
658.5—dc22
2007039012

AVP/Executive Editor: Mark Pfaltzgraff
AVP/Editor-in-Chief: Eric Svendsen
Product Development Manager: Ashley Santora
Project Manager: Susan Abraham
Editorial Assistant: Vanessa Bain
Media Project Manager: Denise Vaughn
Marketing Manager: Anne Howard
Marketing Assistant: Susan Osterlitz
Senior Managing Editor, Production: Judy Leale
Production Manager: Kerri Tomasso
Permissions Coordinator: Charles Morris
Senior Operations Supervisor: Arnold Vila
Operations Specialist: Michelle Klein
Interior Design: Kevin Kall / Jodi Notowitz
Senior Art Director: Janet Slowik
Cover Design: Laura Gardner
Cover Photo: Corbis
Illustration (Interior): GGS Book Services
Director, Image Resource Center: Melinda Patelli
Manager, Rights and Permissions: Zina Arabia
Manager: Visual Research: Beth Brenzel
Manager, Cover Visual Research & Permissions: Karen Sanatar
Image Permission Coordinator: Jan Marc Quisumbing
Composition/Full-Service Project Management: GGS Book Services
Printer/Binder: Courier/Kendallville

Credits and acknowledgments borrowed from other sources and reproduced, with permission, in this textbook appear on appropriate page within text.

Photo credits: **Pages 2, 4, 420, 471**: AGE Fotostock America, Inc. **Page 152 (top left and bottom right)**: American Honda Motor Co. Inc. **Pages 10, 22, 193, 461**: AP Wide World Photos. **Page 538**: Carrier Corporation. **Page 179**: Cecil Bozarth. **Page 476**: Chris Corsmeier Photography. **Page 436**: CORBIS-NY. **Page 85**: Corbis RF. **Pages 6, 91, 268, 374**: Corbis/Bettmann. **Page 3 (top left)**: Corbis/Stock Market. **Page 483**: Creative Eye/MIRA.com. **Page 161**: Forma Design. **Page 177 (left and right)**: Geri Engberg Photography. **Pages 340, 342**: Getty Images. **Pages 129, 254, 400**: Getty Images Inc.—Image Bank. **Page 362**: Getty Images Inc.—Liaison. **Page 124**: Getty Images Inc.—Stone Allstock. **Pages 1, 21, 43, 81, 123, 149, 173, 213, 249, 265, 317, 339, 361, 399, 435, 475, 515, 525**: Getty Images/Digital Vision. **Pages 35, 366**: Highway Images. **Page 119**: Index Stock Imagery, Inc. **Page 3 (bottom)**: INDITEK. **Pages 53, 103, 220**: Jupiter Images Picturequest - Royalty Free. **Page 526 (left and right)**: Kyodo News. **Page 89**: National Institute of Standards and Technology. **Page 533**: Pearson Education/PH College. **Pages 3 (top right), 5, 30, 48, 174, 214, 230, 291, 330, 404, 421**: PhotoEdit Inc. **Page 44**: Procter and Gamble Company. **Page 453**: Robert Harding Picture Library Ltd. **Page 283**: The Image Works. **Page 318**: The Stock Connection. **Page 9**: Wal Mart. **Page 150**: Whirlpool Corporation. **Page 152 (top right and bottom left)**: ww.HondaNews.com.

Pearson Education LTD. London
Pearson Education Singapore, Pte. Ltd
Pearson Education, Canada, Ltd
Pearson Education–Japan
Pearson Education Australia PTY, Limited
Pearson Education North Asia Ltd
Pearson Educación de Mexico, S.A. de C.V.
Pearson Education Malaysia, Pte. Ltd.

10 9 8 7 6 5 4 3 2 1
ISBN-13: 978-0-13-179103-9
ISBN-10: 0-13-179103-6

In memory of Donna Ellison Bozarth

About the Authors

Professor Cecil Bozarth is an Associate Professor at the College of Management at N.C. State University where he has received awards for teaching excellence at both the undergraduate and graduate levels. He is a former chair of the Operations Management Division of the Academy of Management, and in 1999 was recognized by APICS as a subject matter expert (SME) in the area of supply chain management. His particular areas of interest are operations and supply chain strategy and supply chain information systems. Cecil's consulting experience cuts across a wide range of industries, including such companies as ABB, Bayer Biological Products, Daimler-Benz, John Deere, Duke Energy, Ford Motor Company, GKN, IBM, GlaxoSmithKline, Longistics, Milliken, Progress Energy, Sonoco, and others. Cecil is an Associate Editor for the *Journal of Operations Management* and has also served as a guest editor for the *Academy of Management Journal*, as well as the *Journal of Operations Management*.

Professor Robert Handfield is the Bank of America Professor and a Distinguished University Professor at N.C. State University, Rob has extensive consulting experience with companies such as American Airlines, Duke Energy, Bank of America, Federal Express, General Motors, BMW, Steelcase, Herman Miller, Honda of America, Johnson Controls, Bechtel, GlaxoSmithKline, John Deere, Chevron Texaco, Shell, British Petroleum, Union Pacific, Milliken, and others, and is a world-renowned expert in the area of Purchasing and Logistics. Rob is the former Editor-in-Chief of the *Journal of Operations Management* and has written several books on SCM topics, including *Introduction to Supply Chain Management* (Prentice Hall, with Ernest L. Nichols; translated into Japanese, Korean, Chinese, and Indonesian), *Supply Chain Redesign* (Prentice Hall Financial Times), and *Purchasing and Supply Chain Management*, 3rd edition (South-Western College Publishing, with Robert M. Monczka and Robert J. Trent).

BRIEF CONTENTS

CONTENTS

14 *Managing Inventory throughout the Supply Chain* 435

15 *Managing Production across the Supply Chain* 475

15S *Supply Chain Information Systems* 515

16 *JIT/Lean Production* 526

PREFACE

Still the only introductory text to provide an integrated treatment of operations and supply chain management. When we set out to write the first edition of this book, we wanted to create an introductory text that provided an integrated and comprehensive treatment of both operations *and* supply chain management. That goal hasn't changed.

This book is unique among introductory texts because it provides substantial coverage of the major operations management (OM) topics and tools, and it extends the coverage to include core supply chain management (SCM) issues. The second edition now includes three chapters not included in other introductory OM texts. These chapters—Chapter 10, "Sourcing Decisions"; Chapter 11, "Purchasing"; and Chapter 12, "Logistics"—highlight the importance of sourcing decisons, purchasing activities and logistics to the total operations and supply chain picture.

In addition to new and updated content, the book now includes a feature that allows instructors to create different homework problems for different class sections and even different students. This is ideal for instructors teaching large sections of an Introductory Operations/Supply Chain course. With these homework problems, professors have an extra measure to guard against plagiarism in homework assignments. Here's how it works:

1. Students go to the book Web site and open an Excel spreadsheet listed under the chapter of interest.
2. Students type their name and **a *four-digit number chosen by the instructor*** into the spreadsheet. The four-digit number creates new parameters for the problems.
3. Students print out their customized homework sets and solve the problems.
4. The instructor then uses an **Excel-based key** that use the same four-digit number to generate the correct answers.

CONTENT NEW TO THE SECOND EDITION

In this second edition, we have sought to deepen our coverage of important operations and supply chain topics while still maintaining a trim, integrated book.

Chapter 1, "Introduction to Operations and Supply Chain Management," now includes an introduction to the **Supply-Chain Operations Reference (SCOR) model**, as well as updated information on key professional groups in the operations and supply chain management areas. These updates reinforce the connections between the book's content and real-world practice.

Chapter 3, "Business Processes," now includes extended coverage of the **Six Sigma methodology**, including the **DMAIC (Define-Measure-Analyze-Improve-Control**) process. We have also moved the discussion of **continuous improvement tools** into this chapter, where it belongs. Last, we look in more depth at the various types of business processes found in the SCOR model.

The revamped **Chapter 4, "Quality Management,"** explains the linkages between total quality management (TQM) and the Six Sigma methodology. The chapter also includes a new opening case study illustrating how quality problems in the supply chain can affect all parties.

Chapter 5, "Managing Projects," introduces readers to the **Project Management Institute** and the **Project Management Body of Knowledge** (PMBOK®). This is in keeping with our theme of strengthening the connections between the book and real-world practice.

Chapter 6, "Developing Products and Services," contains two major changes. First, we have added a discussion of the **DMADV (Define-Measure-Analyze-Design-Verify)** process, which outlines the Six Sigma approach to creating completely new business processes or products. Second, we have responded to calls for more discussion of green issues by including a discussion of **design for the environment** (DFE), including DFE guidelines put forth by Hewlett-Packard.

Chapter 7, "Process Choice and Layout Decisions in Manufacturing and Services," now includes a discussion of **service blueprinting**, including an extended example that connects back to Chapter 3's discussion of process mapping.

At the request of several users, we have added a supplement to **Chapter 8, "Managing Capacity,"** that deals with **advanced waiting line theory** and **simulation modeling**. This will provide more complete coverage for those instructors who cover these topics in their courses.

Chapter 9, "Forecasting," includes updated coverage of **Collaborative Planning, Forecasting, and Replenishment** (CPFR).

In this second edition, sourcing and purchasing topics are now covered in two chapters rather than one:

Chapter 10, "Sourcing Decisions," includes extended coverage of sourcing strategies, including **portfolio analysis**, **sustainable supply issues**, and **supply chain disruptions**.

Chapter 11, "Purchasing," now includes a section on **spend analysis**. To provide greater realism for the students, the spend analysis problems for Chapter 11 require students to manipulate data contained in a large Excel file. Instructors and students can access the Excel file, problems, and instructions by going to the book's Web site.

To **Chapter 12, "Logistics,"** we have added a discussion of **reverse logistics** as well as more in-depth descriptions of logistics information systems, including **radio-frequency identification** (RFID). We have also updated the transportation statistics to reflect the most current information.

For **Chapter 14, "Sales and Operations Planning (Aggregate Planning),"** we have extended our discussion of cash flow analysis to show how the timing of production can affect a firm's cash position.

Chapter 15, "Managing Production across the Supply Chain," contains several changes. We revamped our description of **available-to-promise** (ATP) in master scheduling to make it clearer. We also included more discussion on how supply chain partners can synchronize production through better planning. Last, we included a chapter supplement that provides an overview of supply chain information systems, including **enterprise resource planning** (ERP) **applications**.

Chapter 16, "JIT/Lean Production," now spends more time discussing the managerial perspectives of lean theories and how they interrelate with other topics in the book. In particular, we describe **Lean Six Sigma** and show how lean concepts can be applied in a services (hospital) environment.

COVERAGE OF ANALYTICAL TOOLS AND TECHNIQUES

Even with the extended focus on SCM, the book does not overlook the important role of analytical tools and techniques. In fact, these subjects are covered in a way that is both comprehensive and integrated throughout the text. The key tools developed in the text are the ones most frequently mentioned by professors and represent a fundamental "tool kit" that can be applied in any manufacturing or service environment. Highlights of the coverage are as follows:

- The book contains **comprehensive coverage** of the tools and techniques in the traditional OM areas (quality, capacity, queuing, forecasting, inventory, planning and control, and project management), as well as the purchasing and logistics areas.
- Tools and techniques are always introduced **within the context** of the OM and SCM issues at hand. For example, a capacity analysis tool kit is woven into a discussion of sales and operations planning across the supply chain rather than being treated separately.
- Throughout the book, students are shown how tools and techniques can be applied using **Microsoft Excel spreadsheets**. Learning is reinforced through homework problems that provide the students with a template and hints for checking their answers.
- **Optimization modeling** is discussed and illustrated at two points in the book. Specifically, students are shown in a step-by-step fashion how to develop and solve the assignment problem in Chapter 11 and the sales and operations problem Chapter 12 using Excel's Solver function. Learning is reinforced through homework problems that provide the students with a template and hints for checking their logic.

Tools and Techniques Integrated Throughout

TOOLS AND TECHNIQUES	SOLVED EXAMPLES	HOMEWORK PROBLEMS	EXCEL EXAMPLES/ PROBLEMS
Chapter 2: Operations and Supply Chain Strategies			
Value index	X	X	X
Chapter 3: Business Processes			
Performance measures (productivity, efficiency, cycle time, percent value-added time)	X	X	
Process mapping	X	X	
Six Sigma methodology and DMAIC process	X		
Continuous improvement tools (root cause analysis, scatter plots, check sheets, Pareto charts)	X	X	
Cause-and-effect diagrams	X		
Chapter 4: Managing Quality			
Process capability ratio	X	X	
Process capability index	X	X	
Six Sigma quality	X	X	
X and *R* charts	X	X	X
p charts	X	X	X
Acceptance sampling	X		

(continued)

TOOLS AND TECHNIQUES	SOLVED EXAMPLES	HOMEWORK PROBLEMS	EXCEL EXAMPLES/ PROBLEMS
Chapter 5: Managing Projects			
Gantt charts	X	X	
Activity on node (AON) diagrams and critical path method (CPM)	X	X	Microsoft project example
Project crashing	X	X	
Chapter 6: Developing Products and Services			
Quality function deployment (QFD)	X		
Chapter 7: Process Choice and Layout Decisions in Manufacturing and Services			
Service blueprinting	X		
Line balancing	X	X	
Assigning department locations	X	X	
Chapter 8: Managing Capacity			
Expected value analysis	X	X	X
Decision trees	X	X	
Break-even analysis	X	X	X
Indifference point	X	X	X
Theory of constraints	X		
Waiting lines (queuing analysis)	X	X	
Learning curves	X	X	
Simulation analysis	X		X
Chapter 9: Forecasting			
Moving average model	X	X	X
Exponential smoothing model	X	X	X
Adjusted exponential smoothing model	X	X	X
Linear regression	X	X	X
Seasonal adjustments	X	X	X
Multiple regression	X	X	X
MAD, MFE, and tracking signal	X	X	X
Chapter 10: Sourcing Decisions			
Total cost analysis	X	X	
Weighted-point evaluation system	X	X	X

(continued)

TOOLS AND TECHNIQUES	SOLVED EXAMPLES	HOMEWORK PROBLEMS	EXCEL EXAMPLES/ PROBLEMS
Chapter 11: Purchasing			
Profit leverage	X	X	
Spend analysis	X	X	X
Chapter 12: Logistics			
Shipment consolidation	X	X	X
Perfect order calculation	X	X	
Landed costs	X	X	
Weighted center of gravity model	X	X	X
Optimization modeling (assignment problem using Excel Solver function)	X	X	X
Chapter 13: Sales and Operations Planning (Aggregate Planning)			
Top-down sales and operations planning	X	X	X
Bottom-up sales and operations planning	X	X	
Cash flow analysis	X	X	
Load profiles	X	X	
Optimization modeling (top-down sales and operations planning using Excel Solver function)	X	X	X
Chapter 14: Managing Inventory throughout the Supply Chain			
Periodic review systems	X	X	
Economic order quantity	X	X	X
Reorder points and safety stock	X	X	X
Quantity discounts	X	X	
Single-period inventory systems (newsboy problem)	X	X	
Pooling safety stock	X	X	X
Chapter 15: Managing Production across the Supply Chain			
Master scheduling	X	X	
Material requirements planning (MRP)	X	X	
Job sequencing rules	X	X	
Distribution requirements planning (DRP)	X	X	
Chapter 16: JIT/Lean Production			
Kanban sizing	X	X	
Linking MRP and kanban	X	X	

Faculty Resources

Instructor's Resource Center:
www.prenhall.com/irc is where instructors can access a variety of print, media, and presentation resources available with this text in downloadable, digital format. For most texts, resources are also available for course management platforms such as Blackboard, WebCT, and Course Compass.

It gets better. Once you register, you will not have additional forms to fill out or multiple usernames and passwords to remember to access new titles and/or editions. As a registered faculty member, you can log in directly to download resource files, and receive immediate access and instructions for installing Course Management content on your campus server.

Need help? Our dedicated Technical Support team is ready to assist instructors with questions about the media supplements that accompany this text. Visit **http://247.prenhall.com/** for answers to frequently asked questions and toll-free user support phone numbers. The following supplements are available to adopting instructors.

For detailed descriptions of all of the supplements listed below, please visit: www.prenhall.com/irc

Instructor's Resource Center (IRC)—ISBN 0-13-158327-1
Printed Instructor's Solutions Manual—ISBN 0-13-613734-2
Printed Test-Item File—ISBN 0-13-234088-7
TestGen (test-generating software)—ISBN 0-13-613735-0
PowerPoints—ISBN 0-13-158325-5

Student Resources

Companion Web Site:
www.prenhall.com/bozarth contains free access to an Online Study Guide, PowerPoint presentations, and Excel problems.

ACKNOWLEDGMENTS

We would like to thank the following reviewers:

R. C. Baker, University of Texas at Arlington
Kimball Bullington, Middle Tennessee State University
Cem Canel, University of North Carolina at Wilmington
Christopher W. Craighead, University of North Carolina at Charlotte
Richard E. Crandall, Appalachian State University
Sime Curkovic, Western Michigan University
Eduardo C. Davila, Arizona State University
Kenneth H. Doerr, University of Miami
Ike C. Ehie, Kansas State University
Lawrence P. Ettkin, University of Tennessee at Chattanooga
Donavon Favre, North Carolina State University
Geraldo Ferrar, University of North Carolina at Chapel Hill
Bruce G. Ferrin, Western Michigan University
Tom Foster, Brigham Young University

Ram Ganeshan, University of Cincinnati
Janet L. Hartley, Bowling Green State University
Ray M. Haynes, California Polytechnic State University—San Luis Obispo
Seung-Lae Kim, Drexel University
Timothy J. Kloppenborg, Xavier University
Terry Nels Lee, Brigham Young University
Binshan Lin, Louisiana State University in Shreveport
Rhonda R. Lummus, Iowa State University
Daniel S. Marrone, State University of New York at Farmingdale
Mark McKay, University of Washington
Mohammad Meybodi, Indiana University—Kokomo
Philip F. Musa, Texas Tech University
Barbara Osyk, University of Akron
Fariborz Y. Partovi, Drexel University
Charles Petersen, Northern Illinois University
Carl J. Poch, Northern Illinois University
Robert F. Reck, Western Michigan University
Richard A. Reid, University of New Mexico
Shane J. Schvaneveldt, Weber State University
Harm-Jan Steenhuis, Eastern Washington University
Joaquin Tadeo, University of Texas at El Paso
V. M. Rao Tummala, Eastern Michigan University
Elisabeth Umble, Baylor University
Enrique R. Venta, Loyola University Chicago
Y. Helio Yang, San Diego State University

PART I CREATING VALUE THROUGH OPERATIONS AND SUPPLY CHAINS

CHAPTER 1

Introduction to Operations and Supply Chain Management

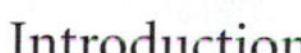

CHAPTER OUTLINE

Chapter Objectives

By the end of this chapter, you will be able to:

- Describe what the operations function is and why it is critical to an organization's survival.
- Describe what a supply chain is and how it relates to a particular organization's operations function.
- Discuss what is meant by operations management and supply chain management.
- Identify some of the major operations and supply chain activities, as well as career opportunities in these areas.
- Make a case for studying both operations management and supply chain management.

INTRODUCTION

Let's start with a question: What do the following organizations have in common?

- **Wal-Mart**, which not only is a leading retailer in the United States, but also has built a network of world-class suppliers, such as GlaxoSmithKline, Sony, and Mattel;
- **Federal Express**, a service firm that provides supply chain solutions and transportation services;
- **Flextronics**, a contract manufacturer that assembles everything from Hewlett-Packard printers to television decoding boxes; and
- **SAP**, the world's largest provider of enterprise resource planning (ERP) software.

Though these firms may appear to be very different, they have at least one thing in common: a strong commitment to superior operations and supply chain management.

In this chapter, we kick off our study of operations and supply chain management. We begin by examining what operations is all about and how the operations of an individual organization fit within a larger supply chain. We then talk about what it means to *manage* operations and supply chains. As part of this discussion, we will introduce you to the Supply-Chain Operations Reference (SCOR) model, which is used by many businesses to understand and structure their supply chains.

In the second half of the chapter, we discuss several trends in business that have brought operations and supply chain management to the forefront of managerial thinking. We also devote a section to what this all means to you. We discuss career opportunities in the field, highlight some of the major professional organizations that serve operations and supply chain professionals, and look at some of the major activities that operations and supply chain professionals are involved in on a regular basis. We end the chapter by providing a roadmap of this book.

Operations management and supply chain management cover a wide range of activities, including transportation services, manufacturing operations, retailing, and consulting.

1.1 WHY STUDY OPERATIONS AND SUPPLY CHAIN MANAGEMENT?

So why should you be interested in operations and supply chain management? There are three simple reasons.

1. Every organization must make a product or provide a service that someone values. Otherwise, why would the organization exist? Think about it. Manufacturers produce physical goods that are used directly by consumers or other businesses. Transportation companies provide valuable services by moving and storing these goods. Design firms use their expertise to create products or even corporate images for customers. The need to provide a valuable product or service holds true for nonprofit organizations as well. Consider the variety of needs met by government agencies, charities, and religious groups, for example.

Operations function
Also called *operations*. The collection of people, technology, and systems within an organization that has primary responsibility for providing the organization's products or services.

The common thread is that each of these organizations has an operations function, or *operations*, for short. The **operations function** is the collection of people, technology, and systems within an organization that has primary responsibility for providing the organization's products or services. Regardless of what career path you might choose, you will need to know something about your organization's operations function.

As important as the operations function is to a firm, few organizations can—or even want to—do everything themselves. This leads to our second reason for studying operations and supply chain management.

Supply chain
A network of manufacturers and service providers that work together to convert and move goods from the raw materials stage through to the end user. These manufacturers and service providers are linked together through physical flows, information flows, and monetary flows.

2. Most organizations function as part of larger supply chains. A **supply chain** is a network of manufacturers and service providers that work together to convert and move goods from the raw materials stage through to the end user. These manufacturers and service providers are linked together through physical flows, information flows, and monetary flows. Put another way, supply chains link together the operations functions of many different organizations.

Consider a store at the local mall that sells athletic shoes. Although the store doesn't actually make the shoes, it provides valuable services for its customers—a convenient location and a wide selection of products. Yet the store is only one link in a much larger supply chain that includes:

- Plastic and rubber producers that provide raw materials for the shoes;
- Manufacturers that mold and assemble the shoes;
- Wholesalers that decide what shoes to buy and when;
- Transportation firms that move the materials and finished shoes to all parts of the world;
- Software firms and Internet service providers (ISPs) that support the information systems that coordinate these physical flows; and
- Financial firms that help distribute funds throughout the supply chain, ensuring that the manufacturers and service firms are rewarded for their efforts.

So where does this lead us? To our third reason for studying operations and supply chain management—and the premise for this book.

3. Organizations must carefully manage their operations and supply chains in order to prosper, and, indeed, survive. Returning to our example, think about the types of decisions facing a shoe manufacturer. Some fundamental operations decisions that it must make include the following: "How many shoes should we make and in what styles and sizes?", "What kind of human resource skills and equipment do we need?", "Should we locate our plants to take advantage of low-cost labor or to minimize shipping costs of the finished shoes?"

In addition to these operations issues, the shoe manufacturer faces many decisions with regard to its role in the supply chain: "From whom should we buy our materials—the lower-cost supplier or the higher-quality one?" "Which transportation carriers will we use to ship our shoes?" The right choices can lead to higher profitability and increased market share, while the wrong choices can cost the company dearly, or even put it out of business.

Athletic shoes at a retailer represent the last stage in a supply chain that crosses the globe and involves many different companies.

Operations Management

Let's begin our detailed discussion of operations and supply chain management by describing operations a little more fully and explaining what we mean by operations management. As noted earlier, all organizations must make products or provide services that someone values, and the operations function has the primary responsibility for making sure this happens.

The traditional way to think about operations is as a *transformation process* that takes a set of inputs and transforms them in some way to create outputs—either goods or services—that a customer values (Figure 1.1). Consider a plant that makes wooden chairs. Even for a product as simple as a chair, the range of activities that must occur to transform raw lumber into a finished chair can be overwhelming at first. Raw lumber arrives as an input to the plant, perhaps by truck or even train car. The wood is then unloaded and

FIGURE 1.1
Viewing Operations as a Transformation Process

Inputs
- Materials
- Intangible needs
- Information

→

Transformation Process
- Manufacturing operations
- Service operations

→

Outputs
- Tangible goods
- Fulfilled needs
- Satisfied customers

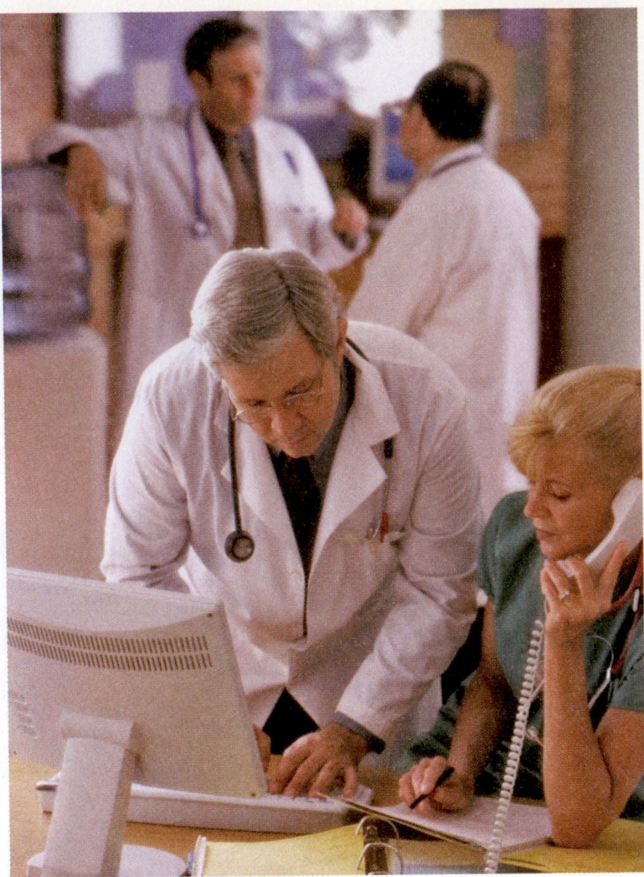

Health care services use highly skilled individuals as well as specialized equipment to provide physiological transformation processes for their patients.

moved onto the plant floor. Planing machines cut the lumber to the right thickness. Lathes shape pieces of wood into legs and back spindles for the chairs. Other machines fabricate wood blanks, shaping them into seats and boring holes for the legs and back spindles.

In addition to the equipment, there are people who run and load the machines, conveyors, and forklifts that move materials around the plant, and there are other people who assemble the chairs. Once the chairs are finished, still more people pack and move the chairs into a finished goods warehouse or onto trucks to be delivered to customers. In the background, supervisors and managers use information systems to plan what activities will take place next.

The operations function can also provide intangible services, as in the case of a law firm. A major input, for example, might be the need for legal advice—hardly something you can put your hands around. The law firm, through the skill and knowledge of its lawyers and other personnel, transforms this input into valuable legal advice, thereby fulfilling the customer's needs. How well the law firm accomplishes this transformation goes a long way in determining its success.

Figure 1.1 makes several other points. First, inputs to operations can come from many places and take many different forms. They can include raw materials, intangible needs, and even information, such as demand forecasts or detailed intelligence on supply market conditions. Also, operations are often highly dependent on the quality and availability of inputs. Consider our chair plant again. If the lumber delivered to it is of poor quality or arrives late, management might have to shut down production. In contrast, a steady stream of good-quality lumber can assure high production levels and superior products. Second, nearly all operations activities require coordination with other business functions, including engineering, marketing, and human resources. We will revisit the importance of cross-functional decision making in operations throughout the book. Third, operations management activities are information and decision intensive. You do not have to be able to assemble a product yourself to be a successful operations manager—but you *do* have to make sure the right people and equipment are available to do the job; the right materials arrive when needed; and the product is shipped on time, at cost, and to specifications!

Operations management
"The planning, scheduling, and control of the activities that transform inputs into finished goods and services."

Upstream
A term used to describe activities or firms that are positioned *earlier* in the supply chain relative to some other activity or firm of interest. For example, corn harvesting takes place upstream of cereal processing, while cereal processing takes place upstream of cereal packaging.

Downstream
A term used to describe activities or firms that are positioned *later* in the supply chain relative to some other activity or firm of interest. For example, sewing a shirt takes place downstream of weaving the fabric, while weaving the fabric takes place downstream of harvesting the cotton.

Operations management, then, is "the planning, scheduling, and control of the activities that transform inputs into finished goods and services."[1] Operations management decisions can range from long-term, fundamental decisions about what products or services will be offered and what the transformation process will look like to more immediate issues, such as determining the best way to fill a current customer order. Through sound operations management, organizations hope to provide the best value to their customers while making the best use of resources.

Supply Chain Management

The traditional view of operations management illustrated in Figure 1.1 still puts most of the emphasis on the activities a particular organization must perform when managing its own operations. But, as important as a company's operations function is, it is not enough for a company to focus on doing the right things within its own four walls. Managers must also understand how the company is linked in with the operations of its suppliers, distributors, and customers—what we refer to as the supply chain.

As noted earlier, organizations in the supply chain are linked together through physical flows, information flows, and monetary flows. These flows go both up and down the chain. Let's extend our discussion and vocabulary using a product many people are familiar with: a six-pack of beer. Figure 1.2 shows a simplified supply chain for Anheuser-Busch. From Anheuser-Busch's perspective, the firms whose inputs feed into its operations are positioned **upstream**, while those firms who take Anheuser-Busch's products and move them along to the final consumer are positioned **downstream**.

When the typical customer goes to the store to buy a six-pack, he probably does not consider all of the steps that must occur beforehand. Take cans, for example. Alcoa extracts

FIGURE 1.2
A Simplified View of Anheuser-Busch's Supply Chain

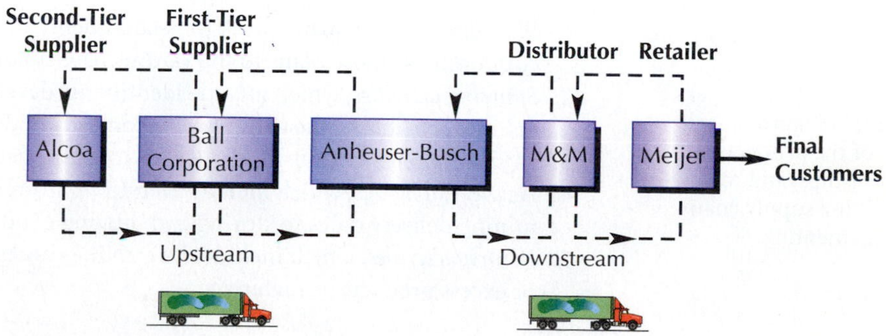

[1] J. F. Cox and J. H. Blackstone, eds., *APICS Dictionary*, 11th ed. (Falls Church, VA: APICS, 2004).

First-tier supplier
A supplier that provides products or services directly to a particular firm.

Second-tier supplier
A supplier that provides products or services to a firm's first-tier supplier.

the aluminum from the ground and ships it to Ball Corporation, which converts the aluminum into cans for Anheuser-Busch. In the supply chain lexicon, Ball Corporation is a **first-tier supplier** to Anheuser-Busch because it supplies materials directly to the brewer. By the same logic, Alcoa is a **second-tier supplier**; it provides goods to the first-tier supplier.

The cans from Ball Corporation are combined with other raw materials, such as cartons, grain, hops, yeast, and water, to produce the packaged beverage. Anheuser-Busch then sells the packaged beverage to M&M, a wholesaler that, in turn, distributes the finished goods to Meijer, the retailer. Of course, we cannot forget the role of transportation carriers, which carry the inputs and outputs from one place to the next along the supply chain.

As Figure 1.2 suggests, the flow of goods and information goes both ways. For instance, Ball Corporation might place an order (information) with Alcoa, which, in turn, ships aluminum (product) to Ball. Anheuser-Busch might even return empty pallets or containers to its first-tier suppliers, resulting in a flow of physical goods back *up* the supply chain.

Of course, there are many more participants in the supply chain than the ones shown here—Anheuser-Busch has hundreds of suppliers and the number of retailers is even higher. We could also diagram the supply chain from the perspective of Alcoa, M&M, or any of the other participants. The point is that most of the participants in a supply chain are both customers and suppliers. Finally, the supply chain must be very efficient, as the final price of the goods must cover all of the costs involved plus a profit for each participant in the chain.

While you were reading through the six-pack example, you might have thought to yourself, "Supply chains aren't new"—and you'd be right. Yet most organizations historically performed their activities independently of other firms in the chain, which made for disjointed and often inefficient supply chains. In contrast, **supply chain management** is the *active* management of supply chain activities and relationships in order to maximize customer value and achieve a sustainable competitive advantage. It represents a conscious effort by a firm or group of firms to develop and run supply chains in the most effective and efficient ways possible.

Supply chain management
The *active* management of supply chain activities and relationships in order to maximize customer value and achieve a sustainable competitive advantage. It represents a conscious effort by a firm or group of firms to develop and run supply chains in the most effective and efficient ways possible.

Supply-Chain Operations Reference (SCOR) model
A framework developed and supported by the Supply-Chain Council that seeks to provide standard descriptions of the processes, relationships, and metrics that define supply chain management.

But what exactly *are* these supply chain activities? To answer this, we turn to the **Supply-Chain Operations Reference (SCOR) model** The SCOR model is a framework, developed and supported by the Supply-Chain Council, that seeks to provide standard descriptions of the processes, relationships, and metrics that define supply chain management.[2] We will explore the SCOR model in more detail in Chapter 3, but for now, Figure 1.3 provides a high-level view of the framework. According to the SCOR model, supply chain management covers five broad areas:

1. *Planning activities*, which seek to balance demand requirements against resources, and communicate these plans to the various participants;
2. *Sourcing activities*, which include identifying, developing, and contracting with suppliers, and scheduling the delivery of incoming goods and services;
3. *"Make" or production activities*, which cover the actual production of a good or service;
4. *Delivery activities*, which include everything from entering customer orders and determining delivery dates to storing and moving goods to their final destination; and
5. *Return activities*, which include the activities necessary to return and process defective or excess products or materials.

[2]Supply-Chain Council, **www.supply-chain.org**.

FIGURE 1.3
The Supply-Chain Operations Reference (SCOR) Model
Copyright Supply-Chain Council, 2007.

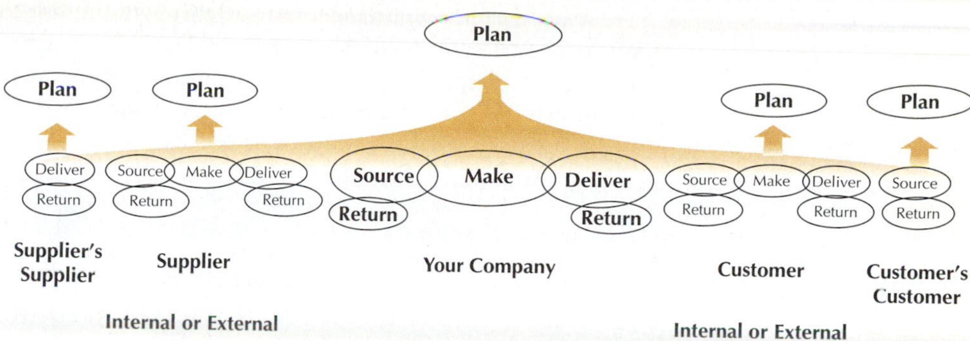

Notice too that Figure 1.3 shows the supply chain management task extending from the company's supplier's suppliers, all the way to the customer's customer. As you can imagine, coordinating the activities of all these parties is challenging.

To illustrate, let's consider Wal-Mart, one of the earliest proponents of supply chain management.[3] What Wal-Mart was doing in the late 1980s and early 1990s was nothing short of revolutionary. Individual stores sent daily sales information to Wal-Mart's suppliers via satellite. These suppliers then used the information to plan production and ship orders to Wal-Mart's warehouses. Wal-Mart used a dedicated fleet of trucks to ship goods from warehouses to stores in less than 48 hours and to replenish store inventories about twice a week. The result was better customer service (because products were nearly always available), lower production and transportation costs (because suppliers made and shipped only what was needed), and better use of retail store space (because stores did not have to hold an excessive amount of inventory).

Wal-Mart was an early proponent of superior supply chain performance. Other companies have now adopted many of the practices Wal-Mart pioneered in the 1980s.

[3]G. Stalk, P. Evans, and L. E. Shulman, "Competing on Capabilities: The New Rules of Corporate Strategy," *Harvard Business Review* 70, no. 2 (March–April 1992): 57–69.

Wal-Mart has continued to succeed through superior sourcing and delivery, and many of the practices it helped pioneer have taken root throughout the business world. To illustrate how widespread supply chain management thinking has become, consider the example of Panera Bread in the *Supply Chain Connections* feature.

SUPPLY CHAIN CONNECTIONS

PANERA BREAD

"A Loaf of Bread in Every Arm"

There is a good chance that you have either heard of or visited a Panera Bread bakery-cafe. Panera Bread is a specialty food retailer that has built its business on providing consumers with fresh artisan bread products served at strategically located, distinctive bakery-cafes. Between December 2003 and the end of 2006, the number of Panera locations grew from 602 to 1027. Financial results were equally impressive; 2006 fourth-quarter revenues and profits were up over the same quarter in 2005 by 25% and 8%, respectively.[4]

But have you ever thought about the upstream supply chain activities that must be accomplished in order to support the company's mission statement, "A loaf of bread in every arm"? In the case of Panera Bread, keeping up with the growth in the number of bakery-cafes—while still maintaining a high-quality, consistent product—presents a special challenge. The company has responded by investing heavily in its supply chain. As a recent article put it:[5]

> *During the past 10 years, Panera Bread's manufacturing and supply chain team has built a fresh dough manufacturing system that consists of 17 facilities with more than 800 employees. In excess of 200 million pounds of dough are delivered by 110 trucks that travel 9.7 million miles annually. Oh, and the team also manages vendor contracts, controls the distribution system for the retail bakery-cafes and supports the company's baking activities. The team is responsible for everything that comes through the back doors of Panera Bread bakery-cafes.*

Even in this short description, we can see how Panera Bread's supply chain activities cover everything from sourcing to production to delivery. It's a safe bet that Panera Bread's interest in effective supply chain management will continue to "rise" along with its products.

[4]Panera Bread, 4th Quarter 2006 Earnings Report, **www.panera.com/about/investor/reports.php**.

[5]L. Gorton, "Fresh Ideas," *Baking and Snack*, December 1, 2004.

Supply chain management efforts can range from an individual firm taking steps to improve the flow of information between itself and its supply chain partners to a large trade organization looking for ways to standardize transportation and billing practices. In the case of Wal-Mart, a single, very powerful firm took primary responsibility for improving performance across its own supply chain. As an alternative, companies within an industry often form councils or groups to identify and adopt supply chain practices that will benefit all firms in the industry. One such group is the Automotive Industry Action Group (AIAG, **www.aiag.org**), whose mission is, in part, to "provide an open forum where members cooperate in developing and promoting solutions that enhance the prosperity of the automotive industry."[6] The Grocery Manufacturers of America/Food Products Association (GMA/FPA, **www.gmabrands.com** and **www.fpa-food.org/index.asp**) serves a similar function. Other organizations, such as the Supply-Chain Council (SCC, **www.supply-chain.org**), seek to improve supply chain performance across many industries.

1.2 IMPORTANT TRENDS

As we will see, operations management and supply chain management are as much philosophical approaches to business as they are bodies of tools and techniques, and thus they require a great deal of interaction and trust between companies. For right now, however, let's talk about three major developments that have brought operations and supply chain management to the forefront of managers' attention:

- Electronic commerce
- Increasing competition and globalization
- Relationship management

Electronic Commerce

Today a laptop computer exceeds the storage and computing capacities of mainframe computers made only 15 years ago. With the emergence of the personal computer, wireless networks, and the Internet, the cost and availability of information resources allow easy linkages and eliminate information-related time delays in any supply chain network.

Electronic commerce
Also called *e-commerce*. The use of information technology (IT) solutions to automate business transactions. Electronic commerce promises to improve the speed, quality, and cost of business communication.

Electronic commerce (or e-commerce, for short) refers to the use of information technology (IT) solutions to automate business transactions. Electronic commerce promises to improve the speed, quality, and cost of business communication. The late 1990s and early 2000s, for example, saw the emergence of Internet-based "trading communities" that put hundreds of buyers and sellers in touch with one another.[7] Now, instead of looking through a catalog, filling out a paper order form, and faxing it to a supplier, buyers in many companies can search for what they need via their computer and, with a couple of clicks, place an order. Many paper transactions are becoming increasingly obsolete. At the same time, the proliferation of new telecommunications and computer technology has made instantaneous communications a reality. Such information systems—for example, Wal-Mart's satellite network—can link together suppliers, manufacturers, distributors, retail outlets, and, ultimately, customers, regardless of location. These systems can also provide visibility into incoming shipments, delays, and can even tell planners how many units of product are on any given store shelf in any given location in the world!

[6] Available at **www.aiag.org/about** (accessed February 14, 2007).

[7] For an example, read about SciQuest at **www.sciquest.com**.

Increasing Competition and Globalization

The second major trend is the increasing level of competition and globalization in the world economy. The rate of change in markets, products, and technology is escalating, leading to situations where managers must make decisions on shorter notice, with less information, and with higher penalty costs if they make a mistake. Customers are demanding quicker delivery, state-of-the-art technology, and products and services better suited to their individual needs. At the same time, new competitors are entering into markets that have traditionally been dominated by "domestic" firms.

Despite these challenges, many organizations are thriving. In later chapters, for example, you will read how such companies as Caterpillar, Honda, Procter & Gamble, and Hewlett Packard have embraced the changes facing today's markets and have put a renewed emphasis on improving their operations and supply chain performance. In some ways, the increased competition and globalization of businesses have given many firms the chance to break away from the pack.

Relationship Management

The information revolution of the last 20 years has given companies a wide range of technologies for better management of their operations and supply chains. Furthermore, increasing customer demands and global competition have given firms the incentive to improve in these areas. But this is not enough. Any efforts to improve operations and supply chain performance are likely to be inconsequential without the cooperation of other firms. As a result, more companies are putting an emphasis on relationship management.

Of all the activities operations and supply chain personnel perform, relationship management is perhaps the most difficult, and therefore the most susceptible to breakdown. Poor relationships within any link of the supply chain can have disastrous consequences for all other supply chain members. For example, an unreliable supplier can "starve" a plant, leading to inflated lead times and resulting in problems across the chain, all the way to the final customer.

To avoid such problems, organizations must manage the relationships with their upstream suppliers as well as their downstream customers. In many United States–based industries, strong supply chain relationships like those found in Japan might not develop readily. Firms can be geographically distant, and there are not as many small, family-owned suppliers as there are in Japan. In the case of high-tech firms, many components can be purchased only from overseas suppliers who are proprietary owners of the required technology. In such environments, it becomes more important to choose a few, select suppliers, thereby paving the way for informal interaction and information sharing.

1.3 OPERATIONS AND SUPPLY CHAIN MANAGEMENT AND YOU

At this point, you might be asking yourself, "If I choose to work in operations or supply chain management, where am I likely to end up?" The answer: Anywhere you like! Operations and supply chain personnel are needed in virtually every business sector. Salaries and placement opportunities for operations and supply chain personnel also tend to be highly competitive, reflecting the important and challenging nature of the work, as well as the relative scarcity of qualified individuals. You also might be asking yourself, "What would my career path look like?" Many operations and supply chain managers find that over their career, they work in many different areas. Table 1.1 lists just a few of the possibilities.

TABLE 1.1
Potential Career Paths in Operations and Supply Chain Management

Career Path	Description
Analyst	Uses analytical and quantitative methods to understand, predict, and improve processes within the supply chain.
Commodity manager	Acquires knowledge in a specific market in which the organization purchases significant quantities of materials and services. Helps formulate long-term commodity strategies and manage long-term relationships with selected suppliers.
Customer service manager	Plans and directs customer service teams to meet the needs of customers and support company operations. Works closely with marketing and sales, logistics, and transportation departments.
International logistics manager	Works closely with manufacturing, marketing, and purchasing to create timely, cost-effective import/export supply chains.
Logistics services salesperson	Markets transportation, warehousing, and specialized services to other companies.
Production manager	Supervises production in a manufacturing setting. Responsible for a wide range of personnel.
Sourcing analyst	Identifies global sources of materials, selects suppliers, arranges suppliers' contracts, and manages ongoing suppliers' relationships.
Sourcing manager	Measures supplier performance, identifies suppliers requiring improvement, and facilitates efforts to improve suppliers' processes.
Logistics and Material Planner	Reviews existing procedures and examines opportunities to streamline production, purchasing, warehousing, distribution, and financial forecasting to meet product distribution needs.
Systems support manager (Management Information Systems)	Provides analytical support in the management of logistics information, supplier performance data, materials requirements, and scheduling processes.
Transportation manager	Manages private, third-party, and contract carriage systems to assure timely and cost-efficient transportation of all incoming and outgoing shipments.

Professional Organizations

If you decide to pursue a career in operations or supply chain management, you will find a number of professional organizations willing to help you. These organizations have professional certification programs that establish an individual as a professional within his or her particular area. Most organizations also have regular meetings at the local level, as well as national and international meetings once or twice a year. We highlight some of these organizations here.

APICS—American Production and Inventory Control Society (**www.apics.org**) describes itself as "the educational society for resource management." It is a widely recognized professional society for persons interested in operations and supply chain management. APICS currently has more than 67,000 members and 250 chapters throughout the United States and its territories.

ISM—The Institute for Supply Management (ISM, **www.ism.ws**) provides national and international leadership in purchasing and materials management, particularly in the areas of education, research, and standards of excellence. Established in 1915, ISM has grown to 40,000 members.

CSCMP—The Council of Supply Chain Management Professionals (CSCMP, **www.cscmp.org**) seeks to be the preeminent professional association providing worldwide leadership for the evolving logistics profession through the development, dissemination, and advancement of logistics knowledge.

ASQ—The American Society for Quality (ASQ, **www.asq.com**) is a leader in education and all aspects of quality improvement, including the Baldrige Award, ISO 9000, and continuous improvement activities.

If you are a student, it is not too early to start thinking of joining one of these organizations. In fact, many of them provide scholarships for college education and can help defray education costs.

Cross-functional and Interorganizational Linkages

Even if you decide that a career in operations and supply chain management is not for you, chances are you will still find yourself working with people in these areas. This is because *none* of the major operations and supply chain activities takes place in a vacuum. Rather, these activities require the input and feedback of other functions within the firm, as well as suppliers and customers. Table 1.2 lists some major operations and supply chain activities,

TABLE 1.2

Major Operations and Supply Chain Activities

OPERATIONS AND SUPPLY CHAIN ACTIVITIES	PURPOSE	KEY INTERFUNCTIONAL PARTICIPANTS	KEY INTERORGANIZATIONAL PARTICIPANTS
Process selection	Design and implement the transformation processes that best meet the needs of the customer and the firm.	Engineering Marketing Finance Human resources IT	Customers
Forecasting	Develop the planning numbers needed for effective decision making.	Marketing Finance Accounting	Suppliers Customers
Capacity planning	Establish strategic capacity levels ("bricks and mortar") and tactical capacity levels (workforce, inventory).	Finance Accounting Marketing Human resources	Suppliers Customers
Inventory management	Manage the amount and placement of inventory within the company and the supply chain.	IT Finance	Suppliers Customers
Planning and control	Schedule and manage the flow of work through an organization and the supply chain; match customer demand to supply chain activities.	Marketing IT	Suppliers Customers
Purchasing	Identify and qualify suppliers of goods and services; manage the ongoing buyer-supplier relationships.	Engineering Finance Marketing	Suppliers
Logistics	Manage the movement of physical goods throughout the supply chain.	Marketing Engineering	Suppliers Customers

as well as some of the key outside participants. Look, for example, at process selection. Engineering and information technology (IT) personnel help identify and develop the technologies needed, while human resources personnel identify the people skills and training programs necessary to make the system work. Involving marketing personnel and customers will assure that the process meets the customers' needs. Finally, finance personnel will need to be involved if the process requires a substantial investment in resources.

1.4 PURPOSE AND ORGANIZATION OF THIS BOOK

Now that we have defined operations and supply chain management, it's time to discuss the purpose and organization of this book. Simply put, the purpose of this book is to give you a solid foundation in the topics and tools of *both* operations management and supply chain management. This is a significant departure from most operations management textbooks, which are dominated by internal operations issues and treat supply chain management as a subdiscipline. Our decision to emphasize both areas is based on two observations. First, more organizations are demanding students who have been exposed to traditional supply chain areas such as purchasing and logistics, as well as more traditional operations topics. Students who have had a course only in operations management are seen as not fully prepared. Second, our years of experience in industry, education, and consulting tell us that supply chain management is here to stay. While a strong internal operations function is vital to a firm's survival, it is not sufficient. Firms must also understand how they link in with their supply chain partners. With this in mind, we have organized the book into four main parts (Table 1.3).

TABLE 1.3
Organization of the Book

I. Creating Value through Operations and Supply Chains
Chapter 1: Introduction to Operations and Supply Chain Management
Chapter 2: Operations and Supply Chain Strategies
Chapter 3: Business Processes
Chapter 4: Managing Quality
II. Establishing the Operations Environment
Chapter 5: Managing Projects
Chapter 6: Developing Products and Services
Chapter 7: Process Choice and Layout Decisions in Manufacturing and Services
Chapter 8: Managing Capacity
III. Establishing Supply Chain Linkages
Chapter 9: Forecasting
Chapter 10: Sourcing Decisions
Chapter 11: Purchasing
Chapter 12: Logistics
IV. Planning and Controlling Operations and Supply Chains
Chapter 13: Sales and Operations Planning (Aggregate Planning)
Chapter 14: Managing Inventory throughout the Supply Chain
Chapter 15: Managing Production across the Supply Chain
Chapter 16: JIT/Lean Production

Part I, *Creating Value through Operations and Supply Chains*, introduces some basic concepts and definitions that lay the groundwork for future chapters. Chapter 2 deals with the topic of operations and supply chain strategies, including what they are, how they support the organization's overall strategy, and how they help a firm provide value to the customer. Chapter 3 is devoted to the topic of business processes, which can be thought of as the "molecules" that make up all operations and supply chain flows. Chapter 3 will introduce you to some of the approaches companies use to design and improve their business processes, including the Six Sigma methodology. Quality control is a particularly important part of process management, and so we devote Chapter 4 to the topic.

Part II, *Establishing the Operations Environment*, deals with fundamental choices that define an organization's internal operations environment. Chapter 5 sets the tone by describing how organizations manage projects, such as new product development efforts and capacity expansions. Chapter 6 addresses the product and service development process, while Chapter 7 deals with the manufacturing and service processes that firms put in place to provide these products or services, as well as layout decisions. In Chapter 8, we discuss the concept of capacity: How much and what types of capacity will an organization need? Decisions in these last three areas—product and service development, manufacturing and services processes, and capacity—set clear boundaries on what an organization can do and how the operations function will be managed. As such, we address them early in the book.

Part III, *Establishing Supply Chain Linkages*, turns the spotlight away from the internal operations function to how organizations link up with their supply chain partners. Forecasting, covered in Chapter 9, is a prime example. By forecasting downstream customer demand and sharing it with upstream suppliers, organizations can do a better job of planning for and controlling the flow of goods and services through the supply chain. Chapters 10, 11, and 12 cover the core supply chain areas of sourcing decisions, purchasing, and logistics. Through sourcing decisions and purchasing activities, organizations establish supply chain relationships with other firms. In fact, nearly all firms play the role of upstream supplier or downstream customer at one time or another. Chapter 10 describes the factors and analyses that will affect a firm's decision to source a product or service from an outside partner. Chapter 11 describes the actual purchasing process, while Chapter 12 deals with the physical flow of goods throughout the supply chain and covers such areas as transportation, warehousing, and logistics decision models.

The last part of the book, Part IV, *Planning and Controlling Operations and Supply Chains*, focuses on core topics in planning and control. These topics can be found in any basic operations management book. But in contrast to more traditional books, we have deliberately extended the focus of each chapter to address the implications for supply chain management. For example, in Chapter 13, we discuss not only how firms can develop tactical sales and operations plans, but also how they can link these plans with supply chain partners. In Chapter 14, we don't just cover basic inventory models; we discuss *where* inventory should be located in the supply chain; *how* transportation, packaging, and material-handling issues affect inventory decisions; and *how* inventory decisions by one firm affect its supply chain partners. Similarly, in Chapters 15 and 16, we don't just cover basic production planning topics; we show how such techniques as distribution requirements planning (DRP) and kanban can be used to synchronize the flow of goods between supply chain partners.

The chapters in Part I provide the foundation knowledge, while Part II deals with fundamental choices that serve to define the capabilities of a firm's operations area. Forecasting, purchasing, and logistics—the topics of Part III—establish linkages between a firm and its supply chain partners. Finally, through the planning and control activities described in Part IV, firms and their partners manage the flow of goods and information across the supply chain.

CHAPTER SUMMARY

Operations and supply chains are pervasive in business. *All* organizations must provide a product or service that someone values. This is the primary responsibility of the operations function. Furthermore, most organizations do not function independently, but find that their activities are linked with those of other organizations through supply chains. Careful management of operations and supply chains is therefore vital to the long-term health of nearly every organization.

Because operations and supply chain activities cover everything from planning and control activities to purchasing and logistics, there are numerous career opportunities for students interested in the area. Trends in information systems and global competition, as well as the growing importance of maintaining good relationships with other supply chain partners, will only increase these opportunities. Fortunately, there are many professional organizations, including APICS, CSCMP, and ISM, that cater to the career development of professionals in operations and supply chain management.

KEY TERMS

Downstream 7
Electronic commerce 11
First-tier supplier 8
Operations function 4
Operations management 7
Second-tier supplier 8
Supply chain 4
Supply chain management 8
Supply-Chain Operations Reference (SCOR) model 8
Upstream 7

DISCUSSION QUESTIONS

1. When a customer calls Dell Computers to order a PC, Dell builds a PC based on the customer's unique requirements and ships it directly to the customer—all in a matter of hours. What do you think Dell Computers' supply chain looks like? How important are Dell's suppliers and transportation partners to the success of the supply chain?
2. One of your friends states that "operations management and supply chain management are primarily of interest to *manufacturing* firms." Is this true or false? Give some examples to support your answer.
3. Think of all the different services provided by a typical college. How many can you name? What resources are required to perform these services? What are the important performance considerations—quality, cost, and so on—for these services?
4. Early in the chapter, we argued that "every organization must make a product or provide a service that someone values." Can you think of an example where poor operations or supply chain management undercut a business?

PROBLEMS

1. Visit the Web sites for the professional organizations listed in the chapter. Who are their target audiences? Are some more focused on purchasing professionals, or logistics professionals? Which of the careers listed in these Web sites are mentioned in the chapter? Which ones sound appealing to you?
2. Draw out the transformation process similar to Figure 1.1 for a simple operations function, such as a health clinic or a car repair shop. What are the inputs? The outputs?
3. Visit the Web site for the Supply-Chain Council at **www.supply-chain.org**. What is the purpose of the council? Who are some of the members?

CASE STUDY

Supply Chain Challenges at LeapFrog[8]

Introduction

Early in the morning on Monday, August 11, 2003, toy executive Kevin Carlson checked his nationwide weekend sales numbers and got a surprising glimpse of Christmas future. Stores had sold 360 of his company's LittleTouch LeapPads in the product's introductory weekend. Parents hunting for an educational toy for infants and toddlers were reaching for the new gadget, which makes noises when a child touches parts of an illustrated book. That small number had huge implications. Forecasting software told Mr. Carlson that he would need about 700,000 units to meet projected holiday demand—twice as many as he had planned to ship.

So his company, LeapFrog Enterprises Inc., did something unusual. At a time when other toy companies were unloading their final Christmas shipments from cargo ships out of China, LeapFrog began placing what would turn into a huge new order for LeapPads. Its factory, privately held Capable Toys Ltd. of Zhongshan, China, scrambled for extra plastic molds, custom-designed electronics, and scarce baby-drool-proof paper and pumped out LeapPads around the clock.

LeapFrog's frantic race against the holiday deadline shows how technology and global supply chains are meeting a great business challenge. For years, toy makers would place their entire holiday orders in January and February, blindly betting on demand for their products. By Christmas, they would have shortages of their hit products and huge stockpiles of their duds. In 1984, parents camped outside stores for Cabbage Patch Dolls, followed by Teenage Mutant Ninja Turtles in 1988 and the Little Mermaid in 1989. In 1993, executives at Bandai Inc. were slow to react to the popularity of Mighty Morphin Power Rangers. Only 600,000 of an estimated demand for 12 million made it to stores by Christmas. In 1996, Tyco Toys Inc. was also caught short on Tickle Me Elmo. The company rolled out about 1 million units of the giggly plush toy, but could have sold almost a million more.

Electronic Commerce, Relationship Management, and Forecasting

The shift that let LeapFrog make its August forecast came just a few years ago with the Internet, as major retailers, including Target, Kmart, and Toys "R" Us—which sell two-thirds of LeapFrog's toys—became less guarded about their market data and allowed suppliers real-time access to their sales databases. These days a LittleTouch sale at any U.S. Wal-Mart appears in LeapFrog's databases overnight. With new data-tracking systems, manufacturers know which stores sold the most products and the buyers' demographics, including whether the shopper is more likely to speak English or Spanish.

With this data, Mr. Carlson can make various extrapolations, even from sales as small as 360 units. In his small cubicle in LeapFrog's California headquarters, Mr. Carlson crunched the LittleTouch sales numbers through four computer models. They are designed to weed out unusual explanations for sales spikes—everything from discounts and TV advertising to where in stores the product was displayed. In the case of LittleTouch, he couldn't find an anomaly: It was a genuine hit. During the next five weeks, LittleTouch sales took off, surpassing those of LeapFrog's other top sellers during their own introductory periods.

After six weeks on the market, LittleTouch retail sales reached 5,000 units at LeapFrog's four major accounts. Based on that rate, forecast models were predicting sales of more than 700,000 in 2003, double LeapFrog's initial projections.

Global Sourcing, Capacity Decisions, and Manufacturing Processes

It took 12 months to produce the first 350,000 LittleTouch toys. LeapFrog eventually would want to make the same number again in just four months. In Zhongshan, an industrial town 60 miles north of Hong Kong, managers at the Capable Toys factory had expected to wrap up production of LittleTouch for the year in early fall. But soon after the sale projections emerged in August, "every day the LeapFrog marketing people said to us, 'Can we have a few more?' " says Capable's chief executive, Kenneth So, 51. As the requests grew larger, Mr. So set up a special task force that met daily to prepare for an all-out LittleTouch emergency.

There was very little Capable could do immediately to increase production. The molds that make the plastic parts of the toy can pump out only about one piece every 40 seconds. The factory needed to find more raw materials and custom-made parts, such as microchips and special paper. The plant needed to hire more workers. Not long ago these issues would have made a last-minute request to increase production hopeless, Mr. So says. But Mr. So's factory isn't

[8] Adapted from G. A. Fowler and J. Pereira, "Christmas Sprees: Behind Hit Toy, a Race to Tap Seasonal Surge," *The Wall Street Journal* (December 18, 2003).

like the simple sweatshops that first sprouted up in China in the 1980s. To compete against low-cost, low-end competitors today, he markets his factory as a specialist in design and supply chain efficiencies that can dramatically speed up manufacturing processes.

The showpiece of his 14-acre, five-building campus is the mechanical-design studio, where about 50 uniformed technicians and engineers use computer-automated-design software to create and improve toy parts and manufacturing processes. Here engineering supervisor Huang Hengbin, 32, made a breakthrough on the molds for the toy's plastic parts. The LittleTouch's 41 metal molds, also called tools, are a critical part of the production process. The factory runs the tools 24 hours a day, in three 8-hour shifts, to produce enough plastic parts to keep the assembly line running during regular hours. "When we design the product from the ground up, we know the limitations," says Mr. Huang. "So with the LittleTouch, we knew immediately that the limit was the tools," he says. One set could produce a maximum of 1,750 toys per day.

The factory, which had two sets of tools running around the clock, got the OK from LeapFrog for a third set of tools in late August when Mr. Bender, LeapFrog's global retail president, was sure that LittleTouch was a bona fide hit. A week later LeapFrog approved the making of a fourth set of tools. Work on those was started in mid-October, when the third set was ready. Mr. Huang's contribution was not only to produce the extra sets, which take weeks to make and cost hundreds of thousands of dollars—but also to ensure that each new set was more than a mere duplicate. "Every single [toy] part can be improved to save time," he says. He did just that: The original two sets of molds produced 3,500 toys a day; the third improved output to 6,300. His design improvements reduced the toys' fail rate to just 0.3 percent today from an initial 5 percent. That means hundreds more finished LittleTouch toys in the same amount of time.

Material Sourcing

LeapFrog and Capable also had to hustle to find the specialized materials and parts they needed. Each toy is equipped with a mini-speaker and three microchips, as well as a specially designed electronic membrane that translates a child's touch into a signal for the toy's "brain." The Capable Toys factory initially had trouble finding a supplier for touch-sensitive membranes, but then Mr. So's staff tapped its network of suppliers to hunt down a second vendor. Another material that caused headaches was the clothlike paper called Tyvek used in the LittleTouch books and made by DuPont Co. Home builders use the material as part of the insulation process because it is water-resistant and still breathes. LeapFrog needed something that would be drool-resistant and still absorb ink. The only way to get the material was through a third-party supplier—a book-printing firm—in the United States, says Andy Murer, LeapFrog's vice president of operations. That meant hiring the U.S. company to do the printing as well. That decision added 50 cents to 60 cents per book in production costs, but it was worth it to preserve the company's long-term image, Mr. Murer says.

Logistics

The toughest and most costly decision for LeapFrog was to use air freight to respond to shortages. That happened around September 21, when retail sales of the $35 LittleTouch began to flatten because of scarce inventory. After Mr. Bender started air-shipping the toys, sales picked up again. But at $10 to $15 per lightweight, but bulky, toy, air shipping sliced the company's profit on those LittleTouch shipments to almost nothing.

As of late December 2003, retailers were again lean on LittleTouch products. The day after Thanksgiving, about 30 percent of retailers were out of stock. The toy was still being either flown in or put on special fast boats, which take 14 days from Hong Kong to Los Angeles without standard stopovers elsewhere.

QUESTIONS

1. Draw a map of the supply chain for LeapFrog, including the retailers, Capable Toys, and suppliers of key materials (such as Tyvek). Which supply chain partners are "upstream" of LeapFrog? Which are "downstream"? Which partners are first-tier suppliers? Second-tier suppliers?
2. What data ultimately led to LeapFrog's decision to increase production levels of the LittleTouch LeapPads? Where did these data come from? How long after interpreting these data did LeapFrog start talking with Capable Toys about increasing production levels? Days, weeks, months?
3. What part of the production process limited output levels at Capable Toys? How did Capable respond to the challenge?
4. What were some of the material sourcing challenges facing LeapFrog and Capable Toys? How did they resolve these problems?
5. What type of logistics solutions did LeapFrog use to get the toys to the stores on time? What are the strengths and weaknesses of these solutions? If it had been August rather than December, what other options might LeapFrog have used?

REFERENCES

Books and Articles

Cox, J. F., and J. H. Blackstone, eds. *APICS Dictionary*. 11th ed. Falls Church, VA: APICS, 2004.

Fowler, G. A. and J. Pereira. "Christmas Sprees: Behind Hit Toy, a Race to Tap Seasonal Surge." *The Wall Street Journal*, December 18, 2003.

Gorton, L. "Fresh Ideas." *Baking and Snack*, December 1, 2004.

Stalk, G., P. Evans, and L. E. Shulman. "Competing on Capabilities: The New Rules of Corporate Strategy." *Harvard Business Review* 70, no. 2 (March–April 1992): 57–69.

Internet

American Society for Quality (ASQ), **www.asq.com**

APICS, **www.apics.org**

Automotive Industry Action Group (AIAG), **www.aiag.org**

Council of Supply Chain Management Professionals (CSCMP), **www.cscmp.org**

Grocery Manufacturers of America/Food Products Association (GMA/FPA), **www.gmabrands.com** and **www.fpa-food.org/index.asp**

Institute for Supply Management (ISM), **www.ism.ws**

Panera Bread, **www.panera.com/about/investor/reports.php**

SciQuest, **www.Sciquest.com**

Supply-Chain Council (SCC), **www.supply-chain.org**

CHAPTER 2

Operations and Supply Chain Strategies

CHAPTER OUTLINE

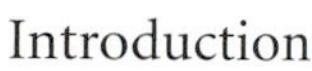

Chapter Objectives

By the end of this chapter, you will be able to:

- Explain the relationship between business strategies and functional strategies and the difference between structural and infrastructural elements of the business.
- Describe some of the main operations and supply chain decision categories.
- Explain the concept of customer value and calculate a value index score.
- Differentiate between customers' order winners and qualifiers and explain why this difference is important to developing the operations and supply chain strategy for a firm.
- Discuss the concept of trade-offs among performance dimensions and give an example.
- Define core competencies and give an example of how core competencies in the operations and supply chain areas can be used for competitive advantage.
- Explain the importance of strategic alignment and describe the four stages of alignment between the operations and supply chain strategy and the business strategy.

APPLE IPOD

Since its introduction in October 2001, Apple's iPod has come to dominate the market for portable media players. Apple has kept ahead of the competition through constant renewal of the product line. For example, Apple introduces a new generation of the full-sized iPod about every year, and in 2005, Apple rolled out two new products, the iPod nano and shuffle. Each iPod generation has been lighter, has incorporated more features, and, more often than not, has sold for less than the previous version.

Sales results have been spectacular, with total sales surpassing 88,701,000 units as of January 2007. Figure 2.1 shows the sales history for the iPod.[1] As the numbers suggest, in addition to rapid growth, iPod demand also experienced large seasonal "bumps" in the last quarters of 2005 and 2006.

These "bumps" can be attributed to the introduction of new generations of products combined with the holiday shopping season.

Not only has the iPod been a marketing success, it's been a supply chain success. This is because Apple put in place a supply chain strategy that addressed both physical flows and information flows. Consider the following:

- On the upstream side, Apple has partnered with suppliers capable of providing both the *quantity* and *quality* of components Apple needs to assemble the iPod. These suppliers are located around the globe, and include Samsung, Wolfson Microelectronics, SigmaTel, and Hitachi. Having suppliers who can respond quickly to new requirements is crucial for products with short life cycles and variable demand levels, such as the iPod.
- On the downstream side, Apple has worked with a wide range of logistics service providers and retailers, including Wal-Mart and Best Buy, to get iPods into the hands of consumers. Accomplishing this task without incurring excessive transportation costs, excessive inventories, or shortages is quite a challenge. This is especially true when you consider that demand can be highly seasonal and the life cycle for each iPod generation is around one year (who wants last year's model once the new one comes out?).
- Finally, in addition to managing the physical flow of iPods to the consumers, Apple has established an *information* supply chain that allows users to download music and videos for a small fee. In some ways, this is arguably the most revolutionary part of the iPod's success. The old, physical supply chain of burning, packaging, and shipping CDs to warehouses or stores has been replaced by a virtual one that allows the user to buy and instantly receive only the music and videos he or she wants.

[1]Apple Corporation Annual Reports, 2005–2007.

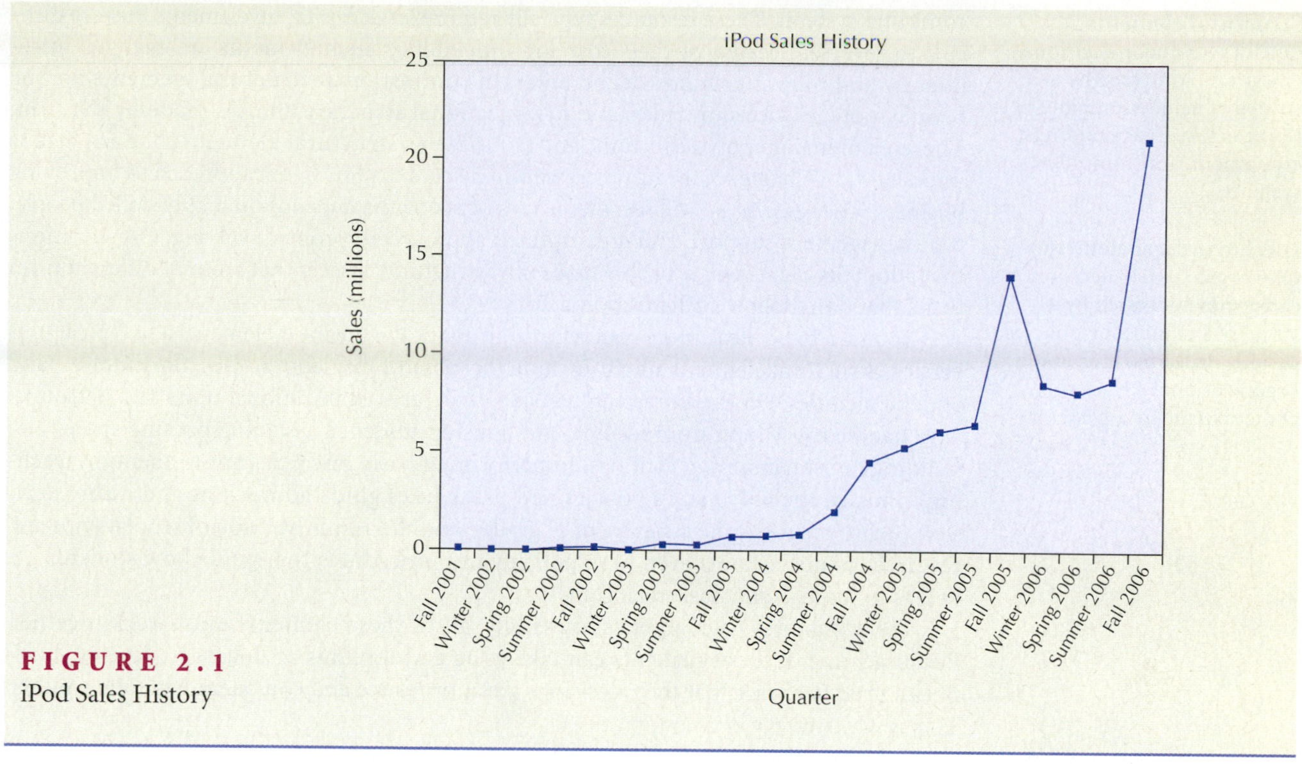

FIGURE 2.1
iPod Sales History

INTRODUCTION

Discussing operations or supply chain management without someone mentioning the word *strategy* is almost impossible. But what does that term really mean? What constitutes an operations or supply chain strategy, and how does it support a firm's overall efforts? In this chapter, we will describe how businesses actually create strategies and how operations and supply chain strategies fit within the larger process.

The second half of the chapter is devoted exclusively to the topic of operations and supply chain strategy. We will discuss the three main objectives of operations and supply chain strategy and consider some of the decisions managers face in developing and implementing their strategies. Throughout this discussion, we will stress the key role operations and supply chains play in creating value for the customer.

2.1 ELEMENTS OF THE BUSINESS

Before we begin our main discussion, let's take a moment to consider the business elements that, together, define a business. These elements include structural and infrastructural elements. **Structural elements** are tangible resources, such as buildings, equipment, and

Structural elements
One of two major decision categories addressed by a strategy. Includes tangible resources, such as buildings, equipment, and computer systems.

Infrastructural elements
One of two major decision categories addressed by a strategy. Includes the policies, people, decision rules, and organizational structure choices made by a firm.

computer systems. These resources typically require large capital investments that are difficult to reverse. Because of their cost and inflexibility, such elements are changed infrequently and only after much deliberation. In contrast, **infrastructural elements** are the people, policies, decision rules, and organizational structure choices made by the firm. These elements are, by definition, not as visible as structural elements, but are just as important. In Chapter 3, for instance, we will discuss the Six Sigma approach to improving business processes. As we will see, the success of Six Sigma depends on highly skilled people, top management support, and a disciplined approach to problem solving. Organizations that adopt Six Sigma will probably make infrastructural choices that are very different from firms that don't follow such an approach.

To make these ideas more concrete, think about the business elements at a typical university. Structural elements might include the classrooms, laboratories, dormitories, and athletic facilities. On the infrastructure side, there are organizational units and personnel who handle everything from feeding and housing students, assigning parking spaces and building and maintaining facilities, to performing basic research (not to mention teaching). Finally, the university's policies and procedures guide admissions and hiring decisions, tenure reviews, the assignment of grades, and the administration of scholarships and research grants. Schools even have policies and procedures that guide how students get tickets to football and basketball games.

For a business to compete successfully, all of these elements must work together. Because some of these elements can take years and millions of dollars to develop, businesses need to ensure that their decisions are appropriate and consistent with one another. This is why strategy is necessary.

2.2 STRATEGY

Strategies
The mechanisms by which businesses coordinate their decisions regarding structural and infrastructural elements.

Mission statement
A statement that explains why an organization exists. It describes what is important to the organization, called its core values, and identifies the organization's domain.

Business strategy
The strategy that identifies the firm's targeted customers and sets time frames and performance objectives for the business.

Strategies are the mechanisms by which businesses coordinate their decisions regarding their structural and infrastructural elements. Strategies can be thought of as long-term game plans, that are focused on achieving a specific set of business objectives at a specific time in the future. They provide direction on what people in the organization must do now to ensure that the firm reaches these objectives. What is considered *long term* can differ from one industry to the next, but generally the phrase covers several years or more.

As Figure 2.2 suggests, most organizations have more than one level of strategy, from upper-level business strategies to more detailed, functional-level strategies. (When organizations have *multiple* distinct businesses, they often distinguish between an overall *corporate* strategy and individual *business unit* strategies.) The **mission statement** explains why an organization exists. It describes what is important to the organization, called its core values, and identifies the organization's domain.

Much has been written on what a business strategy should accomplish. To keep things simple, we will focus only on those parts of a business strategy that are directly relevant to the development of successful operations and supply chain strategies. In this vein, the **business strategy** must:

- Clearly identify the firm's targeted customers and broadly indicate what the operations and supply chain functions need to do to provide value to these customers;
- Set time frames and performance objectives that managers can use to track the firm's progress toward fulfilling its business strategy; and
- Identify the role of supply chain partners;
- Identify and support the development of core competencies in the operations and supply chain areas.

FIGURE 2.2
A Top-Down Model of Strategy

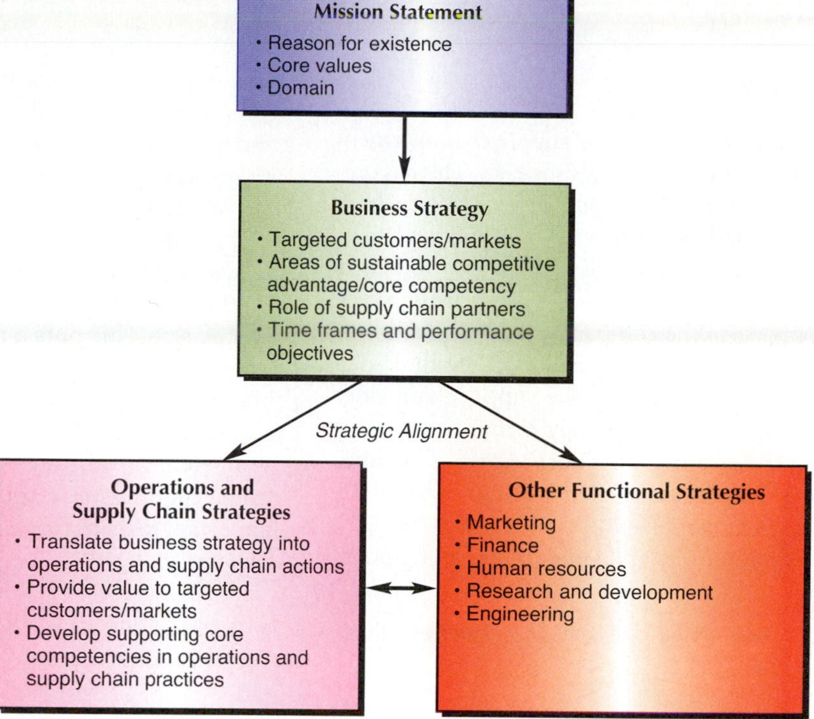

Core competencies
Organizational strengths or abilities, developed over a long period, that customers find valuable and competitors find difficult or even impossible to copy.

The concept of core competencies deserves special attention because of the implications for operations and supply chain strategies. **Core competencies** are organizational strengths or abilities, developed over a long period of time, that customers find valuable and competitors find difficult or even impossible to copy. Honda, for example, is recognized for having core competencies in the engineering and manufacture of small gas-powered engines. Those core competencies have helped Honda stake a claim in numerous markets, including the markets for motorcycles, boat engines, cars, lawn mowers, jet skis, home generators, and soon, small jet aircraft.

Core competencies can take many forms and even shift over time. IBM used to be known as a computer hardware company. Today IBM's core competency is arguably its ability to provide customers with integrated information solutions and the consulting services needed to make them work. As one magazine article noted, "[g]ood IT staffers are hard to find, but IBM Global Services alone has 150,000. That makes IBM the world's largest IT services provider."[2] You can imagine how hard it would be for other firms to try to duplicate IBM's advantage. In some cases, the ability of a firm to manage its supply chain partners may in itself be considered a core competency (see *Supply Chain Connections: Dell Computers*).

Functional strategy
Translates a business strategy into specific actions for the functional areas such as marketing, human resources, and finance. Functional strategies should align with the overall business strategy and with each other.

Functional strategies translate a business strategy into specific actions for the functional areas, such as marketing, human resources, and finance. An operations and supply chain strategy might address the manufacturing or service processes needed to make a specific product, how suppliers will be evaluated and selected, and how the products will be distributed.

---

[2]D. Kirpatrick, "The Future of IBM," *Fortune Magazine*, 145, no. 4 (February 18): 2002, 60–68.

SUPPLY CHAIN CONNECTIONS

DELL COMPUTERS

The ability of a firm to manage its supply chain partners may in itself be considered a core competency. This has certainly been the case for Dell Computer Corporation, which practices what Michael Dell calls "virtual integration."[3]

Dell's operations strategy is based on a build-to-order production system. This means that Dell assembles computers only when the company has actual customer orders. Yet Dell is still able to maintain two- to three-day lead times to its customers. On the supply chain side, Dell buys only the latest technology components—and then just a few days' or even hours' worth at a time. Not only does this minimize Dell's inventory holding costs, but also it reduces Dell's exposure to potentially obsolete parts inventories. (Imagine the poor computer manufacturer who has 100 days' worth of a particular computer chip when the latest version comes out.) Dell also taps into the supply chain to outsource its after-sales service as well as delivery of computers.

While not all organizations are as dependent on their supply chain partners as Dell is, current industry trends suggest that many organizations are focusing on developing only a few core competencies while outsourcing the rest. This puts a premium on an organization's ability to select good partners and coordinate the flow of information and material between partners. It also creates risks, especially if the organization's selected core competencies fall out of favor in the future. In fact, insourcing/outsourcing decisions are becoming so important to firms that we deal with the topic in detail in Chapter 10.

[3]J. Magretta, "The Power of Vertical Integration: An Interview with Dell Computer's Michael Dell," *Harvard Business Review* 76, no. 2 (March–April 1998): 73–84.

The model in Figure 2.2 shows how the mission statement, business strategy, and functional strategies are related to one another. Managers should be able to pick any specific strategic action at the functional level (for example, "Develop a European source for raw material X") and trace it back to the business strategy ("Increase our European business presence") and, ultimately, to the firm's mission statement ("Become a world-class competitor in our industry"). When the different levels of the strategic planning process fit together well, an organization is said to have good strategic alignment.

A firm's strategies should also be aligned *across* the functional areas. Continuing with the previous example, operations and supply chain efforts aimed at developing a European supply base should be matched by marketing, finance, and human resource efforts aimed at expanding the firm's global presence. Indeed, many so-called functional-level strategies—such as new product development and information technology—are really better described as *cross*-functional, as the responsibility, authority, and resources for these activities often reside in multiple areas.

2.3 OPERATIONS AND SUPPLY CHAIN STRATEGIES

Now that we have some understanding of the relationship between business strategies and functional strategies, let's turn our attention to operations and supply chain strategies in particular. The **operations and supply chain strategy** is a functional strategy that indicates how structural and infrastructural elements within the operations and supply chain areas will be acquired and developed to support the overall business strategy. Table 2.1 lists some of the major structural and infrastructural decisions that must be addressed by an

TABLE 2.1
Operations and Supply Chain Decision Categories

STRUCTURAL DECISION CATEGORIES	INFRASTRUCTURAL DECISION CATEGORIES
Capacity (*Chapter 8*) • Amount of capacity • Type of capacity • Timing of capacity changes (lead, lag, or match market demands) *Facilities (Chapters 7, 8, 11)* • Service facilities • Manufacturing plants • Warehouses • Distribution hubs • Size, location, degree of specialization *Technology* (*Chapters 7, 12, 15*) • Manufacturing processes • Services processes • Material handling equipment • Transportation equipment • Computer systems	*Organization* • Structure—centralization/decentralization • Control/reward systems • Workforce decisions *Sourcing decisions and purchasing process* (Chapters 10, 11) • Procurement Systems • Sourcing strategies • Supplier selection • Supplier performance measurement *Planning and control (Chapters 9, 12–16)* • Forecasting • Tactical planning • Inventory management • Production planning and control *Business processes and quality management* (*Chapters 3, 4*) • Six Sigma • Continuous improvement • Business process mapping *Product and service development* (*Chapter 6*) • Development process • Organizational and supplier roles

Adapted from R. Hayes and S. Wheelwright, *Restoring Our Competitive Edge* (New York: John Wiley, 1984), p. 31.

Operations and supply chain strategy
A functional strategy that indicates how structural and infrastructural elements within the operations and supply chain areas will be acquired and developed to support the overall business strategy.

operations and supply chain strategy, as well as where they are discussed in this book. From this table, you can easily see how pervasive infrastructural decisions are in the operations and supply chain strategy. This list of decisions is by no means exhaustive, and it would be much longer and more detailed for an actual business. However, the point is this: Executing successful operations and supply chain strategies means choosing and implementing the right mix of structural and infrastructural elements.

What constitutes the best mix of these structural and infrastructural elements is a subject of ongoing debate among business and academic experts alike. Nevertheless, we can identify three primary objectives of an operations and supply chain strategy:

1. Help managers choose the right mix of structural and infrastructural elements, based on a clear understanding of the performance dimensions valued by customers and the trade-offs involved;
2. Ensure that the firm's structural and infrastructural choices are strategically aligned with the firm's business strategy; and
3. Support the development of core competencies in the firm's operations and supply chains.

These three objectives bring up a whole list of concepts: performance dimensions and customer value, trade-offs, strategic alignment, and core competencies in the operations and supply chain areas. In the remainder of this chapter, we describe these concepts more fully.

Customer Value

As noted in Chapter 1, operations and supply chains help firms provide products or services that someone values. But how should we define value? To begin, most customers evaluate products and services based on multiple performance dimensions, such as performance quality, delivery speed, after-sales support, and cost. The organization that provides the best mix of these dimensions will be seen as providing the highest value. Example 2.1 shows how one might assess the value of a product or service.

Example 2.1

Calculating a Value Index for Two Competing Products

John wants to buy a laptop computer to use for his school assignments. He decides to evaluate the choices on four dimensions:

1. *Performance quality.* How much memory does each computer have? How fast is the processor? How much storage space does each computer have?
2. *Delivery speed.* How quickly can John receive the computer?
3. *After-sales support.* Will the provider help John resolve any technical problems? Will John be able to get help 24 hours a day or just at certain times?
4. *Cost.* What is the total cost to own the computer?

John rates the importance of each of these dimensions on a scale from 1 ("completely unimportant") to 5 ("critical"), coming up with the following values:

DIMENSION	IMPORTANCE
Performance quality	3
Delivery speed	1
After-sales support	2
Cost	4

The campus store carries two different laptops, one made by WolfByte Computers and the other by Dole Microsystems. WolfByte's laptop has a relatively fast processor and plenty of memory, can be delivered in a week, includes around-the-clock technical support for a full year, and costs $1,500. Dole Microsystems' laptop is a little slower and has less memory. However, it is available immediately, comes with a month of technical support, and costs $750. John uses this information to rate the performance of each offering with regard to the four dimensions on a scale from 1 ("poor") to 5 ("excellent"), as follows:

DIMENSION	IMPORTANCE	WOLFBYTE PERFORMANCE	DOLE MICROSYSTEMS PERFORMANCE
Performance quality	3	4	3
Delivery speed	1	3	5
After-sales support	2	4	2
Cost	4	2	4

Value index
A measure that uses the performance and importance scores for various dimensions of performance for an item or service to calculate a score that indicates the overall value of an item or service to a customer.

To find which laptop provides the greater value, John calculates a value index for each. A **value index** is a measure that uses the performance and importance scores for various dimensions of performance for an item or service to calculate a score that indicates the overall value of an item or service to a customer. The formula for the value index is:

$$V = \sum_{i=1}^{n} I_n P_n \quad [2\text{–}1]$$

where:

V = Value index for product or service

I_n = Importance of dimension n

P_n = Performance with regard to dimension n

For WolfByte, the value index equals ($3\times4 + 1\times3 + 2\times4 + 4\times2 = 31$); for Dole Microsystems, it is ($3\times3 + 1\times5 + 2\times2 + 4\times4 = 34$). So even though the Dole laptop has less performance quality and after-sales support, its lower cost makes it a better value for John.

Quality
The characteristics of a product or service that bear on its ability to satisfy stated or implied needs.

Performance quality
A subdimension of quality, addressing the basic operating characteristics of the product or service.

Conformance quality
A subdimension of quality addressing whether the product was made or the service performed to specifications.

Reliability quality
A subdimension of quality addressing whether a product will work for a long time without failing or requiring maintenance.

Delivery speed
A performance dimension that refers to how quickly the operations or supply chain function can fulfill a need, once it has been identified.

Four Performance Dimensions

Operations and supply chains can have an enormous impact on business performance. Experience suggests that four generic performance dimensions are particularly relevant to operations and supply chain activities. These are:

1. Quality
2. Time
3. Flexibility
4. Cost

Let's look at each of these performance dimensions in depth.

QUALITY. **Quality** is defined as the characteristics of a product or service that bear on its ability to satisfy stated or implied needs.[4] The concept of quality is broad, with a number of subdimensions, including **performance quality** (What are the basic operating characteristics of the product or service?), **conformance quality** (Was the product made or the service performed to specifications?), and **reliability quality** (Will a product work for a long time without failing or requiring maintenance? Does a service operation perform its tasks consistently over time?). Chapter 4 provides a comprehensive list of the various quality dimensions and discusses them in detail. The relative importance of these quality dimensions will differ from one customer to the next. One buyer may be more interested in performance, another in reliability. To compete on the basis of quality, a firm's operations and supply chain must consistently meet or exceed customer expectations or requirements on the most critical quality dimensions.

TIME. Time has two basic characteristics: speed and reliability. **Delivery speed** generally refers to how quickly the operations or supply chain function can fulfill a need, once it

[4]American Society for Quality, "Glossary," **www.asq.org/info/glossary/a.html**.

Delivery reliability
A performance dimension that refers to the ability to deliver products or services when promised.

has been identified. **Delivery reliability** refers to the ability to deliver products or services when promised. Note that a firm can have long lead times, yet still maintain a high degree of delivery reliability. Typical measures of delivery reliability include the percentage of orders that are delivered by the promised time and the average tardiness of late orders.

Delivery window
The acceptable time range in which deliveries can be made.

Delivery reliability is especially important to companies that are linked together in a supply chain. Consider the relationship between a fish wholesaler and its major customer, a fish processing facility. If the fish arrive too late, the processing facility may be forced to shut down. On the other hand, fish that arrive too early may go bad before they can be processed. Obviously, these two supply chain partners must coordinate their efforts so that the fish will arrive within a specific **delivery window**, which is defined as the acceptable time range in which deliveries can be made. One automobile manufacturer charges suppliers a penalty fee of $10,000 for every minute a delivery is late. That practice may seem extreme until one considers that late deliveries may shut down an entire production line.

Another measure of delivery reliability is the accuracy of the quantity shipped. For example, Sam's Club demands 95% accuracy in stock deliveries from suppliers. If suppliers ship more than the quantity ordered, they are still considered to be in error. Some firms will consider a partial shipment to be on time if it arrives by the promised date, but others will accept only complete shipments, delivered within the scheduled window.

Flexibility
A performance dimension that considers how quickly operations and supply chains can respond to the unique needs of different customers.

FLEXIBILITY. Many operations and supply chains compete by responding to the unique needs of different customers. Both manufacturing and service firms can demonstrate **flexibility**. A full-service law firm, for instance, will handle any legal issue a client faces. (Some law firms specialize in only real estate transactions or divorce settlements.) A full-service hotel will go to great lengths to fulfill a guest's every need. For example, a staff

Delivery reliability and delivery speed are critical performance dimensions for perishable goods such as fruits and vegetables.

member at the Ritz-Carlton in Dearborn, Michigan, once noticed a guest standing outside the gift shop, waiting for it to open. The employee found out what the guest wanted, picked it up when the shop opened, and waited outside a conference hall to deliver it to the guest. Many firms distinguish among several types of flexibility, including **mix flexibility** (the ability to produce a wide range of products or services), **changeover flexibility** (the ability to provide a new product with minimal delay), and **volume flexibility** (the ability to produce whatever volume the customer needs).

Mix flexibility
The ability to produce a wide range of products or services.

Changeover flexibility
The ability to provide a new product with minimal delay.

Volume flexibility
The ability to produce whatever volume the customer needs.

Consider the case of Solectron, a company that buys components and manufactures goods for many original equipment manufacturers (OEMs) in the electronics industry. Because the electronics industry is notorious for short product life cycles and unpredictable demand, Solectron must be able to adjust the mix and volume of the products it produces quickly. Solectron's supply chain partners must be equally flexible. For instance, Solectron might order 10,000 units of Product A on Friday for delivery on Monday and then call back on Monday and ask the supplier to take back the 10,000 units and deliver 8,000 units of Product B instead.

Flexibility has become particularly valuable in new product development. Some firms compete by developing new products or services faster than their competitors, a competitive posture that requires operations and supply chain partners who are both flexible and willing to work closely with designers, engineers, and marketing personnel. A well-known example is the "motorcycle war" between Honda and Yamaha, which took place in the early 1980s.[5] In 18 months, Honda introduced over 80 new motorcycle models to the Japanese market, while Yamaha introduced just 34. The ability to quickly produce fresh models gave Honda a significant competitive advantage. In another case, Intel's CEO once noted that the company tries to introduce a new chip about once every two years—a pace designed to keep competitors in perpetual catch-up mode. Chapter 6 includes a detailed discussion of how operations and supply chains can support new product development.

COST. Cost is always a concern, even for companies that compete primarily on some other dimension. However, "cost" covers such a wide range of activities that companies commonly categorize costs in order to focus their cost management efforts. Some typical cost categories include:

- Labor costs
- Material costs
- Engineering costs
- Quality-related costs (including failure costs, appraisal costs, and prevention costs)

This is just the tip of the iceberg: Firms have developed literally thousands of different cost categories, many of which are specific to the issues facing a particular firm. The point is that operations and supply chain activities are natural targets for cost management efforts because they typically account for much of an organization's costs. As such, cost is an important performance dimension, and we will return to it frequently throughout this book.

---

[5]G. Stalk, "Time—The Next Source of Competitive Advantage," *Harvard Business Review* 66, no. 4 (July–August 1988): 41–51.

Trade-Offs among Performance Dimensions

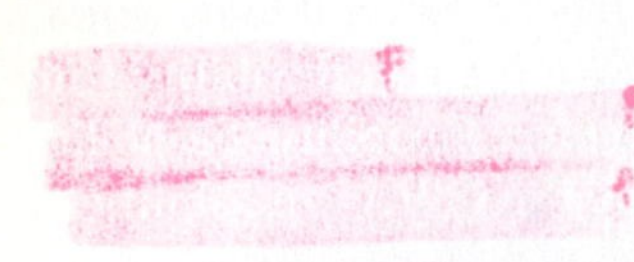

Take a moment to think about the differences between a world-class sprinter and a marathon runner. The sprinter has trained for explosive speed off the line, whereas the marathon runner has trained for paced distance running. Both athletes are in peak condition, yet neither would dream of competing in both events.

The same is true in business. In a competitive marketplace, no firm can sustain an advantage on *all* performance dimensions indefinitely. Excellence in some dimensions may conflict with excellence in others, preventing any one firm from becoming the best in all. In such cases, firms must make **trade-offs**, or decisions to emphasize some dimensions at the expense of others. Nearly all operations and supply chain decisions require such trade-offs. To make logical and consistent decisions, operations and supply chain managers must understand which performance dimensions are most valued by the firm's targeted customers and act accordingly.

Trade-off
The decision by a firm to emphasize one performance dimension over another, based on the recognition that superior performance on some dimensions may conflict with superior performance on others.

Consider some of the trade-offs Delta Airlines might face in scheduling flights between Raleigh and Orlando. More flights mean greater flexibility for the customer, but higher costs for the company. Similarly, larger, more comfortable seats will improve the quality of the service, but also raise costs and reduce the number of passengers a plane can carry. Delta managers know that business flyers will pay a premium for flexibility and comfortable seats, but casual flyers (such as families on their way to Disney World) will be more price sensitive.

Now suppose a competitor of Delta's decides to offer flights between Raleigh and Orlando. Given this move, Delta's flight schedule and seat design take on added importance. If managers choose frequent flights and larger seats, costs may climb higher than the competitor's; if they choose fewer flights and smaller seats, flexibility and quality may suffer. Delta's managers must decide whose needs—those of business flyers or those of casual flyers—will guide their operational decisions.

Order Winners and Order Qualifiers

Some managers use the concepts of order winners and order qualifiers to highlight the relative importance of different performance dimensions.[6] **Order winners** are performance dimensions that differentiate a company's products and services from those of its competitors. Firms win the customer's business by providing superior levels of performance on order winners. **Order qualifiers** are performance dimensions on which customers expect a minimum level of performance. Superior performance on an order qualifier will not, by itself, give a company a competitive advantage.

Order winners
Performance dimensions that differentiate a company's products and services from its competitors'. Firms win the customer's business by providing superior levels of performance on order winners.

Order qualifiers
Performance dimensions on which customers expect a minimum level of performance. Superior performance on an order qualifier will not, by itself, give a company a competitive advantage.

The industrial chemical market offers an example to illustrate the difference between order winners and order qualifiers. Buyers of industrial chemicals expect a certain level of purity (i.e., conformance quality) before they will even consider purchasing a chemical from a particular source. Because all potential sources must meet this minimum requirement, purity is incredibly important. Once the purity requirement has been satisfied, however, other performance dimensions—such as cost, delivery speed, and flexibility—will be used to determine the best source. From the supplier's perspective, product quality is the order qualifier; cost, delivery speed, and flexibility are order winners.

Now suppose we have two suppliers, A and B, that are competing head-to-head in this industry. Figure 2.3 illustrates how the order winner/qualifier logic can be used to evaluate the two suppliers. Supplier A meets the minimum requirements on quality, but falls below Supplier B on all but one of the remaining dimensions (volume flexibility). Supplier B, however, has purity levels below the minimum requirement. So even though Supplier B is

[6] T. Hill, *Manufacturing Strategy: Text and Cases* (Boston: Irwin McGraw-Hill, 2000).

FIGURE 2.3
Performance of Two Chemical Suppliers vis-à-vis Customers' Orders: Winners and Qualifiers

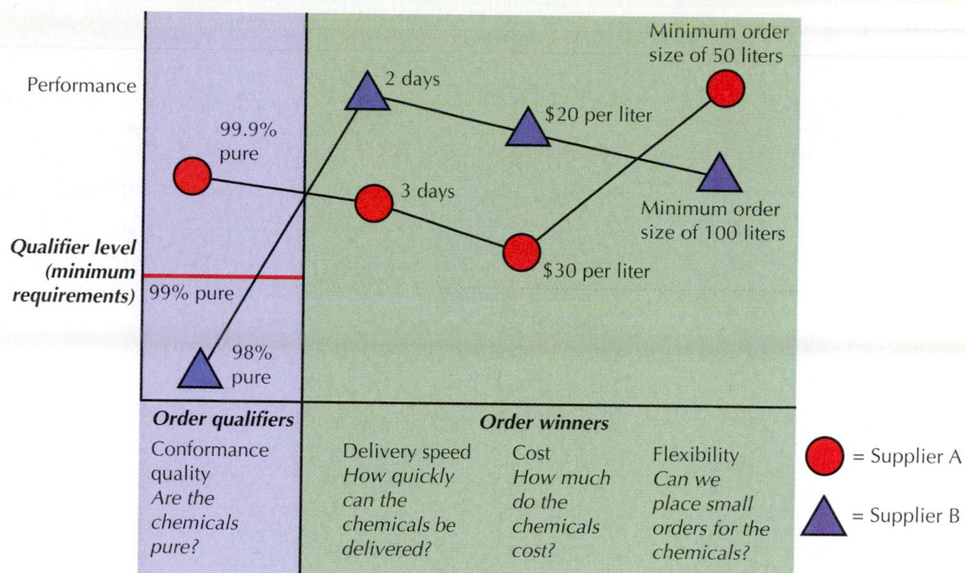

superior to supplier A on two performance dimensions, Supplier B will be dropped from consideration because it fails to qualify on one of the dimensions.

Understanding what the relevant order qualifiers and order winners are helps operations and supply chain managers to formulate strategy in three ways. First, it helps identify potential problem areas, as well as strengths. Second, it clarifies the issues surrounding decisions on trade-offs. Finally, it helps managers to prioritize their efforts.

Take a look again at Supplier B. Supplier B must immediately address its quality problems if it wants to compete at all. After that, the company might look for ways to protect or even increase its delivery and cost advantages. Furthermore, if improving purity involves increasing costs (for example, buying new equipment), Supplier B should understand what the appropriate trade-off is.

Stages of Alignment with the Business Strategy

The ultimate goal of any firm is to develop an operations and supply chain strategy that supports its business strategy. Management should be able to state how each operations and supply chain structural or infrastructural choice supports the customers' order winners and qualifiers and what trade-offs had to be considered when making these choices. However, as Bob Hayes and Steven Wheelwright recognized over 20 years ago,[7] some organizations are further along toward achieving this than are others. They described four stages of alignment, and although the stages originally referred to manufacturing, their descriptions apply equally well to the operations and supply chain areas of today. The four stages are as follows:

Stage 1—Internally neutral. In this stage, management seeks only to minimize any negative potential in the operations and supply chain areas. There is no effort made to link these areas with the business strategy.

Stage 2—Externally neutral. Here industry practice is followed, based on the assumption that what works for competitors will work for the company. Still, there is no effort made to link the operations and supply chain areas with the overall business strategy.

[7]R. Hayes and S. Wheelwright, *Restoring Our Competitive Edge* (New York: John Wiley, 1984).

TABLE 2.2
Aligning Business and Operations and Supply Chain Strategies

	DOLE MICROSYSTEMS	WOLFBYTE COMPUTERS
Business strategy	Assemble, sell, and support PCs targeted at price-sensitive buyers who require adequate, but not exceptional, performance, delivery, and after-sales support.	Assemble, sell, and support PCs targeted at buyers who are willing to pay for excellent performance, delivery, and after-sales support.
Operations and supply chain strategy	• Buy components from the *lowest-cost* suppliers who meet minimum quality and delivery capabilities. • Keep minimum levels of inventory in factories to *hold down inventory costs.* • Hire and train support staff to provide *acceptable* customer service. • Use three-day ground shipment to *keep costs low.*	• Buy components from *state-of-the-art* suppliers. Price is important, but not the critical factor. • Keep enough inventory in factories to *meet rush orders* and *shorten lead times.* • Hire and train support staff to provide *superior* customer service. • Use overnight air freight to *minimize lead time* to customer.

Stage 3—Internally supportive. At this stage, the operations and supply chain areas participate in the strategic debate. Management recognizes that the operations and supply chain structural and infrastructural elements must be aligned with the business strategy.

Stage 4—Externally supportive. At this stage, the operations and supply areas do more than just support the business strategy—the business strategy actively seeks to exploit the core competencies found within these areas.

To illustrate how a firm's operations and supply chain strategies might achieve Stage 3 alignment, let's revisit Dole Microsystems and WolfByte Computers. Suppose that as part of its business strategy, Dole decides to target price-sensitive buyers who need adequate, but not exceptional, performance, delivery, and after-sales support. In contrast, WolfByte decides to focus on buyers who want excellent performance, delivery, and after-sales support. Table 2.2 shows how managers might begin to align their operations and supply chain strategies with the business strategies of these two distinctive companies.

Notice how the operations and supply chain decisions outlined in Table 2.2 seem to naturally flow from the different business strategies. Table 2.2 vividly illustrates how operations and supply chain decisions that are appropriate in one case may be inappropriate in another. Purchasing low-cost components, for example, would make sense for Dole, given its business strategy, but would run counter to WolfByte's emphasis on excellent performance.

Core Competencies in Operations and Supply Chains

Before firms can think about progressing to the fourth stage of alignment (externally supportive), they must develop core competencies within the operations and supply chain areas. Consider the example of Lowe's, a national hardware retailer headquartered in North Carolina. Lowe's uses large distribution centers (called DCs) to coordinate shipments between suppliers and retail stores. The DCs receive large truckload shipments from suppliers, a strategy that allows Lowe's to save on item costs as well as transportation costs. Employees at the DCs then remix the incoming goods and deliver them to individual stores, as often as twice a day.

But that isn't all. The DCs use computer-based information systems to closely coordinate incoming shipments from suppliers with outgoing shipments to individual

Many companies use cross-docking systems to simultaneously lower transportation and inventory costs. Such systems illustrate how supply chain management can provide a competitive advantage.

retail stores. In fact, more than half the goods that come off suppliers' trucks are immediately put onto other trucks bound for individual stores, a method known as *cross-docking*. The result is that both the DCs and the retail stores hold minimal amounts of inventory, yet Lowe's receives the cost breaks associated with large shipments from suppliers (see Figure 2.4).

Why has Lowe's spent millions of dollars developing this distribution system? One reason is that it helps to keep costs low and the availability of goods high—performance dimensions that its targeted customers value highly. Just as important, Lowe's distribution system has emerged as a core competency that will serve the company well, even as the marketplace changes. Their ability to get the right product on the shelf, at the right time of the year, at a cost that the customer is willing to pay, has earned them a strong brand name and a competitive advantage in the marketplace.

Finally, we mentioned earlier in the chapter how core competencies at the functional level can feed back into the business strategy. This is exactly what Hayes and Wheelwright meant by the fourth stage of alignment. Some experts also refer to this as *closing*

FIGURE 2.4 Building Core Competencies at the Operations and Supply Chain Level: Lowe's Distribution System

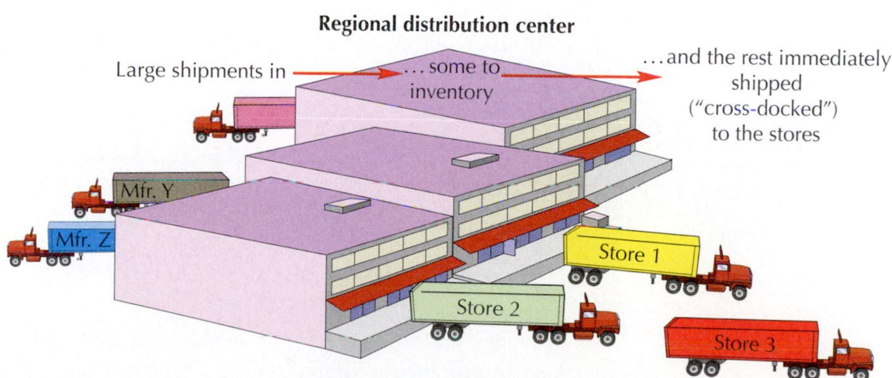

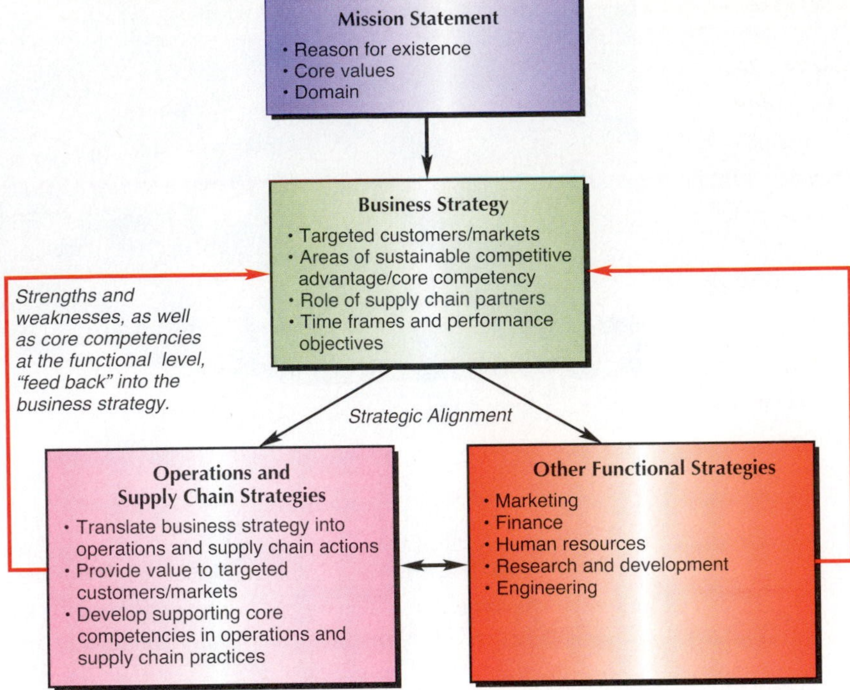

FIGURE 2.5
Closing the Loop between Business Strategy and Functional Area Strategies

the loop. Figure 2.5 illustrates the idea. Firms such as Apple, Lowe's, Honda, and others have developed significant core competencies at the functional level. It makes sense, then, for top managers to look for ways to exploit these strengths. More generally, by closing the loop, top managers assure that the business strategy adequately considers the current capabilities—both positive and negative—within the functional areas.

CHAPTER SUMMARY

The operations and supply chain areas are important providers of value in any organization. To assure that managers make sound operations and supply chain decisions, firms must develop strategies for these functions that are tied to the overall business strategy. This chapter has presented a top-down model of the strategic planning process, with particular attention to the concepts of value, competitive advantage, and core competency.

In the second half of the chapter, we defined the major operations and supply chain decision variables, outlined the four generic performance dimensions (quality, time, flexibility, and cost), and discussed the need to make trade-offs between these key dimensions. We showed how order winner and order qualifier information can help managers understand exactly what their customers demand, so they can make trade-offs in a logical fashion. We ended the chapter with a discussion of the four stages of alignment in operations and supply chain strategy, showing how firms can exploit core competencies in the operations and supply chain areas.

KEY FORMULAS

Value index (page 29):

$$V = \sum_{i=1}^{n} I_n P_n \qquad [2\text{-}1]$$

where:

I_n = Importance of dimension n
P_n = Performance with regard to dimension n

KEY TERMS

Business strategy 24
Changeover flexibility 31
Conformance quality 29
Core competencies 25
Delivery reliability 30
Delivery speed 29
Delivery window 30
Flexibility 30
Functional strategy 25
Infrastructural elements 24
Mission statement 24
Mix flexibility 31
Operations and supply chain strategy 27
Order qualifiers 32
Order winners 32
Performance quality 29
Quality 29
Reliability quality 29
Strategies 24
Structural elements 24
Trade-off 32
Value index 29
Volume flexibility 31

SOLVED PROBLEM

Problem

Calculating Value Indices at WarsingWare

WarsingWare produces specialized shipping containers for food products. The shipping containers help protect the food and keep it from spoiling. In addition, the shipping containers have security devices to ensure that the food is not tampered with. WarsingWare is not the fastest or the cheapest; however, the company prides itself on its ability to provide a wide range of styles to its customers, its strong conformance quality, and its ability to ship products on time. WarsingWare management has rated the firm's performance as shown in Table 2.3.

TABLE 2.3 Performance Dimension Ratings for WarsingWare

DIMENSION	PERFORMANCE (1 = "POOR" TO 5 = "EXCELLENT")
Performance quality	4
Conformance quality	5
Delivery speed	2
Delivery reliability	4
Mix flexibility	5
Cost	2
Volume flexibility	3

WarsingWare has two main customers, Sonco Foods and Gregg Groceries. The relative importance (1 = "completely unimportant" to 5 = "critical") each of these customers places on the dimensions is shown in Table 2.4.

1. According to the value index, which customer—Sonco Foods or Gregg Groceries—currently gets more value out of WarsingWare's products?
2. Suppose WarsingWare decides to reduce its costs by offering fewer design variations. Cost performance will rise to 4, and mix flexibility will fall to 2. Will the customers be more satisfied? Explain.

TABLE 2.4 Importance Ratings for Two Major Customers

DIMENSION	SONCO FOODS	GREGG GROCERIES
Performance quality	4	1
Conformance quality	5	4
Delivery speed	1	5
Delivery reliability	4	3
Mix flexibility	3	2
Cost	4	4
Volume flexibility	4	1

Solution

Table 2.5 shows the value indices for Sonco Foods and Gregg Groceries. Sonco is currently receiving greater value from WarsingWare than Gregg is. This is due in part to the fact that Sonco places a fairly high degree of importance on the dimensions that WarsingWare is particularly good at—performance quality, conformance quality, delivery reliability, and mix flexibility. On the other hand, Gregg does not value any of these four dimensions as highly as Sonco.

TABLE 2.5 Value Indices for Two Major Customers

		Importance		*Value Index*	
	PERFORMANCE	SONCO	GREGG	SONCO	GREGG
Performance quality	4	4	1	16	4
Conformance quality	5	5	4	25	20
Delivery speed	2	1	5	2	10
Delivery reliability	4	4	3	16	12
Mix flexibility	5	3	2	15	10
Cost	2	4	4	8	8
Volume flexibility	3	4	1	12	3
Totals:				**94**	**67**

Now suppose WarsingWare reduces its costs, but does this by reducing its mix flexibility. The *new* value indices are shown in Table 2.6.

According to Table 2.6, the value index for Gregg rises to 69, but Sonco's value index actually falls to 93. Whether or not this is an acceptable trade-off will depend on the relative importance of these two customers to WarsingWare, and WarsingWare's position vis-à-vis competitors.

TABLE 2.6 New Value Indices for Two Major Customers

		Importance		*Value Index*	
	PERFORMANCE	SONCO	GREGG	SONCO	GREGG
Performance quality	4	4	1	16	4
Conformance quality	5	5	4	25	20
Delivery speed	2	1	5	2	10
Delivery reliability	4	4	3	16	12
Mix flexibility	2	3	2	6	4
Cost	4	4	4	16	16
Volume flexibility	3	4	1	12	3
Totals:				**93**	**69**

DISCUSSION QUESTIONS

1. Consider the sales history for the iPod, shown in Figure 2.1. Apple's business strategy has been to introduce a new iPod generation around October, just in time for the holiday season. What are the advantages of doing this? From a supply chain perspective, what are the challenges? How might Apple's business strategy affect the level of emphasis Apple places on delivery speed and volume flexibility when choosing suppliers?
2. Go to the Web and see if you can find the mission statement for a business or school you are familiar with. Is it a useful mission statement? Why or why not? From what you can tell, are the operations and supply chain strategies consistent with the mission statement?
3. We have talked about how operations and supply chain strategies should be based on the business strategy. But can strategy flow the other way? That is, can operations and supply chain capabilities drive the business strategy? Can you think of any examples in industry?
4. Is it enough to just write down the business strategy of a firm? Why or why not? Conversely, what are the limitations of not writing down the strategy, and instead depending on the firm's actions to define the strategy?
5. Chances are you are a college student taking a course in operations or supply chain management. What were the order winners and qualifiers you used in choosing a school? A degree program?
6. Different customers can perceive the value of the same product or service very differently. Explain how this can occur. What are the implications for developing successful operations and supply chain strategies?
7. Go back and look at Hayes and Wheelwright's four stages of alignment. Do firms actually have to develop and then exploit core competencies in the operations and supply chain areas in order to be successful? That is, do all firms need to reach Stage 4?

PROBLEMS

Additional homework problems are available at www.prenhall.com/bozarth. These problems use Excel to generate customized problems for different class sections or even different students.

(* = easy; ** = moderate; *** = advanced)

1. (*) You have just graduated from college and are looking to buy your first car. Money is tight right now, so you are concerned with initial cost as well as ongoing expenses. At the same time, you don't want to drive a slow, ugly car like your parents do. You have narrowed your choices down to two vehicles: a Honda Enigma and a Porsche Booster. Based on the numbers below, calculate the value index for each car. Which car provides you with the greatest value?

DIMENSION	IMPORTANCE TO YOU	HONDA ENIGMA	PORSCHE BOOSTER
Fuel economy	3	5	2
Reliability	5	5	2
Speed and handling	4	2	5
Aesthetics	4	2	5
After-sales support	2	4	4
Purchase price	4	4	1

2. A Chicago-based manufacturer is looking for someone to handle its shipments to the West Coast. In order to evaluate potential transportation providers, the manufacturer has developed the following criteria.

   At a minimum, a shipper must be able to:

   a. Pick up shipments in less than eight hours from the time it is notified (the manufacturer doesn't have enough space for shipments to sit around at the dock).
   b. Deliver shipments in 72 hours or less.

   Beyond this, shippers will be evaluated according to cost and the percentage of shipments that arrive undamaged.

   Three shippers—McAdoo, Klooless, and Big Al—have put in bids for the business. The relevant performance information for the shippers is shown in the following chart:

	MCADOO	KLOOLESS	BIG AL
Pickup time	6 hours	8 hours	9 hours
Shipping time	48 hours	72 hours	36 hours
Cost per 100 lbs. shipped	$20	$30	$15
% of shipments that arrive undamaged	98%	95%	99%

   a. (**) Using Figure 2.3 as a guide, graph how well each of the shippers performs with regard to the order winners and qualifiers.

b. (**) Who is most likely to win the business? Why?
c. (**) What's going on with Big Al? What does Big Al need to do in order to compete successfully for the business?
d. (**) Comment on Klooless's competitive position. Does it meet the minimum requirements? Is the company very competitive? Why or why not?

3. Reconsider Figure 2.3. Suppose Supplier B improves its conformance quality so that the chemicals it produces are now 99.9% pure. The figure at the middle of this page shows the new competitive situation:
   a. (*) Will this be enough to make Supplier B competitive? Which supplier do you think will win the business?
   b. (**) Managers at Supplier A have determined that if they increase the minimum order size to 80 liters, they can decrease their costs to $18 per liter. Should they do it? Explain your logic. (*Hint:* There is no single right answer to this problem.)

4. (***) (*Microsoft Excel problem*) The chart at the bottom of the page shows an Excel spreadsheet that calculates the value index for two alternative suppliers. Re-create this spreadsheet in Excel. You should develop the spreadsheet so that the results will be recalculated if any of the values in the highlighted cells are changed. Your formatting does not have to be exactly the same, but the numbers should be. (As a test, see what happens if you change all of the importance scores to 3. Your new value indices for Supplier 1 and Supplier 2 should be 72 and 63, respectively.)

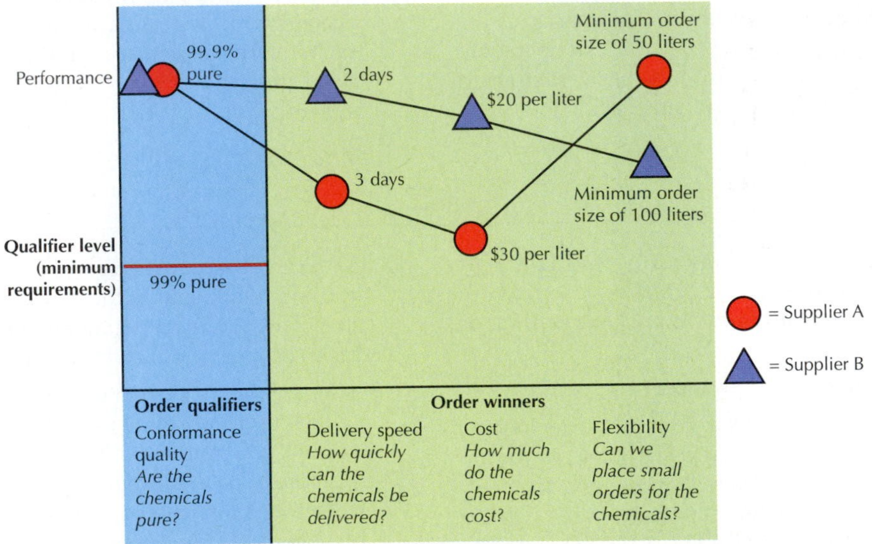

	A	B	C	D	E	F	G
1	**Calculating the Value Index for Two Alternative Suppliers**						
2							
3	Performance: 1 = "poor" to 5 = "excellent"						
4	Importance: 1 = "completely unimportant" to 5 = "critical"						
5							
6				Performance		Value Index	
7			Importance	Supplier 1	Supplier 2	Supplier 1	Supplier 2
8	Performance quality		5	4	3	20	15
9	Conformance quality		4	5	4	20	16
10	Delivery reliability		2	5	4	10	8
11	Delivery speed		3	1	3	3	9
12	Cost		2	3	5	6	10
13	Mix flexibility		2	2	1	4	2
14	Volume flexibility		3	4	1	12	3
15					**Totals:**	**75**	**63**

CASE STUDY

CATHERINE'S CONFECTIONARIES

Catherine Horton was an expert cook, and she enjoyed immensely the creative freedom of developing new dishes. Her specialty was desserts—for years, her friends had raved about her creations, and many had suggested she go into business for herself.

About seven years ago, Catherine took the plunge. At first, she worked out of her home, generating sales through word of mouth and a small advertisement in the Yellow Pages. Most of her initial sales were for special occasions, such as weddings and banquets. Catherine would plan with the customer, usually weeks in advance. This gave her plenty of time to order the ingredients and prepare the desserts beforehand.

Soon Catherine found that she was making the majority of sales to other businesses, such as restaurants and specialty grocery stores. These business customers would order more regularly, but they also wanted Catherine to quickly adjust the mix and quantity of items she made for them. These customers also were more price sensitive than individual customers.

As sales continued to increase, Catherine outgrew the ability to use her own kitchen. She thought that if she could increase sales just a little more, she could quit her regular job and work full time in the dessert business.

Things didn't work out exactly as planned. In order to find a kitchen suitable for her needs, Catherine leased a space that had been previously used as a restaurant. Even though this space was less than ideal, she could not afford to build and equip the perfect site for the business. Not only was the lease payment more than Catherine anticipated, but also there was a large space she had no real use for (the former eating space). Catherine decided to use the space to generate extra revenue by making extra desserts and selling them on a piece-by-piece basis to walk-in customers. This forced her to add two salespeople.

Catherine had hoped that hiring the salespeople would free her from the walk-in business, but this was not the case. Because the walk-in business was fairly small, especially at first, she could afford to pay only minimum wage. Catherine found she was spending much of her time training and supervising these folks, and because the minimum wage caused high employee turnover rates, the hiring and training never stopped.

Catherine soon found that she did not have enough time to manage both the make-to-order customers and her new walk-in business. So Catherine hired a local homemaker (Mary) part time to help make the desserts and a recent business school graduate (Tom) to keep the books and manage the walk-in business. While the extra help was greatly appreciated, it made Catherine's financial situation even more tenuous.

While taking a rare day off, Catherine reflected on her situation. After almost seven years, she was getting burned out, was no longer enjoying her work, and was putting in 15-hour days at least six days a week, and the business was still barely profitable. She felt she had been pulled away from the original focus of the business (the focus that she enjoyed) and now found almost no time to be creative and attempt new recipes.

QUESTIONS

1. What are the three major types of customers Catherine serves? How do they differ from one another? What do you think the order winners are for each group?
2. Consider Catherine's decision to lease the restaurant space (a structural decision). Was this decision consistent with the needs of her different customers? Why? How did this decision change Catherine's business?
3. Consider Catherine's initial decision to hire unskilled labor to help with the walk-in business (an infrastructural decision). Was this decision consistent with the needs of her different customers? Why?
4. Catherine is clearly unhappy with the way things are going right now. What would you suggest she do? What information would you like to have before making a decision?

REFERENCES

Books and Articles

Hayes, R., and S. Wheelwright. *Restoring Our Competitive Edge.* New York: John Wiley, 1984.

Hill, T. *Manufacturing Strategy: Text and Cases.* Boston: Irwin McGraw-Hill, 2000.

Kirpatrick, D. "The Future of IBM." *Fortune Magazine* 145, no. 2 (February 18, 2002): 60–68.

Magretta, J. "The Power of Virtual Integration: An Interview with Dell Computer's Michael Dell." *Harvard Business Review* 76, no. 2 (March–April 1998): 73–84.

Stalk, G. "Time—The Next Source of Competitive Advantage." *Harvard Business Review* 66, no. 4 (July–August 1988): 41–51.

Internet

American Society for Quality, "Glossary," **www.asq.org/info/glossary/a.html**

Apple Corporation, Annual Reports, 2005–2007.

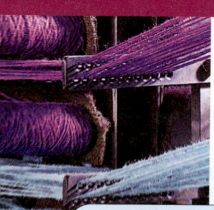

CHAPTER 3

Business Processes

CHAPTER OUTLINE

Chapter Objectives

By the end of this chapter, you will be able to:

- Explain what a business process is and how the business perspective differs from a traditional, functional perspective.
- Create process maps for a business process and use these to understand and diagnose a process.
- Calculate and interpret some common measures of process performance.
- Discuss the importance of benchmarking and distinguish between competitive benchmarking and process benchmarking.
- Describe the Six Sigma methodology, including the steps of the DMAIC process.
- Use and interpet some common continuous improvement tools.
- Explain what the Supply-Chain Operations Reference (SCOR) model is, and why it is important to businesses.

PROCTER & GAMBLE[1]

Procter & Gamble (P&G) is one of the world's largest consumer-goods firms, with such well-known brands as Tide detergent, Crest toothpaste, and Pampers disposable diapers. In the mid-1990s, P&G was organized around five business sectors: laundry and cleaning, paper goods, beauty care, food and beverages, and health care. To the folks within P&G, this made a lot of sense. Dividing such a large organization along product lines allowed each business sector to develop product, pricing, and promotion policies, as well as supply chain strategies, independent of one another.

But to the distributors and retailers who were P&G's direct customers, the view was quite different. Each of these customers had to deal with five separate billing and logistics processes—one for each business sector (Figure 3.1). As Ralph Drayer, vice president of Efficient Consumer Response for Procter & Gamble, noted, this created a wide range of problems:

> *P&G did not allow customers to purchase all P&G brands together for delivery on the same truck. Some customers might go several days without receiving an order, only to have several trucks with P&G orders arrive at the receiving dock at the same time on the same morning.*

FIGURE 3.1 Procter & Gamble Prior to Streamlined Logistics Initiative

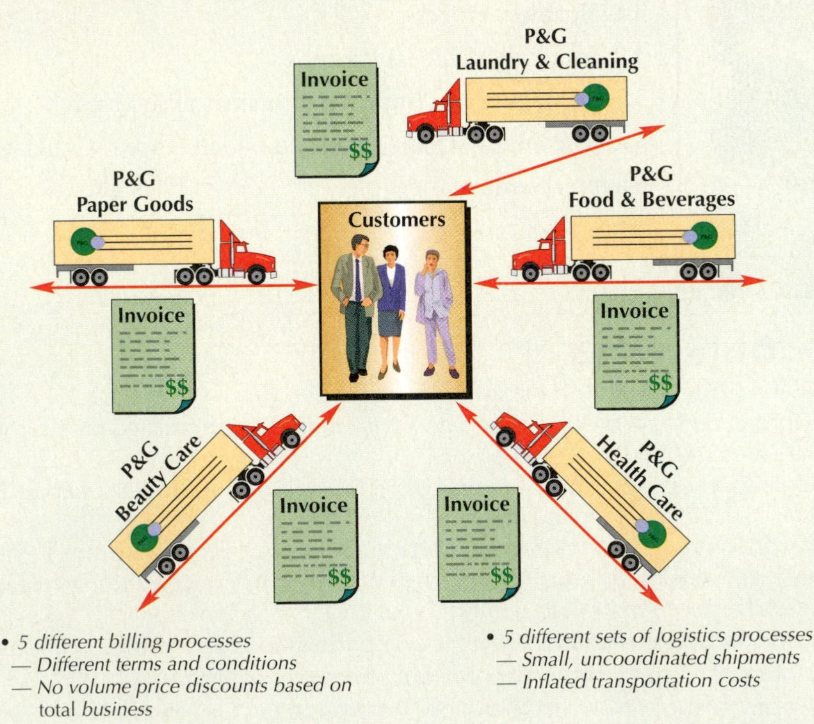

[1] R. Drayer, "Procter & Gamble's Streamlined Logistics Initiative," *Supply Chain Management Review* 3, no. 2 (Summer 1999): 32–43.

Different product categories were shipped on different trucks with different invoices. The trade promotions process was so complex that more than 27,000 orders a month *required manual corrections . . . The separate pricing and promotion policies, coupled with noncoordinated management of logistics activities across the five business sectors, resulted in as many as nine prices per item and order quantities of less-than-full truckloads.*

In 1994, P&G launched its Streamlined Logistics initiative. Among many other things, it drastically reduced the number of new products being introduced (many of which only served to confuse consumers) and simplified the pricing and promotion structure. But, more important, P&G redesigned the information and physical flows across the business sectors so that customers had to deal with only *one* P&G billing process and *one* set of logistics processes (Figure 3.2). The effort required significant collaboration between the logistics team as well as marketing, finance, operations, human resources, and information systems. The results were dramatic:

- Full truckloads were shipped 98% of the time, resulting in dramatically lower transportation costs.
- The number of invoices customers had to handle fell from 25% to 75%. At a processing cost of $35 to $75 for each invoice, this represented a substantial savings to P&G's customers.
- Customers were able to get volume discounts from P&G based on their *total* purchase volume. Under the previous system, this had been difficult, if not impossible, to do.

Procter & Gamble's Streamlined Logistics initiative not only improved profitability for P&G and its customers, but also served as a model for other manufacturers in the industry who have made similar efforts to simplify and streamline their own business processes.

FIGURE 3.2 Procter & Gamble after Streamlined Logistics Initiative

• One integrated billing process
— Administrative cost savings passed on to customers
— Volume discounts applied across all purchases

• One set of logistics processes
— Full-truckload quantities shipped 98% of the time, resulting in substantial transportation cost savings

INTRODUCTION

In recent years, corporate executives and management theorists alike have recognized the importance of putting in place business processes that effectively manage the flow of information, products, and money across the supply chain. One reason is the dollars involved: Experts estimate that total supply chain costs represent the majority of the total operating budget for most organizations; in some cases they may be as high as 75%.[2]

Another reason is the increased emphasis on providing value to the customer. Look again at Procter & Gamble's Streamlined Logistics initiative. P&G used the customer as a

[2]F. Quinn, "What's the Buzz? Supply Chain Management: Part 1," *Logistics Management* 36, no. 2 (February 1997): 43.

focal point for reinventing and simplifying its billing and logistics processes. Because of these efforts, customers found their relationship with P&G to be more rewarding.

The purpose of this chapter is to give you a solid understanding of what business processes are and how the business process perspective differs from more traditional perspectives. We will describe various tools and techniques companies use to manage and improve business processes. In paticular, we will introduce you to the Six Sigma methodology, including the DMAIC (Define-Measure-Analyze-Improve-Control) approach to business process improvement. We end the chapter with a discussion of the Supply-Chain Operations Reference (SCOR) model, which gives companies a common language and model for designing, implementing, and evaluating supply chain business processes.

3.1 BUSINESS PROCESSES

Business process
"A set of logically related tasks or activities performed to achieve a defined business outcome."

Primary process
A process that addresses the main value-added activities of an organization.

Support process
A process that performs necessary, albeit non-value-added, activities.

Development process
A process that seeks to improve the performance of primary and support processes.

So, just what do we mean by the term *business process*? APICS defines a **business process** as "a set of logically related tasks or activities performed to achieve a defined business outcome."[3] For our purposes, these outcomes can be physical, informational, or even monetary in nature. Physical outcomes might include the manufacture and delivery of goods to a customer; an informational outcome might be registering for college courses; and, finally, a monetary outcome might include payment to a supply chain partner for services rendered. Of course, many business processes have elements of all three.

Primary processes address the main value-added activities of an organization. They include activities such as delivering a service and manufacturing a product. These processes are considered "value-added" because some customer is willing to pay for the resulting outputs. In contrast, **support processes** perform necessary, albeit non-value-added, activities. An example is tuition billing. No student wants to pay tuition, and the university would rather not spend the overhead required to collect it, but the university would not be able to sustain itself for very long without monetary flows from the students. Last, **development processes** are those that improve the performance of primary and support processes.[4] Table 3.1 gives examples of primary, support, and development processes.

As with our discussion of supply chains in Chapter 1, you may be saying to yourself that "business processes aren't new," and, once again, you'd be right. What *is* new is the level of attention these processes have attracted in recent years. Prior to the 1990s, most managerial attention was on the activities within specific business *functions*, such as marketing, operations, logistics, and finance. The assumption was that if companies concentrated on how these functions were organized, how individuals were trained, and how the individual functional strategies lined up with the overall business strategy (Chapter 2), then everything would be fine.

TABLE 3.1
Examples of Business Processes

PRIMARY PROCESSES	SUPPORT PROCESSES	DEVELOPMENT PROCESSES
Providing a service	Evaluating suppliers	Developing new products
Educating customers	Recruiting new workers	Performing basic research on improving product
Manufacturing a product	Developing a sales and operations plan (S&OP)	Training new workers

[3]J. F. Cox and J. H. Blackstone, eds., *APICS Dictionary*, 11th ed. (Falls Church, VA: APICS, 2004).
Note: All references to APICS dictionary are for the online dictionary at **www.apics.org**.

[4]B. Andersen, *Business Process Improvement Toolbox* (Milwaukee, WI: ASQ Quality Press, 1999).

FIGURE 3.3
Examples of Business Processes That Cut across Functions and Organizations

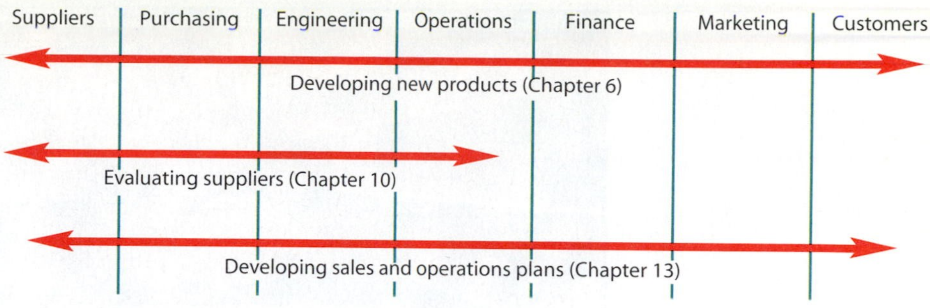

The problem was, however, that managing functions is not the same as managing what a business *does*. Look again at the business processes listed in Table 3.1. Nearly every one of these processes spans multiple functional areas and even multiple supply chain partners. Every function must be aware of the impact of their actions and decisions on other functions, since they all "touch" the process at different times. All too often, people are unaware of the impact of their decisions and actions on other functions, leading to problems with the process.

Figure 3.3 shows three of the business processes we will discuss in this book and how they cut across both functions and organizations. There are other processes that we have not shown here, but our point is this: For many business processes, no single function or supply chain partner has a complete view or complete control of the situation. Developing superior business processes therefore requires a cross-functional and cross-organizational perspective that actively looks at the logical flow of activities that make up a business process. We will expand on this idea in the next section.

Improving Business Processes

Let's illustrate the idea of improving business processes with an example many college students are familiar with: enrolling in classes each semester. Not too long ago students had to interact with three distinct functional areas in order to register: the individual colleges or departments (which granted permission to take classes), the registrar's office (which managed the actual enrollment process), and the cashier's office (which handled tuition payments). A student would first visit his home college or department to pick up the proper permission forms, then schedule his classes, and finally pay tuition. Of course, any problem in the system could force the student to revisit one or more of these areas.

This process was convenient for everyone but the students. Now many colleges and universities have reorganized these activities into a single process with a focus on speed, accuracy, and convenience to the students. Students can now register and pay tuition all with one phone call or visit to a Web site. In some cases, students can even purchase their books and have them automatically delivered to them. The key point is this: Improving the enrollment process required the different functional areas to look beyond their own activities and see the process through the *customers'* (i.e., students') eyes.

Improving business processes is at the very core of operations and supply chain management. For one thing, the performance level of most processes tends to decrease over time unless forces are exerted to maintain it. In addition, even if an organization does not feel a need to improve its business processes, it may be forced to due to competitive pressures. Procter & Gamble's Streamlined Logistics initiative forced competitors, such as Kraft

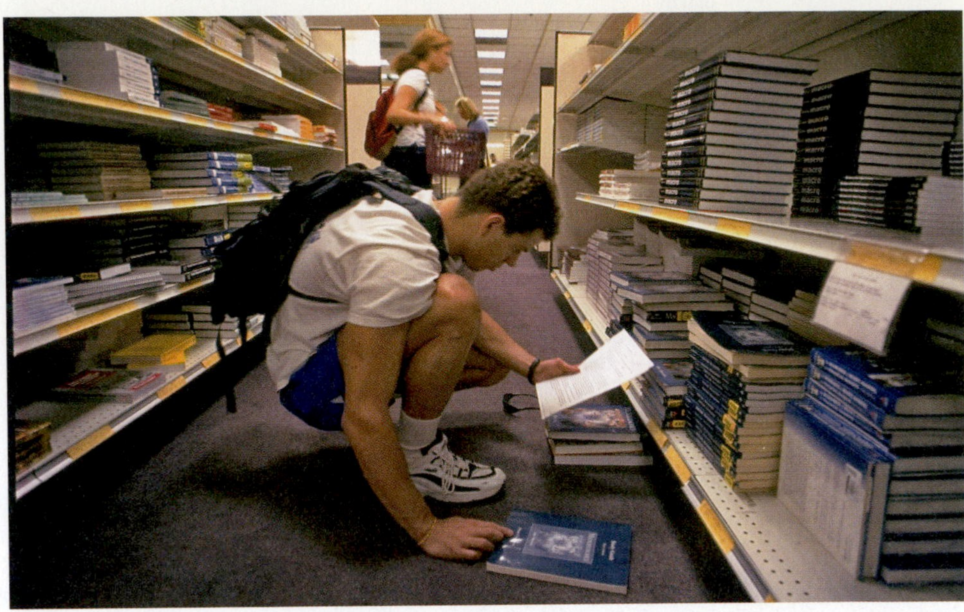

Many universities have already combined course registration and tuition payments into a single, integrated process. How could the purchase of textbooks and other materials be brought into the process?

Foods, to undertake similar process improvement efforts.[5] Finally, today's customers are becoming more and more demanding—what a customer might have considered quite satisfactory a few years ago might not meet his or her requirements today.

3.2 MAPPING BUSINESS PROCESSES

Mapping
The process of developing graphic representations of the organizational relationships and/or activities that make up a business process.

Process map
A detailed map that identifies the specific activities that make up the informational, physical, and/or monetary flows of a process.

Before firms can effectively manage and improve a business process, they must understand it. One way to improve understanding is by developing graphic representations of the organizational relationships and/or activities that make up a business process. This is known as **mapping**. Done properly, mapping serves several purposes:

- It creates a common understanding of the content of the process: its activities, its results, and who performs the various steps.
- It defines the boundaries of the process.
- It provides a baseline against which to measure the impact of improvement efforts.

Process Maps

A **process map** identifies the specific activities that make up the information, physical, or monetary flows of a process. Process maps often give managers their first complete picture of how the process works. Experts have developed a set of graphical symbols to

[5] S. Tibey, "How Kraft Built a 'One-Company' Supply Chain," *Supply Chain Management Review* 3, no. 3 (Fall 1999): 34–42.

FIGURE 3.4
Common Process Mapping Symbols

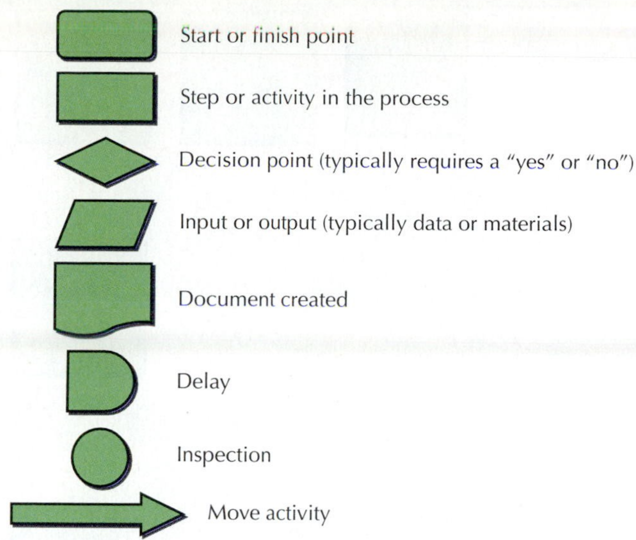

represent different aspects of the process. Figure 3.4 shows some of the more common symbols used.

Because of the level of detail required, process flowcharts can quickly become overly complex or wander off the track unless some conscious effort is made to maintain focus. Some useful rules for maintaining this focus include:

1. **Identify the entity that will serve as the focal point.** This may be a customer, an order, a raw material, or the like. The mapping effort should then focus on the activities and flows that are associated with the movement of this entity through the process.
2. **Identify clear boundaries and starting and ending points.** Recall our earlier example about a manufacturer who wanted to "better understand how it processes customer orders." To develop the process map, the manufacturer must decide on the starting and ending points. Will the starting point be when the customer places the order or when the manufacturer receives it? Similarly, will the flowchart end when the order is shipped out of the plant or when the order is actually delivered to the customer? The manufacturer might also decide to focus only on the physical and information flows associated with the order, and not the monetary flows.
3. **Keep it simple.** Most people developing process maps for the first time tend to put in *too much* detail. They develop overly complex maps, often subdividing major activities into several smaller ones that don't provide any additional insight or including logical branches to deal with every conceivable occurrence, even ones that very rarely occur. There are no simple rules of thumb for avoiding this trap, other than to ask whether the additional detail is important to understanding the process and whether it is worth the added complexity.

Let's illustrate these ideas with an example we are all familiar with: a customer visiting a restaurant. The customer is greeted by a host, who then seats the customer. A waitress takes the customer's order, delivers the drinks and food, and writes up and delivers the check. Finally, a cashier takes the customer's money.

Figure 3.5 shows a simplified map of the process for this restaurant, which we will call the Bluebird Café. In this example, the focal point is the customer—the process begins when the customer enters the Bluebird Café and ends when she leaves. Notice too that many activities that occur in the restaurant are *not* included in this particular map—scheduling

FIGURE 3.5
Process Map for the Bluebird Café

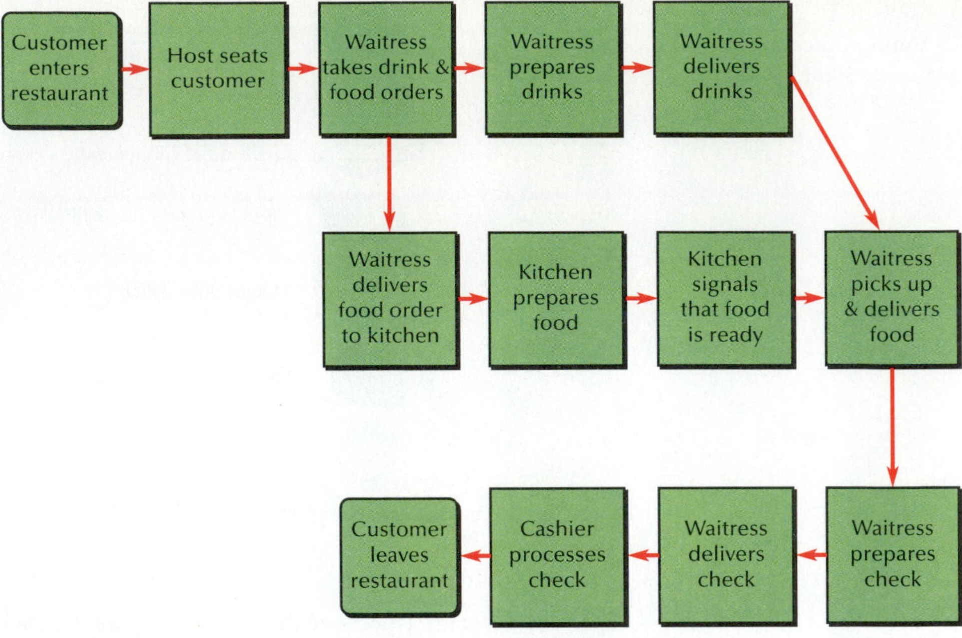

employee work hours, planning deliveries from suppliers, prepping food, and so forth. This is because our current focus is on the customer's interactions with the restaurant. Even so, our "simplified" map still has 11 distinct steps.

With the major customer interaction points laid out, we can start to see how important each of the steps is to the customer's overall satisfaction with her dining experience. We might also start to ask how the Bluebird Café can measure and perhaps improve its performance. Example 3.1 illustrates a somewhat more complex process map for a fictional distribution center. As you read through the example, ask yourself the following questions:

- What is the focal point of the process mapping effort?
- What are the boundaries and the start and stop points for the process map?
- What detail is not included in this example?

Example 3.1

Process Mapping at a Distribution Center

A San Diego distribution center (DC) has responsibility for supplying products to dealers located within a 30-mile radius. Lately, the DC has been receiving a lot of complaints from dealers regarding lost orders and the time required to process orders for items that are already in stock at the DC. A process improvement team has decided to study the process in more detail by tracing the flow of a dealer order through the DC, starting from when the dealer faxes in the order and ending with the order's delivery to the dealer. The team has collected the following information:

- The dealer faxes an order to the DC. Sometimes the paper gets jammed in the fax machine or an order gets thrown away accidentally. Employees estimate that about 1 in 25 orders is "lost" in this manner.
- The fax sits in an inbox anywhere from zero to four hours, with an average of two hours, before the fax is picked up by the DC's internal mail service.
- It takes the internal mail service one hour, on average, to deliver the order to the picking area (where the desired items are picked off the shelves). The range is 0 to 1.5 hours.

In addition, 1 out of 100 orders is accidentally delivered to the wrong area of the DC, resulting in additional "lost" orders.

- Once an order is delivered to the picking area, it sits in the clerk's inbox until the clerk has time to process it. The order might wait in the inbox anywhere from zero to two hours, with an average time of one hour.
- Once the clerk starts processing the order, it takes her about five minutes to determine whether the item is in stock.
- If the requested product is in stock, a worker picks the order and puts it into a box. Average picking time is 20 minutes, with a range of 10 minutes to 45 minutes.
- Next, an inspector takes about two minutes to check the order for correctness. Even with this inspection, 1 out of 200 orders shipped has the wrong items or quantities.
- A local transportation firm then takes the completed order and delivers it to the dealer (average delivery time is two hours, but can be anywhere from one to three hours). The transportation firm has an exemplary performance record: Over the past five years, the firm has never lost or damaged a shipment or delivered to the wrong dealer.
- If the item being ordered is out of stock, the clerk notifies the dealer and passes the order on to the plant, which will arrange a special shipment directly to the dealer, usually within a week.

Using the symbols from Figure 3.4, the process improvement team draws the process map for the order-filling process of in-stock items (Figure 3.6). The map includes detailed information on the times required at each step in the process, as well as various quality problems. Adding up the times at each process step, the team can see that the average time between ordering and delivery for an in-stock item is about 6.45 hours (387 minutes) and can be as long as 11.37 hours (682 minutes). If an item is not in stock, it will take even longer to be delivered.

Of the 6.45 hours an order spends on average in the process, a full 3 hours is waiting time. Finally, 5% of the orders are "lost" before they even get to the picking area. For the orders that do survive to this point, 1 out of 200 will be shipped with the incorrect items or quantities. Clearly there is room for improvement.

FIGURE 3.6 Order-Filling Process for In-Stock Items

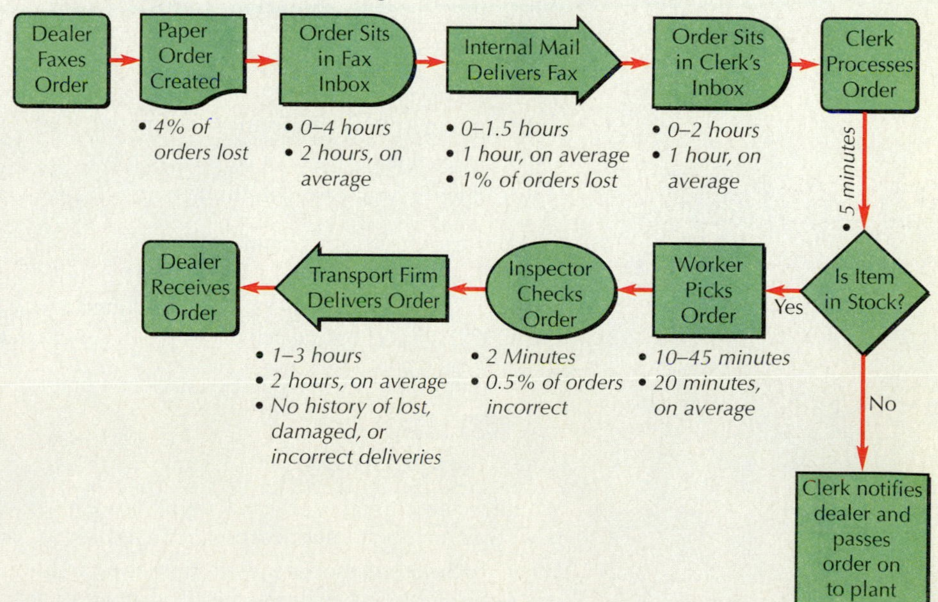

Once the process has been mapped, the team considers ways to improve the process. It is clear that the order-filling process is hampered by unnecessary delays, "lost" paperwork, and an inspection process that yields less-than-perfect results. One potential improvement is to have dealers place orders electronically, with this information sent directly to the picking area. Not only would this cut down on the delays associated with moving the fax through the DC, but also it would cut down on the number of "lost" orders. Errors in the picking and inspection process will require additional changes.

Keep in mind that the idea is to document the process, *as it is*, not the way people remember it. In some cases, employees might need to physically walk through the process, "stapling themselves" to a document or a product. Second, management will need to decide which parts of the process to look at. Areas that are beyond a manager's control or are not directly related to the problem at hand can be omitted from the process mapping effort. In Example 3.1, the focus was on *in-stock* items, so the flowchart did not go into detail regarding what happens if the product is out of stock.

Table 3.2 lists some guidelines to use in identifying opportunities to improve a process. In general, personnel should critically examine each step in the process. In many cases, steps can be improved dramatically or even eliminated.

Swim Lane Process Maps

Sometimes we are interested in understanding not only the steps in a process, but *who* is involved and how these parties interact with one another. In the restaurant example, at least four people were involved in serving the customer—the host, the waitress, the cook, and

TABLE 3.2
Guidelines for Improving a Process

1. Examine each delay symbol
   What causes the delay? How long is it?
   How could we reduce the delay or its impact?
2. Examine each activity symbol
   Is this an unnecessary or redundant activity?
   What is the value of this activity relative to its cost?
   How can we prevent errors in this activity?
3. Examine each decision symbol
   Does this step require an actual decision (Example—"Do we want to accept this customer's order?"), or is it a simple checking activity (Example—"Is the inventory in stock?")? If it is a checking activity, can it be automated or eliminated? Is it redundant?
4. Look for any loops (arrows that go back to a previous point in the process)

   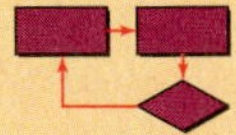

   Would we need to repeat these activities if we had no failures? (Example—cooking a new steak for a customer because the first one was cooked incorrectly.)
   What are the costs associated with this loop (additional time, resources consumed, etc.)? Can this loop be eliminated? If so, how?

Process mapping can be critical to understanding and managing the complex flows of information in many service environments such as healthcare.

Swim lane process map
A process map that graphically arranges the process steps so that the user can see who is responsible for each step.

the cashier. **Swim lane process maps** graphically arrange the process steps so that the user can see who is responsible for each step. As John Grout of Berry College puts it, "The advantage of this mapping approach is that process flows that change 'lanes' indicate hand-offs. This is where lack of coordination and communication can cause process problems. It also shows who sees each part of the process."[6]

Example 3.2 illustrates a swim lane process map that Professor Grout developed to show the process experienced by a patient undergoing a surgical procedure. Notice that there is a "lane" for each of the nine entities involved in the process, and that two errors occurred, one of which could have had serious ramifications.

Example 3.2

Swim Lane Process Map for a Medical Procedure[7]

Professor John Grout
Campbell School of Business, Berry College

Figure 3.7 shows the swim lane process map for a patient undergoing a lumpectomy (the surgical removal of a small tumor from the breast). Nine parties, including the patient, were involved in the process. In this case, the patient detected two errors in the process. Error 1 occurred when the surgeon intended to employ a needle locator to identify the location of the tumor, but failed to forward an order to that effect to the hospital. The patient identified the omission prior to surgery. No harm occurred. Error 2 was a typographic error on the pathology report indicating that the tumor was 1.6 *millimeters* in diameter, when in fact it was 1.6 *centimeters*. While this could have been a more serious mistake, a phone call to confirm the correction avoided any harm.

---

[6] John Grout, Campbell School of Business, Berry College, Mount Berry, Georgia, **http://csob.berry.edu/faculty/jgrout/processmapping/Swim_Lane/swim_lane.html.**
[7] Ibid.

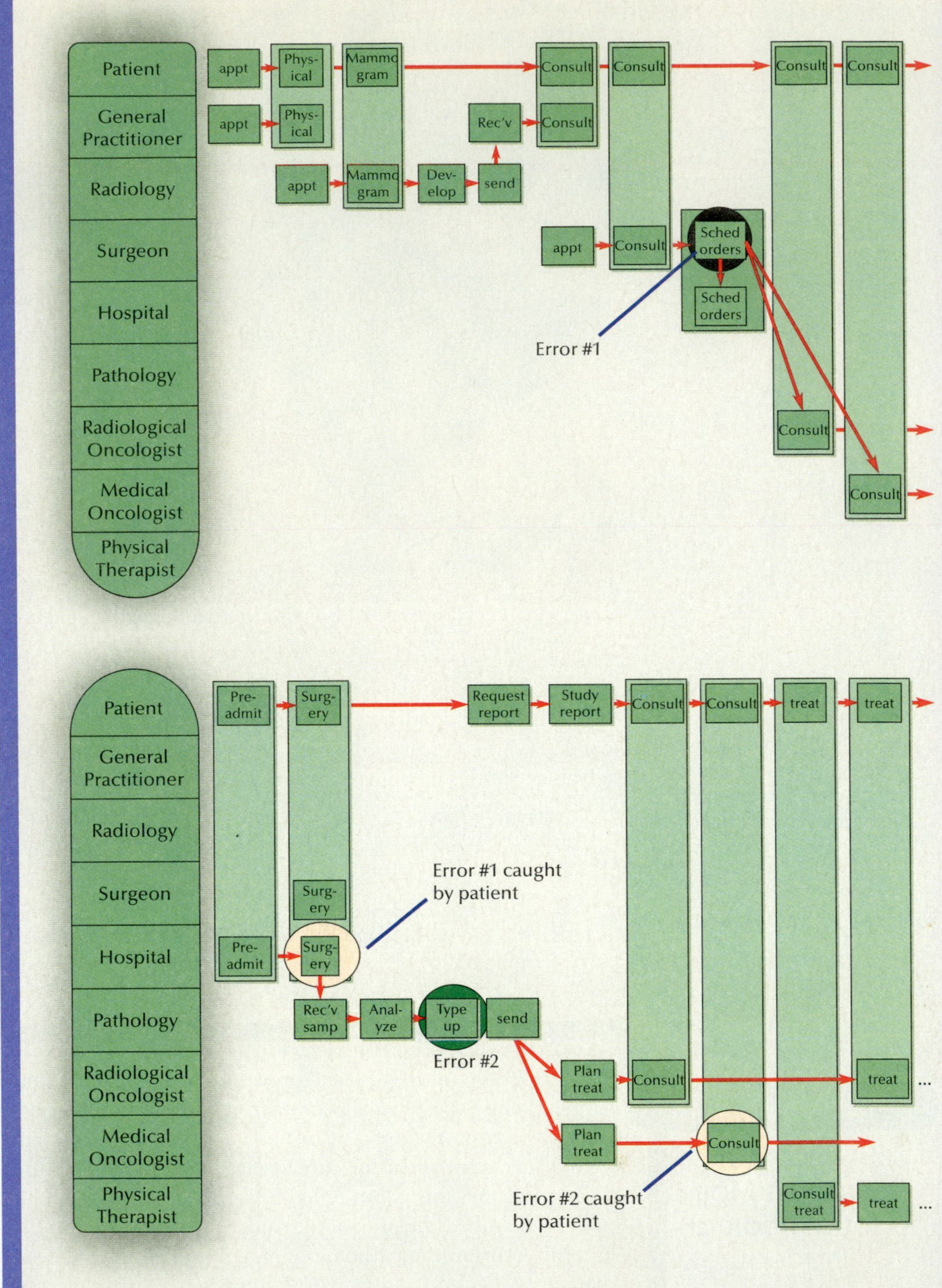

FIGURE 3.7 Swim Lane Process Map for a Surgical Procedure
(*Source:* John Grout, Campbell School of Business, Berry College, Mount Berry, Georgia. **http://csob.berry.edu/faculty/jgrout/processmapping/Swim_Lane/swim_lane.html**)

3.3 MANAGING AND IMPROVING BUSINESS PROCESSES

By now, you should appreciate how critical business processes are to the success of an organization. But you still might wonder how businesses should go about managing and improving these processes. For instance:

- How do we know if a business process is meeting the customers' needs? Even if the customers' needs are being met, how do we know whether the business process is being run efficiently and effectively?
- How should we organize for business process improvement? What steps should we follow? What roles should people play?
- What types of tools and analytical techniques can we use to rigorously evaluate business processes? How can we make sure we manage based on fact and not opinion?

Organizations have been asking these same questions for years. As a result, experts have developed various measures, methodologies, and tools for managing business processes. In fact, the body of knowledge continues to evolve as more is learned about what works and what doesn't. In this section, we will introduce you to current thinking in the area.

Measuring Business Process Performance

Before we can answer the question, "How is the process performing?," we must first understand what it is the customer wants and calculate objective performance information for the process. Let's reconsider the process mapping exercise in Example 3.1 for a moment. Suppose one of the San Diego DC's key customers has told DC management that:

1. All deliveries for in-stock items must be made within eight hours from when the order was placed.
2. Order conformance quality must be 99% or higher. That is, 99% of the orders must be delivered with the right items in the right quantities.

Furthermore, the customer has told DC management that these are *order qualifiers*—if the DC cannot meet these minimum requirements, then the customer will take his business elsewhere. In Example 3.1, the DC managers determined that the time between ordering and delivery for an in-stock item could be as long as 11.37 hours and that less than 95% of the orders were processed properly. Clearly, there is a gap between what the customer needs and what the process is currently able to provide.

There are countless possible measures of process performance, many of which are derived from the four performance dimensions described in detail in Chapter 2:

1. *Quality*, which can be further divided into dimensions such as performance quality, conformance quality, and reliability quality. Chapter 4 includes a comprehensive discussion of the various dimensions of quality.
2. *Cost*, which can include such categories as labor, material, and quality-related costs, to name just a few.
3. *Time*, which includes such dimensions as delivery speed and delivery reliability.
4. *Flexibility*, including mix, changeover, and volume flexibility.

That said, some specific measures that are frequently used to evaluate process performance are productivity, efficiency, and cycle (or throughput) time. Productivity and efficiency measures are particularly important to managers because they evaluate business process performance from the perspective of the firm. We discuss each of these in more detail.

Productivity

Productivity
A measure of process performance; the ratio of outputs to inputs.

One measure that often comes up in discussions is **productivity**. Productivity is a ratio measure, defined as follows:

$$\text{Productivity} = \text{outputs/inputs} \quad \textbf{[3-1]}$$

Productivity measures are always expressed in terms of units of output per unit of input. The outputs and inputs can be expressed in monetary terms or in some other unit of measure. In general, organizations seek to improve productivity by raising outputs, decreasing inputs, or both. Some examples of productivity measures include the following:

(Number of customer calls handled)/(support staff hours)

(Number of items produced)/(machine hours)

(Sales dollars generated)/(labor, material, and machine costs)

Single-factor productivity
A productivity score that measures output levels relative to a single input.

Multifactor productivity
A productivity score that measures output levels relative to more than one input.

The first two examples represent single-factor productivity measures. **Single-factor productivity** measures output levels relative to a single input. In the first example, we are interested in the number of calls handled per support staff hour, while the second measure looks at the number of items produced per machine hour. The assumption is that there is a one-to-one relationship between the output and input of interest that can be managed. In contrast, when it's hard to separate out the effects of various inputs, **multifactor productivity** measures should be used. Look at the last example. "Sales dollars generated" is an output that depends on multiple factors, including labor, material, and machine costs. Considering just labor costs may be inappropriate, especially if labor costs could be driven down by driving some other cost up (such as machine costs). In situations like this, multifactor productivity measures may be preferable.

Though there are some common productivity measures used by many firms, often organizations develop productivity measures that are tailored to their particular needs. Firms use productivity measures to compare their performance to that of other organizations, as well as to compare performance against historic levels or set targets.

Example 3.3

Measuring Productivity at BMA Software

For the last 15 weeks, a project team at BMA Software has been working on developing a new software package. Table 3.3 shows the number of programmers assigned to the project each week, as well as the resulting total lines of computer code generated.

Susan Clarke, the project manager, has heard rumblings from other managers that her programmers aren't being as productive as they were a few weeks earlier. In order to determine whether this is true, Susan develops a measure of programmer productivity, defined as (*lines of code*)/(*total number of programmers*). Using this measure, Susan calculates the productivity numbers in Table 3.4 for the first 15 weeks of the project.

The results indicate that the programmers have actually been *more* productive over the last few weeks (weeks 13–15) than they were in the weeks just prior. In fact, the weekly productivity results for weeks 13–15 are higher than the average weekly productivity for all 15 weeks (1,992.70). Of course, Susan recognizes that there are other performance measures to consider, including the quality of the lines coded (whether they are bug-free) and the difficulty of the lines being coded (which would tend to hold down the number of lines generated).

TABLE 3.3
Programming Results for First 15 Weeks of Project

WEEK	LINES OF CODE	NO. OF PROGRAMMERS
1	8,101	4
2	7,423	4
3	8,872	4
4	8,483	4
5	8,455	5
6	10,100	5
7	11,013	5
8	8,746	5
9	13,710	7
10	13,928	7
11	13,160	7
12	13,897	7
13	12,588	6
14	12,192	6
15	12,386	6

TABLE 3.4
Productivity Results for First 15 Weeks of Project

WEEK	LINES OF CODE	NO. OF PROGRAMMERS	PRODUCTIVITY (LINES OF CODE PER PROGRAMMER)
1	8,101	4	2,025.25
2	7,423	4	1,855.75
3	8,872	4	2,218.00
4	8,483	4	2,120.75
5	8,455	5	1,691.00
6	10,100	5	2,020.00
7	11,013	5	2,202.60
8	8,746	5	1,749.20
9	13,710	7	1,958.57
10	13,928	7	1,989.71
11	13,160	7	1,880.00
12	13,897	7	1,985.29
13	12,588	6	2,098.00
14	12,192	6	2,032.00
15	12,386	6	2,064.33
		Average Productivity:	**1,992.70**

Efficiency

Efficiency
A measure of process performance; the ratio of actual outputs to standard outputs. Usually expressed in percentage terms.

Standard output
An estimate of what should be produced, given a certain level of resources.

While measures of productivity compare outputs to inputs, measures of **efficiency** compare *actual* outputs to some standard—specifically:

$$\text{Efficiency} = 100\%(\text{actual outputs}/\text{standard outputs}) \qquad [3\text{-}2]$$

The **standard output** is an estimate of what should be produced, given a certain level of resources. This standard might be based on detailed studies or even historical results. The efficiency measure, then, indicates actual output as a percent of the standard. An efficiency score of less than 100% suggests that a process is not producing up to its potential.

To illustrate, suppose each painter on an assembly line is expected to paint 30 units an hour. Bob actually paints 25 units an hour, while Casey paints 32. The efficiency of each painter is therefore calculated as follows:

$$Efficiency_{Bob} = 100\%\left(\frac{25}{30}\right) = 83\% \qquad Efficiency_{Casey} = 100\%\left(\frac{32}{30}\right) = 107\%$$

Currently, Bob is performing below the standard. If his efficiency were to remain at this level, management might either intervene with additional training to raise his hourly output level or reassign Bob to another area.

Example 3.4
Measuring Efficiency at BMA Software

Based on the results of her productivity study, Susan Clarke decides to set a standard for her programmers of 1,800 lines of code per programmer per week. Susan consciously set the standard slightly below the average productivity figure shown in Table 3.4. Her reasoning is that she wants her programmers to be able to meet the standard, even when they are dealing with particularly difficult code.

In week 16, Susan hires a new programmer, Charles Turner. After five weeks on the job, Charles has recorded the results in Table 3.5. Susan calculates Charles's efficiency by dividing the actual lines of code produced each week by the standard value of 1,800. Therefore, Charles' efficiency for week 16 is calculated as:

$$\text{Efficiency}_{\text{Week16}} = 100\%(1{,}322/1{,}800) = 73.4\%$$

Results for all five weeks are shown in Table 3.6.

TABLE 3.5
Programming Results for Charles Turner

WEEK	LINES OF CODE
16	1,322
17	1,605
18	1,770
19	1,760
20	1,820

TABLE 3.6
Efficiency Results for Charles Turner

WEEK	LINES OF CODE	EFFICIENCY
16	1,322	73.4%
17	1,605	89.2%
18	1,770	98.3%
19	1,760	97.8%
20	1,820	101.1%

Although Charles started off slowly, his efficiency has steadily improved over the five-week period. Susan is pleased with the results, recognizing that Charles needs some time to become familiar with the project. Nonetheless, she will continue to track Charles's efficiency performance.

Cycle Time

Cycle time
The total elapsed time needed to complete a business process. Also called *throughput time.*

The last measure of process performance we will discuss is cycle time. **Cycle time** (also called *throughput time*) is the total elapsed time needed to complete a business process. Many authors have noted that cycle time is a highly useful measure of process performance.[8] For one thing, in order to reduce cycle times, organizations and supply chains typically must perform well on other dimensions, such as quality, delivery, productivity, and efficiency.

Consider the order-filling process in Figure 3.6. In this case, cycle time is the time that elapses from when the dealer faxes the order until she receives the product. Notice how the process suffers from delays due to waiting, lost orders, and incorrect orders. Therefore, in order to reduce cycle time, the San Diego DC must address these other problems as well. Notice, too, that reducing cycle times does not mean "fast and sloppy." The process cannot be considered "complete" until the dealer receives a *correctly filled* order.

A second advantage of cycle time is that it is a straightforward measure. In comparison to cost data, quality levels, or productivity measures—all of which may be calculated and interpreted differently by various process participants—the time it takes to complete a business process is unambiguous.

Percent value-added time
A measure of process performance; the percentage of total cycle time that is spent on activities that actually provide value.

In addition to measuring cycle time in absolute terms, it is often useful to look at the **percent value-added time**, which is simply the percentage of total cycle time that is spent on activities that actually provide value:

$$\text{Percent value-added time} = 100\%(\text{value-added time})/(\text{total cycle time}) \qquad [3\text{-}3]$$

For example, what is the percent value-added time for the typical "quick change" oil center? Even though the customer may spend an hour in the process, it usually takes only about 10 minutes to actually perform the work. According to Equation 3.3, then:

$$\text{Percent value-added time} = 100\%(10 \text{ minutes})/(60 \text{ minutes}) = 16.7\%$$

[8] J. Blackburn, *Time-Based Competition: The Next Battle Ground in American Manufacturing* (Homewood, IL: Irwin, 1991); G. Stalk and T. Hout, *Competing against Time: How Time-Based Competition Is Reshaping Global Markets* (New York: Free Press, 1990); C. Meyer, *Fast Cycle Time: How to Align Purpose, Strategy, and Structure for Speed* (New York: Free Press, 1993).

Of course, cycle time is not a perfect measure. Our discussion in Chapter 2 of trade-offs between performance measures applies here as well. It might not be cost effective, for example, to drive down cycle times at the drivers' license bureau by quadrupling the number of officers (*but don't you wish they would?*). Therefore, organizations that use cycle time to measure process performance should also use other measures to make sure cycle time is not being reduced at the expense of some other key performance dimension.

Benchmarking

Benchmarking
"The process of identifying, understanding, and adapting outstanding practices from within the same organization or from other businesses to help improve performance."

Competitive benchmarking
The comparison of an organization's processes with those of competing organizations.

Process benchmarking
The comparison of an organization's processes with those of noncompetitors that have been identified as superior processes.

Organizations often find it helpful to compare their business processes against those of competitors or even other firms with similar processes. This activity is known as benchmarking. Cook defines **benchmarking** as "the process of identifying, understanding, and adapting outstanding practices from within the same organization or from other businesses to help improve performance."[9] Benchmarking involves comparing an organization's practices and procedures to those of the "best" in order to identify ways in which the organization or its supply chain can make improvements.

Some experts make a further distinction between competitive benchmarking and process benchmarking. **Competitive benchmarking** is the comparison of an organization's processes with those of competing organizations. In contrast, **process benchmarking** refers to the comparison of an organization's processes with those of noncompetitors that have been identified as having superior processes. As an example of the latter, many organizations have carefully studied Dell Computer's supply chain practices, even though Dell is not a direct competitor.

To give you an idea of the power of benchmarking, let's look at some classic competitive benchmarking data from the late 1980s that highlighted the quality and productivity leads built up by Japanese automotive manufacturers at the time. Table 3.7 contains two sets of results. The first column compares the quality of the assembly processes for Japanese, U.S., and European plants. The second column compares the labor and machine hours required per vehicle for the same three groups.

The hard-nosed nature of this benchmarking data served as a wake-up call to U.S. and European companies, which then started to study the Japanese system in earnest and subsequently improved their quality and productivity levels.

Now let's look at some 2005 competitive benchmarking data put out by Harbour Consulting that compares North American automotive plant performance across different manufacturers (Table 3.8). The results suggest that while the productivity gap is closing among the various manufacturers, Japanese producers still enjoy a significant per-vehicle profit advantage.

TABLE 3.7
Competitive Benchmarking Data from the Automotive Industry, 1989

	NUMBER OF ASSEMBLY DEFECTS PER 100 VEHICLES	LABOR AND MACHINE HOURS PER VEHICLE
Average Japanese plant	34.0	16.9
Average U.S. plant	64.6	35.7
Average European plant	76.8	57

Source: From J. Womack, D. Jones, and D. Roos, *The Machine That Changed the World: How Japan's Secret Weapon in the Global Auto Wars Will Revolutionize Western Industry* (New York: HarperPerennial, 1991).

---

[9]S. Cook, *Practical Benchmarking: A Manager's Guide to Creating a Competitive Advantage* (London: Kogan Page, 1995), 13.

TABLE 3.8
2005 Competitive Benchmarking Results for North American Automakers

MANUFACTURER	TOTAL ASSEMBLY HRS PER VEHICLE	HOURS PER ENGINE	PRE-TAX PROFIT PER VEHICLE
DaimlerChrysler	23.77	3.79	$223
Ford	23.73	4.77	−$590
GM	22.42	3.60	−$2,496
Honda	21.43	3.27	$1,215
Toyota	21.33	2.90	$1,587
Nissan	18.93	3.67	$2,249

Source: From Harbour Consulting, "Harbour Report North America 2006," **www.harbourinc.com.**

The Six Sigma Methodology

Of all the various approaches to organizing for business process improvement, the Six Sigma methodology arguably best respresents current thinking. It certainly is popular, with many top companies, such as GE, Motorola, and Bank of America, citing it as a key element of their business strategy. Six Sigma has its roots in the quality management discipline (quality management is such an important topic to operations and supply chain managers that we have devoted Chapter 4 to the subject).

Six Sigma methodology
"A business improvement methodology that focuses an organization on understanding and managing customer requirements, aligning key business processes to achieve those requirements, utilizing rigorous data analysis to understand and ultimately minimize variation in those processes, and driving rapid and sustainable improvement to business processes."

The term *Six Sigma* refers to both a quality metric and a methodology. In *statistical terms*, a process that achieves Six Sigma quality will generate just 3.4 defects per one million opportunites (DPMO). As a *methodology* for process improvement, Six Sigma has a much broader meaning. Motorola describes the **Six Sigma methodology** as "a business improvement methodology that focuses an organization on:

- Understanding and managing customer requirements
- Aligning key business processes to achieve those requirements
- Utilizing rigorous data analysis to understand and ultimately minimize variation in those processes
- Driving rapid and sustainable improvement to business processes"[10]

Let's consider this definition for a moment. The first two points reinforce the idea that business process improvement efforts need to be driven by the needs of the customer. In this case, the "customer" can be someone inside the organization as well as someone from outside the organization. The third point emphasizes the use of rigorous data analysis tools to ensure that any diagnoses or recommendations are based on *fact* and not just opinion. Finally, there must be an organizational mechanism in place for carrying out these efforts in a timely and efficient manner.

Champions
Senior-level executivies who "own" Six Sigma projects and have the authority and resources needed to carry them out.

Master black belts
"Full-time Six Sigma experts who are responsible for Six Sigma strategy, training, mentoring, deployment and results."

Black belts
"Fully-trained Six Sigma experts with up to 160 hours of training who perform much of the technical analyses required of Six Sigma projects, usually on a full-time basis."

SIX SIGMA PEOPLE. Six Sigma process improvement efforts are carried out by project teams consisting of people serving specialized roles. In the lexicon of Six Sigma, the teams consist of champions, master black belts, black belts, green belts, and team members. **Champions** are typically senior-level executivies who "own" the projects and have the authority and resources needed to carry them out. This can be particularly important if a Six Sigma effort requires large investments of time or money, or if multiple functional areas or supply chain partners are affected. **Master black belts** are "full-time Six Sigma experts who are responsible for Six Sigma strategy, training, mentoring, deployment and results."[11] These individuals often work across organizations and consult with projects on an as-needed basis, but are not permanently assigned to the projects.

Black belts are "fully-trained Six Sigma experts with up to 160 hours of training who perform much of the technical analyses required of Six Sigma projects, usually on a full-time

[10]Motorola University, **www.motorola.com/motorolauniversity.jsp.**

[11]J. Evans and W. Lindsay, *The Management and Control of Quality* (Mason, OH: Thomson South-Western, 2005).

Green belts
Individuals who have some basic training in Six Sigma methodologies and tools and are assigned to projects on a part-time basis.

Team members
Individuals who are not trained in Six Sigma, but are included on a Six Sigma project team due to their knowledge or direct interest in a process.

DMAIC (Define-Measure-Analyze-Improve-Control) A Six Sigma process that outlines the steps that should be followed to improve *existing* business processes.

DMADV (Define-Measure-Analyze-Design-Verify) A Six Sigma process that outlines the steps needed to create *completely new* business processes or products.

Continuous improvement
The philosophy that small, incremental improvements can add up to significant performance improvements over time.

Root cause analysis
A process by which organizations brainstorm about possible causes of problems (referred to as "effects") and then, through structured analyses and data-gathering efforts, gradually narrow the focus to a few root causes.

basis."[12] **Green belts** have some basic training in Six Sigma methodologies and tools and are assigned to projects on a part-time basis. Finally, there are **team members**, who are individuals with knowledge or direct interest in a process and can also be included on a Six Sigma project team, but are not trained in Six Sigma.

SIX SIGMA PROCESSES. The Six Sigma methodology has its own specialized business processes that project teams follow. The first of these is the **DMAIC (Define-Measure-Analyze-Improve-Control)** process, which outlines the steps that should be followed to improve an *existing* business processes. The steps are as follows:

Step 1. *Define* the goals of the improvement activity. The Six Sigma team must first clarify how improving the process will support the business, and establish performance targets. This ensures that the team doesn't waste time on efforts that will not see a pay-off to either the customer or the business.

Step 2. *Measure* the existing process. The second step requires the team members to develop a basic understanding of how the process works. What are the process steps? Who are the parties who carry out or are otherwise touched by the process? How is the process currently performing? What data do we need to analyze the process and evaluate the impact of any changes?

Step 3. *Analyze* the process. Next, the Six Sigma team will identify the relationships and factors that cause the process to perform the way it does. In doing so, the team members must make sure they identify the true underlying causes of the process's performance. We talk later about two approaches for accomplishing this: cause-and-effect diagrams and the "Five Whys."

Step 4. *Improve* the process. Here, the team identifies ways to eliminate the gap between the current performance level and the performance targets established in Step 1.

Step 5. *Control* the new process. The Six Sigma team must then work with the individuals affected to maintain the process improvements. This may involve such activities as developing process control charts (described in Chapter 4), training workers in any new procedures, and updating information systems to monitor ongoing performance.

The second Six Sigma process is **DMADV (Define-Measure-Analyze-Design-Verify)**, which outlines the steps needed to create *completely new* business processes or products. We review DMADV in the chapter on product and service design (Chapter 6).

Continuous Improvement Tools

Organizations interested in process improvement have a broad collection of data analysis tools to help guide their efforts. Many of these tools, which first appeared in the engineering and quality management disciplines, were specifically designed to help users apply logical thinking and statistical concepts to process improvement efforts.The term **continuous improvement** refers to a managerial philosophy that small, incremental improvements can add up to significant performance improvements over time.

Already in this chapter we have talked about one such tool—process mapping. This section highlights some additional tools: root cause analysis, cause-and-effect diagrams, scatter plots, check sheets, and Pareto charts. As the DMAIC steps suggest, firms need to follow a more formal process to make sure that they have indeed diagnosed the problem(s) correctly. **Root cause analysis** is a process by which organizations brainstorm about possible causes of problems (referred to as "effects") and then, through structured analyses and data-gathering efforts, gradually narrow the focus to a few root causes. Root cause analysis fills the gap between the realization that a problem exists and the proposal and implementation of solutions to the problem.

---

[12]Ibid.

FIGURE 3.8
Cause-And-Effect Diagram

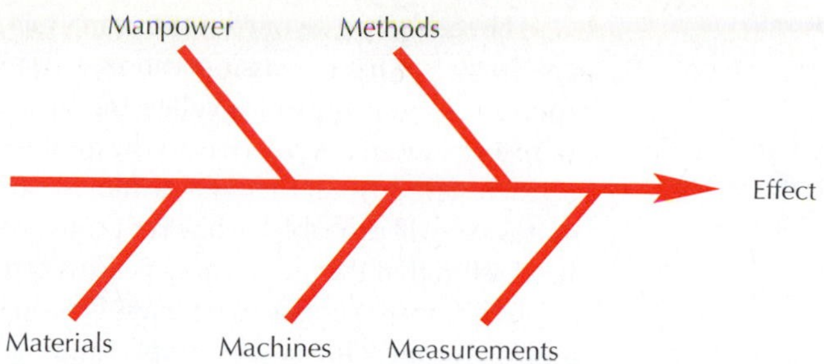

Open phase
The first phase of root cause analysis, devoted to brainstorming.

Cause-and-effect diagram
A graphical tool used to categorize the possible causes for a particular result.

Five M's
The five main branches of a typical cause-and-effect diagram: Manpower, Methods, Materials, Machines, and Measurements.

Organizations often divide root cause analysis into three distinct phases: open, narrow, and closed. The **open phase** is devoted to brainstorming. All team members should be free to make suggestions, no matter how far-fetched they might seem at the time. Teams often use a **cause-and-effect diagram** (also known as a *fishbone* or *Ishikawa diagram*) to organize their thoughts at this stage. Figure 3.8 shows a generic format for a cause-and-effect diagram.

To construct such a diagram, the team members must first describe the "effect" they are seeking a cause for, such as late deliveries, high defect rates, or lost orders. This effect is written on a large poster or chalkboard, at the end of a long arrow. Next the team categorizes the possible causes and places them at the ends of branches drawn along the shaft of the arrow. These branches are often organized around five categories known as the **Five M's**:

- Manpower (people who do not have the right skills, authority, or responsibility)
- Methods (poor business practices; poor process, product, or service designs)
- Materials (poor-quality inputs)
- Machines (equipment that is not capable of doing the job)
- Measurements (performance measurements that are not geared toward eliminating the problem)

Example 3.5

Cause-and-Effect Diagram for a Pump Manufacturer

A Six Sigma team investigating variations in pump shaft dimensions at a pump manufacturer decided to develop a cause-and-effect diagram to identify the possible causes. The resulting diagram is shown in Figure 3.9. The team did not identify any potential causes along the "Measurements" branch; hence, it was left off. Notice that some of the branches are further subdivided in an effort to get to the true underlying causes. For example, "Low motivation" is listed as a possible cause under "Manpower." But why are employees unmotivated? One possible cause, "Low pay," is shown as a branch off of "Low motivation."

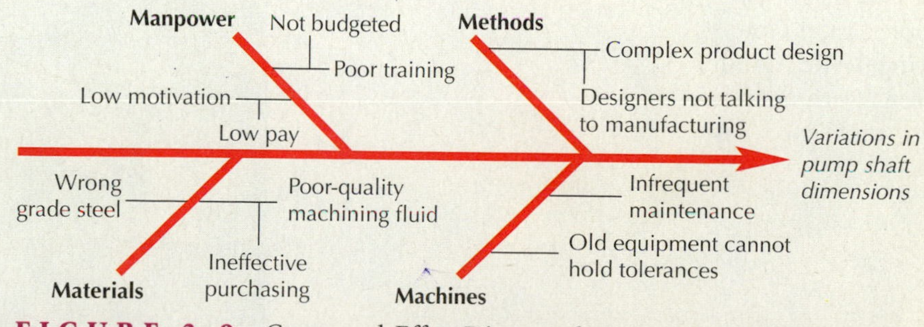

FIGURE 3.9 Cause-and-Effect Diagram for a Pump Manufacturer

The second phase of root cause analysis is known as the *narrow phase*. Here participants pare down the list of possible causes to a manageable number. Some teams formalize this process using an approach called the **Five Whys**. With this approach, the team members brainstorm successive answers to the question, "Why is this a cause of the original problem?" For each new answer, they repeat the question until they can think of no new answers. The last answer will probably be one root cause of the problem. The name comes from the general observation that the questioning process can require up to five rounds.

Five Whys
An approach used during the narrow phase of root cause analysis, in which teams brainstorm successive answers to the question, "Why is this a cause of the original problem?" The name comes from the general observation that the questioning process can require up to five rounds.

To illustrate, suppose a business is trying to understand why a major customer won't pay its bills on time. One possible explanation generated during the open phase is that by delaying payment, the customer is getting a free loan at the business's expense ("Methods"). Using the Five Whys approach, the team members might ask the following series of questions:

Q1: WHY does the customer use our credit as a free loan?
A1: Because there are no penalties for doing so.

Q2: WHY are there no penalties for late payment of our invoices?
A2: Because we charge no penalty fees.

Q3: WHY don't we charge penalty fees?
A3: Because we have never encountered this problem before.

Process improvement efforts must be based on facts, not opinions. Although team members may *think* they have discovered the root cause of a problem, they must verify it before moving on to a solution. In the *closed phase* of root cause analysis, the team validates the suspected root cause(s) through the analysis of available data. Three commonly used data analysis tools are scatter plots, check sheets, and Pareto charts. A **scatter plot** is a graphic representation of the relationship between two variables, typically the root cause and the effect of interest. To illustrate, the scatter plot in Figure 3.10 shows how the defect rate at a manufacturer seems to increase as the amount of weekly overtime increases.

Scatter plot
A graphical representation of the relationship between two variables.

Check sheet
A sheet used to record how frequently a certain event occurs.

Pareto chart
A special form of bar chart that shows frequency counts from highest to lowest.

Bar graph
A graphical representation of data that places observations into specific categories.

Figure 3.10 shows a strong relationship between the two variables of interest. But would the lack of a pattern in a scatter plot mean that a Six Sigma team has failed in its effort to identify a root cause? Not at all. In fact, a scatter plot that shows no relationship between a particular root cause and the effect of interest simply shortens the list of potential root causes that need to be investigated.

Whereas scatter plots highlight the relationship between two variables, check sheets and Pareto charts are used to assess the frequency of certain events. Specifically, **check sheets** are used to record how frequently certain events occur, while **Pareto charts** plot out the resulting frequency counts in **bar graph** form, from highest to lowest.

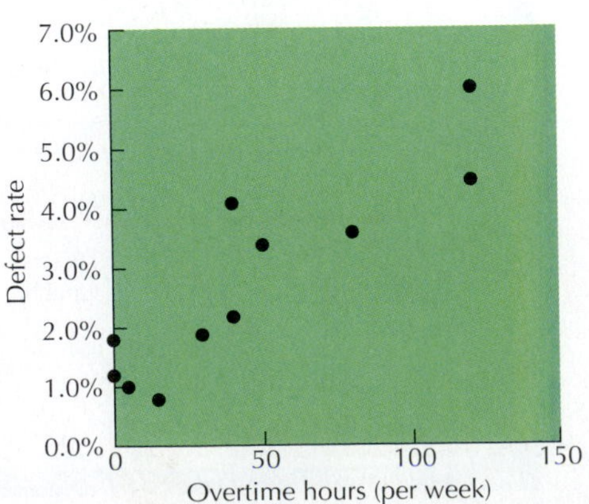

FIGURE 3.10
Example Scatter Plot Showing the Relationship between Overtime Hours (Cause) and Defect Rate (Effect)

Example 3.6

Check Sheets and Pareto Charts at Healthy Foods

The Healthy Foods grocery store is attempting to isolate the root causes of unexpected delays at the checkout counters. The open and narrow phases have resulted in a long list of possible causes, including the register being out of money, price checks, and customers who go back to get items they forgot. In the closed phase, the quality team at Healthy Foods sets up check sheets at each checkout counter. Each time an unexpected delay occurrs, the clerk records the reason for the delay. This process continues until the managers feel they have enough data to draw some conclusions. Table 3.9 shows summary results for 391 delays occurring over a one-week period:

TABLE 3.9 Check Sheet Results for Healthy Foods

CAUSE	FREQUENCY
Price check	142
Register out of money	14
Bagger unavailable	33
Register out of tape	44
Customer forgot item	12
Management override needed due to incorrect entry	86
Wrong item	52
Other	8
Total Delays	**391**

To create the Pareto chart, the Six Sigma team ranks the causes in Table 3.9 from most frequent to least frequent and graphs the resulting data in bar graph form. The Pareto chart for Healthy Foods is shown in Figure 3.11.

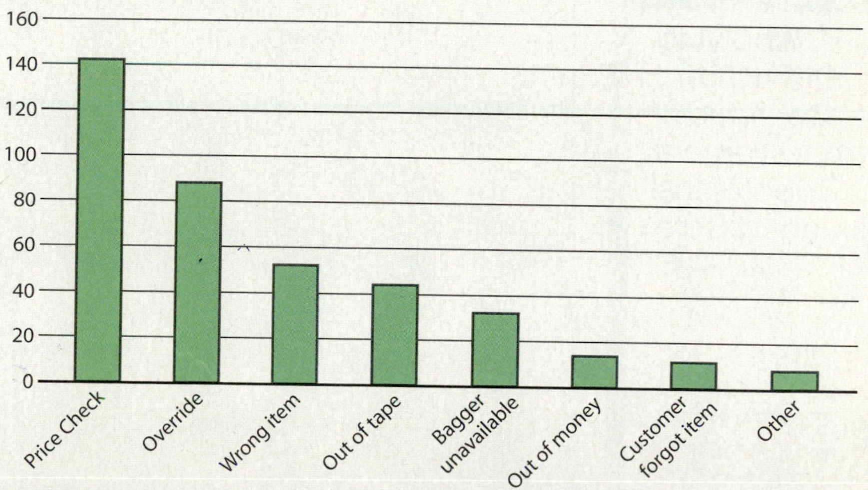

FIGURE 3.11 Pareto Chart Ranking Causes of Unexpected Delays at Checkout Counter

The check sheets and Pareto chart provide the process improvement team with some powerful information. Rather than complaining about customers who forget items (a small problem), the results suggest that Healthy Foods should concentrate on creating more comprehensive and accurate price lists and training clerks to properly use the cash registers. In fact, these two causes alone account for nearly 60% of the delays.

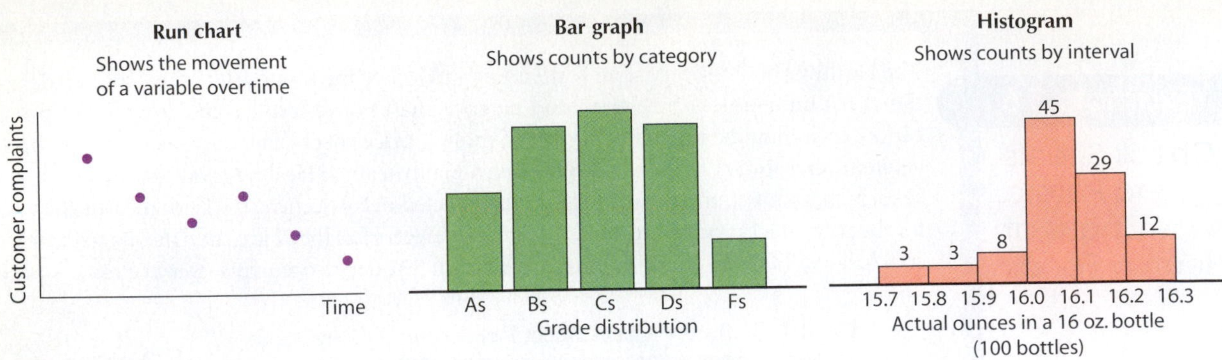

FIGURE 3.12 Additional Data Analysis Tools

Histogram
A special form of bar chart that tracks the number of observations that fall within a certain interval.

Run chart
A graphical representation that tracks changes in a key measure over time.

To complete our discussion of visual tools, Figure 3.12 contains examples and brief descriptions of run charts, bar graphs, and **histograms**. **Run charts** track changes in a key measure over time.

In Example 3.7, we return to the Bluebird Café. The example demonstrates how the DMAIC process and continuous improvement tools can be used to address a customer satisfaction problem.

Example 3.7

Applying DMAIC and Continuous Improvement Tools at the Bluebird Café

Katie Favre, owner of the Bluebird Café, is browsing a Web site that allows individuals to rate restaurants on a 1 to 5 scale, with 1 = "Highly Dissatisfied" and 5 = "Highly Satisfied." Katie is disappointed to learned that, based on several hundred responses, the average rating for the Bluebird Café is only 3.83, and that 12% of respondents actually rated their dining experience as a 1 or 2. Unfortunately, the Web site does not provide any specific information about *why* the customers rated the café as they did. Katie takes great pride in the reputation of the Bluebird Café, and she decides to employ the DMAIC process and continuous improvement tools to tackle the customer satisfaction issue.

STEP 1. *DEFINE* THE GOALS OF THE IMPROVEMENT ACTIVITY. At a meeting with the management team, Katie emphasizes the importance of customer satisfaction to the ongoing success of the business—the Bluebird Café is located in a college town and has plenty of competition. Local customers can go elsewhere if they are dissatisfied, and out-of-town visitors often depend on Internet-based ratings to decide where they will dine. With this in mind, Katie and the management team set a target average rating of 4.5 or greater for any future Internet ratings, with no more than 2% of respondents giving a rating of 1 or 2.

STEP 2. *MEASURE* THE EXISTING PROCESS. Katie already has a process map that identifies the major steps required to serve a customer (Figure 3.5). While this is a good start, the team feels more data is needed. Katie spends a week measuring the time it takes to perform various activities, as well as the percentage of time certain process steps are completed correctly. Figure 3.13 shows the updated process map.

The management team also wants to know what process characteristics lead customers to rate the restaurant as satisfactory or unsatisfactory. To get this information,

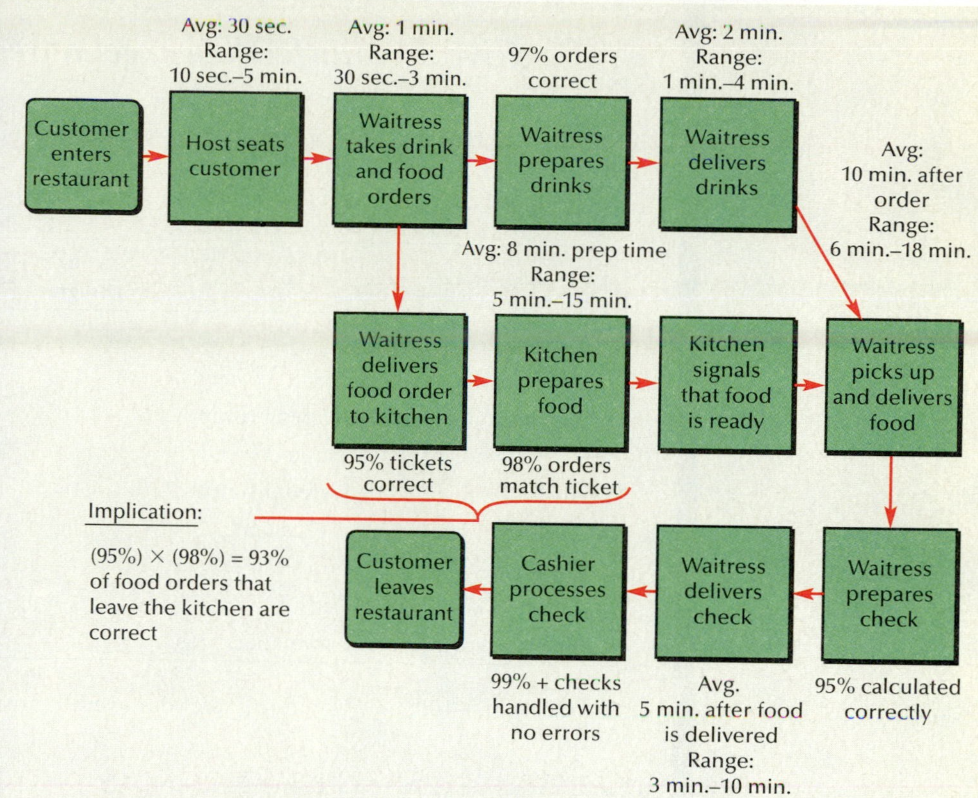

FIGURE 3.13 Process Map for Bluebird Café, Updated to Show Performance Results for Various Steps

Katie puts together a survey card (see Figure 3.14) that is given out to a random sample of customers over several weeks. The survey cards are similar to check sheets, in that they allow the customer to identify particular areas of the café's performance that they are uncomfortable with. Fifty customers fill out the cards.

STEP 3. *ANALYZE* THE PROCESS. Katie and her team are now ready to begin analyzing the process in earnest. Among the tools they use are scatter plots. Figure 3.15 takes the data from the 50 survey cards and plots each customer's overall satisfaction score against his or her response to Question 4 ("My food order was prepared correctly"). Figure 3.16 is similar, except now overall satisfaction scores are plotted against Question 5 results ("My food order was delivered promptly").

Both scatter plots suggest that there is a relationship between customer satisfaction and how correctly and promptly the order is filled, but the results seem particularly strong with regard to order correctness. Put another way, whether or not the food order was prepared correctly appears to have a significant impact on whether the customers are satisfied with their dining experience.

Katie and the team now use the open phase of root cause analysis to brainstorm about possible causes of the orders being prepared incorrectly. The team documents their ideas on a cause-and-effect diagram, from which they identify some potential causes, including "cook not properly trained," "waitress takes incorrect order information," and "food doesn't match menu."

Give us your feedback, get a free Cup of Joe!

The Bluebird Café is always looking for ways to improve your dining experience. Please take a few moments to let us know how we are doing, and **your coffee (or tea or soda) will be on us!**

	Strongly Disagree				**Strongly Agree**
1. I was seated quickly.	1	2	3	4	5
2. My drink order was prepared correctly.	1	2	3	4	5
3. My drink order was delivered promptly.	1	2	3	4	5
4. My food order was prepared correctly.	1	2	3	4	5
5. My food order was delivered promptly.	1	2	3	4	5
6. The menu selection was excellent.	1	2	3	4	5
7. The prices represent a good value.	1	2	3	4	5
8. The café was clean and tidy.	1	2	3	4	5
9. The café has a pleasant ambiance.	1	2	3	4	5

On a scale of 0–100, how would you rate your **overall satisfaction** with your dining experience?

____

Are there any other ideas or comments you'd like to share with us?

____

____

____

FIGURE 3.14 Customer Survey Card for the Bluebird Café

Entering the closed phase of root cause analysis, Katie develops a check sheet and, over the next few weeks, has the staff fill these sheets out each time a customer complains about an incorrect order. The check sheet data is then arranged into a Pareto chart, shown in Figure 3.17.

STEP 4. *IMPROVE* THE PROCESS. In looking at the Pareto chart, the team quickly realizes that the two highest ranked items are really communications problems—the waitress gets the order wrong and the cook hears it incorrectly. Together, these problems account for roughly 62% of the incidences recorded. The third- and fourth-ranked items make up another 30% of the total, and are tied to the failure of the kitchen staff to cook the food properly and match what's put on the plates to what's on the menu.

Armed with this information, the team makes some simple improvements aimed at bringing down the number of orders prepared incorrectly:

1. Waitresses no longer take orders orally, but write them down on an order ticket. The waitresses also repeat the orders back to the customers to verify that the orders are correct.

FIGURE 3.15 Scatter Plot Showing the Relationship between Survey Question 4 ("My food order was prepared correctly") and Customer's Overall Satisfaction Score

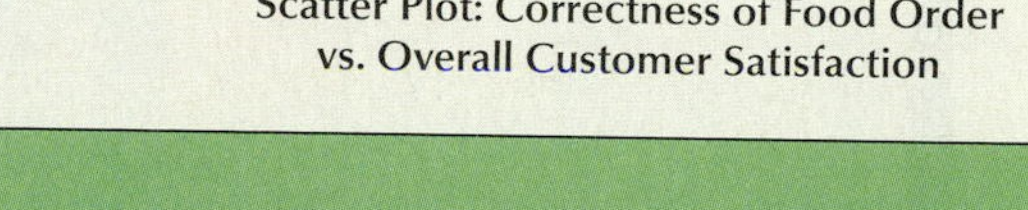

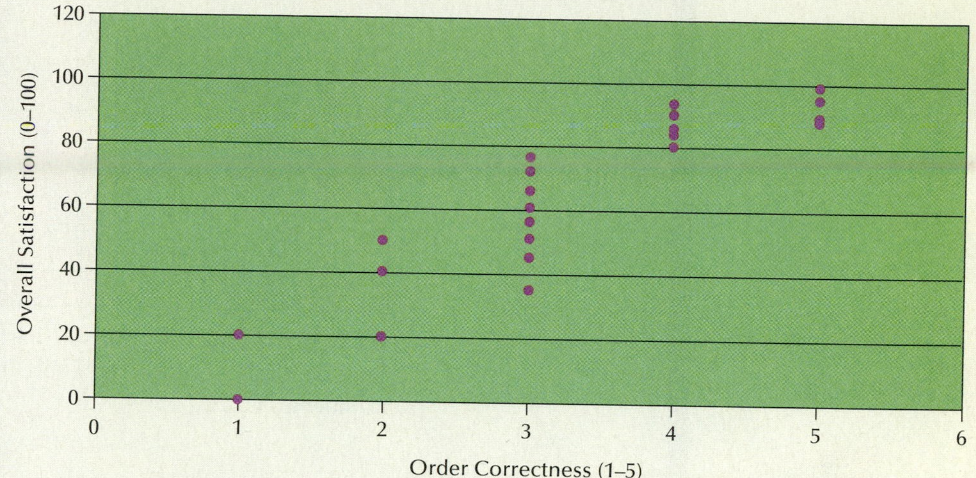

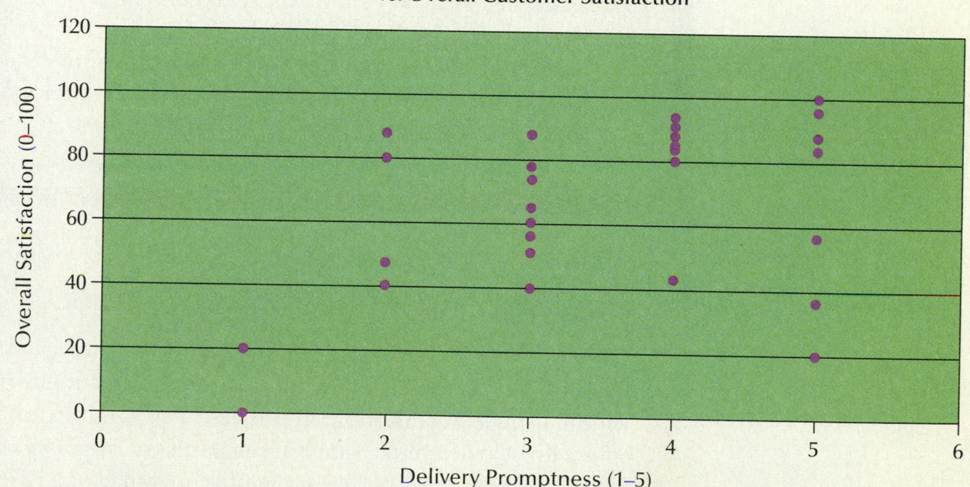

FIGURE 3.16 Scatter Plot Showing the Relationship between Survey Question 5 ("My food order was delivered promptly") and Customer's Overall Satisfaction Score

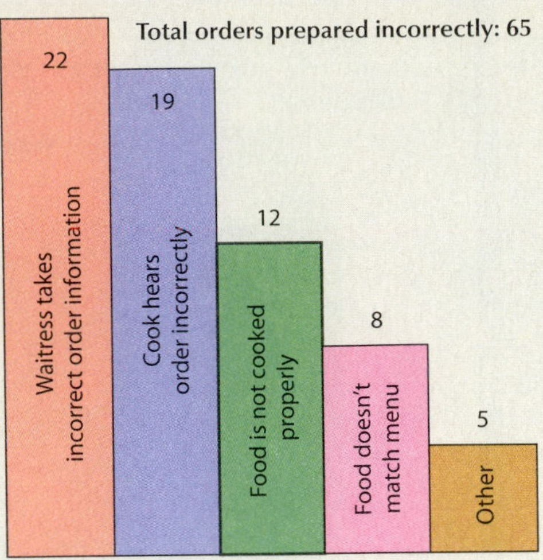

FIGURE 3.17 Pareto Chart Ranking Causes of Incorrect Food Orders at Bluebird Café

2. Cooks are given a written copy of the order ticket.
3. Waitresses compare the prepared dishes against the order ticket, prior to taking it to the customer.
4. Cooks now refer to printed posters hanging on the wall that highlight important cooking steps and show pictures of how each dish should look.

STEP 5. *CONTROL* THE NEW PROCESS. With the changes in place, the café staff make sure that all employees are familiar with the changes and follow the new procedures. Meanwhile, Katie continues to monitor the performance of the Bluebird Café using the Internet-based ratings as well as customer survey cards. After four months, she is pleased to see that the average Internet rating for the Bluebird Café has risen to 4.25—not where she wants to be, but it's on the right track.

Coordinating Process Improvement Efforts across the Supply Chain

In Example 3.7, the Six Sigma process improvement effort was focused on the activities within a single organization, in this case a café. But many times, firms must extend their efforts to include external supply chain partners. The *Supply Chain Connections* feature highlights the experiences of one automotive manufactuer. Extending process management to include external partners is an important step, as significant opportunities for improvement often lie at the interfaces between various partners. But doing so adds greater complexity, given that multiple organizations and their representatives are now participating in the effort.

Business process reengineering (BPR)
"A procedure that involves the fundamental rethinking and radical redesign of business processes to achieve dramatic organizational improvements in such critical measures of performance as cost, quality, service, and speed."

Business Process Reengineering (BPR)

An alternative approach to Six Sigma and the DMAIC process is **business process reengineering (BPR)**. As APICS notes, BPR is "a procedure that involves the fundamental rethinking and radical redesign of business processes to achieve dramatic organizational improvements in

SUPPLY CHAIN CONNECTIONS[13]

CHRYSLER DISCOVERS A PROBLEM

Several years ago Chrysler Corporation began receiving a number of complaints from its dealer network. Apparently, many customers who had purchased Jeep Cherokees were bringing their vehicles in with a serious complaint: While being driven, the Jeeps were running out of gas, yet the fuel gauge showed the tank half-full. Not only was this inconvenient to the customer, it was dangerous, particularly if a vehicle ran out of gas on a busy interstate highway or if weather conditions were poor.

Chrysler investigations revealed that the fuel gauges were indeed showing an incorrect fuel level. Chrysler checked its internal manufacturing processes, but was unable to find the source of the problem. Chrysler then checked its first-tier supplier, who provided the dashboard assembly, but was unable to find the root cause of the problem. Finally, purchasing managers discovered that a third-tier supplier who manufactured the ink for the dashboard gauges had changed the formulation of its ink, which had, in turn, affected the magnetic properties of the dashboard. The supplier had failed to report this change, as no one imagined that this engineering change would have such implications. Unfortunately, the result of this engineering change was that Chrysler's end customers, who were several links down the chain, were now running out of gas with the needle stuck at half-full. Although Chrysler quickly fixed this problem, this illustrates the challenges of managing both the physical and informational flows throughout the supply chain.

[13]Based on a presentation by Jeffrey Trimmer, Vice President of Purchasing, Chrysler Corporation, Michigan State University, East Lansing, June 1998.

such critical measures of performance as cost, quality, service, and speed."[14] Proponents of BPR suggest that organizations should start the BPR process with a "blank sheet" of paper, rather than trying to understand and modify processes that may be severely outdated or dysfunctional. Which approach a firm uses—Six Sigma or BPR—will depend on several factors, including how severe the problems are with the current business process and the ability of process participants to make radical changes.

3.4 THE SUPPLY-CHAIN OPERATIONS REFERENCE (SCOR) MODEL

SCOR model
Supply-Chain Operations Reference model. A comprehensive model of the core management processes and individual process types that together define the domain of supply chain management.

We end this chapter with a discussion of the Supply-Chain Operations Reference (SCOR) Model.[15] The **SCOR model** is a comprehensive model of the core management processes and individual process types that together define the domain of supply chain management. The SCOR model is supported by the Supply-Chain Council, an industry group consisting of hundreds of companies and academics.

Why would companies spend time and money to develop a reference model such as SCOR? Actually, there are several good reasons. For one, a reference model gives individuals a common language for discussing and comparing supply chain business processes. This can be especially important when benchmarking performance or coordinating with other firms to build a supply chain. Second, a reference model provides a template to guide the design and implementation of an organization's own supply chain processes. Third, seeing the processes laid out in a single, comprehensive model helps some managers better understand what supply chain management is all about.

[14]Cox and Blackstone, *APICS Dictionary*.

[15]Supply-Chain Council, 2007, **http://www.supply-chain.org/page.ww?section=SCOR+Model&name=SCOR+Model.**

The SCOR model consists of three levels that describe supply chain processes in increasing detail. Level 1 views SCM as structured around five core management processes:

1. Source—processes that procure goods and services to meet planned or actual demand.
2. Make—processes that transform product to a finished state to meet planned or actual demand.
3. Deliver—processes that provide finished goods and services to meet planned or actual demand. These processes include order management as well as logistics and distribution activities.
4. Return—processes associated with returning or receiving returned products for any reason.
5. Plan—processes that balance aggregate resources with requirements.

Level 2 of the SCOR model further divides SCM activities into what are referred to as process types:

- Planning—a process that aligns expected resources to meet expected demand requirements. Examples include sales and operations planning, master scheduling, and material planning.
- Execution—a process triggered by planned or actual demand that changes the state of material goods.

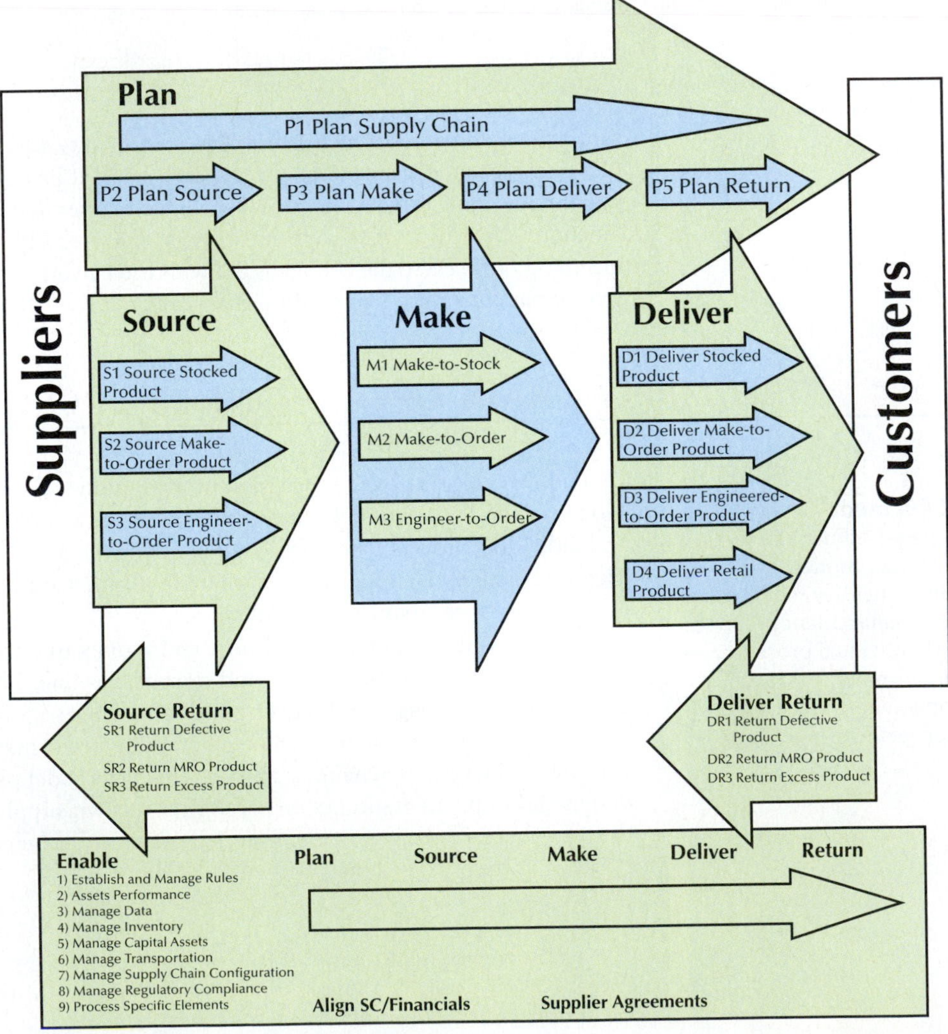

FIGURE 3.18 Overview of the SCOR Model Showing the Five Core Management Processes and the Individual Process Types
(*Source:* Supply-Chain Council, **www.supply-chain.org.**)

- Enable—a process that prepares, maintains, or manages information or relationships on which planning and execution processes rely. Enable processes support the primary value-added activities of an organization, but are not directly involved in them.

Figure 3.18 shows the relationship between the five core management processes and the process types. Note that the SCOR model explicitly recognizes that the information and physical flows required to source, make, deliver, and return a product will differ according to the product's level of customization. For example, make-to-stock products are essentially "off-the-shelf" items completed prior to a specific customer order, whereas engineer-to-order products are custom items that are designed, developed, and manufactured in response to a specific customer request. For an engineer-to-order product, both "source" and "make" activities must wait for the demand signal. Figure 3.18 also shows how "enable" activities fall outside of the five core management processes, but nevertheless perform necessary supporting functions.

FIGURE 3.19
Detailed Process Map for SCOR's "Make Engineer-to-Order"
(*Source:* Phios Product Process Directory for SCOR, **http://repository.phios. com/SCOR/Activity.asp?ID=5394**)

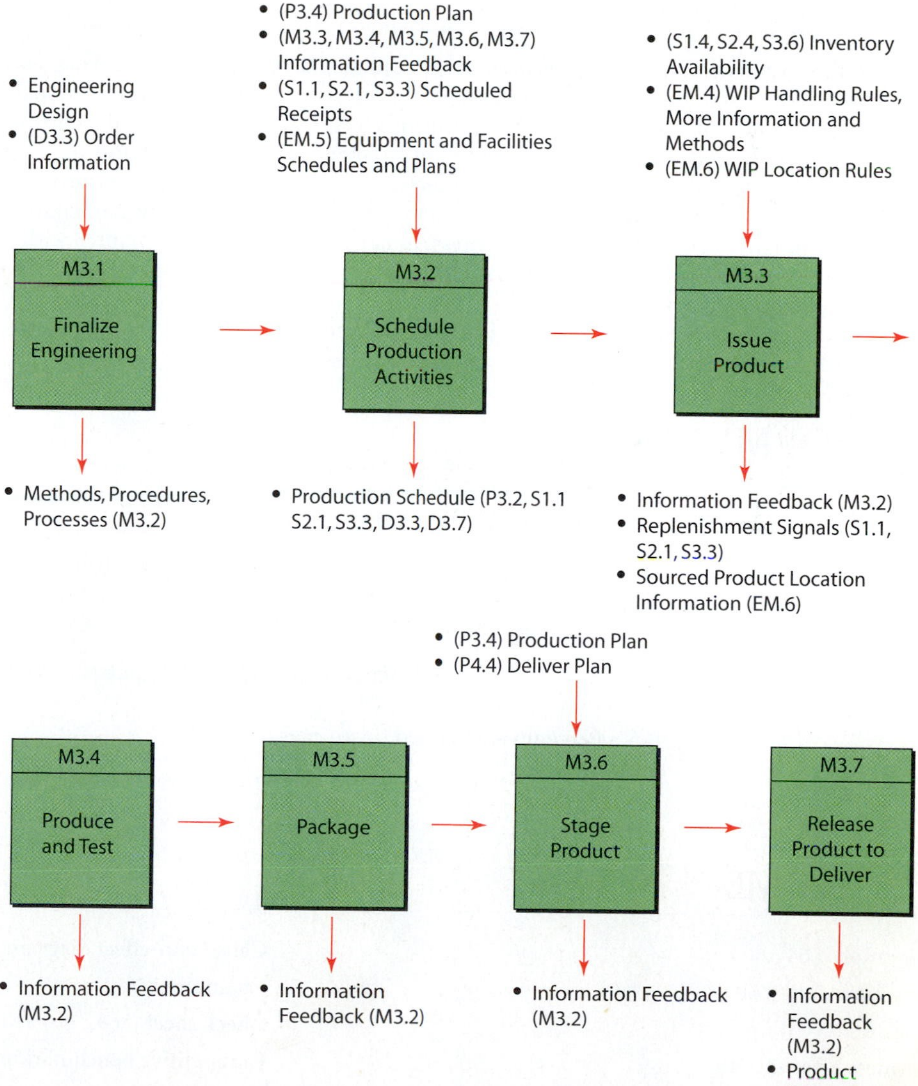

Level 3 of the SCOR model contains generic process maps for the individual process types. Companies can use these maps as a rough guide for developing their own unique processes, or for identifying gaps. Consider the example in Figure 3.19, which shows the process map for one particular process type, "Make Engineer-to-Order Product" (M3).

The process map suggests that manufacturing an engineer-to-order product should consist of seven sequential process "elements," labeled M3.1 through M3.7. The map also shows the prescribed information inflows and outflows to these elements. For example, the second element, "Schedule Production Activities," should take place in response to information inflows, including the production plan, scheduled receipts, feedback from downstream "make" elements, and equipment and facilities schedules and plans. In turn, the information outflow of this element should be an updated production schedule used by the production, sourcing, and distribution areas. Note too that the entire "make engineer-to-order" process, as prescribed by the SCOR model, should contain information links to all five of the core management processes.

CHAPTER SUMMARY

Although the term *business processes* has been in the management lexicon for years, not all organizations clearly understand the importance of business processes and their effects on operations and supply chain performance. In this chapter, we defined the concept of business processes and showed how the business process perspective is different from the traditional, functionally oriented view of business. Business processes change the focus from "How is the business organized?" to "What does the business do?"

Fortunately, practitioners and theorists continue to develop various tools and approaches for managing business processes. In this chapter, we described two process mapping approaches and demonstrated how they could be used. We also spent considerable time talking about various approaches to managing and improving business processes, including performance measurement and benchmarking, the Six Sigma methodology, and continuous improvement tools. We concluded the chapter with a discussion of the SCOR model, which represents an attempt by industry partners to develop a comprehensive model of the various business processes that define supply chain management.

KEY FORMULAS

Productivity (page 56):

$$\text{Productivity} = \text{outputs/inputs} \qquad [3\text{-}1]$$

Efficiency (page 58):

$$\text{Efficiency} = 100\%(\text{actual outputs/standard outputs}) \qquad [3\text{-}2]$$

Percent value-added time (page 59):

$$\text{Percent value-added time} = 100\%(\text{value-added time})/(\text{total cycle time}) \qquad [3\text{-}3]$$

KEY TERMS

Bar graph 64
Benchmarking 60
Black belts 61
Business process 46
Business process reengineering (BPR) 70
Cause-and-effect diagram 63
Champions 61
Check sheet 64
Competitive benchmarking 60
Continuous improvement 62

SOLVED PROBLEM

Problem

Biosphere Products makes and sells environmental monitoring devices for use in industry. These devices monitor and record air quality levels and issue an alarm whenever conditions warrant.

If a monitoring device should fail, Biosphere will repair the device as part of the customer's service agreement. The repair process consists of the following steps:

1. Once the device arrives at Biosphere's repair center, a work order is immediately entered into the computer system. This step takes five minutes.
2. A device will then wait, on average, 24 hours before a technician has a chance to run diagnostics and disassemble the device. The diagnostics procedure usually takes about 30 minutes, while disassembly takes around one hour.
3. Next the technician orders replacements for any broken/worn parts from the main plant. Though it takes only five minutes to order the parts, it usually takes 48 hours for them to arrive from the main plant.
4. After the parts come in, the device will usually wait another 24 hours until a technician has time to reassemble and test the device. The reassembly and testing process takes, on average, three hours.
5. If the device still fails to work, the technician will repeat the process, starting with diagnostics and disassembly. The first time through, 10% of the devices aren't fixed; however, virtually all of them work by the time a second pass has been completed.
6. Once the device has been tested and passed, it is immediately boxed up (10 minutes) and a call is made to UPS, which picks up the package, usually within one hour.

Map the current process. How long will it take, on average, to move a device through the system, assuming everything "works" the first time? How long will it take if the device has to be repaired a second time? What is the percent value-added time under each scenario?

Solution

Figure 3.20 shows the process map, starting with the arrival of the device at the repair facility and ending when UPS picks it up. If the device has to be repaired only once, the total cycle time is 101 hours and 50 minutes. However, if the device has to be "repaired again," we must add another 76 hours and 35 minutes, resulting in a total cycle time of 178 hours and 25 minutes.

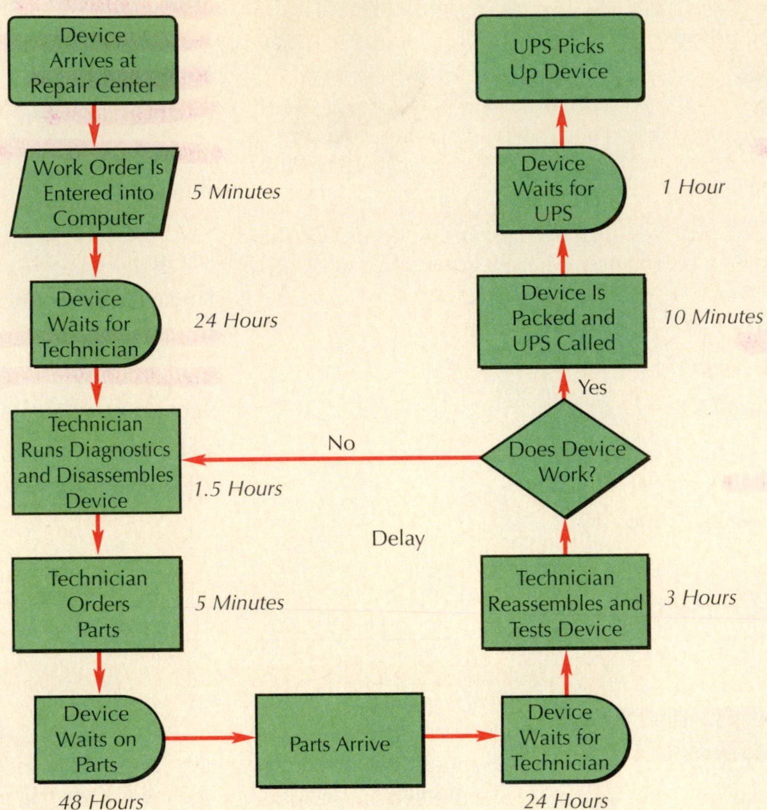

FIGURE 3.20 Process Map for Biosphere Products—Device Repair Process

It gets worse. One could argue that the only value-added activities are running the diagnostics, disassembling and reassembling the device, and testing. These activities total 4.5 hours. Therefore, if Biosphere correctly repairs the device the first time:

$$\text{Percent value-added time} = 100\%(4.5 \text{ hours}/101.83 \text{ hours}) = 4.4\%$$

If the device has to be repaired a second time:

$$\text{Percent value-added time} = 100\%(4.5 \text{ hours}/178.42 \text{ hours}) = 2.5\%$$

In other words, over 95% of the time is spent on non-value-added activities. A careful reader will notice that in the second calculation, we didn't add in any more time for diagnostics, disassembling and reassembling the device, and testing. This was intentional: Our argument is that if these activities did not fix the device the first time, then the first pass through was *wasted* time, not value-added time.

So what should Biosphere do? Looking at the process map, it becomes clear that the vast majority of the time is spent waiting on a technician or on parts or looping through activities because a device wasn't fixed right the first time. If, for example, Biosphere could keep spare parts at the repair center, it could chop 48 hours off of the cycle time. Management might also investigate why it takes technicians so long to get around to working on a device. Are they busy working on other devices, or are they involved in other activities that can wait? Management might even decide that more technicians are needed.

With regard to the relatively high failure rate of "repaired" devices, Biosphere might have to do some more detailed analysis: Are the technicians being trained properly? Are they making the same mistakes over and over again? If so, why? Clearly, Biosphere is an ideal candidate for DMAIC improvement efforts.

DISCUSSION QUESTIONS

1. Use the P&G example at the beginning of the chapter to explain the benefits to the customer of adopting a business processes perspective. Why might a traditional functional perspective have "blinded" P&G to the problems with the old system?
2. We noted that cycle time, though an important measure of process performance, is not the only factor to be considered. Give an example where focusing exclusively on reducing cycle times might hurt other, equally important measures of process performance.
3. Consider the course registration process at your college. Is this a good candidate for a Six Sigma DMAIC effort or business process reengineering? What are the pros and cons of each approach?
4. In the chapter, we stated that "there are countless possible measures of process performance, many of which are derived from the four core measures" of quality, cost, time, and flexibility. In the following table, identify how you think the three measures we described (productivity, efficiency, and cycle time) relate to the four core measures. Specifically:
   - If you think the measure always has a positive impact on a core measure, mark the square with a "+."
   - If you think the measure always has a negative impact, mark the square with "–."
   - If you think the measure can have either a positive or a negative impact, depending on the circumstances, mark the square with "+/–."

   Be ready to justify your answers. What are the implications for using performance measures to evaluate processes?

	QUALITY	COST	TIME	FLEXIBILITY
Productivity				
Efficiency				
Cycle time				

PROBLEMS

Additional homework problems are available at www.prenhall.com/bozarth. These problems use Excel to generate customized problems for different class sections or even different students.

(* = easy; ** = moderate; *** = advanced)

1. Marci spends 15 hours researching and writing a 20-page report for her philosophy class. Jack brags that he has a "streamlined process" for performing the researching and writing. Jack takes just eight hours to research and write the paper, but his report is only 15 pages long.
   a. (*) Calculate Marci's and Jack's productivity. What is the output? What is the input? Is this a single-factor or multifactor productivity measure?
   b. (**) What are the limitations of using productivity measures to evaluate their performance? What other performance measures might the instructor use?
2. (**) Consider the output and labor hour figures shown in the following table. Calculate the labor productivity for each week, as well as the average labor productivity for all six weeks. Do any of the weeks seem "unusual" to you? Explain.

WEEK	OUTPUT (IN UNITS)	LABOR HOURS
1	1,850	200
2	1,361	150
3	2,122	150
4	2,638	250
5	2,599	250
6	2,867	300

3. Smarmy Sales, Inc. (SSI), sells herbal remedies through its Web site and through phone reps. Over the past six years, SSI has started to depend more and more on its Web site to generate sales. The following table shows total sales, phone rep costs, and Web site costs for the last six years.

YEAR	TOTAL SALES	PHONE REP COSTS	WEB SITE COSTS
1999	$4,790,000	$200,000	$50,000
2000	$5,750,000	$210,000	$65,000
2001	$6,900,000	$221,000	$85,000
2002	$8,280,000	$230,000	$110,000
2003	$9,930,000	$245,000	$145,000
2004	$11,920,000	$255,000	$190,000

   a. (*) Calculate productivity for the the phone reps for each of the past six years. Interpret the results.
   b. (*) Calculate the productivity for the Web site for each of the past six years. Interpret the results.
   c. (**) Compare your results in Parts a and b. What are the limitations of these single-factor productivity measures?

d. (**) Now calculate a multifactor productivity score for each year, where the "input" is the total amount spent on both the phone reps and the Web site. Interpret the results. What can you conclude?

4. (*) A word processing job requires workers to complete a particular form in 60 seconds. Les can finish the form in 70 seconds. What is his efficiency? What other performance measures might be important here?

5. (**) Precision Machinery has set standard times for its field representatives to perform certain jobs. The standard time allowed for routine maintenance is two hours (i.e., "standard output" = 0.5 jobs per hour). One of Precision's field representatives records the following results. Calculate the rep's efficiency for each customer and her average efficiency. Interpret the results.

CUSTOMER	ACTUAL TIME REQUIRED TO PERFORM ROUTINE MAINTENANCE
ABC Company	1.8 hours
Preztel	2.4 hours
SCR Industries	1.9 hours
BeetleBob	1.8 hours

6. Gibson's Bodywork does automotive collision work. An insurance agency has determined that the standard time to replace a fender is 2.5 hours (i.e., "standard output" = 0.4 fenders per hour) and is willing to pay Gibson $50 per hour for labor (parts and supplies are billed separately). Gibson pays its workers $35 per hour.

a. (**) Suppose Gibson's workers take four hours to replace a fender. What is Gibson's labor hour efficiency? Given Gibson's labor costs, will the company make money on the job?

b. (***) What does Gibson's labor hour efficiency have to be for Gibson to break even on the job? Show your work.

7. (**) When a driver enters the license bureau to have his license renewed, he spends, on average, 45 minutes in line, 2 minutes having his eyes tested, and 3 minutes having his photograph taken. What is the percent value-added time? Explain any assumptions you made in coming up with your answer.

8. Average waiting times and ride times for two of Dizzy World's rides are as follows:

RIDE	AVERAGE WAITING TIME	LENGTH OF RIDE	TOTAL PROCESS TIME
Magical Mushroom	30 minutes	10 minutes	40 minutes
Haunted Roller Coaster	40 minutes	5 minutes	45 minutes

a. (*) Calculate the percent value-added time for each ride.

b. (**) Now suppose DizzyWorld puts in place a reservation system for the Haunted Roller Coaster ride. Here's how it works: The customer receives a coupon that allows him to come back in 40 minutes and immediately go to the front of the line. In the meantime, the customer can wait in line and then ride the Magical Mushroom. Under this new system, what is the customer's total time waiting? Total time riding? What is the new percent value-added time?

9. (**) Consider Example 3.1 and the accompanying Figure 3.6. Calculate the percent value-added time for the current process. Which activities do you consider to be value-added? Why?

10. Returning to Example 3.1 and Figure 3.6, suppose management actually *does* put a system in place that lets dealers enter orders electronically, with this information sent directly to the picking area.

a. (***) Redraw the process map to illustrate the changes. What is the new cycle time for the process? What is the new percent value-added time?

b. (**) What do you think the impact would be on the number of lost orders? On customer satisfaction?

11. (**) Billy's Hamburger Barn has a single drive-up window. Currently, there is one attendant at the window who takes the order (30–40 seconds), gathers up the food and bags it (30–120 seconds), and then takes the customer's money (30–40 seconds) before handing the food to the customer. Map the current process. What is the minimum cycle time? The longest cycle time?

12. (***) Suppose Billy's Hamburger Barn redesigns the process described in the Problem 11 so that there are now two attendants. The first attendant takes the order. Once this step is finished, the first attendant then takes the money while the second one gathers up and bags the food. Because two of the process steps can now run in parallel (gathering the food and taking the money), what is the new minimum cycle time? What is the longest cycle time? What potential problems could arise by splitting the process across two individuals?

13. Faircloth Financial specializes in home equity loans, loans that customers can take out against the equity they have in their homes. ("Equity" represents the difference between the home's value and the amount a customer owns on any other loans.) The current process is as follows:

- The customer downloads the loan application forms from the Web, fills them in, and mails them to Faircloth (three to five days).
- If there are any problems with the forms (and there usually are), a customer sales representative calls up the customer and reviews these problems. It may take one to two days to contact the customer. After reaching the customer, resolving the problem can take anywhere from

5 minutes to 30 minutes. If the customer needs to initial or sign some new forms, it takes five to seven days to mail the forms to the customer and have her send them back.

- Every Monday morning, the customer sales representatives take a batch of completed, correct application forms to the loan officers. This means that if a correct loan application comes in on Tuesday, the soonest it can get to a loan officer is the following Monday. The loan officers then take two to three days to process the batch of loans, based on information on the forms and information available from credit rating bureaus. Customers are advised by e-mail and regular mail regarding the final decision.

a. (***) Map out the current process. Identify any rework loops and delays in the process. What causes these? What is the impact on cycle times? How might this affect customers' willingness to do business with Faircloth?

b. (***) What changes might you recommend to redesign this process with the needs of the customer in mind? You might start by imagining how the "perfect" process would look to the customer and base your recommendations on that.

CASE STUDY

ZEPHTREX FABRIC

Introduction

Zephtrex fabric is a specialized product made by Ellison Textiles and used exclusively by CMX Corporation. The current demand level is just one-third of Ellison's manufacturing capacity, but the business is expected to grow substantially over the next year.

Order-Entry Process

CMX sends an order to Ellison Textiles 15 business days before CMX needs the Zephtrex fabric. However, CMX would like to shrink this to 10 days. As one CMX manager noted, "Fifteen days doesn't give us the flexibility we need to respond to changes in the marketplace. Sure, we could hold extra inventory here, but I'm not sure this is necessary, especially given the capacity situation at Ellison."

CMX sends the order to the Ellison sales rep, Ed Stevens, via e-mail. Ed supports multiple plants and generally checks his e-mail twice a day. However, if he is on the road and does not have access to the Internet, it may take 24 hours to receive and acknowledge the order. (CMX has been very good in the past about following up on orders that weren't confirmed within a day.) Ed passes these orders to the production planner, Rosemary Wilkins, at the next production planning and status meeting, which occurs every Tuesday and Friday morning at 7:00 A.M. via a conference call.

Production Planning Process

During the semiweekly planning and status meetings, Ed and Rosemary schedule new orders for production. On average, it takes four days to actually produce an order. Orders are scheduled in weekly "time buckets." That is, Rosemary schedules all orders to start on Monday and finish on Friday. Therefore, an order due at the customer on Thursday would need to be scheduled and completed by the prior Friday. Similarly, a customer order that came in on Tuesday would not be started until the following Monday. "Of course, we'll start and end a job on different days if we absolutely have to, but it's easier to interpret the schedule if we stick to the Monday–Friday schedule," says Rosemary.

QUESTIONS

1. Map out the order entry and production planning processes. How long do these processes take? How much of this time is "value-added"? What is the percent value-added time? What accounts for the remainder of the time?
2. Will Ellison be able to meet CMX's lead time requirements under the current processes?
3. Suppose Ellison Textiles would like to use the Six Sigma methodology to structure the improvement effort. How would you describe the "D" step of DMAIC for this particular effort? What kinds of improvements do you think would satisfy the "I" stage? Be creative. Why might it make sense to follow the DMAIC methodology here, even though we might think we "know" what the problem and the solutions are?

REFERENCES

Books and Articles

Andersen, B. *Business Process Improvement Toolbox.* Milwaukee, WI: ASQ Quality Press, 1999.

Blackburn, J. *Time-Based Competition: The Next Battle Ground in American Manufacturing.* Homewood, IL: Irwin, 1991.

Cook, S. *Practical Benchmarking: A Manager's Guide to Creating a Competitive Advantage.* London: Kogan Page, 1995.

Cox, J. F., and J. H. Blackstone, eds. *APICS Dictionary,* 11th ed. Falls Church, VA: APICS, 2004.

Drayer, R. "Procter & Gamble's Streamlined Logistics Initiative." *Supply Chain Management Review* 3, no. 2 (Summer 1999): 32–43.

Evans, J., and W. Lindsay. *The Management and Control of Quality*. Mason, OH: Thomson South-Western, 2005.

Meyer, C. *Fast Cycle Time: How to Align Purpose, Strategy, and Structure for Speed*. New York: Free Press, 1993.

Quinn, F. "What's the Buzz? Supply Chain Management: Part 1." *Logistics Management* 36, no. 2 (February 1997): 43.

Stalk, G., and T. Hout. *Competing against Time: How Time-Based Competition Is Reshaping Global Markets*. New York: Free Press, 1990.

Tibey, S. "How Kraft Built a 'One-Company' Supply Chain." *Supply Chain Management Review* 3, no. 3 (Fall 1999): 34–42.

Trimmer, J. Presentation on "Chrysler Discovers a Problem," Michigan State University, East Lansing, June, 1998.

Womack, J., D. Jones, and D. Roos. *The Machine That Changed the World: How Japan's Secret Weapon in the Global Auto Wars Will Revolutionize Western Industry*. New York: HarperPerennial, 1991.

Internet

Grout, J., Campbell School of Business, Berry College Mount Berry, Georgia, **http://csob.berry.edu/faculty/jgrout/processmapping/Swim_Lane/swim_lane.html**

Harbour Consulting, "Harbour Report North America 2006," **www.harbourinc.com**

Motorola University, **www.motorola.com/motorolauniversity.jsp**

Phios Process Directory for SCOR, **http://repository. phios.com/SCOR/Activity.asp?ID=5394**

Supply-Chain Council, 2007, **www.supply-chain.org/page.ww?section=SCOR+Model&name=SCOR+Model**

CHAPTER 4

Managing Quality

CHAPTER OUTLINE

Chapter Objectives

By the end of this chapter, you will be able to:

- Discuss the various definitions and dimensions of quality and why quality is important to operations and supply chains.
- Describe the different costs of quality, including internal and external failure, appraisal, and prevention costs.
- Explain what TQM is, along with its seven core principles.
- Calculate process capability ratios and indices and set up control charts for monitoring continuous variables and attributes.
- Describe the key issues associated with acceptance sampling, as well as the use of Operating Characteristics (OC) curves.
- Distinguish between Taguchi's quality loss function and the traditional view of quality.

Dell Computers Burned by Poor Quality[1]

Dell Computers has long been recognized as a leader in supply chain management. But as Dell found out, even successful companies are vulnerable when quality problems arise. In August 2006, Dell received a black eye when the company was forced to recall 4.1 million battery packs used in its laptops. The battery packs were overheating, and in some cases leading to fires. Analysts estimated that the resulting recall would cost Dell $200 to $400 million. To make things worse, dramatic photographs of burnt-up laptops were posted on the Web, and Dell became the brunt of a seemingly endless stream of cartoons and jokes.

As experts learned more about the problem, it became clear that several quality issues were at play. The first was a conformance quality problem. The battery packs, which were actually made by Sony, were not being built to specifications. A faulty crimping process on the Sony production line had contaminated the cathodes in the affected battery packs, making them more likely to combust when the battery got too hot.

The second was a potential reliablity problem traced back to the design architecture of the laptop itself: "Dell laptops frequently place the battery toward the front of the laptop—near the two hottest components of the computer—the CPU and graphics process." Such a layout was more likely to result in premature failure of the battery pack. Finally, experts noted that even if the battery packs had been built to specifications, the performance characteristics of the materials within the battery were not up to the demands of newer, more powerful laptops. As a Sony spokesman put it:

> *Our analysis thus far shows that a tiny metal particle that contaminated the electrolyte inside the battery cell caused a short-circuit. Usually, that alone would not cause a fire, because the battery just goes dead at that point. We believe the fire was caused by the combination of batteries and system architecture.*

[1] J. Enoch, "Dell Battery Recall May Not Be the Answer," Consumeraffairs.com., August 21, 2006.

INTRODUCTION

Quality has been a mainstay of the operations and supply chain areas for nearly a century. Quality is a broad and complex topic, covering everything from companywide practices to the application of specific statistical tools. The purpose of this chapter is to give you an overview of the different perspectives of quality found in today's business environment, as well as some of the tools and techniques companies use to improve and monitor quality levels.

Because the topic of quality is so broad, we have deliberately organized this chapter to flow from high-level descriptions of quality issues to more detailed tools and techniques for controlling quality. As you go through this chapter, pay attention to the flow from high-level perspectives to specific tools and techniques. Wherever you end up in an organization, you will be required to discuss and understand quality issues at *all* these levels. You may also notice that there are strong similarities between quality management and business process management, which was the focus of Chapter 3. This is no accident—many of the perspectives, tools, and techniques used to manage business processes first appeared in the quality management area.

4.1 QUALITY DEFINED

Quality
(a) The characteristics of a product or service that bear on its ability to satisfy stated or implied needs. (b) A product or service free of deficiencies.

Value perspective
A quality perspective that holds that quality must be judged, in part, by how well the characteristics of a particular product or service align with the needs of a specific user.

When we talk about quality, it's important to realize there are really two distinct, yet mutually dependent perspectives on quality: the *value perspective* and the *conformance perspective.* The American Society for Quality recognizes this dichotomy in its two-part definition of **quality**:[2]

1. The characteristics of a product or service that bear on its ability to satisfy stated or implied needs [the value perspective]
2. A product or service free of deficiencies [the conformance perspective]

The **value perspective** holds that quality must be judged, in part, on how well the characteristics of a particular product or service align with the needs of a specific user. This is consistent with the views of noted quality expert Joseph Juran, who defines quality as "fitness for use."[3]

Consider how you might use the value perspective to evaluate the quality of a meal at a fast-food restaurant. You might consider such factors as the accuracy of the order-filling process (Did you get what you thought you would?), the speed with which you were served, whether or not the food was fresh, and the price. On the other hand, the dimensions by which you evaluate quality will be quite different for a meal served in a four-star restaurant. What constitutes quality can differ from one situation to the next, as well as from one individual to the next.

In an effort to provide some structure to the value perspective, David Garvin of the Harvard Business School identified eight dimensions on which users evaluate the quality of a product or service:[4]

1. **Performance**—What are the basic operating characteristics of the product or service?
2. **Features**—What extra characteristics does the product or service have, beyond the basic performance operating characteristics?
3. **Reliability**—How long can a product go between failures or the need for maintenance?
4. **Durability**—What is the useful life for a product? How will the product hold up under extended or extreme use?
5. **Conformance**—Was the product made or service performed to specifications?
6. **Aesthetics**—How well does the product or service appeal to the senses?
7. **Serviceability**—How easy is it to repair, maintain, or support the product or service?
8. **Perceived quality**—What is the reputation or image of the product or service?

Table 4.1 illustrates how these dimensions might be applied to both a manufactured good and a service.

As Table 4.1 indicates, not all of the dimensions will be relevant in all situations, and the relative importance will vary from one customer to the next. Furthermore, Garvin's list should really be viewed as a starting framework. There may be other dimensions of quality that would be unique to specific business situations.

---

[2]American Society for Quality, "Glossary," **www.asq.org/info/glossary/a.html.**

[3]J. M. Juran and A. B. Godfrey, eds., *Juran's Quality Control Handbook*, 5th ed. (San Francisco: McGraw-Hill, 1998).

[4]D. Garvin, "Competing on the Eight Dimensions of Quality," *Harvard Business Review* 65, no. 6 (November–December 1987): 101–109.

TABLE 4.1
Dimensions of Quality for a Good and a Service

QUALITY DIMENSION	NEW CAR	TAX PREPARATION SERVICE
Performance	Tow capability; maximum number of passengers	Cost and time to prepare taxes
Features	Accessories; extended warranty	Advance on refund check; automatic filing
Reliability	Miles between required major service visits	Not applicable
Durability	Expected useful life of the engine, transmission, body	Not applicable
Conformance	Number of defects in the car	Number of mistakes on the tax return
Aesthetics	Styling, interior appearance, look and feel of instrumentation	Neatness of the return; manner of presentation to the customer
Serviceability	Are there qualified mechanics in the area? What is the time and cost for typical maintenance procedures?	Will the tax preparation firm talk with the IRS in case of an audit?
Perceived quality	How do prices for used vehicles hold up?	What is the reputation of the firm?

Conformance perspective
A quality perspective that focuses on whether or not a product was made or a service was performed *as intended.*

While the value-based perspective on quality focuses on accurately capturing the end user's needs, the **conformance perspective** focuses on whether or not a product was made or a service was performed *as intended*. Conformance quality is typically evaluated by measuring the actual product or service against some preestablished standards.

Look again at Table 4.1. The "number of defects in the car" and "number of mistakes on the tax return" are two measures of conformance quality. A defect or mistake, by definition, means that the product or service failed to meet specifications.

From these two perspectives on quality, we can start to see what an organization must do in order to provide high-quality products and services to users. Specifically, the organization must:

1. Understand what dimensions of quality are most important to users.
2. Develop products and services that will meet the users' requirements.
3. Put in place business processes capable of meeting the specifications driven by the users' requirements.
4. Verify that the business processes are indeed meeting the specifications.

Consider Steve Walton's experiences with Decatur Trust Bank (Example 4.1) in light of the four points just listed. By keeping the bank open on Saturdays and offering a wide range of customer services, Decatur Trust seems to have done a fair job on the first two points—understanding the dimensions of quality important to users and developing services to meet them. However, on points 3 and 4, Decatur Trust falls really short. No signs were in place to guide customers to the correct line or waiting area, and Decatur Trust failed to provide adequate training to the staff on hand. As a result, Steve Walton had to wait an excessively long time, and even then his IRA certificate was filled out incorrectly.

Example 4.1

Decatur Trust Bank

Recently, the management at Decatur Trust Bank decided to keep its branch offices open on Saturday mornings. Only selected services would be offered, including withdrawals and deposits, the opening of new checking accounts, the purchase of certificates of deposit (CDs), and the establishment of individual retirement accounts (IRAs).

One Saturday morning Steve Walton arrived at the bank. He wanted to (1) cash in a $2,000 CD that had matured; (2) withdraw $1,000 from his checking account; and (3) roll the combined $3,000 into an IRA, to be credited against his 2007 taxes. No signs were posted to indicate which employees could offer these specific services. After waiting in line for 10 minutes to see a teller, Steve learned that one of the two employees seated at desks would need to take care of his transactions. There was no formal waiting area for customers who wanted to see those employees. After two customers walked in front of Steve and obtained service, he finally spoke up and requested that he be served next.

After sitting down, Steve explained the three transactions he wanted to make to the employee, Nina Lau. Nina hesitated and then told Steve she had never opened an IRA before. When Steve suggested that someone else help him, Nina said there would not be a problem; if she made a mistake, the bank had up to seven days to correct it. Someone would call Steve about the matter.

Nina began to fill out various documents, repeatedly asking other employees for help. After 35 minutes of paperwork, including changes, additions, and deletions, Steve became visibly annoyed. Nina sensed his displeasure and became nervous. She apologized for the delay, explaining, "They told me to sit here today, but they never explained what I was supposed to do."

Nina finally finished the paperwork and handed it to Steve. Looking the documents over, he could not find any indication that his deposit was supposed to apply to his 2007 taxes. He asked Nina about the omission, but she didn't think it would make a difference. Steve then insisted that someone else review the document. When Jim Young, the bank manager, looked at it, he agreed that "IRA-2007" should be typed across the top of the CD form. As Steve got up to leave, over an hour after he had arrived, Nina assured him once again that he needn't worry about mistakes because they could be corrected within a week.

On Tuesday, Steve received a letter from Nina, stating: "When you purchased the above-referenced IRA CD on Saturday, December 11, the certificate was inadvertently typed with both your name and your wife's. This, of course, is not permissible on an IRA. Please bring the original certificate in to the bank and we will type a new one for you. This will not affect the account in any way."

4.2 TOTAL COST OF QUALITY

Pioneers in the quality area attempted to quantify the benefits associated with improving quality levels. One such pioneer was Joseph Juran, who edited the widely recognized *Quality Control Handbook*.[5] Juran argued that there are four quality-related costs: internal failure costs, external failure costs, appraisal costs, and prevention costs.

Internal failure costs
Costs caused by defects that occur prior to delivery to the customer, including money spent on repairing or reworking defective products, as well as time wasted on these activities.

Internal failure costs are costs caused by defects that occur prior to delivery to the customer, including money spent on repairing or reworking defective products (or scrapping them if they are completely ruined), as well as time wasted on these activities. As you might have guessed, this cost is not small. A *Business Week* study[6] found that the typical American factory spent 20% to 50% of its operating budget on finding and fixing mistakes. In fact, as many as one out of four factory employees didn't produce anything new that year because they were too busy reworking units not done right the first time.

External failure costs
Costs incurred by defects that are not detected until a product or service reaches the customer.

If defects are not detected until a product or service reaches the customer, the organization incurs an **external failure cost**. These costs are difficult to estimate, but they are inevitably large, for they include not only warranty costs, but also the cost of lost future business and, in some cases, costly litigation. The problems Dell experienced due to the overheating battery packs are a good example.

Appraisal costs
Costs a company incurs to assess its quality levels.

Balanced against failure costs are appraisal and prevention costs. **Appraisal costs** are costs a company incurs to assess its quality levels. Typical appraisal costs are the costs for inspections, the sampling of products or services, and customer surveys.

Prevention costs
The costs an organization incurs to actually prevent defects from occurring to begin with.

Note that appraising quality is *not* the same as preventing defects. For example, a manufacturer might inspect goods before they are shipped, but unless it takes steps to *improve* the production process, defect levels will not change. In contrast, **prevention costs** refer to the costs an organization incurs to actually prevent defects from occurring in the first place. Examples include the costs for employee training, supplier certification efforts, and investment in new processes, not to mention equipment maintenance expenditures. Figure 4.1 shows how these various costs behave as defect levels decrease.

FIGURE 4.1
Total Cost of Quality (Traditional View)

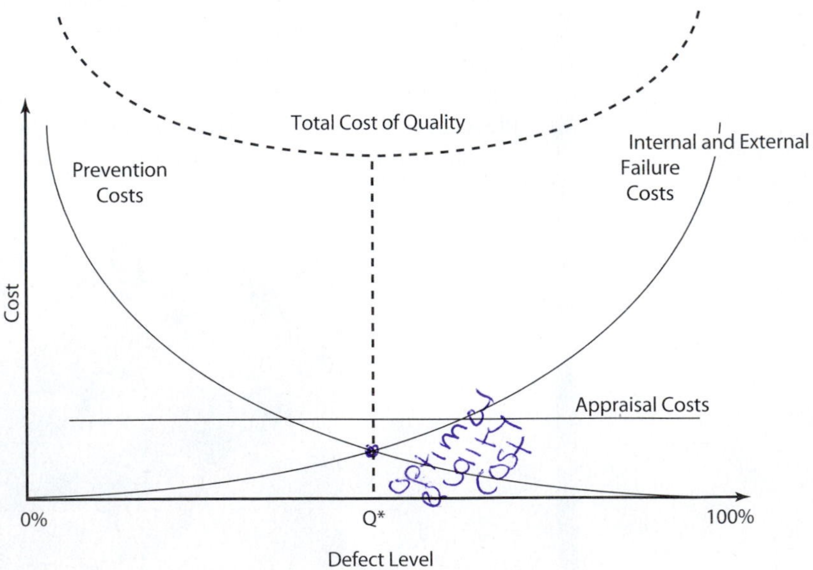

[5]Now in its fifth edition. See Note 3.

[6]D. Greising, "Quality: How to Make It Pay," *Business Week* (August 8, 1994): 54–59.

According to Figure 4.1, as the level of defects is reduced from 100% to 0%, internal and external failure costs fall to zero, and prevention costs rise exponentially. The rationale behind the steeply rising prevention costs is this: As the defect level drops, it becomes even harder to find and resolve the remaining quality problems. Notice, too, that appraisal costs are flat across the various defect levels, as there is no direct relationship between appraising quality and defect levels. Therefore, while appraising quality levels may be necessary, appraisal by itself will not improve quality.

When we add internal and external failure, prevention, and appraisal costs together, we get a **total cost of quality curve**. This curve suggests that there is some optimal quality level, Q^*, that minimizes the total cost of quality. For defect levels higher than this level, exponentially increasing failure costs cause total quality costs to rise; for defect levels below Q^*, increases in prevention costs outstrip decreases in failure costs.

Total cost of quality curve
A curve that suggests there is some optimal quality level, Q^*. The curve is calculated by adding costs of internal and external failures, prevention costs, and appraisal costs.

But as Juran continued his work, he began to notice something that contradicted the pattern shown in Figure 4.1. In particular, Juran noticed that as a business's processes improved to the point where products and services were defect-free, the cost of appraisal fell. In effect, there was no need to inspect products or services for defects. Furthermore, prevention costs held steady (or even decreased) as managers and employees became more skillful at identifying and resolving problems. With the changing appraisal and prevention cost curves, the total cost of quality curve began to look more like the one in Figure 4.2. Note that in this graph, the lowest total cost of quality occurs at the 0% defect level.

Figure 4.3 offers another perspective on how quality costs change over time as an organization gains more experience in managing quality. At first, the organization is spending very little on prevention and appraisal, and internal and external failure costs are high. As the organization ramps up its prevention and appraisal efforts, failure costs begin to drop. Over time, quality management culture and practices become a part of the day-to-day operations, and the organization is able to continue improving quality levels while simultaneously decreasing prevention and appraisal costs.

But how could this be? Let's consider an example from industry. Many companies have supplier certification programs where they work with key suppliers to improve the quality of purchased goods. As the suppliers become better at providing high-quality goods, the purchasing companies do not need to spend as much money on appraising the quality of incoming shipments. Furthermore, good-quality practices become embedded in the

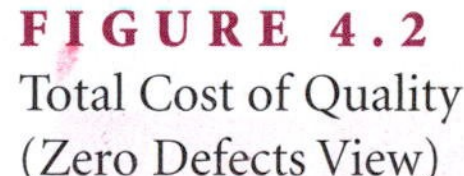
FIGURE 4.2
Total Cost of Quality (Zero Defects View)

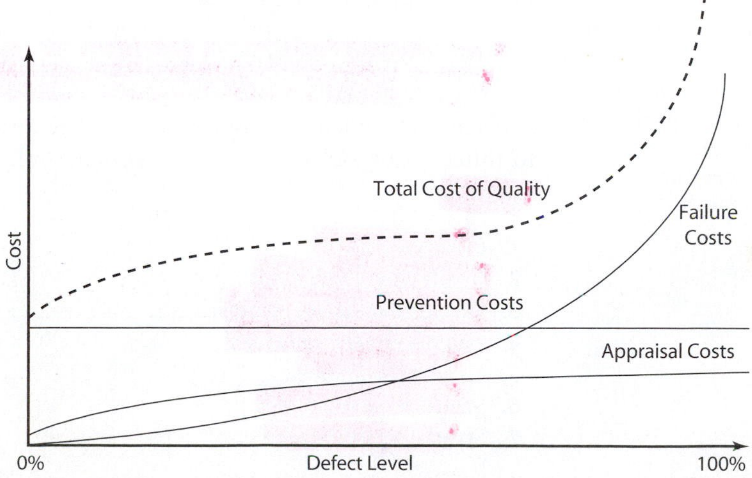

FIGURE 4.3
Quality Cost Improvements Over Time

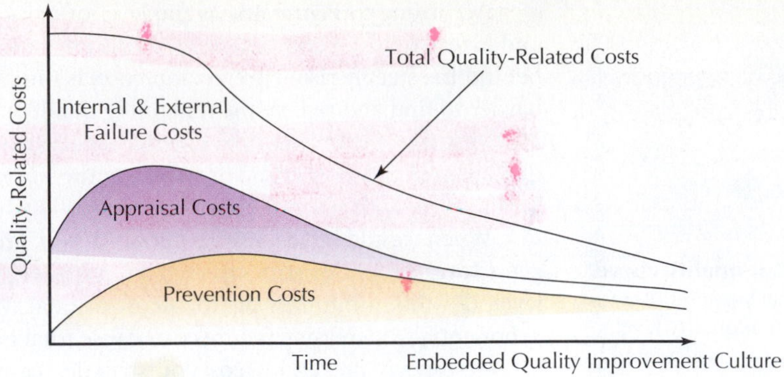

supplier's business processes, and prevention costs decrease as well. Moving to the right on Figure 4.3 is not always easy, but as the total cost curve suggests, it can pay off in the long term.

4.3 TOTAL QUALITY MANAGEMENT

Of course, quality management involves more than just managing to the "optimum" defect level. As noted earlier, to fully address both the value and the conformance perspectives on quality, organizations must:

1. Understand what dimensions of quality are most important to users.
2. Develop products and services that will meet the users' requirements.
3. Put in place business processes capable of meeting the specifications driven by the users' requirements.
4. Verify that the business processes are indeed meeting the specifications.

To accomplish this, all individuals within an organization must address quality within all of an organization's business processes. From design through purchasing, manufacturing, and distribution, the organization must have processes and people capable of delivering quality products and services.

Total quality management (TQM)
A managerial approach in which the entire organization is managed so that it excels in all quality dimensions that are important to customers.

This managerial approach is often referred to as total quality management. **Total quality management (TQM)** is the management of an entire organization so that it excels in all quality dimensions that are important to customers. TQM is such a broad concept that students often have a hard time understanding what it is. Indeed, one way to think about TQM is as a business philosophy centered around seven core ideas, or *principles*:

1. Customer focus
2. Leadership involvement
3. Continuous improvement
4. Employee empowerment
5. Quality assurance
6. Supplier partnerships
7. Strategic quality plan

Exhibit 4.1

The Malcolm Baldrige National Quality Award

The Malcolm Baldrige National Quality Award is given annually by the President of the United States to business, education, and health care organizations that apply and are judged to be outstanding in seven areas:

- Leadership
- Strategic planning
- Customer and market focus
- Measurement, analysis, and knowledge management
- Human resource focus
- Process management
- Business results

Congress established the award program in 1987 to recognize U.S. organizations for their achievements in quality and performance and to raise awareness about the importance of quality and performance excellence. The U.S. Commerce Department's National Institute of Standards and Technology (NIST) manages the Baldrige National Quality Program in close cooperation with the private sector. The Baldrige performance excellence criteria are a framework that any organization can use to improve overall performance.

The Malcolm Baldrige National Quality Award.

Source: "Frequently Asked Questions about the Malcolm Baldrige National Quality Award," **www.nist.gov/public_affairs/factsheet/baldfaqs.htm**.

Customer Focus. TQM starts with employees who are willing to place themselves in the customer's shoes. If employees do not understand how customers really feel about a product or service, they risk alienating customers. In some cases, an employee might not have direct contact with an *external* customer. But every employee has a "customer" whose expectations must be met, even if that customer is *internal* to the organization.

Leadership Involvement. If companies are serious about adopting a TQM mind-set, then change must begin at the top. Managers should carry the message that quality counts to everyone in the company. To inspire and guide managers, W. Edwards Deming presented "Fourteen Points for Management," a set of guidelines for managers to follow if they are serious about improving quality:[7]

1. Demonstrate consistency of purpose toward product improvement.
2. Adopt the new philosophy [of continuous improvement].
3. Cease dependence on mass inspection; use statistical methods instead.
4. End the practice of awarding business on the basis of price tag.
5. Find and work continually on problems.
6. Institute modern methods of training.
7. Institute modern methods of supervision.
8. Drive out fear—promote a company-oriented attitude.
9. Break down barriers between departments.
10. Eliminate numerical goals asking for new levels of productivity without providing methods.
11. Eliminate standards prescribing numerical quotas.
12. Remove barriers that stand between the hourly worker and his right to pride of workmanship.
13. Institute a program of education and retraining.
14. Create a corporate and management structure that will promote the above 13 points.

In promoting his ideas, Deming stressed that managers bear the ultimate responsibility for quality problems. To succeed, they must focus on the entire organization so as to excel in all dimensions that are important to the customer.

Continuous improvement
A principle of TQM that assumes there will always be room for improvement, no matter how well an organization is doing.

Continuous Improvement. **Continuous improvement** means never being content with the status quo, but assuming there will always be room for improvement, no matter how well an organization is doing.

Employee empowerment
Giving employees the responsibility, authority, training, and tools necessary to manage quality.

Employee Empowerment. The traditional business view has been that the executives at the top of a company do the thinking, the middle managers do the supervising, and the remaining employees are paid to work, not to think. However, in a TQM organization, quality is everybody's job, from the CEO to the entry-level employees. **Employee empowerment** means giving employees the responsibility, authority, training, and tools necessary to manage quality. An excellent example of this is training employees in the Six Sigma methodology and continuous improvement tools described in Chapter 3.

Quality assurance
The specific actions firms take to ensure that their products, services, and processes meet the quality requirements of their customers.

Quality Assurance. **Quality assurance** refers to the specific actions a firm takes to ensure that its products, services, and processes meet the quality requirements of its

[7] W. E. Deming, *Quality, Productivity, and Competitive Position* (Boston: MIT Center for Engineering Study, 1982).

W. Edwards Deming was a pioneer in Total Quality Management. His ideas have had a lasting impact on business practice.

Quality function development (QFD)
A technique used to translate customer requirements into technical requirements for each stage of product development and production.

Statistical quality control (SQC)
The application of statistical techniques to quality control.

customers. Quality assurance activities take place throughout the organization. For example, during the design phase, many companies use a technique called **quality function deployment (QFD)** to translate customer requirements into technical requirements for each stage of product development and production (see Chapter 6 for a more detailed discussion of QFD).

Another approach that falls under the quality assurance banner is **statistical quality control (SQC)**, which we will describe in detail later in the chapter. SQC uses basic statistics to help organizations assess quality levels. Other quality assurance efforts can include "error-proofing," which is the deliberate design of a process to eliminate the possibility of an error, and quality auditing of suppliers by carefully trained teams.

SUPPLIER PARTNERSHIPS. As you would expect, companies must extend their TQM efforts to include supply chain partners. If members of the supply chain do not share the same commitment to TQM, quality will suffer because suppliers' materials and services ultimately become part of the company's product or service. The problem with the Sony battery packs found in Dell laptops is a prime example. To ensure that suppliers are willing to meet expectations, managers must monitor their performance carefully and take steps to ensure improvement when necessary.

Strategic quality plan
An organizational plan that provides the vision, guidance, and measurements to drive the quality effort forward and shift the organization's course when necessary.

Process owner
A team or individual who has the authority and responsibility for improving the organization's business processes and who is rewarded accordingly.

STRATEGIC QUALITY PLAN. Finally, TQM cannot be achieved without significant, sustained efforts over time. A well-developed **strategic quality plan** provides the vision, guidance, and measurements to drive the quality effort forward and shift the organization's course when necessary. Such a plan generally extends several years into the future and stipulates a broad set of objectives. However, it should also establish measurable quarterly (three-month) goals for the short term.

Every quarter, executives should review the company's quality performance against its goals and take action to sustain successes and remedy failures. Cross-functional teams consisting of **process owners** then implement their action plans. Process owners are held responsible for achieving specific goals by certain dates, and at every team meeting, members measure their progress against preestablished measures and deadlines.

TQM and the Six Sigma Methodology

As you read through the previous section, you might have noticed a lot of overlap between TQM and the Six Sigma methodology, which we introduced in Chapter 3. Some practitioners and researchers have even gone as far as to say that TQM is passé and has been replaced by Six Sigma. But this is misleading—the fundamental principles behind TQM took decades to develop and are still valid today. The main differences are:

- TQM is a managerial approach in which the entire organization is managed so that it excels in all quality dimensions that are important to customers. The "seven core principles" of TQM and Deming's 14 points illustrate the approach.
- The Six Sigma methodology builds upon TQM and makes use of both the TQM philosophy and continuous improvement tools.
- Six Sigma includes *specific* processes for guiding process improvement and new process/product development efforts. The first of these, DMAIC (Define-Measure-Analyze-Improve-Control), outlines the steps that should be followed to improve an *existing* business processes. The second, DMADV (Define-Measure-Analyze-Design-Verify), outlines the steps needed to create *completely new* business processes or products. DMAIC is described in Chapter 3; DMADV is discussed in Chapter 6.
- Six Sigma defines specific organizational roles and career paths. We discussed five of these in Chapter 3: champions, master black belts, black belts, green belts, and team members.
- Six Sigma has an expanded tool kit that includes computer simulation, optimization modeling, data mining, and other advanced analytical techniques. Typically, master black belts and black belts provide teams with the expertise required to use these tools.

To put it another way, TQM encapsulates the managerial vision behind quality management; Six Sigma builds upon this to provide organizations with the processes, people, and tools required to carry out this vision.

4.4 STATISTICAL QUALITY CONTROL

At the start of the chapter, we noted that organizations must:

1. Understand what dimensions of quality are most important to users.
2. Develop products and services that will meet the users' requirements.

3. Put in place business processes capable of meeting the specifications driven by the users' requirements.
4. Verify that the business processes are indeed meeting the specifications.

Statistical quality control (SQC) is directly aimed at the fourth issue—making sure that a business's current processes are meeting the specifications. Simply put, SQC is the application of statistical techniques to quality control. In this section, we describe some of the more popular SQC applications and illustrate how basic statistical concepts can be applied to quality issues.

Process Capability

Process capability ratio (C_p) A mathematical determination of a process's capability to meet certain quality standards. A $C_p \geq 1$ means the process is capable of meeting the standard being measured.

How does an organization know whether or not its business processes are capable of meeting certain quality standards? One way organizations do this is by comparing the requirements placed on a process to the actual outputs of the process. A simple measure of process capability is the **process capability ratio**, or C_p:

$$C_p = \frac{UTL - LTL}{6\sigma} \quad [4\text{-}1]$$

where:

UTL = upper tolerance limit

LTL = lower tolerance limit

σ = process standard deviation for the variable of interest

Upper tolerance limit (UTL) The highest acceptable value for some measure of interest.

Lower tolerance limit (LTL) The lowest acceptable value for some measure of interest.

The **upper tolerance limit (UTL)** and **lower tolerance limit (LTL)** (sometimes called the *upper* and *lower specification limits*) indicate the acceptable range of values for some measure of interest, such as weight, temperature, or time. Engineering, customers, or some other party typically sets *UTL* and *LTL* values. In contrast, σ is the standard deviation of the process with regard to the same measure. Because the true value of σ is rarely known, it is typically estimated from a sample of observations. This estimated value, $\hat{\sigma}$, is calculated as follows:

$$\hat{\sigma} = \sqrt{\frac{\sum_{i=1}^{n} (\overline{\overline{X}} - X_i)^2}{n - 1}} \quad [4\text{-}2]$$

where:

$\overline{\overline{X}}$ = sample mean

X_i = value for the ith observation

n = sample size

Wider tolerance limits and/or smaller values of σ will result in higher C_p values, while narrower tolerance limits and/or larger σ values will have the opposite result. Thus, higher C_p values indicate a more capable process.

To illustrate, suppose that the output values of a process are normally distributed. If this is the case, statistical theory says that individual observations should fall within $\pm 3\sigma$ of the process mean, μ, 99.7% of the time. The normal distribution given in Figure 4.4 illustrates this idea.

FIGURE 4.4
Normal Distribution

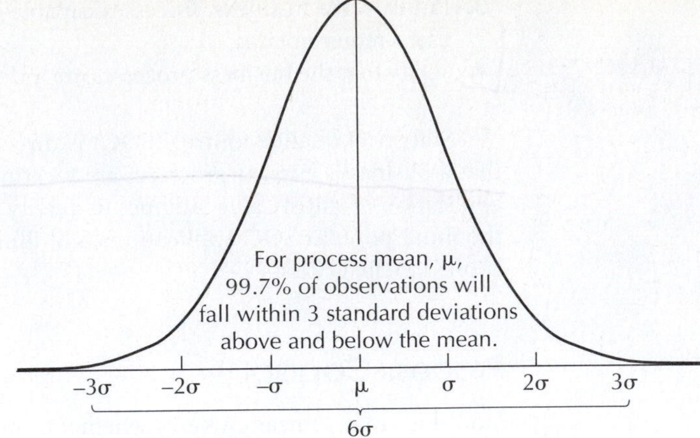
For process mean, μ, 99.7% of observations will fall within 3 standard deviations above and below the mean.
−3σ
−2σ
−σ
μ
σ
2σ
3σ
6σ

Now suppose that the difference between the upper and lower tolerance limits ($UTL - LTL$) just happens to equal 6σ. This suggests that the process is capable of producing within the tolerance limits 99.7% of the time and $C_p = 1$. However, if the tolerance limits are tighter than 6σ, $C_p < 1$ (Figure 4.5).

Process capability index (C_{pk}) A mathematical determination of a process's capability of meeting certain tolerance limits.

In some cases, the process mean, μ, is not exactly centered on the target value. In this case, we use the **process capability index**, C_{pk}, to determine whether or not the process is capable of meeting the tolerance limits 99.7% of the time:

$$C_{pk} = \min\left[\frac{\mu - LTL}{3\sigma}, \frac{UTL - \mu}{3\sigma}\right] \quad [4\text{-}3]$$

where:

μ = process mean
UTL = upper tolerance limit
LTL = lower tolerance limit
σ = standard deviation

FIGURE 4.5
C_p Values for Different Tolerance Limits

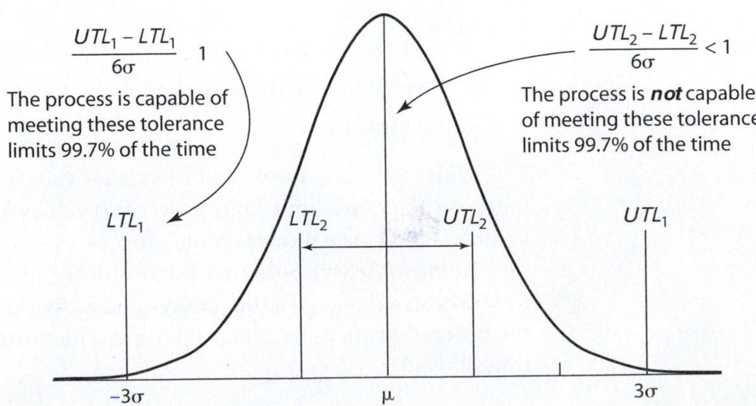
$\frac{UTL_1 - LTL_1}{6\sigma}$ 1
The process is capable of meeting these tolerance limits 99.7% of the time
$\frac{UTL_2 - LTL_2}{6\sigma} < 1$
The process is not capable of meeting these tolerance limits 99.7% of the time
LTL_1
LTL_2
UTL_2
UTL_1
−3σ
μ
3σ

Example 4.2

Calculating and Interpreting the Process Capability Ratio at Big Bob's Axles

Big Bob's Axles has a customer that requires axles with a diameter of 25 cm., ±0.02 cm. The customer has stated that Big Bob must be able to meet these requirements 99.7% of the time in order to keep the business. Currently, Big Bob is able to make axles with a process mean of exactly 25 cm and a standard deviation of 0.005 cm. Is Big Bob capable of meeting the customer's needs?

Notice that the *UTL* and *LTL* are 25.02 cm and 24.98 cm, respectively. Therefore, the process capability ratio is:

$$C_p = \frac{UTL - LTL}{6\sigma} = \frac{25.02 - 24.98}{6(0.005)} = \frac{0.04}{0.03} = 1.33$$

Because the process capability ratio is greater than 1, Big Bob's process is more than capable of providing 99.7% defect-free axles.

Example 4.3

Calculating and Interpreting the Process Capability Index at Milburn Textiles

Engineers at Milburn Textiles have developed the following specifications for a key dyeing process:

Target value for process mean = 140 degrees
Upper tolerance limit (*UTL*) = 148 degrees
Lower tolerance limit (*LTL*) = 132 degrees

The *UTL* and *LTL* are based on the engineers' observations that results are acceptable as long as the temperature remains between 132 and 148 degrees. Currently, the dyeing process has a mean temperature of 139.8 degrees, with a standard deviation of 2.14 degrees. Because the process mean is slightly off from the target value of 140 degrees, the quality team uses the process capability index to evaluate the process's capability:

$$C_{pk} = \min\left(\frac{\mu - LTL}{3\sigma}, \frac{UTL - \mu}{3\sigma}\right)$$

$$= \min\left[\frac{139.8 - 132}{3(2.14)}, \frac{148 - 139.8}{3(2.14)}\right]$$

$$= \min\,[1.21, 1.28] = 1.21$$

Even with the process mean being off-center, the process is still capable of meeting the tolerance limits more than 99.7% of the time.

FIGURE 4.6
Six Sigma Quality

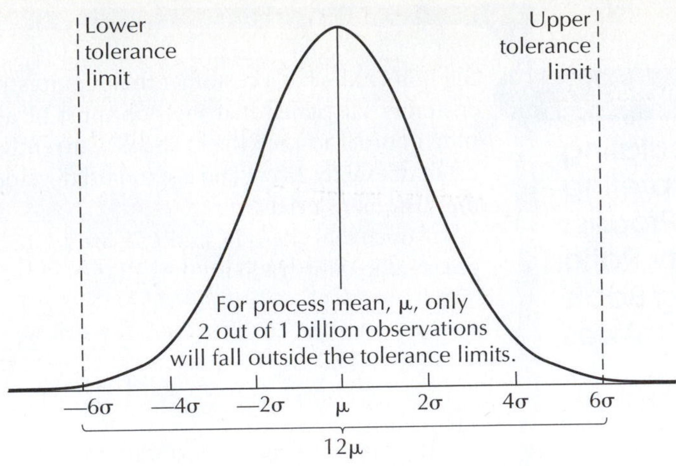

Six Sigma Quality

Six Sigma quality
"A term used generally to indicate that a process is well controlled, i.e., tolerance limits are ±6 sigma (standard deviations) from the centerline in a control chart. The term is usually associated with Motorola, which named one of its key operational initiatives Six Sigma Quality."

In this book, we have already talked about the Six Sigma methodology; now we turn our attention to the quality measure of the same name. The idea behind **Six Sigma quality** is to reduce the variability of a process so that 12 standard deviations can now be squeezed between the tolerance limits. Mathematically, this can be expressed as follows:

$$\text{Six Sigma } C_p = \frac{UTL - LTL}{12\sigma} \geq 1 \qquad \textbf{[4-4]}$$

where:

UTL = upper tolerance limit
LTL = lower tolerance limit
σ = standard deviation

For a *perfectly* centered process with normally distributed output, this translates into around *2 defects per billion* (Figure 4.6).

In reality, most processes are not perfectly centered, resulting in a higher number of observations falling outside the tolerance limits. Practitioners therefore use a working definition of Six Sigma quality that allows for a possible shift in the process mean of ±1.5 standard deviations. The effect is to increase the allowable defect level to *3.4 defects per million*. Either way, you can begin to see why many firms like the term—Six Sigma quality levels serve as a quantifiable, if far-reaching, objective for many organizations.

Example 4.4

Evaluating Six Sigma Quality at Milburn Textiles

Milburn Textiles has recalibrated its dyeing process so that the process mean is now exactly 140 degrees, with a new, lower standard deviation of 1.40 degrees. Given upper and lower tolerance limits of 148 and 132 degrees, does the dyeing process provide Six Sigma quality levels?

Calculating the process capability ratio for Six Sigma quality levels:

$$\text{Six Sigma } C_p = \frac{UTL - LTL}{12\sigma} = \frac{148 - 132}{12(1.40)} = 0.95$$

Because $C_p < 1$, the process is still not capable of providing Six Sigma quality. To achieve Six Sigma quality, Milburn will have to reduce the standard deviation even further.

Control Charts

Control chart
A specialized run chart that helps an organization track changes in key measures over time.

In contrast to the process capability ratio and index, **control charts** are specialized run charts that help organizations track changes in key measures over time. By using control charts, organizations can quickly determine whether a process is "in control" and take action if it is not. Before we describe the different types of control charts in more detail, however, we must first review the concepts of sampling and variable types.

SAMPLING. The idea behind sampling is that businesses do not have to examine *every* process outcome to assess how well a process is doing. Instead, they can use carefully selected samples to get a fairly good idea of how well a process is working. In fact, control charts are based on samples. In general, a good sample is one in which:

- Every outcome has an equal chance of being selected into the sample. This is typically accomplished by taking a random sample from the entire population.
- The sample size is large enough to not be unduly swayed by any single observation.

Continuous variable
A variable that can be measured along a continuous scale, such as weight, length, height, and temperature.

Attribute
A characteristic of an outcome or item that is accounted for by its presence or absence, such as "defective" versus "good" or "late" versus "on time."

Sample average ($\overline{\overline{X}}$)
A key measure that represents the central tendency of a measure of interest in a specific sample; used in conjunction with range (R).

Range (R)
A key measure that represents the variation of a specific sample group; used in conjunction with sample average ($\overline{\overline{X}}$).

Proportion
A measure of the percent of the sample that does or does not have a particular characteristic.

VARIABLE TYPES. Most measures of interest fall into one of two types: continuous variables or attributes. **Continuous variables** are ones that can be measured along a continuous scale, such as weight, length, height, or temperature. **Attributes**, in contrast, refer to the presence or absence of a particular characteristic. To illustrate, suppose a pizza delivery chain promises to deliver a "hot, 16-inch, thick-crust pizza in 30 minutes or less." The first three variables—temperature, diameter, and thickness—can all be measured on a continuous scale and are therefore continuous variables. However, on-time delivery is an attribute. The pizza is either delivered within the allotted time or it isn't.

When firms take samples of a continuous variable, two key measures of interest are the sample average and the range of values. The **sample average** and the **range** for a continuous variable are defined as follows:

$$\text{Sample average for a continuous variable} = \overline{X} = \frac{\sum_{i=1}^{n} X_i}{n} \quad [4\text{-}5]$$

where:

n = number of observations in the sample

X_i = value of the ith observation

$$\text{Sample Range for a continuous variable} = R = (\text{highest value in the sample}) - (\text{lowest value in the sample}) \quad [4\text{-}6]$$

The sample average tells us the central tendency for the measure of interest, while the range tells us something about the variation.

Because attributes refer to the presence or absence of a particular characteristic, the variable of interest is the proportion of the sample with the characteristic. The **proportion** of a sample with a particular characteristic (attribute) is calculated as:

$$p = \frac{\sum_{i=1}^{n} a_i}{n} \quad [4\text{-}7]$$

where:

n = number of observations in the sample

a_i = 0 if the attribute is not present for the ith observation and 1 if it is

Example 4.5

Calculating the Sample Average and Range for a Continuous Variable at DanderNo Shampoo Company

DanderNo Shampoo Company has taken a sample of 15 shampoo bottles and measured the number of ounces in each bottle (Table 4.2).

TABLE 4.2 Sample Results at DanderNo Shampoo Company

SAMPLE OBSERVATION	OUNCES
1	16.41
2	16.12
3	16.57
4	16.88
5	16.86
6	17.02
7	15.85
8	16.43
9	16.83
10	16.17
11	16.29
12	15.99
13	15.95
14	16.21
15	16.27
Sum:	**245.85**

The sample average, $\overline{\overline{X}}$, is 245.85/15 = 16.39 ounces. The range, R, is 17.02 − 15.85 = 1.17.

Control limits
The upper and lower limits of a control chart. They are calculated so that if a sample result falls inside the control limits, the process is considered under control.

With this background, we can begin to describe control charts in more detail. As we said earlier, control charts are specialized run charts that help organizations track changes in key measures over time. Control charts have a central line showing the expected value for a sample measure, as well as upper and lower control limits. **Control limits** are derived using statistical techniques. They are calculated so that if a sample result falls inside

Example 4.6

Estimating the Proportion of Dissatisfied Customers at the Estonia Hotel

The hotel manager at the Estonia Hotel has heard some rumblings that service is "not what it used to be." She would like to estimate what proportion of its guests are dissatisfied with the service they received. To accomplish this, the hotel manager asked a random sample of 100 guests if they were satisfied with their stay. Fourteen of the guests indicated they were dissatisfied. The hotel manager then assigned a value of 1 to those guests who said they were dissatisfied. Therefore, the estimated proportion of the entire population dissatisfied is:

$$p = \frac{14}{100} = 0.14, \text{ or } 14\%$$

the control limits, the process is considered "under control." If a sample result falls outside the control limits, the process is considered "out of control."

In the following sections, we will discuss the development of three different control charts: $\overline{\overline{X}}$ and R charts (for continuous variables) and p charts (for attributes). Regardless of the variable type, the process for setting up control charts is the same:

1. Take m samples of size n each while the process is under control.
2. Use the sample results to set up the control chart using the tables or formulas provided.
3. Continue to take samples of size n, and plot them against the control charts.
4. Interpret the results and take appropriate action.

$\overline{\overline{X}}$ chart
A specific type of control chart for a continuous variable that is used to track the average value for future samples.

***R* chart**
A specific type of control chart for a continuous variable that is used to track how much the individual observations within each sample vary.

We cannot overemphasize two points about control charts. First, control charts *should not* be employed until the process is capable of providing acceptable performance on a regular basis. Second, control charts, by themselves, *will not* result in improved quality levels. Rather, control charts are used to catch quality problems early, before they get out of hand. As such, the use of control charts falls under the appraisal activities of a firm's quality efforts (Figures 4.1 through 4.3).

$\overline{\overline{X}}$ AND *R* CHARTS. For continuous variables, we need two types of control charts. An **$\overline{\overline{X}}$ chart** is used to track the average value for future samples (Equation 4.5), while an ***R* chart** is used to track how much the individual observations within each sample vary (Equation 4.6). Table 4.3 summarizes the calculations required to set up these control charts, while Table 4.4 includes values needed to complete the control limit calculations.

TABLE 4.3 Calculations for $\overline{\overline{X}}$ and R Charts

CHART TYPE	CENTRAL LINE	CONTROL LIMITS
$\overline{\overline{X}}$ chart	$\overline{\overline{X}} = \frac{\sum_{j=1}^{m} \overline{X}_j}{m}$ [4-8] where: $\overline{\overline{X}}$ = grand mean m = number of samples used to develop the $\overline{\overline{X}}$ chart $\overline{X}_j$ = average for the jth sample	($A2$ values are given in Table 4.4) Upper control limit = $UCL_{\overline{X}} = \overline{\overline{X}} + A2(\overline{R})$ [4-10] Lower control limit = $LCL_{\overline{X}} = \overline{\overline{X}} - A2(\overline{R})$ [4-11]
R chart	$\overline{R} = \frac{\sum_{j=1}^{m} R_j}{m}$ [4-9] where: m = number of samples used to develop the control charts R_j = range for the jth sample	($D3$ and $D4$ values are given in Table 4.4) Upper control limit = $UCL_R = D4(\overline{R})$ [4-12] Lower control limit = $LCL_R = D3(\overline{R})$ [4-13]

TABLE 4.4
$A2$, $D3$, $D4$ Values for Developing $\overline{\overline{X}}$ and R Charts

SAMPLE SIZE N	$A2$	$D3$	$D4$
2	1.88	0	3.27
3	1.02	0	2.57
4	0.73	0	2.28
5	0.58	0	2.11
6	0.48	0	2.00
7	0.42	0.08	1.92
8	0.37	0.14	1.86
9	0.34	0.18	1.82
10	0.31	0.22	1.78
11	0.29	0.26	1.74
12	0.27	0.28	1.72

Example 4.7

Developing and Interpreting $\overline{X}$ and R Charts at Milburn Textiles

A quality team at Milburn Textiles has been charged with setting up control charts to monitor the key dyeing process first described in Examples 4.3 and 4.4. Recall that the ideal temperature for the dyeing process is 140 degrees. If the temperature is too high, the fabric will be too dark; if the temperature is too low, streaks can develop. Either condition can ruin large rolls of expensive fabric.

Because temperature is a continuous variable, the quality team decides to set up $\overline{X}$ and R charts to monitor the temperature of the dyeing process. As a first step, the quality team measures the temperature five times a day during a 10-day period. Because these samples are going to be used to set up the control charts, the team makes sure that the process is behaving normally during the 10-day period.

The resulting 10 samples ($m = 10$) of five observations each ($n = 5$) are shown in Table 4.5.

The team calculates $\overline{\overline{X}}$ and R values for each of the 10 samples and then takes the average values across all samples to calculate $\overline{\overline{X}}$ and $\overline{R}$ (Table 4.6).

TABLE 4.5 Sample Temperature Results for the Dyeing Process

	Observation				
DAY	1	2	3	4	5
1	136	137	144	141	138
2	143	138	140	140	139
3	140	141	144	137	135
4	139	140	141	139	141
5	137	138	143	140	138
6	142	141	140	139	138
7	143	141	143	140	140
8	139	139	141	140	136
9	140	138	143	141	139
10	139	141	142	140	136

TABLE 4.6 Calculating $\overline{\overline{X}}$, R, $\overline{X}$, and $\overline{R}$ Values for the Dyeing Process

	Observation (n = 5)						
DAY	1	2	3	4	5	$\overline{X}$	R
1	136	137	144	141	138	139.2	8
2	143	138	140	140	139	140.0	5
3	140	141	144	137	135	139.4	9
4	139	140	141	139	141	140.0	2
5	137	138	143	140	138	139.2	6
6	142	141	140	139	138	140.0	4
7	143	141	143	140	140	141.4	3
8	139	139	141	140	136	139.0	5
9	140	138	143	141	139	140.2	5
10	139	141	142	140	136	139.6	6
					Sum	1398	**53**

$$\overline{\overline{X}} = \frac{1,398}{10} = 139.8 \text{ degrees} \qquad \overline{R} = \frac{53}{10} = 5.3 \text{ degrees}$$

The team then calculates the upper and lower control limits for the $\overline{\overline{X}}$ and R charts by selecting the $A2$, $D3$, and $D4$ values corresponding to samples of five observations each (Table 4.4). The resulting control charts are shown in Figure 4.7.

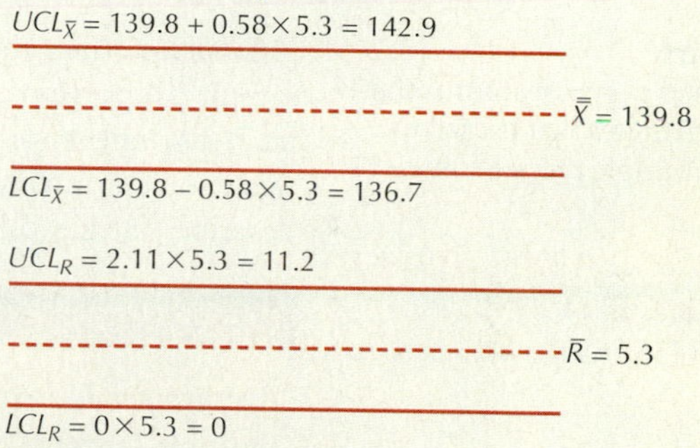

$UCL_{\overline{X}} = 139.8 + 0.58 \times 5.3 = 142.9$

$\overline{\overline{X}} = 139.8$

$LCL_{\overline{X}} = 139.8 - 0.58 \times 5.3 = 136.7$

$UCL_R = 2.11 \times 5.3 = 11.2$

$\overline{R} = 5.3$

$LCL_R = 0 \times 5.3 = 0$

FIGURE 4.7 Blank Control Charts for the Dyeing Process

Note that the $A2$, $D3$, and $D4$ values have been specifically calibrated so that there is a 99.7% chance that future sample $\overline{X}$ and R values will plot within the control limits, *but only if the true mean and standard deviation have not changed.* Put another way, as long as the dyeing process temperature behaves as it has in the past, there is only a 0.3% probability that either the $\overline{X}$ or the R result for a future sample will fall outside of these limits.

Therefore, if an $\overline{X}$ or R value *does* fall outside the control limits, the quality team can assume one of two things:

1. The process has not changed, and the result is simply a random, albeit highly unlikely outcome, or
2. The process has indeed shifted.

Either way, the team should investigate further. After setting up the control charts, the quality team continues to take samples following the same routine as before. Sample results for the next six days are shown in Figure 4.8.

On day 13, both the $\overline{X}$ and the R values fall outside the control limits. Because it is highly unlikely that this occurred due to random chance, the quality team immediately

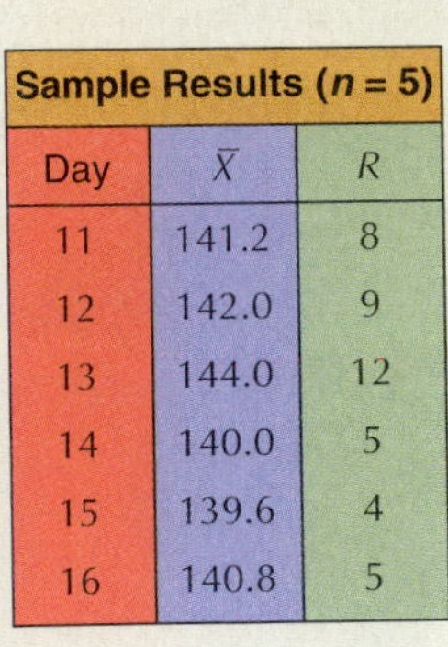

Sample Results (n = 5)		
Day	$\overline{X}$	R
11	141.2	8
12	142.0	9
13	144.0	12
14	140.0	5
15	139.6	4
16	140.8	5

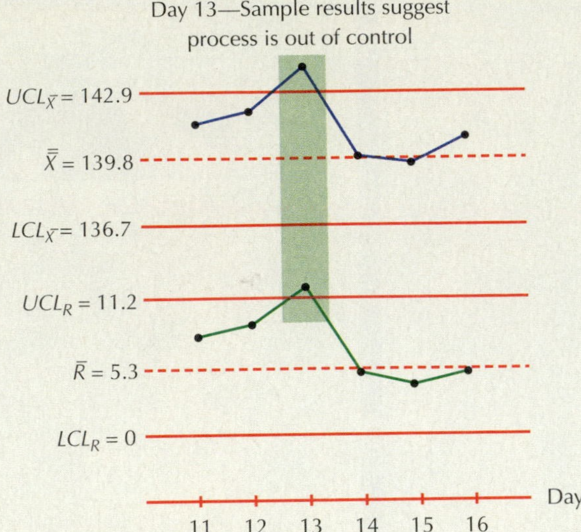

FIGURE 4.8
Control Chart Results for Days 11 through 16

shuts down the process to determine the cause. After replacing a faulty thermostat, the process starts back up. The results for days 14 through 16 suggest that the dyeing process is again functioning normally. By catching the temperature problem early, the quality team is able to take corrective action before the problem gets out of hand.

***p* chart**
A specific type of control chart for attributes that is used to track sample proportions.

***p* CHARTS.** When the measure of interest is an attribute, firms use p charts to track the sample proportions. As with $\overline{\overline{X}}$ and R charts, the p chart has upper and lower control limits. If a sample p value falls outside of these limits, management should immediately investigate to determine whether or not the underlying process has somehow changed. Table 4.7 describes the key calculations for developing a p chart.

TABLE 4.7
Calculations for p Charts

CENTRAL LINE	CONTROL LIMITS
Average p value across multiple samples: $\overline{p} = \dfrac{\sum_{j=1}^{m} p_j}{m}$ **[4-14]** where: $p_j = p$ for the jth sample; m = number of samples used to develop the control chart	Upper control limit = $UCL_p = \overline{p} + 3(S_p)$ **[4-15]** Lower control limit = $LCL_p = \overline{p} - 3(S_p)$ **[4-16]** where: S_p = standard deviation for attribute samples; $S_p = \sqrt{\dfrac{\overline{p}(1-\overline{p})}{n}}$ **[4-17]** where: n = size of each sample

Example 4.8

Developing and Interpreting *p* Charts at Gonzo's Pizza

Since on-time delivery is a key order winner in the pizza business, the manager of Gonzo's Pizzas has decided to set up a control chart to track the proportion of deliveries that take longer than 30 minutes. The manager's first step is to take some samples of deliveries when things are working normally. As a general rule, when sampling by attribute, the sample size (n) should be large enough that:

$$\text{Min}[n(p), n(1-p)] \geq 5 \qquad [4\text{-}18]$$

So if Gonzo's manager expects 10% of the pizzas to be late, he should choose a sample size of at least 50 observations ($50 \times 0.10 = 5$), with an even larger sample size being preferable.

Suppose then that the manager takes samples of 50 deliveries each ($n = 50$) over the next 15 days ($m = 15$). The manager is careful to select these deliveries at random in order to ensure that the sample data are representative of his business. The resulting p values for the 15 samples are shown in the following table:

Sample Results (n = 50)	
DAY	P
1	0.16
2	0.20
3	0.00
4	0.14
5	0.10
6	0.20
7	0.10
8	0.06
9	0.14
10	0.16
11	0.00
12	0.04
13	0.00
14	0.10
15	0.10
Sum	1.50

$$\bar{p} = \frac{1.50}{15} = 0.10 \qquad S_p = \sqrt{\frac{(\bar{p})(1-\bar{p})}{n}} = 0.042$$

Based on the results of his first 15 samples, Gonzo's manager sets up the control chart as follows:

$UCL_p = 0.10 + 3 \times 0.042 = 0.226$

$\bar{p} = 0.10$

$LCL_p = 0.10 - 3 \times 0.042 = -.026$, or 0

p-charts are ideal for tracking the on-time performance of a pizza delivery service.

Like those for the $\overline{\overline{X}}$ and R charts, the formulas for the p chart are set up so that sample p values should fall within the control limits 99.7% of the time, but *only if* the process itself has not changed. Note in this example that the *calculated* lower control limit calculation is actually negative. Because a negative p value is meaningless (Would this mean pizzas were delivered before they were ordered?), the lower control limit is effectively zero.

As long as the percentage of late deliveries in a sample stays below 22.6%, Gonzo's manager can assume the process is behaving normally. However, Gonzo's manager might not be pleased with this definition of "normal." Indeed, he might decide to add more drivers or even shrink the store's delivery area in an effort to increase the proportion of on-time deliveries. If so, Gonzo's manager will need to recalculate the control charts based on the new p value.

As the previous discussion suggests, results that fall outside the control limits might or might not signal trouble. Even so, it is highly unlikely (3 out of 1,000) that a sample $\overline{\overline{X}}$, R, or p value will fall outside the control limits unless something about the process has indeed changed.

There are also patterns *within the control limits* that should be investigated. Two consecutive sample values near one of the control limits could indicate a process that is about to go out of control. Similarly, a run of five or more points on either side of the center line should be investigated, as should a definite upward or downward trend in the measures. The point is that managers do not have to wait until a sample point falls outside the control limits before taking action.

Acceptance Sampling

Even under the best of circumstances, defects can occur and be sent on to the customer. Companies must therefore have some way to determine whether an incoming lot of material or products is of acceptable quality or not and to take action based on the results. One way to determine the quality levels is through 100% inspection (i.e., inspection of each and every item). While this may be necessary in some critical circumstances (for example, donated blood or tiles on the space shuttle), it has its drawbacks.

First, 100% inspection can be extremely expensive and time consuming, especially if there are hundreds or even thousands of items to inspect. Moreover, some quality inspection requires that goods be destroyed or otherwise used up in order to be tested. Wooden matches would be a good example. When 100% inspection is not an option, companies depend on acceptance sampling to determine whether or not an incoming lot of items meets specifications. APICS defines **acceptance sampling** as "the process of sampling a portion of goods for inspection rather than examining the entire lot. The entire lot may be accepted or rejected based on the sample even though the specific units in the lot are better or worse than the sample."[9]

Acceptance sampling
"The process of sampling a portion of goods for inspection rather than examining the entire lot."

In the following example, we illustrate how acceptance sampling works and define operating characteristics (OC) curves, producer's risk, and consumer's risk.

[9]J. F. Cox and J. H. Blackstone, eds., *APICS Dictionary*, 11th ed. (Falls Church, VA: APICS, 2004).

Example 4.9

Acceptance Sampling at Chapman Industries

Chapman Industries has received a shipment of 5,000 parts, each of which can be categorized as "good" or "defective." Rather than inspect all 5,000 parts, Chapman would like to make a decision based on a randomly selected sample of 10 parts ($n = 10$). If more than one part is found to be defective ($c = 1$), Chapman will reject the entire lot.

In addition, Chapman would like to accept all lots with a defect rate $\leq$5%. This is known as the **acceptable quality level (AQL)**. However, because Chapman will be making its decision based on a small sample of parts, there is always the possibility that the company will accidentally accept a lot with a much higher defect level. After much debate, management has agreed to risk accepting lots with defect levels as high as 30%. This upper limit is referred to as the **lot tolerance percent defective (LTPD)**.

Acceptable quality level (AQL)
A term used in acceptance sampling. A cut-off value, representing the maximum defect level at which a consumer would always accept a lot.

Lot tolerance percent defective (LTPD)
A term used in acceptance sampling; represents the highest defect level a consumer is willing to "tolerate."

Consumer's risk (β)
A term used in acceptance sampling; represents the probability of accepting a lot with quality worse than the LTPD level.

Producer's risk (α)
A term used in acceptance sampling; represents the probability of rejecting a lot with quality equal or better than the AQL level.

Operating characteristics (OC) curve
Used in acceptance sampling. Shows the probability of accepting a lot, given the actual fraction defective in the entire lot and the sampling plan being used. Different sampling plans will result in different OC curves.

Using random samples to make decisions about an entire lot has risks. On the one hand, Chapman may accept a lot that is even worse than the LTPD level. The probability of this occurring is called the **consumer's risk** (β). On the other hand, Chapman may actually reject a lot that meets its AQL. The probability of this outcome is known as the **producer's risk** (α).

Figures 4.9 and 4.10 illustrate these concepts. Under 100% inspection, the probability of accepting a "good" lot (defect level of 5% or less) is 100%, while the probability of accepting a bad lot is 0%. In contrast, the **operating characteristics curve (OC)** in Figure 4.9 shows the probability of accepting a lot, given the *actual* fraction defective in the entire lot and the sampling plan being used ($n = 10, c = 1$). It is important to note that different n and c values will result in differently shaped curves.[10]

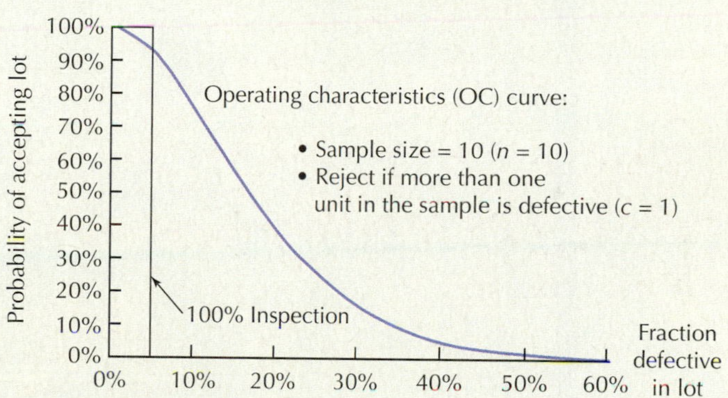

FIGURE 4.9 OC Curve for Chapman Industries

According to the OC curve in Figure 4.9, there is an 80% chance that Chapman will accept a lot that is 90% defect-free, but only a 5% chance that it will accept a lot that is around 40% defect-free. Figure 4.10 shows the actual producer's risk and consumer's risk faced by Chapman under the current sampling plan. Specifically, for an AQL of 5%, the probability of rejecting a good lot (producer's risk) is around 8%. More important from Chapman's perspective, the probability of accepting a lot that doesn't meet Chapman's LTPD level (consumer's risk) is approximately 15%.

What can Chapman do to reduce these risks? In Figure 4.11, we show a new OC curve based on a sample plan that calls for a sample size of 20 ($n = 20$) and $c = 2$. Because the

[10] A. J. Duncan, *Quality Control and Industrial Statistics*, 5th edition (Homewood, IL: Irwin, 1986), pp. 214–248.

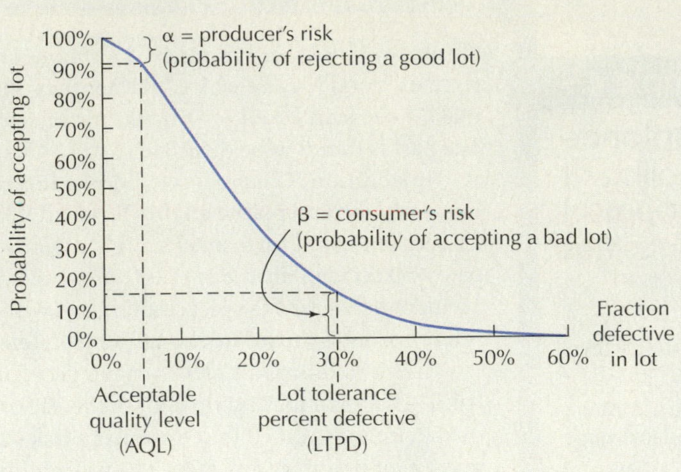

FIGURE 4.10 Producer's and Consumer's Risks

larger sample size is more representative of the entire lot and less likely to be overly influenced by a single observation, the result is a steeper OC curve, which lowers both the consumer's risk *and* the producer's risk. In fact, under the new OC curve, with the same AQL and LTPD values, producer's risk drops to around 7%, and consumer's risk falls dramatically to less than 5%. This highlights a general rule about acceptance sampling: The larger the sample size, the lower the producer's and consumer's risks. Of course, this greater accuracy must be balanced against the increased sampling costs.

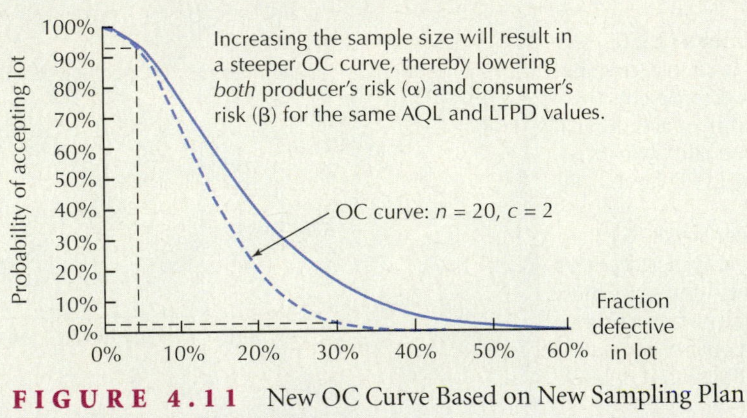

FIGURE 4.11 New OC Curve Based on New Sampling Plan

Taguchi's Quality Loss Function

As you read through the previous sections, you may have thought to yourself, "Is a unit slightly within tolerances really of better quality than one just outside of the tolerances?" After all, an axle with a diameter of 25.019 cm (within tolerances) is only slightly better than one with a diameter of 25.021 cm, and both are larger than the target value of 25 cm.

In fact, upper and lower tolerance limits are really just convenient fictions. If we were to take tolerance limits at face value, we would have to assume that there is no failure cost associated with units that fall within the tolerance limits, while units outside the tolerance limits immediately result in failure costs (Figure 4.12).

FIGURE 4.12
Implied Failure Costs Associated with Tolerance Limits

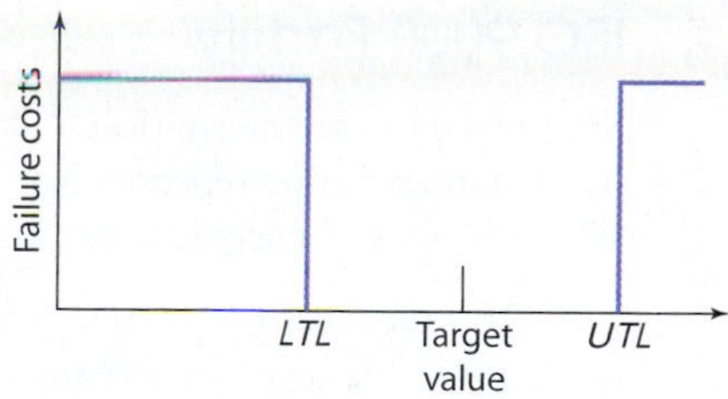

FIGURE 4.13
Taguchi's Quality Loss Function

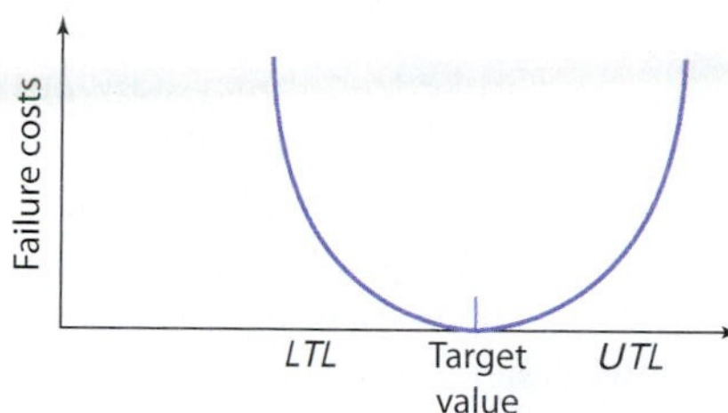

The reality is that the quality of any good or service starts to fall off as soon as the measure of interest drifts from the target value. Examples abound:

- The temperature of a cup of coffee
- The length of a pair of pants
- The total flight time for an commercial airline

Taguchi's quality loss function, shown in Figure 4.13, reflects the idea that any deviation from the target value results in some failure cost. The parabolic shape suggests that these costs start to accrue as soon as there is any deviation from the target value and that they grow exponentially as actual results drift even farther away.

Why do we mention Taguchi's quality loss function? First, it supports the continuous improvement philosophy we described earlier in the chapter. Figure 4.13 suggests that as long as there is *any* variability in the process, there is room for improvement. Taguchi's quality loss function is also consistent with our description of the total costs of quality—failure costs do not disappear completely until the defect level is zero.

4.5 MANAGING QUALITY ACROSS THE SUPPLY CHAIN

So far, much of our attention has been devoted to managing and improving the quality of processes, products, and services within an organization. But the interdependent nature of supply chains suggests that quality management must extend beyond the four walls of the organization. In this section, we talk about two ways in which organizations manage quality across the supply chain. The first, ISO 9000, is a highly successful program that has helped spread quality management practices worldwide. Companies seek ISO 9000 certification both as a way to proactively address quality issues and as a way to signal to potential supply chain partners that they are serious about managing quality. In the second part, we consider how companies deal with external failures in the supply chain.

ISO 9000 Family

ISO 9000
A family of standards, supported by the International Organization for Standardization, representing an international consensus on good quality management practices. ISO 9000 addresses business processes, rather than specific outcomes.

Supported by the International Organization for Standardization (ISO), **ISO 9000** is a family of standards that represents an international consensus on good management practices. ISO 9000 seeks to help organizations deliver products or services that:

- Meet the customer's quality requirements and
- Applicable regulatory requirements, while aiming to
- Enhance customer satisfaction and
- Achieve continual improvement of their performance in pursuit of these objectives.[11]

Unlike traditional standards, ISO 9000 focuses more on practices than outcomes. Companies following ISO 9000 standards will often have independent auditors "certify" that their business processes are ISO 9000 compliant. In some industries, certification is a requirement for doing business, and industry-specific standards may also apply. In others, ISO 9000 may simply signal potential supply chain partners that an organization has quality systems in place.

The ISO 9000 family of standards has been regularly updated to reflect developments in managerial thought since it was first introduced in 1987. ISO 9000 currently consists of two major sets of standards. *ISO 9001:2000* is used by companies seeking to establish a management system that provides confidence in the conformance of their products and services to established or specified requirements. *ISO 9004:2000* is used to extend the benefits obtained from ISO 9001:2000 to all parties who are interested in or affected by a business's operations. The following example illustrates how ISO 9000 was applied in a services environment:

> *A firm of international lawyers wanted to improve their client management processes and to achieve registration/certification to ISO 9001:2000. Their quality management system provides for the design and development of new services such as international tax planning and modifying traditional services to meet the requirements of new or amended legislation. They included purchasing control to cover the selection of computer hardware and software, as well as purchasing the services of specialist lawyers as needed. After successfully implementing ISO 9001:2000, they used the self-assessment guidelines of ISO 9004:2000 to monitor their progress as they improved their quality management system.*[12]

External Failures in the Supply Chain

Even with the best quality programs, companies still need to put into place processes to catch defective products once they have left the organization and entered the supply chain. How quickly and effectively companies handle this can have a large impact on the resulting external failure costs. Tracking systems, lot identification numbers, and explicit procedures for returning or destroying defective (and potentially harmful) goods are all examples of solutions that are employed to deal with such problems. In *Supply Chain Connections*, we consider how one pharmaceutical firm dealt with the potential problems caused by mislabeled drugs.

---

[11]International Organization for Standardization, **www.iso.org/iso/en/iso9000-14000/understand/inbrief.html**.

[12]International Organization for Standardization, **www.iso.org/iso/en/iso9000-14000/understand/selection_use/examplesofiso9000.html**.

SUPPLY CHAIN CONNECTIONS

REMOVING MISLABELED DRUGS FROM THE SUPPLY CHAIN

In May 2004, McNeil Consumer & Specialty Pharmaceuticals realized that it had made a serious mistake—it had accidentally put Adult-Strength Tylenol in bottles meant to hold Children's Motrin. What made this mistake especially worrisome is that the bottles had been released into the supply chain. In an effort to help retailers and consumers track down the defective bottles before anyone was seriously injured, McNeil released a notice that was listed on the Food and Drug Administration (FDA) Web site.[13] The notice gave information regarding:

- The actual manufacturing lots affected (information readily found on the carton);
- The dates the bottles were distributed;
- The visible differences between the two drugs (specifically, Children's Motrin Grape Chewable Tablets are round, purple-colored, scored tablets that have a grape smell, while the Tylenol 8-Hour Geltabs are hard, round, gelatin coated, and shiny); and
- A contact number for anyone finding a bottle or having a question.

At the time of the press release, no one had been injured. Through its quick actions, McNeil hoped to avoid any future injuries. Clearly, McNeil's job would have been much harder if it had not kept track of the manufacturing lot numbers or the shipping dates for the bottles in question.

[13]U.S. Food and Drug Administration, **www.fda.gov/medwatch/SAFETY/2004/safety04.htm#motrin.**

CHAPTER SUMMARY

As an area of intense business interest, quality is here to stay. Operations and supply chain personnel in particular need to be familiar with the major quality topic areas, including the different philosophical perspectives on quality and the tools used to manage quality levels on a day-to-day basis. In this chapter, we gave you a solid introduction to quality topics, ranging from high-level discussions of quality issues to detailed descriptions of tools and techniques. We started by defining quality and describing a total cost of quality model. We then presented an overview of total quality management (TQM), as well as a section on statistical quality control (SQC). We ended the chapter with a discussion of how organizations manage quality across the supply chain and some of the issues they face.

We encourage you not to let your quality education end here. The American Society for Quality (**www.asq.org**), the Juran Institute (**www.juran.com**), the W. Edwards Deming Institute (**www.Deming.org**), and the ISO (**www.iso.org**) are four organizations among many that provide a wealth of information for those interested in quality. Regardless of what you do, you can be assured that you will deal with quality issues in your career.

KEY FORMULAS

Process capability ratio (page 93):

$$C_p = \frac{UTL - LTL}{6\sigma} \qquad [4\text{-}1]$$

where:

UTL = upper tolerance limit
LTL = lower tolerance limit
σ = process standard deviation for the variable of interest

Process capability index (page 94):

$$C_{pk} = \min\left[\frac{\mu - LTL}{3\sigma}, \frac{UTL - \mu}{3\sigma}\right] \qquad [4\text{-}3]$$

where:

μ = process mean
UTL = upper tolerance limit
LTL = lower tolerance limit
σ = standard deviation

Sample average for a continuous variable (page 95):

$$\overline{X} = \frac{\sum_{i=1}^{n} X_i}{n} \qquad [4\text{-}5]$$

where:

n = number of observations in the sample
X_i = value of the ith observation

Sample range (R) for a continuous variable (page 95):

$$R = (\text{highest value in the sample}) - (\text{lowest value in the sample}) \qquad [4\text{-}6]$$

Sample proportion (page 95):

$$p = \frac{\sum_{i=1}^{n} a_i}{n} \qquad [4\text{-}7]$$

where:

n = number of observations in the sample
a_i = 0 if the attribute is not present for the ith observation and 1 if it is

Average sample mean for a continuous variable (page 99):

$$\overline{\overline{X}} = \frac{\sum_{j=1}^{m} \overline{X}_j}{m} \qquad [4\text{-}8]$$

where:

$\overline{\overline{X}}$ = grand mean
m = number of samples used to develop the $\overline{X}$ chart
$\overline{X}_j$ = average for the jth sample

Average range value for samples of a continuous variable (page 99):

$$\overline{R} = \frac{\sum_{j=1}^{m} R_j}{m} \qquad [4\text{-}9]$$

where:

m = number of samples used to develop the control charts
R_j = range for the jth sample

Upper control limit for $\overline{X}$ chart (page 99):

$$\text{Upper control limit} = UCL_{\overline{X}} = \overline{\overline{X}} + A2(\overline{R}) \quad [4\text{-}10]$$

Lower control limit for $\overline{X}$ chart (page 99):

$$\text{Lower control limit} = LCL_{\overline{X}} = \overline{\overline{X}} - A2(\overline{R}) \quad [4\text{-}11]$$

Upper control limit for R chart (page 99):

$$\text{Upper control limit} = UCL_R = D4(\overline{R}) \quad [4\text{-}12]$$

Lower control limit for R chart (page 99):

$$\text{Lower control limit} = LCL_R = D3(\overline{R}) \quad [4\text{-}13]$$

Average sample proportion for an attribute (page 102):

$$\overline{p} = \frac{\sum_{j=1}^{m} p_j}{m} \quad [4\text{-}14]$$

where:

p_j = p value for the jth sample
m = number of samples used to develop the control chart

Upper control limit for p chart (page 102):

$$\text{Upper control limit} = UCL_p = \overline{p} + 3(S_p) \quad [4\text{-}15]$$

where:

S_p = standard deviation for attribute samples

Lower control limit for p chart (page 102):

$$\text{Lower control limit} = LCL_p = \overline{p} - 3(S_p) \quad [4\text{-}16]$$

where:

S_p = standard deviation for attribute samples

Standard deviation for attribute samples (page 102):

$$S_p = \sqrt{\frac{(\overline{p})(1-\overline{p})}{n}} \quad [4\text{-}17]$$

where:

n = size of each sample

KEY TERMS

Acceptable quality level (AQL) 105
Acceptance sampling 104
Appraisal costs 86
Attribute 97
Conformance perspective 84
Consumer's risk (β) 105
Continuous improvement 90
Continuous variable 97
Control chart 97
Control limits 98
Employee empowerment 90
External failure costs 86
Internal failure costs 86
ISO 9000 108
Lot tolerance percent defective (LTPD) 105
Lower tolerance limit (LTL) 93
Operating characteristics (OC) curve 105
p chart 102
Prevention costs 86
Process capability ratio (C_p) 93
Process capability index (C_{pk}) 94
Process owner 92
Producer's risk (α) 105
Proportion 97
Quality 83
Quality assurance 90
Quality function development (QFD) 91
R chart 99
Range (R) 99
Sample average ($\overline{X}$) 97
Six Sigma quality 96
Statistical quality control 91
Strategic quality plan 92
Total cost of quality curve 87
Total quality management (TQM) 88
Upper tolerance limit (UTL) 93
Value perspective 83
$\overline{X}$ chart 99

USING EXCEL IN QUALITY MANAGEMENT

Spreadsheet applications such as Microsoft Excel are ideally suited to performing the large numbers of calculations needed to support statistical quality control efforts. The following spreadsheet calculates the average sample proportion and standard deviation for 30 samples (the sample results are arranged in two columns to save space). The highlighted cells represent the input values. The calculated cells are as follows:

Cell D23 (average sample proportion): = AVERAGE(B7:C21)/C4

Cell D24 (standard deviation): = SQRT(D23*(1-D23)/C4)

	A	B	C	D	E	F	G
1	**Calculating the average sample proportion from 30 samples**						
2	**and standard deviation, S_p, from 30 samples**						
3							
4		Sample size:	150				
5							
6	***No. of observations in each sample displaying the attribute***						
7		17	13				
8		10	10				
9		13	20				
10		12	6				
11		16	16				
12		17	21				
13		16	6				
14		13	10				
15		13	3				
16		12	10				
17		13	13				
18		12	7				
19		13	16				
20		10	16				
21		12	14				
22							
23			**Average sample proportion:**	**0.08444**			
24			**Standard deviation, S_p:**	**0.0227**			
25							

SOLVED PROBLEM

Problem

Pulley Engineering manufactures needle bearings for use in high-tech machinery. The target diameter for one particular bearing is 0.125 inches. The quality control staff has taken 15 samples of five observations each when the manufacturing processes were under control and has measured the diameter. The results are as follows:

	Observation				
SAMPLE	1	2	3	4	5
1	0.1253	0.1262	0.1254	0.1240	0.1230
2	0.1242	0.1247	0.1251	0.1238	0.1241
3	0.1225	0.1258	0.1229	0.1242	0.1255
4	0.1249	0.1259	0.1249	0.1240	0.1257
5	0.1245	0.1252	0.1261	0.1238	0.1225
6	0.1273	0.1234	0.1248	0.1241	0.1260
7	0.1226	0.1239	0.1227	0.1252	0.1259
8	0.1244	0.1238	0.1254	0.1261	0.1260
9	0.1236	0.1262	0.1250	0.1247	0.1250
10	0.1251	0.1264	0.1233	0.1233	0.1246
11	0.1253	0.1248	0.1237	0.1252	0.1226
12	0.1232	0.1251	0.1259	0.1263	0.1257
13	0.1231	0.1242	0.1256	0.1252	0.1257
14	0.1256	0.1240	0.1246	0.1250	0.1252
15	0.1243	0.1240	0.1239	0.1262	0.1246

Use these data to develop control limits for the $\bar{X}$ and R charts. In addition, suppose engineering has established upper and lower tolerance limits of 0.129 inches and 0.121 inches, respectively. Calculate the process capability ratio and interpret the results.

Solution

The first step is to calculate the $\bar{X}$ and R values for each sample and then the $\bar{\bar{X}}$ and $\bar{R}$ values:

	OBSERVATION						
SAMPLE	1	2	3	4	5	$\bar{X}$	R
1	0.1253	0.1262	0.1254	0.1240	0.1230	0.1248	0.0032
2	0.1242	0.1247	0.1251	0.1238	0.1241	0.1244	0.0013
3	0.1225	0.1258	0.1229	0.1242	0.1255	0.1242	0.0033
4	0.1249	0.1259	0.1249	0.1240	0.1257	0.1251	0.0019
5	0.1245	0.1252	0.1261	0.1238	0.1225	0.1244	0.0036
6	0.1273	0.1234	0.1248	0.1241	0.1260	0.1251	0.0039
7	0.1226	0.1239	0.1227	0.1252	0.1259	0.1241	0.0033
8	0.1244	0.1238	0.1254	0.1261	0.1260	0.1251	0.0023
9	0.1236	0.1262	0.1250	0.1247	0.1250	0.1249	0.0026
10	0.1251	0.1264	0.1233	0.1233	0.1246	0.1245	0.0031
11	0.1253	0.1248	0.1237	0.1252	0.1226	0.1243	0.0027
12	0.1232	0.1251	0.1259	0.1263	0.1257	0.1252	0.0031
13	0.1231	0.1242	0.1256	0.1252	0.1257	0.1248	0.0026
14	0.1256	0.1240	0.1246	0.1250	0.1252	0.1249	0.0016
15	0.1243	0.1240	0.1239	0.1262	0.1246	0.1246	0.0023
					Average:	**0.1247**	**0.0027**

Combining these results with the appropriate $A2$, $D3$, and $D4$ values from Table 4.4 yields the following control chart limits:

$$UCL_{\bar{X}} = 0.1247 + 0.58 \times 0.0027 = 0.1263$$
$$LCL_{\bar{X}} = 0.1247 - 0.58 \times 0.0027 = 0.1231$$

$$UCL_R = 2.11 \times 0.0027 = 0.0057$$
$$LCL_R = 0 \times 0.0027 = 0$$

To calculate the process capability ratio, we must first estimate the standard deviation of the individual observations, $\hat{\sigma}$. We can quickly do this using the = STDEV(number1, number2, ...) function of Microsoft Excel, where the values in parentheses represent the raw diameter measurements. Doing so results in the following estimate:

$$\hat{\sigma} = 0.0011$$

Therefore, the process capability ratio is

$$C_p = \frac{0.129 - 0.121}{6(0.0011)} = \frac{0.008}{0.0066} = 1.21$$

The results suggest that the current process is capable of meeting the tolerance limits more than 99.7% of the time.

DISCUSSION QUESTIONS

1. What dimensions of quality were highlighted in the Dell battery pack opening case study? Would statistical quality control tools, such as control charts or acceptance sampling, be enough to resolve quality shortcomings along all these dimensions? Explain. What are the implications for managing quality at Dell?
2. Why can two people perceive the same product or service as having different quality levels? From a business perspective, why is it important then to "know your customer"?
3. Several years ago a major automotive manufacturer was sued because the latch on a minivan's rear door failed after the vehicle was hit from the side at 30 miles per hour. The plaintiff argued that the latch was of poor quality because it didn't hold up under the stress. The manufacturer disagreed, noting that the latch had met all government requirements and had been made to specifications. According to our definition of quality, can both sides be right?
4. Recall the DMAIC process described in Chapter 3. At what stage would statistical quality control tools be used?
5. Suppose the actual range for a sample falls *below* the lower control limit for the R chart. Is this a good thing or a bad thing? Explain.

PROBLEMS

Additional homework problems are available at www.prenhall.com/bozarth. These problems use Excel to generate customized problems for different class sections or even different students.

(* = easy; ** = moderate; *** = advanced)

1. (*) Tyler Apiaries sells bees and beekeeping supplies. Bees (including a queen) are shipped in special packages

according to weight. The target weight of a package is 1.4 kgs. Historically, Tyler's shipments have weighed on average 1.4 kgs, with a standard deviation of 0.15 kgs. Calculate the process capability ratio, assuming the lower and upper tolerance limits are 1.1 kgs and 1.7 kgs, respectively. Is Tyler Apiaries currently able to meet the tolerance limits 99.7% of the time?

2. (*) Refer to Problem 1. Suppose Tyler changes its processes so that the average package weight is now 1.5 kgs with a new standard deviation of 0.6 kgs. Tyler still markets the packages of bees as weighing 1.4 kgs, and the tolerance limits remain as before. Calculate the process capability index for the weight of the bee packages. Is Tyler able to meet the tolerance limits?

3. (**) Referring back to Problem 1, what would the standard deviation have to be for Tyler Apiaries to achieve Six Sigma quality levels with regard to the weight of the bee packages?

4. (**) Refer to Problem 1. The average bee weighs 0.1 grams. Use this information to convert the target package weight and tolerance limits into number of bees. How might Tyler Apiaries use this information to better control the package weights? Should Tyler Apiaries think about resetting the tolerance limits?

5. (*) Leah's Toys produces molded plastic baby rattles. These rattles must be completely smooth. That is, there can be no rough edges where the molded halves fit together. Rattles are judged to be either acceptable or defective with regard to this requirement. Leah's has determined that the current process has an underlying p value of 0.01, meaning that, on average, 1 out of 100 rattles is currently judged to be defective. Calculate the standard deviation for the process and the resulting control limits for samples of 200 rattles each.

6. (*) Leah's Toys also makes rubber balls. The current process is capable of producing balls that weigh, on average, 3 ounces, with a standard deviation of 0.25 ounces. What is the process capability ratio, assuming upper and lower tolerance limits of 3.5 and 2.5 ounces? Is Leah's able to meet the tolerance limits 99.7% of the time? Explain.

7. (**) Reconsider the data in Problem 6. What would the standard deviation have to be to *exactly* meet the tolerance limits 99.7% of the time?

8. (**) Suppose Leah's Toys invests in process improvements that lower the standard deviation in Problem 6 to just 0.10 ounces. Is this enough for Leah's to achieve Six Sigma quality levels with regard to the weight of the balls? Explain.

9. Leah's Toys guarantees to ship customer orders in 24 hours or less. The following chart contains results for five samples of nine customer orders each.

SAMPLE	SAMPLE CUSTOMER ORDERS (HOURS TO SHIP)								
1	3	5	21	4	15	9	7	3	6
2	22	16	8	16	11	38	11	25	15
3	9	2	5	17	2	19	4	2	4
4	6	7	18	9	16	18	7	10	1
5	11	10	20	18	1	6	3	18	9

a. (**) Based on these results, estimate the $\bar{p}$ and S_p values.

b. (**) Another student comments, "Time is a continuous variable. We should really be looking at the $\bar{\bar{X}}$ and $\bar{R}$ values." Do you agree or disagree? Explain your rationale.

10. (**) BlueBolt Bottlers has a bottle-filling process with a mean value of 64 ounces and a standard deviation of 8 ounces. Suppose the upper tolerance limits and lower tolerance limits are 71 and 57 ounces, respectively. What is the process capability ratio? What would the standard deviation have to be in order for the process to meet the tolerance limits 99.7% of the time?

11. (***) Now suppose BlueBolt Bottlers makes some process improvements, thereby lowering the standard deviation of the process to 1.5 ounces, rather than 8 ounces. Using the data in Problem 10 and the new standard deviation, calculate the process capability ratio. Is the filling process able to meet the tolerance limits 99.7% of the time? Does the process provide six-sigma quality levels? Explain.

12. (*) The River Rock Company sells 200-lb. decorative rocks for landscaping use. The current bagging process yields samples with $\bar{\bar{X}}$ and $\bar{R}$ values of 200 lbs. and 12 lbs., respectively. Each sample consists of 12 observations. Develop the appropriate control charts.

13. (**) LaBoing produces springs, which are categorized as either acceptable or defective. During a period in which the manufacturing processes are under control, LeBoing takes multiple samples of 100 springs each, resulting in a calculated $\bar{p}$ value of 0.07. Develop the appropriate control chart for the springs.

14. AnderSet Laboratories produces rough lenses that will ultimately be ground into precision lenses for use in laboratory equipment. The company has developed the following thickness measures, based on 15 samples of four lenses that were taken when the process was under control:

MEAN (MICRONS) ($n = 4$)	MINIMUM	MAXIMUM
3.900	3.617	3.989
4.206	3.971	4.302
4.214	4.062	4.400
3.890	3.749	3.937
4.036	3.501	4.084
4.134	3.543	4.584
3.037	2.935	3.929
5.082	3.797	5.695
3.404	2.837	4.255
5.246	5.106	6.382
4.197	4.085	4.239
4.312	3.949	4.356
4.302	3.989	4.400
3.867	3.617	3.900
4.170	4.046	4.206

a. (**) Use the above data to calculate $\overline{\overline{X}}$ and $\overline{R}$ and set up the appropriate control charts.

b. (**) Can the process be "under control" in statistical terms, but still fail to meet the needs of AnderSet's customers? Explain using a numerical example.

15. (**) Refer to Problem 4. Suppose AnderSet Laboratories takes some additional samples of the same size, yielding the following results. Plot these samples on the control charts, and circle any observations that appear to be out of control.

MEAN (MICRONS) ($n = 4$)	MINIMUM	MAXIMUM
4.134	4.011	4.612
3.913	3.891	4.474
4.584	4.499	5.145
4.009	3.934	4.891
4.612	4.085	4.983
5.627	5.183	6.080

16. (**) Lazy B Ranch produces leather hides for use in the furniture and automotive upholstery industry. The company has taken 10 samples of nine observations each, measuring the square footage of each hide. Summary data are as follows:

MEAN (SQ. FT.) ($n = 9$)	MINIMUM	MAXIMUM
13.2	12.7	13.5
12.8	12.5	13.3
13.3	12.6	13.7
13.1	12.5	13.5
12.7	12.2	13.0
12.9	12.5	13.3
13.2	12.9	13.5
13.0	12.6	13.6
13.1	12.7	13.4
12.7	12.3	13.5

Use the data to set up control limits for the hides. Why would it be important for the Lazy B Ranch to track this information? Why might it be harder for the Lazy B Ranch to reduce process variability than it would be for a more typical "manufacturer"?

17. An Internet service provider has an online help service for its customers. Customer queries that take more than five minutes to resolve are categorized as "unsatisfactory" experiences. To evaluate the quality of its service, the company takes 10 samples of 100 calls each while the process is under control. The resulting p values for unsatisfactory calls are as follows:

p VALUES ($n = 100$)
0.08
0.11
0.12
0.06
0.13
0.09
0.16
0.09
0.18
0.15

a. (**) Calculate the $\overline{p}$ and S_p values, and set up control limits so that future sample p values should fall within the control limits 99.7% of the time.

b. (**) Suppose the Internet service provider in Part a takes four additional samples, yielding the following p values: 0.9, 0.12, 0.25, and 0.10. Plot the results and circle all values that suggest the process is "out of control." Is it possible that a sample result could fall outside of the control limits due to pure chance? Explain.

c. (**) Now suppose that the sample size is actually 50, not 100. Recalculate the control limits for the p chart. What happened? Explain.

18. EK Chemical Company sells a specialty chemical in packages marked 100 grams. In reality, EK has set the process mean at 100.5 grams, and the process currently has a standard deviation of 0.50 grams. Suppose the customer will accept anywhere from 98 to 102 grams as long as the average package has at least 100 grams.

a. (**) Calculate the process capability index for the current manufacturing process. Is the process capable of meeting the tolerance limits more than 99.7% of the time? Explain.

b. (***) Now suppose EK recenters the manufacturing process so that the process mean is exactly 100 grams, while the standard deviation remains the same. Calculate the process capability ratio. Is the process still capable of meeting the tolerance limits more than 99.7% of the time? Explain.

19. Crawford Pharmaceuticals has developed a new drug, Vaxidene. The target amount for a single dose of Vaxidene is 100 mg. Patients can receive as little as 98 mg or as much as 102 mg without experiencing any ill effects. Because of potential liability issues, Crawford has determined that it is absolutely imperative that manufacturing be able to provide Six Sigma quality levels. At present, the manufacturing process has a process mean of 100 mg and a standard deviation of 0.25 mg.

a. (*) What are the upper and lower tolerance limits for Vaxidene?

b. (**) Is Crawford's manufacturing process currently able to meet the dosage specifications at least 99.7% of the time? Show your work.

c. (**) What would the standard deviation for the process have to be in order for Crawford to achieve Six Sigma quality levels?

20. BHC produces bags of cement. The stated weight for a bag of cement is 100 lbs. Customers will accept an occasional bag weighing as little as 96 lbs. as long as the average weight is at least 100 lbs. At the same time, BHC doesn't want to give away cement, so it has set an upper tolerance limit of 104 lbs. The current filling process has an actual process mean of 101 lbs. and a standard deviation of 0.65 lb.

a. (**) Calculate the process capability index for BHC. In this example, why should we use the process capability index, rather than the process capability ratio, to assess capability?

b. (**) Can you think of any reason why BHC might want a process mean higher than the target value?

21. Central Airlines would like to set up a control chart to monitor its on-time arrival performance. Each day over a 10-day period Central Airlines chose 30 flights at random and tracked the number of late arrivals in each sample. The results are as follows:

DAY	SAMPLE SIZE	NO. OF LATE-ARRIVING FLIGHTS
1	30	2
2	30	3
3	30	4
4	30	0
5	30	1
6	30	6
7	30	4
8	30	2
9	30	3
10	30	5

a. (*) Calculate $\overline{p}$.

b. (**) Set up a p chart to track the proportion of late arrivals. (*Note:* Each sample consists of 30 observations.)

c. (***) Airline travel is characterized by busy and slow seasons. As a result, what is "normal" during one time of the year wouldn't be "normal" at some other time. What difficulties might arise as a result of using a single control chart to track the proportion of late arrivals? What could Central Airlines do about this?

22. The Oceanside Apparel Company manufactures men's knit shirts. The production process requires material to be cut into large patterned squares, which are then sewn together. If the squares are not the correct length, the final shirt will be either too large or too small. The target length is 36 inches. In order to monitor the cutting process, Oceanside managers took 22 samples of four squares each and measured the lengths. For each sample, they then calculated the sample mean and range. Finally, they calculated the average sample mean (36.0 inches) and average range value (1.8 inches) for the 22 samples. Managers felt that these values were acceptable; that is, the process was in control.

a. (**) Develop the appropriate control chart(s) to monitor the fabric length.

b. (**) Using the control chart(s) you developed in part a, plot the following samples. Circle any that appear to be out of control.

SAMPLE ($n = 4$)	MEASUREMENTS (IN INCHES)			
1	37.3	36.5	38.2	36.2
2	33.4	35.8	37.9	36.2
3	32.1	34.8	39.1	35.3
4	36.1	37.2	36.7	34.2
5	32.1	34.0	35.6	36.1

23. (***) (*Microsoft Excel problem*) The following Excel spreadsheet calculates the upper and lower control limits for a continuous variable. **Recreate this spreadsheet in**

Excel. You should develop the spreadsheet so that the results will be recalculated if any of the values in the highlighted cells are changed. Your formatting does not have to be exactly the same, but the numbers should be. (As a test, see what happens if all five observations in Sample 1 are 40. Your new upper and lower control limits for the sample means should be 36.06 and 34.28, respectively.)

	A	B	C	D	E	F	G	H	I	J	K
1	**Calculating upper and lower control limits for a continuous variable (sample size = 5)**										
2											
3				***** Observations *****							
4	*Sample*	*1*	*2*	*3*	*4*	*5*	$\overline{X}$	*R*			
5	*1*	*34.26*	*34.66*	*35.53*	*34.62*	*35.87*	*34.99*	*1.61*			
6	*2*	*34.75*	*35.10*	*34.00*	*35.48*	*36.64*	*35.19*	*2.64*			
7	*3*	*34.11*	*35.17*	*34.54*	*35.25*	*34.97*	*34.81*	*1.14*			
8	*4*	*34.31*	*34.56*	*35.36*	*35.38*	*34.30*	*34.78*	*7.08*			
9	*5*	*34.65*	*35.39*	*34.87*	*34.90*	*35.70*	*35.10*	*6.05*			
10	*6*	*33.78*	*35.26*	*35.79*	*34.52*	*34.51*	*34.77*	*2.01*			
11	*7*	*35.13*	*35.42*	*34.73*	*36.27*	*34.67*	*35.24*	*1.60*			
12	*8*	*35.23*	*34.06*	*35.50*	*34.96*	*35.43*	*35.04*	*1.44*			
13	*9*	*34.80*	*34.60*	*34.69*	*32.94*	*33.87*	*34.18*	*1.86*			
14	*10*	*35.16*	*33.26*	*35.92*	*34.08*	*33.33*	*34.35*	*2.66*			
15	*11*	*33.81*	*34.81*	*34.27*	*34.54*	*35.17*	*34.52*	*1.36*			
16	*12*	*35.70*	*33.74*	*34.59*	*35.38*	*34.34*	*34.75*	*1.96*			
17	*13*	*33.97*	*34.81*	*34.93*	*34.27*	*35.47*	*34.69*	*1.50*			
18	*14*	*35.36*	*34.47*	*35.67*	*35.86*	*34.34*	*35.14*	*1.52*			
19	*15*	*35.39*	*35.41*	*35.06*	*34.52*	*34.27*	*34.93*	*1.14*			
20						*Average:*	*34.83*	*1.64*			
21											
22		**Upper control limit for sample means:**				**35.78**					
23		**Lower control limit for sample means:**				**33.88**					
24											
25		**Upper control limit for sample ranges:**				**3.46**					
26		**Lower control limit for sample ranges:**				**0.00**					

24. (***) (*Microsoft Excel problem*) The Excel spreadsheet to the right calculates the upper and lower control limits for an attribute (in this case, the proportion of dissatisfied customers). **Recreate this spreadsheet in Excel.** You should develop the spreadsheet so that the results will be recalculated if any of the values in the highlighted cells are changed. Your formatting does not have to be exactly the same, but the numbers should be. (As a test, see what happens if you change the sample size to 200. The new *UCL* and *LCL* values should be .1542 and .0312, respectively.)

	A	B	C	D	E	F	G	H
1	**Setting Up 99.7% Control Limits, Sampling by Attribute**							
2								
3		No. of dissatisfied		Sample size =			100	
4	Sample	customers	*p*-value		$\overline{p}$	=	0.0927	
5	1	9	0.0900		S_p	=	0.0290	
6	2	11	0.1100					
7	3	13	0.1300					
8	4	8	0.0800	*UCL* for sample p values:				0.1797
9	5	9	0.0900	*LCL* for sample p values:				0.0057
10	6	10	0.1000					
11	7	9	0.0900					
12	8	8	0.0800					
13	9	11	0.1100					
14	10	12	0.1200					
15	11	10	0.1000					
16	12	7	0.0700					
17	13	8	0.0800					
18	14	9	0.0900					
19	15	8	0.0800					
20	16	8	0.0800					
21	17	9	0.0900					
22	18	10	0.1000					
23	19	6	0.0600					
24	20	9	0.0900					
25	21	11	0.1100					
26	22	8	0.0800					
27	23	11	0.1100					
28	24	6	0.0600					
29	25	9	0.0900					
30	26	9	0.0900					
31	27	8	0.0800					
32	28	12	0.1200					
33	29	9	0.0900					
34	30	11	0.1100					

CASE STUDY

DITTENHOEFER'S FINE CHINA

Introduction

Overall, Steve Edwards, Vice President of Marketing at Dittenhoefer's Fine China, is very pleased with the success of his new line of *Gem-Surface* china plates. *Gem-Surface* plates are different from regular china in that the plates have a special polymer coating that makes them highly resistant to chipping and fading. Not only are the plates more durable, but also they are completely dishwasher safe.

In order to manufacture the new plates, Dittenhoefer's has leased a special machine to apply the coating and has put in place a drying system to "cure" the coating on the plates. The research and development (R&D) lab has determined that in order to prevent defective plates, it is important that the machine apply the polymer coating at the proper temperature and in the proper thickness. Specifically, R&D has written up the following guidelines:

Coating thickness. The optimal polymer coating thickness is 4 microns. If the coating is > 5 microns, the plates will take too long to dry. If the coating is < 3 microns, the plates will be inadequately protected.

Coating temperature. The polymer coating needs to be applied at a temperature between 160 degrees Fahrenheit and 170 degrees Fahrenheit, with the target temperature being 165 degrees Fahrenheit. If the temperature is lower than 160°, the polymer will not adhere properly and will flake off. If the temperature is higher than 170°, the polymer coating will fade the design on the plates.

Quality Problems

Traditionally, quality control at Dittenhoefer's has consisted of visually inspecting finished items for defects (chips, cracks, etc.) as they are being packed for shipment. This was acceptable in the past, when defects were few and far between. With the new polymer-coating technology, however, this has caused some serious problems.

For instance, on one Friday during the Christmas season, the packers noticed that nearly all of the plates they were getting ready to ship had faded designs, which suggested that the temperature of the polymer-coating machine might be too high. Sure enough, when a supervisor went back to check on the polymer-coating machine, he found that the thermostat was set at 190 degrees. Apparently, someone had set the temperature higher to clean the machine, but had forgotten to reset it back to 165 degrees. The good news was that the problem was easily fixed. The bad news was that the machine had been running at 190 degrees since *Wednesday*. In the interim, 2,400 plates had been run through the coating machine. In the end, Dittenhoefer's had to destroy all 2,400 plates and was late making shipments to several important customers.

In another instance, a worker just happened to notice that the polymer-coating machine was not using as much raw material as expected. When the worker measured the thickness of the coating being applied to the plates, she found out why—the coating thickness was only 2.4 microns. A quick check of plates being dried and those being packed revealed that they, too, had a coating thickness of around 2.4 microns. While manufacturing was able to correct the problem and save *these* plates, no one knew how many plates had been shipped before the problem was discovered.

The Customer Service Department

The customer service office is responsible for pricing and entering customer orders, tracking the progress of orders, and making sure orders are shipped when promised. If an order is going to be late or there is some other problem, the customer service office is also responsible for notifying the customer. In addition, the customer service office handles customer complaints.

As would be expected, Steve Edwards often visits the larger dealers to find out how satisfied they are with the products and service they have received. It is during one of these trips that Steve realizes there might be problems with the customer service office. When visiting Nancy Sanders, owner of Lenoir Home Furnishings, Steve gets an earful:

> *Steve, I understand that you have been busier ever since you introduced the new line of plates. However, I feel that the service quality has deteriorated and no one seems to care! Just last week, I found that an order I had expected in on Monday was not even ready to ship. No one called me—I just happened to find out when I was calling to place another order. Your information system also seems to be antiquated. The sales assistant apologized for the shipment delay and tried to be helpful, but she couldn't tell me the status of my order or even when I had placed it! It seemed that the previous sales assistant had changed jobs, and no one knew where her notes were. Notes!? Why isn't this stuff on a computer? It makes me have serious reservations about doing business with you.*

Steve is caught flat-footed by the criticism. When he gets back to the office, he puts together a letter to his top 200 customers. In the letter, he gives customers a self-addressed stamped postcard and asks them to list any problems they have had dealing with the sales office. He gets back responses from 93 of the customers. Their responses are summarized here:

PROBLEM	NUMBER OF RESPONDENTS PROBLEM CITING PROBLEMS
Incorrect pricing	23
Lost the order	8
Did not notify customer with regard to change in delivery date	54
Did not know status of customer's order	77
Order incorrect—wrong products shipped	4
Slow response to inquiries	80
Other problems, not listed above	11

QUESTIONS

1. On which dimensions of quality does Dittenhoefer's compete? How are these dimensions being threatened by the problems in the manufacturing and customer service areas?
2. What do you think are the problems with the current manufacturing process as a whole, and with the polymer-coating machine in particular? How might you use process mapping and root cause analysis to get to the bottom of these problems?
3. Develop a Pareto chart based on the customer survey results for the customer service office. What seem to be the key problems? How might you use the DMAIC process to go about resolving these problems?
4. Suppose the polymer-coating machine currently provides the following results:

VARIABLE	PROCESS MEAN	PROCESS STANDARD DEVIATION
Temperature	165 degrees	2.55 degrees
Thickness	4 microns	0.42 micron

   Calculate the process capability ratio (C_p) for both the temperature and the thickness variables. Is the polymer-coating process able to meet the engineering standards 99.7% of the time? Explain.
5. After making numerous process improvements, Steve Edwards decides to set up control charts to monitor the temperature and thickness results for the polymer-coating machine. Sample temperature and thickness data are shown in the following table. Set up the appropriate control charts.

Polymer-Coating Machine:
Sample Temperature and Thickness Measurements
(taken when the process was under control)

SAMPLE	TEMP/ THICK	TEMP/ THICK	TEMP/ THICK	TEMP/ THICK	TEMP/ THICK
June 10	165/4.2	169/3.9	165/4.0	164/4.0	169/3.9
June 15	161/3.8	165/4.2	166/4.0	167/4.8	165/4.2
June 20	169/3.9	161/3.8	167/4.8	164/4.0	167/4.8
June 25	164/4.1	168/4.0	166/4.0	165/4.0	163/3.5
June 30	166/4.0	168/4.0	169/3.9	163/4.3	166/3.7
July 5	168/4.0	163/3.5	167/4.8	164/4.0	166/4.0
July 10	162/4.5	164/4.1	169/3.9	167/4.8	163/3.9
July 15	163/3.5	168/4.0	165/4.0	165/4.0	167/4.8
July 20	167/4.8	167/3.2	164/4.1	167/4.8	164/4.1
July 25	167/3.2	163/3.5	168/4.0	165/3.8	168/4.0
July 30	163/4.0	165/3.8	165/4.2	169/3.9	163/4.0
August 5	163/3.8	165/4.2	169/3.8	165/4.2	163/3.5

REFERENCES

Books and Articles

Cox, J. F., and J. H. Blackstone, eds. *APICS Dictionary*, 11th ed. Falls Church, VA: APICS, 2004.

Deming, W. E. *Quality, Productivity, and Competitive Position.* Boston: MIT Center for Engineering Study, 1982.

Duncan, A. J. *Quality Control and Industrial Statistics*, 5th ed. Homewood, IL: Irwin, 1986.

Garvin, D. "Competing on the Eight Dimensions of Quality." *Harvard Business Review* 65, no. 6 (November–December 1987): 101–109.

Greising, D. "Quality, How to Make It Pay." *Business Week* (August 8, 1994): 54–59.

Juran, J. M., and A. B. Godfrey, eds. *Juran's Quality Control Handbook*, 5th ed. San Francisco: McGraw-Hill, 1998.

Internet

American Society for Quality. **www.asg.org**.

American Society for Quality, "Glossary," **www.asq.org/info/glossary/a.html**

Enoch, J., "Dell Battery Recall May Not Be the Answer," **Consumeraffairs.com**, August 21, 2006.

"Frequently Asked Questions about the Malcolm Baldrige National Quality Award," **www.nist.gov/public_affairs/factsheet/baldfaqs.htm**.

International Organization for Standardization, **www.iso.org/iso/en/iso9000-14000/understand/inbrief.html**.

International Organization for Standardization, **www.iso.org/iso/en/iso9000-14000/understand/selection_use/examplesofiso9000.html**

Juran Institute, **www.juran.com**.

U.S. Food and Drug Administration, **www.fda.gov/medwatch/SAFETY/2004/Safety04.htm#motrin**.

W. Edwards Deming Institute, **www. Deming. org**.

CHAPTER **5**

Managing Projects

CHAPTER OUTLINE

Chapter Objectives

By the end of this chapter, you will be able to:

- Explain the difference between routine business activities and projects.
- Describe the five major phases of a project.
- Construct a Gantt chart and interpret the results.
- Construct a project network diagram and calculate the earliest and latest start and finish times for all activities.
- Identify the critical activities and paths in a network.
- Crash a project.

Building Mega Refineries in Record Time[1]

JAMNAGAR, India, August 2006.—For one billionaire and 150,000 manual workers here on the Indian seacoast, America's gasoline-thirsty motorists mean opportunity. The drivers want more gasoline. U.S. companies that refine it from crude oil are minting money. But they have turned away from building new refineries in the United States because the numbers work better abroad, where costs and red tape are reduced and where expected demand growth is even higher than in the United States.

Into that economic mix sailed Mukesh Ambani, the chairman of India's largest private-sector company, Reliance Industries Ltd. On India's northwest coast near Pakistan, Mr. Ambani is building the world's largest refinery complex. When it's finished, he plans to load 40% of the fuel it turns out onto huge tankers for a 9000-mile trip to America. Mr. Ambani's project in India is among the most ambitious. At $6 billion, it is in keeping with a tradition at Reliance Industries of proposing massive projects and getting them built.

In the 1990s, the company plunged into oil refining after Mr. Ambani noticed that India was importing millions of tons of oil products each year. Reliance soon built one of the world's largest refineries at the Jamnagar site, one that can process 660,000 barrels a day of crude oil. The plant is also one of the most sophisticated, able to process heavy crude, an advantage not only because light, sweet crude is getting harder to come by but also because heavy crude is cheaper.

Reliance put up the refinery on time and within budget. When it was complete in 2000, it let India meet its fuel demands domestically and become a net exporter of refined products. The job of building at Jamnagar entailed an over-the-top project. To attract foreign experts to live and work at the arid site, Reliance built a residential complex that included villas for 2500 families, a nine-hole golf course, a large swimming pool, and an irrigated, 2000-acre farm with 100,000 mango trees, guava, and a flavorful fruit called chiku.

Mr. Ambani soon was mulling over an expansion. Again, the vision was large: a 582,000-barrel-a-day refinery next to the one just built. It would have even greater ability to process heavy crude and make the most expensive types of fuel. Together, the plants would create the largest refinery complex in the world; able to process 1.2 million barrels of oil a day.

With refining profits currently high and many other projects under way, speed was of the essence. Oil analysts say that in five or so years, there likely will be much new capacity, especially in Asia, while U.S. demand growth will slow. Mr. Ambani is pushing to get the second refinery functioning while the profit window is open. He's speeding it along in part by using an extra-large workforce. The goal is to have the plant in operation by December 2008, two years ahead of many projects that others are planning.

As of August 2006, 20,000 workers were at the coastal site, beginning the refinery's superstructure, despite the start of India's monsoon season. Their numbers were expected to eventually reach about 150,000. The goal of fast construction is the reason for using so many workers, says crew chief Sridhar Vaidyanadhan. To avoid wasted time, he says, each welder will have a half-dozen helpers, "so he is always welding and the others bringing him what he needs." Says Mr. Ambani: "We are building the refinery at half the cost and in half the time" possible in America. "I don't know that you could get 150,000 people together to build a refinery" there.

[1]Adapted from S. Levine and P. Barta, "Fuel Lines: Giant New Oil Refinery in India Shows Forces Roiling Industry," *The Wall Street Journal* (Eastern Edition) (August 29, 2006): p. A1.

INTRODUCTION

Project
"A temporary endeavor undertaken to create a unique product, service, or result." Unlike more typical business activities, projects have clear starting and ending points, after which the people and resources dedicated to the project are reassigned.

Much of this book deals with how businesses should develop and manage ongoing operations and supply chain processes. Examples include the purchasing cycle, forecasting, master scheduling and MRP, kanban systems, reorder point inventory systems, and systems for tracking quality levels, to name just a few.

But in addition to these day-to-day activities, all businesses, at one time or another, must embark on projects. A **project** is "a temporary endeavor undertaken to create a unique product, service, or result."[2] Unlike more typical business activities, projects have clear starting and ending points, after which the people and resources dedicated to the project are reassigned.

Not all projects are as dramatic or large as the the oil refineries built by Reliance. More typical ones include developing a new product or service, making long-term process or capacity decisions, and even implementing a new software system. All of these represent nonroutine activities that are vital to a business's survival.

Projects are distinct from "typical" business activities in several ways. We've already noted that projects are nonroutine. For example, a company may schedule employees' work hours every month or reorder inventory items every week. These are routine business activities. On the other hand, projects such as moving headquarters, breaking into a new geographic market, implementing a new software system, and developing a new passenger jet may happen only once in a decade and have a significant impact on a firm's competitive position.

Second, the nonroutine nature of projects often makes them very difficult to manage. Consider a new product development project. At the start of the project, no one is quite sure what the final product will look like, how long it will take to complete, what resources will be needed, and what the final costs will be. This is not to say that developing a new product is more complex than, say, building a car, but at least the auto manufacturer has an idea what it is building!

Third, projects typically require significant levels of cross-functional and interorganizational coordination—more, in fact, than routine business activities, which can often be formalized enough to be managed by a small group of people. The cross-functional and interorganizational nature of projects presents unique organizational challenges. For example, an engineer working on a jet development team may have to report to two managers: his functional (engineering) manager and a project manager charged with getting the jet developed on time. Many working groups will need to interact, so a good project plan will seek to identify the nature and timing of these interactions.

Fourth, projects, unlike routine activities, have a defined ending point, at which time the project is complete. Bridges are opened. New information systems are brought online. New products or services are launched. When this occurs, the people and resources involved must be assigned to new projects.

For many organizations, such as construction firms and software developers, projects actually account for the bulk of business activity. Routine business processes pale in comparison to the time and effort these firms must spend on developing new software products on budget, on time, and as bug-free as possible. The firms that succeed under these conditions typically are highly competent at managing projects.

---

[2] *A Guide to the Project Management Body of Knowledge: Preface to the Third Edition*, **www.pmi.org/prod/groups/public/documents/info/pp_pmbokguidethirdexcerpts.pdf**.

5.1 THE GROWING IMPORTANCE OF PROJECT MANAGEMENT

Project management
"The application of knowledge, skills, tools and techniques to project activities to meet project requirements."

The Project Management Institute (PMI; **www.pmi.org**) defines **project management** as "the application of knowledge, skills, tools and techniques to project activities to meet project requirements."[3] However, until recently, project management was often treated more as an art than an actual management discipline; when projects were completed on time and on budget, it was attributed primarily to good luck. And when things didn't go right (which often happened), managers wrote it off as the inevitable consequence of managing complex, nonroutine activities.

But this is no longer the case. For one thing, companies no longer accept the premise that projects are too complex to manage well. Second, professional organizations, such as PMI, have emerged to educate practicing managers on state-of-the-art tools and techniques. As a management discipline, project management is quickly maturing.

Industry trends have also pushed project management to the forefront. Two trends of particular interest are:

- The faster pace of strategic change and
- The changing role of middle management.

Let's talk about each of these in turn, starting with the pace of strategic change. New product lines must be introduced more often to fight off hungry competitors. Software systems that used to last 10 years are now out of date after five, and customer and supplier networks quickly change, requiring new supply chain solutions. The result of all this is that companies find themselves involved in many more projects with strategic ramifications than they did just a few years earlier. As the number of projects increases, the case for improved project management becomes even stronger for a firm.

Project management has also received more attention as the traditional role of middle management has shrunk. Advanced information systems now handle many of the data analysis tasks that middle managers used to perform. At the same time, many companies have taken the authority and responsibility for work outcomes away from middle managers and pushed them down to direct supervisors and workers.

Though the result has been a dramatic decrease in the number of middle managers, those that are left find themselves more involved in managing projects—areas in which their decision-making ability and flexibility are put to better use. Simply put, those middle managers who hope to keep their jobs, much less advance, will need to learn how to manage projects.

5.2 PROJECT PHASES

Because of the unique characteristics of projects, a whole set of tools has been developed to plan and control projects. Before we get to these tools, however, let's look at the five phases of a generic project. (You might want to compare and contrast these phases with the detailed description of the product development process in Chapter 6.) Though the amount of time and resources spent on each phase will differ from one situation to the next, nearly all projects go through these phases. Figure 5.1 emphasizes two other points: the finite nature of a project and the typically high level of resources needed to both plan and carry out the project activities.

---

[3]Ibid.

FIGURE 5.1
Five Phases of a Generic Project

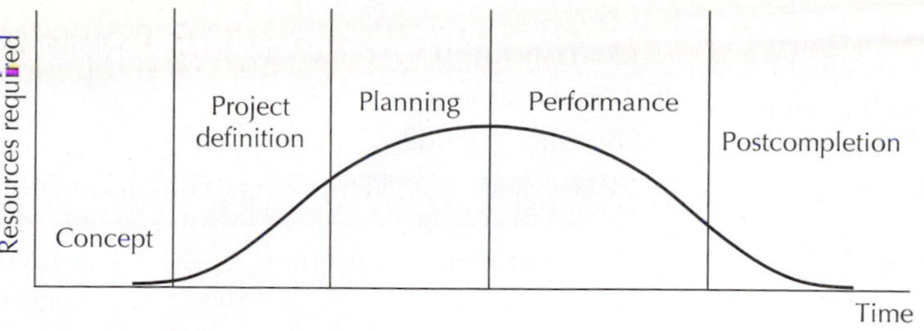

Concept Phase

Concept phase
The first of five phases of a project. Here, project planners develop a broad definition of what the project is and what its scope will be.

In the **concept phase**, project planners develop a broad description of what the project is and what its scope will be. For example, project planners might describe the project as "Develop a Web site where students can order textbooks online" or "Open up a new support center in Michigan." Once the project has been broadly described, planners identify key resources, budget requirements, and time considerations. Key outputs of this phase include initial budget estimates, estimates of personnel needed, and required completion dates. Experience suggests that budget estimates made during the concept phase are usually accurate to ±30% compared to the actual final budget. Planners use this information not only to get an early fix on the scope of the project, but also in many cases to determine whether a project is even feasible. This is particularly important for new product or service development projects.

Project Definition Phase

Project definition phase
The second of five phases in a project. Here, project planners identify how to accomplish the work, how to organize for the project, the key personnel and resources required to support the project, tentative schedules, and tentative budget requirements.

If project planners believe the project is feasible, they proceed to the **project definition phase**. Project definition provides greater detail than the concept phase. The project definition identifies how to accomplish the work, how to organize for the project, the key personnel and resources required to support the project, tentative schedules, and tentative budget requirements. Budget estimates begin to become more exact, with a target of ±5% to 10% compared to the actual final budget.

Planning Phase

Planning phase
The third of five phases of a project. Here, project planners prepare detailed plans that identify activities, time and budget targets, and the resources needed to complete each ask. This phase also includes putting in place the organization that will carry out the project.

Milestone
A performance or time target for each major group of activities in a project.

The **planning phase** entails preparing detailed plans that identify activities, time and budget targets, and the resources needed to complete each task. This phase also includes putting in place the organization that will carry out the project. Firms often create project teams to perform the day-to-day tasks required to complete the project. The planning phase is particularly critical because there is a strong relationship between effective planning and successful project outcomes.

Detailed planning provides an opportunity to discuss each person's role and responsibilities throughout the project. A key part of this phase is developing performance and time targets for major groups of activities, known as **milestones**. These milestones will be used to track the progress of the project. An organization must also define how the different tasks and activities that make up the project come together to result in a completed project. The detailed plan serves as a reference that enables everyone to determine how the project is progressing at various points in time. Later we will address project planning and control tools and techniques in more detail.

Table 5.1 shows an example of some of the detail that might come out of this phase. In this example, Activity Group 3 of a larger project has been broken down into specific activities. In addition to an overall budget and a time milestone of 7/9/08, the table indicates personnel assignments and responsibilities, budgets, and due dates for each of the five individual activities.

TABLE 5.1
Example of Detailed Project Information, Including Budget and Time Milestones

Activity Group 3: Build and deliver product to the customer
Time milestone: 7/9/08
Budget: $70,000

SPECIFIC ACTIVITIES	PERSONNEL	BUDGET	DUE DATE
3.1 Complete specifications	John C.* Chester B.	$15,000	6/4/08
3.2 Complete Subassembly A	Maria G.* Tom T. Debra V.	$20,000	6/19/08
3.3 Complete Subassembly B	Philip B.* Emily W.	$24,000	6/19/08
3.4 Final assembly and testing	John C.* Chester B. Anne I.	$9000	7/2/08
3.5 Deliver and train customer	Anne I.*	$2000	7/9/08

*Indicates person with primary responsibility.

Performance Phase

Performance phase
The fourth of five phases of a project. In this phase, the organization actually starts to execute the project plan.

In the **performance phase**, the organization actually starts to execute the project plan. It is here that the value of the previous phases really becomes apparent. Specifically, effective planning increases the likelihood that actual performance outcomes will meet expectations. Project managers play a particularly important role here in coordinating and directing the work effort and in ensuring that time and performance milestones are met. Depending on the type of project, this may be the longest phase.

Postcompletion Phase

Postcompletion phase
The fifth of five phases of a project. This is the phase in which the project manager or team confirms the final outcome, conducts a postimplementation meeting to critique the project and personnel, and reassigns project personnel.

The **postcompletion phase** is the "wrap-up" phase of project management, which includes several important tasks. During this phase, the project manager or team:

- Confirms that the final outcome of the project meets the expectations of management or the customers. This usually entails a comparison of actual outcomes (time, cost, etc.) to the expected outcomes established during planning.
- Conducts a postimplementation meeting to discuss the strengths and weaknesses of the project effort and personnel. As we saw in our discussion of continuous improvement in Chapters 3 and 4, an effective organization learns from its experiences.
- Reassigns project personnel to other positions or projects. One of the primary characteristics of projects as a form of work is the movement of personnel from project to project.

5.3 PROJECT MANAGEMENT TOOLS

Practitioners and academics have developed a host of tools to aid organizations in their project management efforts. Project management tools are used to plan, measure, and track a project's progress. In this section, we introduce two well-accepted tools: Gantt charts and network diagrams. These tools help managers understand which activities need to be completed, who is responsible for various activities, and when the activities should be completed. These tools also allow managers to track the time it takes to complete activities as well as costs. With the proper planning and control information, managers can take corrective actions when necessary to meet project objectives.

Gantt chart
A graphical tool used to show expected start and end times for project activities, and to track actual progress against these time targets.

Gantt Charts

Gantt charts are graphical tools used to show expected start and end times for project activities and to track actual progress against these time targets. As such, the Gantt chart provides both a planning and a control function.

Example 5.1

Gantt Chart for the Gina3000 Project

Courter Corporation makes high-end speakers that are used with home entertainment systems. Courter has designed a new speaker, the Gina3000, that is louder and more reliable than Courter's earlier model. Before Courter goes any further, however, it wants to give its customers—the home entertainment system manufacturers—the chance to test and critique the Gina3000.

Management has outlined 10 activities that must be completed before the Gina3000 speakers can be released for regular production. These 10 activities are listed in Table 5.2.

The Gina3000 Speaker.

TABLE 5.2 List of Activities for the Gina3000 Project

ACTIVITY		DURATION (WEEKS)	PREDECESSORS
A	Legal department approves prototype use	2	None
B	R&D* builds prototype speakers	3	None
C	Customer uses and approves prototypes	3	A, B
D	New equipment is ordered and installed	5	C
E	Manufacturing produces sample speakers	2	D
F	R&D* writes up product specifications	3	C
G	Customer tests and approves sample speakers	3	E, F
H	QC** tests and approves sample speakers	3	E
I	Manufacturing finalizes process	3	E
J	Management approves product for regular production	2	G, H, I

*Research and Development. **Quality Control.

There are a couple of interesting things to note about Table 5.2. First, some activities, such as Activity A (Legal department approves prototype use) and Activity B (R&D builds prototype speakers) can occur simultaneously. Courter Corporation should consider this when planning the expected time for the project's completion. Second, some activities have predecessors that must be completed beforehand. Take Activity H, for example. Obviously, one can't test sample speakers before they have been made (Activity E). Likewise, Activity E can't be completed until the new equipment has been ordered and installed (Activity D).

Figure 5.2 shows a Gantt chart for the Gina3000 project. For simplicity, each activity is referred to by its corresponding letter in Table 5.2. The Gantt chart provides a lot of useful information at a glance. First, according to the chart, the project should be completed by the end of week 18. Second, the chart tells us when specific activities should start and finish. Note that Activity C has a planned start date of week 4. Why week 4? Because this is the first week in which *both* Activity A and Activity B (Activity C's predecessors) are finished.

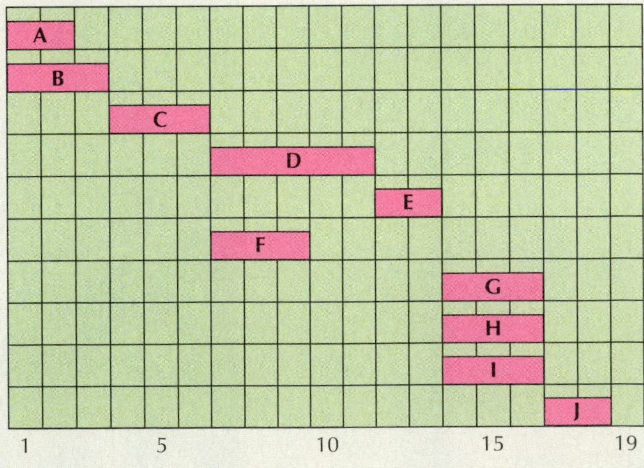

FIGURE 5.2 Initial Gantt Chart for the Gina3000 Project

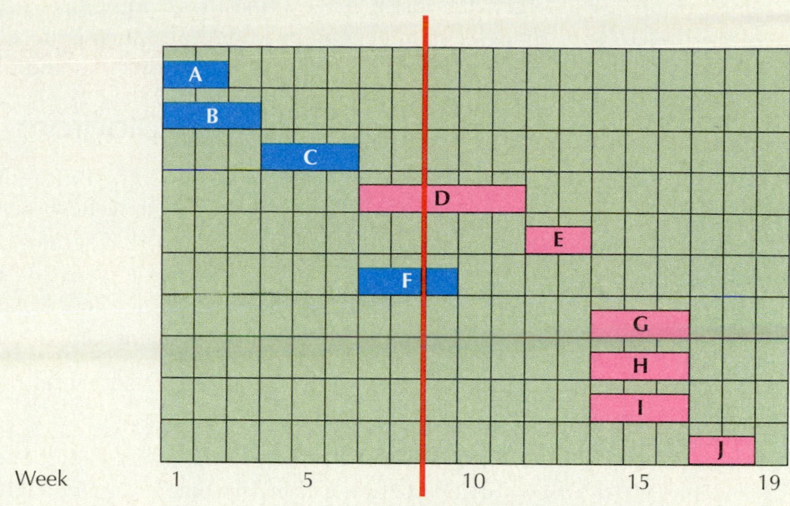

FIGURE 5.3 Gantt Chart at End of Week 8

As time goes on, Courter can use a Gantt chart to check its progress against the plan. In Figure 5.3, we use shading to show how much of each activity has been completed. Figure 5.3 shows that by the end of week 8, Activity F has been completed one week ahead of schedule (i.e., the entire activity has been shaded in), while Activity D is already two weeks late getting started (none has been shaded in). Based on this information, Courter Corporation has several options, including rescheduling the project or expediting activities to finish within the 18-week plan.

Network diagram
A graphical tool that shows the logical linkages between activities in a project.

Critical path method (CPM)
A network-based technique in which there is a single time estimate for each activity. An alternative approach is PERT, which has multiple time estimates for each activity.

Program evaluation and review technique (PERT)
A network-based technique in which there are multiple time estimates for each activity. An alternative approach is CPM, which has a single time estimate for each activity.

Network Diagrams

Gantt charts have one major weakness: They fail to explicitly show precedence relationships. For example, it is not clear from Figures 5.2 and 5.3 whether or not Activity F is a predecessor of Activity G (it is). This can be a real limitation for larger projects involving dozens or even hundreds of activities.

Network diagrams improve on Gantt charts by visually showing the linkages between various activities. The **critical path method (CPM)** and the **program evaluation and review technique (PERT)** are two popular network-based techniques. Like Gantt charts, these techniques require the user to identify the activities that make up a project and to determine their sequence and interrelationships.

Both CPM and PERT allow project managers to monitor progress over time while managing costs across all activities. CPM is used for projects where there is a single time estimate for each activity. PERT is used when the time estimates are less certain and it makes more sense to provide several estimates—most likely a pessimistic and an optimistic estimate. These estimates are combined to arrive at a single time estimate for each project activity.

PERT users can also determine the probability of completing a project by a certain target date using normal distribution curve statistics.[4] In reality, PERT is rarely used in

[4]For a detailed description of these methods, see L. Krajewski and L. Ritzman, *Operations Management: Strategy and Analysis*, 6th ed. (Upper Saddle River, NJ: Prentice Hall, 2002).

practice. Most managers find that coming up with a single best estimate of an activity's time is difficult enough without introducing the added complexity of multiple estimates. As such, we will focus our attention on CPM and the use of single time estimates.

Constructing a Network Diagram

Activity on node (AON) diagram
A network diagram in which each activity is represented by a node, or box, and the precedence relationships between various activities are represented with arrows.

Critical activities
Project activities for which the earliest start time and latest start time are equal. Critical activities cannot be delayed without lengthening the overall project duration.

Network path
A logically linked sequence of activities in the network diagram.

Critical path
The longest path in the project network. There may be more than one critical path.

Regardless of whether one uses CPM or PERT, the underlying logic is the same. Each approach uses a network diagram to show how each individual activity relates in time and sequence to all other activities. Network diagrams show at a glance how separate activities come together to form an entire project.

There are several ways to construct network diagrams, but the process is much the same in both CPM and PERT. The major steps are as follows:

1. Identify each unique activity in a project by a capital letter that corresponds only to that activity.
2. Represent each activity in the project by a node that shows the estimated length. This style of network diagram is known as an **activity on node (AON) diagram**.
3. If an activity has an immediate predecessor(s), show the relationship by connecting the two activities with an arrow. The network diagram consists of all the activity nodes and arrows linking them together.
4. Determine the earliest start time (*ES*) and earliest finish time (*EF*) for each activity by performing what is called a forward pass.
5. Determine the latest finish time (*LF*) and latest starting time (*LS*) for each activity by doing a backward pass.
6. Determine the critical activities and path(s) in the project. **Critical activities** are activities for which the earliest start time and the latest start time are equal. Critical activities cannot be delayed without lengthening the overall project duration. **Network paths** are logically linked sequences of activities in the network diagram. A path is a **critical path** if it is the longest path in the network (or tied for longest path). The duration of the project is equal to the duration of the critical path(s).

Example 5.2
Network Diagram for the Gina3000 Project

Courter Corporation decides to follow the six steps just outlined to create a network diagram of the Gina3000 project.

STEP 1. *Identify each unique activity in a project by a capital letter that corresponds only to that activity.* This has already been done in Table 5.2.

STEP 2. *Represent each activity in the project by a node that shows the estimated length.* To illustrate, "Customer uses and approves prototypes" (Activity C) is estimated to take three weeks. Courter represents this as follows:

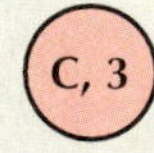

STEP 3. *If an activity has an immediate predecessor, show that relationship by connecting the two activities with an arrow.* Activity A immediately precedes Activity C. This is shown as follows:

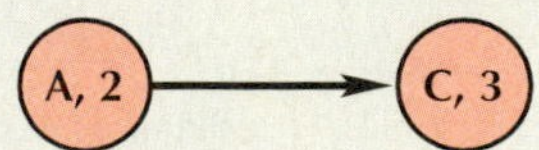

The same logic is used to link all the activities in the project. The result is the AON network diagram for the Gina3000 project shown in Figure 5.4. Note that there is one arrow for every predecessor relationship listed in Table 5.2.

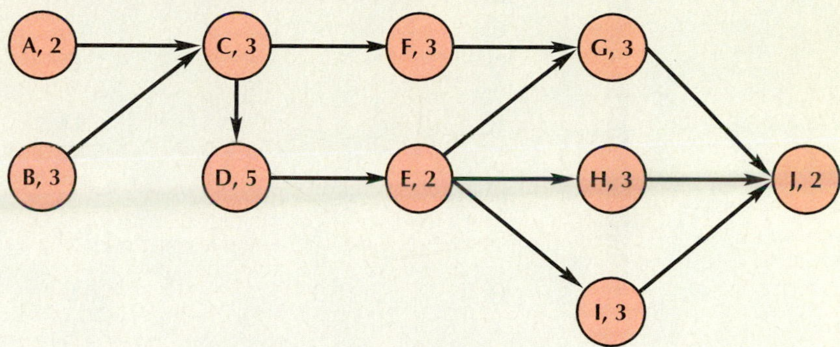

FIGURE 5.4 AON Network Diagram for the Gina3000 Project

Now consider the following: Even though Activity A is not listed as an *immediate* predecessor for any activity except C, it must still be completed before all other activities, except for Activity B. That is, all the activities except B are on a network path in which Activity A is the first activity that must be completed. One path through the network is the sequence A–C–F–G–J. This path implies that Activity A must be completed before Activity C; C before F, and so on. Paths are the key to understanding the relationship between activities and determining the length of a project. There are a total of eight different paths in this network. Can you find all of them?

Forward pass
The determination of the earliest start and finish times for each project activity.

Earliest start time (ES)
The earliest an activity can be started, as determined by the earliest finish time for all immediate predecessors.

Earliest finish time (EF)
The earliest an activity can be finished, calculated by adding the activity's duration to its earliest start time.

STEP 4. *Determine the earliest start time (ES) and earliest finish time (EF) for each activity.* This step is also known as the **forward pass** through the network. In general, the **earliest start time (ES)** is defined as follows:

$$ES = \text{earliest time by which } all \text{ immediate predecessors could be finished}$$
$$= \text{latest } EF \text{ for all immediate predecessors} \quad [5\text{-}1]$$

Neither Activity A nor Activity B has any predecessors, so their $ES = 0$. But what about Activity C? The earliest time C can start is based on the earliest time that *both* A and B will be finished. Because the EF for A = 2 and B = 3, the earliest start time for C = 3.

The **earliest finish time (EF)** is calculated as follows:

$$EF = ES + \text{activity's duration} \quad [5\text{-}2]$$

For Activity A, then, $ES = 0$ and $EF = 0 + 2 = 2$ (that is, the end of week 2). For Activity C, $EF = 3 + 3 = 6$. Table 5.3 shows the earliest start (ES) and earliest finish (EF) times for each activity in our speaker development project. There are several interesting pieces of information in Table 5.3. First, the table indicates that the entire project can be completed by the end of week 18. That is because the highest EF value for any activity in the table is 18. This finding is consistent with the Gantt chart shown in Figure 5.2.

Second, look at the earliest start times for Activities G and J. Activity G has two immediate predecessors, E and F. Even though Activity F can be completed as early as week 9, Activity E won't be completed until week 13. Therefore, week 13 is the earliest we can start Activity G. Similarly, Activity J must wait until Activities G, H, and I are *all* finished.

TABLE 5.3 Earliest Start (ES) and Earliest Finish (EF) Times for Gina3000 Project

ACTIVITY	DURATION	PREDECESSORS	ES	EF
A	2	None	0	2
B	3	None	0	3
C	3	A, B	3	6
D	5	C	6	11
E	2	D	11	13
F	3	C	6	9
G	3	E, F	13	16
H	3	E	13	16
I	3	E	13	16
J	2	G, H, I	16	18

Backward pass
The determination of the latest finish and start times for each project activity.

Latest finish time (LF)
The latest an activity can be finished and still finish the project on time, as determined by the latest start time for all immediate successors.

Latest start time (LS)
The latest an activity can be started and still finish the project on time, calculated by subtracting the activity's duration from its latest finish time.

STEP 5. *Determine the latest finish time (LF) and latest start time (LS) for each activity.* This step is also known as the **backward pass.** Calculating the *LS* and *LF* times indicates how late specific activities can be performed and still get the project done by a certain time. This step is particularly important when trying to determine what impact a delay might have on the length of a project.

Latest finish time (LF) is defined as follows:

$$LF = \text{latest time by which } all \text{ immediate successors must be started in order to finish the project on time} = \text{earliest } LS \text{ for all immediate successors} \quad [5\text{-}3]$$

The **latest start time (LS)** is calculated as follows:

$$LS = LF - \text{activity's duration} \quad [5\text{-}4]$$

The backward pass is best illustrated by example. Activity J has the latest *EF* of any activity (end of week 18). Setting the latest finish time for Activity J equal to 18, the latest start time is as follows:

$$LS = LF - \text{activity's duration} = 18 - 2 = 16$$

The latest start time answers the question "How late can this activity be started and still complete the project on time?" Having calculated the *LF* and *LS* for Activity J, we work backward (hence the term *backward pass*) to those activities immediately preceding Activity J: Activities G, H, and I. Having completed the calculations for those activities, we then work backward to Activities E and F. Table 5.4 summarizes the results of the forward and backward passes.

STEP 6. *Determine the critical activities and path(s) in the project.* Combined with the network diagram (Figure 5.4), the values in Table 5.4 provide Courter management with some valuable information. First, look at Activities B, C, D, E, G, H, I, and J (marked with asterisks). In each case, $ES = LS$. This means that the *latest* these activities can be started and still

TABLE 5.4 Results of Forward and Backward Passes on the Gina3000 Project

ACTIVITY	DURATION (WEEKS)	PREDECESSORS	*ES*	*EF*	*LS*	*LF*
A	2	None	0	2	1	3
B*	3	None	0	3	0	3
C*	3	A, B	3	6	3	6
D*	5	C	6	11	6	11
E*	2	D	11	13	11	13
F	3	C	6	9	10	13
G*	3	E, F	13	16	13	16
H*	3	E	13	16	13	16
I*	3	E	13	16	13	16
J*	2	G, H, I	16	18	16	18

*Critical activity.

get the project done on time is *also the earliest* they can be started. Because *any* delay in these activities will cause the entire project to be late, these activities are critical activities.

Activities A and F, in contrast, are not critical activities. The amount of allowable delay, or **slack time**, is calculated as follows:

Slack time
The difference between an activity's latest start time (*LS*) and earliest start time (*ES*). Slack time indicates the amount of allowable delay. Critical activities have a slack time of zero.

$$\text{Slack time} = LS - ES \qquad [5\text{-}5]$$

For Activity A, $1 - 0 = 1$ week of slack time; for Activity F, $10 - 6 = 4$ weeks of slack. Now try to calculate the slack time for one of the critical activities. The answer should be zero, reinforcing the notion that critical activities cannot be delayed without delaying the entire project.

Figure 5.5 marks the critical activities in red, thereby showing the critical paths in the project. Critical paths are always the longest paths in the network, as there is no slack time in any of the activities they link together. In this case, there are three critical paths: B–C–D–E–G–J, B–C–D–E–H–J, and B–C–D–E–I–J. By adding up the times for the individual activities in each path, Courter realizes that each critical path takes 18 weeks. This result is consistent with the Gantt charts (Figures 5.2 and 5.3) and Table 5.4. A final point: Though a project may have many critical paths, it must always have at least one critical path. After all, some path has to be the longest!

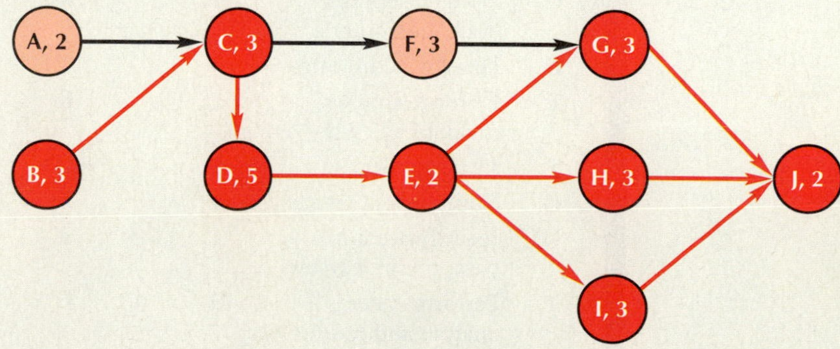

FIGURE 5.5 AON Network Diagram for the Gina3000 Project (critical activities and paths marked in red)

Crashing a Project

In many instances, the initial estimate of the time required to complete a project might be unacceptable. For high-tech products, even a few months of delay can often result in a significant loss of market share. And any city hosting the Olympics has no choice but to complete construction before the games begin; there is no room for negotiation. Alternatively, managers may be offered financial or other incentives for completing a project early.

Crashing
Shortening the overall duration of a project by reducing the time it takes to perform certain activities.

Crashing is an effort to shorten the overall duration of a project by reducing the time it takes to perform certain activities. As with the initial development of the network diagram, there is a series of steps to follow when crashing a project:

1. List all network paths and their current lengths. Mark all activities that can be crashed.
2. Focus on the critical path or paths. Working on one period at a time, choose the activity or activities that will shorten all critical paths at the least cost. The one rule is this: Never crash an activity that is *not* on a critical path, regardless of the cost. Doing so will not shorten the project; it will only add costs.
3. Recalculate the lengths of all paths, and repeat step 2 until the target project completion time is reached or until all options have been exhausted.

Example 5.3

Crashing a Project at Courter Corporation

Nearly 60% of the cost of Courter Corporation's products comes from components provided by outside suppliers. As a result, management would like to:

- Develop a set of performance criteria and an evaluation system for assessing potential suppliers;

TABLE 5.5 List of Activities for Supplier Selection and Evaluation Project

ACTIVITY		ORIGINAL LENGTH (WEEKS)	PREDECESSORS	NUMBER OF WEEKS ACTIVITY CAN BE CRASHED	CRASH COST PER WEEK
A	Assemble project team	2	None	—	
B	Identify potential suppliers	6	A	1	$500
C	Develop supplier evaluation criteria	4	A	—	
D	Develop audit form	3	C	1	$800
E	Perform supplier financial analysis	2	B	—	
F	Visit suppliers	8	E, D	2	$2,000
G	Compile visit results	5	F	1	$700
H	Identify needs for computerized system	4	A	—	
I	Perform systems analysis and coding	10	H	2	$300
J	Test system	3	I	—	
K	Select final suppliers	2	G	—	

- Identify, evaluate, and select suppliers for critical components; and
- Develop a computerized system that will evaluate the performance of the selected suppliers on a continuous basis.

Management requires that the entire project be completed within *23 weeks*. Table 5.5 lists the various activities that must be completed. In addition to the estimated duration and predecessors for each activity, the table shows how many weeks each activity can be crashed and the crash cost for each week. For example, the expected duration of Activity B is six weeks. However, for an additional $500, Activity B can be squeezed down, or crashed, by one week. Note that not all activities can be crashed. For instance, testing of the computerized supplier evaluation system (Activity J) and final selection (Activity K) cannot be crashed at all.

Figure 5.6 shows the network diagram for this project. Notice that there are three paths: A–B–E–F–G–K, A–C–D–F–G–K, and A–H–I–J. It is interesting to note that there are *two* final activities, K and J. That is because the development of the computerized system (A–H–I–J) is essentially independent of the supplier selection effort.

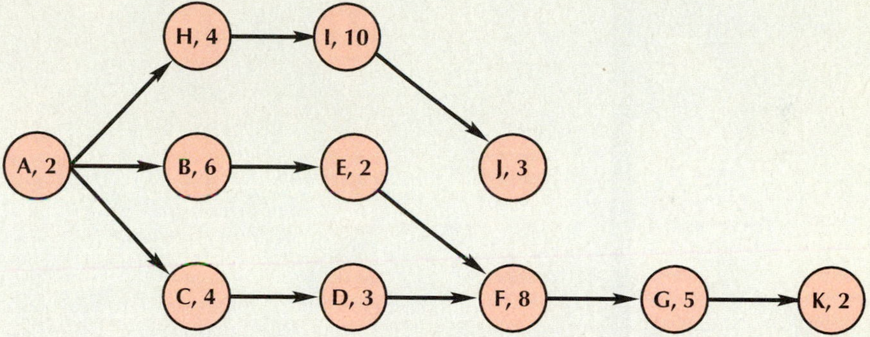

FIGURE 5.6 Network Diagram for Project

Table 5.6 contains the results of the forward and backward passes for this project. (You might want to calculate the *ES*, *EF*, *LS*, and *LF* values yourself in order to convince yourself that you understand how they were obtained.) Of the three paths, only A–B–E–F–G–K is

TABLE 5.6 Results of Forward and Backward Passes for Project

ACTIVITY	DURATION (WEEKS)	PREDECESSORS	*ES*	*EF*	*LS*	*LF*
A*	2	None	0	2	0	2
B*	6	A	2	8	2	8
C	4	A	2	6	3	7
D	3	C	6	9	7	10
E*	2	B	8	10	8	10
F*	8	E, D	10	18	10	18
G*	5	F	18	23	18	23
H	4	A	2	6	8	12
I	10	H	6	16	12	22
J	3	I	16	19	22	25
K*	2	G	23	25	23	25

*Critical activity.

critical because the activities on this path are the only ones for which $ES = LS$. Based on Table 5.6, we can conclude that the project will take 25 weeks.

Yet the project must be completed in *23* weeks, not 25. Can it be done, and if so, what is the cheapest way to accomplish the task? Crashing, like network development, can be divided into several steps.

Step 1. *List all network paths and their current lengths. Mark all activities that can be crashed.* Table 5.5 shows the duration, crash time, and crash cost for each activity in this project. The current length of each path, therefore, is as shown in Table 5.7 (all activities that can be crashed appear in color).

TABLE 5.7 Network Paths for Project*

	LENGTH
A–B–E–F–G–K	25**
A–C–D–F–G–K	24
A–H–I–J	19

*Activities that can be crashed appear in **color**.
**Critical path.

Step 2. *Focus on the critical path or paths. Working one period at a time, choose the activity or activities that will shorten all critical paths at the least cost.* We will need to shorten two paths, A–B–E–F–G–K and A–C–D–F–G–K to meet the 23-week deadline. Table 5.7 shows that there are several options for crashing each.

As noted earlier, it never makes sense to crash a noncritical activity. Look at Activity **I**. Courter could crash that activity for only $300 per week, but the path it is on is already shorter than necessary—just 19 weeks. And crashing it would have no effect on the length of the critical path, A–B–E–F–G–K. Courter would be out $300 per week, and the project would still take 25 weeks.

Because A–B–E–F–G–K is the longest path, management should start there. Shortening this one path by 1 week will reduce the length of the entire project to 24 weeks. The cheapest way to shorten it is to crash Activity **B** by one week at a cost of $500. The new path lengths are shown in Table 5.8. Notice that neither of the other two paths is affected because Activity **B** is not on them.

TABLE 5.8 Updated Network Path Lengths

	LENGTH	LENGTH AFTER CRASHING B
A–B–E–F–G–K	25*	24*
A–C–D–F–G–K	24	24*
A–H–I–J	19	19

Crashing cost: $500.

*Critical path.

Step 3. *Recalculate the lengths of all paths, and repeat Step 2 until the target project completion time is reached or until all options have been exhausted.* After Activity **B** has been crashed, two paths become critical: A–B–E–F–G–K and A–C–D–F–G–K. Any further crashing efforts must consider both of these paths. The next cheapest crashing option, therefore, is to crash Activity G at a cost of $700 (see Table 5.5). Doing so will bring down the lengths of both A–B–E–F–G–K and A–C–D–F–G–K to the required 23 weeks. Table 5.9 shows the final results.

TABLE 5.9 Final Results of Crashing Activities B and G

	ORIGINAL LENGTH	LENGTH AFTER CRASHING B	LENGTH AFTER CRASHING G
A–B–E–F–G–K	25*	24*	23*
A–C–D–F–G–K	24	24*	23*
A–H–I–J	19	19	19

Crashing cost: $500 + $700 = $1200.

*Critical path.

If Courter wanted to collapse the project any further, it would have to reduce Activity F by two weeks at a cost of $4,000. Crashing Activity D wouldn't be enough, because it affects only path A–C–D–F–G–K. And crashing Activity I wouldn't help at all, because it isn't on any critical path.

5.4 PROJECT MANAGEMENT SOFTWARE

The advent of cheap computer power has resulted in an explosion in the number of project management software packages. What we did by hand in the previous section—drawing networks, determining critical paths, crashing projects—can now be done automatically. These software packages are also far more sophisticated than anything discussed here. Nearly every package, for instance, allows users to evaluate the impact of resource constraints or to consider multiple estimates of activity time, as is done in PERT. In addition, nearly every software package offers resource utilization reports and exception reports on activities that are in danger of falling behind or becoming critical. This latter feature can be particularly valuable in managing complex projects with hundreds of activities because it highlights the critical few that managers need to pay attention to.

To give you a flavor for how these packages work, this section includes screenshots from one popular package, Microsoft Project. Figure 5.7 shows how we might set up the Gina3000 project (discussed in Examples 5.1 and 5.2) in the software package. Compare the activities ("tasks") listed here with those in Table 5.2. Also, as you can see by the toolbar on the left side of the screen, the software package offers some fairly sophisticated resource management tools.

Figure 5.8 shows the Gantt chart that was automatically generated for the project. Note the similarities to Figures 5.2 and 5.3. Microsoft Project has the added advantage that it shows precedence relationships using arrows.

Figure 5.9 shows the AON diagram for the project. As with other software packages of this type, Microsoft Project automatically calculates starting and ending times and identifies the critical activities and paths. In this case, the critical activities and paths are highlighted in red. Once again, you might compare this network diagram with those we showed earlier in Figures 5.4 and 5.5. While slightly different, they contain the same basic information. Of course, the software package has the added advantage that these diagrams are automatically updated as activities are added or deleted or as time estimates change.

Microsoft Project - Gina3000 - Business Management

Legal department okays prototype use

ID	Task Name	Duration	Start	Finish	Predecessors	Resource Names
1	Legal department okays prototype use	10 days	Mon 9/6/04	Fri 9/17/04		Legal
2	R&D builds prototype speakers	15 days	Mon 9/6/04	Fri 9/24/04		R&D
3	Customer uses & approves prototypes	15 days	Mon 9/27/04	Fri 10/15/04	1,2	Customer
4	New equipment is ordered & installed	25 days	Mon 10/18/04	Fri 11/19/04	3	Ind. Engineering
5	Mfg. produces sample speakers	10 days	Mon 11/22/04	Fri 12/3/04	4	Mfg.
6	R&D writes up product specs	15 days	Mon 10/18/04	Fri 11/5/04	3	R&D
7	Customer tests & approves samples	15 days	Mon 12/6/04	Fri 12/24/04	5,6	Customer
8	QC tests & approves samples	15 days	Mon 12/6/04	Fri 12/24/04	5	QC Dept.
9	Mfg. finalizes process	15 days	Mon 12/6/04	Fri 12/24/04	5	Mfg.
10	Mgmt. Oks product for regular productio	10 days	Mon 12/27/04	Fri 1/7/05	7,8,9	Top mgmt.

Tasks are numbered sequentially.

Task numbers are used to define precedence relationships.

The software allows users to closely manage resources.

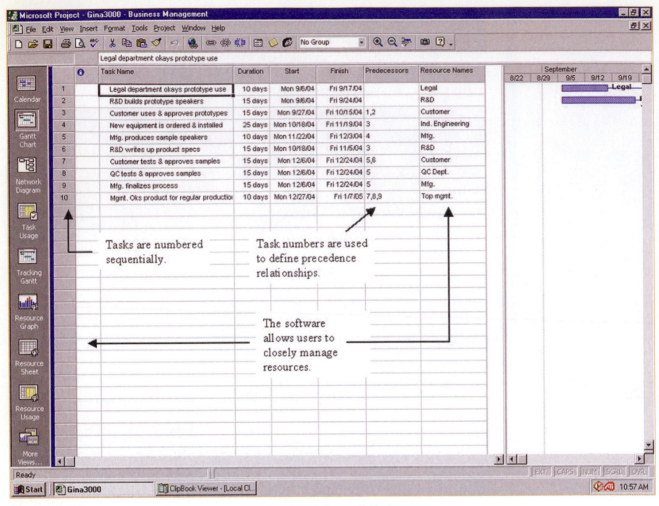

FIGURE 5.7 Entering the Gina3000 Project into Microsoft Project

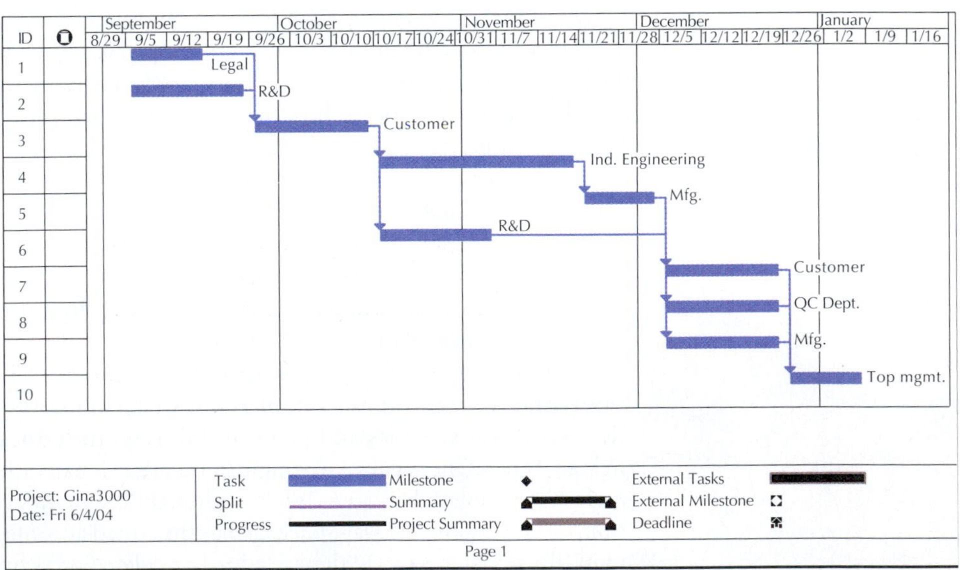

FIGURE 5.8 Computer-Generated Gantt Chart for the Gina3000 Project

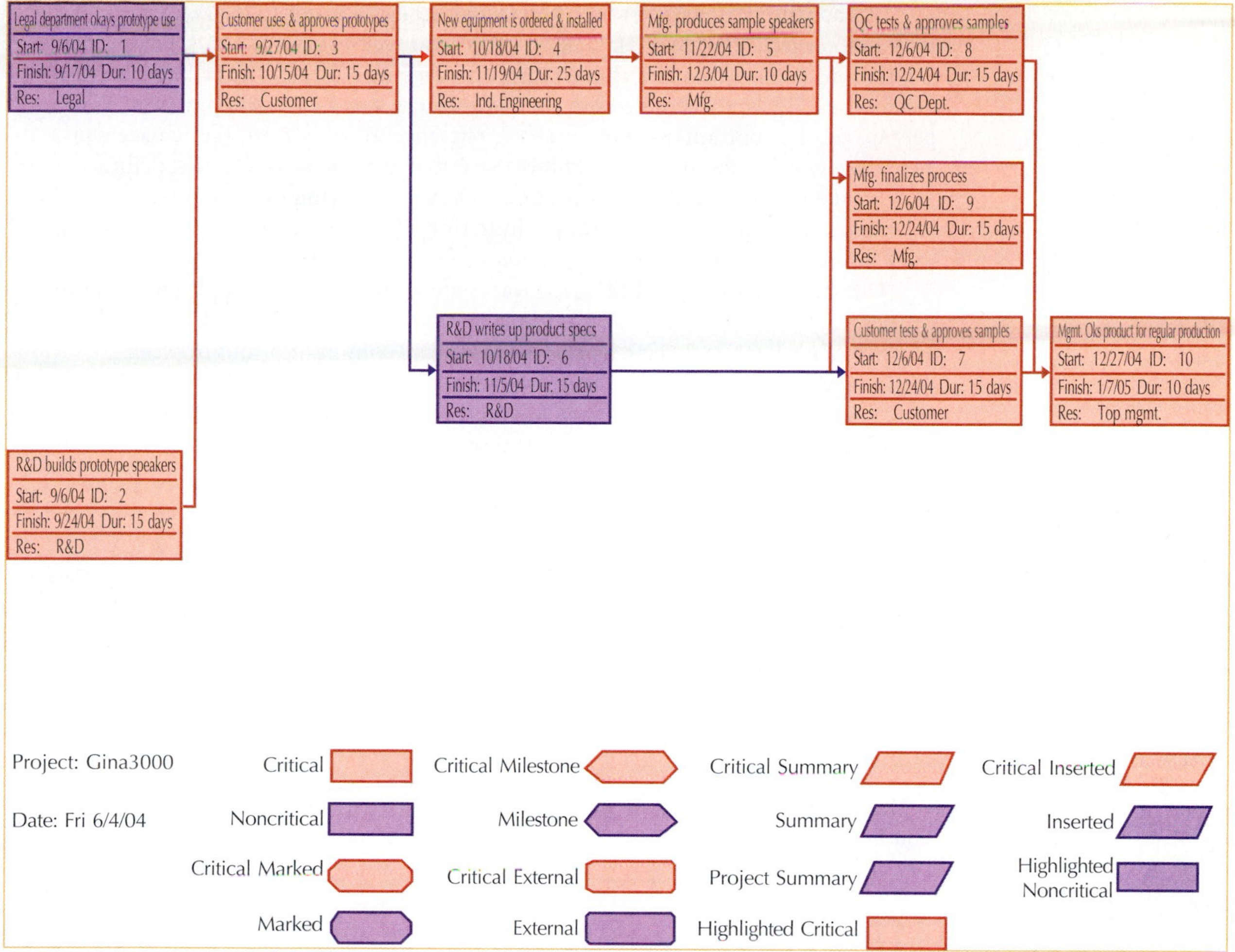

FIGURE 5.9 Computer-Generated Network Diagram for the Gina3000 Project

Even with almost unlimited computer power, it's still the responsibility of managers to make sure that project information is updated on a regular basis, particularly when activities or time estimates change frequently. Sophisticated users of project management software update project information on a weekly or even a daily basis to keep on top of changes that could affect the timing or cost of a project.

5.5 PMI AND THE PROJECT MANAGEMENT BODY OF KNOWLEGEDGE (PMBOK®)

Throughout this book, we have identified numerous professional organizations dedicated to the advancement of operations and supply chain practices. The Project Management Institute (PMI) is one such organization. PMI serves the needs of project management professionals from a wide range of industries, including software development, construction, finance, and manufacturing. In addition to certification and other educational offerings, PMI also sponsers conferences, research, and special interest groups for individuals interested in various aspects of project management.

Perhaps the organization's best-known output is the *Guide to the Project Management Body of Knowledge* (PMBOK®).[5] The PMBOK guide serves several needs. First, it provides a common language for discussing project management issues. Second, it identifies and disseminates generally accepted project management knowledge and practices. Third, and perhaps most important, it serves as a basic reference source for project management.

The guide divides the body of knowledge into two main parts. The first defines the various business processes that organizations follow in carrying out projects. The PMBOK recognizes five major process groups: Initiating, Planning, Executing, Controlling and Monitoring, and Closing projects.

The second part of the PMBOK covers nine knowledge areas applicable to nearly all projects. These knowledge areas include such topics as managing the scope, quality, time, and cost of projects, managing human resources and communications between the various parties, and managing project risk. It's interesting to note that while the PMBOK deals with these knowledge areas within the context of project management, it draws heavily from other managerial disciplines such as organizational behavior and finance.

CHAPTER SUMMARY

Projects represent nonroutine business activities that often have long-term strategic ramifications for a firm. In this chapter, we examined how projects differ from routine business activities and discussed the major phases of projects. We noted how environmental changes have resulted in increased attention being paid to projects and project management over the last decade.

In the last half of the chapter, we introduced some basic tools that businesses can use when planning for and controlling projects. Both Gantt charts and network diagrams give managers a visual picture of how the project is going. Network diagrams have the added advantage of showing the precedence between activities, as well as the critical paths. We wrapped up the chapter by showing how these concepts are embedded in inexpensive, yet powerful, software packages such as Microsoft Project.

If you want to learn more about project management, we encourage you to take a look at the Web site for the Project Management Institute (PMI) at **www.pmi.org**.

KEY FORMULAS

Earliest start time for a project activity (page 133):

$$ES = \text{latest } EF \text{ for all immediate predecessors} \quad [5\text{-}1]$$

Earliest finish time for a project activity (page 133):

$$EF = ES + \text{activity's duration} \quad [5\text{-}2]$$

Latest finish time for a project activity (page 134):

$$LF = \text{earliest } LS \text{ for all immediate successors} \quad [5\text{-}3]$$

Latest start time for a project activity (page 134):

$$LS = LF - \text{activity's duration} \quad [5\text{-}4]$$

Slack time for a project activity (page 135):

$$\text{Slack time} = LS - ES \quad [5\text{-}5]$$

[5]*A Guide to the Project Management Body of Knowledge (PMBOK® Guide)*, 3rd ed., Project Management Institute, 2004.

KEY TERMS

SOLVED PROBLEM

Problem

Lance Thompson is opening a new restaurant in Collegetown called the GriddleIron. The first football game of the fall is in 15 weeks, and Lance wants to be open in time to serve visiting alumni and other fans.

Table 5.10 lists all of the activities that Lance needs to complete, as well as crashing options for two of the activities. How long will the project take if Lance doesn't crash any activities? Can Lance meet his 15-week deadline? If so, what will the cost be?

TABLE 5.10 Activity List for GriddleIron Project

ACTIVITY	ORIGINAL LENGTH (WEEKS)	PREDECESSORS	NUMBER OF WEEKS ACTIVITY CAN BE CRASHED	CRASH COST PER WEEK
A Get city council permission and permits	4	None	—	
B Get architect to draw up renovation plans	4	A	—	
C Hire manager	3	A	—	
D Hire staff	3	C	—	
E Train staff	1	D	—	
F Select and order kitchen equipment	2	B	—	
G Select and order dining room and bar furnishings	1.5	B	—	
H Renovate dining area	4	G	1	\$2000
I Renovate kitchen area	5	F	2	\$1000
J Perform fire inspection	1	H, I	—	
K Perform health inspection	1	H, I	—	
L Grand opening	1	J, K		

Solution

Figure 5.10 shows the network diagram for the GriddleIron project, while Table 5.11 shows the results of the forward and backward passes.

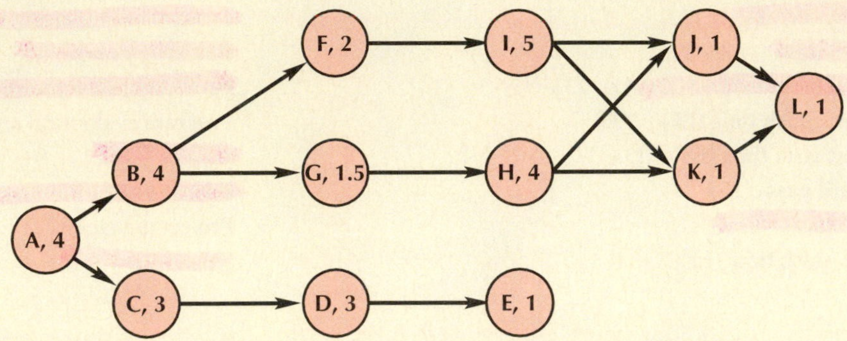

FIGURE 5.10 Network Diagram for GriddleIron Project

TABLE 5.11 Forward and Backward Pass Results for GriddleIron Project

ACTIVITY	EARLIEST START	EARLIEST FINISH	LATEST START	LATEST FINISH
A*	0	4	0	4
B*	4	8	4	8
C	4	7	10	13
D	7	10	13	16
E	10	11	16	17
F*	8	10	8	10
G	8	9.5	9.5	11
H	9.5	13.5	11	15
I*	10	15	10	15
J*	15	16	15	16
K*	15	16	15	16
L*	16	17	16	17

*Critical activity.

Looking at the results, we can see that there are two critical paths: A–B–F–I–J–L and A–B–F–I–K–L. The critical paths are 17 weeks long, with the next longest paths being 15.5 weeks.

To meet the 15-week deadline, Lance must make sure that *all* paths are less than or equal to 15 weeks. Table 5.12 shows the crashing logic. First, Lance crashes Activity I by 1 week, bringing both critical paths down to 16 weeks. Next Lance crashes Activity I by another week and Activity H by one week. If Lance did not crash Activity H, then two new paths (A–B–G–H–J–L and A–B–G–H–K–L) would become critical at 15.5 weeks, and the project would miss the deadline. The total crashing costs are \$1,000 + \$1,000 + \$2,000 = \$4,000.

TABLE 5.12 Crashing Logic for GriddleIron Project

PATH	ORIGINAL LENGTH (WEEKS)	CRASH I 1 WEEK	CRASH I ANOTHER WEEK, AND CRASH H 1 WEEK
A–B–F–I–J–L	17*	16*	15*
A–B–F–I–K–L	17*	16*	15*
A–B–G–H–J–L	15.5	15.5	14.5
A–B–G–H–K–L	15.5	15.5	14.5
A–C–D–E	11	11	11

*Critical path.

DISCUSSION QUESTIONS

1. Visit the Web site for the Project Management Institute at **www.pmi.org**. What types of educational material are available for project managers? What types of professional certification programs? What do you think a professional project manager does?
2. In what businesses would you expect project management skills to be most important? In what businesses would you expect them to be least important?
3. What are the main advantages of using a network-based approach to project management rather than a Gantt chart? Under what circumstances might a Gantt chart be preferable to a network-based approach?
4. Why do you think it is important for project planners to revisit the network diagram as time goes on?

PROBLEMS

Additional homework problems available at www. prenhall .com/bozarth. These additional problems use Excel to generate customized problems for different class sections or even different students.

(* = easy; ** = moderate; *** = advanced)

1. Consider the following project activities:

ACTIVITY	DURATION (DAYS)	PREDECESSORS
A	3	None
B	2	None
C	6	A
D	1.5	A, B
E	2.5	C, D
F	3.5	D
G	4	E, F

   a. (*) Draw the project network diagram.
   b. (*) Identify all the paths through the network and their lengths.
   c. (**) Identify all the critical activities and path(s). How long will the entire project take?

2. (**) Reconsider the project outlined in Problem 1. Management would like to complete the project in less than 12 days. They have determined that Activity C can be crashed four days for a total cost of $10,000. No other activities can be crashed. Will crashing Activity C meet management's goal of less than 12 days? Why or why not?

3. Consider the following project activities:

ACTIVITY	DURATION (DAYS)	PREDECESSORS
A	1	None
B	2	None
C	1.5	None
D	3	A, B
E	2.5	C
F	1.5	D, E
G	4	F
H	2	F

a. (*) Draw the project network diagram.
b. (*) Identify all the paths through the network and their lengths. Are there any activities that are on *all* paths?
c. (**) Identify all the critical activities and path(s). How long will the entire project take?

4. (**) Now reconsider the project in Problem 3. Every day the project goes on costs the company $5,000 in overhead costs. One of the managers responsible for carrying out Activity E feels she can crash the activity by 1 day through the use of overtime. The cost would be only $2,500. Should the company do it? Why or why not?

5. Consider the following project activities:

ACTIVITY	(DAYS)	PREDECESSORS
A	4	None
B	3	A
C	7	A
D	9	A
E	8	A
F	7	B
G	6	C
H	13	C
I	4	D, E
J	12	E
K	1	E
L	5	F, G, H
M	4	I, J, K
N	5	L, M

a. (*) Draw the project network diagram.
b. (*) Identify all the paths through the network and their lengths.
c. (**) Identify all the critical activities and path(s). How long will the entire project take?
d. (**) After completing part b, and before you perform the forward and backward passes, you should already be able to tell that Activities A and N are on the critical path(s). Why?

6. (**) After constructing the project network diagram in Problem 5, management comes up with the following information regarding how many days certain activities can be crashed, and at what cost.

ACTIVITY	NUMBER OF DAYS ACTIVITY CAN BE CRASHED	CRASH COST PER DAY
C	3	$1,000
D	3	$2,500
E	2	$5,000
G	1	$1,000
H	3	$3,000
J	2	$2,000

Suppose that every day the project goes on costs the company $3,500. How many days should management crash the project? What activities should it crash? What is the new project length?

7. Consider the following project activities:

ACTIVITY	DURATION (WEEKS)	PREDECESSORS
A	4	None
B	5	None
C	7	B
D	3	A, C
E	6	B
F	6	D
G	8	D
H	4	E, G

a. (*) Draw the project network diagram.
b. (*) Identify all the paths through the network and their lengths.
c. (**) Identify all the critical activities and path(s). How long will the entire project take?
d. (**) Which activity or activities have the most slack? What are the practical implications of this slack?

8. (**) Just before starting the project described in Problem 7, someone points out that (1) Activity A really needs to be done before Activity C, and (2) Activity C needs to be completed before Activity G can start. What is the impact on the expected length of the project?

9. (**) Reconsider Problem 7 (prior to any changes in Problem 8). Management has determined that the project must be completed in 25 weeks or less, and that "cost is no object." How many paths will need to be crashed in order to meet this goal? Which activities do not need to be considered for crashing?

10. Spartan Cabinets is thinking of offering a new line of cabinets. The project activities are as follows:

ACTIVITY	DURATION (WEEKS)	PREDECESSORS
A Hire workers	8	None
B Install equipment	6	None
C Order materials	3	None
D Test equipment	4	B
E Train workers	6	A, B
F Run pilot tests	5	C, D

a. (**) Identify all the paths through the network and their lengths. Which activities "start" one or more paths? Which activities "end" a path? How will those activities affect *ES*/*EF* and *LS*/*LF* calculations?

b. (**) Identify all the critical activities and path(s). How long will the entire project take?

11. Suppose management at Spartan Cabinets has developed additional information for the project described in Problem 10.

ACTIVITY	DURATION (WEEKS)	NUMBER OF WEEKS ACTIVITY CAN BE CRASHED	CRASH COST PER WEEK
A Hire workers	8	3	$2,000
B Install equipment	6	1	4,000
C Order materials	3	1	1,000
D Test equipment	4	2	2,500
E Train workers	6	2	5,000
F Run pilot tests	5	3	3,000

To illustrate, Activity **A** can be crashed by up to three weeks at a cost of $2,000 per week. Therefore, Activity **A** can be 8, 7, 6, or 5 weeks long, depending on how much money Spartan Cabinets decides to spend to crash the activity.

a. (***) What is the cheapest way to crash the project by two weeks?

b. (***) What is the shortest time in which the project can be completed? (Assume that cost is not a concern.)

12. After graduation, you and several of your friends decide to start a new software company. As the vice president of operations, you are in charge of several production steps, including the process that records software onto a CD. You have identified several activities that must take place before this "burn-in" process is ready to use:

ACTIVITY	DURATION (WEEKS)	PREDECESSORS
A Consult with engineering	3.5	None
B Determine equipment layout	2	None
C Install equipment	4.5	A, B
D Order materials	2	A
E Test equipment	2	C
F Train employees	3	D, E
G Perform pilot runs	2	F
H Get OSHA approval	4	E

a. (**) Draw the project network and calculate all *ES*, *EF*, *LS*, and *LF* times.

b. (**) Every week of delay in the project costs your company $3,000. Suppose you know the following: (1) Activity **G** can be crashed by 1 week at a cost of $1,500, (2) Activity **F** can be crashed by 1 week at a cost of only $50, and (3) Activity **H** can be crashed by 1 week at a cost of $2,000. Should you try to crash the project? If not, why not? If so, how much money will the company save?

13. For this question, consider the Gina3000 project described in Examples 5.1 and 5.2.

a. (***) Consider Table 5.4 and Figure 5.5. Every week the project continues costs the Courter Corporation an additional $5,000 in lost profits. The quality control manager says she can crash Activity **H** from three weeks down to 2 weeks by working overtime. Doing so would cost an additional $2,000. Should Courter do it?

b. (***) Writing up the product specifications (Activity **F**) is taking longer than expected. Assuming that no other activities have been delayed or crashed, how many weeks can Activity **F** be delayed without delaying the entire project?

CASE STUDY

VIVA ROMA!

Certe, toto, sentio nos in kansate non iam adesse.

Robert Curtis had just been hired into his first academic job as an assistant professor in the Classics Department at Topeka State University. One day in September 2008, not long after Robert had started, the department head came to talk to him.

"Bob, I know it's a little sudden and we usually don't ask new assistant professors to handle such a task, but I'd like you to put together our summer study abroad program in Rome. Professor Wurst has done it for the past 10 years, but he won't be able to this year. Plan on about 15 to 20 students. The program usually lasts about a month, going from mid-June to mid-July, but the college is usually flexible on the exact dates. So what do you think?"

Even though he was new, Robert thought it would be a great opportunity, and sitting down at his desk, he started to think about what he should do next. He had never put together such a trip before, so it made sense to start by listing all the different activities that had to take place to get the trip planned in time. Robert wanted to post the complete information packet by March 31, 2008, which would give prospective students plenty of time to plan for the trip and meet the May 15 registration deadline.

The first thing Robert had to do was negotiate the exact starting and ending dates with the college, as well as make a rough estimate of the per-student costs. Specifically, Robert needed to know when the students would leave and when they would be expected to return to the United States. Robert felt he could do all this within 1 week.

Once Robert had these date and cost targets, he would then need to develop a daily schedule of the sites to visit, including any trips outside of the Rome area (such as to Florence or Naples). Robert knew this would take a little time—museums and historical sites in Italy do not keep typical business hours, and some sites might even be closed for repair. Robert felt that this would take at least 3 weeks.

With a detailed schedule in hand, Robert would then have to make air transportation arrangements (1 week), and local transportation arrangements (about 1 week) and select the accomodations to stay in during the trip (3 weeks). Because Robert knew a lot of the time would be spent playing "telephone tag" with various people, all three of these activities could go on simultaneously.

Finally, Robert thought he would need to give himself a few weeks to finalize any loose ends. For example, he might learn that there were no rooms available during the time he wanted to schedule a side trip to Herculaneum, resulting in the need to adjust the schedule and other arrangements. With the finalized plans and costs in place, Robert would then need to develop and post the online information packet for students (1 week).

QUESTIONS

1. What are the important time milestones for this project?
2. Given these time milestones, when should Robert start on the project? Draw a network diagram and determine the earliest and latest starting and finishing times for all activities. From a scheduling perspective, which activities are critical?
3. Comment on the time estimates for the various activities: Should Robert give himself more time? What are the pros and cons of doing so? Are there any pitfalls to starting too early? Where might he get good estimates of these times?

REFERENCES

Books and Articles

A *Guide to the Project Management Body of Knowledge (PMBOK® Guide),* 3rd ed. Newton Square, Pennsylvania: Project Management Institute, 2004.

Krajewski, L., and L. Ritzman. *Operations Management: Strategy and Analysis,* 6th ed. Upper Saddle River, NJ: Prentice Hall, 2002.

Levine, S., and P. Barta. "Fuel Lines: Giant New Oil Refinery in India Shows Forces Roiling Industry." *The Wall Street Journal* (Eastern Edition) (August 29, 2006): p. A1.

Internet

Project Management Institute, **www.pmi.org**

CHAPTER 6

Developing Products and Services

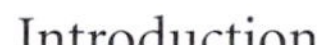

CHAPTER OUTLINE

Chapter Objectives

By the end of this chapter, you will be able to:

- Explain why product design is important to a business's success.
- Describe the six dimensions of product design that are of particular interest to operations and supply chain managers.
- Describe the five phases of product and service development and explain the difference between sequential development and concurrent engineering.
- Discuss the different roles played by such areas as engineering and accounting during the development process.
- Describe some of the more common approaches to improving product and service designs, including the Define-Measure-Analyze-Design-Verify (DMADV) process, quality function deployment (QFD), design for manufacturability (DFM), and target costing.

Whirlpool[1]

Rio Claro, Brazil—Silvia Oliveira calls her "my second mother." Lourdes Silva caresses her contours adoringly. The two Brazilian housewives aren't fawning over a person. The object of their adoration is a washing machine. Whirlpool Corporation has launched what it bills as the world's cheapest automatic washer, with an eye on low-income consumers who never thought they could afford one. "Before she came along I spent hours bent over the washing tub," says Mrs. Oliveira, a mother of six whose husband, a freelance mason, earns about $200 a month. Referring to the washer by its name in Brazil, she adds, "Now, I can put Ideale to work and do other things, like tend to my children, cook dinner and even visit my sick mother."

Whirlpool invested $30 million over 18 months to develop the washing machine in Brazil. But the Ideale washer is a global project because it is also being manufactured in China and India. The washer was launched in October 2003 in Brazil and China (where its Chinese name means Super Hand-Washing Washer). It was set to debut in India in 2004, followed by debuts in other developing countries. The target retail price: $150 to $200. That compares with the average washer price in the United States of $461, Whirlpool Corporation says. The people's washing-machine project shows how Whirlpool has decentralized its operations, shifting more design work to developing countries. Brazil boasts some of Whirlpool brand's most advanced factories and a growing technology staff, where highly skilled, low-cost engineers and industrial designers not only "Latinize" U.S. designs, but create entirely new products for consumers worldwide. "It's the second wave of globalization," says Nelson Possamai, manufacturing director of the Whirlpool refrigerator plant in the southern Brazilian city of Joinville, where products are developed for Indian homes as well as U.S. college dormitories.

Whirlpool has long dominated the appliance market in Brazil thanks to its purchase of two established brands, Brastemp and Consul. But its products catered mainly to well-to-do Brazilians. Sales of a basic washer launched in 1998 didn't take off because the model, which cost about $300, still was unaffordable to low-income consumers.

Whirlpool was convinced that it had to start from scratch to make a product that was affordable and appealing to the average Brazilian worker, who earns about $220 a month. "It wasn't a matter of stripping down an existing model," says Marcelo Rodrigues, a Whirlpool Corporation top washing-machine engineer in Latin America. "We had to innovate for the masses," said Mr. Rodrigues, who is director of laundry technology at Multibras SA Eletrodomesticos, the Brazilian unit of Whirlpool.

His team developed a cost-effective technology, for which it has applied for patents in key markets. Washing machines normally work a bit like cars, shifting gears for different functions. But for Ideale, Brazilian engineers built a single-drive system by which clothes are washed and spun without switching gears. That is the biggest cost-saving device. To be sure, the spinning is slower than in more sophisticated machines, so clothes may be a bit damper, but Whirlpool studies show that it is good enough for the target consumers.

Whirlpool also found that Brazilians prefer cheery and rounded styling over sleek and square. Housewives approved when the company changed a gray-and-black control panel to one that incorporated color, such as a yellow start button and blue lettering. Like wealthy Brazilians, however, low-income women also strongly associate white with cleanliness; Ideale comes only in white, as does the vast majority of appliances in Brazil. In China, white is disdained because it dirties easily. There, the washer comes in light blue and gray. In India, it will be produced in green, blue, and white.

Whirlpool's Ideale washing machine is specifically targeted at consumers in developing countries. Designed in Brazil, it is also manufactured in China and India.

[1]M. Jordan and J. Karp, "Machines for the Masses: Whirlpool Aims Cheap Washer at Brazil, India and China," *The Wall Street Journal*, December 9, 2003. (Photograph used with permission from Whirlpool Corporation.)

INTRODUCTION

Whirlpool Corporation's experiences highlight some of the issues companies face when developing new products and services. But how do companies like Whirlpool go about managing the development process, and what roles do various parties within and outside the firm play? These questions are the subject of this chapter. First, we discuss the role of product and service development in today's businesses, emphasizing the impact new and enhanced products and services have on a firm's ability to compete.

We then turn our attention to the actual process by which companies develop new products and services or modify existing ones. We pay special attention to operations and supply chain perspectives on product and service design: What are the important considerations? What role do the purchasing function and suppliers play? What tools and techniques are companies using to enhance the product development effort?

Product Design and the Development Process

Product design
The characteristics or features of a product or service that determine its ability to meet the needs of the user.

Product development process
The overall process of strategy, organization, concept generation, product and marketing plan creation and evaluation, and commercialization of a new product.

Before we get started, it's important for us to distinguish between product design and the product development process. **Product design** can be thought of as the characteristics or features of a product or service that determine its ability to meet the needs of the user. In contrast, the **product development process** is "the overall process of strategy, organization, concept generation, product and marketing plan creation and evaluation, and commercialization of a new product."[2] In this chapter, we focus on how product and service design affects operations and supply chain activities and what role operations and supply chains play in the development process. We use the term *product design* to refer to the development of both intangible services and physical products. As you can probably guess, product development is by necessity a cross-functional effort affecting operations and supply chain activities, as well as engineering, marketing, and finance.

Four Reasons for Developing New Products and Services

There are least four reasons why a company might develop new products or services or update its existing ones. The first is straightforward: *New products or services can give firms a competitive advantage in the marketplace.* Consider the problem facing H&R Block a few years ago: How do you attract customers when faced with increasing competition from other tax preparation firms as well as PC-based software packages that can help people do their tax returns on their own? You do it by providing new and distinctive services, such as PC-based will kits, refund anticipation loans (RALs), and a Web page that provides customers with valuable information in multiple languages.

Not all product development efforts *directly* benefit the customer, however. This leads to our second reason for developing new products or services—*new products or services provide benefits to the firm.* Hewlett-Packard might redesign one of its desktop printers so it has fewer parts and is easier to assemble. Even though the printer might look and function exactly as before, the result is improved assembly productivity and lower purchasing and production costs. Hewlett-Packard might or might not share these savings with the customer.

Third, *companies develop new products or services to exploit existing capabilities.* An excellent example is Honda. As noted in Chapter 2, Honda progressed from making and selling motorcycles, to automobiles, and, most recently, to lawn equipment, jet skis, and

[2]Product Development and Management Association, "Glossary of New Product Development Terms," **www.pdma.org/library/glossary.html.**

Honda is a leader in the design and manufacture of gas-powered engines. These strengths have allowed the company to enter a wide range of markets.

small jet airplanes. In retrospect, it is easy to see that Honda has built on its core competencies in the design and production of gas-powered vehicles. It will be interesting to see how Honda maintains its advantage as more products shift to alternative fuels.

Fourth, *companies can use new product development to block out competitors*. Consider the case of Gillette.[3] By the early 1990s, Gillette had grown tired of spending millions to develop a new razor blade, only to have competitors introduce cheaper (and poorer-quality) replacement blades within a few months. Gillette made a point of designing its Sensor razor so that it not only provided customers with a superior shave, but also would be difficult for competitors to copy. Developing the Sensor razor therefore required a great deal of coordination with the manufacturing arm of the firm. Of course, a firm might have multiple reasons for developing a new product or service, or for updating existing ones. But regardless of the underlying reasons, the development effort must be consistent with the strategy of a firm.

---

[3]L. Ingrassia, "Taming the Monster: How Big Companies Can Change: Keeping Sharp: Gillette Holds Its Edge by Endlessly Searching for a Better Shave," *The Wall Street Journal*, December 10, 1992.

Just how important are new products and services to firms? Consider the following figures. In a sample of 383 companies from a wide range of industrial settings, the Product Development and Management Association (PDMA) found the following:

- On average, about 30% of revenues and profits come from products introduced in the last five years. For the most successful firms, these figures rise to nearly 50%.
- In the past 10 years, the time it takes to develop new products in many industries had dropped from about 31 months to about 24 months—a reduction of about 30%.
- Over 84% of the more innovative development projects use cross-functional development teams.
- Despite the shorter development times, the percentage of new product development efforts deemed successful by the firms has held steady at 59%.

6.1 OPERATIONS AND SUPPLY CHAIN PERSPECTIVES ON DESIGN

If someone asked you, as a consumer, what the important dimensions of product design are, you might mention such aspects as functionality, aesthetics, ease of use, and cost. Operations and supply chain managers also have an interest in product design because ultimately these managers will be responsible for providing the products or services on a day-to-day basis. To understand the operations and supply chain perspective, think about a new electronic device. It is one thing for a team of highly trained engineers to build a working prototype in a lab. It's quite another thing to make millions of devices each year using skilled and semi-skilled labor, coordinate the flow of parts coming from all over the world, and ship the devices so that they arrive on time, undamaged, and at the lowest possible cost. Yet, as you might recall from the opening case study for the iPod in Chapter 2, this is exactly what the operations and supply chain managers at companies like Apple are doing.

The interest of operations and supply chain management in *service* design is even greater. This is because the service design is often the operations process itself. To take an example from physical distribution, when a transportation firm agrees to provide global transportation services to a large customer, it has to make decisions regarding the number of trucks, ships, or airplanes required, the size and location of any warehousing facilities, and the information systems and personnel needed to support the new service. This type of activity is also called **supply chain design**, in that it involves designing the flow of goods and materials between multiple locations.

Supply chain design
The process of designing the flow of goods and materials between multiple locations.

With this in mind, the operations and supply chain perspective on product design will usually center on six dimensions:

1. Repeatability
2. Testability
3. Serviceability
4. Product volumes
5. Product costs
6. Match between the design and existing capabilities

Repeatability, Testability, and Serviceability

Repeatability, testability, and serviceability are dimensions of product design that affect the ability of operations to deliver the product in the first place and to provide ongoing support afterward. *Repeatability* deals with the question, Are we capable of making the product over and over again, in the volumes needed? This is addressed through robust design.

Robust design
The design of products to be less sensitive to variations, including manufacturing variation and misuse, increasing the probability that they will perform as intended.

Testability
The ease with which critical components or functions can be tested during production.

Serviceability
The ease with which parts can be replaced, serviced, or evaluated.

PDMA describes **robust design** as "the design of products to be less sensitive to variations, including manufacturing variation and misuse, increasing the probability that they will perform as intended."[4] Product designs that are robust are better able to meet tolerance limits (see Chapter 4), making it easier for the operations and supply chain functions to provide good products on an ongoing basis.

Testability refers to the ease with which critical components or functions can be tested during production. Suppose for a moment that your company manufactures expensive electronics equipment. The manufacturing process consists of a series of steps, each of which adds parts, costs, and value to the product. If a $5 circuit board has gone bad, you want to find this out before you assemble it with some other component or put together the final product.

Serviceability is similar to testability. In this case, serviceability refers to the ease with which parts can be replaced, serviced, or evaluated. Many modern automobiles require that the engine be unbolted from the car frame and tilted forward before the spark plugs can be changed—hardly a plus for shade-tree mechanics! On the other hand, all new cars have computer diagnostics systems that allow mechanics to quickly troubleshoot problems.

Serviceability is of particular interest to organizations that are responsible for supporting products in the field. When products are easy to service, costs can be contained and service times become more predictable, resulting in higher productivity and greater customer satisfaction. Some of the ways in which ease of service can be improved are by using standard parts, improving access to important parts of the product, and standardizing the service work.

Product Volumes

Once a company decides to go forward with a new product or service, it becomes the job of operations and supply chain managers to make sure that the company can handle the resulting volumes. This responsibility might mean expanding the firm's own operations by building new facilities, hiring additional workers, and buying new equipment. It might also require joint planning with key suppliers.

As we will see in Chapter 7, the expected volume levels for a product or service also affect the *types* of equipment, people, or facilities needed. Highly automated processes that are too expensive and inflexible for low-volume custom products can be very cost effective when millions of units will be made.

Product Costs

A study conducted by Computer-Aided Manufacturing International (CAM–I) concluded that 80% of the cost for a typical product is "locked in" at the design stage. In other words, any effort to "tweak" costs later on will be limited by decisions that were made early in a product's life. Given the importance of costs in operations and supply chain activities, it is not surprising that operations and supply chain managers have a vested interest in addressing cost before the product design has been finalized.

For our purposes, we can think of products and services as having obvious and hidden costs. Obvious costs include such things as the materials required, the labor hours needed, and even the equipment costs needed to provide a particular service or product. These costs are usually the easiest ones to see and manage (i.e., we can track material usage, machine time, and the amount of direct labor that goes into our products or services).

Hidden costs are not as easy to track, but can have a major impact nonetheless. Hidden costs are typically associated with the overhead and support activities driven by some

[4]Product Development and Management Association, "Glossary."

aspect of design. There are numerous drivers of hidden costs, but we will talk about three to make the point:

1. The number of parts in a product;
2. Engineering changes; and
3. Transportation costs.

Think about the activities that are driven by the number of parts used in a product, such as a washing machine. Engineering specifications must be developed for each part. The manufacturer must identify a supplier for each part and then place and track orders. Furthermore, the manufacturer must monitor the inventory levels of each part in its manufacturing plants and service support centers. Even if the manufacturer stops selling the washing machine after five years, it must continue to stock each part for years to come. All these activities represent hidden costs driven by the number of parts. Clearly, the manufacturer has an incentive to reduce the number of parts in a washing machine and to share parts across as many products as possible.

Engineering change
A revision to a drawing or design released by engineering to modify or correct a part.

There are also hidden costs associated with engineering changes to a product. An **engineering change** is a revision to a drawing or design released by engineering to modify or correct a part.[5] Returning to our washing machine example, suppose the manufacturer decides to make improvements to a part once the washing machine has been on the market for a few years. Suppliers, plants, and service support centers have to be notified of the change, and inventories have to be switched over from the old part to the new one. Yet the manufacturer will still have to keep track of information on both parts for years to come. Clearly, the manufacturer has a real financial incentive to design the part right the first time.

Products can also be designed to minimize transportation costs. Oddly shaped or fragile products can quickly drive up transportation costs. In contrast, products that can be shipped in standardized containers to take advantage of lower transportation rates can hold down the costs of distribution. NordicTrack engineers designed the Walk-Fit treadmill so that the electronics could be shipped to the customer separately from the treadmill. This was important because these components were made in different facilities. By separating the electronics from the treadmill, engineers allowed the bulky treadmill to be shipped at a lower per-pound cost rate. If the relatively fragile electronics had been included with the bulkier treadmill, the entire product would have had to be shipped at a much higher cost rate.

Match with Existing Capabilities

Finally, operations and supply chain managers are always concerned with how well new products or services match up with existing products or capabilities. A new product or service that allows a manufacturer to use existing parts and manufacturing facilities is usually easier to support than one that requires new ones. Similarly, services that exploit existing capabilities are especially attractive. An excellent example is the online tracking service that FedEx provides to its customers. In fact, this "new" service was built on an existing capability supported by FedEx's internal tracking software.

It may *seem* obvious that companies should consider such factors as production volumes and existing capabilities when designing new products or services. But what happens if they don't? Well, Nabisco ran into this exact problem back in 1993 when it introduced its new SnackWell's Devil's Food Cookie Cakes. The *Supply Chain Connections* feature reveals a classic example of what can happen when the operations and supply chain perspective is not adequately considered when designing a new product.

---

[5] J. F. Cox and J. H. Blackstone, eds., *APICS Dictionary*, 10th ed. (Falls Church, VA: APICS, 2002).

SUPPLY CHAIN CONNECTIONS

HOW DIFFICULT CAN IT BE TO MAKE A COOKIE?[6]

If you think only high-tech companies face difficulties when developing and launching new products, consider the situation faced by Nabisco back in 1993. The following excerpt taken from an article written at the time describes some of the challenges Nabisco faced after introducing its SnackWell's Devil's Food Cookie Cakes.

More than a year after the launch of the fat-free chocolate-and-marshmallow cookies, Nabisco is still unable to meet consumer demand. Supermarkets nationwide say supplies of the cookie are tightly rationed, and that the shortage has created a buying frenzy among some consumers who view the fat-free cookies as the perfect food: healthy sweets.

So why can't Nabisco, which will bake some 600 million pounds of cookies this year, simply make more of the scarce sweets? The Devil's Food Cookie Cake, it turns out, is one tough cookie to produce. Whipping up confections that require only shaping and baking, such as Lorna Doone shortbread or Chips Ahoy! chocolate chip cookies, is a breeze by comparison, according to Brian Beglin, senior director of operations services for Nabisco. "There is no such thing as a simple cookie," Mr. Beglin says. "But the Devil's Food Cookie Cake is the hardest one we make."

The main culprit: Marshmallow cream. Less complex confections, such as Mallomars or Pinwheels, have the sticky stuff only on one side of the cookie center. Hence, they may be placed on a conveyor belt after they are coated with chocolate—"enrobed" in cookie lingo—and whisked along toward a waiting box or bag. The SnackWell's cookie center, by contrast, is covered on all sides with marshmallow. Then it is completely drenched with chocolate icing, followed by a separate chocolate glaze. Because the cookie is completely enrobed, it would stick to a conveyor belt. That means devil's food cookies require custom-made machinery. That equipment is currently available in just one bakery, in Sioux City, South Dakota, owned by Interbake Foods Inc.

Adding capacity would be difficult and expensive. The Sioux City bakery uses a method, called a pin trolley system, that has not changed much since the 1920s, when the devil's food cookie was created. After baking for six minutes, each cookie-cake center is placed on an upright pin—actually a tiny, two-pronged fork—that is mounted on a trolley. The whole contraption is pulled by a chain along a mile-long track that snakes around the bakery for four hours, passing through the marshmallow and chocolate coatings en route.

Further complicating matters: Because the chocolate covering is fat-free, it cannot be chilled to speed the setting process. Instead, it must be allowed to air-dry between coats. That means the entire process takes four hours, compared to only about 30 minutes from the time Chips Ahoy! dough is sliced to the time the venerable chocolate-chip product is packaged.

Nabisco says it currently has three production lines running overtime to produce the Devil's Food Cookie Cakes, and is about to add a fourth—all the capacity currently available at the Interbake plant, rivals say. Until Nabisco can accurately gauge demand for the new product, it is being sold only in northeastern states. Says a company spokesman, "We've learned our lesson."

6.2 THE DEVELOPMENT PROCESS

In the previous section, we talked about some product design dimensions of particular interest to operations and supply chain managers. But there are other perspectives to consider, including those of the final customer, marketing, engineering, and finance, to list just a few. How do firms go about designing products and services that incorporate all these perspectives and, just as important, how do they move from the idea stage to the actual launch of a new product or service? This section describes a model of the product development process and discusses the organizational roles played by different functional areas and supply chain partners.

[6]K. Deveny, "Man Walked on the Moon But Man Can't Make Enough Devil's Food Cookie Cakes," *The Wall Street Journal*, September 28, 1993.

A Model of the Development Process

All of us have experienced products or services that for some reason stood out from the competition—a hand tool that was easier to use or more powerful than previous models, an airline seat that was more comfortable, or maybe even online financial services that allowed us to check our portfolios and initiate trades 24 hours a day.

Good design does not happen by accident. Rather, it requires a coordinated effort supported by many individuals, both within and outside of the firm. Table 6.1 offers one view of the development process. The table divides the development process into five phases, paying particular attention to the roles played by the operations and supply chain functions, as well as by marketing and engineering.

Concept development phase
The first phase of a product development effort. Here a company identifies ideas for new or revised products and services.

Planning phase
The second phase of a product development effort. Here the company begins to address the feasibility of a product or service.

In the **concept development phase**, a company identifies ideas for new or revised products and services. As Table 6.1 suggests, these ideas can come from a variety of sources, not just from customers. For example, engineering might identify a new material that can reduce the weight and cost of a product, even before marketing or the customer knows about it. The operations and supply chain functions have a role to play here as well—purchasing personnel might look at potential suppliers to see if they have any promising new technologies or capabilities that could be turned into a new product or service.

If a concept is approved, it will pass on to the **planning phase**, where the company begins to address the feasibility of a product or service. Customers are often brought in at this stage to evaluate ideas. Engineering might begin to identify the general performance characteristics of the product or service and the process technologies needed to produce it. Marketing will start to estimate sales volumes and expected profit margins. Operations and

TABLE 6.1 Phases of Product and Service Development

FUNCTIONAL ACTIVITIES	CONCEPT DEVELOPMENT	PLANNING	DESIGN AND DEVELOPMENT	COMMERCIAL PREPARATION	LAUNCH
Engineering	Propose new technologies; Develop product ideas	Identify *general* performance characteristics for the product or service; Identify underlying technologies	Develop *detailed* product specifications; Build and test prototypes	Resolve remaining technical problems	Evaluate field experience with product or service
Marketing	Provide market-based input; Propose and investigate product or service concepts	Define target customers' needs; Estimate sales and profit margins; Include customers in development effort	Conduct customer tests; Evaluate prototypes; Plan marketing rollout	Train sales force; Prepare sales procedures; Select distribution channel	Fill downstream supply chain; Sell and promote
Operations and supply chain functions	Scan suppliers for promising technologies/ capabilities	Develop initial cost estimates; Identify key supply chain partners	Develop *detailed* process maps of the operations and supply chain flows; Test new processes	Build pilot units using new operations; Train personnel; Verify supply chain flows work as expected	Ramp up volumes; Meet targets for quality, cost, and other performance goals

Source: Adapted from S. Wheelwright and K. Clark, *Revolutionizing Product Development* (New York: Free Press, 1992).

supply chain personnel might start identifying the key supply chain partners to be involved. Many ideas that look good in the concept development phase fail to pass the hurdles set at the planning phase. A product may be too costly to make, may not generate enough revenues, or may simply be impossible to produce in the volumes needed to support the market.

Design and development phase
The third phase of a product development effort. Here the company starts to invest heavily in the development effort and builds and evaluates prototypes.

Those that do clear the hurdles go on to the **design and development phase**, during which the company starts to invest heavily in the development effort. In this phase, the company builds and evaluates prototypes of the product or service. Product prototypes can range from simple Styrofoam mock-ups to fully functional units. Service prototypes can range from written descriptions to field tests using actual customers. At the same time, operations and physical distribution begin to develop detailed process maps of the physical, information, and monetary flows that will need to take place in order to provide the product or service on a regular basis (Chapter 3). They may even start to develop quality levels for key process steps (Chapter 4). The design and development phase is complete when the company approves the final design for the product and related processes.

Commercial preparation phase
The fourth phase of a product development effort. At this stage, firms start to invest heavily in the operations and supply chain resources needed to support the new product or service.

The **commercial preparation phase** is characterized by activities associated with the introduction of a new product or service. At this stage, firms start to invest heavily in the operations and supply chain resources needed to support the new product or service. This may mean new facilities, warehouses, personnel, and even information systems to handle production requirements. Obviously, this phase will go more smoothly if the new product or service can build on existing operations and supply chain systems. If new supply chain partners are required or if new technologies are needed, commercial preparation and launch can be much more difficult and expensive.

Launch phase
The final phase of a product development effort. For physical products, this usually means "filling up" the supply chain with products. For services, it can mean making the service broadly available to the target marketplace.

The last phase is the **launch phase**. For physical products, this usually means "filling up" the supply chain with products. For services, it can mean making the service broadly available to the target marketplace, as in the case of cell phone service. In either case, operations and supply chain managers must closely monitor performance results to make sure that quality, cost, and delivery targets are being met and must take corrective action when necessary.

Sequential Development versus Concurrent Engineering

Sequential development process
A process in which the product or service idea must clear specific hurdles before it can go on to the next development phase.

The development model in Table 6.1 outlines a sequential development process. A **sequential development process** is one in which the product or service idea must clear specific hurdles before it can go on to the next development phase. The result is that while many ideas may be considered at the relatively cheap concept development phase, few make it to the commercial preparation and launch phases (where significant resources have to be invested). Steven Wheelright and Kim Clark of the Harvard Business School describe this process as the *development funnel* (Figure 6.1).

FIGURE 6.1
The Development Funnel
Source: K. Clark, and S. Wheelwright, *Managing New Product and Process Development: Text and Cases* (New York: Free Press, 1993), p. 294.

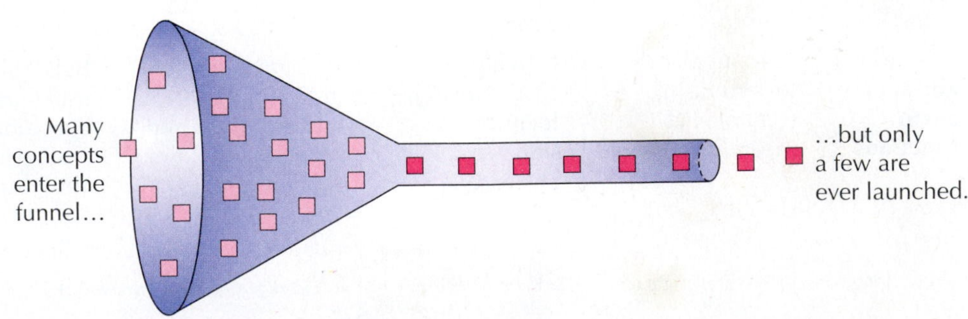
Many concepts enter the funnel...
...but only a few are ever launched.

FIGURE 6.2
Concurrent Engineering

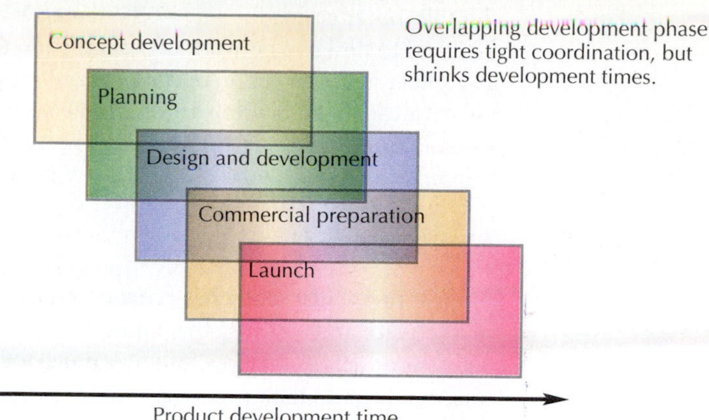

Concurrent engineering An alternative to sequential development in which activities in different development stages are allowed to overlap with one another, thereby shortening the total development time.

An alternative to sequential development is concurrent engineering. As the name implies, **concurrent engineering** allows activities in different development stages to overlap with one another, thereby shortening the total development time. For example, engineering may begin to build and test prototypes (design and development phase) even before the general product characteristics have been finalized (planning phase). In contrast to a sequential development process, in which there is a clear "hand-off" from one stage to the next, concurrent engineering requires constant communication between participants at various stages in the development effort. Figure 6.2 illustrates the idea.

Concurrent engineering helps reduce development times by forcing development teams to agree on critical product and process characteristics *early* in the development process, usually in the concept through design and development phases. These broad characteristics—costs, size, materials, markets to be served, and so on—provide clear guidance and boundaries for later activities. Returning to our engineering example, the *only way* engineers can start to build prototypes before the product characteristics are finalized is if there is *general* agreement regarding the characteristics of the new product (size, basic features, etc.). When this isn't the case, firms will need to follow a more sequential approach.

6.3 ORGANIZATIONAL ROLES IN PRODUCT AND SERVICE DEVELOPMENT

Product or service development is almost always a cross-functional effort. Table 6.1 shows how various parties contribute to the development effort in different ways. How well the different functions coordinate their efforts goes a long way toward determining the success of any development effort. Marketing, for example, might need to work with engineering to know what product features are technologically feasible. Purchasing then might help identify outside sources for needed inputs or services. Let's take a moment to discuss how different functions contribute to the development effort.

Engineering

Engineering provides the expertise needed to resolve many of the technological issues associated with a firm's products or services. Some of these issues center on the actual design of a product or service. A product engineer might be asked to design a lightweight, yet durable, outer casing for a new cell phone. Or a team of civil and electrical engineers might be asked to design a network of transmission towers for the relay of cell phone signals.

Other issues center on operational and supply chain considerations. Industrial engineers, for instance, might develop specifications for the manufacturing equipment needed to make the cell phone casings or transmission towers. Packaging engineers might be asked to develop shipping containers that strike a balance between cost and protection against damage.

Marketing

In most firms, marketing has primary responsibility for understanding what goes on in the marketplace and applying that knowledge to the development process. Who buys our company's products or services, and how much will they pay? Who are our company's competitors, and how do their products and services stack up against ours? How large is the market for a particular product or service? Marketing professionals use a variety of research techniques to answer such questions, including surveys, focus groups, and detailed market studies. When it comes to really understanding what customers want, many companies would be lost without marketing's input.

But marketing's role goes beyond that of providing information in the early phases of the development process. Marketing also has to select distribution channels, train sales personnel, and develop selling and promotional strategies.

Accounting

Accounting plays the role of "scorekeeper" in many companies. Not only do accountants prepare reports for the government and outside investors, but they are also responsible for developing the cost and performance information many companies need to make intelligent business decisions. How much will a new product or service cost? How many hours of labor or machine time will be needed? The answers to these types of questions often require input from the firm's accountants.

Finance

The role of finance in product and service development is twofold. First, finance establishes the criteria used to judge the financial impact of a development effort. How much time will pass before our company recoups its investment in a product or service? What is the expected rate of return? How risky is the project?

Once a company decides to proceed with the development of a product or service, it is the responsibility of finance to determine exactly how the company will acquire the needed capital. Several years ago Sprint spent $400 million to launch a new networking service and $8.3 billion to update its existing services.[7] Sprint's financial managers were charged with funding this growth.

Designers

Designers can come from a variety of educational backgrounds—from engineering, design, and business schools, to name a few. Their role is one of the least understood aspects of the development process. One myth is that designers only do *product* design, but they do much more than that. They create identities for companies (logos, brochures, etc.), environments (such as buildings, interiors, and exhibits), and even service experiences.

[7]S. Mehta and J. Keller, "Sprint to Integrate Voice, Data," *The Wall Street Journal*, June 3, 1998.

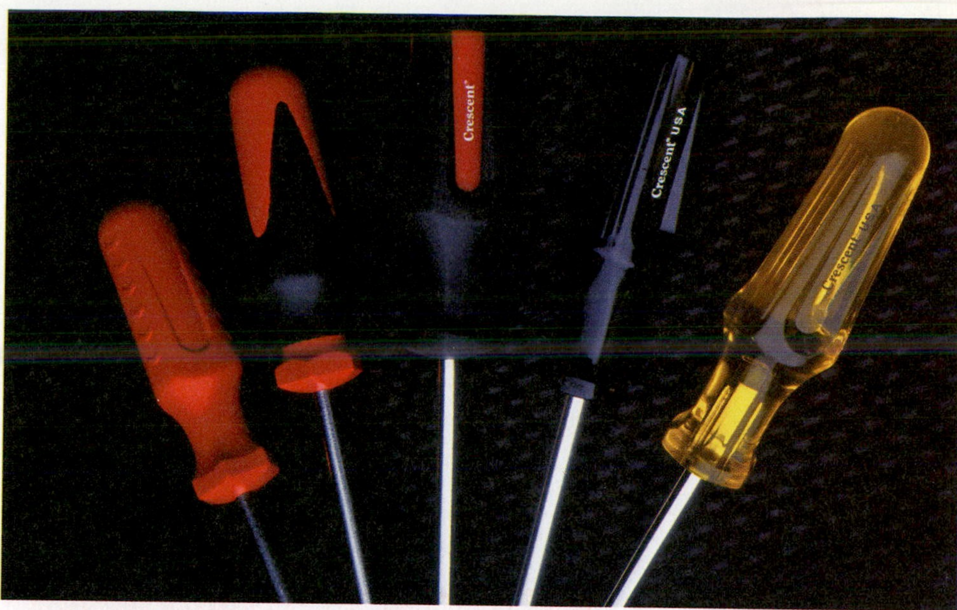

Forma Designs of Raleigh, North Carolina, improved the grips for a customer's line of screwdrivers. Even small changes such as this can make a big difference in the marketplace.

To make cell phone towers blend in with the environment, for example, designers have camouflaged the giant poles as trees or added decorative latticework.

A second myth is that designers simply make something "look good." This suggests that design is all form and no content. Yet consider an apparently simple handheld tape measure redesigned by Forma Design of Raleigh, North Carolina. As part of the redesign effort, Forma changed the tape measure so that the thumb pressed against the index finger to work the tape measure's locking mechanism. Before that, users had to apply force between the thumb and *little* finger. If you try pushing your thumb against your little finger and then your index finger, you can see for yourself that the new design results in considerably less hand fatigue. Designers also work with schedules and constraints, just like other professionals. For example, in the redesign of the tape measure, Forma was not allowed to change any of the internal mechanisms.

Purchasing

Purchasing deserves special mention because it plays several important roles in product development. As the main contact with suppliers, purchasing is in a unique position to identify the best suppliers and sign them up early in the development process. Many purchasing departments even have databases of preapproved suppliers. The process of preapproving suppliers for specific commodities or parts is known as **presourcing**. As part of this process, purchasing professionals will carefully examine the capabilities and capacity levels of different suppliers to meet future needs.

Presourcing
The process of preapproving suppliers for specific commodities or parts.

Another role purchasing plays is that of a consultant with special knowledge of material and service supply markets. Purchasing personnel might recommend substitutes for high-cost or volatile materials, or standard items instead of more expensive custom-made parts. In some cases, they may even ask suppliers to meet with the product development team, and provide advice and share their intellectual property in order to help the team make the most effective design decisions. This type of interaction can substantially improve product cost, quality, and technical performance. Finally, purchasing plays the role of monitor, tracking forecasts of the prices and long-term supply of key materials or monitoring technological innovations that might affect purchasing decisions.

Suppliers

Suppliers can bring a fresh perspective to the table, thereby helping organizations see opportunities for improvement they might otherwise miss. Teaming up with suppliers can also help organizations divide up the development effort, thereby saving time and reducing financial risks. Boeing, for instance, uses outside suppliers to develop many of the key components and subassemblies for its jets. If Boeing tried to develop the jet on its own, the project would cost considerably more money and take much longer.

Bringing suppliers into the development effort goes beyond just sharing information with them. Important suppliers should be included early in the development of a new product, perhaps even as part of the project team. The benefits of such early inclusion include gaining a supplier's insight into the development process, allowing comparisons of proposed production requirements with a supplier's existing capabilities, and allowing a supplier to begin preproduction work early on.

Gray box design
Used to describe a situation in which the supplier works with the customer to jointly design the product.

Black box design
Used to describe a situation in which suppliers are provided with general requirements and are asked to fill in the technical specifications.

The degree of supplier participation can also vary. At one extreme, the supplier is given blueprints and told to produce to the specifications. In a hybrid arrangement, called **gray box design**, the supplier works with the customer to jointly design the product. At the highest level of supplier participation, known as **black box design**, suppliers are provided with general requirements and are asked to fill in the technical specifications.

Black box design is best when the supplier is the acknowledged "expert." For example, an automotive manufacturer may tell a key supplier that it wants an electric window motor that costs under $15, pulls no more than 5 amps, fits within a certain space, and weighs less than 2 pounds. Given these broad specifications, the supplier is free to develop the best motor that meets the automotive manufacturer's needs.

Who Leads?

Ultimately, someone or some group has to have primary responsibility for making sure the product development process is a success. But who? The answer depends largely on the nature of the development effort and the industrial setting. In high-tech firms, scientists and engineers will typically take the lead. Their scientific and technological expertise is essential to developing safe, effective products that can be made in the volumes required. In contrast, at a toy producer, the technical questions usually aren't nearly as interesting as the consumers and markets themselves: What toys will be "hot" next December? How many will be sold? Marketing is therefore likely to have primary responsibility for managing the development effort.

6.4 APPROACHES TO IMPROVING PRODUCT AND SERVICE DESIGNS

Coordinating a product development effort while ensuring all dimensions of performance are adequately considered is no easy task. As a result, organizations have developed useful approaches to help them accomplish these goals. The purpose of this section is to introduce you to some of the more common approaches.

DMADV (Define-Measure-Analyze-Design-Verify) A Six Sigma process that outlines the steps needed to create *completely new* business processes or products.

DMADV (Define-Measure-Analyze-Design-Verify)

Chapter 3 introduced the Six Sigma methodology and the DMAIC (Define-Measure-Analyze-Improve-Control) approach to improving *existing* business processes. The Six Sigma methodology also includes a process called **DMADV (Define-Measure-Analyze-Design-Verify)**, which outlines the steps needed to create *completely new* business processes or products. As with DMAIC, the DMADV process places a premium on rigorous data analysis, and depends on teams of black belts, green belts, and champions to carry it out. The five steps of DMADV are as follows:

Step 1. *Define* the project goals and customer deliverables. Because the focus is on a *new* process or product, the Six Sigma team must properly scope the project to ensure that the effort is carried out in a timely and efficient manner. What products or services do we want to provide and to whom? How will we know when we have completed the project successfully?

Step 2. *Measure* and determine customer needs and specifications. The second step requires the team to develop a clear picture of what the targeted customers want in terms of quality, delivery, cost, or other measures of interest. Market research techniques as well as quality function deployment (QFD), which we describe in the following section, are employed here.

Step 3. *Analyze* the product or process options to meet the customer needs. In this step, the Six Sigma team evaluates how the various options available stack up against the customers' requirements.

Step 4. *Design* the product or process. Here, the hard work of designing the product or process, as outlined in the "Design and Development Phase" of Table 6.1, takes place.

Step 5. *Verify* the new product or process. Last, the team must verify the results. Does the product or process perform as intended? Does it meet the needs of the targeted customers?

Quality Function Deployment (QFD)

Quality function deployment (QFD)
A graphical tool used to help organizations move from vague notions of what customers want to specific engineering and operational requirements. Also called the "house of quality."

One of the greatest challenges firms face when designing new products or services is moving from vague notions of what the customer wants to specific engineering or operational requirements. **Quality function deployment (QFD)** is one tool that has been developed to formalize this process. First introduced in Japan in the early 1970s, QFD became very popular in the late 1980s and continues to be used by companies.[8]

Figure 6.3 shows a simplified example of a QFD matrix for a cell phone. This matrix is sometimes called the "house of quality," due to its obvious resemblance to a house. The left

FIGURE 6.3
QFD Matrix for a Cell Phone

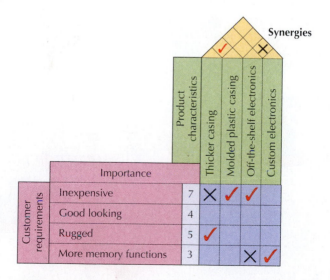

Synergies

Customer requirements	Importance	Thicker casing	Molded plastic casing	Off-the-shelf electronics	Custom electronics
Inexpensive	7	✗	✓	✓	
Good looking	4				
Rugged	5	✓			
More memory functions	3			✗	✓

(Product characteristics: Thicker casing, Molded plastic casing, Off-the-shelf electronics, Custom electronics)

[8]J. Hauser and D. Clausing, "The House of Quality," *Harvard Business Review*, 66, no. 3 (May–June 1988): 63–73.

side of the matrix lists general customer requirements and their relative importance (1–10) to the target customers. Note that these requirements are stated in terms of how the product performs, not specific characteristics. Along the top is a list of specific product characteristics. The main body of the matrix shows how each of the product characteristics does or does not support the customer requirements. As you can see, there are some potential conflicts. For example, the off-the-shelf electronics characteristic is consistent with an inexpensive unit, but conflicts with customers' desires for more memory functions. Ultimately, a trade-off may need to be made. Finally, the "roof" of the matrix shows synergies between some of the features. Obviously, off-the-shelf electronics conflicts with customized ones. On the other hand, a molded plastic casing and a thicker casing are two product characteristics that can easily be combined.

The matrix in Figure 6.3 moves the organization from customer requirements to broad product characteristics. But the process doesn't end here. The ultimate goal is to identify the specific manufacturing and service process steps needed to meet the customers' requirements. As a result, an organization may develop a series of QFD matrices that make the following logical linkages:

1st Matrix: Customer requirements → product characteristics
2nd Matrix: Product characteristics → product specifications
3rd Matrix: Product specifications → process characteristics
4th Matrix: Process characteristics → process specifications

Figure 6.4 illustrates this idea.

Returning to our example, we identified "Rugged" as an important customer requirement in Figure 6.3 and "Thicker Casing" as one product characteristic that would support this need. To move to *product specifications*, we need to translate "Thicker Casing" into more detailed information regarding the materials needed and the actual thickness value. Next we have to describe the *process characteristics* needed to meet these product specifications regularly. This might include information on tolerance limits and acceptable process variability. Finally, we need to identify the specific manufacturing resources needed (e.g., "an injection molding device with computer controls") to support the process characteristics.

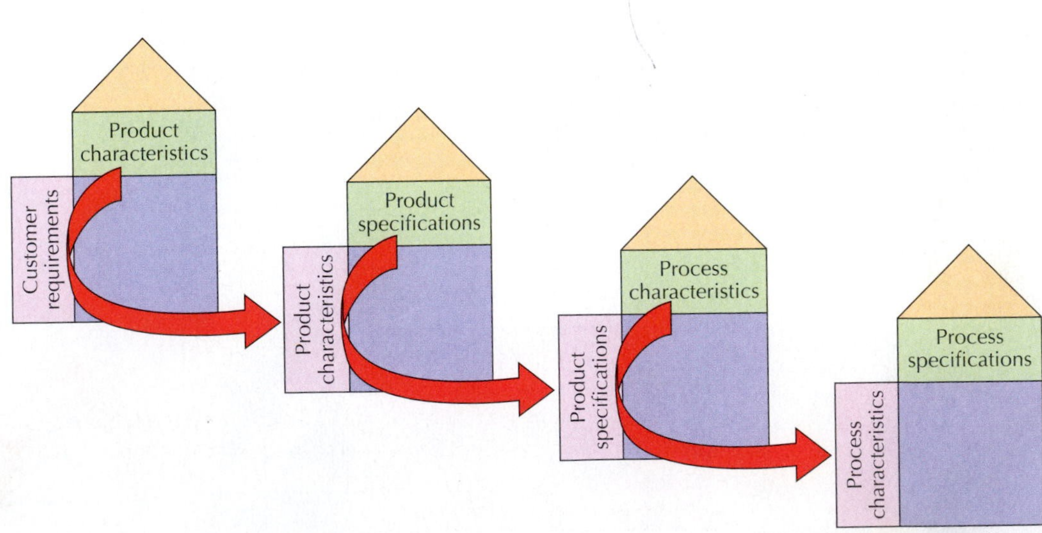

FIGURE 6.4
Using QFD Matrices to Move from Customer Requirements to Process Specifications

Computer-Aided Design (CAD) and Computer-Aided Design/Computer-Aided Manufacturing (CAD/CAM)

Advancements in information systems have also transformed the development process. In particular, **computer-aided design (CAD) systems** allow engineers to develop, modify, share, and even test designs in a virtual world. By doing so, CAD systems help organizations avoid the time and expense of paper-based drawings and physical prototypes.

Computer-aided design/computer-aided manufacturing (CAD/CAM) systems take the process a step further. Here CAD-based designs are translated into machine instructions, which are then fed automatically into computer-controlled manufacturing equipment. Such systems allow for rapid prototyping and reduce the time and costs associated with producing one-of-a-kind pieces.

Computer-aided design (CAD) systems
Information systems that allow engineers to develop, modify, share, and even test designs in a virtual world. CAD systems help organizations avoid the time and expense of paper-based drawings and physical prototypes.

Computer-aided design/computer-aided manufacturing (CAD/CAM) systems
An extension of CAD. Here, CAD-based designs are translated into machine instructions, which are then fed automatically into computer-controlled manufacturing equipment.

The "Design for . . ." Approaches

At a minimum, products and services must be designed to meet the needs of the customers. But beyond this, organizations also want products and services to be easy to make, easy to maintain, virtually defect-free (to reduce their costs as well as improve customer satisfaction), and environmentally sound. This has led to what can be called the "design for..." approaches to product and service design. Four critical ones are design for manufacturability (DFM), design for maintainability (DFMt), design for Six Sigma (DFSS), and design for the environment (DFE).

Design for manufacturability (DFM) is the systematic consideration of manufacturing issues in the design and development process, facilitating the fabrication of the product's components and their assembly into the overall product.[9] In general, the goal of DFM is to design a product that can be produced at consistently high quality levels, at the lowest cost, and, when possible, with existing processes.

Two ways in which organizations accomplish DFM are parts standardization and modularity. **Parts standardization** refers to the planned elimination of superficial, accidental, and deliberate differences between similar parts in the interest of reducing part and supplier proliferation.[10] By standardizing and sharing parts across various products, companies can reduce the time and cost of developing new products and reduce the cost of the final products (see *Supply Chain Connections: Standardization at Ford*).

Modular architecture is another way in which organizations implement DFM. A **modular architecture** is a product architecture in which each functional element maps into its own physical chunk. Different chunks perform different functions; the interactions between the chunks are minimal, and they are generally well defined.[11] To illustrate, consider the typical Windows-compatible PC. Suppose a PC retailer sells PCs that are assembled from the following module options:

- four different system units
- two different graphics cards
- five different displays
- three different printers

The visual functionality of the PC is contained within the graphics cards and displays, while the print functionality is contained within the printer. The remainder of the PC's

Design for manufacturability (DFM)
The systematic consideration of manufacturing issues in the design and development process, facilitating the fabrication of the product's components and their assembly into the overall product.

Parts standardization
The planned elimination of superficial, accidental, and deliberate differences between similar parts in the interest of reducing part and supplier proliferation.

Modular architecture
A product architecture in which each functional element maps into its own physical chunk. Different chunks perform different functions; the interactions between the chunks are minimal, and they are generally well defined.

[9] Product Development and Management Association, "Glossary."
[10] Cox and Blackstone, *APICS Dictionary*.
[11] Product Development and Management Association, "Glossary."

functionality is within the system unit itself. What makes this product truly "modular" is the fact that the PC retailer can easily swap modules to make a different final configuration, as PCs use standard interfaces for plugging in displays, printers, and the like. In fact, the 14 modules can theoretically be configured into $4 \times 2 \times 5 \times 3 = 120$ different combinations.

Design for maintainability (DFMt)
The systematic consideration of maintainability issues over the product's projected life cycle in the design and development process.

In contrast to DFM, **design for maintainability (DFMt)** is the systematic consideration of maintainability issues over the product's projected life cycle in the design and development process.[12] Here the focus is on how easy it is to maintain and service a product after it has reached the customer. DFMt directly supports an organization's efforts to improve the serviceability of its products and services.

Design for Six Sigma (DFSS)
An approcah to product and process design that seeks to ensure the organization is capable of providing products or services that meet Six Sigma quality levels—in general, no more than 3.4 defects per million opportunities.

Design for Six Sigma (DFSS), as the name implies, seeks to ensure that the organization is capable of providing products or services that meet Six Sigma quality levels—in general, no more than 3.4 defects per million opportunities. DFSS is often mentioned in conjunction with DMADV, with DMADV serving as the process for achieving DFSS.

Design for the environment (DFE)
An approach to new product design that addresses environmental, safety, and health issues over the product's projected life cycle in the design and development process.

Finally, **design for the environment (DFE)** addresses environmental, safety, and health issues over the product's projected life cycle in the design and development process.[13] DFE is becoming increasingly important for companies seeking to both reduce potential legal liabilities and respond to regulatory requirements. To illustrate how companies are implementing DFE, consider some of Hewlett-Packard design guidelines:[14]

- Place environmental stewards on every design team to identify design changes that may reduce environmental impact throughout the product's life cycle.
- Reduce the number and types of materials used, and standardize on the types of plastic resins used.
- Use molded-in colors and finishes instead of paint, coatings, or plating whenever possible.
- Help customers use resources responsibly by minimizing the energy consumption of HP's printing, imaging, and computing products.
- Increase the use of pre- and postconsumer recycled materials in product packaging.
- Minimize customer waste burdens by using fewer product and packaging materials overall.
- Design for disassembly and recyclability by implementing solutions such as the ISO 11469 plastics labeling standard, minimizing the number of fasteners and the number of tools necessary for disassembly.

Target costing
The process of designing a product to meet a specific cost objective. Target costing involves setting the planned selling price and subtracting the desired profit, as well as marketing and distribution costs, thus leaving the required target cost.

Design to cost
See Target costing.

Target Costing and Value Analysis

Cost is such an important aspect of product and service design that organizations have developed approaches specifically focused on this dimension. In this section, we talk about two of them: target costing and value analysis. In general, target costing is done during the initial design effort, whereas value analysis is applied to both new and existing products and services. **Target costing**, also called **design to cost**, is the process of designing a product to meet a specific cost objective. Target costing involves setting the planned selling price and subtracting the desired profit, as well as marketing and distribution costs, thus

[12]Ibid.

[13]Ibid.

[14]Hewlett-Packard, DFE Guidelines, **www.hp.com/hpinfo/globalcitizenship/environment/productdesign/design.html**.

SUPPLY CHAIN CONNECTIONS

STANDARDIZATION AT FORD[15]

In February 2002, Phil Martens, head of Ford's new product development group, woke up in the middle of the night and had a revelation that would help solve Ford's problems in producing new vehicles that cost too much for the U.S. market: "Copy with pride. That's our mantra." In effect, what he was suggesting was for vehicle design teams to share designs and technologies among similar vehicles.

Martens emphasized this approach to Nick Sheele, president and chief operating officer, noting that if Ford was to be as cost efficient as its Japanese affiliate, Mazda Motor Company, it would mean fixing the vehicle creation process. Ford should rely on successful existing designs, Martens argued, instead of using competing groups within the company to, in effect, reinvent the wheel.

He pointed out that Ford, which takes about three years to develop a vehicle, is at least 25% or so slower than the industry's most efficient developers. Why? Because each project was prone to "free-wheeling," as engineering organizations were built around five teams working independently: "Tough Trucks," "Outfitters," "Ford Family Vehicles," "Ford Living Legends," and Lincoln-Mercury. The teams often created their own unique body frames, suspensions, brakes, engines, and transmissions, in effect having to "move" down the learning curve of experience every time. For example, the Ford F-150 truck frame was being redesigned at the same time as the Expedition and Navigator, each of which had a different independent rear-suspension system. This made the SUVs more expensive to produce than the models they replaced, and the three frames are so different that they require different suppliers, components, and parts. In contrast, GM has used one basic truck architecture to turn out models as diverse as the Chevy Silverado pickup and the Hummer H2, which is one reason why GM is outearning Ford.

The new platform teams at Ford will mean that the number of platforms used by Ford will be reduced to 12 from 18, and each team will use common components. This allows Ford to tap the same Mazda suppliers to produce its new vehicles, cutting engineering time and saving money. As Mr. Martens points out: "You don't need a whole army to do a ground-up vehicle."

leaving the required target cost.[16] *Supply Chain Connections: Target Costing at NEC* describes how NEC worked with a key supplier to implement target costing for a new product.

Value analysis (VA) A process that involves examining all elements of a component, assembly, end product, or service to make sure it fulfills its intended function at the lowest total cost.

Value analysis (VA) is a process that involves examining all elements of a component, assembly, end product, or service to make sure it fulfills its intended function at the lowest total cost. The primary objective of value analysis is to increase the value of an item or service at the lowest cost without sacrificing quality. In equation form, value is the relationship between the function of a product or service and its cost:

$$\text{Value} = \text{function}/\text{cost}$$

There are many variations of function and cost that will increase the value of a product or service. The most obvious ways to increase value include increasing the functionality or use of a product or service while holding cost constant, reducing cost while not reducing functionality, and increasing functionality more than cost (e.g., offering a five-year warranty versus a two-year warranty with no price increase raises the value of a product to the customer).

A common approach for implementing value analysis is to create a VA team composed of professionals with knowledge about a product or service. Many functional groups can contribute to the value analysis team, including engineering, marketing, purchasing,

[15]Cox and Blackstone, *APICS Dictionary*.

[16]N. Shirouzu, "Copy That—Ford's New Development Plan: Stop Reinventing Its Wheels," *The Wall Street Journal*, April 16, 2003.

SUPPLY CHAIN CONNECTIONS

TARGET COSTING AT NEC[17]

NEC makes many business machines, but its plant in Abiko, Japan, manufactures only fax and copy machines. Early in the development cycle for the NEFAX 880e, NEC purchasing managers visited Sato Electronics, one of NEC's major suppliers. NEC wanted to determine whether Sato could make the parts NEC needed for the 880e at a specified or target cost. A target cost for the entire product was developed based on marketing's input, and it was then broken down for different categories of parts based on historical costs. The target cost for the mechanical parts was further broken down into a target cost for each metal part needed to make the fax machine. When it was determined that Sato Electronics could supply almost all of the parts for the 880e at or below NEC's target costs, the two companies were able to move into the development and engineering phases.

At first, there was no detailed design for the 880e. After general discussion, Sato submitted an initial design for the machine. As the development cycle evolved, the design became progressively tighter and more detailed. It started out with a basic frame and shape, and eventually it was reduced to a set of detailed design specifications. At each stage in the design evolution, engineers from both companies worked together, with purchasing acting as a liaison. While engineering provided the technical information and specifications, purchasing personnel helped to coordinate meetings and provided information on business volumes, pricing, cost management strategies, and contract specifics.

The joint venture has also paid off for Sato Electronics. In return for Sato's cooperation and support, NEC mechanical design engineers have been using some of the same components for future generations of the product, and Sato will have the first opportunity at new business. Sato Electronics and NEC understand their interdependencies. They also understand the importance of relying on purchasing as an integrating function.

production, and key suppliers. Value analysis teams ask a number of questions to determine if opportunities exist for item, product, or service improvement. Some typical questions include the following:

1. Is the cost of the final product proportionate to its usefulness?
2. Does the product need all its features or internal parts?
3. Is there a better production method to produce the item or product?
4. Can a lower-cost standard part replace a customized part?
5. Are we using the proper tooling considering the quantities required?
6. Will another dependable supplier provide material, components, or subassemblies for less cost?
7. Are there equally effective but lower-cost materials available?
8. Are packaging cost reductions possible?
9. Is the item properly classified for shipping purposes to receive the lowest transportation rates?
10. Are design or quality specifications too tight, given customer requirements?
11. If we are making an item now, can we buy it for less (and vice versa)?

The most likely VA improvements include modifying product design and material specifications, using standardized components in place of custom components, substituting lower-cost for higher-cost materials, reducing the number of parts that a product contains, and developing better production or assembly methods.

---

[17] R. Monczka, R. Handfield, G. Ragatz, D. Frayer, and T. Scannell, *Supplier Integration into New Product/Process Development: Best Practices* (Milwaukee, WI: ASQ Press, 2000).

CHAPTER SUMMARY

Product and service development is critical to the success of many firms. Points to take away from this chapter include the following:

- The importance of a well-managed development process, whether it is a sequential process or one based on concurrent engineering; and
- The need to consider operations and supply chain perspectives when developing new products and services, including repeatability, testability, and serviceability of the design; product volumes; product costs; and the match with a company's existing capabilities.

As the last section of this chapter made clear, organizations have developed various tools and techniques for ensuring that the development process not only goes smoothly, but also results in "good" designs.

KEY TERMS

Black box design 162
Commercial preparation phase 158
Computer-aided design (CAD) systems 165
Computer-aided design/computer-aided manufacturing (CAD/CAM) systems 165
Concept development phase 157
Concurrent engineering 159
(DMADV) Define-Measure-Analyze-Design-Verify 162
Design and development phase 158
Design for maintainability (DFMt) 166
Design for manufacturability (DFM) 165
Design for the environment (DFE) 166
Design for Six Sigma (DFSS) 166
Design to cost 166
Engineering change 155
Gray box design 162
Launch phase 158
Modular architecture 165
Parts standardization 165
Planning phase 157
Presourcing 161
Product design 151
Product development process 151
Quality function deployment (QFD) 163
Robust design 154
Sequential development process 158
Serviceability 154
Supply chain design 153
Target costing 166
Testability 154
Value analysis (VA) 167

DISCUSSION QUESTIONS

1. In this chapter, we described several approaches to product design, including parts standardization and modularity. How do these two approaches relate to the dimensions of product design described earlier in the chapter?
2. We talked about concurrent engineering as an alternative to sequential development. What are the advantages of concurrent engineering? Under what circumstances might sequential development be preferable?
3. Consider some of the dimensions of product design that we listed as important to operations and supply chain managers. Are these dimensions more or less important than whether the product or service meets the customers' needs? Can you think of situations in which there might be conflict between these different perspectives?
4. Consider the phases of product and service development shown in Table 6.1. Why is it important to include customers early on in the development process?
5. Which type of product development effort would be better suited to concurrent engineering: a radically new product involving cutting-edge technologies or the latest version of an existing product? Why?
6. What are some of the benefits of including suppliers in the product development process? Can you think of any risks?

CASE STUDY

GILLETTE[18]

Introduction

BOSTON, 1992—Several mornings a week, Alfred M. Zeien performs an odd ritual. After lathering his face, he shaves with two razors—one for each side of his face. Then he runs his fingers over his cheeks to check the closeness of the shave. "That's the only way to really compare shaves," declares Mr. Zeien, chairman and chief executive officer of Gillette Co., who tests both his company's razors and competitors'. Gillette is a company obsessed with shaving. "We spend more time than you can imagine studying facial hair growth—which is quite different from the growth of other hair on your head—because that's the way to improve your product," explains the very clean-shaven Mr. Zeien, who keeps a drawer full of experimental Gillette blades in his office for trying out.

In the annals of American business, few companies have dominated an industry so much and for so long as this one. Gillette so dominates shaving worldwide that its name has come to mean a razor blade in some countries. It is the leader in Europe with a 70% market share and in Latin America with 80%. Indeed, for every blade it sells at home, it sells five abroad, a figure likely to grow as joint ventures expand sales in China, Russia, and India. Retaining its dominance in razors also has meant spending hundreds of millions of dollars to develop the innovative twin-blade Trac II razor in 1972, the pivoting-head Atra in 1977, and the hugely successful Sensor, with independently suspended blades, in 1989. It also meant rushing out—albeit reluctantly—a disposable razor in 1976 to fend off French rival Societe Bic SA, even though the cheap throwaways cut into sales of higher-profit Gillette products.

Coated Stainless Steel Blades

But Gillette is one of America's noteworthy corporate successes not just because it has done so well, but also because it once blundered so remarkably—and came back. Back in 1962, Gillette's U.S. market share had just reached its highest point ever—72%. "We have," an executive boasted to *Forbes* magazine in 1962, "no complaints on how things are going."

They soon would. Wilkinson Sword, which forged the famous swords for British cavalry at the height of the empire, but by the 1960s mostly made garden tools, decided to get into razor blades. Its Super SwordEdge stainless-steel blade, coated with a thin chemical film to protect the edge, lasted up to 12 shaves, or two or three times as many as Gillette's own coated Super Blue Blade, made of softer carbon steel.

Gillette was stunned. "They were the talk of the town," recalls shaving-division vice president Scott Roberts, then a salesman in New York. "Our leadership was threatened." Gillette knew stainless steel was harder than carbon steel. It also knew about stainless blade coatings—in fact, Wilkinson later had to license technology for making its coated blade from Gillette, which had a patent. But making a stainless steel blade would have made much of Gillette's manufacturing equipment obsolete.

It was tempted to do what many big companies do: Ignore its rival, hoping the market niche would remain small, or improve its existing carbon-blade technology. Eventually, Gillette decided it had no choice and introduced a stainless steel blade in late 1963. By then, two other small players had introduced stainless steel blades, and Gillette's U.S. market share had begun a precipitous drop that would bottom out at around 50% in 1965.

In retrospect, Gillette was lucky Wilkinson didn't have the firepower to exploit its weakness. "I had nightmares thinking that someone at Procter & Gamble would shave with a stainless blade and decide to get in the business or buy out Wilkinson," confesses William G. Salatich, a retired Gillette executive. (Unable to duplicate the breakthrough it made with stainless blades, Wilkinson has become a minor player in most countries; Gillette, in fact, eventually bought Wilkinson's blade business outside Europe and the United States.)

Disposable Razors

Though short-lived, the Wilkinson Sword debacle galvanized Gillette in a way a lesser threat wouldn't have. Russell B. Adams Jr., author of a corporate biography for the company, says, "It has become part of the myth and folklore: This is what happens to you if you're not up there keeping ahead of the market." Indeed, the ordeal prepared Gillette for the next major challenge to its razor and blade business—disposable razors. In 1974, Bic sold its first inexpensive disposables in Greece. There was skepticism at Gillette about the product because it offered a worse shave, not a better one. "We'd get samples and I would try them and wonder why anybody would compromise their shave to save a little money," remembers Mr. Scott, the Gillette vice president.

Moreover, why come out with a new razor that cost more to make (because disposables had a handle and blade, as opposed to a cartridge that fit on an existing razor) but sold for less—especially when it might take sales from more profitable brands? It was similar to the issue Detroit would face when the Japanese invaded the U.S. with small cars.

[18]Ingrassia, "Taming the Monster."

"There was sizable debate whether we should or shouldn't make a disposable," says Robert E. Ray, a former overseas manager at Gillette. "If you sit down with pencil and paper, you conclude, 'This ain't such a hot idea, we're going to make less money.' But after a while you didn't have to be a rocket scientist to figure out that consumers wanted disposables." With the 1960s disaster in mind, Gillette began a crash program to develop a disposable. Gillette rolled out its Good News disposable—using the Trac II twin-blade technology, compared with Bic's single blade—nationwide in April 1976, months before Bic introduced its razor regionally. Says former president Stephen Griffin: "We were giving up profitability, but we had to do that to maintain our customers."

Blocking Out Competitors

One of the savvy developments of Gillette researchers over the past 20 years has been to design razors that are hard for competitors to make. In the days of the double-edge blade, it was easy for others to make blades that fit Gillette's razors; Trac II and other twin-blade razors changed that. Rivals generally come out with cartridges compatible with new Gillette razors, but only after a lag.

At any given time, Gillette has up to 20 experimental razors in development. One promising prototype has been in the works for four years—and won't be ready for eight more. And in another move from the Japanese playbook, the next generation razor isn't likely to be introduced first in the United States, says Mr. Zeien, the chairman. "This is what the auto companies learned from the Japanese," he says. "If you want to be a leader on a global basis, you can't just be a leader in your home market."

QUESTIONS

1. With regard to developing and introducing new products, what lessons did Gillette learn from the Wilkinson Sword and Bic experiences?
2. Why do you think Gillette was so slow in introducing coated stainless steel blades, even though the company was familiar with the technology? What are the implications for firms faced with making long-term investments in manufacturing and supply chain resources?
3. Why is it not enough for Gillette to simply design a razor that gives the "best shave possible"? How does manufacturing help Gillette maintain its market share and profitability? What are the implications of having operations and supply chain personnel involved early on in the development effort?

REFERENCES

Books and Articles

Clarke, K. and S. Wheelwright. *Managing New Product and Process Development: Text and Cases*. New York: Free Press, 1993.

Cox, J. F., and J. H. Blackstone, eds. *APICS Dictionary*, 10th ed. Falls Church, VA: APICS, 2002.

Deveny, K. "Man Walked on the Moon But Man Can't Make Enough Devil's Food Cookie Cakes." *The Wall Street Journal*, September 28, 1993.

Hauser, J., and D. Clausing. "The House of Quality." *Harvard Business Review* 66, no. 3 (May–June 1988): 63–73.

Ingrassia, L. "Taming the Monster: How Big Companies Can Change: Keeping Sharp: Gillette Holds Its Edge by Endlessly Searching for a Better Shave." *The Wall Street Journal*, December 10, 1992.

Jordan, M., & J. Karp. "Machines for the Masses: Whirlpool Aims Cheap Washer at Brazil, India and China." *The Wall Street Journal*, December 9, 2003.

Mehta, S., and J. Keller. "Sprint to Integrate Voice, Data." *The Wall Street Journal*, June 3, 1998.

Monczka, R., R. Handfield, G. Ragatz, D. Frayer, and T. Scannell. *Supplier Integration into New Product/Process Development: Best Practices*. Milwaukee, WI: ASQ Press, 2000.

Shirouzu, N. "Copy That—Ford's New Development Plan: Stop Reinventing Its Wheels." *The Wall Street Journal*, April 16, 2003.

Wheelwright, S., and K. Clark. *Revolutionizing Product Development*. New York: Free Press, 1992.

Internet

Product Development and Management Association, "Glossary of New Product Development Terms," **www.pdma.org/library/glossary.html**

Hewlett-Packard, DFE Guidelines, **www.hp.com/hpinfo/globalcitizenship/environment/productdesign/design.html**

CHAPTER 7

Process Choice and Layout Decisions in Manufacturing and Services

CHAPTER OUTLINE

Chapter Objectives

By the end of this chapter, you will be able to:

- Describe the characteristics of the five classic types of manufacturing processes.
- Explain how different manufacturing processes can be linked together via the supply chain.
- Describe the critical role of customization in manufacturing, including the degree and point of customization, and upstream versus downstream activities.
- Discuss the three dimensions that differentiate services from one another—the service package, customization, and customer contact—and explain the different managerial challenges driven by these dimensions.
- Create and interpet a service blueprint.
- Position a service on a conceptual model and explain the underlying managerial challenges.
- Develop product-based and functional process layouts.

Bliven Furniture Company

A few years back Bliven Furniture Company[1] faced a tough decision. Bliven needed additional capacity for making solid wooden seats. The company's engineering team came up with the following two manufacturing process options:

	SADDLER/SHAPER MACHINES PROCESS OPTION	5-AXIS ROUTER PROCESS OPTION
Setup time	6 hours	10 minutes
Time to make a seat (after process is set up)	1.1 minutes	3.5 minutes

The first option used special saddler and shaper machines to cut and form blocks of wood to the proper seat shape. Though these machines worked very quickly once they had been properly set up (1.1 minutes per seat), skilled machinists had to reset the machines every time the seat style changed. The "setup time" took about six hours—nearly an entire shift.

The second option was an advanced technology called a 5-axis router. The router used a robotic arm to do all the tasks the saddler and shaper machines did. The router's arm movements, including tool changes, were controlled by a computer that ran a different program for each seat style.

The main advantage of the 5-axis router was its ability to handle a wide range of seats. In only 10 minutes, it could be converted from one seat style to the next. However, the 5-axis router took much longer to make individual seats (3.5 minutes) and required skilled programmers.

The "best" process option depended on the variety and volumes of seats Bliven Furniture made and the relative availability of skilled machinists and programmers. Whichever decision Bliven managers made, however, it had to be the right one: Each option required an investment of hundreds of thousands of dollars and would have a direct impact on the firm's product offerings for years to come.

[1]The company name has been changed to protect the company's confidentiality.

INTRODUCTION

In Chapter 3, we introduced you to the general topic of business processes. In this chapter, we look in more depth at specific types of manufacturing and service processes. Manufacturing and service process decisions are very important to firms for at least two reasons. First, they tend to be expensive and far-reaching. The decision to put in a production line, for example, will dictate the types of workforce and equipment that are needed, the types of products that can be made, and the kinds of information systems that are required to run the business. Because of the financial commitment, it is not a decision that can be easily reversed.

Second, process decisions deserve extra attention because different processes have different strengths and weaknesses. Some processes are particularly good at supporting a wide variety of goods or services, while others are better at providing standardized products or services at the lowest possible cost. But no process is best at everything. Managers must therefore carefully consider the strengths and weaknesses of different processes and make sure that the process they choose best supports their overall business strategy and, in particular, the needs of their targeted customers.

We start this chapter by describing manufacturing processes. We first review the five classic types and then discuss the concepts of hybrid and linked manufacturing processes. We pay particular attention to the roles product standardization, production volumes, and customization play in determining the best process choice.

In the second half of the chapter, we turn our attention to service processes. How do they differ from one another? What are the key managerial challenges and capabilities of the different service process types? How can service firms position themselves for strategic advantage? The special role services play in supply chains will also be discussed.

We then end the chapter by introducing you to two approaches that firms use to develop layouts. As you will see, the approach will differ dramatically depending on the type of layout one is dealing with.

7.1 MANUFACTURING PROCESSES

Managers face a plethora of choices when deciding on a specific manufacturing process. The choice facing Bliven Furniture was just a quick example of the technical and business issues that can arise. Here are a few general principles to keep in mind when selecting and implementing a manufacturing process:

1. Selecting an effective manufacturing process means much more than just choosing the right equipment. Manufacturing processes also include people, facilities and physical layouts, and information systems. These pieces must work together for the manufacturing process to be effective.
2. Different manufacturing processes have different strengths and weaknesses. Some are best suited to making small numbers of customized products, while others excel at making large numbers of standard items. Companies must make sure that their manufacturing processes support the overall business strategy.
3. The manufacture of a particular item might require many different types of manufacturing processes, spread over multiple sites and organizations in the supply chain. Effective operations and supply chain managers understand how important it is for these processes to work well together.

Much has changed in manufacturing over the past 20 years. High quality is no longer a way for manufacturers to differentiate themselves from competitors, but rather a basic requirement of doing business. At the same time, many customers are demanding smaller quantities, more frequent shipments, and shorter lead times—not to mention lower prices. Add to this list of challenges the increasingly important role of information technologies, and you can see that the hallmark of manufacturing in the early twenty-first century will be change.

Even so, there is a basic truth about manufacturing that will not change: *No manufacturing process can be best at everything.* The choice of one manufacturing process over another will always bring trade-offs. **Flexible manufacturing systems (FMSs)**, for instance, are highly automated batch processes (discussed later) that can reduce the cost of making groups of similar products. But as efficient as they are, a production line dedicated to making a smaller number of standard products will still be cheaper, if not as flexible. Similarly, today's high-volume line processes might be more flexible than their counterparts of just 20 years ago, but they will never be as flexible as skilled laborers with general-purpose tools.

Flexible manufacturing systems (FMSs)
Highly automated batch processes that can reduce the cost of making groups of similar products.

Obviously, the selection of a manufacturing system is a complex process. However, experienced managers find that several questions crop up regularly in the selection process:

- What are the physical requirements of the company's product?
- How similar are the products the company makes?
- What are the company's production volumes?
- Where in the value chain does customization take place (if at all)?

We will use these criteria to describe five classic manufacturing processes: production lines, continuous flow processes, job shops, batch manufacturing, and fixed-position layout.

Production Lines and Continuous Flow Manufacturing

When most people think about manufacturing, they think about production lines. A **production line** is a type of manufacturing process used to produce a narrow range of standard items with identical or highly similar designs.[2] Production lines have several distinct characteristics. First, they follow a **product-based layout** (Figure 7.1), where resources are arranged sequentially according to the steps required to make a product. The various steps are usually linked by some system that moves the items from one step to the next, such as a conveyor belt. A production line for battery-powered hand tools might divide the assembly into three steps—mounting the motor inside the right half of the casing, putting the left and right halves together, and putting a warning sticker on the outside of the casing. All

Production line
A type of manufacturing process used to produce a narrow range of standard items with identical or highly similar designs.

Product-based layout
A type of layout where resources are arranged sequentially according to the steps required to make a product.

FIGURE 7.1
Production Line and Continuous Flow Processes

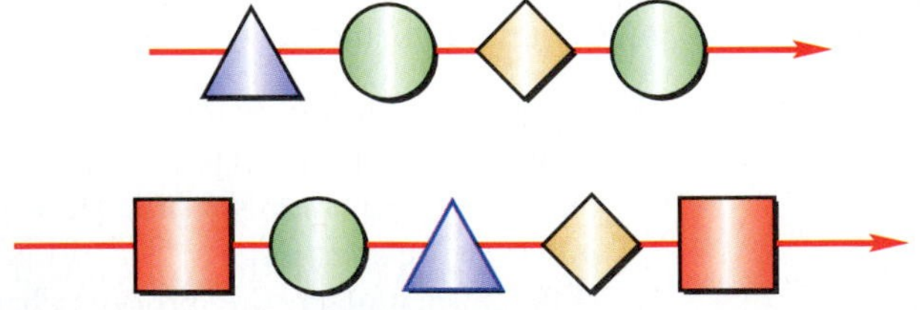

- Product-based layout: Equipment and people are highly specialized and arranged sequentially according to the steps required to make a product or product family.
- Production is often "paced."
- Best suited to high-volume production of standardized products.

[2] J. F. Cox and J. H. Blackstone, eds., *APICS Dictionary*, 10th ed. (Falls Church, VA: APICS, 2002).

three steps are done continuously, so as one hand tool is having its motor mounted, another is having its warning sticker put on.

Second, items typically move through the production line at a predetermined pace. A line might, for example, complete 60 units an hour, or 1 every minute. The time between completions of successive units is known as the **cycle time** of the line. At each step in the process, equipment or people have a set amount of time to finish each task. By dividing the manufacturing process into a series of discrete, carefully timed steps, production lines achieve high degrees of equipment and worker specialization, as well as consistent quality and high efficiency.

Cycle time
For a line process, the actual time between completions of successive units on a production line.

Production lines are ideally suited to the high-volume production of a single product or of products characterized by similar design attributes, such as size, material, or manufacturing steps. An auto assembly line can handle the same model car with different transmissions, different engines, and even different interiors, one right after the other, because the line was designed to fit all possible options of the car model it produces.

Production lines have two drawbacks, however. First, high volumes are required to justify the required investment in specialized equipment and labor. Second, lines are inflexible with regard to products that do not fit the design characteristics of the production line. When production volumes are low or product variety is high, other solutions are needed.

Continuous flow process
A type of manufacturing process that closely resembles a production line process. The main difference is the *form* of the product, which usually *cannot* be broken into discrete units. Examples include yarns and fabric, food products, and chemical products such as oil or gas.

Continuous flow processes closely resemble production line processes in that they produce highly standardized products using a tightly linked, paced sequence of steps. The main difference is the *form* of the product, which usually *cannot* be broken into discrete units. Examples include chemical processing and fiber formation processes. In many ways, a continuous flow process is even less flexible than a production line. The nature of the product tends to make shutdowns and start-ups expensive, which discourages flexibility and encourages product standardization. And the highly technical nature of many continuous flow processes means that specialists are needed to control operations. The only responsibilities of direct laborers might be to load and unload materials and monitor the process. Continuous flow processes also tend to be highly capital intensive and very inflexible with respect to changes in output levels. Examples include an oil or chemical refinery, in which there is very little labor (other than in maintenance of the equipment).

Scharffen Berger Chocolates uses both batch and continuous flow manufacuring processes to make its chocolates. The first picture shows a batch of semisweet chocolate being prepared in a vat; the second photo shows chocolate bars on a conveyor belt, near the end of the process.

FIGURE 7.2
Job Shop Processes

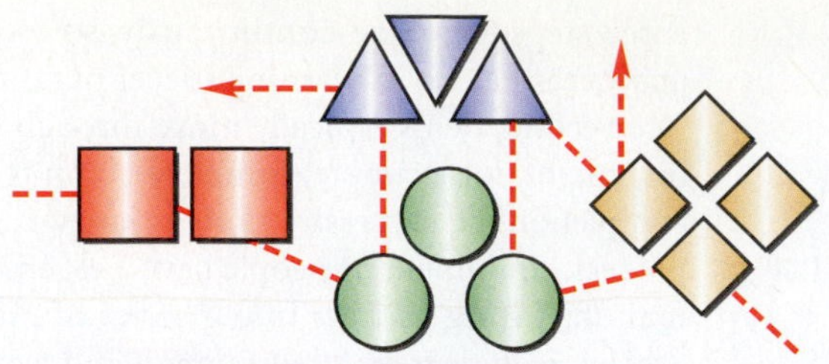

- General-purpose equipment and broadly skilled people.
- Functional layout: Work areas are arranged by function.
- Requirements can change dramatically from one job to the next.
- Best suited to low-volume production of one-of-a-kind products.
- Highly flexible, but not very efficient.

Job Shops

Job shop
A type of manufacturing process used to make a wide variety of highly customized products in quantities as small as one. Job shops are characterized by general-purpose equipment and workers who are broadly skilled.

In contrast, a **job shop** is a type of manufacturing process used to make a wide variety of highly customized products in quantities as small as one. Job shops are characterized by general-purpose equipment and broadly skilled workers. The main emphasis in a job shop is meeting a customer's unique requirements, whatever they may be. Products made in job shops include custom furniture, specialized machine tools used by manufacturers, and restoration and refurbishing work. In a job shop, the product design is *not* standardized. In fact, the shop may need to work closely with the customer to identify just what the product's characteristics should be, and these characteristics may even change once manufacturing starts. Obviously, estimating the time, cost, and specific production requirements for such products is not easy!

Functional layout
A type of layout where resources are physically grouped by function.

Job shops depend on highly flexible equipment and personnel to accomplish their tasks. Personnel in job shops commonly handle several stages of production. Job shops typically follow a **functional layout**, where resources are physically grouped by function (molding, welding, painting, etc.). This makes sense because the process steps required can change dramatically from one job to the next (Figure 7.2). Finally, job shops must be very flexible in their planning. Whereas the manager of a paced assembly line might have clear expectations of what the output level should be (e.g., 200 ovens an hour), the manager of a job shop does not have that luxury. Manufacturing requirements can change dramatically from one job to the next. And the lack of a clear, predictable product flow means that some areas of a job shop can be idle while other areas are backed up.

Batch Manufacturing

Batch manufacturing
A type of manufacturing process where items are moved through the different manufacturing steps in groups, or "batches."

Batch manufacturing gets its name from the fact that items are moved through the different manufacturing steps in groups, or "batches." This process fits somewhere between job shops and production lines in terms of production volumes and flexibility. Batch manufacturing covers a wide range of environments and is probably the most common type of manufacturing process.

To illustrate a typical batch process, let's return to the opening case, Bliven Furniture. Workers might run 200 seats through the saddler machine, stacking the semifinished seats on a pallet. After all 200 seats have completed this step, the entire batch will be moved to the shaper machine, where the 200 seats will wait their turn to be processed. This sequence of processing, moving, and waiting will continue throughout the production process.

Even though this 1937 Lincoln-Zephyr coupe was originally produced on an assembly line, its restoration will take place in a job shop characterized by broadly skilled workers and general-purpose tools.

Though production volumes are higher in a batch process than in a job shop, the sequence of steps is not so tightly linked that units are automatically passed, one at a time, from one process step to the next, as they are on a production line. Thus, batch manufacturing strikes a *balance* between the flexibility of a job shop and the efficiency of a production line.

Fixed-Position Layout

Fixed-position layout
A type of manufacturing process in which the position of the product is fixed. Materials, equipment, and workers are transported to and from the product.

The final classic manufacturing process type is what is known as **fixed-position layout.** The distinguishing characteristic here is that the position of the product, due to size or other constraints, is fixed. Materials, equipment, and workers are transported to and from the product. Fixed-position layouts are used in industries where the products are very bulky, massive, or heavy and movement is problematic.[3] Examples include shipbuilding, construction projects, and even traditional home construction.

Hybrid Manufacturing Processes

Hybrid manufacturing processes
A general term referring to manufacturing processes that seek to combine the characteristics, and hence advantages, of more than one of the classic processes. Examples include flexible manufacturing systems, machining centers, and group technology.

Not all manufacturing processes fall cleanly into the categories just listed. **Hybrid manufacturing processes** seek to combine the characteristics, and hence advantages, of more than one of the classic processes. We already mentioned flexible manufacturing systems earlier in the chapter. Flexible manufacturing systems are highly automated (like line processes), but are able to handle a wider range of products (like batch processes).

Though there are literally hundreds of hybrid manufacturing processes out there, we will illustrate the point by discussing two common types: machining centers and group

[3]Cox and Blackstone, eds., *APICS Dictionary*.

Machining center
A type of manufacturing process that completes several manufacturing steps without removing an item from the process.

technology. **Machining centers** are typically found in batch manufacturing environments. What makes them different, however, is that a machining center will complete several manufacturing steps without removing an item from the process. The 5-axis router we talked about at the beginning of the chapter is a perfect example. It trims the outside edges of the seat, "scoops" out the seating area, and even bores holes for the legs and back spindles before it is finished with one seat and moves to the next. Once all of the seats in the batch have been processed by the 5-axis router, the entire batch moves on to the next step. By combining steps, a machining center tries to achieve some of the efficiencies of a production line, while still maintaining the flexibility of a batch process.

Group technology
A type of manufacturing process that seeks to achieve the efficiencies of a line process in a batch environment by dedicating equipment and personnel to the manufacture of products with similar manufacturing characteristics.

Cellular layout
A type of layout typically used in group technology settings; resources are physically arranged according to the dominant flow of activities for the product family.

Product family
In group technology, a set of products with very similar manufacturing requirements.

Similarly, **group technology** is a type of manufacturing process that seeks to achieve the efficiencies of a line process in a batch environment by dedicating equipment and personnel to the manufacture of products with similar manufacturing characteristics. Group technology cells typically follow a **cellular layout**, in which the resources are physically arranged according to the dominant flow of activities for the product family. To illustrate, a batch manufacturer might find that, while it makes 3,000 different items, 25% of these are products with very similar manufacturing requirements. These products might therefore be grouped together into a **product family**. Because of the relatively high percentage of production accounted for by the product family, management might find it worthwhile to dedicate specific equipment and personnel to just these products. The resulting group technology work cell should be able to improve its efficiencies, but at the expense of lower flexibility (Figure 7.3).

Linking Manufacturing Processes across the Supply Chain

A manufacturing system may actually consist of several different types of processes linked across multiple supply chain partners. Consider the sequence of manufacturing processes needed to produce a sweater. Yarn production has all the characteristics of a continuous flow process: It is capital intensive, turns out a standardized product at a predetermined pace, and requires little or no user interaction. The finished yarn is then fed into a loom that weaves the yarn into fabric, also a continuous flow process. At this point, the rolls of woven fabric might be sent to another facility where the fabric is cut into patterns and sewn into sweaters. The final sewing operation is highly labor intensive, requiring a classic batch process in which individual workers are responsible for

FIGURE 7.3
Group Technology Work Cell

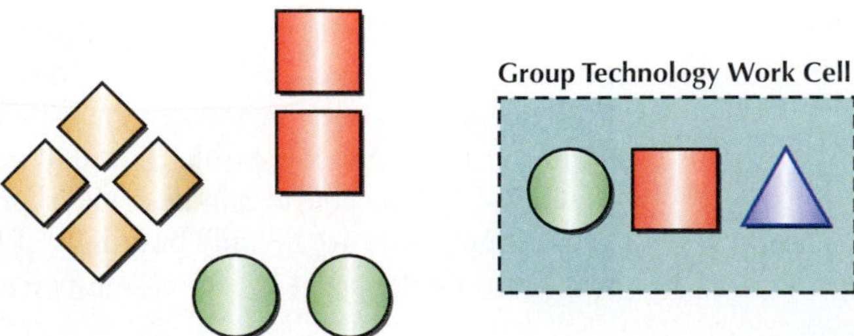

- Equipment and personnel are dedicated to the production of a product family.
- Cellular layout: Resources are physically arranged according to the dominant flow of activities for the product family.

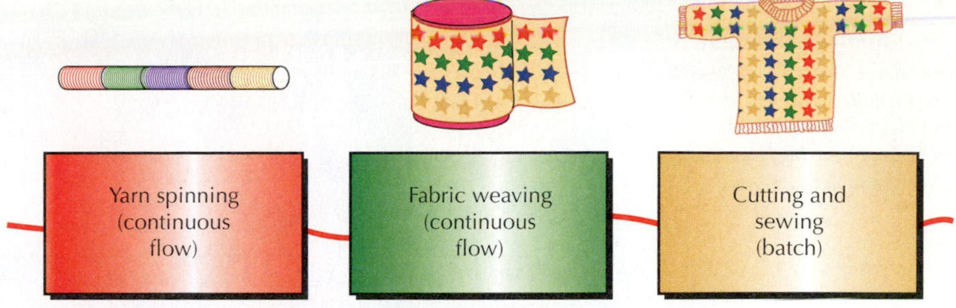

FIGURE 7.4
Linking Processes Together to Make a Sweater

completing a lot of 50 or more garments. When the garments are finished, they might move on to another station for additional processing, followed by a packing operation. Figure 7.4 illustrates this idea.

Selecting a Manufacturing Process

With the exception of fixed-position layouts and continuous flow manufacturing (which are essentially dictated by the physical characteristics of the product), managers face several choices when selecting a manufacturing process. Table 7.1 compares the major characteristics of three of these: job shops, batch manufacturing, and production lines. Each process type has its own strengths and weaknesses. Job shops have a clear advantage when production volumes are low, customization levels are high, and the manufacturer is not competing on the basis of cost. Production lines excel when production volumes are high, products are standard rather than customized, and cost is important. Batch systems tend to fall somewhere in between these extremes.

The Product-Process Matrix

The product-process matrix (Figure 7.5) makes the preceding points graphically. When the characteristics of a company's manufacturing processes line up with the products' characteristics, as shown by the points on the diagonal line in Figure 7.5, there is a strategic match.

TABLE 7.1
Characteristics of Three Manufacturing Processes

	JOB SHOP	BATCH	PRODUCTION LINES
Products			
Product types	Special, highly customized	______________	Standard
Product range	Very wide	______________	Narrow
Process Characteristics			
Technology	General purpose	______________	Dedicated
Key resource	Skilled labor	______________	Equipment, materials
Process flexibility	High	______________	Low
Production volumes	Low	______________	High
Key manufacturing task	Meet the customers' unique requirements	______________	Keep production costs low
What the company sells	Capability	______________	Products

Source: Adapted from T. Hill, *Manufacturing Strategy: Text and Cases* (Homewood, IL: Irwin, 1994), p. 127.

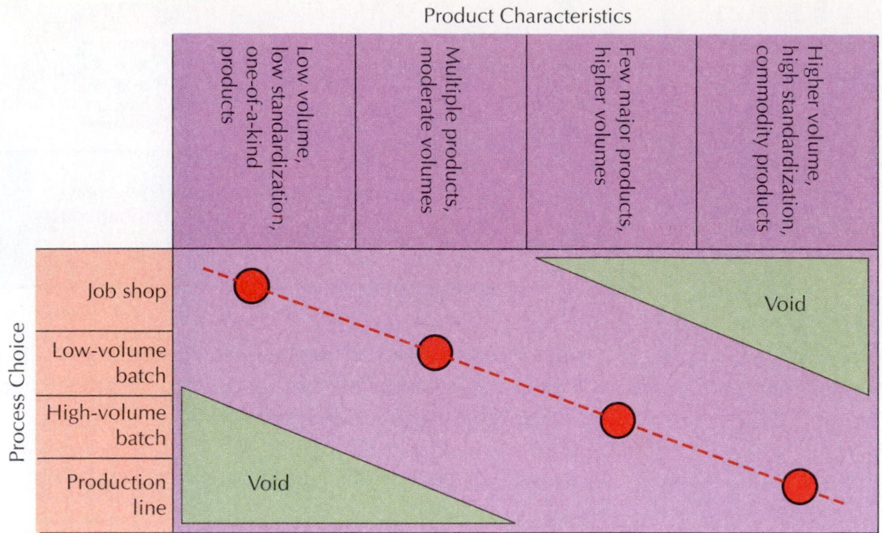

FIGURE 7.5
The Product-Process Matrix
Source: Adapted from R. Hayes and S. Wheelwright, *Restoring Our Competitive Edge: Competing through Manufacturing* (New York: John Wiley and Sons, 1984), p. 209.

But consider the two shaded areas labeled "Void." The area in the top right corner occurs when a job shop tries to support high-volume, standardized products. Although such products *could* be built in a job shop, it would be an unwise use of resources, and the job shop could never hope to compete on a cost basis with production lines.

In contrast, the shaded area in the bottom left corner suggests an organization trying to produce low-volume or one-of-a-kind products using a high-volume batch or production line process. Once again, there is a strategic mismatch—these processes can't possibly meet the flexibility or broad skill requirements needed here. The point is that companies must choose the right manufacturing process, given their markets and product requirements.

7.2 PRODUCT CUSTOMIZATION WITHIN THE SUPPLY CHAIN

A word commonly heard in discussions of manufacturing is *customization*. But what does this term mean? True customization requires *customer-specific* input at some point in the supply chain. For instance, manufacturers of specialized industrial equipment often start with an *individual customer's* specifications, which drive subsequent design, purchasing, and manufacturing efforts. And hardware stores mix ready-made paints to match a customer's particular color sample. In both cases, the product is customized. However, the *degree* and *point* of customization differ radically between the two.

Four Levels of Customization

Manufacturers typically talk about four levels of product customization. From least to greatest customization, these are:

- Make-to-stock (MTS) products
- Assemble- or finish-to-order (ATO) products
- Make-to-order (MTO) products
- Engineer-to-order (ETO) products

Make-to-stock (MTS) products
Products that require no customization. They are typically generic products and are produced in large enough volumes to justify keeping a finished goods inventory.

Make-to-stock (MTS) products involve no customization. They are typically generic products and are produced in large enough volumes to justify keeping a finished goods inventory. Customers typically buy these products "off the shelf." Examples include basic tools (hammers, screwdrivers), consumer products sold in retail stores, and many raw materials.

Assemble- or finish-to-order (ATO) products
Products that are customized only at the very end of the manufacturing process.

Assemble- or finish-to-order (ATO) products are products that are customized only at the very end of the manufacturing process. And even then, the customization is typically limited in nature. A T-shirt with a customer's name airbrushed on it is a simple example. The T-shirt itself is generic until the very last step. Many automobiles are also ATO products because the final set of options—deluxe or standard interior, power locks and windows, and so on—is not determined until the very last stage, based on the dealer's or customer's order. Another example of a finish to order system is a "late pack customization" process, in which a standard product is put into a customized package which may have a different language, promotion, co-packaging promotion, or some other feature. For example, soda is a standard product, but may be bottled in a special "NASCAR" or "Superbowl" package to coincide with these events at different times of the year.

Make-to-order (MTO) products
Products that use standard components, but the final *configuration* of those components is customer-specific.

Like ATO products, **make-to-order (MTO) products** use standard components, but the final *configuration* of those components is customer-specific. To illustrate, Balley Engineered Structures builds an endless variety of customized walk-in industrial coolers or refrigerators from a standard set of panels.[4] MTO products push the customization further back into the manufacturing process than ATO products do.

Engineer-to-order (ETO) products
Products that are designed and produced from the start to meet unusual customer needs or requirements. They represent the highest level of customization.

The fourth and most highly customized products are **engineer-to-order (ETO) products.** These products are designed and produced from the start to meet unusual customer needs or requirements. Though these products might include standard components, at least some of these components are specifically designed with the help of the customer. One can imagine, for example, that a major component for the Hubble telescope would fit nicely into this category.

The Customization Point

To manufacturing personnel, the key difference between these four product types is not so much the degree of customization, but the *point* at which it occurs. That is, *when and where* do the customers' specific requirements affect operations and supply chain activities? Consider Figure 7.6.

For ETO products, the customer's needs become apparent at the design stage (at the far left in Figure 7.6). The exact content and timing of all subsequent activities, from design through distribution, are determined only after the customer's order arrives. Not surprisingly, ETO products are often found in job shop environments. In contrast, MTS products (at the far right in Figure 7.6) move along from the design stage to finished goods inventory, the warehouse, or even the retail outlet without direct input from the final customer. The timing and volume of production activities for MTS products are more likely to be driven by internal efficiency or capacity utilization goals. As a result, production lines or even high-volume batch processes are usually the best choice for MTS products.

[4]B. J. Pine II, *Mass Customization: The New Frontier in Business Competition* (Boston: Harvard Business School Press, 1993).

FIGURE 7.6
Where Does Customization Occur in the Supply Chain?

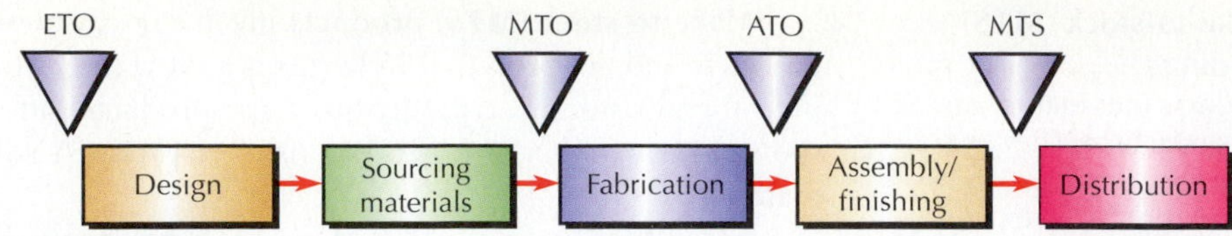

Upstream activities
In the context of manufacturing customization, activities that occur prior to the point of customization.

Downstream activities
In the context of manufacturing customization, activities that occur at or after the point of customization.

Law of variability
The greater the random variability either demanded of the process or inherent in the process itself or in the items processed, the less productive the process is. This law is relevant to customization because completing upstream activities off-line helps isolate these activities from the variability caused by either the timing or the unique requirements of individual customers.

Drawing attention to the point at which customization occurs allows us to make crucial distinctions between manufacturing activities that occur on either side of the customization point. We refer to activities that take place prior to the customization point as **upstream activities**, while those that occur at or after the customization point are called **downstream activities**.

By definition, upstream activities are not affected by the particular nuances of an individual customer order. Thus, they can be completed off-line, or prior to the arrival of a customer order. Completing activities off-line has two advantages. First, it reduces lead time to the customer, as only the downstream activities remain to be completed. This can be particularly important in competitive situations where delivery speed is critical. At Dell Computers, all value chain activities in the manufacturing system except final assembly and shipping, which are downstream activities, take place before the customer order arrives. Upstream activities include the ordering, manufacturing, shipping, and stocking of standardized components. The result is two- to three-day lead times for the customer.[5]

A second advantage has to do with the **law of variability**, described by Roger Schmenner and Morgan Swink (1998). According to the authors, "the greater the random variability either demanded of the process or inherent in the process itself or in the items processed, the less productive the process is."[6] Completing upstream activities off-line helps isolate these activities from the variability caused by either the timing or the unique requirements of individual customers.

But in ETO, MTO, and ATO environments, some activities can be completed only online, or once the customer's needs are known. This tends to increase lead times to the customer. The *Supply Chain Connections* feature describes how TimberEdge Cabinets changed from an MTO manufacturer to an ATO manufacturer. The change had dramatic implications for the efficiency of its manufacturing processes and TimberEdge's ability to meet customer needs in a timely manner.

To summarize, when customization occurs *early* in the supply chain,

- Flexibility in response to unique customer needs will be greater;
- Lead times to the customer will tend to be longer; and
- Products will tend to be more costly.

When customization occurs *late* in the supply chain,

- Flexibility in response to unique customer needs will be limited;
- Lead times to the customer will tend to be shorter; and
- Products will tend to be less costly.

---

[5]J. Magretta, "The Power of Virtual Integration: An Interview with Dell Computer's Michael Dell," *Harvard Business Review* 76, no. 2 (March–April 1998): 73–84.

[6]R. Schmenner and M. Swink, "On Theory in Operations Management," *Journal of Operations Management* 17, no. 1 (1998): p. 101.

SUPPLY CHAIN CONNECTIONS

TIMBEREDGE CABINETS

TimberEdge Cabinets[7] illustrates what can happen when a manufacturing organization changes its customization point. Originally, TimberEdge manufactured custom-fit cabinets for home kitchens and bathrooms. Manufacturing was make-to-order. Specifically, the customization point occurred in TimberEdge's fabrication area, where the cabinet sides and back and front panels were actually cut to a customer's exact specifications (Figure 7.7).

While the make-to-order system provided considerable flexibility, it also created several problems. First, lead times to the customer often ran several weeks or more because cabinet panels could not be fabricated in advance. The long lead times also made it more difficult to coordinate the completion of cabinets with the construction schedules of new homes. In addition, the slight dimensional differences from one job to the next forced TimberEdge to use highly flexible, albeit less efficient, equipment and labor in the fabrication area.

Management concluded that a selection of standard-sized panels (sized in 2-inch increments) would provide enough product range to satisfy their customers' needs. As a result, management transformed the product into an assemble-to-order one (Figure 7.8). Under this arrangement, the fabrication area now became an *upstream* activity. New manufacturing equipment was used in the fabrication area to produce large batches of standard-sized panels *before* the actual customer orders arrived. Customization now took place in the assembly and finishing steps, which were organized around a job shop style of manufacturing process.

The results were impressive. The switch from MTO to ATO allowed greater efficiency in the fabrication area. Because fabrication—the longest and most labor-intensive value chain activity—was now off-line, lead times to the customer shrank from weeks to days. Inventory levels were cut in half, and the workforce was decreased by 25%. Quality actually increased due to the focus on standard-sized panels.

FIGURE 7.7 TimberEdge Cabinets Before: Make-to-Order Manufacturing

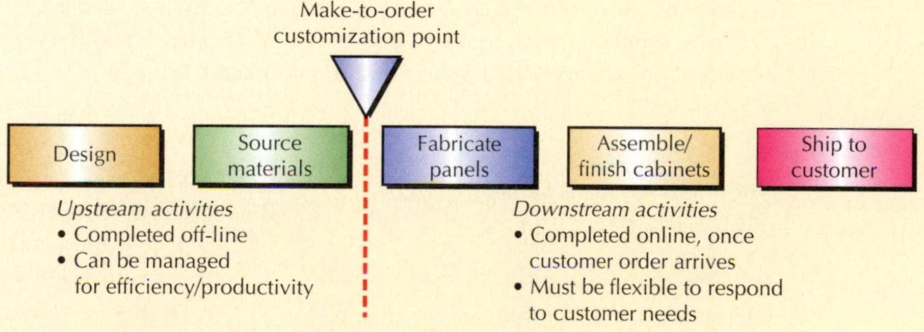

FIGURE 7.8 TimberEdge Cabinets After: Assemble-to-Order Manufacturing

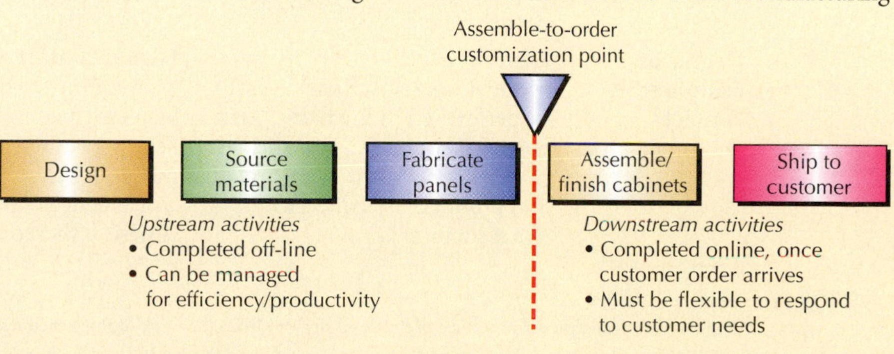

[7]The company name has been changed to protect the company's confidentiality.

7.3 SERVICE PROCESSES

Business textbooks have traditionally differentiated between manufacturing and service operations. The reason for this distinction was that manufacturers produce tangible, physical products, whereas service operations provide intangible value. Unfortunately, this distinction has led some readers to assume that service operations are somehow "softer" or more difficult to pin down than manufacturing operations.

In reality, service operations are more diverse than manufacturing operations. Some service operations even have more in common with manufacturing than they do with other services. Consider mail sorting at the post office. Letters and packages are sorted using highly specialized sorting and reading equipment. This activity occurs "behind the scenes," out of the customer's view. Furthermore, the equipment is arranged sequentially, following a product-based layout. One can readily see that mail sorting has more in common with batch manufacturing than it does with other services such as consulting or teaching.

To begin our discussion of services, then, let's consider three dimensions on which services can *differ*: the nature of the service package, the degree of customization, and the level of customer contact.[8] These dimensions have a great deal to do with how different services are organized and managed. Table 7.2 summarizes the different managerial challenges faced by services organizations, depending on the nature of the service package, the degree of customization, and the degree of customer contact.

The Service Package

Service package
Includes all the value-added *physical* and *intangible* activities that a service organization provides to the customer.

The **service package** includes all the value-added *physical* and *intangible* activities that a service organization provides to the customer. For some service operations, the primary sources of value are physical activities, such as the storage, display, or transportation of goods or people. Airlines move passengers from one city to another; hotels provide travelers with rooms and meeting facilities. Retailers add value by providing customers with

TABLE 7.2
Managerial Challenges in Service Environments

Nature of the service package	**Primarily physical activities →** Greater emphasis on managing physical assets (Airline, trucking firm)	**Primarily intangible activities →** Greater emphasis on managing people and knowledge assets (Law firm, software developer)
Degree of customization	**Lower customization →** Greater emphasis on closely controlling the process and improving productivity (Quick-change oil shop)	**Higher customization →** Greater emphasis on being flexible and responsive to customers' needs (Full-service car repair shop)
Degree of customer contact	**Lower contact →** More of the service package can be performed in the back room. Service layout, location, and hours will be based more on cost and productivity concerns. (Mail sorting)	**Higher contact →** More of the service package must be performed in the front room. Service layout, location, and hours must be designed with customer convenience in mind. (Physical therapist)

[8]Our discussion and model of service processes is derived from the work of Roger Schmenner and, in particular, from R. Schmenner, "How Can Service Businesses Survive and Prosper?" *Sloan Management Review* 27, no. 3 (Spring 1986): 21–32.

TABLE 7.3
Sample Activities in Two Distinct Service Packages

SERVICE	INTANGIBLE ACTIVITIES	PHYSICAL ACTIVITIES
University	Teaching Conducting research Performing service and outreach	Supporting the "physical plant" Providing transportation services Providing dining services
Logistics services provider	Finding the best transportation solution for the customer Handling government customs issues	Providing housing Moving goods Storing goods

convenient access to a wide range of products at a fair price. Many of the same rules and techniques that are used to manage physical goods in a manufacturing setting apply equally well to these services, even though airlines, hotels, and retail stores do not actually "make" products.

For other services, the service package consists primarily of intangible activities. A lawyer or editor, for example, creates value primarily through the knowledge he or she provides. The fact that this knowledge might be captured on paper or in an electronic file is secondary.

Most service packages include a mix of physical and intangible value-added activities. Table 7.3 lists some of the activities in the service package offered by a university and a logistics services provider.

Though the primary source of value that logistics companies provide might be the movement and storage of goods, such companies also routinely determine the best transportation options for customers and handle customs paperwork. They might also conduct packaging activities, and deal with customer service issues. Airlines are another example of a mix of physical and intangible services. In addition to providing physical transportation, airlines help travelers to plan their itineraries and track their frequent flier miles, and even put them in touch with service providers such as hotels and rental car agencies.

The greater the emphasis on physical activities is, the more management's attention will be directed to capital expenditures (buildings, planes, and trucks), material costs, and other tangible assets. Retailers, for instance, frequently spend more than 60 cents of every sales dollar on products. These products must be moved, stored, displayed, and in some cases returned. Hotel and airline executives also spend a great deal of time managing expensive tangible assets.

The greater the emphasis on intangible activities is, the more critical is the training and retention of skilled employees and the development and maintenance of the firm's knowledge assets. Labor cost tends to be quite a high percentage of total cost in such environments. In some intellectually intensive services, such as consulting, labor costs may far outstrip expenditures on buildings and other physical assets.

Knowledge assets generally refer to the intellectual capital of the firm, which may be embedded in the people, the information systems, or even the copyrights and patents owned by a firm. For example, Oracle spends an enormous amount of time developing, refining, and protecting its software offerings. Oracle's market intelligence about competitors' products and customer needs can also be viewed as a key knowledge asset.

Service Customization

Customization has an enormous impact on how services are designed and managed. *As the degree of customization decreases*, the service package becomes more standardized. To deliver a standardized service, managers can hire workers with more narrow skills and employ special-purpose technology. Within the same business sector, for instance, one law firm might specialize in divorce or traffic cases, while another might offer a full range of legal services, depending on the customer's needs. Law firms that specialize in divorces can use special software packages designed to help clients reach a quick and equitable settlement.

Controlling the degree of customization also allows better measurement and closer control over the service process. In some cases, managers might draw up a precise, step-by-step process map of the service and establish standard times for performing each step. Many fast-food restaurants follow such an approach. Not surprisingly, businesses that offer less customized services have more opportunity to focus on cost and productivity. A classic example is an automotive shop dedicated only to oil changes. Employees in this type of business do not need to be master mechanics or skilled electricians, nor do they need a broad range of expensive equipment and tools. Furthermore, customers can be handled at a predictable and relatively fast rate. The standardized nature of the service allows many such shops to guarantee that a customer's car will be serviced within some precise period, usually an hour or less.

As the degree of customization increases, the service package becomes less predictable and more variable. Efficiency and productivity, though they are important, become much more difficult to measure and control, as each customer may have unique needs. Organizations that offer customized services tend to compete less on cost and more on their ability to provide customers with exactly what they need.

Consider, for example, a general hospital that offers a full range of health care services, from pediatrics to surgery. On any given day, the mix of patients and ailments the hospital must treat is only partially predictable. The breadth and depth of skills required to deal with any and every eventuality are high, and labor costs are therefore high as well. Such a hospital also needs to invest in a wide range of technologies, some of which might be quite expensive.

Customer Contact

A third consideration in managing service processes is the level of customer contact. Contact is *not* the same as customization. A fast-food restaurant provides a high degree of customer contact, but little customization. On the other hand, a health clinic provides a high degree of contact *and* customization: Physicians may need to see patients frequently to make a diagnosis, prescribe a treatment, and monitor the treatment's effectiveness.

Front room
The physical or virtual point where the customer interfaces directly with the service organization.

The degree of customer contact determines the relative importance of front-room and back-room operations in a service process. The **front room** in a service organization is the point (either physical or virtual) where the customer interfaces directly with the service organization. It may be the sales floor in a retail store, the help desk for a software provider, or even the Web home page for a company. The front-room operations of an airline include the reservation desk, baggage check-in, and terminal gate, as well as the planes themselves. As a rule, *as the degree of customer contact increases*, more of the service package is provided by front-room operations.

In designing front-room operations, managers must consider how the customer interfaces with the service. Layout, location, and convenience become key. The physical layout must be comfortable, safe, and attractive and the location convenient. And front-room service must be available when the customer needs it. Kinko's is one example of a high-contact service: Its copying and personal computer services are available 24 hours a day at locations convenient to colleges and universities.

Back room
The part of a service operation that is completed without direct customer contact.

As the degree of customer contact decreases, more of the service package is provided by back-room operations. The **back room** refers to that part of a service operation that is completed without direct customer contact. The back room is often hidden from the customer's view. Package sorting at FedEx or UPS is a classic example of a back-room operation, as is the testing of medical samples. Such services can be located to reduce transportation costs and laid out to improve productivity. Because back-room personnel do not deal directly with customers, the hours of operation are not as crucial as they are in front-room operations, and employees do not have to be skilled in dealing with customers. FedEx and UPS personnel sort packages in the middle of the night while customers are sleeping. As you might expect, back-room service operations are usually easier to manage than front-room operations.

Service blueprinting A specialized form of business process mapping that allows the user to better visualize the degree of customer contact. The service blueprint lays out the service process from the viewpoint of the customer. It parses out the organization's service actions based on (1) the extent to which an action involves direct interaction with the customer, and (2) whether or not an action takes place as a direct response to a customer's needs.

Service blueprinting is a specialized form of business process mapping that allows the user to better visualize the degree of customer contact.[9] The service blueprint does this in two ways. First, it lays out the service process from the viewpoint of the customer. It then parses out the organization's service actions based on (1) the extent to which an action involves direct interaction with the customer, and (2) whether or not an action takes place as a direct response to a customer's needs.

Figure 7.9 provides a template for the service blueprint. The blueprint has four layers. The first layer represents specific *customer actions*, such as placing an order, calling up a service support hotline, or entering a service facility, such as a doctor's office or a retail store. The second layer represents *onstage actions* carried out by the service provider. Onstage actions provide a point of direct interaction with the customer. Some proponents of service blueprinting reserve this layer for activities that involve direct *physical* interaction with the customer. Others argue that any form of direct interaction, whether it be a phone call or even a visit to a Web site, would appear here. In this sense, onstage activities are synonymous with front-room operations. Because onstage actions involve direct interaction with the customer, they cross the *line of interaction* and occur above the *line of visibility*.

The third layer of the service blueprint consists of *backstage actions*. These take place in direct response to a customer action, but the difference is that the customer does not "see" these activities carried out. As such, they take place below the line of visibility and are analogous to back-room operations. An example would be the activities required to pick, pack,

FIGURE 7.9 Service Blueprinting Template

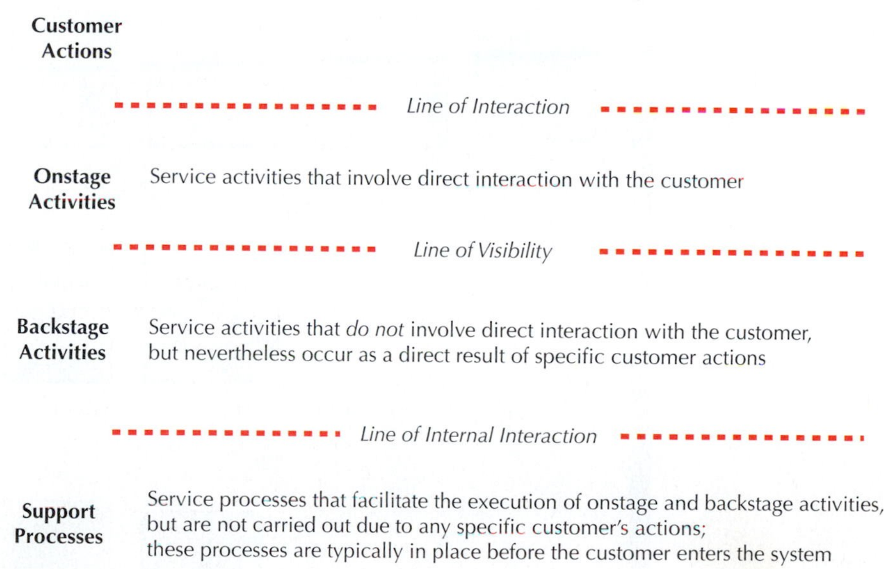

Customer Actions
Line of Interaction
Onstage Activities
Service activities that involve direct interaction with the customer
Line of Visibility
Backstage Activities
Service activities that do not involve direct interaction with the customer, but nevertheless occur as a direct result of specific customer actions
Line of Internal Interaction
Support Processes
Service processes that facilitate the execution of onstage and backstage activities, but are not carried out due to any specific customer's actions; these processes are typically in place before the customer enters the system

[9]M. J. Bitner, "Managing the Evidence of Service," in *The Service Quarterly Handbook*, eds. E. E. Scheuing and W. F. Christopher (New York: AMACOM, 1993).

and ship the books and videos you order from Amazon.com. You don't "see" these activities take place, but nevertheless they occur as a direct result of your order being placed.

The fourth layer of the service blueprint contains *support processes*. Unlike onstage and backstage actions, these processes do not occur as a result of any particular customer's actions. Rather, these processes facilitate the execution of onstage and backstage actions. In the language of service blueprinting, they do this by crossing the *line of internal interaction*. Continuing with our example, Amazon's Web site development and inventory management processes ensure that there is a Web site that can take your order (and credit card information) and that the books and videos you want are in stock.

Example 7.1

Service Blueprinting at the Bluebird Café

In Chapter 3, we described how Katie Favre, owner of the Bluebird Café, used process mapping to map the steps that occur when a customer visits the café. The resulting process map is shown in Figure 7.10.

Katie feels that it would be valuable to remap this process using service blueprinting so that she can better see how the customer interacts with her staff. Furthermore, Katie would like to understand what support processes are critical to carrying out the onstage and backstage actions. Figure 7.11 presents the resulting service blueprint.

Looking at the service blueprint provides Katie with new insights into her business. First, Katie notes that there are six points at which the customer directly interacts with her staff. Furthermore, four of these six interactions occur between the waitress and the customer. Katie has usually had her friendliest and most efficient people serve as hosts or cashiers, but the service blueprint makes her wonder about the wisdom of this policy.

Katie also observes that the ability of the kitchen to prepare food (a backstage activity) depends in part on two support processes: the food system inventory management, which makes sure that the right quantities of food are on hand and properly stored; and the

FIGURE 7.10 Process Map for the Bluebird Café

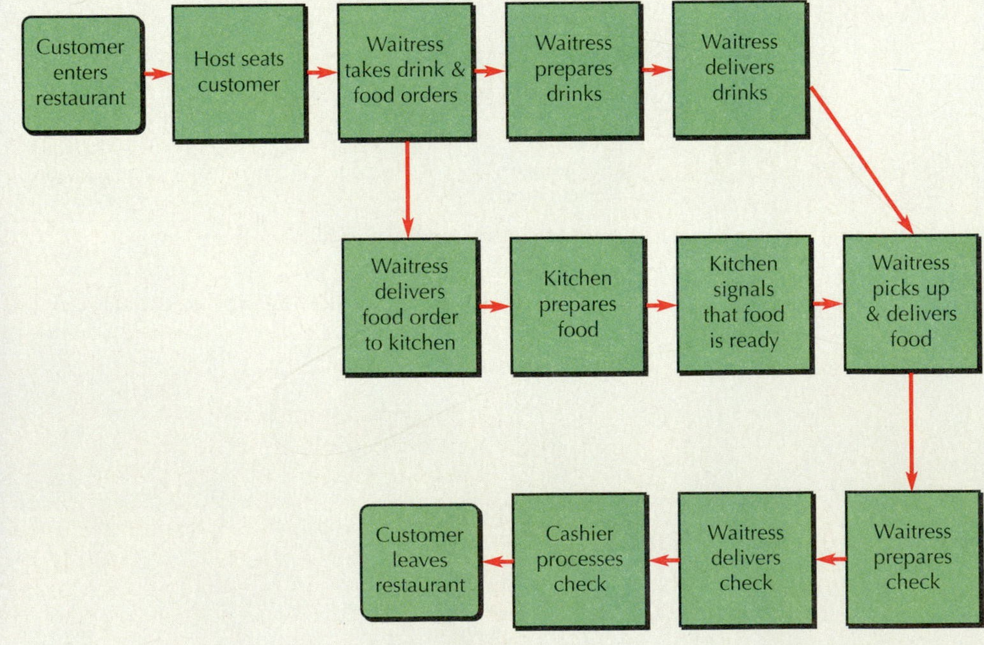

FIGURE 7.11 Service Blueprint for the Bluebird Café

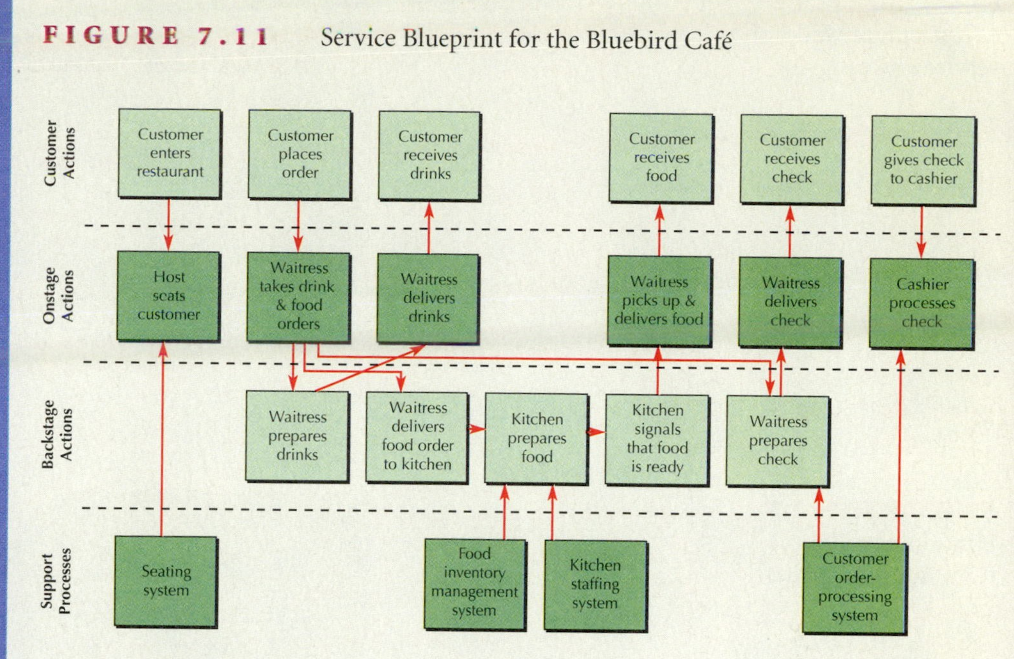

kitchen staffing system, which makes sure the proper number and mix of personnel are available.

Katie has heard grumblings in the past about the kitchen staffing system (really just an informal sign-up sheet). She had dismissed this as a problem for the kitchen management staff to resolve, but now she begins to think about how this "invisible," indirect support process might potentially undermine key backstage and onstage actions.

Service Positioning

Service operations compete and position themselves in the marketplace based on the three dimensions—nature of the service package, degree of customization, and degree of customer contact—that were just discussed. Figure 7.12 shows a conceptual model of service processes containing these three dimensions. The three dimensions of the cube represent the nature of the service package, the degree of customization, and the level of contact with the customer.

To illustrate how positioning works, consider the case of public hospitals. Such community-sponsored hospitals are typically chartered to provide a wide selection of health services to the local population. These hospitals are characterized by:

- High levels of service customization;
- High levels of customer contact; and
- A mix of physical and intangible service activities.

These characteristics make community hospitals very expensive to run, and very challenging to manage. The position of such service operations is shown graphically in Figure 7.13.

Now compare this to a birthing center that specializes in low-risk births. All the center's personnel and equipment are focused on a single activity. While customer contact is high, customization of the service package is relatively low.

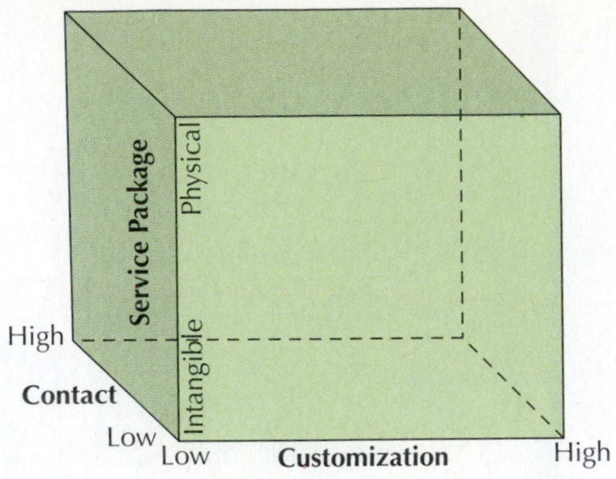

FIGURE 7.12
A Conceptual Model of Service Process

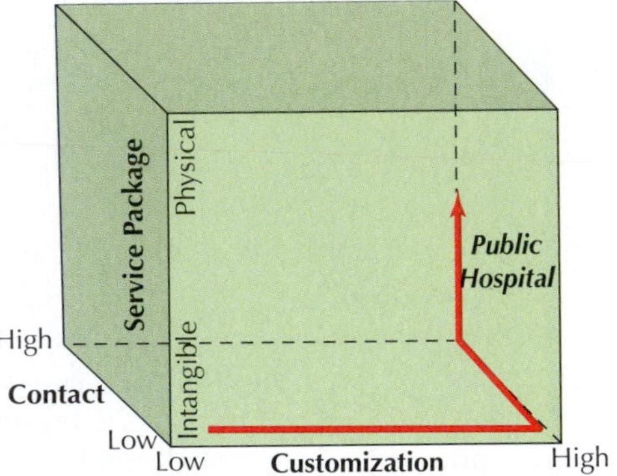

FIGURE 7.13
Positioning a Typical Community Hospital

A birthing center competes by staking out a position quite different from that of the traditional public hospital (see Figure 7.14). As a result, the birthing center and the hospital face different managerial challenges and meet different customer needs. Though the typical birthing center competes by offering greater efficiency and a more "family-friendly" atmosphere than the typical public hospital, it cannot meet the broad range of health care needs found in a community hospital. A birthing center may "steal" some business from the local hospital, but it cannot replace it.

Services within the Supply Chain

Many people view supply chains as being dominated by manufacturers. However, take a moment to look back at the beginning of Chapter 1, which starts with a description of four companies: Wal-Mart, Federal Express, SAP, and Flextronics. Note that two of these companies, Wal-Mart and Federal Express, are service firms that provide both physical and intangible activities. SAP is a service firm that provides software for the management of supply chains. All three companies, in fact, are deeply involved with supply chain management issues. Large retailers like Wal-Mart "pull" products through the supply chain, companies like Federal Express make sure products and materials arrive in a timely and

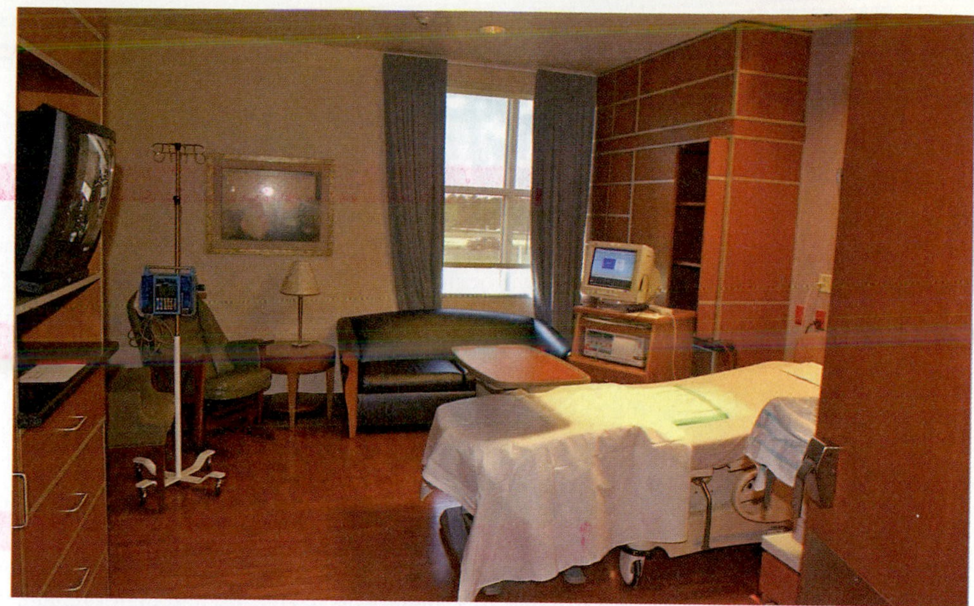

Birthing centers have a high degree of customer contact and represent a mix of physical and intangible activities. But because they focus on one particular health care need, the degree of customization is low.

FIGURE 7.14
Positioning a Birthing Center

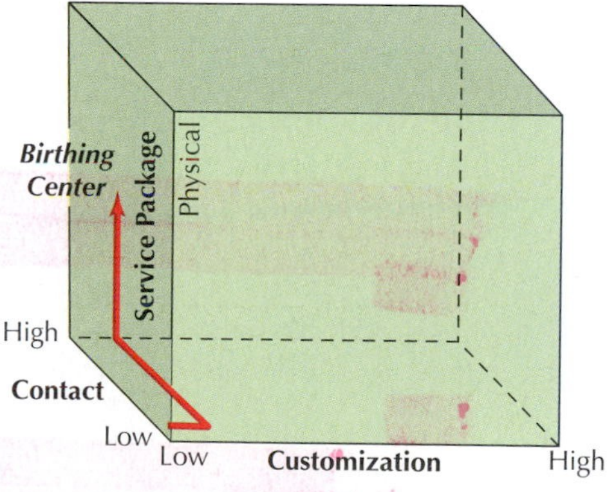

cost-effective manner, and companies like SAP provide the "smarts" needed to run supply chains as effectively as possible.

The point is that services are an integral part of any supply chain. Of course, some services have very little to do with supply chains, due to the nature of the service package. But for others, supply chains are a source of both products and business opportunities.

7.4 LAYOUT DECISION MODELS

An important part of process choice is deciding how the various resources will be logically grouped and physically arranged. We have already described four types of layouts in this chapter: product-based, functional, cellular, and fixed-position layouts. For a fixed-position layout, there is little discretion regarding how the process is laid out because the productive resources have to be moved to where the product is being made or where the service is being provided.

For the remaining three, however, managers do face choices regarding how the processes are laid out. A product-based layout arranges resources sequentially according to the steps required to make a product or provide a service. The security check-in at an airport is an example of a service process that follows a product-based layout (in this case, the "product" is the passenger). Such an arrangement makes sense when the sequence of activities does not change from one period to the next. In contrast, a functional layout physically groups resources by function. A functional layout is better suited to environments where the process steps can change dramatically from one job or customer to the next. An example of this would be a full-service auto repair facility, with inspections done in one area, alignments in another, and major repairs in a third area. Finally, a cellular layout is similar in many ways to a product-based layout. The primary difference is that the cellular layout is used in a group technology cell, where the production resources have been dedicated to a subset of products with similar requirements, known as a product family.

In the remainder of this section, we introduce two approaches that managers use to develop effective product-based and functional layouts.

Line Balancing

Line balancing is a technique used in developing product-based layouts, as would be found in a production line or group technology work cell. The technique works by assigning tasks to a series of linked workstations in a manner that minimizes the number of workstations and minimizes the total amount of idle time at all stations for a given output level.[10] When the amount of work assigned to each workstation is identical, we say the line is perfectly balanced. In reality, most lines are unbalanced, as the actual amount of work varies from one workstation to the next. The six basic steps of line balancing are as follows:

1. Identify all the process steps required, including the time for each task, the immediate predecessor for each task, and the total time for all tasks.
2. Draw a precedence diagram based on the information gathered in step 1. This diagram is used when assigning individual tasks to workstations.
3. Determine the takt time for the line. **Takt time** is computed as the available production time divided by the required output rate:

$$\text{Takt time} = \frac{\text{available production time}}{\text{required output rate}} \quad [7\text{-}1]$$

Takt time
In a production line setting, the available production time divided by the required output rate. Takt time sets the maximum allowable cycle time for a line.

[10] Cox and Blackstone, eds., *APICS Dictionary*.

Simply put, takt time tells us the maximum allowable time between completions of successive units on the line. As we noted earlier, the actual time between completions is referred to as the *cycle time* of a line.

4. Compute the theoretical minimum number of workstations needed. The theoretical minimum number of workstations is defined as:

$$W_{Min} = \frac{\sum_{i=1}^{I} T_i}{\text{takt time}} \quad [7\text{-}2]$$

where:

T_i = time required for the *i*th task

$\sum_{i=1}^{I} T_i$ = total time for all *I* tasks

As you can see, the shorter the required takt time is, the more workstations we will require. This is because the tasks will need to be divided across more workstations to ensure that cycle time, which is determined by the total amount of work in the largest workstation, remains below the takt time.

5. Working on one workstation at a time, use a decision rule to assign tasks to the workstation. Start with the first workstation, and add tasks until you reach the point at which no more tasks can be assigned without exceeding the takt time. If you reach this point and all the tasks have not been assigned yet, close the workstation to any more tasks and open up a new workstation. Repeat the process until all tasks have been assigned.

   Be sure not to assign a task to a workstation unless all direct predecessors (if any) have been assigned. Common decision rules for determining which task to assign next are to (1) assign the largest eligible task that will still fit within the workstation without exceeding the takt time, (2) assign the eligible task with the most tasks directly dependent on it, or (3) assign some combination of the two.

6. Evaluate the performance of the proposed line by calculating some basic performance measures, including:

$$\text{Cycle time} = CT = \text{maximum amount of time spent in any one workstation} \quad [7\text{-}3]$$

$$\text{Idle time} = IT = W_{Actual}CT - \sum_{i=1}^{I} T_i \quad [7\text{-}4]$$

where:

W_{Actual} = actual number of workstations

$$\text{Percent idle time} = PI = 100\%\left[\frac{IT}{W_{Actual}CT}\right] \quad [7\text{-}5]$$

$$\text{Efficiency delay} = ED = 100\% - PI \quad [7\text{-}6]$$

In general, solutions with low idle times and high-efficiency delay values are considered superior. It's important to realize that the decision rules just mentioned will not always generate the best solution; good decision makers, therefore, look for ways to improve the solution.

Example 7.2

Line Balancing at Blackhurst Engineering

Blackhurst Engineering, a small contract manufacturer, has just signed a contract to assemble, test, and package products for another company. The contract states that Blackhurst must produce 500 units per eight-hour day. The list of tasks, including time requirements and immediate predecessors, is as follows:

TASK	TIME (IN SECONDS)	IMMEDIATE PREDECESSOR(S)
A	15	None
B	26	A
C	15	A
D	32	B, C
E	25	D
F	15	E
G	18	E
H	10	E
I	22	F, G, H
J	24	I
Total	**202**	

Now that Blackhurst has won the business, Griffin Blackhurst, founder of the company, has decided to set up a line process to make the units. He knows that he will have to staff each workstation with one of his employees. Therefore, Griffin does not want to have any more workstations than necessary, and he would like to keep their idle time down to a minimum. As a first step, Griffin draws out the precedence diagram for the various tasks (Figure 7.15). Each task is represented by a box, and precedence relationships are shown with arrows.

FIGURE 7.15 Precedence Diagram for Blackhurst Engineering

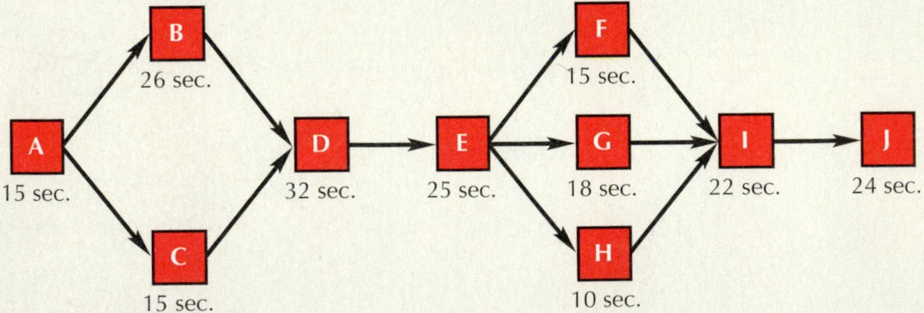

Next Griffin calculates the maximum allowable cycle time, or takt time, for the proposed line. Because there are 28,800 seconds in an eight-hour shift,

$$\text{Takt time} = \frac{\text{available production time}}{\text{required output rate}} = \frac{28{,}800 \text{ seconds}}{500 \text{ units per day}} = 57.6 \text{ seconds per unit}$$

With this information, Griffin calculates the theoretical minimum number of workstations:

$$W_{Min} = \frac{\sum_{i=1}^{I} T_i}{\text{takt time}} = \frac{202 \text{ seconds}}{57.6 \text{ seconds}} = 3.51, \text{ or 4 workstations}$$

Griffin rounds up when determining W_{Min} because there is no such thing as a fractional workstation, and anything less than the calculated value would not be enough. Now that Griffin knows the takt time and the theoretical minimum number of workstations that will be needed, he begins to assign tasks to the workstations. He has decided to use the following decision rules:

1. Assign the largest eligible task that can be added to the workstation without exceeding the takt time.
2. If there is a tie, assign the eligible task with the most tasks directly dependent on it.
3. If there is still a tie, randomly choose among any of the tasks that meet the previous two criteria.

Following these rules, Griffin begins assigning tasks to the first workstation. He assigns Task **A** first, followed by Task **B** and Task **C**. At this point, the first workstation has a total workload of 56 seconds:

WORKSTATION 1	
Task **A**	15 seconds
Task **B**	26 seconds
Task **C**	15 seconds
Total	**56 seconds**

Because there are no more tasks that can be added to workstation 1 without exceeding the takt time of 57.6 seconds, Griffin closes workstation 1 to any further assignments and starts assigning tasks to workstation 2. Ultimately, Griffin ends up with the following assignments to the four workstations:

WORKSTATION 1	
Task **A**	15 seconds
Task **B**	26 seconds
Task **C**	15 seconds
Total	**56 seconds**

WORKSTATION 2	
Task **D**	32 seconds
Task **E**	25 seconds
Total	**57 seconds**

WORKSTATION 3	
Task **G**	18 seconds
Task **F**	15 seconds
Task **H**	10 seconds
Total	**43 seconds**

WORKSTATION 4	
Task **I**	22 seconds
Task **J**	24 seconds
Total	**46 seconds**

Figure 7.16 shows the workstation assignments.

FIGURE 7.16 Workstation Assignments at Blackhurst Engineering

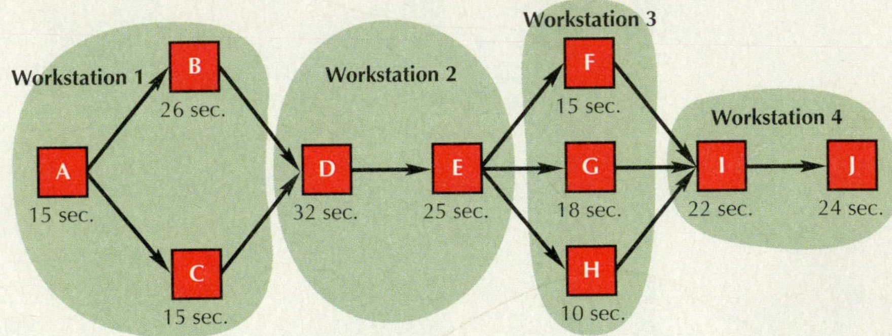

At 57 seconds, workstation 2 has the most task time of any workstation. Because units must be passed from one workstation to the next, units cannot move through the line any faster than the slowest workstation. Workstation 2 effectively dictates that the cycle time for the entire line will be 57 seconds.

The actual number of workstations (W_{Actual}) is the same as the theoretical minimum number (W_{Min}), which makes Griffin think he has developed a good solution. Nevertheless, he calculates the idle time, percent idle time, and efficiency delay for the proposed line:

$$\text{Idle time} = IT = W_{Actual}CT - \sum_{i=1}^{I} T_i$$

$$= 4(57 \text{ seconds}) - 202 \text{ seconds} = 26 \text{ seconds}$$

$$\text{Percent idle time} = PI = 100\%\left[\frac{IT}{W_{Actual}CT}\right] = 100\%\left(\frac{26}{228}\right) = 11.4\%$$

$$\text{Efficiency delay} = ED = 100\% - PI = 88.6\%$$

Interpreting the numbers, the line has an idle time of 26 seconds because not all of the workstations have workloads equal to the cycle time of 57 seconds. In fact, the idle times for the four workstations are as follows:

WORKSTATION	CYCLE TIME – ACTUAL TIME
1	57 – 56=1 second
2	57 – 57=0 seconds
3	57 – 43=14 seconds
4	57 – 46=11 seconds
Total	**26 seconds of idle time**

Looking at the idle times for each workstation, Griffin realizes that the resulting line is not even close to being perfectly balanced. As such, he will probably need to rotate his employees across the workstations to make sure no one feels slighted. The idle time and efficiency delay numbers tell us that a unit going through the process is idle 11.4% of the time. Conversely, the efficiency delay tells us that the assembly line is being utilized 88.6% of the available production time.

Assigning Department Locations in Functional Layouts

Because there is no clearly defined flow of tasks for functional layouts, a different approach to developing layouts is needed. In general, the objective here is to arrange the different functional areas, or *departments*, in such a way that departments that should be close to one another (such as packaging and shipping) are, while departments that don't need to be or shouldn't be near one another aren't.

Though this may sound simple, developing functional layouts can actually be quite complex, especially when there is a large number of departments and the criteria for assigning locations are unclear. Experts have developed a variety of approaches to developing functional layouts. Under one approach, decision makers develop closeness ratings for each possible pairing of departments. These closeness ratings, which can be qualitative ("undesirable," "desirable," "critical," etc.) or quantitative (1, 2, 3, etc.), are then used to guide the layout decision.

Another approach, which we describe here, is to locate departments in such a way as to *minimize the total distance traveled*, given a certain number of interdepartmental trips per time period. The logic is that not only will this cut down on unproductive travel time, but also companies can gain natural synergies by locating highly interactive departments next to one another. As with line balancing, the process can be divided into several basic steps:

1. Identify the potential department locations and distances between the various locations.
2. For each department, identify the expected number of trips between the department and all other departments (interdepartmental trips).
3. Attempt to assign department locations in such a way as to minimize the total distance traveled. There are several heuristics that can be used when making these assignments:
   a. If a particular department can be assigned only to a certain location, do this first. For example, a firm may decide that the client waiting room must be located next to the building entrance. Making such assignments up front reduces the number of potential arrangements to consider.

b. Rank order department pairings by number of interdepartmental trips, and attempt to locate departments with the most interdepartmental trips next to one another.

c. Centrally locate departments that have significant interactions with multiple departments (this will help increase the likelihood that other departments can be located adjacent to them).

d. Finally, see if the solution can be improved by swapping pairs of departments.

In a practical sense, the only way to ensure that one has identified the optimal solution (i.e., the one that minimizes total distance traveled) is to evaluate all possible arrangements. However, this can be prohibitive, as there are *N*! ways of assigning *N* departments to *N* locations. This means that for just five departments, there are 5! − 5*4*3*2*1=120 possible combinations to consider. If there are 10 departments that must be assigned, the possible number of arrangements is a staggering 10!=3,628,800. Therefore, most decision makers seek to identify a viable, if not optimal, solution.

Example 7.3
Assigning Departments at Blackhurst Engineering

Blackhurst Engineering has been so successful that its founder, Griffin Blackhurst, has decided to relocate the company to a new facility. Griffin has five departments that must be located within the facility: Accounting, Marketing, Engineering, Production, and Shipping & Receiving (S&R).

Figure 7.17 shows the layout of the new facility. The facility has five different areas, any of which is large enough to house the various departments. Because Shipping & Receiving needs access to the bay doors, Griffin has already assigned this department to area E. In addition, Griffin has determined that Production will need to be in either area C or area D due to the significant flow of materials between Production and Shipping & Receiving. Beyond this, however, Griffin has not decided where to place the four unassigned departments.

FIGURE 7.17 Layout of New Facility for Blackhurst Engineering

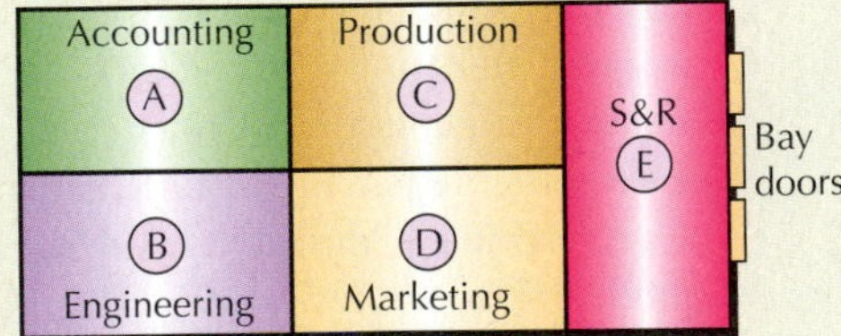

Because material flow has been addressed by locating Production next to Shipping & Receiving, Griffin has decided to base the final layout on the number of trips personnel make between departments. Specifically, he would like to minimize the total distance traveled per day.

In order to accomplish this, Griffin creates two tables. Table 7.4 shows the distance between the five areas shown in Figure 7.17. Table 7.5 shows the number of interdepartmental trips personnel make each day between the various departments.

After ranking the interdepartmental trip data in Table 7.5 from highest to lowest (Table 7.6), Griffin notes that the greatest number of interdepartmental trips is made between Production and Marketing (110 trips) and between Shipping and Production (90). In addition, the smallest number of trips is made between Shipping and Accounting (10) and between Shipping and Engineering (5). Based on this information, Griffin decides

TABLE 7.4 Distances (in meters) between Areas, Blackhurst Engineering

AREA	A	B	C	D	E
A	—				
B	30	—			
C	40	50	—		
D	50	40	30	—	
E	70	70	35	35	—

TABLE 7.5 Numbers of Daily Interdepartmental Trips, Blackhurst Engineering

DEPARTMENT	ACCOUNTING	MARKETING	PRODUCTION	ENGINEERING	SHIPPING
Accounting	—				
Marketing	80	—			
Production	35	110	—		
Engineering	60	40	55	—	
Shipping	10	25	90	5	—

TABLE 7.6 Ranked Number of Daily Interdepartmental Trips, Blackhurst Engineering

DEPARTMENTS	AVERAGE TRIPS PER DAY
Production ⇔ Marketing	110
Shipping ⇔ Production	90
Marketing ⇔ Accounting	80
Engineering ⇔ Accounting	60
Engineering ⇔ Production	55
Engineering ⇔ Marketing	40
Production ⇔ Accounting	35
Shipping ⇔ Marketing	25
Shipping ⇔ Accounting	10
Shipping ⇔ Engineering	5

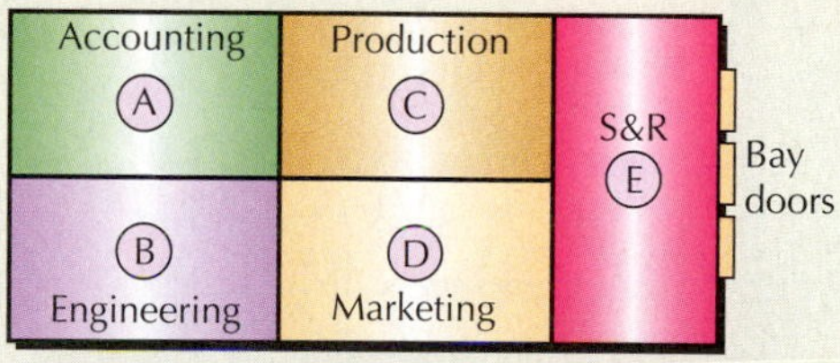

FIGURE 7.18 Initial Layout Assignments at Blackhurst Engineering

to locate Production and Marketing in areas C and D, respectively, and Accounting and Engineering in areas A and B, respectively (see Figure 7.18).

Griffin evaluates his proposed solution by multiplying the number of interdepartmental trips by the distances between departments. As Table 7.7 shows, the proposed solution results in total distance traveled per day of 19,925 meters.

TABLE 7.7 Total Distance Traveled per Day, Initial Solution

INTERDEPARTMENTAL TRAVEL	DISTANCE TRAVELED PER DAY (METERS)
Production ⇔ Marketing	110 trips * 30 = 3300
Shipping ⇔ Production	90 * 35 = 3150
Marketing ⇔ Accounting	80 * 50 = 4000
Engineering ⇔ Accounting	60 * 30 = 1800
Engineering ⇔ Production	55 * 50 = 2750
Engineering ⇔ Marketing	40 * 40 = 1600
Production ⇔ Accounting	35 * 40 = 1400
Shipping ⇔ Marketing	25 * 35 = 875
Shipping ⇔ Accounting	10 * 70 = 700
Shipping ⇔ Engineering	5 * 70 = 350
Total distance traveled	**19,925 meters**

Looking at his solution, Griffin realizes that Production has more interactions with Engineering than Marketing does, while Marketing has more interactions with Accounting than Production does. Griffin wonders if he could improve his results by switching the location of the Accounting and Engineering departments.

Figure 7.19 shows the revised layout. Recalculating the results (Table 7.8), Griffin realizes that this change cuts the total distance traveled by 600 meters (19,925 – 19,325 meters), or about 3%.

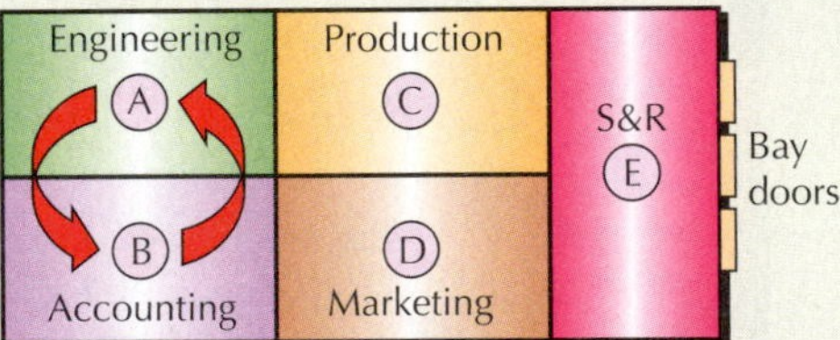

FIGURE 7.19 Revised Layout Assignments at Blackhurst Engineering

TABLE 7.8 Total Distance Traveled per Day, Revised Solution

INTERDEPARTMENTAL TRAVEL	DISTANCE TRAVELED PER DAY (METERS)
Production ⇔ Marketing	110 trips * 30 = 3300
Production ⇔ Shipping	90 * 35 = 3150
Marketing ⇔ Accounting	80 * 40 = 3200
Engineering ⇔ Accounting	60 * 30 = 1800
Engineering ⇔ Production	55 * 40 = 2200
Engineering ⇔ Marketing	40 * 50 = 2000
Production ⇔ Accounting	35 * 50 = 1750
Shipping ⇔ Marketing	25 * 35 = 875
Shipping ⇔ Accounting	10 * 70 = 700
Shipping ⇔ Engineering	5 * 70 = 350
Total distance traveled	**19,325**

CHAPTER SUMMARY

In this chapter, we looked at some of the important issues managers face when selecting a manufacturing or service process. We started with a discussion of manufacturing processes, emphasizing the strengths and weaknesses of different types, and we described the impact of customization on the manufacturing process and the supply chain. As our discussion made clear, managers must be careful in selecting both the manufacturing process and the degree and point of customization.

We then turned our attention to service processes. We looked at three defining dimensions of services: the service package (the mix of physical and intangible activities), service customization, and customer contact. We showed how services face different managerial challenges, depending on where they stand on these dimensions, and demonstrated service blueprinting, a specialized form of process mapping that highlights customer contact points. Finally, we ended the chapter by demonstrating two approaches to developing layouts in manufacturing and service environments.

KEY FORMULAS

Takt time (page 194):

$$\text{Takt time} = \frac{\text{available production time}}{\text{required output rate}} \quad [7\text{-}1]$$

Theoretical minimum number of workstations (page 195):

$$W_{Min} = \frac{\sum_{i=1}^{I} T_i}{\text{takt time}} \quad [7\text{-}2]$$

where:

T_i = time required for the ith task

$\sum_{i=1}^{I} T_i$ = total time for all I tasks

Cycle time for a production line (page 195):

$$CT = \text{maximum amount of time spent in any one workstation} \quad [7\text{-}3]$$

Idle time (page 195):

$$IT = W_{Actual}CT - \sum_{i=1}^{I} T_i \quad [7\text{-}4]$$

where:

W_{Actual} = actual number of workstations

Percent idle time (page 195):

$$PI = 100\%\left[\frac{IT}{W_{Actual}CT}\right] \qquad [7\text{-}5]$$

Efficiency delay (page 195):

$$ED = 100\% - PI \qquad [7\text{-}6]$$

KEY TERMS

Assemble- or finish-to-order (ATO) products 183
Back room 188
Batch manufacturing 178
Cellular layout 180
Continuous flow process 177
Cycle time 177
Downstream activities 184
Engineer-to-order (ETO) products 183
Fixed-position layout 179
Flexible manufacturing systems (FMSs) 176
Front room 188
Functional layout 178
Group technology 180
Hybrid manufacturing processes 179
Job shop 178
Law of variability 184
Machining center 180
Make-to-order (MTO) products 183
Make-to-stock (MTS) products 183
Product-based layout 176
Product family 180
Production line 176
Service blueprinting 189
Service package 186
Takt time 194
Upstream activities 184

SOLVED PROBLEM

Problem

Every Halloween, the sisters of Alpha Delta Pi put together "Monster Bags" for children at the local hospital. Each Monster Bag consists of a paper bag stuffed with candy. Each bag has a character's face drawn on it, with yarn hair and paper arms and legs attached.

For the past three years, several sisters have worked individually, putting together bags on their own. But because some of the women are much better artists than others, the quality of the Monster Bags has varied greatly.

Erika Borders, a supply chain major, has been thinking about this problem. She realizes that making each bag really consists of several steps:

A. Draw the face on the bag.
B. Cut out the arms and legs.
C. Attach the arms and legs.
D. Cut the yarn for the hair.

E. Attach the hair to the bag.
F. Fill the bag with candy.
G. Staple the bag closed.

Erika decides that the ideal solution would be to develop a little production line to make the bags. This way the most talented artists can focus on what they do best—drawing the characters' faces. She has developed the time estimates and predecessor data for the tasks. Alpha Delta Pi needs to make 200 bags, and Erika feels she would have no problem getting volunteers to help if they could get all the bags done in four hours.

TIME TASK	(SECONDS)	IMMEDIATE PREDECESSORS
A	45	None
B	60	None
C	30	B
D	15	None
E	25	A, D
F	10	C, E
G	10	F
Total	195	

Solution

After a couple of tries, Erika draws out the precedence diagram for the tasks:

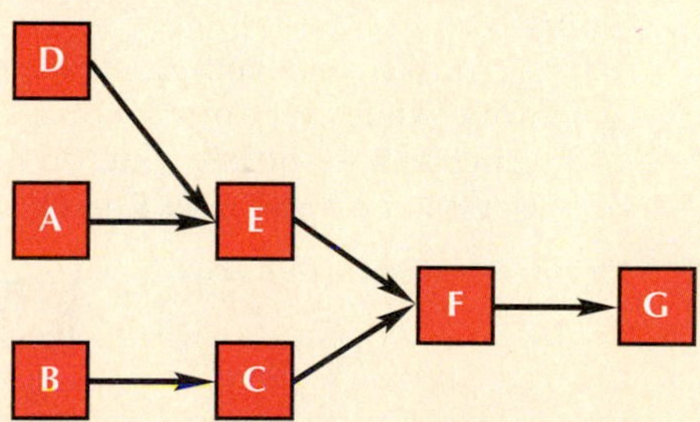

She then calculates the takt time for her production line:

$$\text{Takt time} = \frac{\text{available production time}}{\text{required output rate}} = \frac{14{,}400 \text{ seconds}}{200 \text{ bags}} = 72 \text{ seconds per bag}$$

and the theoretical minimum number of workstations:

$$W_{Min} = \frac{\sum_{i=1}^{I} T_i}{\text{takt time}} = \frac{195 \text{ seconds}}{72 \text{ seconds}} = 2.7, \text{ or } 3 \text{ workstations}$$

Next, Erika begins to assign tasks to the various workstations. The rule she uses is to assign the largest eligible task (i.e., the largest task that has all its predecessors assigned and that will still fit in the workstation without exceeding the takt time). In the case of a tie, she assigns the task with the most tasks depending directly on it. Working on one task at a time, Erika develops an initial solution:

WORKSTATION 1	
Task B	60 seconds
Total	**60 seconds**

WORKSTATION 2	
Task A	45 seconds
Task D	15 seconds
Total	**60 seconds**

WORKSTATION 3	
Task C	30 seconds
Task E	25 seconds
Task F	10 seconds
Total	**65 seconds**

WORKSTATION 4	
Task G	10 seconds
Total	**10 seconds**

Erika is not completely happy with her solution; workstation 4 has only 10 seconds of work, while every other workstation has 60 seconds or more. The current solution would generate a lot of idle time. To balance things out better, she decides to move Task **D** into workstation 3 and Tasks **E** and **F** into workstation 4:

WORKSTATION 1	
Task B	60 seconds
Total	**60 seconds**

WORKSTATION 2	
Task A	45 seconds
Total	**45 seconds**

WORKSTATION 3	
Task D	15 seconds
Task C	30 seconds
Total	**45 seconds**

WORKSTATION	4
Task E	25 seconds
Task F	10 seconds
Task G	10 seconds
Total	**45 seconds**

Although Erika was not able to fit all the tasks into the theoretical minimum number of workstations, the new solution is much better balanced. Total idle time for the line is:

$$\text{Idle time} = IT = 4(60 \text{ seconds}) - 195 \text{ seconds} = 45 \text{ seconds}$$

$$\text{Percent idle time} = PI = 100\%\left[\frac{IT}{W_{Actual}CT}\right]$$

$$= 100\%\left(\frac{45}{240}\right) = 18.8\%$$

$$\text{Efficiency delay} = ED = 100\% - PI = 81.2\%$$

Now all Erika needs to do is to line up four volunteers, including a good artist to handle workstation 2. So where *are* those pledges?

DISCUSSION QUESTIONS

1. Suppose a firm invests in what turns out to be the "wrong" manufacturing or service process, given the business strategy. What will happen? Can you think of an example?
2. In general, would you expect to see production lines upstream or downstream of the customization point in a supply chain? What about job shops? Explain.
3. At many college athletic events, you can find plastic drink cups with the school logo printed on them. Twenty years ago these cups came molded in a variety of colors. Now nearly all the cups are white with only the printed logos containing any color. Use the concept of the customization point to explain what has happened and why.
4. Between 1964 and 1966, Ford made more than 1 million Mustangs. Nowadays car collectors are spending tens of thousands of dollars to restore to "like new" vintage Mustangs that originally sold for around $3,000. What types of manufacturing processes do you think were originally used to produce Mustangs? What types of manufacturing processes do you think are used in the restoration of such cars? Why the difference?
5. How does a group technology process resemble a classic batch process? How does it resemble a classic production line? What are the advantages/disadvantages of such a hybrid manufacturing process?
6. Many universities are beginning to offer Web-based courses in lieu of traditional classes. These courses often contain lecture notes, linkages to videos and other documents, and online testing capabilities. How are Web-based courses positioned vis-à-vis large lecture classes? What are the advantages/disadvantages of Web-based courses? What are the managerial challenges?

PROBLEMS

Additional homework problems are available at www.prenhall.com/bozarth. These problems use Excel to generate customized problems for different class sections or even different students.
(* = easy; ** = moderate; *** = advanced)

1. Burns Boats wants to assemble 50 boats per eight-hour day using a production line. Total task time for each boat is 45 minutes.
   a. (*) What is the takt time? What is the theoretical minimum number of workstations needed?

b. (**) Suppose the longest individual task takes four minutes. Will Burns be able to accomplish its goal? Justify your answer.

2. (*) A production line has four workstations and a 50-second cycle time. The total amount of actual task time across all four workstations is 170 seconds. What is the idle time? The percent idle time? The efficiency delay?

3. (**) Polar Containers makes high-end coolers for camping. The total task time needed to make a cooler is 360 seconds, with the longest individual task taking 50 seconds. Polar Containers would like to set up a line capable of producing 50 coolers per eight-hour day. What is the takt time? What is the maximum output per day? (*Hint:* Consider the longest individual task time.)

4. LightEdge Technologies would like to put in place an assembly line in its Mexican facility that puts together Internet servers. The tasks needed to accomplish this, including times and predecessor relationships, are as follows:

TASK	TIME (MINUTES)	IMMEDIATE PREDECESSOR
A	2.9	None
B	0.2	None
C	0.25	A, B
D	0.4	A, B
E	1.7	C
F	0.1	C, D
G	0.7	D
H	1.7	E, F, G
I	1.2	H
J	2.3	I
K	2.7	I
L	1.5	J, K

a. (*) Draw a precedence diagram for the tasks. Suppose the takt time is 240 seconds (four minutes). What is the theoretical minimum number of workstations?
b. (**) Develop workstation assignments using the "largest eligible task" rule (i.e., assign the largest task that will fit into the workstation without exceeding the takt time).
c. (**) How many workstations does your solution require? What is the cycle time for the line? What is the idle time?

5. The state tax department wants to set up what would amount to a series of identical production lines (running eight hours a day) for processing state tax returns that are submitted on the state's "EZ" form. The various tasks, times, and precedence relationships for each line follows. The director has determined that each line needs to process 150 returns a day. The director has asked you to develop a proposed layout that would be shared across the lines.

TASK	TIME (MINUTES)	DIRECT PREDECESSORS
A. Open return; verify filer's name, address, and taxpayer ID.	0.75	None
B. Make sure W2 and federal information match computer records.	1.25	A
C. Check key calculations on return for correctness.	2.50	B
D. Print report to go with return.	0.50	C
E. Route return to refund, payment, or special handling department, based on the results.	0.30	D
F. Update status of return on computer system.	3.0	D

a. (*) What is the takt time for each line? What is the theoretical minimum number of workstations needed on each line?
b. (**) Make workstation assignments using the "largest eligible task" rule. Calculate the cycle time, idle time, percent idle time, and efficiency delay for the resulting line.
c. (***) Given the task times just listed, what is the minimum cycle time that can be achieved by a line? What is the maximum daily output that could be achieved by a single line?

6. Rayloc rebuilds automotive components. Its main facility has a work cell dedicated to rebuilding fuel pumps. The tasks, times, and predecessor relationships are as follows:

TASK	TIME (SECONDS)	IMMEDIATE PREDECESSOR
A	100	None
B	150	None
C	93	A
D	120	B
E	86	B
F	84	C
G	65	D, E
H	15	F, G

a. (**) Draw a precedence diagram for the tasks. Rayloc would like the cell to be able to handle 100 pumps a day. What is the takt time? What is the theoretical minimum number of workstations needed?
b. (**) Develop workstation assignments using the "largest eligible task" rule.
c. (**) How many workstations does your solution require? What is the cycle time for the line? What is the idle time? What is the percent idle time?
d. (***) Suppose Rayloc would like to double the output to 200 pumps a day. Is this possible, given the tasks just listed? Explain why or why not.

7. The local university has developed an eight-step process for screening the thousands of admissions applications it gets each year. The provost has decided the best way to take a first cut at all these applications is by employing a line process. The following table shows the times and predecessors for the various tasks:

TASK	TIME (MINUTES)	IMMEDIATE PREDECESSOR
A	1.2	None
B	1	A
C	0.65	B
D	1.1	B
E	1.3	C
F	0.7	D
G	0.8	D
H	0.9	E, F, G

a. (**) Draw a precedence diagram for the tasks. Suppose the university needs to process 30 applications an hour during the peak season. What is the takt time? What is the theoretical minimum number of workstations?
b. (**) Develop workstation assignments using the "largest eligible task" rule.
c. (**) How many workstations does your solution require? What is the cycle time for the line? What is the idle time? What are the percent idle time and the efficiency delay?
d. (***) In theory, what is the fastest cycle time possible, given the tasks just listed? How many applications per hour does this translate into?

8. (**) As the new facilities manager at Hardin Company, you have been asked to determine the layout for four departments on the fourth floor of the company's headquarters. Following is a map of the floor with distances between the areas.

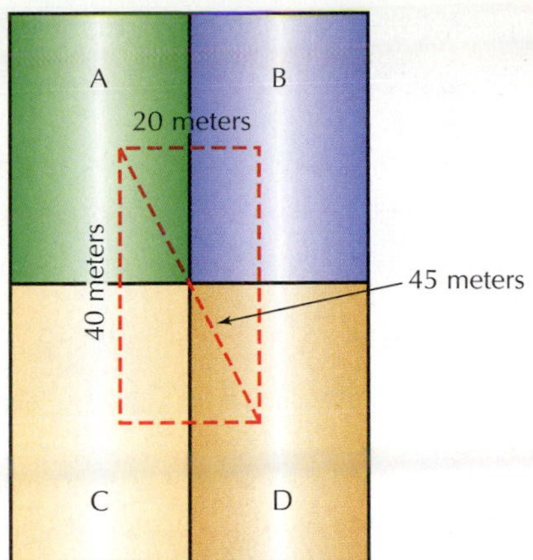

The number of interdepartmental trips made per day is as follows:

DEPARTMENT	1	2	3	4
1	—			
2	10	—		
3	5	60	—	
4	30	.40	50	—

Generate at least *two* alternative layout solutions. What is the maximum possible number of arrangements? Which of your two alternatives is best? Why?

9. Dr. Mike Douvas is opening a new sports clinic and is wondering how to arrange the six different departments of the clinic:

1. Waiting
2. Reception
3. Records and staff lounge
4. Examination
5. Outpatient surgery
6. Physical therapy

A map of the clinic follows. The six marked areas are big enough to handle any of the departments, although Dr. Douvas wants to have Reception near the front door (for obvious reasons). Areas that share a side are approximately 15 feet apart, while those that share a corner are 25 feet apart. The distances between A and E and between B and F are 30 feet, while the distances between A and F and between B and E are approximately 40 feet.

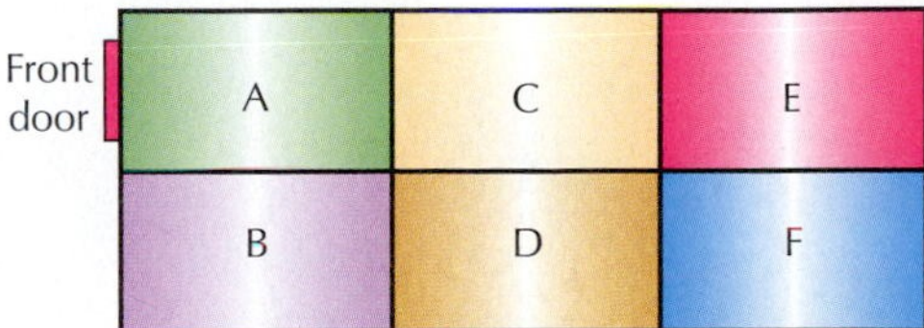

Dr. Douvas also has estimates of the number of trips made by patients and staff between the various departments each day:

	WAITING	RECEPTION	RECORDS/ LOUNGE	EXAMINATION	OUTPATIENT SURGERY	PHYSICAL THERAPY
Waiting	—					
Reception	100	—				
Records/Lounge	0	150	—			
Examination	35	5	10	—		
Outpatient Surgery	15	5	10	5	—	
Physical Therapy	50	10	15	40	0	

a. (**) Given that Dr. Douvas wants Reception assigned to area A, how many possible arrangements are there?

b. (**) Generate the best solution you can, given the information just noted. Calculate the total distance traveled for your solution.

c. (***) Now select two departments to switch (except Reception). By carefully choosing two, can you come up with a better solution? Justify your answer.

10. (***) Omega Design is moving into an old Victorian building with a very unusual floor layout:

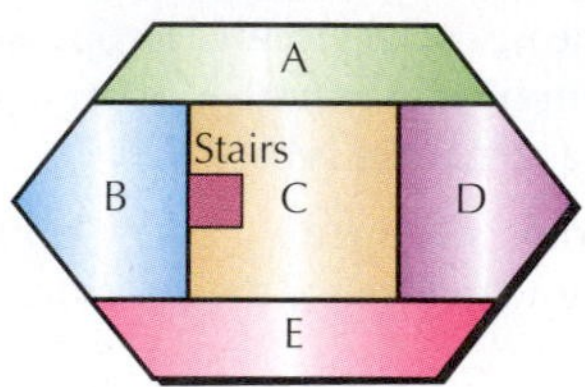

Distances in meters between the areas are as follows:

AREA	A	B	C	D	E
A	—				
B	14	—			
C	8	8	—		
D	14	20	8	—	
E	18	14	8	14	—

and the number of daily interdepartmental trips are as follows:

DEPARTMENT	1	2	3	4	5	6
1	—					
2	23	—				
3	24	52	—			
4	13	5	17	—		
5	21	56	28	25	—	
6	60	15	57	3	42	—

Use the "minimal distance traveled" logic to develop a potential layout for Omega. What other information—including qualitative factors—might you want to know when developing your solution?

11. (**) Consider the process map shown in Figure 3.20 (Chapter 3) for Biosphere Products. In the language of service blueprinting, how many of the process steps represent onstage actions? Backstage actions? Support processes? What information would you need to know to complete a service blueprint that included customer actions?

12. (**) Consider the process steps that occur when you order a video from netflix.com. Where do you interact with Netflix? What other service providers do you interact with? What backstage actions must take place to get the videos to you? Do you ever interact directly with a person?

CASE STUDY

Manufacturing and Service Processes: Loganville Window Treatments

Introduction

For nearly 50 years, Loganville Window Treatments (LWT) of Loganville, Georgia, has made interior shutters that are sold through decorating centers. Figure 7.20 shows some of the various styles of shutters made by LWT.

Past Manufacturing and Service Operations: 2004

Traditionally LWT supported a limited mix of standard products. At any particular point in time, the mix of products might consist of six different styles offered in five predetermined sizes, resulting in 30 possible end products. LWT would produce each of these end products in batches of 500 to 1000 (depending on how popular each style/size combination was) and hold the finished products in the plant warehouse. When a decorating center called in with an order, LWT would either meet the order from the finished goods inventory or hold the order to be shipped when the next batch was finished.

LWT's products were sold through independent decorating centers located across the United States and Canada. LWT would send each of these decorating centers a copy of its catalog, and the decorating centers would use these catalogs to market LWT's products to potential customers. It was the responsibility of the decorating centers to work with customers to price out the shutters, make sure the correct size and style were ordered from LWT, and resolve any problems. As a result, LWT almost never dealt directly with the final customers.

Manufacturing and Service Operations: 2005

By 2004, the influx of low-cost shutters made in China had forced LWT to reconsider its business model. Specifically, because of the low labor costs in China (1/15 of LWT's labor costs), Chinese manufacturers could make exact copies of LWT's products for substantially less and hold them in warehouses across the United States and Canada. LWT's traditional customers—the decorating centers—were turning more and more to these alternative sources.

LWT decided to fight back. As Chuck Keown, president of LWT, put it, "The only permanent advantage that we have over our Chinese competitors is that we are located here in the United States, closer to the final customer. So from now on, we will be a make-to-order manufacturer. We will deal directly with customers and make shutters to whatever specific measurements and finish they need. This means we can no longer count on producing batches of 500 to 1000 shutters at a time and holding them in inventory. Rather, we will need to be able to make a few at a time in one-off sizes, if that's what the customer needs.

"On the service and marketing side of the house, we will now take orders directly from the customer. We will reach them through the Internet and through catalogs. We will work with them to determine what style best suits their needs, and to take the measurements needed to make the shutters. When there is a problem, we will work directly with the customer to resolve them.

"Yes, this will require dramatic changes to our business. But it also means we will be able to charge a premium for our products and create a relationship with the customers that our Chinese rivals will find difficult to emulate. As I see it, this is the only way we can survive."

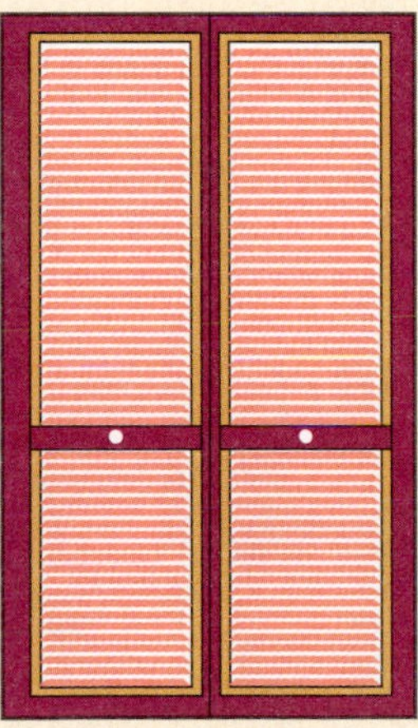

FIGURE 7.20 Sample Products Made by LWT

QUESTIONS

1. As of 2004, what type of manufacturing process did LWT appear to be using? What level of customization was it offering? *Where* was the point of customization?
2. Using Table 7.2 and Figure 7.12 as guides, how would you describe the service side of LWT's business prior to 2005? What were the managerial challenges?
3. What type of manufacturing process is needed to support the changes proposed by Chuck Keown? What level of customization will LWT be offering? *Where* will the point of customization be?
4. Using Table 7.2 and Figure 7.12 as guides, how will the service side of the house change for 2005? What will the *new* managerial challenges be?
5. Develop a list of 8 to 10 things that must happen in order to accomplish the changes Chuck Keown envisions. Will the new business model be more or less difficult to manage than the old one? Justify your answer.

REFERENCES

Books and Articles

Bitner, M. J. "Managing the Evidence of Service," in *The Service Quarterly Handbook*, eds. E. E. Scheuing and W. F. Christopher. New York: AMACOM, 1993.

Cox, J. F., and J. H. Blackstone, eds. *APICS Dictionary*, 10th ed. Falls Church, VA: APICS, 2002.

Hayes, R., and S. Wheelwright. *Restoring Our Competitive Edge: Competing through Manufacturing*. New York: John Wiley and Sons, 1984.

Hill, T. *Manufacturing Strategy: Text and Cases*. Homewood, IL: Irwin, 1994.

Magretta, J. "The Power of Virtual Integration: An Interview with Dell Computer's Michael Dell." *Harvard Business Review* 76, no. 2 (March–April 1998): 73–84.

Pine II, B. J. *Mass Customization: The New Frontier in Business Competition*. Boston Harvard Business School Press, 1993.

Schmenner, R. "How Can Service Businesses Survive and Prosper?" *Sloan Management Review* 27, no. 3 (Spring 1986): 21–32.

Schmenner, R., and M. Swink. "On Theory in Operations Management." *Journal of Operations Management* 17, no. 1 (1998): 97–113.

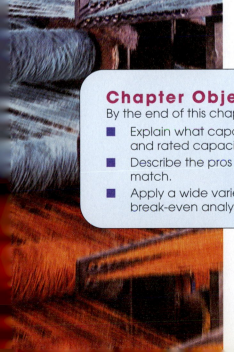

CHAPTER 8

Managing Capacity

CHAPTER OUTLINE

Chapter Objectives

By the end of this chapter, you will be able to:

- Explain what capacity is, how firms measure capacity, and the difference between theoretical and rated capacity.
- Describe the pros and cons associated with three different capacity strategies: lead, lag, and match.
- Apply a wide variety of analytical tools to capacity decisions, including expected value and break-even analysis, decision trees, waiting line theory, and learning curves.

MERCK AND CRIXIVAN[1]

A few years back Merck launched a new AIDS-fighting drug called Crixivan. The following is an excerpt from a *Wall Street Journal* article at the time, highlighting some of the key capacity issues Merck faced.

> *Merck & Co. has spent more than $1 billion over the past decade to create Crixivan, one of the most promising drugs ever to attack AIDS. . . . There is just one problem: The company has been struggling for months to keep ahead of demand. . . . About 90,000 patients world-wide are already on the drug, but there is only enough supply for about 110,000. If too many patients started on the drug, they might find their pharmacies out when they went for refills. Patients who stop taking the drug even for a short time risk developing resistance to it. . . .*
>
> *Merck created some of its own problems. In the face of a world-wide abundance of production capacity, it chose to build its own plants rather than contract out more of the work to outside suppliers. And upon learning that two rivals might beat it to market with similar therapies, Merck requested and got approval of Crixivan—the most complex drug it has ever tried to mass-produce—well before its plants were ready. . . .*
>
> *Merck began testing Crixivan in humans in early 1993, and that summer—long before even knowing whether the drug would work—top scientists met for lunch in the company cafeteria to chart how to mass-produce it. . . . In late 1993, [a development] team began using a prototype production line at a plant in Rahway, NJ, which was able to turn out bigger batches but took up to four months to do it. . . . By September 1995, competitive pressures were intensifying. . . . Under its original timetable Merck was still a year away from launching Crixivan. But it was hell-bent on getting to market at the same time as its competitors. So its top researchers waged a pitched lobbying campaign to have Crixivan considered alongside [a competitor's] drug at a coming meeting of an FDA advisory panel. . . .*
>
> *Meantime, as Merck churned out small quantities of the drug at its prototype plant, construction proceeded at a furious pace at the 45,000-square-foot main plant in Elkton and the satellite in Albany. Finally on May 27, 1996, the big operation was ready. The first Crixivan batch entered the system at 9:30 A.M. For six weeks, Merck engineers and chemists crossed their fingers as 30,000 gallons of liquid trickled through 20 miles of pipes, vats, dryers, pressers and capsule- and bottle-fillers. On July 5, the last of the batch's white capsules were in boxes, ready for shipment. . . .*
>
> *Slowly more Crixivan "runs" are going on-line; the plants will eventually handle 18 batches at once, each lot producing two million capsules. The question now is whether Merck will get the operation up to full-scale production before demand can overtake it. . . . "It wasn't humanly possible to be ahead of where we are, given the history of the project," Dr. Scolnick, head of research and manufacturing, says. But he vows: "Merck isn't going to run out of this drug."*

Though Merck's effort to develop Crixivan and bring it to market is unusual, it does highlight some of the critical issues companies face when making capacity decisions. If Merck developed too much production capacity, the company could lose millions of dollars on idle facilities. On the other hand, with too little capacity, patients could die.

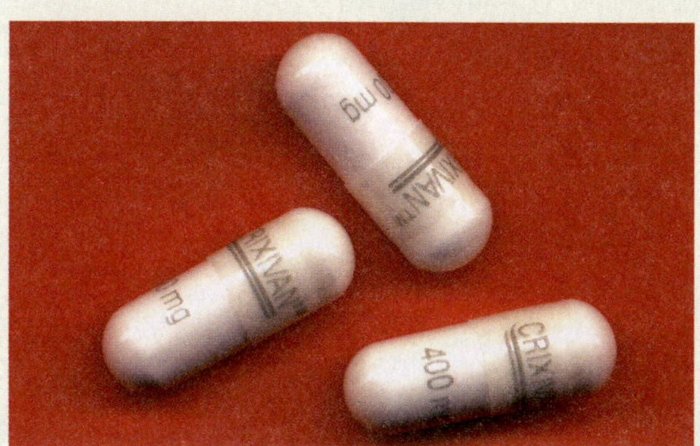

[1]Excerpted from E. Tanouye, "Short Supply: Success of AIDS Drug Has Merck Fighting to Keep Up the Pace," *The Wall Street Journal*, November 5, 1996.

INTRODUCTION

Some of the most important strategic decisions managers face revolve around capacity. *How much* capacity do we need? *When* do we need it? *What form* should the capacity take? This chapter starts with a discussion of capacity and then introduces several tools that managers use to evaluate capacity choices, including break-even analysis and expected value analysis. The last half of the chapter deals with advanced perspectives on capacity, such as the Theory of Constraints (TOC), waiting line theory, and learning curves. As you go through this chapter, keep in mind the following points:

- Capacity can take many different forms, and capacity planning is an important activity in both service and manufacturing organizations.
- Though there are many quantitative tools to help managers make informed capacity decisions, there is some degree of risk inherent in nearly all such decisions.

With that background, let's dive in.

8.1 CAPACITY

Capacity
The capability of a worker, machine, work center, plant, or organization to produce output per time period.

Simply put, **capacity** is the capability of a worker, machine, work center, plant, or organization to produce output per time period.[2] As the definition suggests, there are many forms of capacity in an organization. Operations and supply chain managers must make decisions regarding how much capacity their organizations need and which types. In making these decisions, managers must consider several issues:

- How capacity is measured;
- Which factors affect capacity; and
- The impact of the supply chain on the organization's effective capacity.

Measures of Capacity

Managers are constantly evaluating whether or not their organizations' resources are adequate to meet current or future demands. To do so, they need measures of capacity. Such measurements vary widely. In general, though, companies measure capacity in terms of inputs, outputs, or some combination of the two. The manager of a textile plant that makes thread from raw cotton might express its capacity in terms of the number of spinning hours available each month or the number of square feet of available warehouse space (both of which are inputs) or in terms of the number of finished pounds it can produce in a single period (an output). Similarly, a software development firm might measure capacity based on the number of programmers (an input) or lines of code written (an output).

In organizations that provide standard products or services, capacity is likely to be expressed in terms of outputs because the output doesn't change radically from one period to the next. In organizations that provide customized services or products, capacity is more likely to be expressed in terms of inputs. That is why the managing partners in a consulting firm are more likely to think in terms of available consultant hours (an input) than of projects completed over a certain period. Table 8.1 shows the capacity measures used in a variety of business settings. Note which measures express capacity in terms of inputs and which express it in terms of output. Note, too, that many of the measures have a time element—spinning hours *per shift*, units *per day*.

[2]J. F. Cox and J. H. Blackstone, eds., *APICS Dictionary*, 10th ed. (Falls Church, VA: APICS, 2002).

TABLE 8.1
Examples of Capacity in Different Organizations

ORGANIZATION	CAPACITY MEASURE	FACTORS AFFECTING CAPACITY
Law firm	Billable hours available each month	Number of lawyers and paralegals; education and skill levels; supporting software
Textile-spinning plant	Spinning hours per shift; number of spindles produced per week	Number of machines running; quality of raw materials; maintenance
Automatic car wash	Cars per hour	Availability of water and chemicals; reliability of the car wash (Is it frequently down for repairs?)
Airline	(Seats) × (miles flown)	Number of jets, pilots, terminals

Theoretical capacity
The maximum output capability, allowing for no adjustments for preventive maintenance, unplanned downtime, or the like.

Rated capacity
The long-term, expected output capability of a resource or system.

Organizations also differentiate between theoretical capacity and rated capacity. **Theoretical capacity** is the maximum output capability, allowing no adjustments for preventive maintenance, unplanned downtime, or the like, whereas **rated capacity** represents the long-term, expected output capability of a resource or system.[3] Managers understand that work levels must sometimes exceed levels that are typical, or even desirable, over the long haul. High-tech manufacturers often experience a big surge in demand during the fourth quarter of the year, as customers seek to use up their budgets. For example, a salmon-processing plant might run 24 hours a day during the peak season. And personnel at an accounting firm might work 18 hours a day the week before April 15. Peak periods such as these are usually short in duration and are often characterized by high levels of overtime and reactive "firefighting" (instead of proactive planning). Yet running at or near the theoretical capacity for a short time is often a better option than increasing resource levels permanently. Good managers know the difference between theoretical capacity and more sustainable rated capacity levels, and they use that knowledge when measuring and planning capacity.

Factors That Affect Capacity

Even in seemingly simple environments, many factors affect capacity, and many assumptions must be made. Take the following formula, which describes capacity for an assembly plant with three assembly lines and a maximum of two 8-hour shifts per day:

$$\text{Capacity} = (800 \text{ units per line per shift})(\text{number of lines})(\text{number of shifts})$$

What is the "capacity" of the plant? It could be as low as 800 units per day (one line, one shift) or as high as 4,800 units per day (three lines, two shifts). The number of shifts or lines active at any time is a controllable factor that managers can use to adjust capacity in response to market demands. Other examples of controllable factors include the number of jets an airline keeps on active status, the number of temporary workers, and even the number of public storage facilities, which companies can add or drop as needed.

Product variations are another source of ambiguity in measuring capacity. Suppose our hypothetical factory can assemble several different models, so that 800 units represents an *average* rated capacity. The actual output can range from 700 to 900 units, depending on the complexity of the model being assembled. If that is the case, capacity can range from 700 to 5,400 units.

Another factor that affects capacity is conformance quality, which we discussed in Chapter 4. In general, poor conformance quality reduces available capacity because employees must spend valuable time and resources resolving quality problems or reworking "defective" products or service outcomes. In contrast, quality improvement can increase an organization's effective capacity by reducing the amount of resources needed to provide a product or service.

---

[3]Ibid.

Supply Chain Considerations

A firm's capacity concerns certainly aren't limited to just *its* activities. In many cases, a firm must also consider the capacities of key suppliers and distributors. Suppose Procter & Gamble (P&G) decides to launch a new line of children's shampoos—the fifth phase in our model of new product development (see Chapter 6). According to the model, P&G will need to fill the downstream supply chain with product. Among other things, P&G managers must make sure that suppliers have adequate capacity to provide the necessary raw materials when they are needed. They also must arrange for adequate trucking, warehousing, and shelf space—all forms of capacity—in order to move the products and display the new line in retail stores.

Raw material availability has become a major problem since 2004. For example, a recent visit to a large equipment manufacturer revealed that the factory was only running on one shift, even though there was a three year backlog of orders waiting for the equipment. Why? The company could not purchase steel forgings at a rate that was capable of keeping workers busy on more than one shift. The point is this: A firm's ability to use its own capacity is often directly dependent on capacity up and down the supply chain. We will revisit this point in our discussion of the Theory of Constraints.

SUPPLY CHAIN CONNECTIONS

SERVERS AS HIGH AS AN ELEPHANT'S EYE[4]

There is an increasing shortage of facilities equipped to massage, transmit, and store the data flowing from the surge in Web-based software and services. You may not give it a thought while firing up a Google search, downloading a song from iTunes, or chatting on the phone via Vonage's Internet service. But all those tasks have to be processed on computers somewhere. And there are only so many places that offer the necessary cheap power and access to big fiber-optic networks that can economically host giant rooms full of them.

As more and more of our digital doings take place via Net-based services rather than on software that resides in our home PCs, it's driving up costs for this most unsexy side of techdom. In the past year owners of commercial hosting centers have been able to increase their prices by 20% or more, say some data center operators.

If more server farms aren't built—and a state-of-the-art data center can cost up to $1,000 a square foot, five times the cost of conventional office space—the squeeze might even crimp the ability of Net up-and-comers to bring new innovations to market. "I'm not seeing what I need to see" in terms of new capacity coming online, says Jay Adelson, the CEO of social networking Web site Digg.com, who also started Equinix Inc., a Foster City (California) company that operates data centers. Digg.com secured space in Equinix facilities, but Adelson asks: "There are hundreds of me out there, and where are we all going to go? There isn't [enough] data center space."

Building new data centers can take more than a year, and they're a lot more complex than their warehouse-like exteriors suggest. They must be outfitted with massive air conditioners to prevent the thousands of packed-in servers from overheating, as well as locomotive-sized generators in case of blackouts. "The power goes down more often than you'd like to think," says Margie Backaus, chief business officer for Equinix. It once lost power when a squirrel bit into a power line.

Data center operators must continually devise new tricks to accommodate the power consumed by today's screaming-fast tech gear. So-called blade servers can be packed into cabinets like books on a shelf. But this configuration generates more heat, increasing demand for energy to run cooling systems. In fact, 50% of a center's monthly energy bill can go for cooling. That's why Equinix is replacing the traditional "raised floor" with cables that run overhead in a raised ceiling, allowing much more room for heat to dissipate. Still, any way you slice it, server farms require lots and lots of power. The Equinix center being built near Chicago will consume 20 megawatts, four times that of a typical data center operating today. DuPont Fabros plans to build a 36-megawatt facility. That's enough power to satisfy a small city. This also explains why the techies are converging in Quincy, Washington. Because of nearby dams, power there costs 1.89 cents per kilowatt-hour, versus more than 15 cents in Silicon Valley or Manhattan.

---

[4]Adapted from Peter Burrows, "Servers as High as an Elephant's Eye," *Business Week* (June 12, 2006).

We end this section by pointing you to the *Supply Chain Connections* feature, which offers an interesting twist on how supply chain capacity is affecting Internet-based businesses. Specifically, many Internet-based companies depend on outside commercial hosting centers to run the "server farms" that handle the bulk of their Internet transactions. But as these commercial hosting centers face difficulties adding capacity, their customers might soon find that their own plans for growth are affected.

8.2 THREE COMMON CAPACITY STRATEGIES

Oftentimes capacity decisions are made to accommodate expected growth in demand or product lines. The question managers must deal with is how quickly to increase capacity. Three common strategies for timing capacity expansions are the lead, lag, and match strategies (see Figure 8.1).

Lead capacity strategy
A capacity strategy in which capacity is added in anticipation of demand.

Using a **lead capacity strategy**, capacity is added in anticipation of demand. This strategy has several advantages. First, it assures that the organization has adequate capacity to meet all demand, even during periods of high growth. This is especially important when the availability of a product or service is crucial, as in the case of emergency care. Another example is a hot new product, like Nintendo's Wii in late 2006. For many new products, being late to market can mean the difference between success and failure.

Another advantage of a lead capacity strategy is that it can be used to preempt competitors who might be planning to expand their own capacity. Being the first in an area to open a large grocery or home improvement store gives a retailer a definite edge. Finally, many businesses find that overbuilding in anticipation of increased usage is cheaper and less disruptive than constantly making small increases in capacity.

Of course, a lead capacity strategy can be very risky, particularly if demand is unpredictable or technology is evolving rapidly. Merck's decision to build full-scale production facilities for Crixivan long before trials of the drug were completed and FDA approval was secured is a prime example. If Crixivan had not proved safe and effective, Merck would have invested millions of dollars in potentially unusable capacity.

Lag capacity strategy
A capacity strategy in which capacity is added only after demand has materialized.

The opposite of a lead capacity strategy is a **lag capacity strategy**, whereby organizations add capacity only *after* demand has materialized. Three clear advantages of this strategy are a reduced risk of overbuilding, greater productivity due to higher utilization levels, and the ability to put off large investments as long as possible. Organizations that follow this strategy often provide mature, cost-sensitive products or services. Many government agencies try to avoid adding extra capacity and their requisite costs until it is absolutely necessary. Yet one can easily imagine the drawbacks of a lag capacity strategy, the most evident being the reduced availability of products or services during periods of high demand.

Most organizations do not follow one strategy. For one thing, different products and services require different approaches. Consider a public hospital. If you are the chief executive officer, you

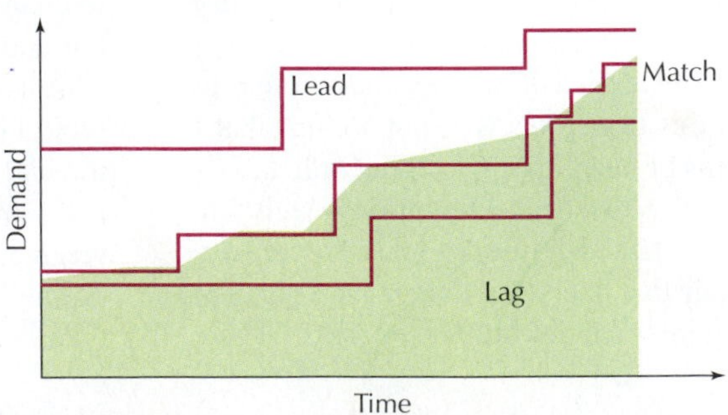

FIGURE 8.1
When to Add Capacity: Lead, Lag, and Match Strategies

Match capacity strategy
A capacity strategy that strikes a balance between the lead and lag capacity strategies by avoiding periods of high under- or overutilization.

Virtual supply chain
A collection of firms that typically exists for only a short period. Virtual supply chains are more flexible than traditional supply chains, but less efficient.

will follow a lead capacity strategy for expanding critical emergency services, especially if yours is the only hospital in the region. You will not apply the same rationale to noncritical services.

A **match capacity strategy** strikes a balance between the lead and lag capacity strategies by avoiding periods of high under- or overutilization. A relatively new concept in capacity planning is the **virtual supply chain**, which is really a collection of firms, each of which does only one or two core activities—design, manufacturing, distribution, marketing, and so on. The firms coordinate their activities by using advanced information systems to share critical data.

Unlike a traditional supply chain, a virtual supply chain might exist for only a short period. The virtual supply chain might be pulled together during the holiday season to produce and market a new toy and then disappear. The members of the virtual supply chain might even change from one week to the next. What virtual supply chains gain in short-term flexibility, however, they lose in long-term efficiency. As a result, traditional supply chains are more likely to prevail in markets in which long-term relationships or costs are critical.

8.3 METHODS OF EVALUATING CAPACITY ALTERNATIVES

An organization usually has many ways to meet its capacity needs. Merck had a choice between building its own facilities and leasing manufacturing capacity from other firms. Airlines debate whether to purchase or lease jets. On the human side, organizations make a choice between full-time employees and temporaries and among different types of skills. An organization might even have to choose between using inventory ("stored" capacity) and using overtime to meet demand during peak seasons. Clearly managers need some help in evaluating these alternatives.

In this section, we discuss several approaches that are useful in evaluating capacity alternatives. They include the concept of fixed versus variable costs, expected value, and break-even analysis. Keep in mind as we describe these approaches that they deal primarily with *financial* considerations—what are the costs and/or revenues associated with a particular capacity option? Nevertheless, they provide a good starting point.

Cost

Fixed costs
The expenses an organization incurs regardless of the level of business activity.

Variable costs
Expenses directly tied to the level of business activity.

To begin, many capacity alternatives have both fixed and variable cost components. **Fixed costs** are the expenses an organization incurs regardless of the level of business activity. Examples include lease payments on equipment, mortgage payments on buildings, and monthly maintenance charges for software. The company must pay these expenses regardless of the number of customers it serves or products it makes. **Variable costs**, on the other hand, are expenses directly tied to the level of business activity. Material costs are a good example. If the fabric cost per pair of jeans is \$2.35, then we can calculate fabric cost as \$2.35 × (number of jeans produced). The general formula for describing the total cost of a capacity alternative is:

$$TC = FC + VC \times X \quad [8\text{-}1]$$

where:

TC = total cost

FC = fixed cost

VC = variable cost per unit of business activity

X = amount of business activity (number of customers served, number of units produced, etc.)

The distinction between fixed and variable costs is important because it shows how the level of business activity affects costs. This kind of information can be critical in choosing between several capacity alternatives.

Example 8.1

Analyzing the Cost of Capacity Alternatives at Ellison Seafood Company

Ellison Seafood Company ships fresh seafood to customers in a nearby city. The logistics manager has identified three shipping alternatives. The first is to call up a common carrier (i.e., a trucking company) each time a shipment is ready to go. This alternative has no fixed cost, but the variable cost per shipment would be about $750. At the other extreme, Ellison Seafood could lease its own refrigerated trucks. The logistics manager has determined that the yearly cost to lease three trucks would be $21,000, including insurance and prepaid maintenance. Because Ellison would have to pay the lease charge regardless of how many shipments were made, the $21,000 would be a fixed expense. On the other hand, the variable cost would drop dramatically to $50 per shipment—just enough to cover the cost of fuel and the driver's wages. Somewhere between these two extremes is the third option: a contractual arrangement with a local carrier. For a yearly fixed charge of $5,000, the local carrier would agree to make all of Ellison's deliveries at a variable cost of just $300 per delivery. Table 8.2 summarizes the three options.

TABLE 8.2 Capacity Alternatives and Costs for Ellison Seafood Company

	COMMON CARRIER	CONTRACT CARRIER	LEASING
Fixed cost	None	$5,000	$21,000
Variable cost	$750	$300	$50

Figure 8.2 shows the total cost (fixed cost + variable cost) of each alternative as the number of shipments increases. By looking at the graph, we can see that the cost of using a common carrier starts out the lowest, but quickly becomes much more expensive than the other two options. As the number of shipments nears 11, using a contract carrier becomes cheaper. The contract carrier remains the cheapest option until the activity level approaches 64 shipments, at which point leasing becomes the cheapest option.

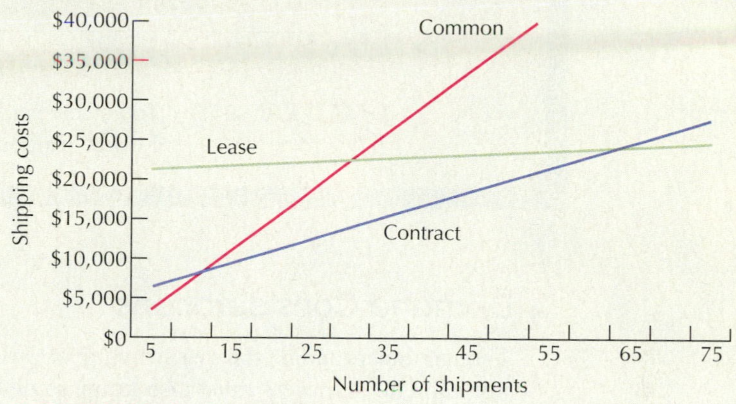

FIGURE 8.2 Total Cost of Three Capacity Alternatives, Ellison Seafood Company

Indifference point
The output level at which two capacity alternatives generate equal costs.

We can find the exact output level at which two capacity alternatives generate equal costs, called the **indifference point**, by setting their two cost functions equal to one another and solving for the number of shipments, X. For instance, the indifference point for the common carrier and contract carrier options would be calculated as follows:

$$\text{Total cost of common carrier option} = \text{total cost of contract carrier option}$$

$$\$0 + \$750X = \$5{,}000 + \$300X$$

$$X = (\$5{,}000 - \$0)/(\$750 - \$300) = 11.11, \text{ or about } \textit{11 shipments}$$

We can use the same logic to find the indifference point for the contract carrier and leasing options:

$$\text{Total cost of contract carrier option} = \text{total cost of leasing}$$

$$\$5{,}000 + \$300X = \$21{,}000 + \$50X$$

$$X = (\$21{,}000 - \$5{,}000)/(\$300 - \$50) = \textit{64 shipments}$$

Figure 8.3 provides a different view of the same three options. In this case, we have plotted the cost *per shipment*, which is calculated by dividing total cost by the number of shipments. Not surprisingly, the cost per shipment for the common carrier option is flat. Notice, however, that as the number of shipments increases, the cost per shipment for the leasing option drops dramatically. This is because the total cost per shipment drops when the fixed cost of $21,000 is spread across more shipments. Finally, note that the cost curves in Figure 8.3 cross at the same levels shown in Figure 8.2—the three indifference points.

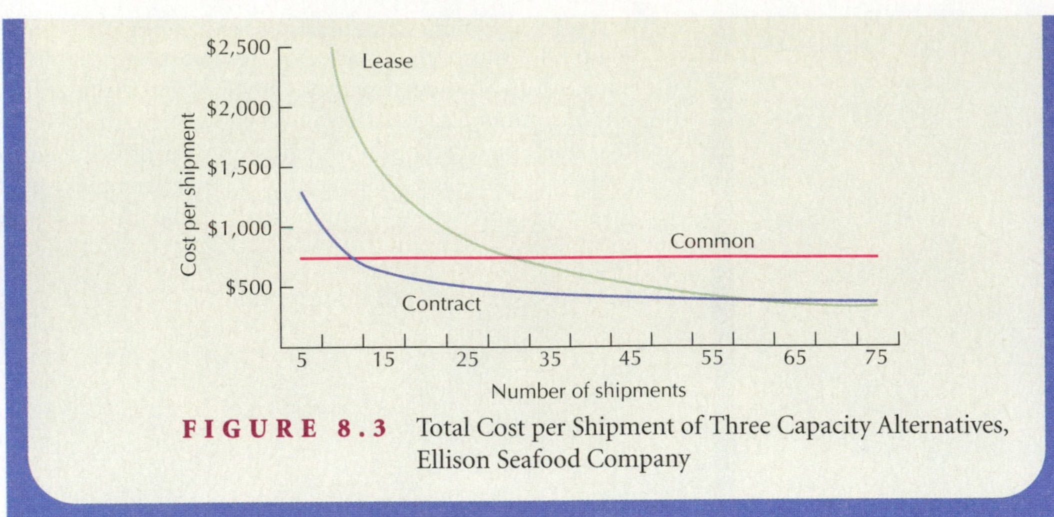

FIGURE 8.3 Total Cost per Shipment of Three Capacity Alternatives, Ellison Seafood Company

Demand Considerations

Though understanding the cost structure of various capacity alternatives is important, it is not enough. Managers must also know something about the expected demand levels. Otherwise, how will they know which capacity alternative will provide the lowest total cost? Table 8.3 makes this point. If Ellison Seafood expects to make 40 shipments per year, the contract carrier option makes the most sense. However, if demand is expected to be as high as 75 shipments per year, leasing is cheaper.

Of course, predicting demand with certainty is rarely easy. In many business situations, it makes more sense to develop *multiple* estimates of demand that capture a range of possibilities, as in Table 8.3. Even so, how should we interpret Table 8.3? Though leasing is the cheapest alternative for a yearly total of 75 shipments, how *likely* is demand to reach that level? Similarly, how likely is the number of shipments to fall in the range in which contracting is cheapest? To tackle this type of problem, managers turn to expected value analysis.

Expected value A calculation that summarizes the expected costs, revenues, or profits of a capacity alternative based on several demand levels, each of which has a different probability.

Expected Value

One way companies evaluate capacity alternatives when demand is uncertain is to use a decision tool called the expected value approach. In a nutshell, **expected value** is a

TABLE 8.3 Total Cost of Three Capacity Alternatives at Different Demand Levels, Ellison Seafood Company

TOTAL COST EQUATION	15 SHIPMENTS (LOW DEMAND)	40 SHIPMENTS (MEDIUM DEMAND)	75 SHIPMENTS (HIGH DEMAND)
Common carrier: $0 + $750*X*	$11,250	$30,000	$56,250
Contract carrier: $5000 + $300*X*	**$9,500**	**$17,000**	$27,500
Leasing: $21,000 + $50*X*	$21,750	$23,000	**$24,750**

calculation that summarizes the expected costs, revenues, or profits of a capacity alternative based on several different demand levels, each of which has a different probability.

The major steps of the expected value approach are as follows:

1. Identify several different demand-level scenarios. These scenarios are not meant to identify all possible outcomes. Rather, the intent is to approximate the *range* of possible outcomes.
2. Assign a probability to each demand-level scenario.
3. Calculate the expected value of each alternative. This is done by multiplying the expected financial result (cost, revenue, or profit) at each demand level by the probability of each demand level and then summing across all levels. The equation is

$$EV_j = \sum_{i=1}^{I} P_i C_i \quad [8\text{-}2]$$

where:

EV_j = expected value of capacity alternative j

P_i = probability of demand level i

C_i = financial result (cost, revenue, or profit) at demand level i

Example 8.2

Expected Value Analysis at Ellison Seafood Company

Suppose Ellison Seafood wants to know the *expected cost* of one of the options, contracting. As a first step, management needs to identify some potential demand scenarios:

Low demand	→	30 shipments per year
Medium demand	→	50 shipments per year
High demand	→	80 shipments per year

Next, management must assign a probability to each. The only stipulation is that the probabilities must sum to 100%.

Low demand	→	30 shipments per year	→	25%
Medium demand	→	50 shipments per year	→	60%
High demand	→	80 shipments per year	→	15%
		Total		100%

Based on Table 8.3, the costs associated with contracting at each demand level are

$$C(\text{low demand}) = \$5{,}000 + \$300(\mathbf{30}) = \$14{,}000$$
$$C(\text{medium demand}) = \$5{,}000 + \$300(\mathbf{50}) = \$20{,}000$$
$$C(\text{high demand}) = \$5{,}000 + \$300(\mathbf{80}) = \$29{,}000$$

And the expected cost of contracting is

$$EV_{Contract} = (14{,}000 \times 25\%) + (\$20{,}000 \times 60\%) + (\$29{,}000 \times 15\%)$$
$$= \$3{,}500 + \$12{,}000 + \$4{,}350 = \$19{,}850$$

Using similar logic, we can calculate the expected costs of using a common carrier or of leasing:

$$EV_{Common} = (\$22,500 \times 25\%) + (\$37,500 \times 60\%) + (\$60,000 \times 15\%)$$
$$= \$37,125$$

$$EV_{Lease} = (\$22,500 \times 25\%) + (\$23,500 \times 60\%) + (\$25,000 \times 15\%)$$
$$= \$23,475$$

The analysis suggests that, on average, the contracting option has the lowest expected costs at $19,850. Intuitively, this result seems consistent with Figures 8.2 and 8.3, which show that the contracting option is cheapest for a fairly wide range of shipping levels.

Decision Trees

Decision tree
A visual tool that decision makers use to evaluate capacity decisions. The main advantage of a decision tree is that the users can see the interrelationships between decisions and possible outcomes.

A **decision tree** is a visual tool that decision makers use to evaluate capacity decisions. The main advantage of a decision tree is that the users can see the interrelationships between decisions and possible outcomes. Decision trees are particularly good at helping users visualize a complex *series* of decisions and outcomes.

The basic rules for using decision trees are as follows:

1. Draw the tree from left to right, starting with a decision point or outcome point, and develop branches from there.
2. Each *decision point* is represented by a square, with the different branches coming out of the square representing alternative choices.
3. *Outcome points* (which are beyond the control of the decision maker) are represented by circles. Each possible outcome is represented by a branch off of the circle. Each branch is assigned a probability, indicating the possibility of that outcome, and the total probability for all branches coming out of an outcome point must equal 100%.
4. For expected value problems, calculate the financial result for each of the smaller branches, and move backward by calculating weighted averages for the branches, based on their probabilities.

Example 8.3

Decision Trees at Ellison Seafood Company

Figure 8.4 shows a decision tree for the transportation decision facing Ellison Seafood (Example 8.2). Reading from left to right, the tree starts with the selection of one of the three transportation options. Once the transportation decision is made, there are three possible demand outcomes: 30 shipments, 50 shipments, and 80 shipments, each with different probabilities. Because the actual demand is an outcome and not a decision, a circle is used to represent these branch points.

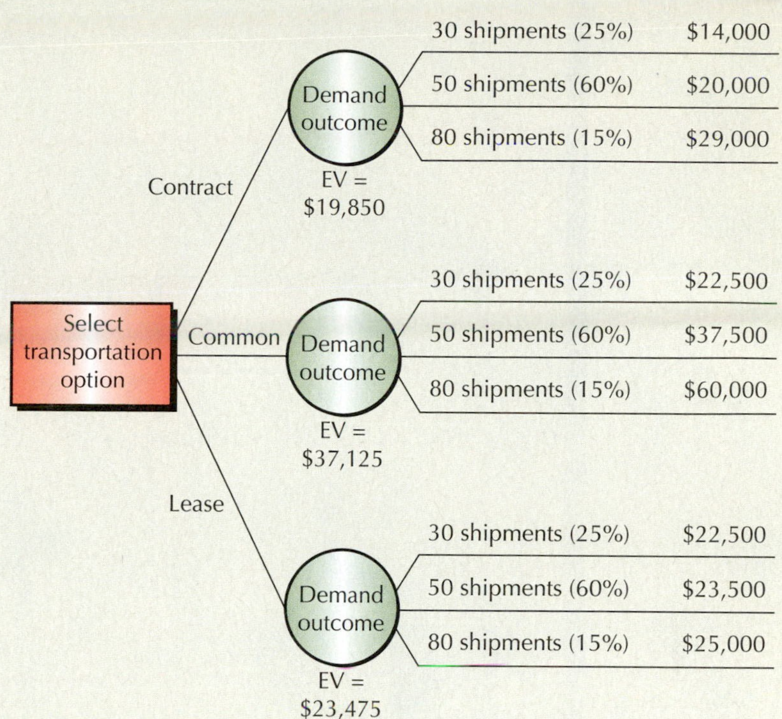

FIGURE 8.4 Decision Tree for Transportation Ellison Seafood Company

The combination of three different transportation options and three demand scenarios results in 3 × 3 = 9 branches, each of which has a resulting cost. Finally, the expected value of each decision branch is calculated as the weighted average of the possible demand outcome branches. Note that the numbers in Figure 8.4 match those in Example 8.2.

Now suppose that a potential new customer, Straley Grocers, has approached Ellison Seafood. Straley wants Ellison to sign a contract promising 30 deliveries a year. These deliveries would be *in addition to* Ellison's normal business. Ellison management would like to develop a decision tree to understand how the Straley contract might affect the transportation decision.

Figure 8.5 shows the updated decision tree. Ellison *first* has to make a decision about whether or not to accept the Straley contract, and, based on that decision, it has to select a transportation option. The added decision point effectively doubles the size of the tree.

Note how the demand levels and resulting costs for each demand outcome branch in the lower half have been updated to show the impact of the additional 30 shipments. Looking at the tree, it becomes clear that if Ellison decides *not* to accept the Straley contract, the lowest expected cost is to go with the contract carrier (this is the same result as in Example 8.2). But if Ellison *does* accept the contract, then the lowest expected cost is to lease a truck.

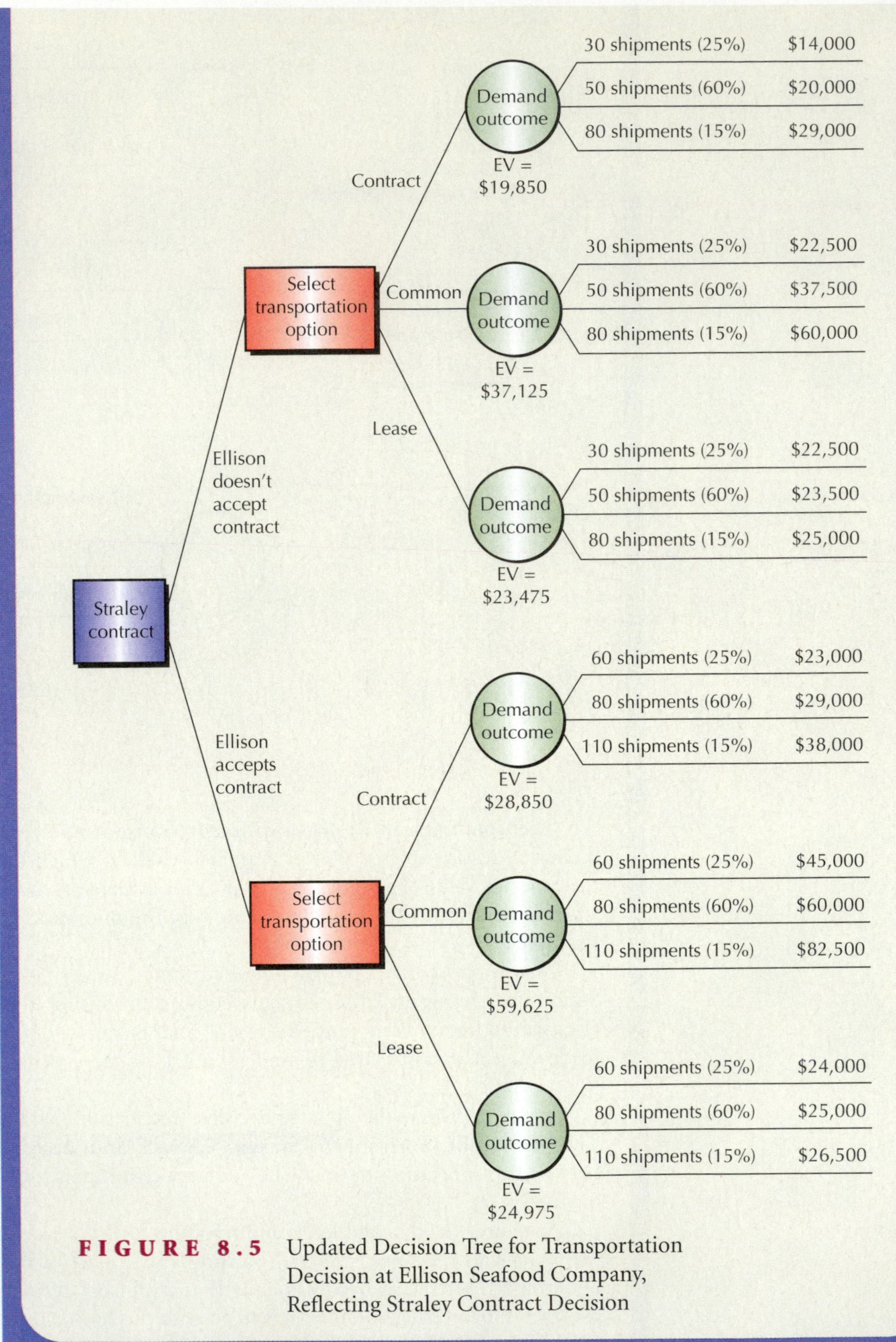

FIGURE 8.5 Updated Decision Tree for Transportation Decision at Ellison Seafood Company, Reflecting Straley Contract Decision

Break-Even Analysis

Break-even point
The volume level for a business at which total revenues cover total costs.

When the focus is on profitability, a key question managers often face is "At what volume level do total revenues cover total costs?" This volume level is referred to as the **break-even point**. Managers are very interested in knowing what the break-even point is because once business volume passes the break-even point, the company begins to make money.

The formula for the break-even point is:

$$BEP = \frac{FC}{R - VC} \quad [8\text{-}3]$$

where:

BEP = break-even point
FC = fixed cost
VC = variable cost per unit of business activity
R = revenue per unit of business activity

Example 8.4
Break-Even Analysis at Ellison Seafood Company

Ellison makes a $1,000 profit on each shipment *before* transportation costs are considered. What is the break-even point for each shipping option?

For the common carrier option:

$$BEP = \frac{FC}{R - VC}$$

$$BEP = \$0/\$250, \text{ or } 0 \textit{ shipments}$$

For the contracting option:

$$BEP = \$5{,}000/\$700 = 7.1, \text{ or rounding up, } 8 \textit{ shipments}$$

And for the leasing option:

$$\$21{,}000 + \$50X = \$1{,}000X$$

$$BEP = \$21{,}000/\$950 = 22.1, \text{ or rounding up, } 23 \textit{ shipments}$$

The common carrier option has the lowest break-even point, which arguably makes it the least risky option. However, Ellison Seafood will clear only ($1,000 − $750) = $250 on each shipment. On the other hand, the leasing option has a break-even point of 23 shipments, yet each additional shipment beyond 23 contributes ($1,000 − $50) = $950 to the bottom line. In choosing the appropriate shipping option, Ellison Seafood must carefully consider the risks as well as the expected demand levels.

Other Considerations

Not all capacity problems can be solved using the quantitative models just described. Other considerations that will affect a firm's choice include:

- The strategic importance of an activity to the firm;
- The desired degree of managerial control; and
- The need for flexibility.

These considerations are usually relevant to the choice between developing internal capacity and outsourcing, a topic we consider in more depth in Chapter 10.

The more strategically important an activity is to a firm, the more likely the firm is to develop the internal capacity to perform the activity. Strategic activities are often called core activities because they are a major source of competitive advantage. Product design at Nortel, a provider of telecommunications equipment, is one example. Nortel spends millions of dollars each year to develop the internal capacity needed to design innovative products. Engineers, designers, equipment, and facilities are crucial to this strategic activity. But while Nortel does not want to depend on outside sources for new technologies or product ideas, the firm's managers will outsource nonstrategic manufacturing activities. For instance, Nortel depends on Flextronics, a contract manufacturer, to assemble many of its products.

Managerial control is another issue in the choice between internal and external capacity. Whenever a firm outsources an activity, it loses some control over it. Consider Nortel's relationship with Flextronics. No doubt Nortel and Flextronics have a contract that establishes expected quality levels, volume levels, delivery times, and cost targets. However, Nortel's managers cannot just pick up the phone and tell Flextronics to stop assembling another firm's products in order to make room for a new Nortel product. Nortel managers lose some control by outsourcing the company's assembly capacity.

The flip side of this is flexibility. A firm might favor the capacity alternative that requires the least commitment on its part, especially if long-term needs are uncertain. Returning to Ellison Seafood, while the common carrier option becomes quite expensive as the number of shipments increases, it is also the most flexible option. Ellison can decide to stop making shipments at any time and will not pay another dime for trucking.

8.4 ADVANCED PERSPECTIVES ON CAPACITY

We now turn our attention to some advanced perspectives on capacity. The Theory of Constraints (TOC) considers how capacity should be managed when products or services flow along a chain of processes. Waiting line theory makes several key points about the interrelationship between capacity levels and waiting line performance. This is especially important in environments where customers are exposed to potentially long waiting times. Finally, learning curves show how effective capacity can increase over time, even though the actual level of resources doesn't change.

Theory of Constraints (TOC)
An approach to visualizing and managing capacity that recognizes that nearly all products and services are created through a series of linked processes, and in every case, there is at least one process step that limits throughput for the entire chain.

Constraint
The process step (or steps) that limits throughput for an entire process chain.

The Theory of Constraints (TOC)

In recent years, a fundamentally different approach to visualizing and managing capacity has emerged. Developed by Eliyahu Goldratt, the **Theory of Constraints (TOC)** is based on the recognition that nearly all products and services are created through a series of linked processes.[4] These process chains can be contained within a single organization or stretched across multiple organizations (i.e., a supply chain). Each process step has a specific capacity to produce output or take in input (as is the case with customers), and in every case, there is at least one process step that limits throughput for the entire chain. This process step is referred to as the **constraint**. Consider Figure 8.6.

FIGURE 8.6
Throughput of a "Pipeline" Is Determined by the Smallest "Pipe"

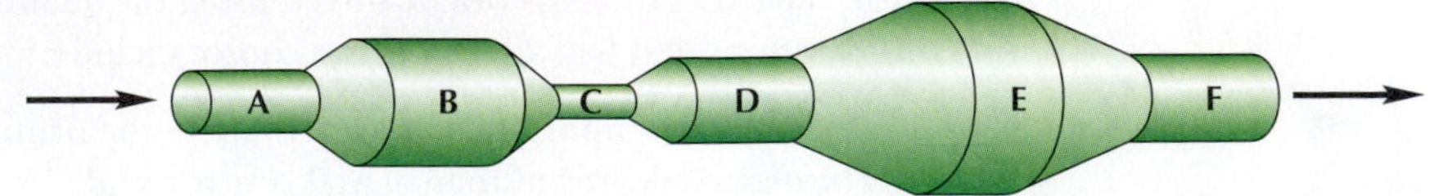

[4]E. Goldratt, *The Goal*, 2nd ed. (Great Barrington, MA: North River Press, 1992).

FIGURE 8.7
Throughput Is Controlled by the Constraint, Process 3

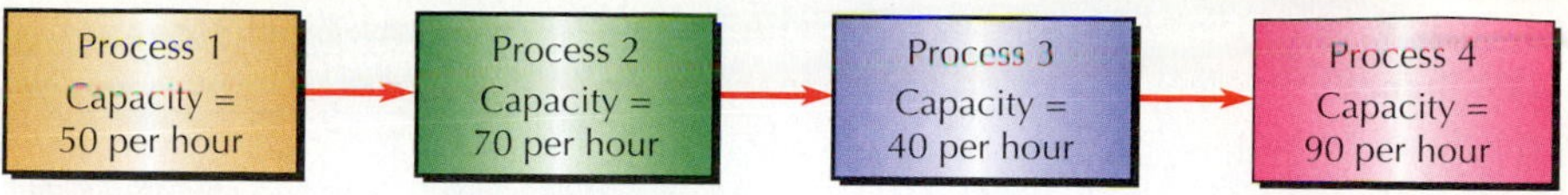

The movement of goods through a process chain is very much like the movement of liquid through a pipeline. Each process step has a certain capacity, analogous to the diameter of a "pipe." In Figure 8.6, process E has the largest capacity, while process C has the smallest capacity. Because process C is the constraint, it will limit the amount of throughput for the entire process chain. Increasing the capacity at any other process step will not increase throughput for the entire process chain.

Figure 8.7 provides a numerical example. It should be clear from this simple illustration that process 3 limits total throughput for the chain to 40 units per hour. Pushing out more than 40 units an hour in processes 1 and 2 will simply create a glut of inventory in front of process 3. Furthermore, output from process 3 will limit process 4 to just 40 units per hour.

TOC experts have suggested a five-step approach to improving the overall throughput of a process chain:

1. **Identify the constraint.** The constraint can be anywhere in the chain—including the customer. Consider Figure 8.7. Suppose customers are buying products at the rate of only 30 per hour. In this case, demand is the constraint and not process 3.
2. **Exploit the constraint.** An hour of throughput lost at the constraint is an hour of throughput lost for the entire chain. It is therefore imperative that organizations carefully manage the constraint to ensure an uninterrupted flow of product.
3. **Subordinate everything to the constraint.** Effective utilization of the constraint is the most important issue. Everything else is secondary.
4. **Elevate the constraint.** Essentially this means to find ways to increase the capacity of the constraint.
5. **Find the new constraint and repeat the steps.** As the effective capacity of the constraint is increased, it may cease to be a constraint. In that case, the emphasis should shift to finding and exploiting the new constraint.

Waiting Line Theory

If you have ever sat in an emergency room waiting for a doctor, you have experienced firsthand the relationship between capacity and waiting lines. Waiting lines are a concern for manufacturers as well. Furniture manufacturers traditionally made customers wait 10 or more weeks for their furniture to be delivered. Even though it was the furniture that actually waited to be made, it was the customer who felt the impact.

The purpose here is twofold. First, we want to highlight the relationship between capacity and waiting lines. Second, we want to introduce you to some common tools that can be used to analyze waiting line performance. To illustrate the relationship between waiting lines and capacity, let's consider an environment we are all familiar with—the drive-up window at a fast-food restaurant. In the language of waiting lines, the drive-up window represents a *single-channel, single-phase system* (Figure 8.8). There is a single channel, or path, through the system. The "single phase" is at the drive-up window, where the employee takes your money and gives you your food.

FIGURE 8.8
Single-Channel, Single-Phase System

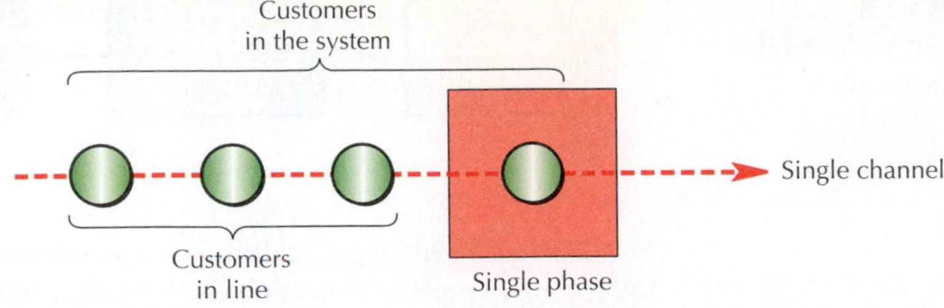

If you have ever sat in line at a drive-up window, you may have thought about (or maybe cursed) the system's performance. Managers have the very same concerns. Some of the specific questions that managers have include the following:

- *What percentage* of the time will the server be busy?
- On average, *how long* will a customer have to wait in line? How long will the customer be in the system (waiting and being served)?
- On average, *how many* customers will be in line?
- *How* will these averages be affected by the arrival rate of customers and the service rate of the drive-up window personnel?

Waiting line theory
A body of theory based on applied statistics that helps managers evaluate the relationship between capacity decisions and such important performance issues as waiting times and line lengths.

Fortunately, researchers have developed a body of theory based on applied statistics to address these types of questions. **Waiting line theory** helps managers evaluate the relationship between capacity decisions and such important performance issues as waiting times and line lengths.

Following are some of the key assumptions and terminology that make up waiting line theory and some basic formulas for determining waiting line performance for a single-channel, single-phase system. We should point out right now that there are many different waiting line environments, most of which are much more complex than the example we will present. In some cases, no formulas exist for estimating waiting line per-

Long wait times can dramatically affect customers' perceptions of service performance. As a result, many service firms use waiting line theory to understand how capacity decisions affect waiting times.

formance. When this occurs, more sophisticated simulation modeling techniques are needed to analyze the systems. The supplement at the end of this chapter discusses simulation modeling in more detail.

ARRIVALS. In most waiting line models, customers are assumed to arrive at random intervals, based on a Poisson distribution. The probability of n arrivals in T time periods is calculated as follows:

$$P_n = \frac{(\lambda T)^n}{n!} e^{-\lambda T} \qquad \textbf{[8-4]}$$

where:

P_n = probability of n arrivals in T time periods

λ = arrival rate

T = number of time periods

Example 8.5

Arrivals at a Drive-Up Window

Customers arrive at the drive-up window at the rate of three per minute ($\lambda = 3$). If the number of arrivals follows a Poisson distribution, what is the probability that two or fewer customers would arrive in one minute?

The probability of two or fewer customers is actually the probability of no arrivals *plus* the probability of one arrival *plus* the probability of two arrivals, or

$$P(\leq 2) = P(0) + P(1) + P(2)$$

$$= 0.050 + 0.149 + 0.224 = 0.423, \text{ or } 42.3\%$$

SERVICE TIMES. Similarly, waiting line models assume that service times will either be constant (a rare occurrence) or vary. Service times often vary because customers require somewhat different services, or because the servers vary in how they perform the tasks involved. In the latter case, modelers often use the exponential distribution to model service times, using the symbol μ to refer to the service rate.

Priority rules
Rules for determining which customer, job, or product is processed next in a waiting line environment.

OTHER ASSUMPTIONS. Finally, we need to make some assumptions about the order in which customers are served, the size of the customer population, and whether or not customers can balk or renege. We will assume that customers are served on a first-come, first-served (FCFS) basis. Other **priority rules** might consider the urgency of the customers' needs (as in an emergency room), the speed with which customers can be served, or even the desirability of different customer types. In addition, we will assume that the population of customers is effectively infinite; that is, we are not likely to run through all the possible customers any time soon. This assumption seems reasonable for a fast-food restaurant next to a busy highway. On the other hand, different formulas are needed if the population is substantially restricted.

We will also assume that customers enter the system and remain there until they are served, regardless of the length of the line or the time spent waiting. They neither balk (decide against entering the system to begin with) nor renege (leave the line after entering).

With that background, we can now apply some basic formulas. Suppose that customers arrive at the rate of four per minute ($\lambda = 4$) and that the worker at the drive-up window is able to handle, on average, five customers a minute ($\mu = 5$). The average utilization of the system is:

$$\rho = \frac{\lambda}{\mu} \qquad [8\text{-}5]$$

where:

ρ = average utilization of the system
λ = arrival rate
μ = service rate

which for the drive-up example = 4/5, or 80%.

"Great!" you say. "It looks like we have plenty of capacity. After all, the drive-up window is not being fully utilized." But there is a catch. Because the actual number of arrivals per minute and the service rate both vary, there can be periods of time where there is no one in line, but other times when significant queues develop. For instance, the drive-up window may go for two minutes without a customer, only to have four SUVs filled with screaming kids pull up at the same time.

In fact, according to waiting line theory, the *average number of customers waiting* (C_W) at the drive-up window can be calculated using the following formula:

$$C_W = \frac{\lambda^2}{\mu(\mu - \lambda)} \qquad [8\text{-}6]$$

And the *average number of customers in the system* (C_S) is

$$C_S = \frac{\lambda}{\mu - \lambda} \qquad [8\text{-}7]$$

Example 8.6

Average Number of Customers Waiting and in the System at a Drive-Up Window

Given an arrival rate of four customers per minute and a service rate of five customers per minute, the average number of customers waiting is

$$C_W = \frac{\lambda^2}{\mu(\mu - \lambda)} = \frac{16}{5(1)} = 3.2 \text{ customers}$$

And the average number of customers in the system is

$$C_S = \frac{\lambda}{\mu - \lambda} = \frac{4}{1} = 4 \text{ customers}$$

But what about the average amount of *time* customers spend waiting and in the system? There are formulas to estimate these values as well:

$$\text{Average time spent waiting} = T_W = \frac{\lambda}{\mu(\mu - \lambda)} \qquad [8\text{-}8]$$

$$\text{Average time spent in the system} = T_S = \frac{1}{\mu - \lambda} \qquad [8\text{-}9]$$

Example 8.7

Average Time a Customer Spends Waiting and in the System at a Drive-Up Window

Returning to the drive-up example, the average time spent waiting is

$$T_W = \frac{\lambda}{\mu(\mu-\lambda)} = \frac{4}{5(1)} = 0.80 \text{ minutes, or 48 seconds}$$

And the average time spent in the system (waiting and being served) is

$$T_S = \frac{1}{\mu-\lambda} = \frac{1}{1} = 1 \text{ minute}$$

The results in Examples 8.5 through 8.7 may not surprise you, but look at what happens as the arrival rate approaches the service rate (Table 8.4). *Even though the utilization level never reaches 100%*, the lines and waiting times get longer and longer—in fact, they grow exponentially. Note that the formulas don't even work for arrival rates greater than or equal to the service rate. This is because, under such conditions, the systems can never reach a steady state, or "average" level.

TABLE 8.4
Waiting Line Performance (service rate = 5 customers per minute)

ARRIVAL RATE (CUSTOMERS PER MINUTE)	AVERAGE UTILIZATION OF THE SYSTEM (ρ)	AVERAGE NUMBER OF CUSTOMERS WAITING (C_W)	AVERAGE TIME SPENT WAITING (MINUTES) (T_W)
3.0	60.0%	0.90	0.30
3.1	62.0%	1.01	0.33
3.2	64.0%	1.14	0.36
3.3	66.0%	1.28	0.39
3.4	68.0%	1.45	0.43
3.5	70.0%	1.63	0.47
3.6	72.0%	1.85	0.51
3.7	74.0%	2.11	0.57
3.8	76.0%	2.41	0.63
3.9	78.0%	2.77	0.71
4.0	80.0%	**3.20**	**0.80**
4.1	82.0%	3.74	0.91
4.2	84.0%	4.41	1.05
4.3	86.0%	5.28	1.23
4.4	88.0%	6.45	1.47
4.5	90.0%	8.10	1.80
4.6	92.0%	10.58	2.30
4.7	94.0%	14.73	3.13
4.8	96.0%	23.04	4.80
4.9	98.0%	48.02	9.80
4.95	99.0%	98.01	19.80
4.995	99.9%	998.00	199.80

The previous example points out an important general truth:

In operations and supply chain environments that must deal with random demand, it is virtually impossible to achieve very high capacity utilization levels and still provide acceptable customer service.

Some organizations get around this by attempting to "de-randomize" demand—doctors' offices make appointments, and manufacturers fit jobs into a preset schedule. But this is not always an option. If you are injured in a car wreck, you need an ambulance now, not three hours from now.

Rather, capacity decisions in such environments often come down to striking the best balance between costs and customer service. Suppose that the fast-food restaurant in our example can add a second worker at the drive-up window for $15,000 a year. The second worker would allow the drive-up window to handle six customers per minute. As Table 8.5 shows, the waiting line performance statistics would improve considerably. Whether or not the restaurant should expand capacity may ultimately depend on whether the additional revenue from shorter lines and happier customers offsets the cost of hiring the second worker.

TABLE 8.5
Waiting Line Performance (service rate = 6 customers per minute)

ARRIVAL RATE (CUSTOMERS PER MINUTE)	AVERAGE UTILIZATION OF THE SYSTEM (ρ)	AVERAGE NUMBER OF CUSTOMERS WAITING (C_W)	AVERAGE TIME SPENT WAITING (MINUTES) (T_W)
3.0	50.0%	0.50	0.17
3.1	51.7%	0.55	0.18
3.2	53.3%	0.61	0.19
3.3	55.0%	0.67	0.20
3.4	56.7%	0.74	0.22
3.5	58.3%	0.82	0.23
3.6	60.0%	0.90	0.25
3.7	61.7%	0.99	0.27
3.8	63.3%	1.09	0.29
3.9	65.0%	1.21	0.31
4.0	66.7%	**1.33**	**0.33**
4.1	68.3%	1.47	0.36
4.2	70.0%	1.63	0.39
4.3	71.7%	1.81	0.42
4.4	73.3%	2.02	0.46
4.5	75.0%	2.25	0.50
4.6	76.7%	2.52	0.55
4.7	78.3%	2.83	0.60
4.8	80.0%	3.20	0.67
4.9	81.7%	3.64	0.74
4.95	82.5%	3.89	0.79
4.995	83.3%	4.14	0.83

Example 8.8

Waiting Line Performance at a Snappy Lube

Snappy Lube is a quick-change oil center with a single service bay. On average, Snappy Lube can change a car's oil in 10 minutes. Cars arrive, on average, every 15 minutes. From these numbers, we can estimate the average arrival rate and service rate:

$$\text{Arrival rate} = \lambda = 60 \text{ minutes}/15 \text{ minutes} = 4 \text{ per hour}$$
$$\text{Service rate} = \mu = 60 \text{ minutes}/10 \text{ minutes} = 6 \text{ per hour}$$

Therefore,

$$\text{Average utilization} = 4/6 = 67\%$$
$$\text{Average number of cars waiting} = 16/(6 \times 2) = 1.33 \text{ cars}$$
$$\text{Average number of cars in the system} = 4/2 = 2 \text{ cars}$$
$$\text{Average time spent waiting} = 4/(6 \times 2) = 0.33 \text{ hour}$$
$$\text{Average time spent in the system} = 1/2 = 0.50 \text{ hour}$$

Learning Curves

Here's a question to ponder: Can the effective capacity of operations or supply chains *increase* even though the level of resources remains the *same*? In many cases, the answer is "yes." Recall that in Chapter 3 we defined *productivity* as follows:

$$\text{Productivity} = \text{outputs/inputs} \quad [8\text{-}10]$$

If organizations can improve their productivity, they can get more output from the same amount of resources or, conversely, the same output from fewer resources. Either way, changes in productivity imply changes in effective capacity. **Learning curve theory** suggests that productivity levels can improve at a predictable rate as people and even systems "learn" to do tasks more efficiently. In formal terms, learning curve theory states that *for every doubling of cumulative output, there is a set percentage reduction in the amount of inputs required*. The learning curve is defined as follows:

Learning curve theory
A body of theory based on applied statistics that suggests that productivity levels can improve at a predictable rate as people and even systems "learn" to do tasks more efficiently. In formal terms, learning curve theory states that for every doubling of cumulative output, there is a set percentage reduction in the amount of inputs required.

$$T_n = T_1 n^b \quad [8\text{-}11]$$

where:

T_n = resources (usually labor) required for the nth unit

T_1 = resources required for the 1st unit

b = ln(Learning percentage)/ln2

The rate at which learning occurs is captured by the learning percentage, where 80% would be expressed as 0.80.

Example 8.9

Learning Curves at a Service Call Center

A video game manufacturer has hired a new service technician to handle customer calls. The times it takes the new service technician to help the first, second, fourth, and eighth callers, as well as the resulting productivity figures, are as follows:

CALL	TIME FOR CALL	PRODUCTIVITY
1	5.00 minutes	0.20 calls per minute
2	4.00 minutes	0.25 calls per minute
4	3.20 minutes	0.31 calls per minute
8	2.56 minutes	0.39 calls per minute

Notice that the second call takes 80% of the time of the first (4/5 = 80%). Similarly, the fourth call takes 80% of the time of the second, and the eighth call takes 80% of the time of the fourth. In effect, for every doubling of cumulative output, the service technician is experiencing a 20% reduction in the amount of time required. This represents an 80% learning curve.

For our service technician, then, we can use Equation [8-11] to estimate the time it will take her to handle her 25th call:

$$T_{25} = T_1(25^{\ln(0.80)/\ln 2}) = (5 \text{ minutes})(25^{-0.32193})$$
$$= (5 \text{ minutes})(0.355)$$
$$= 1.78 \text{ minutes}$$

Figure 8.9 uses the learning curve equation to plot the expected service times for the first 50 calls, based on an 80% learning curve. As you can see, the learning curve is characterized by quick improvements in productivity early on, followed by more gradual improvements.

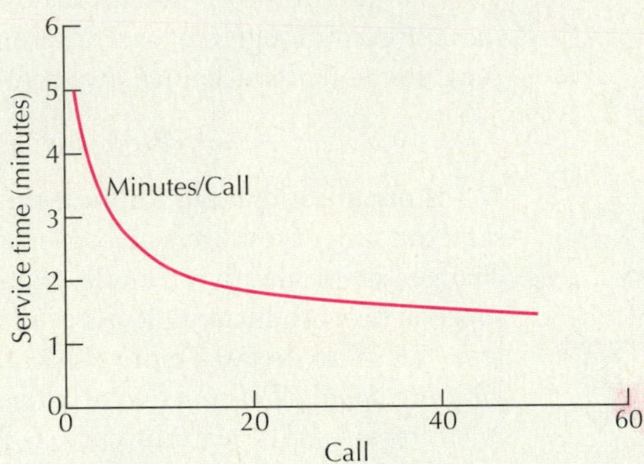

FIGURE 8.9 Learning Curve for Service Technician

Table 8.6 contains calculated n^b values, as well as cumulative n^b values, for a wide range of n values and learning curve percentages.

To see how the table works, suppose the video game manufacturer mentioned earlier hires a second service technician. The second service technician takes 5 minutes for his first call, followed by 4.5 minutes for the second call. Based on this information:

- Estimate the learning rate;
- Calculate the time it should take to handle the 25th call; and
- Calculate the total time it should take to handle *the next 23 calls* (calls 3 through 25).

The estimated learning rate = 4.5 minutes/5 minutes = 90%. Looking at Table 8.6, we can see that we have an entire column of n^b values and cumulative n^b values (Σn^b) for a 90% learning curve. Looking down the table until we find the row for the 25th unit (in this case, a customer call), we find n^b for a 90% learning curve = 0.613. Therefore:

Estimated time for the 25th call = (5 minutes)(0.613) ≈ 3.065 minutes

TABLE 8.6 Selected n^b and $\sum n^b$ Values for Different Learning Curves

UNIT NUMBER	70% LEARNING n^b	70% LEARNING $\sum n^b$	75% LEARNING n^b	75% LEARNING $\sum n^b$	80% LEARNING n^b	80% LEARNING $\sum n^b$	85% LEARNING n^b	85% LEARNING $\sum n^b$	90% LEARNING n^b	90% LEARNING $\sum n^b$
1	1.000	1.000	1.000	1.000	1.000	1.000	1.000	1.000	1.000	1.000
2	0.700	1.700	0.750	1.750	0.800	1.800	0.850	1.850	0.900	1.900
3	0.568	2.268	0.634	2.384	0.702	2.502	0.773	2.623	0.846	2.746
4	0.490	2.758	0.563	2.946	0.640	3.142	0.723	3.345	0.810	3.556
5	0.437	3.195	0.513	3.459	0.596	3.738	0.686	4.031	0.783	4.339
6	0.398	3.593	0.475	3.934	0.562	4.299	0.657	4.688	0.762	5.101
7	0.367	3.960	0.446	4.380	0.534	4.834	0.634	5.322	0.744	5.845
8	0.343	4.303	0.422	4.802	0.512	5.346	0.614	5.936	0.729	6.574
9	0.323	4.626	0.402	5.204	0.493	5.839	0.597	6.533	0.716	7.290
10	0.306	4.932	0.385	5.589	0.477	6.315	0.583	7.116	0.705	7.994
11	0.291	5.223	0.370	5.958	0.462	6.777	0.570	7.686	0.695	8.689
12	0.278	5.501	0.357	6.315	0.449	7.227	0.558	8.244	0.685	9.374
13	0.267	5.769	0.345	6.660	0.438	7.665	0.548	8.792	0.677	10.052
14	0.257	6.026	0.334	6.994	0.428	8.092	0.539	9.331	0.670	10.721
15	0.248	6.274	0.325	7.319	0.418	8.511	0.530	9.861	0.663	11.384
16	0.240	6.514	0.316	7.635	0.410	8.920	0.522	10.383	0.656	12.040
17	0.233	6.747	0.309	7.944	0.402	9.322	0.515	10.898	0.650	12.690
18	0.226	6.973	0.301	8.245	0.394	9.716	0.508	11.405	0.644	13.334
19	0.220	7.192	0.295	8.540	0.388	10.104	0.501	11.907	0.639	13.974
20	0.214	7.407	0.288	8.828	0.381	10.485	0.495	12.402	0.634	14.608
21	0.209	7.615	0.283	9.111	0.375	10.860	0.490	12.892	0.630	15.237
22	0.204	7.819	0.277	9.388	0.370	11.230	0.484	13.376	0.625	15.862
23	0.199	8.018	0.272	9.660	0.364	11.594	0.479	13.856	0.621	16.483
24	0.195	8.213	0.267	9.928	0.359	11.954	0.475	14.331	0.617	17.100
25	0.191	8.404	0.263	10.191	0.355	12.309	0.470	14.801	0.613	17.713
26	0.187	8.591	0.259	10.449	0.350	12.659	0.466	15.267	0.609	18.323
27	0.183	8.774	0.255	10.704	0.346	13.005	0.462	15.728	0.606	18.929
28	0.180	8.954	0.251	10.955	0.342	13.347	0.458	16.186	0.603	19.531
29	0.177	9.131	0.247	11.202	0.338	13.685	0.454	16.640	0.599	20.131
30	0.174	9.305	0.244	11.446	0.335	14.020	0.450	17.091	0.596	20.727
31	0.171	9.476	0.240	11.686	0.331	14.351	0.447	17.538	0.593	21.320
32	0.168	9.644	0.237	11.924	0.328	14.679	0.444	17.981	0.590	21.911
33	0.165	9.809	0.234	12.158	0.324	15.003	0.441	18.422	0.588	22.498
34	0.163	9.972	0.231	12.389	0.321	15.324	0.437	18.859	0.585	23.084
35	0.160	10.133	0.229	12.618	0.318	15.643	0.434	19.294	0.583	23.666
36	0.158	10.291	0.226	12.844	0.315	15.958	0.432	19.725	0.580	24.246
37	0.156	10.447	0.223	13.067	0.313	16.271	0.429	20.154	0.578	24.824
38	0.154	10.601	0.221	13.288	0.310	16.581	0.426	20.580	0.575	25.399
39	0.152	10.753	0.219	13.507	0.307	16.888	0.424	21.004	0.573	25.972
40	0.150	10.902	0.216	13.723	0.305	17.193	0.421	21.425	0.571	26.543
41	0.148	11.050	0.214	13.937	0.303	17.496	0.419	21.844	0.569	27.111
42	0.146	11.196	0.212	14.149	0.300	17.796	0.416	22.260	0.567	27.678
43	0.144	11.341	0.210	14.359	0.298	18.094	0.414	22.674	0.565	28.243
44	0.143	11.484	0.208	14.567	0.296	18.390	0.412	23.086	0.563	28.805
45	0.141	11.625	0.206	14.773	0.294	18.684	0.410	23.496	0.561	29.366
46	0.139	11.764	0.204	14.977	0.292	18.975	0.408	23.903	0.559	29.925
47	0.138	11.902	0.202	15.180	0.290	19.265	0.405	24.309	0.557	30.482
48	0.136	12.038	0.201	15.380	0.288	19.552	0.403	24.712	0.555	31.037
49	0.135	12.173	0.199	15.579	0.286	19.838	0.402	25.113	0.553	31.590
50	0.134	12.307	0.197	15.776	0.284	20.122	0.400	25.513	0.552	32.142

To estimate the time for the next 23 calls, we calculate the expected time for the first 25 calls and subtract out the time for the first two. Working off of the same row of Table 8.6:

$$\text{Estimated time for the next 23 calls} = \text{Estimated time for the first 25 calls} - \text{Time for the first 2 calls}$$
$$= 5 \text{ minutes} (\Sigma n^b) \quad - (5 + 4.5 \text{ minutes})$$
$$= 5 \text{ minutes} (17.713) - 9.5 \text{ minutes}$$
$$= 79 \text{ minutes}$$

When learning occurs in an organization, productivity will improve over time, and the effective capacity of the organization will grow—even if the level of resources remains the same. This has important implications for capacity planning. If managers expect their employees or work systems to experience learning effects, then they must anticipate these effects when making capacity decisions. Otherwise, they may overestimate the capacity needed to meet future requirements.

Of course, in nearly every case, there is a minimum amount of time or resource that will be required, regardless of how many times the task is repeated. This puts an effective limit on the learning curve effect. Also, it is not unusual for learning improvements to not follow a smooth trajectory of improvement, as suggested by Equation [8.11]. Rather, organizations may be able to see the actual improvement only over large numbers of observations.

One final observation about learning curves: In many industrial buyer-supplier settings, buyers *expect* their suppliers to experience productivity improvements due to learning over time. Buyers might even build price reductions based on anticipated learning into long-term purchasing contracts. Wal-Mart, for instance, may purchase a new item from a supplier, expecting overall costs to follow a 90% learning curve. This creates an incentive for the supplier to proactively look for ways to decrease costs through learning or other means.

CHAPTER SUMMARY

Capacity decisions are among the most important strategic decisions operations and supply chain managers make. As the opening case study on Merck suggested, such decisions can have far-reaching effects for a business and its customers. Even though capacity decisions are inherently risky, this chapter showed how managers can think about and analyze these decisions in a logical manner.

Specifically, we talked about three common capacity strategies and also demonstrated various methods for evaluating the financial pros and cons of capacity alternatives. We devoted the last half of the chapter to advanced perspectives on capacity: the Theory of Constraints (TOC), waiting line theory, and productivity and learning curves. These advanced perspectives help us understand how capacity behaves across a supply chain, how waiting lines and capacity interrelate, and what impact learning has on productivity levels and, ultimately, on effective capacity.

KEY FORMULAS

Total cost of a capacity alternative (page 219):

$$TC = FC + VC \times X \qquad \textbf{[8-1]}$$

where:

TC = total cost
FC = fixed cost

VC = variable cost per unit of business activity
VX = amount of business activity (number of customers served, number of units produced, etc.)

Expected value of a capacity alternative (page 223):

$$EV_j = \sum_{i=1}^{I} P_i C_i \qquad [8\text{-}2]$$

where:

EV_j = expected value of capacity alternative j
P_i = probability of demand level i
C_i = financial result (cost, revenue, or profit) at demand level i

Break-even point (page 227):

$$BEP = \frac{FC}{R - VC} \qquad [8\text{-}3]$$

where:

BEP = break-even point
FC = fixed cost
VC = variable cost per unit of business activity
R = revenue per unit of business activity

Probability of *n* arrivals in *T* time periods (page 231):

$$P_n = \frac{(\lambda T)^n}{n!} e^{-\lambda T} \qquad [8\text{-}4]$$

where:

P_n = probability of n arrivals in T time periods
λ = arrival rate
T = number of time periods

Average utilization of a waiting line system (page 232):

$$\rho = \frac{\lambda}{\mu} \qquad [8\text{-}5]$$

where:

λ = arrival rate
μ = service rate

Average number of customers waiting in a waiting line (page 232):

$$C_W = \frac{\lambda^2}{\mu(\mu - \lambda)} \qquad [8\text{-}6]$$

Average number of customers in the waiting line system (page 232):

$$C_S = \frac{\lambda}{\mu - \lambda} \quad [8\text{-}7]$$

Average time spent waiting in a waiting line (page 232):

$$T_W = \frac{\lambda}{\mu(\mu - \lambda)} \quad [8\text{-}8]$$

Average time spent in the waiting line system (page 232):

$$T_S = \frac{1}{\mu - \lambda} \quad [8\text{-}9]$$

Productivity (page 235):

$$\text{Productivity} = \text{outputs/inputs} \quad [8\text{-}10]$$

Resources (usually labor) required to complete the *n*th unit (page 235):

$$T_n = T_1 n^b \quad [8\text{-}11]$$

where:

T_n = resources (usually labor) required for the *n*th unit
T_1 = resources required for the 1st unit
b = ln(Learning percentage)/ln2

KEY TERMS

USING EXCEL IN CAPACITY MANAGEMENT

Many of the capacity decision models we have shown in this chapter can easily be incorporated into a spreadsheet application, such as Microsoft Excel. The following spreadsheet calculates the break-even points and indifference points for three capacity alternatives.

For instance, the break-even point for option B (cell C14) is calculated as follows:

BEP = fixed cost/(revenue per unit − variable cost per unit)
= C8/(D4 − D8) = 14.71

Likewise, the indifference point for options B and C (cell E15) is:

$$= \frac{(\text{option C fixed cost} - \text{option B fixed cost})}{(\text{option B variable cost} - \text{option C variable cost})}$$

= (C9 − C8)/(D8 − D9)

= 366.67

Of course, the key advantage of using the spreadsheet is that we can quickly evaluate new scenarios simply by changing the input values.

	A	B	C	D	E	F
1	**Evaluating Alternative Capacity Options**					
2	**(Enter inputs in shaded cells)**					
3						
4		Revenue per unit of output:		$100.00		
5						
6		Capacity Option	Fixed cost	Variable cost per unit of output	Max. output	
7		Option A	$0.00	$30.00	200	
8		Option B	$1,250.00	$15.00	300	
9		Option C	$4,000.00	$7.50	400	
10						
11				*** Indifference Points ***		
12			*** Break-even point ***	Option A	Option B	Option C
13		Option A	0.00	---		
14		Option B	14.71	83.33	---	
15		Option C	43.24	177.78	366.67	---

SOLVED PROBLEM

Problem

With the market for luxury cruises burgeoning, Auvia Cruise Lines is debating whether or not to invest in a large cruise ship to serve what would be a new market for the company—cruises around Alaska. This is no small investment: Auvia management figures the new 86,000-gross-registered-tons vessel will cost approximately $375 million. Spread over 25 years (the useful life of the ship), this amounts to a fixed cost of $375 million/25 = $15 million per year. The new ship can carry 2000 passengers at a time, or up to 40,000 per year.

Management has determined that the average passenger will generate revenues of $2400 and variable costs of $1300. Furthermore, marketing has put together the following demand estimates for the new cruise:

ANNUAL DEMAND (PASSENGERS)	PROBABILITY
10,000	30%
30,000	50%
38,000	20%

Calculate the yearly break-even point for the new cruise ship. Determine the expected value of the new cruise ship, and draw out the decision tree for Auvia Cruise Lines.

Solution

The break-even point for the new cruise ship is

$$FC + VC(X) = R(X)$$

$$\$15{,}000{,}000 + \$1{,}300X = \$2{,}400X$$

$$X = \$15{,}000{,}000/\$1100, \textit{ or about 13,636 passengers per year}$$

And the expected financial results under the three demand scenarios are as follows:

$$(R - VC) \times X - FC$$

$$\text{10,000 passengers: } (\$2{,}400 - \$1{,}300) \times 10{,}000 - \$15{,}000{,}000 = -\$4{,}000{,}000$$

$$\text{30,000 passengers: } (\$2{,}400 - \$1{,}300) \times 30{,}000 - \$15{,}000{,}000 = \$18{,}000{,}000$$

$$\text{38,000 passengers: } (\$2{,}400 - \$1{,}300) \times 38{,}000 - \$15{,}000{,}000 = \$26{,}800{,}000$$

The expected value is simply the average of these three results, weighted by the respective probabilities:

$$\text{Expected value for the new cruise ship} =$$
$$30\% \times (-\$4{,}000{,}000) + 50\% \times (\$18{,}000{,}000) + 20\% \times (\$26{,}800{,}000) = \$13{,}160{,}000$$

The decision tree follows. Note that the expected value of not investing in the new ship is $0. This reflects the fact that if Auvia does not invest in the new ship, it will incur neither the expenses nor the revenues associated with cruises around Alaska. If Auvia is willing to take the risk of losing up to $4 million a year, the new cruise line looks very promising.

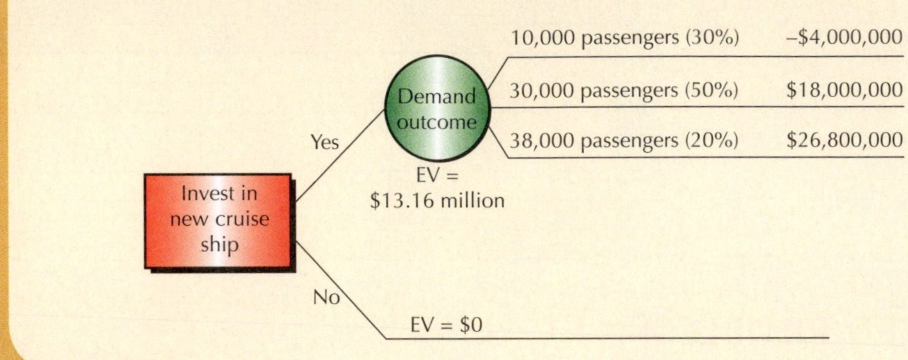

DISCUSSION QUESTIONS

1. Which type of operations and supply chain environment do you think would have a more difficult time managing capacity—an environment supporting standardized products/services or one supporting customized products/services? Why?
2. What kind of capacity strategy—lead, lag, or match—would you expect a fire station to follow? What about a driver's license testing center? Why?
3. Who do you think would benefit more from a "virtual corporation" capacity strategy—a small start-up firm with few resources or an older, more established company? Why? What are the risks associated with such a strategy?
4. When Merck first started to sell Crixivan, it had enough manufacturing capacity to support only 110,000 patients. If patients started using Crixivan and stopped taking it for even short period of time, they risked developing a resistance to the drug. Merck therefore decided to sell the drug through a single distribution channel that was limited to supporting only 90,000 patients. Explain the logic behind this decision using the theory of constraints.
5. The manager at a local bank says to you, "I want my tellers to be busy 100% of the time. I can't afford to have them sit around." How would you use waiting line theory to explain the problems with this thinking? Is there some way to have the tellers do productive work even when they aren't dealing with customers?
6. What are the relationships among learning, productivity, and effective capacity? What are the pros and cons of using learning curves to estimate future resource requirements?

PROBLEMS

Additional homework problems are available at www.prenhall.com/bozarth. These problems use Excel to generate customized problems for different class sections or even different students.
(* = easy; ** = moderate; *** = advanced)

1. (*) The Shelly Group has leased a new copier that costs $700 per month plus $0.10 for each copy. What is the total cost if Shelly makes 5000 copies a month? If it makes 10,000 copies a month? What is the per-copy cost at 5000 copies? At 10,000 copies?

2. Arktec Manufacturing must choose between the following two capacity options:

	FIXED COST (PER YEAR)	VARIABLE COST (PER UNIT)
Option 1	$500,000	$2 per unit
Option 2	$100,000	$10 per unit

a. (*) What would the cost be for each option if the demand level is 25,000 units per year? If it is 75,000 units per year?
b. (**) In general, which option do you think would be better as volume levels increase? As they decrease? Why?
c. (*) What is the indifference point?

3. (*) Suppose the Shelly Group (Problem 1) has identified two possible demand levels for copies per month:

COPIES (PER MONTH)	PROBABILITY
5,000	50%
10,000	50%

What is the expected cost, given the fixed and variable costs in Problem 1?

4. Consider the two capacity options for Arktec Manufacturing, shown in Problem 2. Suppose the company has identified the following three possible demand scenarios:

DEMAND (UNITS PER YEAR)	PROBABILITY
25,000	30%
60,000	40%
100,000	30%

a. (**) What is the expected value of each option? Which option would you choose based on this information?
b. (**) Suppose the lowest and highest demand levels are updated to 40,000 and 110,000, respectively. Recalculate the expected values. What happened?

5. Problem 2 identified two capacity options for Arktec Manufacturing, and Problem 4 identified three possible demand outcomes.
a. (**) Draw the decision tree for Arktec Manufacturing. When drawing your tree, assume that managers must select a capacity option *before* they know what the demand level will actually be.
b. (**) Calculate the expected value for each decision branch. Which option would you prefer? Why?

6. You are the new CEO of DualJet, a company that makes expensive, premium kitchen stoves for home use. You must decide whether to assemble the stoves in-house or to have a Mexican company do it. The fixed and variable costs for each option are as follows:

	FIXED COST	VARIABLE COST
Assemble in-house	$55,000	$620
Contract with Mexican assembler	$0	$880

a. (**) Suppose DualJet's premium stoves sell for $2500. What is the break-even volume point for assembling in-house?
b. (*) At what volume level do the two capacity options have identical costs?
c. (**) Suppose the expected demand for stoves is 3000. Which capacity option would you prefer from a cost perspective?

7. Emily Watkins, a recent college graduate, faces some tough choices. Emily must decide whether to accept an offer for a job that pays $35,000 or hold out for another job that pays $45,000 a year. Emily figures there is a 75% chance she will get an offer for the higher-paying job. The problem is that Emily has to make a decision on the lower-paying job within the next few days and she will not know about the higher-paying job for two weeks.
a. (**) Draw out the decision tree for Emily Watkins.
b. (**) What is the key decision facing Emily? What is the expected value of each decision branch?
c. (**) What other factors might Emily consider, other than expected value?

8. (*) Philip Neilson owns a fireworks store. Philip's fixed costs are $12,000 a month, and each fireworks assortment he sells costs, on average, $8. The average selling price for an assortment is $25. What is the break-even point for Philip's fireworks store?

9. Suppose Philip Neilson (Problem 8) decides to expand his business. His new fixed expenses will be $20,000 per month, but the average cost for a fireworks assortment will fall to just $5 due to Philip's higher purchase volumes.
a. (*) What is the new break-even point?
b. (**) At what volume level is Philip indifferent to the two capacity alternatives outlined in Problems 8 and 9?

10. Merck is considering the launch of a new drug called Laffolin. Merck has identified two possible demand scenarios:

DEMAND LEVEL	PROBABILITY
1,000,000 patients	30%
2,000,000 patients	70%

Merck also has the following information:

Revenue	$140 per patient
Fixed costs to manufacture and sell Laffolin	$70 million
Variable costs to manufacture and sell Laffolin	$80 per patient
Maximum number of patients that Merck can handle	3,000,000

a. (*) How many patients must Merck have in order to break even?
b. (**) How much money will Merck make if demand for Laffolin is 1,000,000 patients? If demand is 2,000,000 patients?
c. (**) What is the expected value of making Laffolin?
d. (**) Draw the decision tree for the Laffolin decision, showing the profits for each branch (Total revenues – total variable costs – total fixed costs) and all expected values.

11. Clay runs a small hot dog stand in downtown Chapel Hill. Clay can serve about 30 customers an hour. During lunchtime, customers randomly arrive at the rate of 20 per hour.
a. (*) What percentage of the time is Clay busy?
b. (*) On average, how many customers are waiting to be served? How many are in the system (waiting and being served)?
c. (*) On average, how long will a customer wait to be served? How long will a customer be in the system?

12. Peri Thompson is the sole dispatcher for Thompson Termite Control. Peri's job is to take customer calls, schedule appointments, and in some cases resolve any service or billing questions while the customer is on the phone. Peri can handle about 15 calls an hour.
a. (*) Typically, Peri gets about 10 calls an hour. Under these conditions, what is the average number of customers waiting, and what is the average waiting time?
b. (**) Monday mornings are unusually busy. During these peak times, Peri receives around 13 calls an hour, on average. Recalculate the average number of customers waiting and the average waiting time. What can you conclude?

13. Benson Racing is training a new pit crew for its racing team. For its first practice run, the pit crew is able to complete all the tasks in exactly 30 seconds—not exactly world-class. The second time around the crew shaves 4.5 seconds off its time.
a. (*) Estimate the learning rate for the pit crew based on the times for the first two practice runs.
b. (**) Mark Benson, owner of Benson Racing, says that the pit crew must be able to complete all the tasks in less than 15 seconds in order to be competitive. Based on your answer to Part a, how many times will the pit crew need to practice before it breaks the 15-second barrier?
c. (**) Is it realistic to expect the pit crew to experience learning improvements indefinitely? Explain.

14. Wake County has a special emergency rescue team. The team is practicing rescuing dummies from a smoke-filled building. The first time the team took 240 seconds (four minutes). The second time it took 180 seconds (three minutes).
a. (*) What is the estimated learning rate for the rescue team based on this information?
b. (**) Suppose the team's learning rate for the rescue exercise is 80%. How many times will the team need to repeat the exercise until its time is *less than 120 seconds* (50% of the original time)?
c. (**) How long will it take the emergency team to perform its 20th rescue if the learning rate is 80%?

Problems 15 through 17: *TriangCom*

15. After graduating from college, your friends and you start an Internet auction service called TriangCom. Business has been fantastic, with 10 million customer visits—or "hits"—to the site in the last year. You have several capacity decisions to consider. One key decision involves the number of computer servers needed. You are considering putting in 10, 20, or 30 servers. Costs and capacity limits are as follows:

NUMBER OF SERVERS	FIXED COST PER YEAR	VARIABLE COST PER HIT	MAXIMUM HITS PER YEAR
10	$50,000	$0.005	20 million
20	$90,000	$0.003	40 million
30	$120,000	$0.002	60 million

In addition, marketing has developed the following demand scenarios:

YEARLY DEMAND	PROBABILITY
15 million hits	30%
30 million hits	60%
45 million hits	10%

Finally, TriangCom generated $5 million last year based on 10 million "hits." Put another way, each "hit" generated, on average, $0.50 in revenue.
a. (**) Calculate the break-even point for each capacity alternative.
b. (**) At what demand level will you be indifferent to having either 10 or 20 servers?

c. (***) Calculate the expected value for each capacity alternative. (*Hint:* Don't forget about capacity constraints that can limit the number of "hits" each capacity alternative can handle.) Which alternative will you prefer if you want to maximize the expected value?

16. TriangCom has hired Donna Olway to code programs. Donna completes her first job in five weeks and her second job in four weeks. Assuming that (1) Donna continues to learn at this rate and (2) her time improvements will follow a learning curve:

a. (**) How long will you expect Donna to take to complete her sixth job?

b. (**) How long will you expect Donna to take to complete the next five jobs (jobs 3 through 7)?

17. With thousands of customers, TriangCom has established a hotline to take customer calls. The hotline is staffed by one person 24 hours a day. You have the following statistics:

Service rate for calls	15 per hour, on average
Arrival rate for calls	11 per hour, on average

As part of your customer service policy, you have decided that the average waiting time should not exceed 2.5 minutes.

a. (*) What is the average number of callers being served?

b. (*) On average, how many callers are waiting to be served?

c. (**) What is the average waiting time for a customer? Is this acceptable, given the customer service policy?

Problems 18 through 20: Sawyer Construction

Rich Sawyer runs a landscaping firm. Each year Rich contracts for labor and equipment hours from a local construction company. The construction company has given Rich three different capacity options:

CAPACITY OPTION	LABOR HOURS	EQUIPMENT HOURS
High capacity	9000	6000
Medium capacity	6750	4500
Low capacity	4500	3000

Cost per labor hour:	$10 per hour
Cost per equipment hour:	$20 per hour

Once Rich has chosen a capacity option, he cannot change it later. In addition, the cost for each capacity option is fixed. That is, Rich must pay for all labor and equipment hours he contracts for, even if he doesn't need them all. Therefore, there are essentially no variable costs. Rich also has information concerning the amount of revenue and the labor and equipment hours needed for the "typical" landscaping job:

Job revenue	$2,000 per job
Labor hours per job	30 hours
Equipment hours per job	20 hours

Finally, Rich has identified three possible demand levels. These demand levels, with their associated probabilities, are as follows:

DEMAND LEVEL	NUMBER OF JOBS	PROBABILITY
High demand	300	30%
Medium demand	200	40%
Low demand	120	30%

18. (***) Determine the total fixed costs and the break-even point for each capacity option. What is the maximum number of jobs that can be handled under each capacity option?

19. (***) Draw a decision tree for Sawyer Construction. What are the nine possible outcomes Rich is facing? (*Hint:* One is "Rich subcontracts for low capacity and demand turns out to be low.") What is the profit (Revenue – fixed costs) associated with each of the nine outcomes? Be sure to consider the capacity limits of each alternative when calculating revenues.

20. (***) Using the information from Problem 19, calculate the expected profit of each capacity alternative. Which option will Rich prefer if he wants to maximize expected profit?

21. (***) (*Microsoft Excel problem*). The following figure shows an expanded version of the Excel spreadsheet described in *Using Excel in Capacity Management* (page 240). In addition to the break-even and indifference points, the expanded spreadsheet calculates financial results for three capacity options under three different demand scenarios. **Re-create this spreadsheet in Excel.** You should develop the spreadsheet so that the results will be recalculated if any of the values in the highlighted cells are changed. Your formatting does not have to be exactly the same, but the numbers should be. (As a test, see what happens if you change the "Max. output" and "Variable cost" for Capacity Option A to 250 units and $35, respectively. Your new expected value for Capacity Option A should be $14,218.75.)

	A	B	C	D	E	F
1	**Evaluating Alternative Capacity Options**					
2	**(Enter inputs in shaded cells)**					
3						
4		Revenue per unit of output:		$100.00		
5						
6		Capacity Option	Fixed cost	Variable cost per unit of output	Max. output	
7		Option A	$0.00	$30.00	200	
8		Option B	$1,250.00	$15.00	300	
9		Option C	$4,000.00	$7.50	400	
10						
11		Demand Scenario	Demand level	Probability		
12		Low	125	25%		
13		Medium	275	55%		
14		High	425	20%		
15			Total:	100%		
16						
17				*** Indifference Points ***		
18			*** Break-even point ***	Option A	Option B	Option C
19		Option A	0.00	---		
20		Option B	14.71	83.33	---	
21		Option C	43.24	177.78	366.67	---
22						
23			*** Results for different capacity/demand combinations ***			
24						
25			Low	Medium	High	*** Expected value ***
26		Option A	$8,750.00	$14,000.00	$14,000.00	$12,687.50
27		Option B	$9,375.00	$22,125.00	$24,250.00	$19,362.50
28		Option C	$7,562.50	$21,437.50	$33,000.00	$20,281.25

CASE STUDY

FORSTER'S MARKET

Introduction

Forster's Market is a retailer of specialty food items, including premium coffees, imported crackers and cheeses, and the like. Last year Forster's sold 14,400 pounds of coffee. Forster's pays a local supplier $3 per pound and then sells the coffees for $7 a pound.

The Roaster Decision

While Forster's makes a handsome profit on the coffee business, owner Robbie Forster thinks he can do better. Specifically, Robbie is considering investing in a large industrial-sized coffee roaster that can roast up to 40,000 pounds per year. By roasting the coffee himself, Robbie will be able to cut his coffee costs down to $1.60 a pound. The drawback is that the roaster will be quite expensive; fixed costs (including the lease, power, training, and additional labor) will run about $35,000 a year.

The roaster capacity will also be significantly more than the 14,400 pounds that Forster's needs. However, Robbie thinks he will be able to sell coffee to area restaurants and coffee shops for $2.90 a pound. Robbie has outlined three possible demand scenarios:

Low demand	18,000 pounds per year
Medium demand	25,000 pounds per year
High demand	35,000 pounds per year

These numbers include the 14,400 pounds sold at Forster's Market. In addition, Robbie thinks all three scenarios are equally likely.

QUESTIONS

1. What are the two capacity options that Robbie needs to consider? What are their fixed and variable costs? What is the indifference point for the two options? What are the implications of the indifference point?
2. Draw the decision tree for the roaster decision. If Forster's does not invest in the roaster, does Robbie need to worry about the different demand scenarios just outlined? Why or why not?
3. Calculate the expected value for the two capacity options. Keep in mind that for the roaster option, any demand above 14,400 pounds will generate revenues of only $2.90 a pound. Update the decision tree to show your results.
4. What is the worst possible financial outcome for Forster's? The best possible financial outcome? What other factors—core competency, strategic flexibility, and so on—should Robbie consider when making this decision?

REFERENCES

Books and Articles

Burrows. P. "Servers as High as an Elephants' Eye."*Business Week* (June 12, 2006).

Cox, J. F., and J. H. Blackstone, eds. *APICS Dictionary,* 10th ed. Falls Church, VA: APICS, 2002.

Engardio, P. "Souping Up the Supply Chain." *Business Week,* August 24, 1998: 110.

Goldratt, E. *The Goal,* 2nd ed. Great Barrington, MA: North River Press, 1992.

Krajewski, L., and L. Ritzman. *Operations Management: Strategy and Analysis,* 6th ed. Upper Saddle River, NJ: Prentice Hall, 2002.

Tanouye, E. "Short Supply: Success of AIDS Drug Has Merck Fighting to Keep Up the Pace." *The Wall Street Journal,* November 5, 1996.

CHAPTER 8 SUPPLEMENT

Advanced Waiting Line Theory and Simulation Modeling

SUPPLEMENT OUTLINE

Supplement Objectives

By the end of this supplement, you will be able to:

- Describe different types of waiting line systems.
- Use statistics-based formulas to estimate waiting line lengths and waiting times for three different types of waiting line systems.
- Explain the purpose, advantages and disadvantages, and steps of simulation modeling.
- Develop a simple Monte Carlo simulation using Microsoft Excel.
- Develop and analyze a system using SimQuick.

INTRODUCTION

Chapter 8 introduced waiting line theory and provided some formulas for calculating waiting times and line lengths for a simple waiting line situation. In this supplement, we describe two additional waiting line environments, and demonstrate how statistically derived formulas can be used to assess the performance of these systems as well.

The second half of this supplement introduces simulation modeling. Simulation is often described in conjunction with waiting lines because many complex waiting line systems cannot be analyzed through neatly derived formulas. That said, simulation can be used in any environment where actual occurrences of interest—arrivals, quality problems, work times, and so on—can be modeled mathematically. We show how Monte Carlo simulation can be used to develop a very simple simulation using Excel. We then use one particular simulation package, SimQuick, to illustrate simulation model building and analysis.

8S.1 ALTERNATIVE WAITING LINES

In Chapter 8, we illustrated how waiting line theory worked using the example of a waiting line environment in which there was a single path through the one-process step, and both the arrival rate and service rate were probabilistic. In the language of waiting line theory, this is known as a **single-channel, single-phase system** (Figure 8S.1).

We then illustrated how statistics-based formulas could be used to answer questions such as:

- What percentage of the time will the process be busy?
- On average, *how long* will a unit have to wait in line? How long will it be in the system (waiting and being served)?
- On average, *how many* units will be in line?
- How will these averages be affected by the arrival rate of units and the service rate at the process step?

Of course, there are many waiting line environments that do not fit this mold. An automatic car wash, for example, may have one line and one process step, but the service time is *constant*. Or we may be interested in a multiple-channel, single-phase system, such as a bank. Here, there is only one process step, but there can be multiple paths through the system, depending on how many tellers are working (Figure 8S.2).

Or we may be interested in a single-channel, multiple-phase system. Examples include a hospital emergency room, where you wait to check in (phase 1), and then you wait to see

FIGURE 8S.1
Single-Channel, Single-Phase System

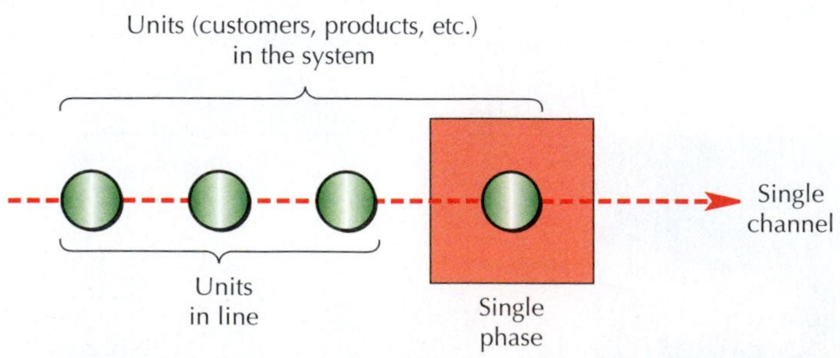

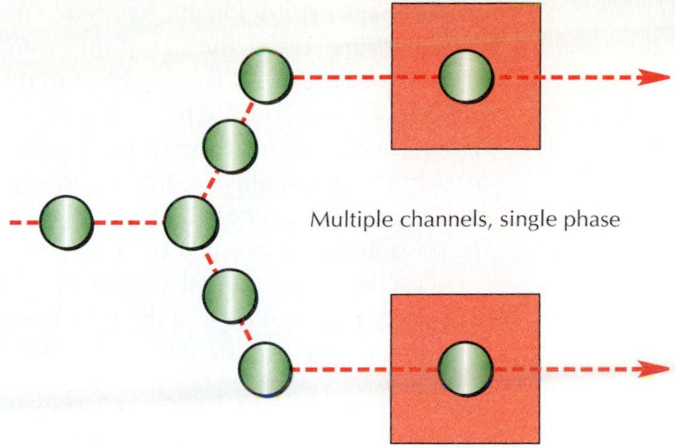

FIGURE 8S.2
Multiple-Channel, Single-Phase System

a doctor or nurse (phase 2). Figure 8S.3 illustrates such a system. We can even have multiple-channel, multiple-phase systems. In general, the more complex the environment is, the less likely we are to be able to analyze it with preestablished formulas.

In the remainder of this supplement, we review some of the key assumptions and terminology that make up waiting line theory, and introduce some formulas for determining waiting line performance for two additional waiting line environments—the single-channel, single-phase system with constant service times, and the multiple-channel, single-phase system. In the second half of the supplement, we introduce simulation modeling, which can be used to model more complex environments.

Assumptions behind Waiting Line Theory

ARRIVALS. In most waiting line models, customers are assumed to arrive at random intervals, based on a Poisson distribution. The probability of *n* arrivals in *T* time periods is calculated as follows:

$$P_n = \frac{(\lambda T)^n}{n!} e^{-\lambda T} \qquad \textbf{[B-1]}$$

where:

P_n = Probability of *n* arrivals in *T* time periods
λ = Arrival rate
T = Number of time periods

SERVICE TIMES. Waiting line models also assume that service times will either be constant or vary. In the latter case, modelers often use the exponential distribution to model service times, using the symbol μ to refer to the service rate.

FIGURE 8S.3
Single-Channel, Multiple-Phase System

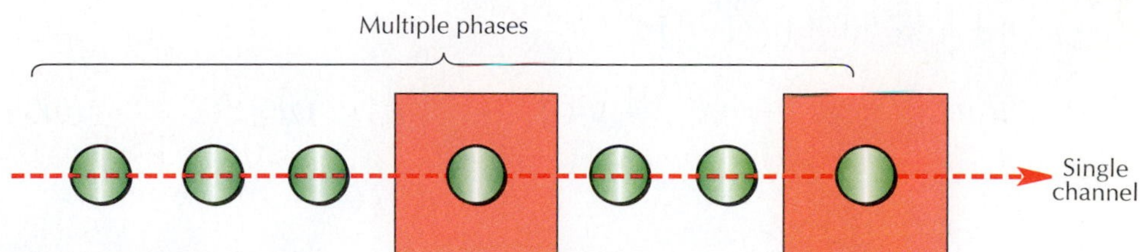

OTHER ASSUMPTIONS. Finally, we need to make some assumptions about the order in which customers are served, the size of the customer population, and whether or not customers can balk or renege. All waiting line formulas assume that customers are served on a first-come, first-served (FCFS) basis. Other priority rules might consider the urgency of the customers' needs (as in an emergency room), the speed with which customers can be served, or even the desirability of different customer types. In addition, we will assume that the population of customers is effectively infinite; that is, we are not likely to run through all the possible customers anytime soon.

Last, we will assume that customers enter the system and remain there until they are served, regardless of the length of the line or time spent waiting. They neither balk (decide against entering the system to begin with) nor renege (leave the line after entering).

TABLE 8S.1 Waiting Line Formulas for Three Different Environments

WAITING LINE ENVIRONMENT: λ = average number of arrivals per period of time; μ = average time each server takes to service a unit; M = Number of channels	AVERAGE NUMBER OF UNITS WAITING, C_W	AVERAGE NUMBER OF UNITS IN SYSTEM, C_S	AVERAGE TIME SPENT WAITING, T_W	AVERAGE TIME SPENT IN SYSTEM, T_S
Single channel, single phase with Poisson arrivals and exponential service times	$\frac{\lambda^2}{\mu(\mu-\lambda)}$ [B-2]	$C_W + \frac{\lambda}{\mu}$ [B-3]	$\frac{\lambda}{\mu(\mu-\lambda)}$ [B-4]	$T_W + \frac{1}{\mu}$ [B-5]
Single channel, single phase with Poisson arrivals and constant service times	$\frac{\lambda^2}{2\mu(\mu-\lambda)}$ [B-6]	$C_W + \frac{\lambda}{\mu}$ [B-7]	$\frac{\lambda}{2\mu(\mu-\lambda)}$ [B-8]	$T_W + \frac{1}{\mu}$ [B-9]
Multiple channel, single phase with Poisson arrivals and exponential service times ("multiserver model")	$C_S - \frac{\lambda}{\mu}$	$\frac{\lambda\mu\left(\frac{\lambda}{\mu}\right)^M}{(M-1)!(M\mu-\lambda)^2}P_0 + \left(\frac{\lambda}{\mu}\right)$	$T_S - \frac{1}{\mu}$	$\frac{\mu\left(\frac{\lambda}{\mu}\right)^M}{(M-1)!(M\mu-\lambda)^2}P_0 + \left(\frac{1}{\mu}\right)$
where: P_0 = Probability of 0 units in the system = $\frac{1}{\left[\sum_{n=0}^{M-1}\frac{1}{n!}\left(\frac{\lambda}{\mu}\right)^n\right]+\frac{1}{M!}\left(\frac{\lambda}{\mu}\right)^M\left(\frac{M\mu}{M\mu-\lambda}\right)}$ [B-10]	[B-11]	[B-12]	[B-13]	[B-14]

Waiting Line Formulas for Three Different Environments

Table 8S.1 contains formulas for estimating performance in three different waiting line environments. In all three cases, the formulas require that we know:

- The average number of arrivals per period of time, λ, and
- The average time each server takes to service a unit, μ.

The first row of formulas is for a single-channel, single-phase system with probabilistic arrivals and service times. The second row is for a single-channel, single-phase system where service times are constant and arrivals are probabilistic. The third row described a multiple-channel, single-phase system (Figure 8S.2). We illustrate how these formulas can be used in Examples 8S.1 through 8S.3.

Example 8S.1

Luc's Deluxe Car Wash, Part 1—Probabilistic Arrivals and Service Times

Luc Shields, an enterprising high school student, runs a car wash where he has a single crew of workers wash cars by hand (i.e., a single-channel, single-phase system). Cars arrive about every eight minutes, on average. Luc's crew can wash, on average, one car every six minutes. Arrivals follow a Poisson distribution, and the service times are exponentially distributed.

Luc would like to estimate (1) the average number of cars waiting and in the system, and (2) the average time a car spends waiting and in the system. From the information provided, we know that:

$$\text{Arrival rate} = \lambda = \frac{60 \text{ minutes}}{8 \text{ minutes}} = 7.5 \text{ cars per hour}$$

$$\text{Service rate} = \mu = \frac{60 \text{ minutes}}{6 \text{ minutes}} = 10 \text{ cars per hour}$$

Therefore, applying Equations [B-2] through [B-5]:

$$\text{Average number of cars waiting } (C_w) = \frac{\lambda^2}{\mu(\mu - \lambda)} = \frac{7.5^2}{10(10 - 7.5)} = 2.25 \text{ cars}$$

$$\text{Average number of cars in the system } (C_S) = C_w + \frac{\lambda}{\mu} = 2.25 + 0.75 = 3 \text{ cars}$$

$$\text{Average time a car spends waiting } (T_w) = \frac{\lambda}{\mu(\mu - \lambda)} = \frac{7.5}{10(10 - 7.5)}$$
$$= 0.3 \text{ hours, or about 18 minutes}$$

$$\text{Average time a car spends in the system } (T_S) = T_w + \frac{1}{\mu} = 0.3 + 0.1$$
$$= 0.4 \text{ hours, or about 24 minutes}$$

Example 8S.2

Luc's Deluxe Car Wash, Part 2—Probabilistic Arrivals and Constant Service Times

Luc is contemplating replacing his work crew with an automated car wash system. Although the automated system is no faster than the current work crew, it can handle cars at a *constant* rate of one car every six minutes. Luc is not sure if this would make any difference with regard to the waiting line performance at his car wash, so he decides to use the equations in Table 8S.1 to find out.

Notice that the arrival rate and service rate are still 7.5 cars and 10 cars per hour, respectively. The difference is that the service rate no longer follows an exponential distribution, but is constant. Applying Equations [B-6] through [B-9], Luc gets the following estimates:

$$\text{Average number of cars waiting } (C_w) = \frac{\lambda^2}{2\mu(\mu - \lambda)} = \frac{7.5^2}{20(10 - 7.5)} = 1.125 \text{ cars}$$

$$\text{Average number of cars in the system } (C_S) = C_w + \frac{\lambda}{\mu} = 1.125 + 0.75 = 1.875 \text{ cars}$$

$$\text{Average time a car spends waiting } (T_w) = \frac{\lambda}{2\mu(\mu - \lambda)} = \frac{7.5}{20(10 - 7.5)}$$
$$= 0.15 \text{ hours, or about 9 minutes}$$

$$\text{Average time a car spends in the system } (T_S) = T_w + \frac{1}{\mu} = 0.15 + 0.10$$
$$= 0.25 \text{ hours, or about 15 minutes}$$

Looking at the results, Luc is surprised to see that the average number of cars waiting and average time waiting are cut in half. The results impress upon Luc the impact of variability on process performance and capacity requirements.

Example 8S.3

Luc's Deluxe Car Wash, Part 3—Adding a Second Crew

Even though Luc likes the fact that an automated car wash system with constant service time would decrease waiting times and line lengths, he doesn't feel he can afford the investment at this point. Rather, Luc is thinking about adding a second crew. This would effectively make his car wash a multiple-channel, single-phase system, where M = 2. Assuming that the second crew has the same service rate numbers as the first ($\mu = 10$; service times are exponentially distributed), Luc can estimate the performance of the system using Equations [B-10] through [B-14]. To use these equations, we must first calculate the probability of zero cars in the system:

$$P_0 = \frac{1}{\left[\sum_{n=0}^{M-1} \frac{1}{n!}\left(\frac{\lambda}{\mu}\right)^n\right] + \frac{1}{M!}\left(\frac{\lambda}{\mu}\right)^M \left(\frac{M\mu}{M\mu-\lambda}\right)}$$

$$= \frac{1}{\left[1+\frac{7.5}{10}\right] + \frac{1}{2!}\left(\frac{7.5}{10}\right)^2\left(\frac{2*10}{2*10-7.5}\right)}$$

$$= \frac{1}{1.75+\frac{1}{2}(0.5625)(1.6)} = \frac{1}{1.75+0.45} = 0.4545$$

Plugging the resulting P_0 value into the formula for C_s:

$$C_S = \frac{\lambda\mu\left(\frac{\lambda}{\mu}\right)^M}{(M-1)!(M\mu-\lambda)^2}P_0 + \left(\frac{\lambda}{\mu}\right) = \frac{7.5*10\left(\frac{7.5}{10}\right)^2}{(2*10-7.5)^2}\times(0.4545)+(7.5\,/\,10)$$

$$= \frac{42.1875}{156.25}\times(0.4545)+(7.5/10) = 0.873 \text{ cars in the system, on average}$$

The average number of cars waiting:

$$C_w = C_S - \frac{\lambda}{\mu} = 0.873 - 0.75 = 0.123 \text{ cars}$$

The average time a car spends in the system:

$$T_S = \frac{\mu\left(\frac{\lambda}{\mu}\right)^M}{(M-1)!(M\mu-\lambda)^2}P_0 + \left(\frac{1}{\mu}\right) = \frac{10\left(\frac{7.5}{10}\right)^2}{(20-7.5)^2}0.4545+0.10$$

$$= \left(\frac{5.625}{156.25}\right)0.4545+0.10 = 0.12 \text{ hours, or about 7 minutes}$$

Finally, we can calculate the average time a car spends waiting:

$$T_w = T_S - \frac{1}{\mu} = 0.12 - 0.10 = 0.02 \text{ hours, or roughly 1 minute.}$$

8S.2 SIMULATION MODELING

APICS defines simulation as "the technique of using representative or artificial data to reproduce in a model various conditions that are likely to occur in the actual performance of a system."[1] Although simulations can include physical re-creations of an actual system, most business simulations are computer-based and use mathematical formulas to represent actual systems or policies. Simulation models have a number of advantages:

1. **Off-line evaluation of new processes or process changes.** Simulation models allow the user to experiment with processes or operating procedures without endangering the performance of real-world systems. For example, the user can test new systems or evaluate the impact of changes to processes or procedures prior to implementing them.
2. **Time compression.** Simulation models allow the user to compress time. Many days, months, or even years of activity can be simulated in a short period of time.
3. **"What if" analyses.** This can be particularly valuable in understanding how processes or procedures would perform under extreme conditions. What if the demand rate was to double? What if one of our key support centers was down? With simulation models, managers can get an idea of the impact prior to an actual occurrence.

Of course, simulations have their disadvantages:

1. **It is still a simulation.** Most simulation models—like the waiting line formulas we reviewed in the first half of the supplement—make simplifying assumptions about how the real world works. While these assumptions make the model easier to develop and understand, they also make it less realistic.
2. **The more realistic a simulation model is, the more costly it will be to develop and the more difficult it will be to interpret.** This is the converse of the first point. Model developers must strike a balance between cost, ease of use, and realism.
3. **Simulation models do not provide an "optimal" solution.** Simulation models only reflect the conditions and rules of the environments they are set up to model.

Monte Carlo Simulation

By far the most common form of simulation modeling is mathematical simulation, where mathematical formulas and statistical processes are used to simulate activities, decisions, and the like. One particularly well-known approach is **Monte Carlo simulation**, a technique in which statistical sampling is used to generate outcomes for a large number of trials. The results of these trials are then evaluated to gain insight into the system of interest.

Monte Carlo simulation is used to simulate all types of systems and many types of statistical distributions. To illustrate the basic principles of the technique, we will take a very simple system everyone is familiar with: flipping a coin. You probably understand that for a fair coin, each outcome—heads or tails—has a 50% chance of occurring. And you probably also understand that the outcome for any particular flip is "memoryless"; that is, the probability of coming up heads or tails is unaffected by what happened previously. Still, you may wonder how the pattern of outcomes might play out over, say, 50 flips.

Figure 8S.4 shows an Excel-based Monte Carlo simulation model for 50 coin flips, or trials. The random numbers for the 50 trials were generated using the following Excel formula:

=RAND()*100

[1]J. F. Cox and J. H. Blackstone (eds.), *APICS Dictionary*, 10th ed. (Falls Church, VA: APICS, 2002).

FIGURE 8S.4
Excel-Based Monte Carlo Simulation of 50 Coin Tosses

	A	B	C	D	E	F	G
1	Monte Carlo simulation of 50 coin tosses						
2	Excel-generated random numbers generated between 0 and 100						
3	v"Tails" if random number <50, "Heads" otherwise						
4							
5	**Trial**	**Random Number**	**Simulated Outcome**		**Trial**	**Random Number**	**Simulated Outcome**
6	1	75.79	Heads		26	41.23	Tails
7	2	54.88	Heads		27	28.41	Tails
8	3	3.20	Tails		28	80.16	Heads
9	4	89.32	Heads		29	79.27	Heads
10	5	64.62	Heads		30	6.34	Tails
11	6	25.56	Tails		31	89.72	Heads
12	7	60.99	Heads		32	14.85	Tails
13	8	77.68	Heads		33	15.76	Tails
14	9	77.14	Heads		34	99.29	Heads
15	10	51.42	Heads		35	40.66	Tails
16	11	14.43	Tails		36	19.91	Tails
17	12	27.02	Tails		37	55.73	Heads
18	13	25.73	Tails		38	83.07	Heads
19	14	43.28	Tails		39	69.75	Heads
20	15	36.91	Tails		40	14.89	Tails
21	16	49.08	Tails		41	45.60	Tails
22	17	88.84	Heads		42	0.40	Tails
23	18	45.94	Tails		43	80.11	Heads
24	19	97.69	Heads		44	16.58	Tails
25	20	27.94	Tails		45	19.35	Tails
26	21	78.90	Heads		46	15.19	Tails
27	22	90.03	Heads		47	32.78	Tails
28	23	64.11	Heads		48	25.08	Tails
29	24	60.71	Heads		49	95.15	Heads
30	25	2.02	Tails		50	45.36	Tails

This Excel formula generates a random number between 0 and 100, with all numbers having an equal probability of being generated. The adjacent column in the spreadsheet then translates these results into heads or tails. For example:

Formula for Cell C6: =IF(B6<50, "Tails", "Heads")

Translated, if the random number in Cell B6 is less than 50, write "Tails" in the cell; otherwise, write "Heads." Looking at the results, we can see that "Tails" came up 27 times and "Heads" came up 23 times—not exactly a 50/50 balance, but close. In addition, we can see that the simulated results do not alternate back and forth between heads and tails. In fact, there are several runs of four or more heads or tails.

Monte Carlo simulation can be used to simulate other statistical distributions as well. Figure 8S.5 shows another Excel-based Monte Carlo simulation model. In this case, we are trying to simulate arrivals, based on a Poisson distribution and an average arrival rate per time period of three arrivals.

First, the spreadsheet calculates the probability of zero through eight arrivals per time period using Equation [B-1]. Notice that the total of these probabilities is essentially 100%. Next, we assigned random numbers between 0 and 100 to each possible arrival quantity. For example, there is a 5% chance of zero arrivals. Therefore, we assigned all numbers (r) that meet the condition ($0 \le r < 5$) to represent zero arrivals. Since the probability of

FIGURE 8S.5
Excel-Based Monte Carlo Simulation of Poisson-Distributed Arrivals

Monte Carlo simulation of Poisson-distributed arrivals			
Arrival rate (λ) = 3			
Arrivals	Probability of *n* arrivals	Cumulative probability	Assigned random numbers (*r*) (0 to 100)
0	5%	5%	$0 \le r < 5$
1	15%	20%	$5 \le r < 20$
2	22%	42%	$20 \le r < 42$
3	22%	64%	$42 \le r < 65$
4	17%	82%	$65 \le r < 82$
5	10%	92%	$82 \le r < 92$
6	5%	97%	$92 \le r < 97$
7	2%	99%	$97 \le r < 99$
8	1%	100%	99 or greater
Time Period	Random no.	Simulated Arrivals	
1	75.60	4	
2	74.03	4	
3	80.70	4	
4	22.18	2	
5	88.12	5	
6	75.95	4	
7	47.38	3	
8	10.63	1	
9	34.96	2	
10	42.99	3	
11	83.14	5	
12	2.68	0	
13	8.21	1	
14	73.41	4	
15	39.71	2	
16	73.79	4	
17	99.70	8	
18	22.89	2	
19	19.32	1	
20	64.51	3	
	Average:	3.1	

drawing such a number using the "=RAND()*100" equation is also 5%, we can use this method to accurately simulate Poisson-distributed arrivals. Arrivals of one through eight units per time period were simulated in a similar fashion.

The bottom half of Figure 8S.5 presents results for 20 simulated time periods. Notice how the simulated arrivals range anywhere from zero to eight. For this particular simulation, the average arrival rate is 3.1, close to the expected arrival rate of 3 per time period.

Building and Evaluating Simulation Models with SimQuick

Developing a useful simulation model can require a great deal of creativity and practice, but the basic process can be divided into four steps:

1. Develop a picture of the system to be modeled. The process mapping material in Chapter 3 of the book can be particularly helpful in this regard.

2. Identify the objects, elements, and probability distributions that define the system. **Objects** are the people or products that move through the system, and **elements** are pieces of the system itself, such as lines, workstations, and entrance and exit points.
3. Determine the experimental conditions and required output information. Many simulation packages provide the user with options regarding the output reports that are generated.
4. Build and test the simulation model for your system, and capture and evaluate the relevant data.

When the process to be modeled is fairly complex, it usually makes sense to use a specialized simulation software package. These packages can range from very sophisticated applications that provide graphics and sophisticated "what if" analyses and make use of existing company databases, to simple stand-alone packages. In the following example, we build and test a simulation model of Luc's Deluxe Car Wash using SimQuick,[2] a highly intuitive, easy-to-learn simulation package that runs under Microsoft Excel.

Example 8S.4

Simulating Operations at Luc's Deluxe Car Wash

While Luc is generally happy with the statistics he was able to generate using the waiting line formulas (Examples 8S.1 through 8S.3), one thing troubles him: All of these statistics describe *averages*—average wait time, average number of cars in the system, and so on. They don't tell Luc how long the lines can actually get, or what the maximum time might look like.

Luc's car wash is pictured in Figure 8S.6. For simulation modeling purposes, there are four elements that make up Luc's car wash: The entrance, the driveway (where cars wait for an available crew), the crew, and washed cars. Two of these elements—cars arriving and the crews washing cars—are controlled by probability distributions.

Figure 8S.7 shows how the same system is defined in SimQuick. The first box is labeled "simulation controls." Luc has set the simulation to cover five iterations of 3600 minutes each. In effect, *each* iteration represents a work week consisting of five 12-hour days, or 3,600 minutes. The fact that Luc can run our simulation in a matter of seconds illustrates the time compression advantages of simulation.

The simulation model has one entrance point, "Cars." Cars arrive based on an exponential distribution, with an average of eight minutes between arrivals. Note that this is the *same* as saying that the arrivals are Poisson-distributed with an average of 60 minutes/8 minutes = 7.5 arrivals per hour.

Once a car "arrives," it then goes to the driveway, which is the first buffer point in the model. *For now*, Luc assumes that there is unlimited room for cars to wait here

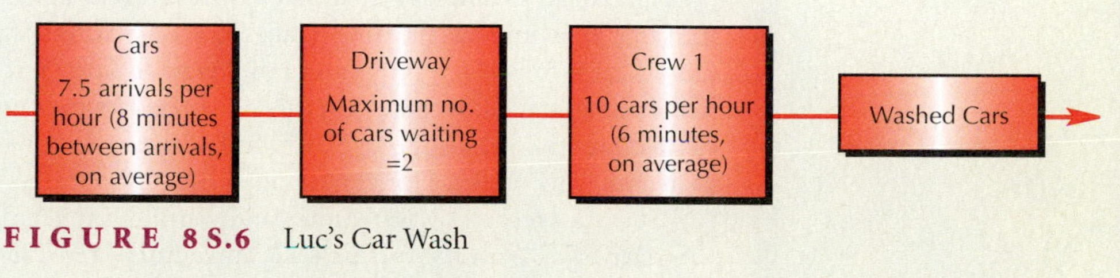

FIGURE 8S.6 Luc's Car Wash

[2] D. Hartvigsen, *SimQuick: Process Simulation in Excel* (Upper Saddle River, NJ: Prentice Hall, 2001).

	A	B	C	D	E	F
1	**Model View**					
2	(Note: Cannot edit model here)					
3						
4		**Simulation Controls:**				
5						
6		Time units per simulation →	3600			
7		Number of simulations →	5			
8						
9						
10		**Entrances:**				
11						
12						
13		**Name** →	Cars			
14		Time between arrivals →	Exp(8)			
15		Num. objects per arrivals →	1			
16		Output				
17		destination(s) ↓				
18		Driveway				
19						
20						
21						
22		**Work Stations:**				
23						
24						
25			**Name** →	Crew 1		
26			Working time →	Exp (6)		
27		Output	# of output	Resource	Resource	
28		destination(s) ↓	objects ↓	name(s) ↓	#units needed ↓	
29		Washed Cars				
30						
31						
32						
33		Buffers:				
34						
35		1			2	
36		**Name** →	Driveway		**Name** →	Washed Cars
37		Capacity →	10000		Capacity →	10000
38		Initial # objects →	0		Initial # objects →	0
39		Output	Output		Output	Output
40		destination(s) ↓	group size ↓		destination(s) ↓	group size ↓
41		Crew 1	1			
42						

FIGURE 8S.7 SimQuick Model Specification for Single-Channel, Single-Phase System, Luc's Deluxe Car Wash

("Capacity → 10,000"). If the washing crew is not busy, the car will immediately proceed to the workstation "Crew 1." Otherwise it will wait in the driveway.

The earlier examples stated that a crew can wash, on average, 10 cars per hour. This is the same as saying that the time it takes to wash a car is six minutes, on average ("Exp(6)"). Once a car is finished, it proceeds to the "Washed Cars" buffer. By modeling the system this way, Luc can track how many cars are completed by the end of each iteration.

Figure 8S.8 shows the overall simulation results for five iterations of 3,600 minutes each (five work weeks, each consisting of five 12-hour days).

Statistics regarding wait times and waiting line lengths can be found by looking at the "Driveway" results. In this case, "inventory" represents cars waiting to be washed. The average inventory is 2.58 cars and the mean cycle (i.e., waiting) time is 20.64 minutes. It's interesting to compare the simulation results to the formula-derived results in Example 8S.1:

Formula-derived estimate of average number of cars waiting $(C_w) = 2.25$ *cars*
Simulation estimate of average number of cars waiting = *2.58 cars*
Formula-derived estimate of average waiting time $(T_w) = 0.3$ hours, or about *18 minutes*
Simulation estimate of average number of cars waiting = *20.64 minutes*

Figure 8S.8 also shows that the average maximum number of cars in line across all five iterations was 15.8, and the fraction of time the washing crew was busy was 0.77, or 77%.

	A	B	C	D	E	F	G	H
1	**Results**							
2								
3	**Element**	**Statistics**	**Overall**	**Simulation Numbers**				
4	**names**		**means**	**1**	**2**	**3**	**4**	**5**
5								
6	Cars	Objects entering process	447.40	460	471	460	424	422
7		Objects unable to enter	0.00	0	0	0	0	0
8		Service level	1.00	1.00	1.00	1.00	1.00	1.00
9								
10	Crew 1	Final status	NA	Working	Working	Working	Working	Working
11		Final inventory (int. buff.)	0.00	0	0	0	0	0
12		Mean inventory (int. buff.)	0.00	0.00	0.00	0.00	0.00	0.00
13		Mean cycle time (int. buff.)	0.00	0.00	0.00	0.00	0.00	0.00
14		Work cycles started	444.20	459	466	453	421	422
15		Fraction time working	0.77	0.77	0.81	0.79	0.75	0.73
16		Fraction time blocked	0.00	0.00	0.00	0.00	0.00	0.00
17								
18	Driveway	Objects leaving	444.20	459	466	453	421	422
19		Final inventory	3.20	1	5	7	3	0
20		Minimum inventory	0.00	0	0	0	0	0
21		Maximum inventory	15.80	13	21	22	13	10
22		Mean inventory	2.57	2.07	3.74	3.84	1.75	1.47
23		Mean cycle time	20.64	16.22	28.89	30.55	15.01	12.54
24								
25	Washed Cars	Objects leaving	0.00	0	0	0	0	0
26		Final inventory	443.20	458	465	452	420	421
27		Minimum inventory	0.00	0	0	0	0	0
28		Maximum inventory	443.20	458	465	452	420	421
29		Mean inventory	219.71	233.76	228.58	223.11	196.72	216.40
30		Mean cycle time	Infinite	Infinite	Infinite	Infinite	Infinite	Infinite

FIGURE 8S.8 Simulation Results for Single-Channel, Single-Phase System

Example 8S.5

Simulating the Impact of Limited Waiting Space at Luc's Deluxe Car Wash

Satisfied that the simulation model adequately reflects his business, Luc decides to modify the model to capture one key characteristic that has not yet been considered. Specifically, *there is only enough room in the driveway for two cars to be waiting.* This means that if the crew is busy washing a car and two cars are already waiting, any other car that drives up will have to go elsewhere. Luc wonders how this would affect the results.

The modified simulation model is identical to the one shown in Figure 8S.7, *except now the capacity for the driveway buffer is set at 2.* Simulation results for this new model are shown in Figure 8S.9.

Looking at the results, Luc can clearly see the impact the small driveway is having on his business. According to the simulation results, on average, 61.4 cars per week are unable to enter the process. Because fewer cars enter the system, the fraction of time the washing crew is busy also suffers. In fact, it drops down to 64%. Finally, the mean cycle time and mean number of cars in the driveway decrease dramatically, but this is only because a large number of cars are *turned away.* In theory of constraints terms (Chapter 8), the driveway is clearly a constraint that limits throughput for the entire system. If Luc can somehow find more space to queue up the cars (and assuming the drivers are willing to wait), he could expect to achieve results closer to those in Figure 8S.8.

	A	B	C	D	E	F	G	H
1	**Results**							
2								
3	**Elements**	**Statistics**	**Overall**	**Simulation Numbers**				
4	**names**		**means**	**1**	**2**	**3**	**4**	**5**
5								
6	Cars	Objects entering process	378.20	386	376	373	−396	360
7		Objects unable to enter	61.40	65	49	62	68	63
8		Service level	0.86	0.86	0.88	0.86	0.85	0.85
9								
10	Crew 1	Final status	NA	Working	Working	Not Working	Working	Not Working
11		Final inventory (int.buff)	0	0	0	0	0	0
12		Mean inventory (int.nuff).	0.00	0.00	0.00	0.00	0.00	0.00
13		Mean cycle time (int.buff.)	0.00	0.00	0.00	0.00	0.00	0
14		Work cycle started	377.60	384	376	373	395	360
15		Fraction time working	0.64	0.65	0.60	0.61	0.69	0.63
16		Fraction time blocked	0.00	0.00	0.00	0.00	0.00	0.00
17								
18	Driveway	Objects leaving	377.60	384	376	373	395	360
19		Final inventory	0.60	2	0	0	1	0
20		Minimum inventory	0.00	0	0	0	0	0
21		Maximum inventory	2.00	2	2	2	2	2
22		Mean inventory	0.49	0.53	0.40	0.43	0.59	0.51
23		Mean cycle time	4.68	4.93	3.85	4.12	5.41	5.10
24								
25	Washed Cars	Objects leaving	0.00	0	0	0	0	0
26		Final inventory	377.00	383	375	373	394	360
27		Minimum inventory	0.00	0	0	0	0	0
28		Maximum inventory	377.00	383	375	373	394	360
29		Mean inventory	187.57	194.89	188.37	188.99	195.84	169.77
30		Mean cycle time	Infinite	Infinite	Infinite	Infinite	Infinite	Infinite

FIGURE 8S.9 Simulation Results for Single-Channel, Single-Phase System—Driveway Capacity is Limited to two Cars

SUPPLEMENT SUMMARY

In this supplement, we described different types of waiting line systems. We also provided formulas for evaluating the steady-state performance of three different systems. The second half of the supplement introduced simulation modeling, including a discussion and examples of Monte Carlo simulation, as well as the development and analysis of a simulation model using SimQuick.

Simulation modeling is a particularly important tool that managers can use to model and gain insight into complex business processes. Simulation is often the only way managers can understand what impact changes in capacity, process flows, or other elements of the business will have on customer performance.

We encourage you not to let your education end here, however. There is much more to both of these topics, and especially simulation modeling, than can be covered in this supplement. In fact, there are books devoted to simulation modeling,[3] and many colleges offer courses or even a series of courses on the topic.

DISCUSSION QUESTIONS

1. All things being equal, why do you think waiting line environments with constant service times have shorter waiting times and lines? Can you think of an example to illustrate your intuition?

2. Consider a supply chain where multiple manufacturers take turns processing a particular product. Which of the waiting line systems shown in Figures 8S.1 through 8S.3 best represent this environment? Explain.

3. We stated earlier that simulation modeling does not provide the user with an optimal solution. What did we mean by this? Explain, using one or more of the simulation examples given in the supplement.

[3]See, for example, J. Banks, J. Carson, B. Nelson, and D. Nicol, *Discrete-Event System Simulation*, 3rd ed. (Upper Saddle River, NJ: Prentice Hall, 2004).

PROBLEMS

Additional homework problems are available at www.prenhall.com/bozarth. These problems use Excel to generate customized problems for different class sections or even different students.
(* = easy; ** = moderate; *** = advanced)

1. Horton Williams Airport is a small municipal airport with two runways. One of these runways is devoted just to planes taking off. During peak time periods, about 8.5 planes per hour radio to the tower that they want to take off. The tower handles these requests in the order they arrive. Once the tower has given the go-ahead, it takes the plane, on average, five minutes to position itself on the runway and take off.
   a. (*) On average, how many planes will be waiting during peak time periods? How many will be in the system (waiting and on the runway)?
   b. (*) How long, on average, will a plane have to wait before it is allowed to take off?

2. The Women's department at Hector's Department Store has a single checkout register. Customers arrive at the register at the rate of 11 per hour. It takes the clerk, on average, four minutes to check out a customer.
   a. (**) On average, how many customers will be waiting to be checked out? In your mind, is this number reasonable? Why or why not?
   b. (**) How long, on average, will customers have to wait before the clerk starts serving them? Again, is this a reasonable time? If Hector's decides to open another register, what are the trade-offs to consider?

3. Parts arrive at an automated machining center at the rate of 100 per hour, based on a Poisson distribution. The machining center is able to process these parts at a fixed rate of 150 per hour. That is, each part will take exactly 60/150 = 0.4 minutes to process.
   a. (*) How many parts, on average, will be waiting to be processed? How many will be in the system (waiting and being processed)?
   b. (*) How long, on average, will a part have to wait before it is processed?

4. To deal with greater demand, Horton Williams Airport (Problem 1) has opened up a second runway devoted just to planes taking off. Peak demand has now been bumped up to 15 planes per hour. Furthermore, each plane still takes about five minutes to position itself and take off, once it has been given the go-ahead.
   a. (***) On average, how many planes will be waiting during peak time periods? How many will be in the system (waiting and on the runway)?
   b. (***) How long, on average, will a plane have to wait before it is allowed to take off?

5. Hector's Department store (Problem 2) has decided to add a second checkout register. This second register works at the same average speed as the first. Customer arrivals are the same as before.
   a. (***) On average, how many customers will be waiting to be checked out? From a business perspective, is this reasonable?
   b. (***) How long, on average, will customers have to wait before the clerk starts serving them? Again, is this a reasonable time?

6. Consider the Monte Carlo simulation shown in Figure 8S.5.
   a. (***) Recalculate the values in the "Probability of *n* arrivals" and "Cumulative probability" columns for an arrival rate of four arrivals. You may need to add some additional rows beyond just eight arrivals.
   b. (***) Based on the results of part a, redo the assigned random numbers column.
   c. (***) Using the same random numbers shown in Figure 8S.5, take the results from Parts a and b, and redo the column labeled "Simulated arrivals." What is the new average number of arrivals per time period?

7. (***) Consider the SimQuick simulation model for Luc's Car Wash, shown in Figure 8S.6. Suppose Luc decides to put in place a second crew. Redraw Figure 8S.6 to reflect this change. What changes to the model specification (Figure 8S.7) would you need to make? (*Hint*: You will not only need to make changes to the workstations, but to the "Driveway" buffer as well.)

REFERENCES

Banks, J., J. Carson, B. Nelson, and D. Nicol. *Discrete-Event System Simulation*, 3rd ed. Upper Saddle River, NJ: Prentice Hall, 2004.

Cox, J. F., and J. H. Blackstone, eds. *APICS Dictionary*. 10th ed. (Falls Church, VA: APICS, 2002).

Hartvigsen, D. *SimQuick: Process Simulation in Excel*. Upper Saddle River, NJ: Prentice Hall, 2001.

CHAPTER 9

Forecasting

CHAPTER OUTLINE

Chapter Objectives

By the end of this chapter, you will be able to:

- Discuss the importance of forecasting and identify the most appropriate type of forecasting approach, given different forecasting situations.
- Apply a variety of time series forecasting models, including moving average, exponential smoothing, and linear regression models.
- Develop causal forecasting models using linear regression and multiple regression.
- Calculate measures of forecasting accuracy and interpret the results.

CHEEZNAX SNACK FOODS, PART 1

It's November 2008, and Jamie Favre, demand planner for Cheeznax Snack Foods, is working away at her desk. In just two days, Jamie will need to provide top management with a forecast of 2009 demand, broken down by month. Cheeznax makes three products: puffed cheese balls, cheese nachos, and cheese-flavored potato chips. Currently, Cheeznax's products are sold through 100 convenience stores owned by Gas N' Grub. Jamie knows how important an accurate demand forecast is to the supply chain:

- *On the downstream side of the supply chain,* Gas N' Grub expects Cheeznax to keep the store shelves stocked with fresh products. If Cheeznax fails to deliver, then Gas N' Grub will take its business elsewhere.
- Within Cheeznax, manufacturing needs the forecast to plan production. While manufacturing doesn't want to underproduce, it also doesn't want to overproduce and end up with excessive inventory levels and spoilage costs. Furthermore, the finance department needs the forecast to project revenues for the upcoming year.
- Finally, *on the upstream side of the supply chain,* Cheeznax's suppliers need the forecast to plan their overall production levels of raw ingredients and packaging material.

Jamie looks at the 2008 Cheeznax sales figures, shown in Table 9.1. Jamie knows the 2008 numbers are a good starting point for developing the 2009 forecast, but she also knows that she needs more information. For instance, Gas N' Grub currently has 100 stores, but how many new stores will it open in 2009? How will this affect demand? Also, in past years Gas N' Grub has launched advertising campaigns for its stores without warning Cheeznax first. Cheeznax was unable meet the unplanned surges in demand, and the result was bickering between Jamie and the Gas N' Grub's purchasing manager. Ultimately, things would get smoothed over, but Jamie couldn't help but think about the lost sales opportunity. As Jamie contemplates all this information, she starts to formulate a plan for developing her forecast.

TABLE 9.1
2008 Monthly Sales Totals for Cheeznax

MONTH	SALES ($)
January	$230,000
February	$230,000
March	$240,000
April	$250,000
May	$240,000
June	$250,000
July	$270,000
August	$260,000
September	$260,000
October	$260,000
November*	$280,000
December*	$290,000
TOTAL:	$3,060,000

* Estimated demand

INTRODUCTION

Forecast
An estimate of the future level of some variable. Common variables that are forecasted include demand levels, supply levels, and prices.

A **forecast** is an estimate of the future level of some variable. The variable is most often demand, but it can also be some other criteria, such as capacity, available supply, or price. As we shall see throughout this book, forecasting is often the very first step organizations must go through when determining long-term capacity needs, yearly business plans, and shorter-term operations and supply chain activities. For example, could you imagine being a hospital administrator and trying to decide on the physical size of a new hospital, the number of doctors and nurses needed, or even the amount of supplies needed *without* forecasting patient demand first?

In practice, most organizations use a number of different forecasting techniques, depending on the situation they face. Some forecasting approaches depend on informal, human judgments; others depend primarily on statistical models and past data. Both types of forecasts are important in predicting the future.

In the first part of this chapter, we discuss the different types of forecasts firms use and the four laws of forecasting. We then differentiate between qualitative and quantitative forecasting techniques. Most of this chapter is devoted to illustrating some of the more common quantitative forecasting methods, as well as measures of model accuracy. Finally, we highlight the role of computer-based forecasting packages and the use of collaborative planning, forecasting, and replenishment (CPFR) programs by some supply chain partners to improve the accuracy of their forecasting efforts.

9.1 FORECAST TYPES

Often organizations need to forecast variables other than demand. In this section, we describe some of the more common forecast types: demand, supply, and price forecasts.

Demand Forecasts

When we talk about demand forecasts, we need to distinguish between overall market demand and firm-level demand. Both types of demand are of interest to businesses, but for different reasons. For instance, the U.S. demand for new cars and light trucks in 2007 is expected to be around 16.5 million. Working from this number, automotive manufacturers must decide what percentage of this overall demand they will capture. But the demand for new trucks is not the only demand the automotive manufacturers face. It will combine with other sources of demand—including warranty repairs, spare parts, and the like—to determine firm-level demand for all assemblies and components that go into trucks. Once firms have accurately forecasted this firm-level demand, they can begin to plan their business activities accordingly.

Supply Forecasts

Supply forecasts can be just as important as demand forecasts, as an interruption in supply can break the flow of goods and services to the final customer. A supply forecast might provide information on the number of current producers and suppliers, projected aggregate supply levels, and technological and political trends that might affect supply. To illustrate, one of the world's largest supplier of manganese is located in central Africa. Because political turmoil in this region has interrupted manganese shipments in the past, companies whose products depend on this mineral need to pay close attention to what is going on in this area of the world.

Price Forecasts

Third, many businesses need to forecast prices for key materials and services they purchase. When commodity prices are expected to increase, a good strategy is forward buying, in which companies buy larger quantities than usual, store them in inventory for future use, and save on the price they pay. If prices are falling, a better strategy is to buy more frequently in smaller quantities than usual, with the expectation that prices will go down over time. But the point is this: In order to decide on a purchasing strategy, firms must first have the price forecasts. Of course, sometimes price forecasting efforts don't always go as planned. The *Supply Chain Connections* box highlights Ford's difficulties with forecasting the price of palladium, a key raw material used in manufacturing antipollution devices.

SUPPLY CHAIN CONNECTIONS

FORD'S PALLADIUM DEBACLE[1]

In January 2002, Ford Motor Co. shocked Wall Street with a $1 billion write-off of the value of its stockpile of precious metals, primarily palladium. All of the big carmakers buy precious metals used in exhaust systems to make emissions cleaner. Ford accumulated an unusually large hoard in recent years, anticipating growing need and fearing unpredictable supplies from Russia. Yet Ford's own engineering innovations were shrinking its need for palladium, even as the purchasing department was loading up on it at near-record prices.

From 1992 to 1996, global auto-industry demand for the metal nearly quintupled, to 2.4 million ounces. Russia had massive stockpiles of palladium built up during the Soviet era, when demand had been slight. The cash-strapped government of then-president Boris Yeltsin seemed likely to remain a willing seller.

But in 1997, the Russians shocked the market by holding up palladium shipments. Outsiders could only speculate on what motivated the move: perhaps internal political or bureaucratic wrangling, or maybe a conscious effort to cause a panic—and higher prices. Whatever lay behind it, the disruption resulted by early 1998 in a price surge to the previously unheard of level of $350 an ounce.

The pressure only continued to grow. Palladium prices jumped again in 1999 amid uncertainty about Russian shipments. By spring 2000, the major metals exchange in Tokyo temporarily froze skyrocketing palladium at $700 an ounce.

Worried by these developments, Ford's top managers in 2000 approved a proposal from the purchasing staff to begin stockpiling palladium and lining up long-term supply. As Ford kept buying in early 2001, continued anxiety about Russian supplies pushed prices to a record of $1,094 an ounce in January of that year.

But by late 2001, Ford's own engineers had developed improved catalytic converters that would allow Ford to cut its use of precious metals in half across its entire North American lineup of cars and trucks, starting with the 2003 models.

But what about all of the palladium Ford had been scooping up? Not only was the company now overstocked in an exotic commodity it had much less need for, but also demand generally began to fall in 2001 as supplies stabilized. Demand was falling in part because other automakers had also succeeded in capping or reducing their use of palladium. Demand from the electronics industry, which also consumes a lot of palladium for use in capacitors, had diminished with the overall weakening of the world economy.

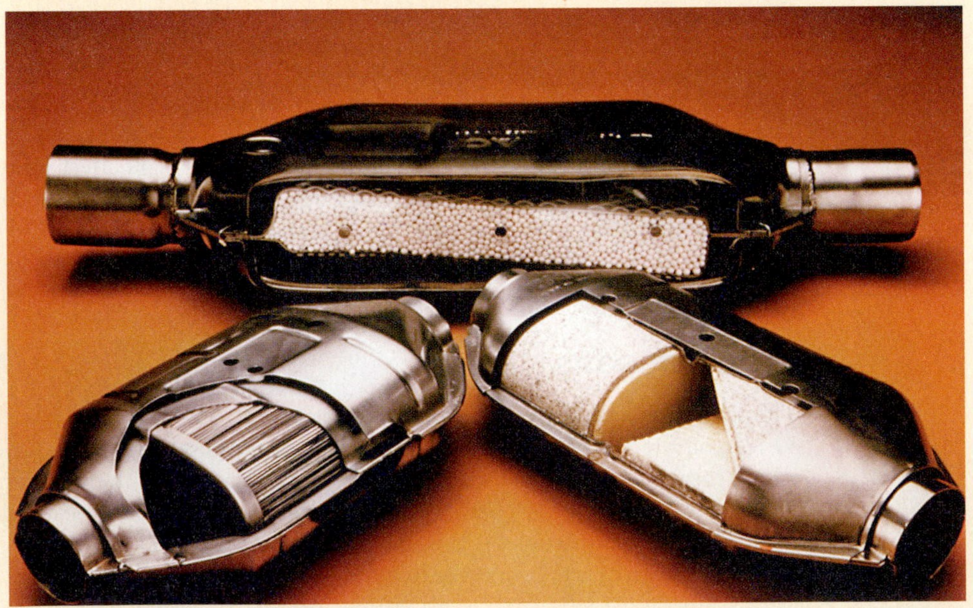

[1]Excerpts from G. White, "Precious Commodity: How Ford's Big Batch of Rare Metal Led to $1 Billion Write-Off," *The Wall Street Journal*, February 6, 2002.

On the supply side, high prices had spurred mine operators in South Africa to increase palladium production. And the unpredictable Russian supply began to stabilize. After reaching their peak above $1,000 in January 2001, palladium prices fell steadily through the summer to their lowest levels since 1999—about $350. Ford executives realized by fall 2001 that their fears about availability had proved to be overblown. "You've got a free supply situation now," said one Ford manager. "In retrospect, did we have too much [palladium]? Yes."

In retrospect—and hindsight is *always* 20/20—Ford's troubles were due in part to its inability to correctly forecast the demand, supply, and price of palladium. First, because the purchasing group did not consult with engineering, they were unaware of engineering breakthroughs that would dramatically cut Ford's demand for palladium. Second, Ford failed to predict how historically high prices would encourage suppliers to increase their output. This led to its third forecasting error—not anticipating that higher prices would encourage increased supply, thereby bringing prices down to more reasonable levels. Had Ford been able to forecast these changes more accurately, it is unlikely it would have been forced to take such an enormous write-off.

9.2 LAWS OF FORECASTING

Now that we have discussed some of the major types of forecasts, let's review the basic laws of forecasting. By keeping these laws in mind, users can avoid the misapplication or misinterpretation of forecast results.

Law 1: Forecasts Are Almost Always Wrong (But They Are Still Useful)

Even under the best of conditions, no forecasting approach can predict the *exact* level of future demand, supply, or price. There are simply too many factors that can ultimately affect these numbers. Rather, businesses should use forecasting methods to get *close* estimates. The degree to which a forecast is *accurate* is a function of forecasting laws 2 and 3.

Law 2: Forecasts for the Near Term Tend to Be More Accurate

This law recognizes that in the near term, the factors that affect the forecast variable are not likely to change greatly. Take, for instance, the price of gas. Given your understanding of current economic and political conditions, as well as the current price, you may feel reasonably comfortable predicting the price of gas for the next month or two. But what about the price of gas 10 or 20 years from now? In addition to economic and political changes, other factors such as technological breakthroughs and demographic changes could radically affect the demand for, and hence the price of, gas.

Law 3: Forecasts for Groups of Products or Services Tend to Be More Accurate

Many businesses have found that it is easier and more accurate to forecast for groups of products or services than it is to forecast for specific ones. The reason is simple: The demand, supply, or price of a *specific* item is usually affected by many more factors. Take, for example, the demand for dark green cars versus *all* cars. Color fashion may affect the precise demand for green cars. However, when we look at *overall* demand, the impact of color fashion disappears—higher or lower demand for green cars is balanced out by demand for cars of other colors.

Law 4: Forecasts Are No Substitute for Calculated Values

Forecasts should be used only when better approaches to determining the variable of interest are not available. To see what can go wrong when this law is not followed, consider the experiences of a plant visited by one of the authors. The plant made rubber products. Every Wednesday the management team would determine how many of each product would be made in the coming week. From this production plan, the plant's buyers could have easily calculated *exactly* how much and what grades of raw rubber would be needed. Instead, the buyers chose to forecast rubber requirements. As a result, sometimes the plant had too much rubber on hand, and at other times, not enough. In effect, the plant forecasted demand when it would have been simpler and more accurate to calculate demand.

9.3 SELECTING A FORECASTING METHOD

Quantitative forecasting models
Forecasting models that use measurable, historical data to generate forecasts. Quantitative forecasting models can be divided into two major types: time series models and causal models.

Forecasting is clearly an important business process. But how should companies go about selecting from the myriad of forecasting methods available? Figure 9.1 provides a road map that highlights the key questions forecasters need to ask, as well as the major categories and types of forecasting models used in practice.

The first set of issues concerns the availability of quantitative, historical data and evidence that this data can be used to predict the future. When these conditions hold, forecasters can use quantitative forecasting models. **Quantitative forecasting models** are forecasting models that use measurable, historical data to generate forecasts. When these

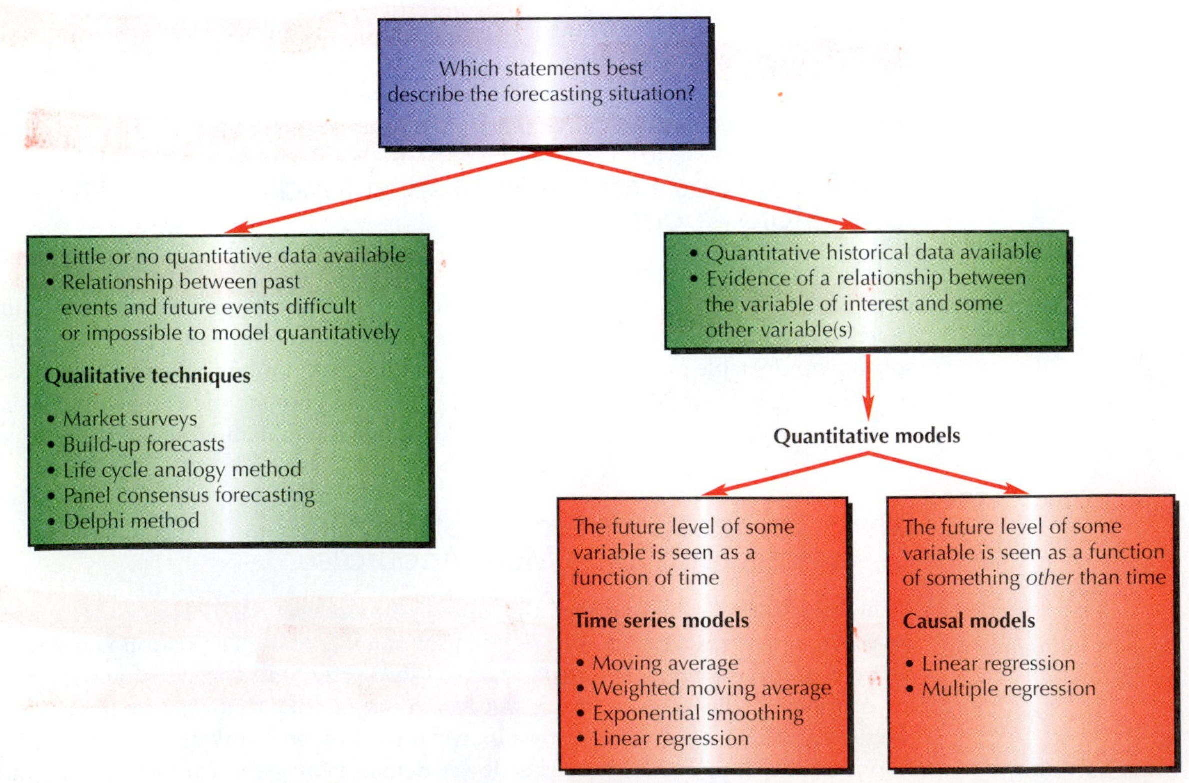

FIGURE 9.1 Selecting a Forecasting Method

conditions don't hold, qualitative forecasting techniques must be used. **Qualitative forecasting techniques** are forecasting techniques based on intuition or informed opinion. These techniques are used when historical data are scarce, not available, or irrelevant.

Qualitative forecasting techniques
Forecasting techniques based on intuition or informed opinion. These techniques are used when data are scarce, not available, or irrelevant.

To illustrate the distinction, consider two forecasting situations facing a large recording company:

- Total CD sales for the year, and
- CD sales for a new recording artist.

Market surveys
Structured questionnaires submitted to potential customers, often to gauge potential demand.

In the first case, last year's total sales may be a good predictor of total CD sales for this year (a classic example of time series modeling). The recording company may even be able to forecast total yearly sales based on the number of 18- to 25-year-olds or average personal disposable income figures (causal forecasting). Quantitative techniques are well suited to this situation.

Panel consensus forecasting
A qualitative forecasting technique that brings experts together to jointly discuss and develop a forecast.

But what about CD sales for a new artist? The recording company might try to draw comparisons to similar artists or even test the new CD with focus groups, but ultimately the company's managers will have to depend more on their opinions than any "hard" data.

9.4 QUALITATIVE FORECASTING METHODS

Delphi method
A qualitative forecasting technique that has experts work individually to develop forecasts. The individual forecasts are then shared among the group, after which each participant is allowed to modify his or her forecast based on information from the other experts. This process is repeated until a consensus is reached.

Even when qualitative forecasting must be used in situations where hard data doesn't exist, it doesn't mean that the forecast cannot be developed in a rational manner. **Market surveys** are structured questionnaires submitted to potential customers. They solicit opinions about products or potential products and often attempt to estimate likely demand. If structured well and administered to a representative sample of the defined population, market surveys can be quite effective. A major drawback is that they are expensive and time consuming to perform.

The Delphi method and panel consensus forecasting both use panels of experts to develop a consensus forecast. The major difference between the two is the process used to collect the data. **Panel consensus forecasting** brings the experts together to jointly discuss and develop forecasts. In contrast, the **Delphi method** has experts work individually to develop forecasts. The individual forecasts are then shared among the group, after which each participant is allowed to modify his or her forecast based on information from the other experts. This process is repeated until a consensus is reached. As you could probably imagine, these methods tend to be quite expensive, primarily due to the time requirements. The advantage is that when done correctly, they can be quite accurate.

Life cycle analogy method
A qualitative forecasting technique that attempts to identify the time frames and demand levels for the introduction, growth, maturity, and decline life cycle stages of a new product or service.

The **life cycle analogy method** is used when the product or service is new. The technique is based on the fact that many products and services have a fairly well-defined life cycle, consisting of an introduction stage, a growth stage, a maturity stage, and a decline stage. The major questions that arise include the following:

- How long will each stage last?
- How rapid will the growth be? How rapid will the decline be?
- How large will the overall demand be, especially during the maturity phase?

Build-up forecasts
A qualitative forecasting technique in which individuals familiar with specific market segments estimate the demand within these segments. These individual forecasts are then added up to get the overall forecast.

One approach is to base the forecast for the new product or service on the actual history of a similar product or service. This can be especially effective if the new product or service is essentially replacing another in the market and is targeted to the same population.

Finally, **build-up forecasts** work by having individuals familiar with specific market segments estimate the demand within these segments. These individual market segment

Time series
A series of observations arranged in chronological order.

forecasts are then added up to get the overall forecast. For instance, a U.S. company with sales offices in each of the 50 states might ask each regional sales manager to estimate per-state sales. Overall U.S. sales would then be calculated as the sum of these individual forecasts.

9.5 TIME SERIES FORECASTING MODELS

Time series forecasting models
Quantitative forecasting models that use time series to develop forecasts. With a time series model, the chronology of the observations, as well as their values, is important in developing forecasts.

Randomness
Within the context of forecasting, unpredictable movement from one time period to the next.

Trend
Long-term movement up or down in a time series.

Seasonality
A repeated pattern of spikes or drops in a time series associated with certain times of the year.

Quantitative forecasting models use statistical techniques and historical data to predict future levels. Such forecasting models are considered objective, rather than subjective, because they follow certain rules in calculating forecast values. The two main types of quantitative forecasting models are time series and causal models.

A **time series** consists of observations arranged in chronological order. **Time series forecasting models**, then, are quantitative forecasting models that analyze time series to develop forecasts. With a time series model, the chronology of the observations, as well as their values, is important in developing forecasts.

For example, suppose the director of an emergency care facility has recorded the number of patients who have arrived at the facility over the last 15 weeks. This demand time series is shown in Table 9.2.

Table 9.2 represents a time series because the values are arranged in chronological order. As Table 9.2 and Figure 9.2 show, the time series has two key characteristics. First, the weekly values tend to hover around 100, although in some weeks the number of patients is higher, and in other weeks, lower. Logic would suggest that, unless there are significant changes in either the population or the number of emergency care facilities in the area, future demand levels should be similar. Therefore, it would make sense to use the past demand numbers to forecast future demand levels. Second, the 15-week demand pattern shows **randomness**, or unpredictable movement from one time period to the next. Even though the average number of patients is approximately 101, actual demand numbers range anywhere from 81 to 127. This randomness makes forecasting difficult.

In some cases, time series might also show trend and seasonality, as well as randomness. **Trend** represents a long-term movement up or down, whereas **seasonality** is a

TABLE 9.2
Time Series Data for an Emergency Care Facility

WEEK	NUMBER OF PATIENTS
1	84
2	81
3	89
4	90
5	99
6	106
7	127
8	117
9	127
10	103
11	96
12	96
13	86
14	101
15	109
Average:	100.73

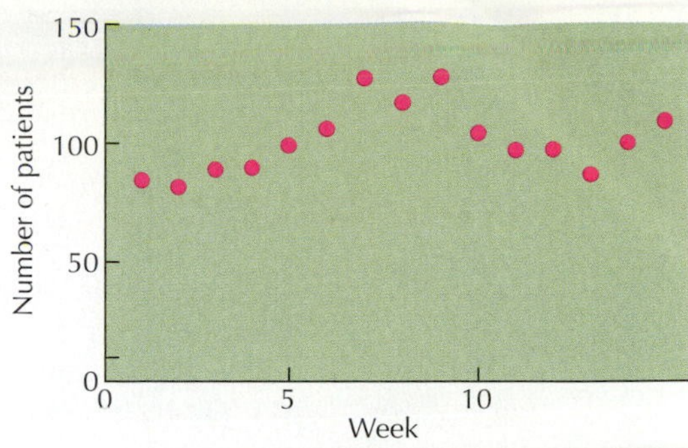

FIGURE 9.2
Time Series of Weekly Demand at an Emergency Care Facility

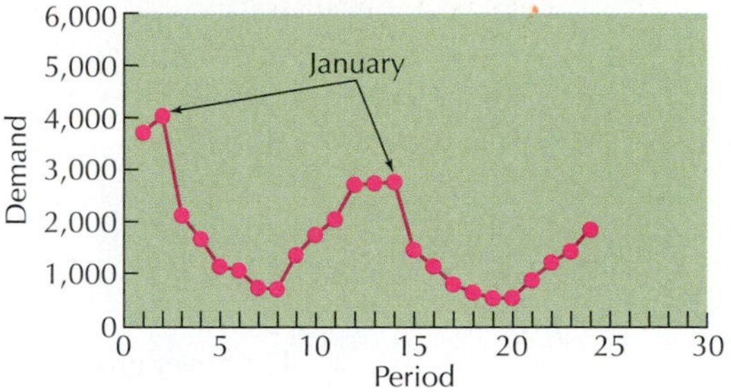

FIGURE 9.3
Time Series Showing Randomness, a Downward Trend, and Seasonality (Higher Demand in the Winter Months)

repeated pattern of spikes or drops in the variable of interest associated with certain times of the year. Figure 9.3 shows the time series for a product experiencing randomness, a downward trend, and seasonality in the demand. By the end of this chapter, we will have presented methods for developing time series forecasts when all three of these characteristics are present.

Last Period

The simplest time series model is a last-period model, which uses demand for the current period as a forecast for the next period. Stated formally:

$$F_{t+1} = D_t \qquad \textbf{[9-1]}$$

where:

F_{t+1} = forecast for the next period, $t + 1$
D_t = demand for the current period, t

Consider the time series listed in Table 9.2 and graphed in Figure 9.2. Suppose the director of the emergency care facility decides to use a last-period forecasting model to predict the number of patients each week. The demand in week 1 becomes the forecast for week 2, the demand in week 2 becomes the forecast for week 3, and so on, as can be seen in Table 9.3.

Figure 9.4 graphs the demand and forecast values from Table 9.3. As the results suggest, the main problem with a last-period model is that it is based on only one observation. This makes it overly susceptible to unusually high or low values. Look at the week 10 forecast, which is based on week 9's demand of 127. The forecast turns out to be much higher than actual demand in week 10. In fact, week 10's demand is actually much closer to the average demand of 100.73.

TABLE 9.3
Last-Period Forecasting for an Emergency Care Facility

WEEK	NUMBER OF PATIENTS	LAST-PERIOD FORECAST
1	84	
2	81	84
3	89	81
4	90	89
5	99	90
6	106	99
7	127	106
8	117	127
9	127	117
10	103	127
11	96	103
12	96	96
13	86	96
14	101	86
15	109	101
16		109

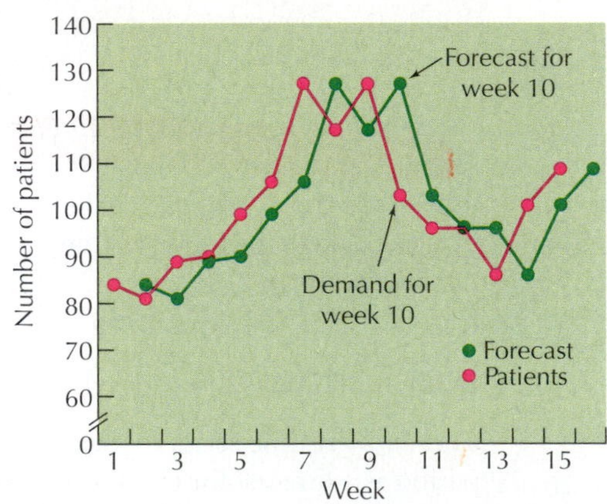

FIGURE 9.4
Last-Period Forecasting for an Emergency Care Facility

Moving Average

Moving average model
A time series forecasting model that derives a forecast by taking an average of recent demand values.

In response to the limitations of a last-period forecasting model, **moving average models** derive a forecast by taking an average of a set of recent demand values. By basing the forecast on more than one observed demand value, the moving average model is less susceptible to random swings in demand. The model is stated as follows:

$$F_{t+1} = \frac{\sum_{i=1}^{n} D_{t+1-i}}{n} \quad [9\text{-}2]$$

where:

F_{t+1} = forecast for time period $t+1$
D_{t+1-i} = actual demand for period $t+1-i$
n = number of most recent demand observations used to develop the forecast

For example, using the data in Table 9.2, the *three*-period moving average forecast for week 16 is derived from the demand figures for the previous three weeks (weeks 13–15):

$$F_{16} = \frac{\sum_{i=1}^{3} D_{16-i}}{3} = \frac{D_{15}+D_{14}+D_{13}}{3} = \frac{109+101+86}{3}$$
$$= 98.7$$

By basing the forecast on multiple values, the moving average model generates "smoothed" forecasts that are less susceptible to random fluctuations in demand. It is because of this that moving average models are sometimes called **smoothing models**.

Smoothing models
Another name for moving average models. The name refers to the fact that using averages to generate forecasts results in forecasts that are less susceptible to random fluctuations in demand.

Table 9.4 shows two-period moving average and four-period moving average results for the emergency medical care center.

The smoothing effect is evident in the minimum and maximum values for the two forecasting models. The same effect can be seen graphically in Figure 9.5. Both the two-period and the four-period models smooth out the peaks and valleys in the raw demand numbers. Because their forecasts are averages based on past data, the forecasts also echo the rises and falls in demand. These smoothing and delayed-reaction characteristics are more pronounced in the four-period model than in the two-period one.

So which is better here, the two-period or four-period model? Generally speaking, the more randomness there is in the raw data, the more attractive the smoothing and delayed-reaction characteristics are. The four-period model would be preferable in such a case. On the other hand, if rises or falls in demand are not random, but really do indicate changes in

TABLE 9.4
Two-Period and Four-Period Moving Average Forecasts

WEEK	NUMBER OF PATIENTS	2-PERIOD MOVING AVERAGE FORECAST	4-PERIOD MOVING AVERAGE FORECAST
1	84		
2	81		
3	89	82.5	
4	90	85.0	
5	99	89.5	86.0
6	106	94.5	89.8
7	127	102.5	96.0
8	117	116.5	105.5
9	127	122.0	112.3
10	103	122.0	119.3
11	96	115.0	118.5
12	96	99.5	110.8
13	86	96.0	105.5
14	101	91.0	95.3
15	109	93.5	94.8
16		105.0	98.0
Average:	100.7	101.0	102.6
Minimum:	81	82.5	86.0
Maximum:	127	122.0	119.3

FIGURE 9.5
Two-Period and Four-Period Moving Average Forecasts for an Emergency Care Facility

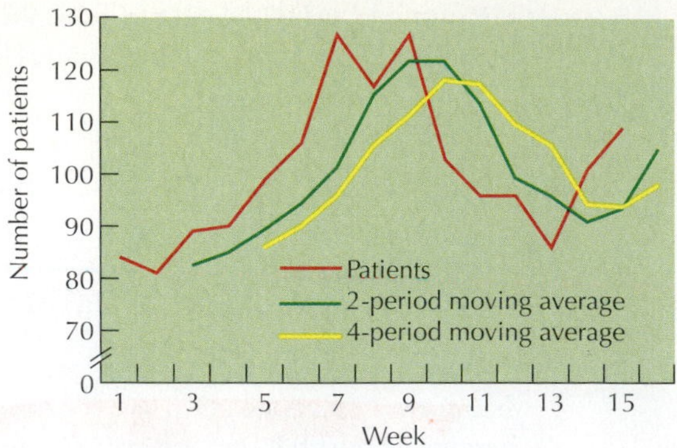

the underlying demand pattern, we would prefer a more reactive model, such as the two-period model. Later in the chapter, we describe measurements that can be used to compare the relative performance of alternative forecasting models.

Weighted Moving Average

Weighted moving average model
A form of the moving average model that allows the actual weights applied to past observations to differ.

A variation of the moving average model is the **weighted moving average model**. In this case, the actual weights applied to past observations are allowed to differ:

$$F_{t+1} = \sum_{i=1}^{n} W_{t+1-i} D_{t+1-i} \qquad \textbf{[9-3]}$$

where:

W_{t+1-i} = weight assigned to the demand in period $t + 1 - i$

$$\sum_{i=1}^{n} W_{t+1-i} = 1$$

As the formulas suggest, the only real restriction is that the weights must add to 1. Allowing the weights to vary lets the user change the emphasis placed on the past observations. Suppose we want to use a three-period weighted moving average model with the following weights:

Weight given to the current time period $= W_t = 0.5$
Weight given to the last time period $= W_{t-1} = 0.3$
Weight given to the time period two periods earlier $= W_{t-2} = 0.2$

The different weights will place more emphasis on the most recent observations. Using the data in Table 9.2, the three-period weighted moving average forecast for week 16 would be:

$$F_{16} = \sum_{i=1}^{3} W_{16-i} D_{16-i} = W_{15}D_{15} + W_{14}D_{14} + W_{13}D_{13}$$

$$= 0.5 + 109 + 0.3 + 101 + 0.2 + 86 = 102$$

Example 9.1

Flavio's Pizza

Flavio's Pizza has recorded the following demand history for each Friday night for the past five weeks. Develop forecasts for week 6 using a two-period moving average model and a three-period moving average model. The weights for the three-period weighted moving average model are 0.4, 0.35, and 0.25, starting with the most recent observation.

WEEK	DEMAND
1	62
2	45
3	55
4	73
5	60

The two-period moving average forecast would be

$$F_6 = (60 + 73)/2 = 66.5 \text{ pizzas}$$

The three-period weighted moving average forecast would be

$$F_6 = 0.4 \times 60 + 0.35 \times 73 + 0.25 \times 55 = 63.3 \text{ pizzas}$$

Exponential Smoothing

Exponential smoothing model
A special form of the moving average model in which the forecast for the next period is calculated as the weighted average of the current period's actual value and forecast.

The **exponential smoothing model** is a special form of the moving average model in which the forecast for the next period is calculated as the weighted average of the current period's actual demand and forecast. The formula for the exponential smoothing model is:

$$F_{t+1} = \alpha D_t + (1 - \alpha) F_t \qquad \textbf{[9-4]}$$

where:

F_{t+1} = forecast for time period $t + 1$ (i.e., the *new* forecast)
F_t = forecast for time period t (i.e., the *current* forecast)
D_t = actual value for time period t
α = smoothing constant used to weight D_t and F_t $(0 \leq \alpha \leq 1)$

There are a couple of things to note about the exponential smoothing model. First, as Equation 9-4 shows, the exponential smoothing model works by "rolling up" the current period's actual and forecasted values into the next period's forecast. Because all forecasts are based on past actual values, all actual demand values back to the first period ultimately end up in the most recent forecast.

To show how it works, suppose the Emerald Pool Company has just started selling above-ground pools. In the first month, Emerald forecasted demand of 40 pools, while actual demand turned out to 50. If we select an α value of 0.3, the exponential smoothing forecast for period 2 becomes:

$$F_2 = 0.3 \times D_1 + (1 - 0.3) F_1$$
$$= 0.3 \times 50 + 0.7 \times 40 = 15 + 28 = 43 \text{ pools}$$

TABLE 9.5
Exponential Smoothing Forecasts for Periods 2–6, Emerald Pool Company

Period	Demand	Forecast
1	50	40
2	46	0.3 * 50 + (1 – 0.3) * 40 = 43
3	52	0.3 * 46 + (1 – 0.3) * 43 = 43.9
4	48	0.3 * 52 + (1 – 0.3) * 43.9 = 46.33
5	47	0.3 * 48 + (1 – 0.3) * 46.33 = 46.83
6		0.3 * 47 + (1 – 0.3) * 46.83 = 46.88

Now suppose period 2 demand turns out to be 46 pools. The forecast for period 3 can now be calculated as:

$$F_3 = 0.3 \times D_2 + (1 - 0.3)F_2$$
$$= 0.3 \times 46 + 0.7 \times 43 = 13.8 + 30.1 = 43.9 \text{ pools}$$

Notice how period 3's forecast (F_3) is derived in part from the forecast in period 2 (F_2). Because F_2 is based in part on demand in period 1, so is the forecast for period 3. Table 9.5 shows this "rolling up" effect over the first six periods. By following the arrows, you can see how period 1's demand ultimately becomes part of the forecast for period 6. The same is true for periods 2 through 5.

Another critical feature of the exponential smoothing model is the smoothing constant, α. According to Equation 9-4, the forecast for the next period, F_{t+1}, is really just a weighted average, with α determining the relative weight put on the current period's actual and forecasted values, D_t and F_t. The closer α is to 1, the greater is the weight put on the *most recent* actual demand value; the closer α is to 0, the more emphasis is put on *past* forecasts. Therefore, we can control how reactive the model is by controlling α.

The general rule for determining the α value is this: The greater the randomness in the time series data, the lower the α value should be. Conversely, the less randomness there is in the time series data, the higher the α value should be.

Figure 9.6 shows a time series of demand data, as well as the resulting forecasts for an exponential smoothing model with a smoothing constant value of α = 0.2. The time series contains a spike in demand in period 11 and a trough in period 18. After each of these periods, the actual demand numbers seem to return to the "normal" range of values between 8 and 12.

In a situation like this, we would not want the forecast model to overreact to the extreme demand levels in periods 11 and 18. And in fact, due to the low weight put on the most recent demand level, D_t, the exponential smoothing forecast values are only slightly affected by periods 11 and 18.

Now consider the demand numbers in Figure 9.7. Here, the demand spike in period 11 is followed by a shift up in the demand numbers. In other words, period 11 is *not* a random result, but an important indicator of a change in the underlying demand pattern. How does the exponential smoothing model perform in this case? Not as well as before. In fact, because of the low α value, the forecasting model still hasn't "caught up" by period 20.

HAVE YOU THOUGHT ABOUT *Customizing* THIS BOOK?

Customizing

The Prentice Hall Just-In-Time Program in Decision Science

You can combine chapters from this book with chapters from any of the Prentice Hall titles listed on the following page to create a text tailored to your specific course needs. You can add your own material or cases from our extensive case collection. By taking a few minutes to look at what is sitting on your bookshelf and the content available on our Web site, you can create your ideal textbook.

The Just-In-Time program offers:

- **Quality of Material to Choose From**—In addition to the books listed, you also have the option to include any of the cases from Prentice Hall Custom Business Resources, which gives you access to cases (and teaching notes where available) from Darden, Harvard, Ivey, NACRA, and Thunderbird. Most cases can be viewed online at our Web site.
- **Flexibility**—Choose only that material you want, either from one title or several titles (plus cases) and sequence it in whatever way you wish.
- **Instructional Support**—You have access to the text-specific CD-ROM that accompanies the traditional textbook and desk copies of your JIT book.
- **Outside Materials**—There is also the option to include up to 20% of the text from materials outside of Prentice Hall Custom Business Resources.
- **Cost Savings**—Students pay only for material you choose. The base price is $6.00, plus $2.00 for case material, plus $.09 per page. The text can be shrink-wrapped with other Pearson textbooks for a 10% discount. Outside material is priced at $.10 per page plus permission fees.
- **Quality of Finished Product**—Custom cover and title page—including your name, school, department, course title, and section number. Paperback, perfect bound, black-and-white printed text. Customized table of contents. Sequential pagination throughout the text.

Visit our Web site at www.prenhall.com/custombusiness and create your custom text on our bookbuildsite or download order forms online.

FIGURE 9.6
Exponential Smoothing Forecast ($\alpha = 0.2$) for Time Series A

α =	0.2	EXPONENTIAL SMOOTHING
PERIOD	DEMAND	FORECAST
1	10	10*
2	11	10.00
3	9	10.20
4	11	9.96
5	10	10.17
6	8	10.14
7	12	9.71
8	9	10.17
9	10	9.94
10	11	9.95
11	**20**	10.16
12	11	**12.13**
13	9	11.90
14	11	11.32
15	10	11.26
16	9	11.01
17	11	10.61
18	4	10.68
19	10	9.34
20	11	9.48

*To start the process,the forecast for Period 1 was set at 10.

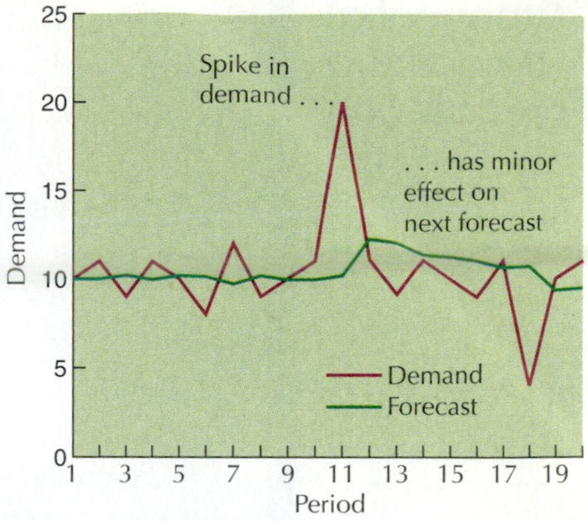

Spike in demand . . .
. . . has minor effect on next forecast
Demand
Forecast
Demand
Period
0
5
10
15
20
25
1 3 5 7 9 11 13 15 17 19

FIGURE 9.7
Exponential Smoothing Forecast ($\alpha = 0.2$) for Time Series B

α =	0.2	EXPONENTIAL SMOOTHING
PERIOD	DEMAND	FORECAST
1	10	10*
2	11	10.00
3	9	10.20
4	11	9.96
5	10	10.17
6	8	10.14
7	12	9.71
8	9	10.17
9	10	9.94
10	11	9.95
11	20	10.16
12	21	12.13
13	19	13.90
14	22	14.92
15	18	16.34
16	20	16.67
17	21	17.34
18	19	18.07
19	20	18.26
20	21	18.60

*To start the process, the forecast for Period 1 was set at 10.

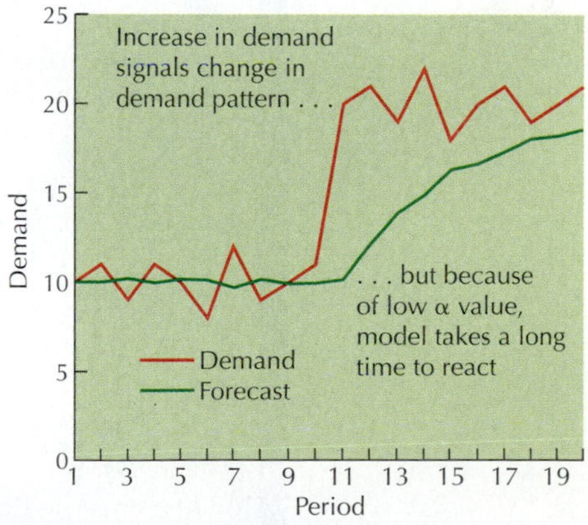

Increase in demand signals change in demand pattern . . .
. . . but because of low α value, model takes a long time to react
Demand
Forecast
Demand
Period
0
5
10
15
20
25
1 3 5 7 9 11 13 15 17 19

Example 9.2

Exponential Smoothing Forecast with $\alpha = 0.8$

Using the time series data in Figure 9.7, calculate an exponential smoothing forecast for periods 2 through 20, using a smoothing constant value of 0.8. Graph the results.

The detailed calculations for F_2 through F_7 are as follows:

$$F_2 = 0.8 \times D_1 + 0.2 \times F_1 = 0.8 \times 10 + 0.2 \times 10 = 10$$
$$F_3 = 0.8 \times D_2 + 0.2 \times F_2 = 0.8 \times 11 + 0.2 \times 10 = 10.8$$
$$F_4 = 0.8 \times D_3 + 0.2 \times F_3 = 0.8 \times 9 + 0.2 \times 10.8 = 9.36$$
$$F_5 = 0.8 \times D_4 + 0.2 \times F_4 = 0.8 \times 11 + 0.2 \times 9.36 = 10.67$$
$$F_6 = 0.8 \times D_5 + 0.2 \times F_5 = 0.8 \times 10 + 0.2 \times 10.67 = 10.13$$
$$F_7 = 0.8 \times D_6 + 0.2 \times F_6 = 0.8 \times 8 + 0.2 \times 10.13 = 8.43$$

Forecasts for periods 8 through 20 are completed in a similar manner. Figure 9.8 shows the complete set of forecast values and graph. Because of the high α value, the exponential smoothing model now reacts quickly to the increase in demand levels.

α =	0.8	EXPONENTIAL SMOOTHING
PERIOD	DEMAND	FORECAST
1	10	10.00*
2	11	10.00
3	9	10.80
4	11	9.36
5	10	10.67
6	8	10.13
7	12	8.43
8	9	11.29
9	10	9.46
10	11	9.89
11	20	10.78
12	21	18.16
13	19	20.43
14	22	19.29
15	18	21.46
16	20	18.69
17	21	19.74
18	19	20.75
19	20	19.35
20	21	19.87

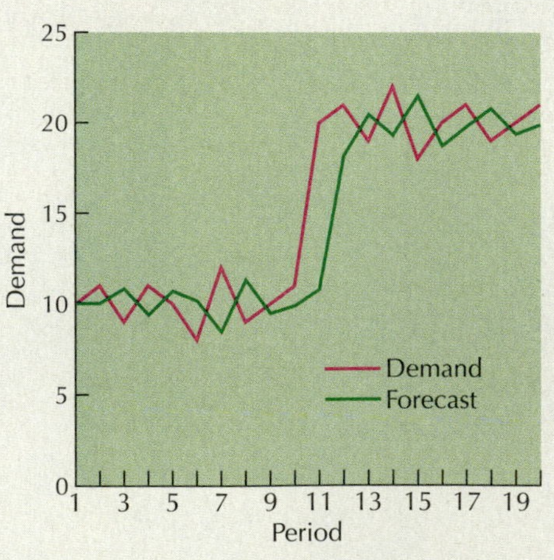

*To start the process,the forecast for Period 1 was set to 10.

FIGURE 9.8 Exponential Smoothing Forecast (α = 0.8) for Time Series B

Adjusted Exponential Smoothing

None of the models we have talked about so far will work when there is a pronounced upward or downward trend in the time series. This is because all of the previous models are just averages of past observations. If there is a strong upward or downward trend, the resulting forecasts will lag.

Adjusted exponential smoothing model
An expanded version of the exponential smoothing model that includes a trend adjustment factor.

In the next two sections, we describe two approaches to dealing with a trend in the time series. The first is the **adjusted exponential smoothing model**, which takes the simple exponential smoothing model and adds a trend adjustment factor to it. Specifically:

$$AF_{t+1} = F_{t+1} + T_{t+1} \quad [9\text{-}5]$$

where:

AF_{t+1} = adjusted forecast for the next period

F_{t+1} = unadjusted forecast for the next period = $\alpha D_t + (1 - \alpha)F_t$

T_{t+1} = trend factor for the next period = $\beta(F_{t+1} - F_t) + (1 - \beta)T_t$ **[9-6]**

T_t = trend factor for the current period

β = smoothing constant for the trend adjustment factor

To illustrate the adjusted exponential smoothing model, consider the demand time series shown in Table 9.6. Using an α value of 0.3, the unadjusted exponential smoothing forecast for period 2, F_2, is calculated as follows:

$$F_2 = 0.3 \times 30 + 0.7 \times 27 = 27.9$$

TABLE 9.6
Adjusted Exponential Smoothing Forecast for a Time Series ($\alpha = 0.3$, $\beta = 0.6$)

PERIOD	DEMAND	UNADJUSTED FORECAST F_t	TREND T_t	ADJUSTED FORECAST AF_t
1	30	27*	0	
2	34	27.90	0.54	28.44
3	37	29.73	1.31	31.04
4	40	31.91	1.83	33.74
5	44	34.34	2.19	36.53
6	48	37.24	2.62	39.86
7	51	40.47	2.99	43.45
8	55	43.63	3.09	46.72
9	58	47.04	3.28	50.32
10	62	50.33	3.29	53.62
11	65	53.83	3.42	57.25
12	66	57.18	3.38	60.56
13	67	59.83	2.94	62.77
14	66	61.98	2.47	64.45
15	67	63.19	1.71	64.90
16	65	64.33	1.37	65.70
17	66	64.53	0.67	65.20
18	67	64.97	0.53	65.50
19	67	65.58	0.58	66.16
20	66	66.01	0.49	66.50

*To start the process, F_1 was set equal to 27.

FIGURE 9.9
Comparing Exponential Smoothing (F_t) and Adjusted Exponential Smoothing (AF_t) Forecasts for a Time Series with a Trend

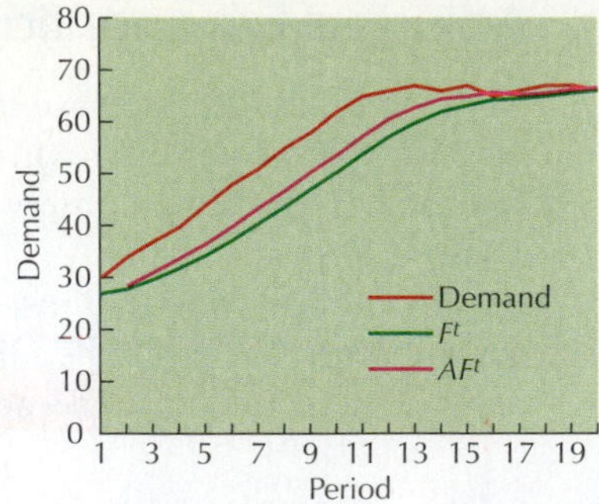

The trend adjustment factor for period 2, T_2, is then calculated as a weighted average of the difference between the last two unadjusted forecasts ($F_2 - F_1$) and the previous trend adjustment factor, T_1. Using a trend smoothing factor of $\beta = 0.6$:

$$T_2 = 0.6 \times (F_2 - F_1) + 0.4 \times T_1$$
$$= 0.6 \times (27.9 - 27) + 0.4 \times 0 = 0.$$

And adding F_2 and T_2 gives us the adjusted forecast for period 2:

$$AF_2 = 27.9 + 0.54 = 28.44$$

As can be seen from the results in Table 9.6 and Figure 9.9, the adjusted exponential smoothing model does a better job of picking up on the upward trend in the data than does the unadjusted model.

Linear Regression

Linear regression
A statistical technique that expresses the forecast variable as a linear function of some independent variable. Linear regression can be used to develop both time series and causal forecasting models.

Another approach to forecasting when there is a trend in the data is linear regression. **Linear regression** is a statistical technique that expresses the forecast variable as a linear function of some independent variable. In the case of a time series model, the independent variable is the time period itself. Linear regression works by using past data to estimate the intercept term and slope coefficient for the following line:

$$\hat{y} = \hat{a} + \hat{b}x \quad [9\text{-}7]$$

where:

$\hat{y}$ = forecast for *dependent* variable, y

x = *independent* variable, x, used to forecast y

$\hat{a}$ = estimated intercept term for the line

$\hat{b}$ = estimated slope coefficient for the line

$\hat{a}$ and $\hat{b}$ are estimated using the raw time series data for variable y (the *dependent* variable) and variable x (the *independent* variable):

$$\hat{b} = \frac{\sum_{i=1}^{n} x_i y_i - \frac{\left(\sum_{i=1}^{n} x_i\right)\left(\sum_{i=1}^{n} y_i\right)}{n}}{\sum_{i=1}^{n} x_i^2 - \frac{\left(\sum_{i=1}^{n} x_i\right)^2}{n}} \quad [9\text{-}8]$$

and

$$\hat{a} = \bar{y} - \hat{b}\bar{x} \quad [9\text{-}9]$$

where:

(x_i, y_i) = matched pairs of observed (x, y) values

$\bar{y}$ = average y value

$\bar{x}$ = average x value

n = number of paired observations

Once the line in Equation 9-7 has been estimated, the forecaster can then plug in values for x, the independent variable, to generate the forecast values, $\hat{y}$.

Example 9.3

Clem's Competition Clutches

Mike Clem, owner of Clem's Competition Clutches, designs and manufactures heavy-duty car clutches for use in drag racing. In his first 10 months of business, Mike has experienced the demand shown in Table 9.7 and Figure 9.10.

TABLE 9.7 Ten-Month Time Series of Demand for Clem's Competition Clutches

MONTH (x)	DEMAND (y)
1	8
2	12
3	25
4	40
5	50
6	65
7	36
8	61
9	88
10	63

Using the month as the independent variable (x) to forecast demand (y), Mike wants to develop a linear regression forecasting model and use the model to forecast demand for months 11, 12, and 13. Following Equations 9-8 and 9-9, the first step is to set up columns to

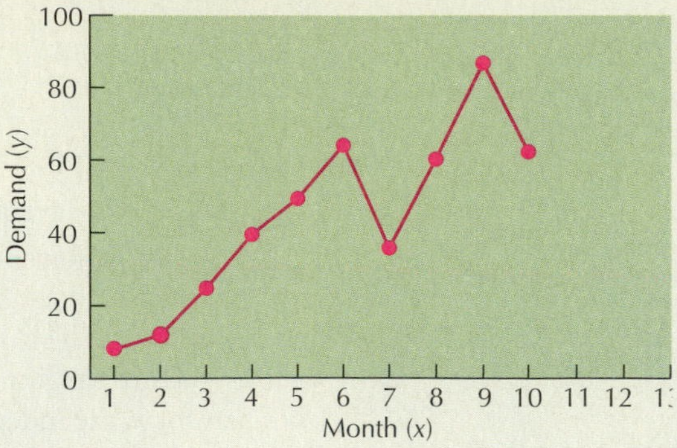

FIGURE 9.10 Ten-month Time Series of Demand for Clem's Competition Clutches

calculate the average x and y values, as well as the sums of the x, y, x^2, and xy values for the first 10 months:

	MONTH x	DEMAND y	x^2	xy
	1	8	1	8
	2	12	4	24
	3	25	9	75
	4	40	16	160
	5	50	25	250
	6	65	36	390
	7	36	49	252
	8	61	64	488
	9	88	81	792
	10	63	100	630
Sum:	55	448	385	3,069
Average:	5.50	44.80		

Plugging these values into the equations gives the estimate of the slope coefficient, $\hat{b}$:

$$\hat{b} = \frac{3{,}069 - \dfrac{55 \times 448}{10}}{385 - \dfrac{55^2}{10}} = \frac{3{,}069 - 2{,}464}{385 - 302.5} = 7.33$$

and the intercept term, $\hat{a}$:

$$\hat{a} = \overline{y} - \hat{b}\overline{x} = 44.80 - 7.33 \times 5.50 = 4.$$

The resulting regression line is:

$$\hat{y} = 4.49 + 7.33x$$

By plugging 11, 12, and 13 in for x, we can generate forecasts for months 11, 12, and 13:

Month 11 forecast: $4.49 + 7.33 \times 11 = 85.12$ clutches

Month 12 forecast: $4.49 + 7.33 \times 12 = 92.45$ clutches

Month 13 forecast: $4.49 + 7.33 \times 13 = 99.78$ clutches

Figure 9.11 plots the regression line forecasts for months 1 through 13 and the first 10 months of demand. The graph shows how the regression line captures the upward trend in the data and projects it out into the future. Of course, these future forecasts are good only as long as the upward trend of around 7.33 additional sales each month continues.

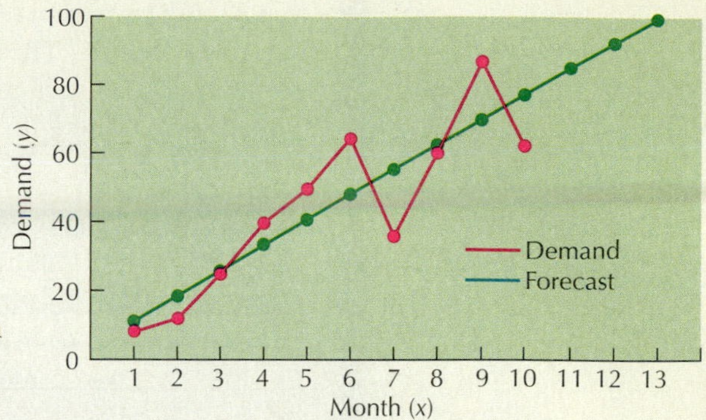

FIGURE 9.11 Regression Forecast for Clem's Competition Clutches

Microsoft Excel has a built-in function for regression analysis. Figure 9.12 shows the demand data for Clem's Competition Clutches, as well as the dialog box for Excel's regression function. The regression function can be accessed by going to the "Tools" menu of Excel, clicking on "Data Analysis," and then clicking on "Regression."

The "Input Y Range" box shows where the y values for the model are located, and "Input X Range" identifies the location of the x values. Also note that we have clicked

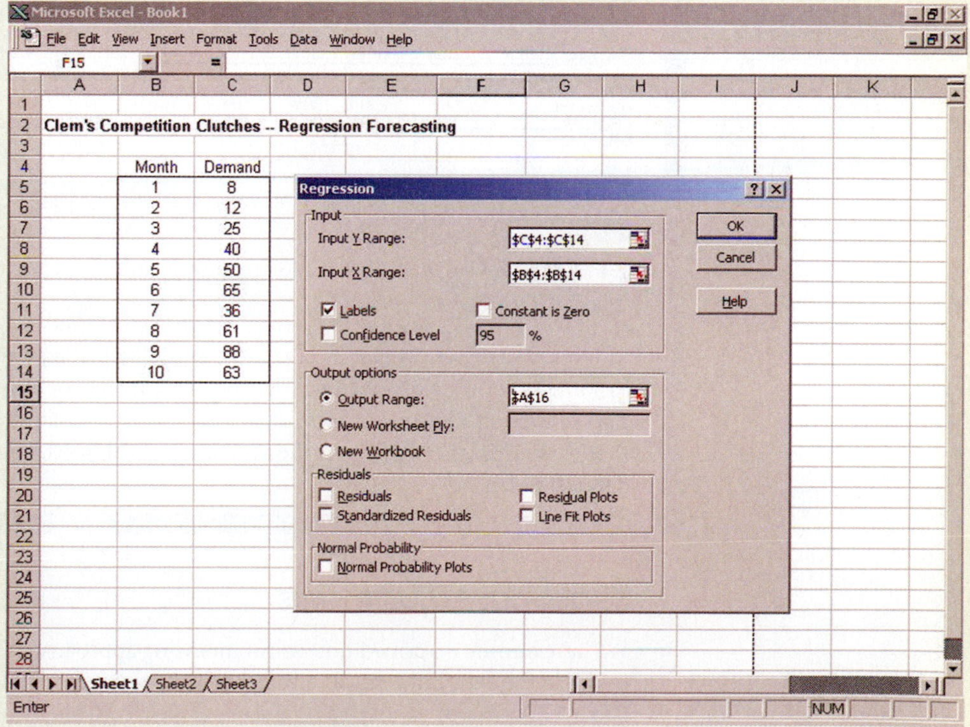

FIGURE 9.12 Using Excel's Regression Function for Clem's Competition Clutches

the "Labels" box, indicating that the first cell in each range contains an identifying label. Finally, we have instructed Excel to print out the results of the regression starting in Cell A16.

After filling out the appropriate boxes and clicking "OK" in the regression dialog box, we get the results shown in Figure 9.13. The "Coefficients" column contains the estimated value for the intercept term, as well as the slope coefficient associated with our independent variable, "Month." These values are 4.467 and 7.333, respectively. Except for some slight rounding differences in the intercept term, these are the same as those generated using Equations 9-8 and 9-9.

Microsoft Excel - Book1

File Edit View Insert Format Tools Data Window Help

A15 =

	A	B	C	D	E	F	G	H	I
1									
2	**Clem's Competition Clutches -- Regression Forecasting**								
3									
4		Month	Demand						
5		1	8						
6		2	12						
7		3	25						
8		4	40						
9		5	50						
10		6	65						
11		7	36						
12		8	61						
13		9	88						
14		10	63						
15									
16	SUMMARY OUTPUT								
17									
18	*Regression Statistics*								
19	Multiple R	0.873							
20	R Square	0.763							
21	Adjusted R Square	0.733							
22	Standard Error	13.138							
23	Observations	10.000							
24									
25	ANOVA								
26		*df*	*SS*	*MS*	*F*	*Significance F*			
27	Regression	1.000	4436.667	4436.667	25.702	0.001			
28	Residual	8.000	1380.933	172.617					
29	Total	9.000	5817.600						
30									
31		*Coefficients*	*Standard Error*	*t Stat*	*P-value*	*Lower 95%*	*Upper 95%*	*Lower 95.0%*	*Upper 95.0%*
32	Intercept	4.467	8.975	0.498	0.632	-16.230	25.164	-16.230	25.164
33	Month	7.333	1.446	5.070	0.001	3.998	10.669	3.998	10.669

Sheet1 / Sheet2 / Sheet3 /

Ready NUM

FIGURE 9.13 Excel's Regression Results for Clem's Competition Clutches

Excel's regression results also include the R^2 ("R square") value for the model, as well as some other tests of statistical significance for the coefficients. R^2 indicates what proportion of the variance in the dependent y variable ("Demand") is explained by the regression model. In this case, 76.3% of the variance is explained, suggesting that the model fits the data very well.

Seasonal Adjustments

We have already described time series modeling approaches for dealing with randomness and trends in the data. But what about seasonality? As we mentioned earlier, seasonality is a repeated pattern of spikes or drops in a time series associated with certain times of the year. Many products and services have seasonal demand patterns (as well as seasonal supply and price patterns). Table 9.8 lists just a few examples of products or services that demonstrate seasonality.

TABLE 9.8
Examples of Products and Services That Experience Seasonality

PRODUCT OR SERVICE	PEAK SEASON(S)
Gasoline	Summer months, as more people are traveling
Caribbean cruises	Winter months
Cub Scout uniforms	Fall, as new scouts are joining up
Emergency medical care	Summer months, as more people are involved in outdoor activities
Fruitcake	November and December holiday season, after which *no one* buys it (or eats it)

When there is seasonality in the demand pattern, we need some way to adjust our forecast numbers to account for this effect. A simple four-step procedure for developing seasonal adjustments is as follows:

1. For each of the demand values in the time series, calculate the corresponding forecast, using the unadjusted forecast model.
2. For each demand value, calculate $\frac{\text{Demand}}{\text{Forecast}}$. If the ratio is less than 1, then the forecast model overforecasted; if it is greater than 1, then the model underforecasted.
3. If the time series covers multiple years, take the average $\frac{\text{Demand}}{\text{Forecast}}$ for corresponding months or quarters to derive the seasonal index. Otherwise, use $\frac{\text{Demand}}{\text{Forecast}}$ calculated in step 2 as the seasonal index.
4. Multiply the unadjusted forecast by the seasonal index to get the seasonally adjusted forecast value.

Example 9.4
Linear Regression with Seasonal Adjustments

In this example, we develop a linear regression forecasting model using the following time series data. Based on the results of the regression model, we then develop a seasonal index for each month, and reforecast months 1 through 24 (January 2004–December 2005), using the seasonal indices.

MONTH	DEMAND	MONTH	DEMAND
January 2004	51	January 2005	112
February	67	February	137
March	65	March	191
April	129	April	250
May	225	May	416
June	272	June	487
July	238	July	421
August	172	August	285
September	143	September	235
October	131	October	222
November	125	November	192
December	103	December	165

The time series, as well as the corresponding regression forecasts for the first 24 months, is shown in Figure 9.14.

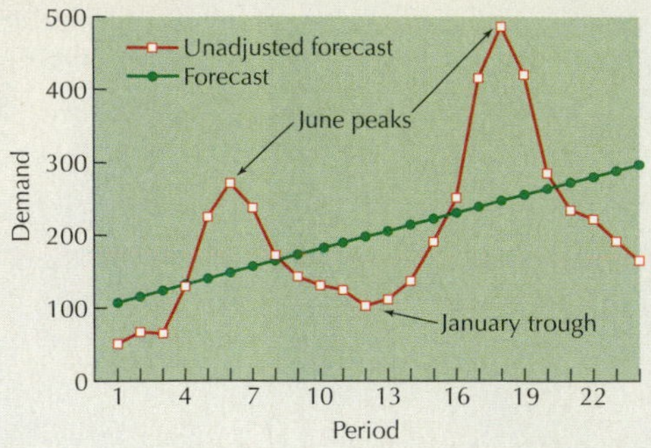

FIGURE 9.14 Plot of Unadjusted Regression Forecast against a Time Series with Seasonality

Notice that the forecast errors (actual demand − unadjusted regression forecast) are all over the place, ranging from −131 to 240.3. The magnitude of these forecast errors implies that the model is only marginally effective.

Regression Forecast Model

Forecasted demand = 98.71 + 8.22 × period

MONTH	PERIOD	DEMAND	UNADJUSTED REGRESSION FORECAST	FORECAST ERROR
January 2004	1	51	106.9	−55.9
February	2	67	115.2	−48.2
March	3	65	123.4	−58.4
April	4	129	131.6	−2.6
May	5	225	139.8	85.2
June	6	272	148.0	124.0
July	7	238	156.3	81.7
August	8	172	164.5	7.5
September	9	143	172.7	−29.7
October	10	131	180.9	−49.9
November	11	125	189.1	−64.1
December	12	103	197.4	−94.4
January 2005	13	112	205.6	−93.6
February	14	137	213.8	−76.8
March	15	191	222.0	−31.0
April	16	250	230.2	19.8
May	17	416	238.5	177.5
June	18	487	246.7	240.3
July	19	421	254.9	166.1
August	20	285	263.1	21.9
September	21	235	271.3	−36.3
October	22	222	279.6	−57.6
November	23	192	287.8	−95.8
December	24	165	296.0	−131.0

In fact, when the unadjusted regression forecasts are plotted against the actual demand values, it becomes clear that the regression model has picked up on the trend in the data, but not the seasonality (Figure 9.14). The result is large, positive forecast errors in the summer months and large, negative forecast errors in the winter months.

In step 2, $\frac{\text{Demand}}{\text{Forecast}}$ is calculated for each of the time periods. For the two January observations, the calculations are

$$\text{January 2004: } \frac{\text{Demand}}{\text{Forecast}} = \frac{51}{106.9} = 0.477$$

$$\text{January 2005: } \frac{\text{Demand}}{\text{Forecast}} = \frac{112}{205.6} = 0.545$$

The results confirm what Figure 9.14 suggests—the unadjusted regression model tends to badly *over*forecast demand in January. In fact, actual January demands were only 48% and 55% of the forecasts for 2004 and 2005, respectively. The effect is just the opposite for June, where the regression model badly *under*forecasts.

In step 3, monthly seasonal indices are calculated by averaging the $\frac{\text{Demand}}{\text{Forecast}}$ values for corresponding months. Continuing with the January example:

$$\text{Monthly seasonal index, January} = (0.477 + 0.545)/2 = 0.511$$

Finally, the seasonally adjusted forecasts are calculated as follows:

$$\text{Seasonally adjusted forecast} = \text{unadjusted forecast} \times \text{seasonal index}$$

$$\text{January 2004: } 106.9 \times 0.511 = 54.63$$

$$\text{January 2005: } 205.6 \times 0.511 = 105.06$$

Table 9.9 shows the complete set of results for this problem. Note that the monthly seasonal indices in 2004 are repeated in 2005. In addition, notice how the new forecast errors (demand − adjusted regression forecast) are much smaller than before. In fact, if we plot actual demand against the adjusted forecast values, we can see how well the new forecast model fits the past data (Figure 9.15).

FIGURE 9.15 Plot of Seasonally Adjusted Regression Forecast against a Time Series Showing Seasonality

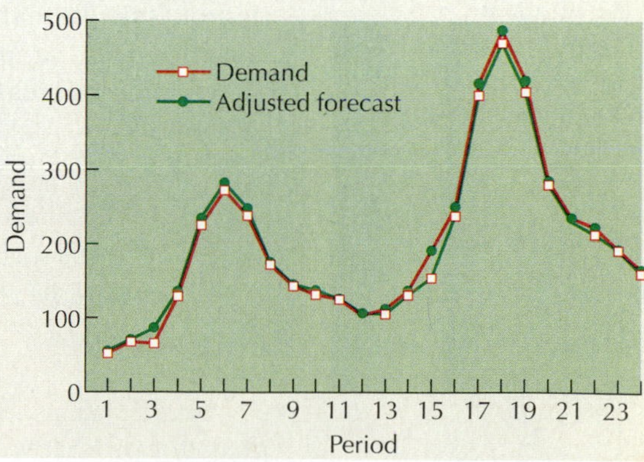

TABLE 9.9 Adjusted Regression Forecast for a Time Series with Seasonality

Regression forecast model:

Forecasted demand = 98.71 + 8.22 x period

The adjusted forecast is calculated by multiplying the unadjusted forecast by the seasonal index. For January 2004: 106.9 x 0.511 = 54.6.

The percentages for January 2004 and 2005 are averaged to develop the monthly seasonal index for January. The procedure follows the same pattern for other months.

Month	Period	Demand	Unadjusted Regression Forecast	Demand/ Forecast	Monthly Seasonal Index	Adjusted Regression Forecast	New Forecast Error
January 2004	1	51	106.9	0.477	0.511	54.6	−3.6
February	2	67	115.2	0.582	0.611	70.4	−3.4
March	3	65	123.4	0.527	0.694	85.6	−20.6
April	4	129	131.6	0.980	1.033	135.9	−6.9
May	5	225	139.8	1.609	1.677	234.5	−9.5
June	6	272	148.0	1.837	1.906	282.1	−10.1
July	7	238	156.3	1.523	1.587	248.0	−10.0
August	8	172	164.5	1.046	1.064	175.1	−3.1
September	9	143	172.7	0.828	0.847	146.3	−3.3
October	10	131	180.9	0.724	0.759	137.3	−6.3
November	11	125	189.1	0.661	0.664	125.6	−0.6
December	12	103	197.4	0.522	0.540	106.5	−3.5
January 2005	13	112	205.6	0.545	0.511	105.0	7.0
February	14	137	213.8	0.641	0.611	130.7	6.3
March	15	191	222.0	0.860	0.694	154.0	37.0
April	16	250	230.2	1.086	1.033	237.8	12.2
May	17	416	238.5	1.745	1.677	399.9	16.1
June	18	487	246.7	1.974	1.906	470.1	16.9
July	19	421	254.9	1.652	1.587	404.6	16.4
August	20	285	263.1	1.083	1.064	280.1	4.9
September	21	235	271.3	0.866	0.847	229.8	5.2
October	22	222	279.6	0.794	0.759	212.2	9.8
November	23	192	287.8	0.667	0.664	191.1	0.9
December	24	165	296.0	0.557	0.540	159.7	5.3

9.6 CAUSAL FORECASTING MODELS

Causal forecasting models A class of quantitative forecasting models in which the forecast is modeled as a function of something other than time.

So far, the forecasting models we have dealt with treat the variable of interest as a function of time. In many cases, however, changes in the variable we want to forecast—demand, price, supply, and so on—are caused by something *other* than time. Under these conditions, **causal forecasting models** should be used. Consider the following examples:

VARIABLE	CAUSE OF CHANGE
Dollars spent on drought relief	Rainfall levels
Mortgage refinancing applications	Interest rates
Amount of food eaten at a party	Number and size of guests

Notice that in all three cases, what happened in the recent past is not necessarily a good predictor of what will happen in the future. If rainfall next year is unusually low, then dollars spent on drought relief will increase even if the last few years saw little money spent on drought relief. Likewise, would a caterer be wise to only bring 10 pounds of barbecue to a party with 50 guests just because the same amount was plenty for yesterday's party of 17 people?

Linear Regression

Linear regression can be used to develop causal forecasting models as well as time series forecasting models. The only difference is that the independent variable, x, is no longer a time period, but some other variable. Other than that, the calculations are the same as before (Equations 9-7 through 9-9).

Example 9.5
SunRay Builders

SunRay Builders is a large, multistate home builder serving the southwestern United States. Table 9.10 shows the quarterly home sales and corresponding mortgage rates for the past four years. The president of SunRay Builders has asked you to develop a forecasting model that predicts the number of home sales based on the mortgage rate. He would then like you to forecast quarterly home sales when mortgage rates are 6% and 8%.

Before applying a forecasting technique, let's look at why a causal forecasting model is better suited here. Figure 9.16 shows the time series for home sales. Note that there appears to be no clear relationship between the time period and home sales. We could try fitting one of the time series models to this data, but the apparent randomness in the data would probably result in a weak model.

Now look at Figure 9.17, which plots mortgage rates against home sales (note that this is *not* a time series, as the data are *not* arranged in order of the time periods). Figure 9.17 shows a strong *negative* relationship between mortgage rates and home sales. Mortgage rates therefore look like an ideal variable for predicting home sales.

TABLE 9.10 Quarterly Home Sales and Mortgage Rate Values

QUARTER	30-YEAR MORTGAGE RATES	HOME SALES
1	7.5%	750
2	7.0%	790
3	6.0%	860
4	6.5%	870
5	7.0%	840
6	7.0%	830
7	8.0%	710
8	8.5%	650
9	9.0%	600
10	8.5%	640
11	8.0%	680
12	8.0%	690
13	6.0%	880
14	7.0%	800
15	6.5%	850
16	7.5%	750

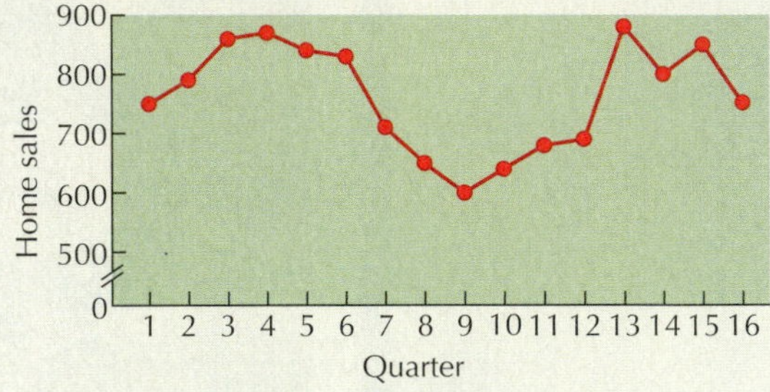

FIGURE 9.16 Plot Showing Weak Relationship between Home Sales and Quarter

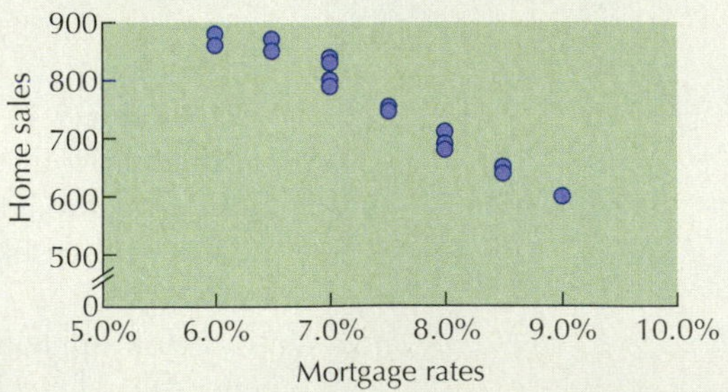

FIGURE 9.17 Plot Showing Strong Relationship between Home Sales and Mortgage Rates

To develop a regression forecasting model using mortgage rates as the independent variable, x, we follow the same procedures outlined earlier. Using Equations 9-8 and 9-9, we first set up columns to calculate the average x and y values, as well as the sums of the x, y, x^2, and xy values for the 16 pairs of observations:

	30-YEAR MORTGAGE RATE x	HOME SALES y	x^2	xy
	0.075	750	0.005625	56.25
	0.070	790	0.004900	55.3
	0.060	860	0.003600	51.6
	0.065	870	0.004225	56.55
	0.070	840	0.004900	58.8
	0.070	830	0.004900	58.1
	0.080	710	0.006400	56.8
	0.085	650	0.007225	55.25
	0.090	600	0.008100	54
	0.085	640	0.007225	54.4
	0.080	680	0.006400	54.4
	0.080	690	0.006400	55.2
	0.060	880	0.003600	52.8
	0.070	800	0.004900	56
	0.065	850	0.004225	55.25
	0.075	750	0.005625	56.25
Sum:	1.180	12,190	0.088250	886.95
Average:	0.0738	761.875		

Plugging these values into Equation 9-8 gives the estimate of the slope coefficient, $\hat{b}$:

$$\hat{b} = \frac{886.95 - \frac{1.18 \times 12{,}190}{16}}{0.08825 - \frac{1.18^2}{16}} = -9{,}846.94$$

and, from Equation 9-9, the intercept term, $\hat{a}$:

$$\hat{a} = \bar{y} - \hat{b}\bar{x} = 761.875 + 9{,}846.94 \times .0738 = 1{,}488.58.$$

The resulting regression model is:

Forecasted home sales = 1,488.58 − 9,846.94(mortgage rate %)

Using the regression model to forecast home sales at 6% and 8% gives us the following results:

Forecasted home sales at 6% mortgage rate: 1,488.58 − 9,846.94(6%) = 898 home sales

Forecasted home sales at 8% mortgage rate: 1,488.58 − 9,846.94(8%) = 701 home sales

The results make intuitive sense: As mortgage rates rise, homes become less affordable, and the number of home sales should go down.

Multiple Regression

Multiple regression
A generalized form of linear regression that allows for more than one independent variable.

In some cases, there may be more than one causal variable. The amount of barbecue eaten at a party may be a function of not only the number of guests, but also the average size of the guests (after all, 20 football players will probably eat more than 20 normal-sized people). In such cases, we can use a generalized form of linear regression that allows for more than one independent variable, called **multiple regression**. The multiple regression forecast model is defined as follows:

$$\hat{y} = \hat{a} + \sum_{i=1}^{k} \hat{b}_i x_i \qquad [9\text{-}10]$$

where:

$\hat{y}$ = forecast for *dependent* variable, y

k = number of independent variables

x_i = ith *independent* variable, where $i = 1 \ldots k$

$\hat{a}$ = estimated intercept term for the line

$\hat{b}_i$ = estimated slope coefficient associated with variable x_i

The formulas for calculating $\hat{a}$ and $\hat{b}_i$ in a multiple regression setting are far too cumbersome to do by hand. Fortunately, many software packages, such as Excel's regression function, can easily handle multiple independent variables. Example 9.6 illustrates how Excel can be used to develop a multiple regression forecasting model.

Example 9.6

Lance's BBQ Catering Service

Lance's BBQ Catering Service is a favorite of sports teams in the Raleigh, North Carolina, area. By counting and surreptitiously weighing each guest as he or she arrived at the party, Lance's BBQ Catering Service was able to capture the amount of barbecue eaten, the number of guests, and the average weight of each guest for 15 recent parties:

BARBECUE EATEN (LBS.)	NUMBER OF GUESTS	AVERAGE WEIGHT (LBS.)
46.00	50	150
40.00	20	175
60.00	30	250
45.00	25	200
44.00	40	150
42.50	15	200
58.50	25	250
43.00	30	175
43.50	15	200
36.00	10	150
49.00	80	250
63.00	70	200
39.00	20	175
46.00	60	150
65.00	40	250

Lance has a party coming up for members of the North Carolina State football team. He expects there to be around 60 guests, with each having an average weight of around 240 pounds. Lance wants to use multiple regression to estimate how much barbecue these guests will eat, based on number of guests and average weight.

Figure 9.18 shows the Excel spreadsheet containing the historical demand data and independent variables, as well as the regression dialog box. In this example, the independent

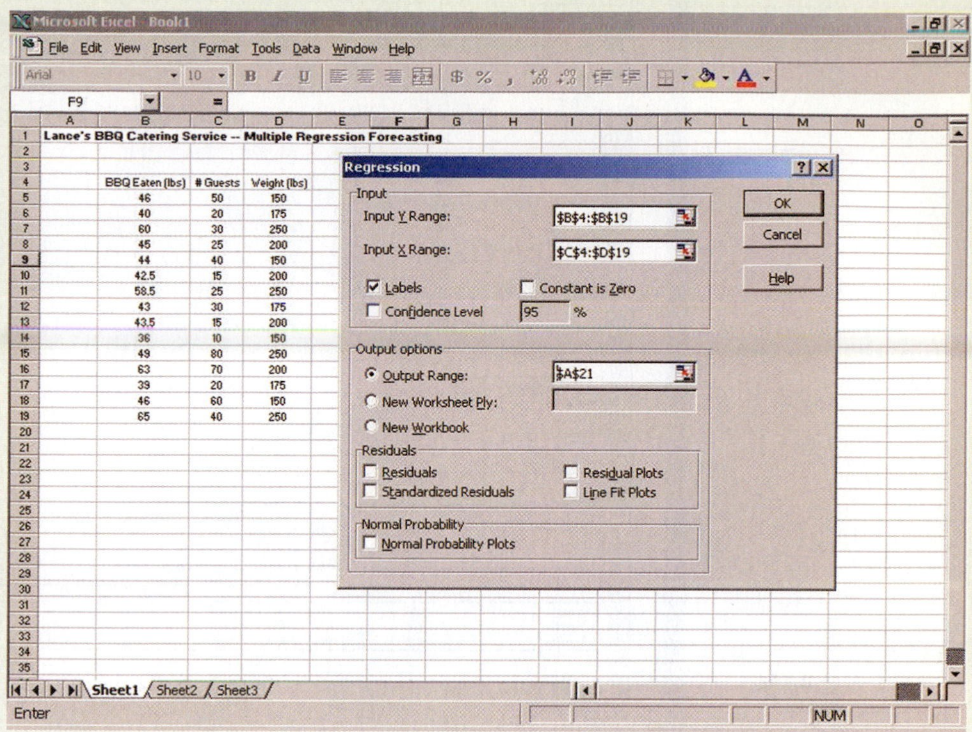

FIGURE 9.18 Multiple Regression Using Excel, Lance's BBQ Catering Service

x variables are found in two columns, C and D ("$C$4:$D$19"), and we have chosen to print the regression results on this worksheet starting in Cell A21.

The multiple regression results are shown in Figure 9.19 (we have scrolled down the spreadsheet to show the entire set of results).

The R^2 value for the model is 0.63, indicating that the model explains 63% of the variance in the dependent variable. The model parameters are:

$$\text{Intercept term} = 12.52$$
$$\text{Slope coefficient for number of guests} = 0.15$$
$$\text{Slope coefficient for average weight} = 0.15$$

Therefore, Lance's forecasting model would be:

$$\text{Barbecue eaten (lbs.)} = 12.52 + 0.15(\text{no. of guests}) + 0.15(\text{average weight})$$

According to the multiple regression model, then, Lance would expect 60 guests with an average weight of 240 pounds to consume

$$12.52 + 0.15(60) + 0.15(240) = 57.52 \text{ lbs. of barbecue}$$

Now for a question: How much barbecue should Lance bring to the party? If you said *more* than 57.52 pounds, you are correct because 57.52 pounds represents Lance's best estimate of what the guests will eat—the actual amount will probably be higher or lower. To ensure that he doesn't run out of barbecue (and anger an entire football team), Lance should plan on taking more than just 57.52 pounds.

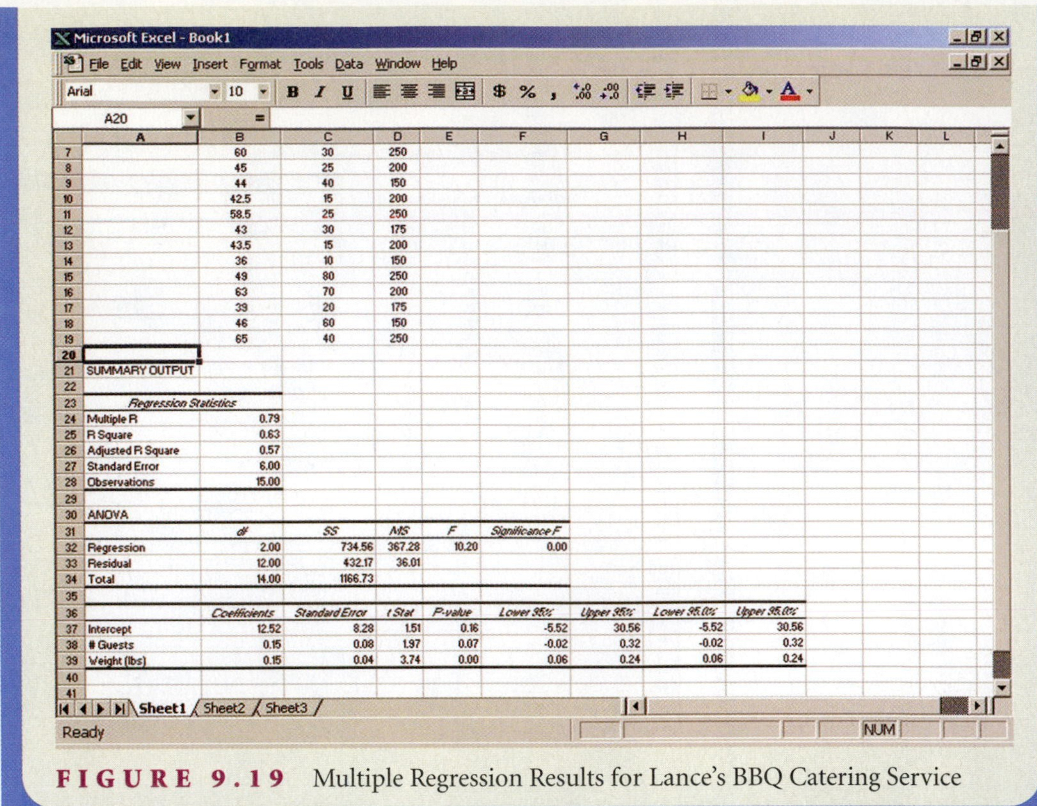

	A	B	C	D
7		60	30	250
8		45	25	200
9		44	40	150
10		42.5	15	200
11		58.5	25	250
12		43	30	175
13		43.5	15	200
14		36	10	150
15		49	80	250
16		63	70	200
17		39	20	175
18		46	60	150
19		65	40	250

SUMMARY OUTPUT

Regression Statistics	
Multiple R	0.79
R Square	0.63
Adjusted R Square	0.57
Standard Error	6.00
Observations	15.00

ANOVA

	df	*SS*	*MS*	*F*	*Significance F*
Regression	2.00	734.56	367.28	10.20	0.00
Residual	12.00	432.17	36.01		
Total	14.00	1166.73			

	Coefficients	*Standard Error*	*t Stat*	*P-value*	*Lower 95%*	*Upper 95%*	*Lower 95.0%*	*Upper 95.0%*
Intercept	12.52	8.28	1.51	0.16	-5.52	30.56	-5.52	30.56
# Guests	0.15	0.08	1.97	0.07	-0.02	0.32	-0.02	0.32
Weight (lbs)	0.15	0.04	3.74	0.00	0.06	0.24	0.06	0.24

FIGURE 9.19 Multiple Regression Results for Lance's BBQ Catering Service

9.7 MEASURES OF FORECAST ACCURACY

In this section, we introduce four simple measures of forecast accuracy. These measures are commonly used to assess how well an individual model is performing or to compare multiple forecast models to one another. The four measures are

$$\text{Forecast error } (FE) = (\text{actual value} - \text{forecasted value}) \quad [9\text{-}11]$$

$$\text{Mean forecast error } (MFE) = \frac{\sum_{i=1}^{n} FE_i}{n} \quad [9\text{-}12]$$

$$\text{Mean absolute deviation } (MAD) = \frac{\sum_{i=1}^{n} |FE_i|}{n} \quad [9\text{-}13]$$

$$\text{Tracking signal} = \frac{\sum_{i=1}^{n} FE_i}{MAD} \quad [9\text{-}14]$$

where:

$$\sum_{i=1}^{n} FE_i = \text{sum of the forecast errors for periods 1 through } n$$

MFE measures the bias of a forecast model, or the propensity of a model to under- or overforecast. A completely unbiased model would have an *MFE* of 0. A model with a negative *MFE* suggests that, on average, the model overforecasts, while a positive *MFE* suggests that the model underforecasts.

By taking the average of the absolute value of the forecast errors, *MAD* tracks the average *size* of the errors, regardless of direction. From the perspective of *MAD*, overforecasting or underforecasting by some value—say, 10—has the same impact. *MAD* will always be ≥0, with the ideal model having a *MAD* value of 0. We need to know *MAD* as well as *MFE* because a model could have, *on average*, forecast errors of 0, but still make large errors in over- and underforecasting.

Finally, the tracking signal is used to flag a forecasting model that is getting out of control. In general, as long as the tracking signal value remains between −4 and 4, the forecasting model is considered to be performing normally. If, however, the tracking signal falls outside of this range, the computer program or person responsible for the forecast will typically try to identify a better-fitting model or at least bring the poor performance of the model to the users' attention.

Example 9.7

Walk-in Advising at Wolf State University

Andi Irby, director of advising at Wolf State University, is trying to decide which of two forecasting models does a better job at predicting walk-in demand for student advising. Once she has selected a model, she would like to establish a tracking signal for it. Suppose Andi has the demand and forecast information for the last 10 weeks shown in Table 9.11.

TABLE 9.11 Forecast Results for Walk-in Advising at Wolf State University

WEEK	ACTUAL WALK-IN DEMAND	FORECAST MODEL 1	FORECAST MODEL 2
1	**18**	20	21
2	**14**	18	21
3	**21**	19	21
4	**26**	21	25
5	**26**	23	25
6	**29**	24	25
7	**19**	25	19
8	**19**	22	19
9	**25**	23	19
10	**15**	24	19

For each model, Andi first calculates the forecast error for each week, as well as the absolute deviation of the forecast error. Next she calculates the *sums* of the forecast errors and absolute deviations for each model:

WEEK	ACTUAL WALK-IN DEMAND	FORECAST MODEL 1	FORECAST ERROR	ABSOLUTE DEVIATION	FORECAST MODEL 2	FORECAST ERROR	ABSOLUTE DEVIATION
1	**18**	20	−2	2	21	−3	3
2	**14**	18	−4	4	21	−7	7
3	**21**	19	2	2	21	0	0
4	**26**	21	5	5	25	1	1
5	**26**	23	3	3	25	1	1
6	**29**	24	5	5	25	4	4
7	**19**	25	−6	6	19	0	0
8	**19**	22	−3	3	19	0	0
9	**25**	23	2	2	19	6	6
10	**15**	24	−9	9	19	−4	4
		Sum:	−7	41		−2	26

To calculate the mean forecast error (*MFE*) for each model, Andi divides the sum of the forecast errors by the number of weeks for which she has observations (10):

$$MFE \text{ for model 1: } -7/10 = -0.70$$

$$MFE \text{ for model 2: } -2/10 = -0.20$$

She then calculates the mean absolute deviation (*MAD*) values:

$$MAD \text{ for model 1: } 41/10 = 4.10$$

$$MAD \text{ for model 2: } 26/10 = 2.60$$

Because model 2 has the *MFE* value closest to 0, it appears to be the least biased. On average, model 2 overforecasted by 0.20 walk-ins, while model 1 overforecasted by 0.70. In addition, model 2 has the lowest *MAD*, with a mean absolute deviation of 2.60. Based on these results, model 2 appears to be the superior forecasting model.

Finally, Andi develops a tracking signal for the first 10 weeks. For each week, she takes the most recent sum of forecast errors and divides it by the most recent estimate of *MAD*. The most recent sum of forecast errors is often called the *running sum of forecast errors* to emphasize the fact that it is updated each period. The results are as follows:

WEEK	ACTUAL WALK-IN DEMAND	FORECAST MODEL 2	FORECAST ERROR	ABSOLUTE DEVIATION	RUNNING SUM OF FORECAST ERRORS	*MAD*	TRACKING SIGNAL
1	18	21	−3	3	−3	3.00	−1.00
2	14	21	−7	7	−10	5.00	−2.00
3	21	21	0	0	−10	3.33	−3.00
4	26	25	1	1	−9	2.75	−3.27
5	26	25	1	1	−8	2.40	−3.33
6	29	25	4	4	−4	2.67	−1.50
7	19	19	0	0	−4	2.29	−1.75
8	19	19	0	0	−4	2.00	−2.00
9	25	19	6	6	2	2.44	0.82
10	15	19	−4	4	−2	2.60	−0.77

Although the tracking signal for model 2 gets dangerously close to −4.0 in week 5, the model has since recovered with a tracking signal for week 10 of −0.77. For future weeks, Andi will continue to update the tracking signal, making sure it doesn't get too high or low.

9.8 COMPUTER-BASED FORECASTING PACKAGES

Though the logic behind the various quantitative forecasting models is straightforward, the amount of data that needs to be tracked, as well as the number of calculations, can grow quickly for realistic business situations. Imagine a national retailer that needs to forecast next month's demand for thousands of different items, and you can see why developing forecasts by hand is not practical.

In such situations, companies use computer-based forecasting packages to develop, evaluate, and even change forecasting models as needed. With enough demand history (i.e., time series data), a computer-based forecasting package could, in relatively quick fashion, evaluate alternative forecasting methods for each item and select the model that best fits the past data. Furthermore, such packages can use preestablished *MFE*, *MAD*, or tracking signal criteria to flag a poor forecasting model and *automatically* kick off a search for a better one. Many companies also use forecasting packages to develop *multiple* forecasts for a single item. These multiple forecasts can then be compared to one another or even combined to come up with a single forecast.

9.9 COLLABORATIVE PLANNING, FORECASTING, AND REPLENISHMENT (CPFR)

Throughout this book, we have made a point of highlighting ways in which practitioners implement the various concepts and tools. For example, in Chapters 3 and 6 we discussed the Six Sigma processes for improving existing processes and for developing new products and services. We also described in Chapter 3 the Supply-Chain Operations Reference (SCOR) model, which outlines the core management processes and individual process types that together define the domain of supply chain management. In Chapter 5, we pointed to the Project Management Body of Knowledge (PMBOK®). This guide, put out by the Project Management Institute, serves as a basic reference source for project management.

Collaborative planning, forecasting, and replenishment (CPFR) A set of business processes, backed up by information technology, in which members agree to mutual business objectives and measures, develop joint sales and operational plans, and collaborate to generate and update sales forecasts and replenishment plans.

We have incorporated these discussions to emphasize a point: Operations and supply chain management is a *practice*, and companies really do use the concepts and tools presented here. It is in this spirit that we introduce **Collaborative Planning, Forecasting and Replenishment (CPFR)**. CPFR is a set of business processes, backed up by information technology, in which supply chain partners agree to *mutual* business objectives and measures, develop *joint* sales and operational plans, and *collaborate* to generate and update sales forecasts and replenishment plans.[2] What distinguishes CPFR from traditional planning and forecasting approaches is the emphasis on *collaboration*—experience shows that

[2] *Collaborative Planning, Forecasting and Replenishment: An Overview.* Voluntary Interindustry Commerce Standards, May 18, 2004, **www.vics.org/committees/cpfr/CPFR_Overview_US-A4.pdf.**

SUPPLY CHAIN CONNECTIONS

CPFR AT BABYBOOM CONSUMER PRODUCTS[3]

Keeping up with consumer demands driven by changing tastes and uncertain economic conditions is an ever-present challenge for vendors and retailers. Effectively managing inventory levels has become the focal point, with forecasting and planning considered a top priority and a critical core competency. "The business has become Darwinian. The importance of forecasting and planning has grown out of the fierce competition taking place in retailing, and the development of new and better technology," notes Chris Cassidy, director of planning, BabyBoom Consumer Products Inc., which produces all types of infant products, including apparel.

In order to properly service its major customers, BabyBoom assigns both a planner and a sales representative who review their shared accounts weekly. They also visit with [the retailers'] buyers and planners together, usually once a quarter, to review results and discuss new programs. These meetings speed up the process and get all parties on the same page, which leads to teamwork and a stronger working relationship. "We've also incorporated a retail format for tracking our own inventory. We manage inventory as an investment and track turn, GMROI,[4] markdowns, gross margin, average inventory, and age of goods by product line. This approach allows us to identify both opportunities and problems faster, and educate all involved on what our retail counterparts are working with," Cassidy concludes.

For Cassidy, the most important ingredient of accurate forecasting is good information from which to make decisions. Forecasts need to be realistic and to be built from the item level up. All items being considered need to have a plan based on some kind of historical information. Included in that plan must be the impact various items within the assortment have on each other. "Our relationships with retail buyers have changed to include planners for both parties at sales meetings. We've found that this greatly improves communication and provides different perspectives from which to make decisions," he says.

supply chains are better at meeting demand and managing resources when the partners synchronize their plans and actions. The increased communication among partners means that when demand, promotions, or policies change, managers can adjust jointly managed forecasts and plans immediately, minimizing or even eliminating costly after-the-fact corrections. The *Supply Chain Connections* feature highlights some of the CPFR efforts at one business, BabyBoom Consumer Products.

Example 9.8

Cheeznax Snack Foods Revisited

We end this chapter by returning to Jamie Favre, the demand manager for Cheeznax Snack Foods. Both Cheeznax and its primary customer, Gas N' Grub, are interested in coordinating their supply chain activities so that Gas N' Grub stores can be stocked with fresh products at the lowest possible cost to both companies. With this in mind, the two supply chain partners enter into a CPFR arrangement. As part of the arrangement, Gas N' Grub agrees to share with Cheeznax its 2009 plans for promotions and new store openings:

[3]Excerpts from T. Haisley, "Survival of the Forecasting and Planning Fittest," *Apparel*, July 1, 2003. Available at **www.apparelmag.com/bobbin/ reports_analysis/article_display.jsp?vnu_content_id=1932000**.

[4]Gross marginal return on investment (GMROI): for each dollar invested in merchandise inventory, the equivalent dollars generated in gross margin. It is usually stated as the gross margin as a percentage of the average inventory investment at cost. American Marketing Association, "Dictionary," **www.marketingpower.com/live/mg-dictionary.php**.

1. Gas N' Grub plans to open 10 new convenience stores each month, starting in **June and ending in September**. This means that by the end of September, Gas N' Grub will have 140 stores.
2. Gas N' Grub will also launch an advertising campaign that is expected to raise sales in all stores by 5%. This advertising campaign will run from **July through September**, at which time individual store sales are expected to settle back down to previous levels.

Jamie now feels she is ready to start developing the monthly sales forecasts for 2009. As a first step, Jamie plots the 2008 sales data to see if there are discernable patterns. The results are shown in Figure 9.20.

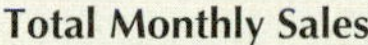

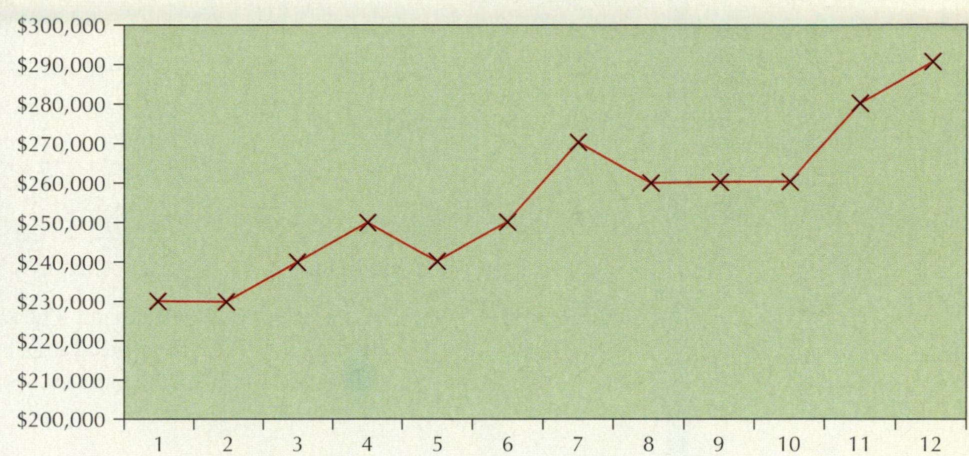

FIGURE 9.20 2008 Sales Data for Cheeznax Snack Foods Company

Jamie notes that sales appear to show a slight upward trend over the year. Based on this information, Jamie uses Equations 9.8 and 9.9 to fit a regression model to the 2008 data. She chooses monthly total sales as her dependent variable, y, and month (January = 1, February = 2, etc.) as her independent variable, x. She then calculates the values she needs to plug into the formulas:

	MONTH (x)	SALES (y)	x^2	xy
	1	230,000	1	230,000
	2	230,000	4	460,000
	3	240,000	9	720,000
	4	250,000	16	1,000,000
	5	240,000	25	1,200,000
	6	250,000	36	1,500,000
	7	270,000	49	1,890,000
	8	260,000	64	2,080,000
	9	260,000	81	2,340,000
	10	260,000	100	2,600,000
	11	280,000	121	3,080,000
	12	290,000	144	3,480,000
Sum:	78	3,060,000	650	20,580,000
Average:	6.5	255,000		

Next, Jamie uses these values to calculate the slope coefficient, $\hat{b}$:

$$\hat{b} = \frac{\sum_{i=1}^{n} x_i y_i - \frac{\left(\sum_{i=1}^{n} x_i\right)\left(\sum_{i=1}^{n} y_i\right)}{n}}{\sum_{i=1}^{n} x_i^2 - \frac{\left(\sum_{i=1}^{n} x_i\right)^2}{n}} = \frac{\$20,580,000 - \frac{78 \times \$3,060,000}{12}}{650 - \frac{78^2}{12}}$$

$$= \$4,825.17$$

And then the intercept term, $\hat{a}$:

$$\hat{a} = \bar{y} - \hat{b}\bar{x} = \$255,000 - \$4,825.17 \times 6.5 = \$223,636.40$$

Resulting in the following regression forecasting model:

Forecasted Total Monthly Sales = \$223,636.40 + \$4,825.17 × (Period)

Jamie compares her model against actual 2008 demand. The results, including MFE and MAD, are shown in Table 9.12. Though the results seem promising, Jamie still remains cautious—she realizes that fitting a model to past data is *not* the same as forecasting future demand.

TABLE 9.12 Comparison of Regression Forecast Model to Historical Demand

Forecasted Total Monthly Sales = \$223,636.36 + \$4,825.17 × (Period)

MONTH	PERIOD	TOTAL SALES	REGRESSION FORECAST	FORECAST ERROR	ABSOLUTE DEVIATION
January	1	\$230,000	**\$228,462**	\$1,538	\$1,538
February	2	\$230,000	**\$233,287**	−\$3,287	\$3,287
March	3	\$240,000	**\$238,112**	\$1,888	\$1,888
April	4	\$250,000	**\$242,937**	\$7,063	\$7,063
May	5	\$240,000	**\$247,762**	−\$7,762	\$7,762
June	6	\$250,000	**\$252,587**	−\$2,587	\$2,587
July	7	\$270,000	**\$257,413**	\$12,587	\$12,587
August	8	\$260,000	**\$262,238**	−\$2,238	\$2,238
Sept.	9	\$260,000	**\$267,063**	−\$7,063	\$7,063
Oct.	10	\$260,000	**\$271,888**	−\$11,888	\$11,888
Nov.	11	\$280,000	**\$276,713**	\$3,287	\$3,287
Dec.	12	\$290,000	**\$281,538**	\$8,462	\$8,462
		\$3,060,000			
			MFE =	\$0	
				MAD =	\$5,804

But Jamie is not done. She still needs to a 2009 forecast that takes into account the 10 stores being added each month from June through September, as well as the advertising campaign that is expected to increase demand by 5% from July through September.

Jamie uses a three-step approach to develop her 2009 forecast. These steps are outlined in Figure 9.21. First, Jamie uses the regression forecast model to develop an initial forecast for January through December of 2009 (Periods 13–24). Next, Jamie reasons that each new

Month	Period	(1) Forecast, Total Monthly Sale	(2) Increase in Stores (Base = 100%)	(2) Advertising Campaign Lift (Base = 100%)	(3) Adjusted Forecast, Total Monthly Sale
January	13	$286,364	100%	100%	$286,364
February	14	$291,189	100%	100%	$291,189
March	15	$296,014	100%	100%	$296,014
April	16	$300,839	100%	100%	$300,839
May	17	$305,664	100%	100%	$305,664
June	18	$310,489	110%	100%	$341,538
July	19	$315,315	120%	105%	$397,297
August	20	$320,140	130%	105%	$436,991
September	21	$324,965	140%	105%	$477,699
October	22	$329,790	140%	100%	$461,706
November	23	$334,615	140%	100%	$468,461
December	24	$339,440	140%	100%	$475,216
					$4,538,978

FIGURE 9.21 Adjusting Cheeznax Forecast to Take Into Account Gas N' Grub's Store Openings and Advertising Campaign

store should generate sales at a level similar to the existing stores. Therefore, if there are 100 stores to start with, adding 10 more stores in June will increase sales by $110/100 = 110\%$ over what the sales would have been otherwise. By the end of the year, there will be 40% more stores than at the beginning of the year. Jamie uses this logic to develop lift factors to account for the new stores. These percentages are shown in the fourth column of Figure 9.21. Similarly, Jamie uses lift factors to reflect the impact of the July–September advertising campaign.

In the third and final step, Jamie multiples the initial monthly forecast by *both* the store and the advertising lift factors to get a final, adjusted forecast. To illustrate, the adjusted forecast for June 2009 is now:

$$(\$310{,}489) \times (110\%) \times (100\%) = \$341{,}538$$

Figure 9.22 plots the adjusted monthly forecasts for 2009. The dashed line shows what the forecasts would be if Jamie did *not* adjust for the store openings and advertising campaign. The impact of the store openings, as well as the advertising campaign, can clearly be seen. Looking at the graph, Jamie realizes that developing this forecast required not just the proper application of quantitative tools, but also the sharing of critical information between Cheeznax and its major customer, Gas N' Grub.

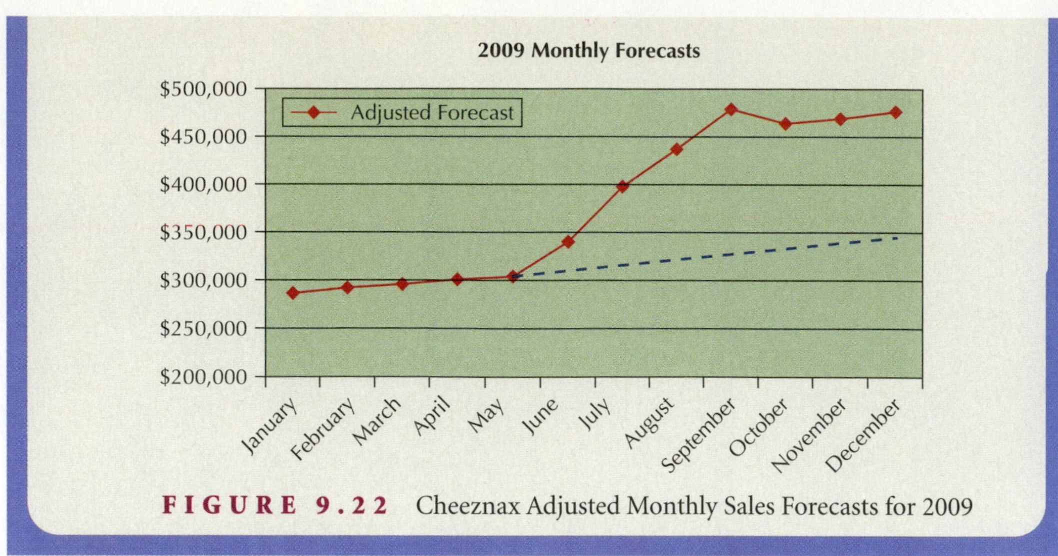

FIGURE 9.22 Cheeznax Adjusted Monthly Sales Forecasts for 2009

CHAPTER SUMMARY

Forecasting is a critical business process for nearly every organization. Whether the organization is forecasting demand, supply, prices, or some other variable, forecasting is often the first step it must go through in planning future business activities. In this chapter, we described the different types of forecasts companies use and the four laws of forecasting. We also talked about when to use qualitative and quantitative forecasting techniques and explained several approaches to developing time series and causal forecasting models.

Of course, forecasting is not just about the "numbers." As the discussion and CPFR examples illustrate, organizations can collaborate with one another to improve the accuracy of their forecasting efforts or even reduce the need for forecasts.

KEY FORMULAS

Last-period forecasting model (page 273):

$$F_{t+1} = D_t \qquad \textbf{[9-1]}$$

where:

F_{t+1} = forecast for the next period, $t + 1$
D_t = demand for the current period, t

Moving average forecasting model (page 274):

$$F_{t+1} = \frac{\sum_{i=1}^{n} D_{t+1-i}}{n} \qquad \textbf{[9-2]}$$

where:

F_{t+1} = forecast for time period $t + 1$
D_{t+1-i} = actual demand for period $t + 1 - i$
n = number of most recent demand observations used to develop the forecast

Weighted moving average forecasting model (page 277):

$$F_{t+1} = \sum_{i=1}^{n} W_{t+1-i} D_{t+1-i} \qquad [9\text{-}3]$$

where:

W_{t+1-i} = weight assigned to the demand in period $t+1-i$ $\sum_{i=1}^{n} W_{t+1-i} = 1$

Exponential smoothing forecasting model (page 281):

$$F_{t+1} = \alpha D_t + (1-\alpha)F_t \qquad [9\text{-}4]$$

where:

F_{t+1} = forecast for time period $t + 1$ (i.e., the *new* forecast)

F_t = forecast for time period t (i.e., the *current* forecast)

D_t = actual demand for time period t

α = smoothing constant used to weight D_t and F_t $(0 \leq \alpha \leq 1)$

Adjusted exponential smoothing forecasting model (page 281):

$$AF_{t+1} = F_{t+1} + T_{t+1} \qquad [9\text{-}5]$$

where:

$F_{t=1} = \alpha D_t + (1-\alpha)F_t$

$$T_{t+1} = \beta(F_{t+1} - F_t) + (1-\beta)T_t \qquad [9\text{-}6]$$

T_{t+1} = trend factor for the next period

T_t = trend factor for the current period

β = smoothing constant for the trend adjustment factor

Linear regression forecasting model (page 282):

$$\hat{y} = \hat{a} + \hat{b}x \qquad [9\text{-}7]$$

where:

$\hat{y}$ = forecast for *dependent* variable, y

x = *independent* variable, x, used to forecast y

$\hat{a}$ = estimated intercept term for the line

$\hat{b}$ = estimated slope coefficient for the line

Slope coefficient $\hat{b}$ and intercept coefficient $\hat{a}$ for linear regression model (pages 282 and 283):

$$\hat{b} = \frac{\sum_{i=1}^{n} x_i y_i - \frac{\left(\sum_{i=1}^{n} x_i\right)\left(\sum_{i=1}^{n} y_i\right)}{n}}{\sum_{i=1}^{n} x_i^2 - \frac{\left(\sum_{i=1}^{n} x_i\right)^2}{n}} \qquad [9\text{-}8]$$

and

$$\hat{a} = \bar{y} - \hat{b}\bar{x} \qquad [9\text{-}9]$$

where:

(x_i, y_i) = matched pairs of observed (x, y) values
$\bar{y}$ = average y value
$\bar{x}$ = average x value
n = number of paired observations

Multiple regression forecasting model (page 294):

$$\hat{y} = \hat{a} + \sum_{i=1}^{k} \hat{b}_i x_i \qquad [9\text{-}10]$$

where:

$\hat{y}$ = forecast for *dependent* variable, y
k = number of independent variables
x_i = the ith *independent* variable, where $i = 1 \ldots k$
$\hat{a}$ = estimated intercept term for the line
$\hat{b}_i$ = estimated slope coefficient associated with variable x_i

Measures of forecast accuracy (page 296):

$$\text{Forecast error } (FE) = (\text{actual value} - \text{forecasted value}) \qquad [9\text{-}11]$$

$$\text{Mean forecast error } (MFE) = \frac{\sum_{i=1}^{n} FE_i}{n} \qquad [9\text{-}12]$$

$$\text{Mean absolute deviation } (MAD) = \frac{\sum_{i=1}^{n} |FE_i|}{n} \qquad [9\text{-}13]$$

$$\text{Tracking signal} = \frac{\sum_{i=1}^{n} FE_i}{MAD} \qquad [9\text{-}14]$$

where:

$\sum_{i=1}^{n} FE_i$ = sum of the forecast errors for periods 1 through n

KEY TERMS

Adjusted exponential smoothing model 281
Build-up forecasts 271
Causal forecasting models 290
Collaborative planning, forecasting, and replenishment (CPFR) 299
Delphi method 271
Exponential smoothing model 277
Forecast 266
Life cycle analogy method 271

SOLVED PROBLEM

Problem

Chris Boote Industries makes rebuild kits for old carbureted snowmobiles (newer snowmobiles have fuel-injected engines). The past two years of demand for the kits are as follows:

Chris would like to develop a model to forecast demand for the upcoming year.

	PERIOD	DEMAND
January 2003	1	3420
February	2	3660
March	3	1880
April	4	1540
May	5	1060
June	6	900
July	7	660
August	8	680
September	9	1260
October	10	1600
November	11	1920
December	12	2400
January 2004	13	2500
February	14	2540
March	15	1300
April	16	1060
May	17	740
June	18	620
July	19	460
August	20	480
September	21	880
October	22	1100
November	23	1340
December	24	1660

Solution

As a first attempt, Chris Boote develops a three-period moving average model to forecast periods 19 through 24 and evaluates the results using *MAD* and *MFE*. The three-period moving average forecast for period 19 is calculated as follows:

$$F_{19} = (620 + 740 + 1060)/3 = 806.67 \text{ rebuild kits}$$

The rest of the forecasts are calculated in a similar manner. The results are shown in the following table:

	PERIOD	DEMAND	FORECAST	FORECAST ERROR	ABSOLUTE DEVIATION
April	16	1060			
May	17	740			
June	18	620			
July	19	460	806.67	−346.67	346.67
August	20	480	606.67	−126.67	126.67
September	21	880	520.00	360.00	360.00
October	22	1100	606.67	493.33	493.33
November	23	1340	820.00	520.00	520.00
December	24	1660	1106.67	553.33	553.33

Mean forecast error $(MFE) = 242.22$

Mean absolute deviation $(MAD) = 400.00$

Because of the relatively large *MFE* and *MAD* values, Chris decides to try another model: a regression model with seasonal adjustments. To keep it simple, Chris wants to develop seasonal indices for the months of January and June and to forecast demand for January and June of 2005.

First, Chris sets up the table to calculate the values that go into Equations 9-8 and 9-9.

	PERIOD	DEMAND		
	x	y	x^2	x^*y
January, 2003	1	3420	1	3420
February	2	3660	4	7320
March	3	1880	9	5640
April	4	1540	16	6160
May	5	1060	25	5300
June	6	900	36	5400
July	7	660	49	4620
August	8	680	64	5440
September	9	1260	81	11,340
October	10	1600	100	16,000
November	11	1920	121	21,120
December	12	2400	144	28,800
January, 2004	13	2500	169	32,500
February	14	2540	196	35,560
March	15	1300	225	19,500
April	16	1060	256	16,960
May	17	740	289	12,580
June	18	620	324	11,160
July	19	460	361	8740
August	20	480	400	9600
September	21	880	441	18,480
October	22	1100	484	24,200
November	23	1340	529	30,820
December	24	1660	576	39,840
Sum:	300	35,660	4900	380,500
Average:	12.50	1485.83		

Plugging these terms into Equations 9-8 and 9-9, Chris gets

$$\hat{b} = \frac{\sum_{i=1}^{n} x_i y_i - \frac{\left(\sum_{i=1}^{n} x_i\right)\left(\sum_{i=1}^{n} y_i\right)}{n}}{\sum_{i=1}^{n} x_i^2 - \frac{\left(\sum_{i=1}^{n} x_i\right)^2}{n}} = \frac{380{,}500 - \frac{300 \times 35{,}660}{24}}{4{,}900 - \frac{300^2}{24}} = -56.74$$

$$\hat{a} = \bar{y} - \hat{b}\bar{x} = 1{,}485.83 + 56.74 \times 12.50 = 2{,}195.07$$

And the resulting forecast model:

$$\text{Demand} = 2{,}195.08 - 56.74(\text{period})$$

Note that the negative slope coefficient suggests that there is a downward trend in demand. To calculate seasonal indices for January and June, Chris needs to generate the *unadjusted* forecasts for the past two years:

January 2003: $2{,}195.08 - 56.74(1) = 2{,}138.34$
January 2004: $2{,}195.08 - 56.74(13) = 1{,}457.46$

June 2003: $2{,}195.08 - 56.74(6) = 1{,}854.64$
June 2004: $2{,}195.08 - 56.74(18) = 1{,}173.76$

and then calculate $\frac{\text{Demand}}{\text{Forecast}}$ values using the unadjusted forecasts:

MONTH	PERIOD	DEMAND	UNADJUSTED FORECAST	DEMAND / FORECAST
January 2003	1	3420	2138.34	1.60
June 2003	6	900	1854.64	0.49
January 2004	13	2500	1457.46	1.72
June 2004	18	620	1173.76	0.53

Next, Chris calculates the seasonal index for January by taking the average of the $\frac{\text{Demand}}{\text{Forecast}}$ ratio for 2003 and 2004:

$$(1.60 + 1.72)/2 = 1.66$$

Following the same logic for June:

$$(0.49 + 0.53)/2 = 0.51$$

Finally, Chris can calculate the adjusted regression forecasts for January 2005 (period 25) and June 2005 (period 30):

January 2005: $[2{,}195.08 - 56.74 \times (25)]\ 1.66 = 1{,}289$ rebuild kits
June 2005: $[2{,}195.08 - 56.74 \times (30)]\ 0.51 = 251$ rebuild kits

An interesting thing to note is that eventually the forecast model will result in negative forecasts as the period count grows higher. In reality, demand will probably level off at some low level.

DISCUSSION QUESTIONS

1. Which forecasting techniques do you think Ford should have used to forecast changes in the demand, supply, and price of palladium? Time series models? Causal models? Qualitative models? Justify your answer.
2. Are time series forecast techniques such as moving average and exponential smoothing models well suited to developing forecasts for multiple periods into the future? Why?
3. What are the advantages of having computer-based forecasting packages handle the forecasting effort for a business? What are the pitfalls?
4. Explain the differences in using linear regression to develop a time series forecasting model and a causal forecasting model.
5. If forecasting is so important, why do firms look to such approaches as CPFR as a way to reduce the need for forecasting?

PROBLEMS

Additional homework problems are available at www.prenhall.com/bozarth. These problems use Excel to generate customized problems for different class sections or even different students.

(* = easy; ** = moderate; *** = advanced)

For Problems 1 through 3, use the following time series data:

PERIOD	DEMAND
10	248
11	370
12	424
13	286
14	444

1. (*) Develop a three-period moving average forecast for *periods 13 through 15.*
2. (*) Develop a two-period weighted moving average forecast for *periods 12 through 15.* Use weights of 0.7 and 0.3, with the most recent observation weighted higher.
3. (*) Develop an exponential smoothing forecast ($\alpha = 0.25$) for *periods 11 through 15.* Assume your forecast for period 10 was 252.

For Problems 4 through 6, use the following time series data:

MONTH	DEMAND	MONTH	DEMAND
January 2006	119	July	111
February	72	August	116
March	113	September	89
April	82	October	95
May	82	November	88
June	131	December	90

4. (**) Develop a three-period moving average forecast for *April 2006 through January 2007.* Calculate the *MFE* and *MAD* values for *April through December 2006.*
5. (**) Develop a two-period weighted moving average forecast for *March 2006 through January 2007.* Use weights of 0.6 and 0.4, with the most recent observation weighted higher. Calculate the *MFE* and *MAD* values for *March through December.*
6. (**) Develop an exponential smoothing forecast ($\alpha = 0.3$) for *February 2006 through January 2007.* Assume your forecast for January 2006 was 100. Calculate the *MFE* and *MAD* values for *February through December 2006.*

For Problems 7 through 9, use the following time series data:

PERIOD	DEMAND
1	221
2	247
3	228
4	233
5	240
6	152
7	163
8	155
9	167
10	158

7. (*) Develop a last-period forecast for *periods 2 through 11.* Calculate the *MFE* and *MAD* values for *periods 2 through 10.* Is this a good model? Why or why not?
8. (**) Develop a three-period weighted moving average forecast for *periods 4 through 11.* Use weights of 0.4, 0.35, and 0.25, with the most recent observation weighted the

highest. Calculate the *MFE* and *MAD* values for *periods 4 through 10*. How do your results compare with those for Problem 7?

9. (**) Develop *two* exponential smoothing forecasts for *periods 2 through 11*. For the first forecast, use $\alpha = 0.2$. For the second, use $\alpha = 0.7$. Assume your forecast for period 1 was 250. Plot the results. Which model appears to work better? Why?

10. After graduating from college, you and your friends start selling birdhouses made from recycled plastic. The idea has caught on, as shown by the following sales figures:

MONTH	DEMAND
March	220
April	2240
May	1790
June	4270
July	3530
August	4990

a. (*) Prepare forecasts for *June through September* using a three-period moving average model.
b. (**) Prepare forecasts for *June through September* using an exponential smoothing model with $\alpha = 0.5$. Assume the forecast for May was 2000.
c. (**) Prepare forecasts for *June through September* using an adjusted exponential smoothing model with $\alpha = 0.5$ and $\beta = 0.3$. Assume the unadjusted forecast (F_t) for May was 2000 and the trend factor (T_t) for May was 700.

11. (**) Your manager has come to you with the following data, showing actual demand for five periods and forecast results for two different models. He has asked you to tell him which forecast model is "best" and why. Using *MFE* and *MAD*, tell him which model is best and why.

PERIOD	ACTUAL DEMAND	FORECAST MODEL 1	FORECAST MODEL 2
8	248	364	486
9	357	280	341
10	423	349	295
11	286	416	364
12	444	354	380

12. (*) Consider the following forecast results. Calculate *MAD* and *MFE* using the data for the months January through June. Does the forecast model under- or over-forecast?

MONTH	ACTUAL DEMAND	FORECAST
January	1040	1055
February	990	1052
March	980	900
April	1060	1025
May	1080	1100
June	1000	1050

13. After graduation, you take a position at Top-Slice, a well-known manufacturer of golf balls. One of your duties is to forecast monthly demand for golf balls. Using the following data, you developed a regression model that expresses monthly sales as a function of average temperature for the month:

$$\text{Monthly sales} = -767.7 + 98.5(\text{average temperature})$$

	MONTHLY SALES	TEMPERATURE
March 2003	4670	52
April	5310	58
May	6320	69
June	7080	75
July	7210	83
August	7040	82
September	6590	78
October	5520	65
November	4640	54
December	4000	48
January 2004	2840	41
February	3170	42

a. (**) Using Equations 9-8 and 9-9 from the text, show how the $\hat{a}$ and $\hat{b}$ values of −767.7 and 98.5 were calculated.
b. (*) Use the regression forecasting model to forecast total golf ball sales for *June and July 2004*. Average temperatures are expected to be 76 degrees in June and 82 degrees in July.
c. (*) Is the regression model just used a time series or a causal forecasting model? Explain.

14. (**) The following table lists the number of home improvement loans approved by a finance company, along with the loan interest rate.

MONTH	INTEREST RATE	NUMBER OF LOANS
1	7%	20
2	5%	30
3	4%	35
4	8%	18
5	10%	15
6	6%	22
7	11%	15
8	9%	20
9	5%	27
10	12%	10

a. Develop a regression forecast model using the interest rate as the predictor (i.e., independent) variable. Is this a time series or a causal forecasting model? Explain.
b. How many loans should the bank expect to make if the interest rate is 10%? 6.5%? Do these results make sense?

15. (**) While searching through your class notes, you stumble across the following forecasting model. Based *only* on this information, answer the following true/false questions. Justify your answers.

Demand = (35,000 + 4.8 × period) seasonal index

SEASONAL INDICES	
Summer	1.25
Fall	0.90
Winter	0.75
Spring	0.90

a. True or false? The forecast model is a time series model.
b. True or false? The forecast model suggests that the variable being forecasted is experiencing an upward trend in demand.
c. True or false? The variable being forecasted experiences a sharp increase during the summer months, followed by lower levels in the winter months.

16. (**) Suppose you are given the following demand and forecast data for the last four quarters.

QUARTER	DEMAND	FORECAST
Winter	285	250
Spring	315	300
Summer	300	350
Fall	400	400

Develop a seasonal index for each of the quarters. Does the fall quarter really need a seasonal adjustment index? Explain.

17. (***) After developing her 2009 forecast (Example 9.8), Jamie Favre gets a visit from Cheeznax's production manager, Mark Mobley. Mark says, "I think the forecast is fine, but I really need estimates of demand broken out by product type. In other words, I need to see how much of each month's demand will consist of cheese balls, cheese nachos, and cheese potato chips." Jamie goes back to the 2008 sales results and finds the following figures:

MONTH	CHEESE BALLS	CHEESE NACHOS	CHEESE POTATO CHIPS	TOTAL SALES
January	$126,500	$69,000	$34,500	$230,000
February	$119,600	$73,600	$36,800	$230,000
March	$115,200	$81,600	$43,200	$240,000
April	$125,000	$70,000	$55,000	$250,000
May	$112,800	$64,800	$62,400	$240,000
June	$115,000	$75,000	$60,000	$250,000
July	$126,900	$75,600	$67,500	$270,000
August	$124,800	$75,400	$59,800	$260,000
September	$135,200	$83,200	$41,600	$260,000
October	$135,200	$78,000	$46,800	$260,000
November	$151,200	$72,800	$56,000	$280,000
December	$142,100	$98,600	$49,300	$290,000
				$3,060,000

Using this information and the 2009 adjusted forecast results shown in Figure 9.21, develop a forecast for each product in each month of 2009. The sum of the individual product forecasts should equal the monthly total sales forecast. (*Hint:* Use the 2008 figures to estimate what percentage of demand is accounted for by each product type.)

18. (***) Consider the time series data shown in Table 9.1. Use an adjusted exponential smoothing model to develop a forecast for the 12 months of 2008 (assume that the unadjusted forecast and trend factor for January are 220,000 and 10,000, respectively). How do your results compare to the regression model results shown in Table 9.12?

Cooper Toys sells a portable baby stroller called the Tot n' Trot. The past two years of demand for Tot n' Trots are shown in the following table. Use this information for Problems 19 and 20.

	PERIOD	DEMAND
January 2007	1	1200
February	2	1400
March	3	1450
April	4	1580
May	5	1796
June	6	2102
July	7	2152
August	8	2022
September	9	1888
October	10	1938
November	11	1988
December	12	1839
January 2008	13	1684
February	14	1944
March	15	1994
April	16	2154
May	17	2430
June	18	2827
July	19	2877
August	20	2687
September	21	2492
October	22	2542
November	23	2592
December	24	2382

19. (***) (*Microsoft Excel problem*) Prepare forecasts for *February 2007 through January 2009* for Cooper Toys, using an adjusted exponential smoothing model with $\alpha = 0.25$ and $\beta = 0.4$. Assume the initial unadjusted forecast (F_1) for January 2007 was 1100 and the trend factor (T_1) was 60.

20. (***) (*Microsoft Excel problem*). Using regression analysis, develop a forecasting model with monthly seasonal indices for Cooper Toys. Forecast demand for each of the months in the six-month period covering *January through June 2009.*

21. (***) (*Microsoft Excel problem*). Wayne Banker is in charge of planning water usage for agriculturally intensive Burke County. August is the peak month of water usage for Burke County. Wayne has collected the following statistics from the past 15 years, showing the total March–June rainfall (in inches), average daily high temperature in July, and number of acre-feet of water used in August by farms in the area. Wayne wants to know if he can predict how much water will be needed in August, given the March–June rainfall and July temperature data.

YEAR	INCHES OF RAINFALL, MARCH–JUNE	AVERAGE PEAK DAILY TEMPERATURE, JULY	ACRE-FEET OF WATER USED, AUGUST
1990	12.5	78.4	39,800
1991	11.2	74.9	43,700
1992	12.2	84.1	45,100
1993	10.6	85.1	54,500
1994	9.3	70.6	32,900

YEAR	INCHES OF RAINFALL, MARCH–JUNE	AVERAGE PEAK DAILY TEMPERATURE, JULY	ACRE-FEET OF WATER USED, AUGUST
1995	11.7	71.0	31,500
1996	10.0	87.4	35,500
1997	13.3	91.4	35,800
1998	8.4	98.3	69,700
1999	14.9	99.6	48,100
2000	10.0	91.7	53,700
2001	12.6	91.6	40,300
2002	10.6	81.5	32,600
2003	7.1	77.0	34,100
2004	11.3	83.9	36,800

Use Excel's regression function to develop a multiple regression forecast for Wayne. What is the R^2 for the model? Use the model to forecast water usage for 1990–2004. Calculate the *MFE* and *MAD* for the model. In your opinion, how good is the model?

22. (***) (*Microsoft Excel problem*). The following figure shows an Excel spreadsheet that calculates a two-period weighted moving average and exponential smoothing model for a set of demand numbers, as well as the resulting *MFE* and *MAD* values. **Re-create this spreadsheet in Excel.** While your formatting does not have to be exactly the same, your answers should be. (*Hint:* Format the cells for the exponential smoothing model to show only two decimal places. Otherwise, the number of decimal places that shows will increase with each new forecast.)

Your spreadsheet should recalculate results whenever any changes are made to the shaded cells. If your logic is correct, changing the initial forecast for the exponential smoothing model to 50 will result in new *MFE* and *MAD* values of 0.76 and 5.62, respectively. Similarly, changing both weights for the two-period model to 0.5 should result in new *MFE* and *MAD* values of −0.077 and 7.692, respectively.

	A	B	C	D	E	F	G	H	I
1	**Comparing a Two-Period Moving Average and an Exponential Smoothing Model**								
2									
3		Two-period moving average model					Exponential smoothing model		
4		Weight on Period t-2:		0.35			Initial forecast:		65
5		Weight on Period t-1:		0.65			Alpha (a):		0.3
6									
7	Period	Demand	Forecast	Forecast Error	Absolute Deviation		Forecast	Forecast Error	Absolute Deviation
8	1	60					65.00	−5.00	5.00
9	2	53					63.50	−10.50	10.50
10	3	65	55.45	9.55	9.55		60.35	4.65	4.65
11	4	72	60.8	11.2	11.2		61.75	10.26	10.26
12	5	72	66.55	2.45	2.45		64.82	7.18	7.18
13	6	74	72	2	2		66.98	7.02	7.02
14	7	50	73.3	−23.3	23.3		69.08	−19.08	19.08
15	8	60	58.4	1.6	1.6		63.36	−3.36	3.36
16	9	72	56.5	15.5	15.5		62.35	9.65	9.65
17	10	53	67.8	−14.8	14.8		65.25	−12.25	12.25
18	11	56	59.65	−3.65	3.65		61.57	−5.57	5.57
19	12	51	54.95	−3.95	3.95		59.90	−8.90	8.90
20	13	51	52.75	−1.75	1.75		57.23	−6.23	6.23
21	14	54	51	3	3		55.36	−1.36	1.36
22	15	55	52.95	2.05	2.05		54.95	0.05	0.05
23			MFE =	−0.008			MFE =	−1.380	
24				MAD =	7.292			MAD =	7.350

CASE STUDY

Top-Slice Drivers

Introduction

Two years ago the Top-Slice Company moved from just making golf balls to also producing oversized drivers. Top-Slice makes three different models: the Bomber, the Hook King, and the Sir Slice-A-Lot. As the names suggest, the last two clubs help correct for golfers who either hook or slice the ball when driving.

While Top-Slice is pleased with the growing sales for all three models (see the following tables), the numbers present Jacob Lee, the production manager, with a dilemma. Jacob knows that the current manufacturing work cell is capable of producing only 2700 drivers per month, and total sales seem to be rapidly approaching that number. Jacob's staff has told him it will take at least three months to plan for and implement an expanded work cell.

MONTH	BOMBER	HOOK KING	SIR SLICE-A-LOT
April 2004	1410	377	343
May	1417	381	344
June	1434	387	346
July	1452	391	349

(continued)

MONTH	BOMBER	HOOK KING	SIR SLICE-A-LOT
August	1466	396	350
September	1483	400	352
October	1490	403	354
November	1505	409	357
December	1521	412	359
January 2005	1536	420	363
February	1547	423	365
March	1554	426	367
April	1562	431	369
May	1574	437	371
June	1587	441	375
July	1595	445	377
August	1613	454	381
September	1631	461	384
October	1642	464	386
November	1656	471	389
December	1673	477	392
January 2006	1685	480	394
February	1703	485	396
March	1720	490	399

QUESTIONS

1. Develop a quantitative forecast model for Jacob Lee. Which modeling technique did you choose, and why? What are the assumptions behind your model?
2. According to your model, when will Top-Slice need to have the expanded work cell up and running? What are the implications for when Jacob should start the expansion effort?
3. Now suppose over lunch the marketing vice president says to Jacob:

   We're feeling a lot of heat from Chinese manufacturers who are offering very similar clubs to ours, but at significantly lower prices. The legal department is working on a patent infringement case, but if we can't block these clubs from entering the market, I expect to see our sales flatten, and maybe even fall, over the rest of the year.

   What questions should Jacob ask? How would the answers to these questions affect the forecast? Does it still make sense to use quantitative forecasting under these circumstances? Why?

REFERENCES

Books and Articles

White, G. "Precious Commodity: How Ford's Big Batch of Rare Metal Led to $1 Billion Write-Off." *The Wall Street Journal*, February 6, 2002.

Internet

American Marketing Association, "Dictionary," **www.marketingpower.com/live/mg-dictionary.php**

Collaborative Planning, Forecasting and Replenishment: An Overview, Voluntary Interindustry Commerce Standards, May 18, 2004, **www.vics.org/committees/cpfr/CPFR_Overview_US-A4.pdf**

T. Haisley, "Survival of the Forecasting and Planning Fittest," *Apparel*, July 1, 2003, **www.apparelmag.com/bobbin/reports_analysis/article_display.jsp?vnu_content_id=1932000**.

CHAPTER 10

Sourcing Decisions

CHAPTER OUTLINE

Chapter Objectives

By the end of this chapter, you will be able to:

- Discuss the various strategic issues surrounding sourcing decisions and identify some of the key factors favoring one approach over the other.
- Perform a simple total cost analysis.
- Explain what a sourcing strategy is, and show how portfolio analysis can be used to identify the appropriate sourcing strategy for a particular good or service.
- Show how multicriteria decision models can be used to evaluate suppliers, and interpret the results.
- Discuss some of the longer-term trends in supply management and why they are important.

Apple's iPod Supply Chain at Risk[1]

how does this volcano in the Philippines threaten Apple's iPod?

At the start of Chapter 2, we described how Apple's supply chain strategy for the iPod product line included sourcing components from around the globe. Yet this strategy is not without its risks. As Nathaniel Forbes puts it, "Could a typhoon in Manila affect what teenagers in Minneapolis find in their Christmas stockings?"

A lot of high-tech gadgets are made in the Philippine Islands, including parts of the iPod. In September 2006, Mr. Forbes reviewed the contingency planning at one Philippines factory that assembles 1.8-inch disk drives for the iPod. The factory is located about 30 miles south of Manila, and ships over 20,000+ disk drives each day. If the factory was destroyed, it would take months, and several hundred million dollars, to build a new assembly line from scratch.

On the plus side, Forbes noted that the factory has a documented, tested emergency-response system, an active emergency team, and a visible, active security force. It is also protected by a municipal fire department. According to Forbes, the factory is reasonably prepared; ready for a fire or a plant-specific event.

But what if a widespread natural catastrophe strikes? Consider the following:

1. The Taal volcano, 18 miles from the factory, is one of 16 volcanoes identified as serious potential hazards to population centers by the International Association of Volcanology and Chemistry of the Earth's Interior (IAVCEI). The Taal volcano recorded 29 volcanic earthquakes in *one day* in September 2006, according to the Philippine Institute of Volcanology and Seismology (PHIVOLCS).
2. There were four earthquakes in the Philippines in one *weekend* in October 2006; one near the factory measured 4.7 on the Richter scale.
3. Tropical storms and typhoons are regular occurrences in the Philippines.
4. The area around the factory is subject to regular flooding from storm water, blocking logistics in and out of the area. The factory even sends people home early when a serious storm is forecast, because of the risk that the roads will be impassable.

The factory has about two days of finished product stored on site, waiting for shipment. The drives are just too valuable to keep around in inventory. Construction of an alternative production line is excruciatingly expensive, and would raise the cost of production, putting the factory at a competitive disadvantage. A disruption at the factory could have a direct and serious impact on Apple's ability to produce iPods, within about 48 hours of its occurrence. If that interruption happened in October, it could drastically reduce the supply of iPods available at retail for Christmas.

[1]Adapted from N. Forbes, "Tuning out Supply Chain Risk," ZD Net Asia, October 28, 2006, **www.zdnetasia.com/blog/bcp/0,39056819,61963177,00.htm**.

INTRODUCTION

Every day, businesses face the question of whether to produce some product or service internally or to source it from an outside supply chain partner. Though nearly every organization depends on sourcing to some extent, the decision to outsource goods or services raises a host of strategic questions, including the following:

- What are the pros and cons of sourcing externally?
- If we do decide to source externally, what sourcing strategy should we follow?
- Are there suppliers capable of meeting our needs? Which supplier is the "best"?
- How many suppliers should be used to ensure supply continuity and maintain competition, yet achieve the benefits of a solid supply relationship?
- What major trends will impact the supply market in the years to come?

This chapter is the first of two dealing with sourcing decisions and purchasing. Our goal in this chapter is to give you a solid understanding of the major issues surrounding sourcing decisions, and to provide you with a high-level view of various sourcing strategies and trends in supply management. With this background, you will be prepared for a more detailed discussion of the purchasing process in Chapter 11.

10.1 THE SOURCING DECISION

Sourcing decisions
High-level, often strategic, decisions regarding what products or services will be provided internally, and which will be provided by external supply chain partners.

Insourcing
The use of resources within the firm to provide products or services.

Outsourcing
The use of supply chain partners to provide products or services.

Make-or-buy decision
See sourcing decisions.

Sourcing decisions are high-level, often strategic, decisions regarding which products and services will be provided using resources within the firm (known as **insourcing**) and which will be provided by a firm's supply chain partners (known as **outsourcing**). The sourcing decision is also called the **make-or-buy decision**. Supply chain managers often make a distinction between sourcing decisions and purchasing activities, which are more tactical in nature.

Quite simply, the sourcing decision is critical to operations and supply chain managers because it defines their responsibilities. Suppose, for example, that a company decides to insource a product or service. In this case, operations and supply chain managers must determine the capacity and resources they need, the most appropriate manufacturing or service processes to use, and the information systems they will rely on to coordinate operations. But if the company decides to outsource the product or service, the emphasis shifts to the purchasing activities associated with identifying the most qualified suppliers and managing the buyer–supplier relationship (Chapter 11).

Advantages and Disadvantages of Insourcing and Outsourcing

Core competencies
Organizational strengths or abilities, developed over a long period, that customers find valuable *and* competitors find difficult or even impossible to copy.

Insourcing gives a company a high degree of control over its operations. This is particularly desirable if the company owns proprietary designs or processes. Insourcing can also lower costs, but *only* if a company enjoys the business volume necessary to achieve economies of scale. So when a company such as Nike decides to outsource the manufacturing of its running shoes, it also makes a conscious decision to retain the design and marketing of these shoes. Why? Because Nike excels at product innovation and marketing. This example points out an important concept: Companies should try to *insource* those processes that are **core competencies**—organizational strengths or abilities, developed over a long period, that customers find valuable *and* competitors find difficult or even impossible to copy.

Products or processes that could evolve into core competencies are prime candidates for insourcing.

On the downside, insourcing can be risky because it decreases a firm's strategic flexibility. Making a product or providing a service internally often requires companies to make long-term capacity commitments that cannot be easily reversed. Finally, if suppliers can provide a product or service more effectively, managers must decide whether to commit scarce resources to upgrading their processes or to outsource the product or service. Attempting to catch up to suppliers technologically can be an expensive proposition, which could restrict a firm's ability to invest in other projects, or even threaten its financial viability.

Outsourcing typically increases a firm's flexibility and access to state-of-the-art products and processes. As markets or technologies change, many firms find changing supply chain partners easier than changing internal processes. With outsourcing, less investment is required up front in the resources needed to provide a product or service. The benefits can be significant. For instance, many firms today are outsourcing their logistics capabilities to companies such as FedEx and UPS. Mike Eskew, CEO of UPS, even described his organization as an "enabler of global commerce," coordinating the movement of goods from its customers' suppliers to their final destinations, and sometimes becoming involved with assembly along the way.[2] Outsourcing is also a critical strategy for Hewlett Packard, which outsources a significant amount of manufacturing of tape drives, printers, servers, and computers to third party "contract manufacturers" such as Flextronics, Solectron, Jabil, and others. HP will typically design the product, test it, and then move production over to the supplier's facility, and might even have their own personnel working on-site in the supplier's location for a year or more during the transition phase.

Of course, outsourcing has its risks. Suppliers might misstate their capabilities: Their process technology might be obsolete or their performance might not meet the buyer's expectations. In other cases, the supplier might not have the capability to produce the product to the quality required (remember the Dell example in Chapter 4?). Outsourcing, particularly to a single supplier, also dramatically increases exposure to unforeseen problems due to unexpected natural disasters. An example of this is is when several auto makers, including Toyota Motor Corp., Honda, Nissan, and Fuji Heavy Industry had to halt production in July, 2007. The supplier (Riken) which made piston rings, had to halt production when their factory was damaged by a powerful earthquake, showing how vulnerable the supply chain is in the auto industry to widespread outsourcing to a single supplier.[3]

Control and coordination are also issues in outsourcing. Buying firms may need to create costly safeguards to regulate the quality, availability, confidentiality, or performance of outsourced goods or services. Coordinating the flow of materials across separate organizations can be a major challenge, especially when time zone differences, language barriers, and even differences in information systems come into play.

Companies who outsource also risk losing key skills and technologies that are part of their core competencies. To counteract such threats, many companies oversee key design, operations, and supply chain activities and keep current on what customers want and how their products or services meet those demands.[4] Table 10.1 summarizes the advantages and disadvantages of insourcing and outsourcing.

---

[2]R. Kapadia, "The Brown Revolution," Smart *Money Magazine, December*, 2005, **www.smartmoney.com/mag/ceo/index.cfm?story=december2005**.

[3]"Japan's Car Makers Stall After Quake Hits Supplier" Amy Chozick, *The Wall Street Journal* (July 19, 2007): A3.

[4]"The Internet Age," *Business Week* (October 4, 1999): 103–104.

TABLE 10.1
Advantages and Disadvantages of Insourcing and Outsourcing

Insourcing	
ADVANTAGES	**DISADVANTAGES**
High degree of control	Reduced strategic flexibility
Ability to oversee the entire process	Required high investment
Economies of scale and/or scope	Potential suppliers may offer superior products and services
Outsourcing	
ADVANTAGES	**DISADVANTAGES**
High strategic flexibility	Possibility of choosing a bad supplier
Low investment risk	Loss of control over the process and core technologies
Improved cash flow	Communication/coordination challenges
Access to state-of-the-art products and services	"Hollowing out" of the corporation
	Increased risk of supply chain disruption

TABLE 10.2
Factors That Affect the Decision to Insource or Outsource

FACTOR	FAVORS INSOURCING	FAVORS OUTSOURCING
Environmental uncertainty	Low	High
Competition in the supplier market	Low	High
Ability to monitor supplier's performance	Low	High
Relationship of product/service to buying firm's core competencies	High	Low

Table 10.2 looks at the debate from another angle: What factors will influence the decision to insource or outsource? As the table suggests, insourcing will generally be more favorable in situations where environmental uncertainty is low (thereby reducing the risk of investing in capacity), supplier markets are not well developed, and the product or service being considered is directly related to the buying firm's core competencies. In contrast, outsourcing becomes more attractive as competition in supplier markets increases, the product or service is not seen as strategically critical, and environmental uncertainty makes internal investment a risky prospect. Given this, it makes sense that a lot of high-tech companies, facing short product life cycles and uncertain market conditions, outsource more often than firms in more stable industries.

Total Cost Analysis

Total cost analysis
A process by which a firm seeks to identify and quantify all of the major costs associated with various sourcing options.

Direct costs
Costs tied directly to the level of operations or supply chain activities, such as the production of a good or service, or transportation.

Managers must understand the cost issues associated with insourcing versus outsourcing. Determining the actual cost of a product or service is a complicated task requiring both good judgment and the application of sound quantitative techniques. In this section we will first examine the different costs managers must consider in making such decisions.

Total cost analysis is a process by which a firm seeks to identify and quantify all of the major costs associated with various sourcing options. Table 10.3 lists some typical costs. As the table shows, these costs are often divided into direct and indirect costs. **Direct costs** are those costs that are tied directly to the level of operations or supply chain activities, such as the production of a good or service, or transportation. If, for example, a product requires 1.3 square feet of sheet metal, and the cost of sheet metal is \$0.90 per square foot, the direct cost of the sheet metal is:

$$\$0.90 \times (1.3 \text{ feet}) = \$1.17$$

TABLE 10.3
Insourcing and Outsourcing Costs

	INSOURCING	OUTSOURCING
Direct Costs	Direct material Direct labor Freight costs Variable overhead	Price (from invoice) Freight costs
Indirect Costs	Supervision Administrative support Supplies Maintenance costs Equipment depreciation Utilities Building lease Fixed overhead	Purchasing Receiving Quality control

Indirect costs
Costs that are not tied directly to the level of operations or supply chain activity.

Indirect costs, as the name implies, are not tied directly to the level of operations or supply chain activity. Building lease payments and staff salaries are classic examples of indirect costs, which in essence represent the cost of doing business. To understand the true total cost of insourcing or outsourcing, managers must allocate indirect costs to individual units of production. That task is not as easy as it may sound, however. Suppose managers are trying to decide whether to make a product in house or outsource it. They estimate they will need to spend $600,000 just to design the new product. If they plan to produce 200,000 units, they might assign the design cost as follows:

$$\$600{,}000/200{,}000 \text{ units} = \$3.00 \text{ per unit.}$$

But what if the results of the design effort could be applied to *future* products? Should part of the design cost be assigned to those future products, and if so, how? For this reason, outsourcing costs are usually easier to determine than insourcing costs. With outsourcing, the indirect costs are included in the direct purchase price shown on the supplier's invoice. Generally, the only additional costs that need to be considered in the outsourcing decision are inbound freight (a direct cost) and administrative costs associated with managing the buyer–supplier relationship (such as purchasing and quality control). In contrast, the bulk of insourcing costs may fall into the indirect category, making the task of estimating the true total cost more difficult.

In determining total costs, managers must also consider the time frame of the sourcing decision. If an insourcing arrangement is expected to be of relatively short duration, as it might be for a product with a limited life cycle, then perhaps only direct costs and some portion of the indirect costs should be applied. In the short run, firms are better off recovering their direct costs and some portion of their indirect costs than risking a significant decline in their business. However, if managers expect an insourcing arrangement to become part of ongoing operations, they should consider all relevant costs that might reasonably be incurred over the long term, including all indirect costs.

Example 10.1

Total Cost Analysis at the ABC Company

One of ABC's Taiwanese suppliers has bid on a new line of molded plastic parts that are currently being assembled at ABC's facility. The supplier has bid $0.10 per part, given a forecasted demand of 200,000 parts in year 1, 300,000 in year 2, and 500,000 in year 3. Shipping and handling of parts from the supplier's facility is estimated at $0.01 per unit. Additional inventory handling charges should amount to $0.005 per unit. Finally, administrative costs are estimated at $20 per month.

Although ABC's facility is capable of producing the part, it would need to invest in another machine that would cost $10,000, depreciated over the life of the product. Direct materials can be purchased for $.05 per unit. Direct labor is estimated at $.03 per unit plus a 50% surcharge for benefits; indirect labor is estimated at $.011 per unit plus 50% for benefits. Up-front engineering and design costs will amount to $30,000. Finally, ABC management has insisted that overhead (an indirect cost) be allocated to the parts at a rate of 100% of direct labor cost.

Table 10.4 shows one possible analysis of the total costs. Of course, different managers might come up with slightly different analyses. For instance, ABC's managers might want to experiment with different allocation rates for overhead and depreciation expense, to see how a change in the rate might affect the decision. They might also want to consider the effect of exchange rates on the supplier's costs. Suppose that the outsourcing costs are based on an exchange rate of 30 Taiwanese dollars to 1 U.S. dollar. If the exchange rate were to fall to 25 to 1, ABC's outsourcing costs could rise by 20%. The point is that even a relatively simple cost analysis requires managerial judgment and interpretation. Total cost analyses are most useful when they are considered jointly with strategic factors.

TABLE 10.4 Total Cost Analysis for the Sourcing Decision at ABC

INSOURCING OPTION		
Operating Expenses		
Direct labor	$0.0300	
Benefits (50%)	$0.0150	
Direct material	$0.0500	
Indirect labor	$0.0110	
Benefits (50%)	$0.0055	
Equipment depreciation	$0.0100	($10,000 absorbed over 1 million units)
Overhead	$0.0300	
Engineering / design costs	$0.0300	($30,000 absorbed over 1 million units)
Total cost per unit	**$0.1815**	
OUTSOURCING OPTION		
Purchase price	$0.1000	
Shipping and handling	$0.0100	
Inventory charges	$0.0050	
Administrative costs	$0.0007	[($20 per month) * (36 months)] / 1 million units
Total cost per unit	**$0.1157**	
Savings per unit	**$0.0658**	
Total savings (1 million units)	**$65,800**	

10.2 SOURCING STRATEGIES

Once the decision has been made to outsource a product or service, the firm still needs to develop and implement a sourcing strategy. But what constitutes a sourcing strategy? Simply put, a good sourcing strategy identifies the tactics and actions a firm should follow when sourcing a particular good or service, based on the sourced item's characteristics and the specific needs of the firm.

Portfolio Analysis

Sourcing professionals and academics have developed a wide range of approaches to help them in identifying the correct sourcing strategy. Figure 10.1 shows one such approach, called portfolio analysis.[5] In *portfolio analysis*, the products or services to be sourced are assigned to one of four strategic quadrants, based on (1) their relative complexity and/or risk impact to the firm, and (2) value potential. In general, the more money a company spends on a particular good or service, the higher its value potential. Depending on what quadrant a product or service is assigned to, the sourcing firm can then identify the most appropriate sourcing strategy, tactics, and actions.

To illustrate, a standardized product available from many sources represents a relatively low level of complexity and sourcing risk to the firm—the product characteristics are well understood, and if one supplier fails to meet the needs of the company, another one will be ready to pick up the business. On the other hand, a highly customized product or service, available from one or a handful of suppliers, introduces greater levels of complexity and risk. Likewise, a service that represents $30 million of annual spending has a greater

FIGURE 10.1
Sourcing Portfolio Analysis

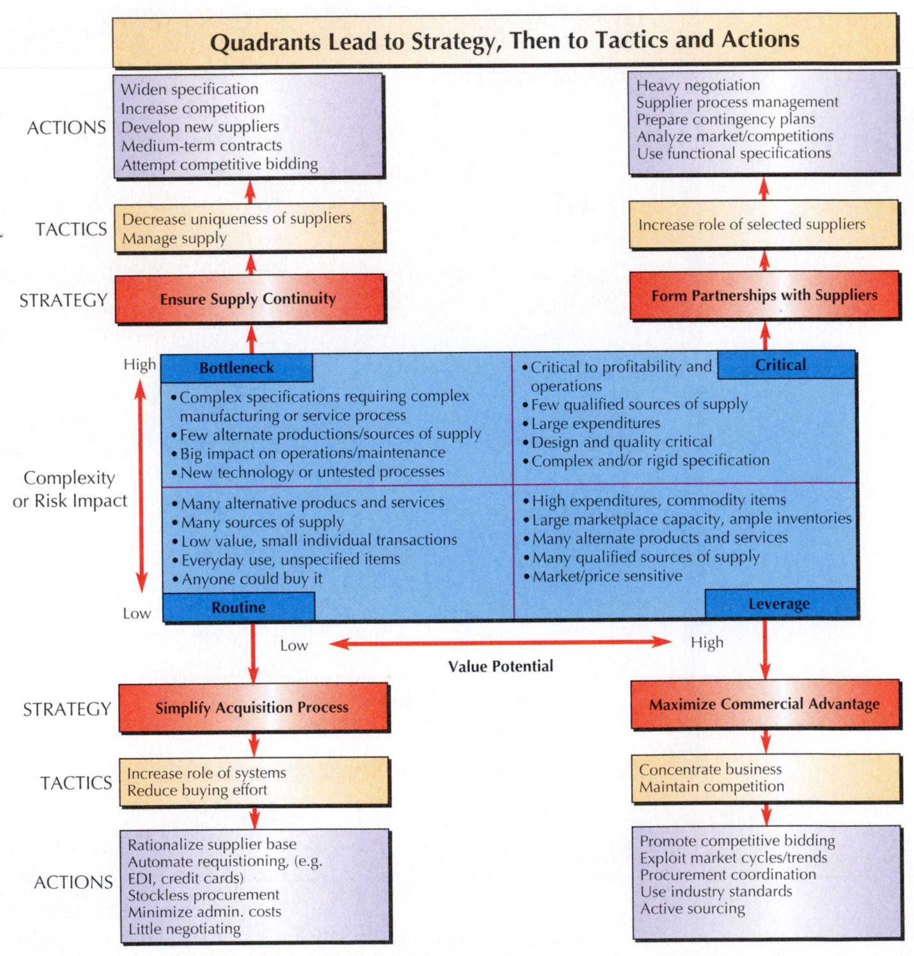

[5]R. Monczka, R. Trent, and R. Handfield, *Purchasing and Supply Chain Management*, 3rd ed. (Cincinnati: Southwestern College Publishing, 2004).

value potential—and hence deserves more attention from the firm—than one with an annual spending amount of just $10,000.

"ROUTINE" QUADRANT. Products or services in this quadrant are readily available, and represent a small portion of a firm's purchasing expenditures. Examples include office supplies, cleaning services, and the like. The sourcing strategy therefore becomes one of simplifying the acquisition process, thereby lowering the costs associated with purchasing items in this quadrant. Specific actions can include automating the purchasing process, reducing the number of suppliers used, and using **electronic data interchange (EDI)** or credit cards to streamline payment.

Electronic data interchange (EDI)
An information technology that allows supply chain partners to transfer data electronically between their information systems.

"LEVERAGE" QUADRANT. Products or services in this quadrant tend to be standardized, readily available, and represent a significant portion of the spending amount. The sourcing strategy therefore focuses on leveraging the firm's spending levels to get the most favorable terms possible. A **preferred supplier** is a supplier that has demonstrated its performance capabilities through previous purchase contracts, and therefore receives preference during the supplier selection process. Preferred suppliers are frequently awarded the business with the understanding that they will reduce the cost of supplying these items in return for significant order volumes and multiyear contracts. A high level of service is also expected, which may include such services as on-site inventory management by the supplier and e-purchasing.

Preferred supplier
A supplier that has demonstrated its performance capabilities through previous purchase contracts, and therefore receives preference during the supplier selection process.

"BOTTLENECK" QUADRANT. "Bottleneck" products or services have unique or complex requirements that can only be met by a few potential suppliers. In this case, the primary goal of the sourcing strategy is to not run out—in effect, to ensure supply continuity. This might involve carrying extra inventory to protect against interruptions in supply or even contracting with multiple vendors to reduce supply chain risks.

"CRITICAL" QUADRANT. Like bottleneck items, products or services in this quadrant have complex or unique requirements coupled with a limited supply base. The primary difference is that these items can represent a substantial level of expenditure for the sourcing firm. The 1.8-inch disk drives that Apple sources from a Philippine plant (described at the beginning of the chapter) fit into this quadrant. In cases such as this, the sourcing firm will spend considerable time negotiating favorable deals and building partnerships with suppliers, as well as preparing contingency plans in case of an interruption in supply.

Single sourcing
The buying firm depends on a single company for all or nearly all of a particular item or service.

Multiple sourcing
A sourcing strategy in which the buying firm shares its business across multiple suppliers.

Single/Multiple Sourcing, Cross Sourcing, and Dual Sourcing

An important part of any sourcing strategy is determining how many suppliers to use when sourcing a good or service. In **single sourcing**, the buying firm depends on a single company for all or nearly all of a particular item. In **multiple sourcing**, the buying firm shares its business across multiple suppliers. The advantages and disadvantages of each are shown in Table 10.5.

In the past, very few North American organizations would have considered voluntarily using a single supplier due to the inherent risks. This perception has changed somewhat because of the example set by Japanese firms who have used single sourcing to achieve continuous price, quality, and delivery improvements.

One way that companies can overcome the dilemma of the single sourcing/multiple sourcing decision is through a compromise known as **cross sourcing**. In this strategy, the

Cross sourcing
A sourcing strategy in which the company uses a single supplier for a certain part or service in one part of the business, and another supplier with the same capabilities for a similar part in another area of the business. Each supplier is then awarded new business based on their performance, creating an incentive for them to improve.

TABLE 10.5 Advantages and Disadvantages of Multiple/Single Sourcing

Multiple Sourcing		*Single Sourcing*	
ADVANTAGES	DISADVANTAGES	ADVANTAGES	DISADVANTAGES
Creates competition	Reduces supplier loyalty—suppliers may not be willing to "go the extra mile" for the purchaser	Volume leveraging as volumes go up, cost per unit decreases as supplier spreads fixed costs over larger volume	Knowing they have the business, suppliers can actually increase prices in the short term
Spreads risk (in event of a fire, strike, etc. at one supplier)	Can increase risk in the event of a shortage—supplier may only supply preferred customers	Transportation economics—fewer shipments and lower per-unit transportation costs	Increased supply risk—if a disaster occurs, the buyer can be left without a source of supply
Required if the purchased volume is too great for one supplier	May result in different product attributes with varying quality	Reduces quality variability; standardized products	Buyer can become "captive" to a supplier's technology—while other suppliers are surging ahead with newer technology that has better performance
Desired if firm wishes to meet obligations to support minority suppliers	Can actually result in increased prices over time, as suppliers are reluctant to provide cost-saving ideas	Builds stronger relationship with supplier, and gains access to design and engineering capabilities	Do not know if you have the "best" supplier available
Can ensure that suppliers do not become "complacent"	Suppliers can let performance slide if volume is not high enough to merit their attention	Required when supplier has a proprietary product	Dangerous strategy if the supplier has limited capacity—may "shut down" the buyer if it takes on too much business
		Required when volume is too small to split between two suppliers	

company uses a single supplier for one product or service, and another supplier with the same capabilities for a similar product or service. Each supplier is then awarded new business based on its performance, creating an incentive for both to improve. This also provides for a backup supplier in case the primary supplier cannot meet the company's needs.

Dual sourcing
A sourcing strategy in which two suppliers are used for the same purchased product or service.

A similar purchasing strategy is **dual sourcing**. This strategy is exactly what it sounds like—two suppliers are used for the same purchased product or service. Typically, the split of the business is 70% to Supplier A and 30% to Supplier B. In this manner, Supplier A is "looking over his shoulder," knowing that if performance suffers, it will lose the business to Supplier B. Dual sourcing in some ways combines the best of both worlds.

10.3 SUPPLIER EVALUATION

While portfolio analysis can help identify the appropriate sourcing strategy for a product or service, the buying firm still needs some way to evaluate potential and current suppliers. Identifying the "best" supplier for a new product or service, or evaluating past supplier performance, is a difficult task. This is especially true when the criteria include not just quantitative measures (such as costs, on-time delivery rates, etc.), but other, more qualitative factors, such as "management stability" or "trustworthiness." Some of the more qualitative criteria that a company might use to evaluate suppliers include:[6]

- **Process and Design Capabilities.** Since different manufacturing and service processes have inherent strengths and weaknesses (Chapter 7), the buying firm must be aware of these characteristics up front. When the buyer expects suppliers to perform component design and production, it should also assess the suppliers' design capability. One way to reduce the time required to develop new products is to use qualified suppliers who are able to perform product design activities.
- **Management Capability.** Different aspects of management capability include management's commitment to continuous process and quality improvement, overall professional ability and experience, ability to maintain positive relationships with its workforce, and management's willingness to develop a closer working relationship with the buyer.
- **Financial Condition and Cost Structure.** Selecting a supplier who is in poor financial condition presents a number of risks. First, there is the risk that the organization will go out of business, disrupting the flow of goods or services. Second, suppliers who are in poor financial condition may not have the resources to invest in required personnel, equipment, or improvement efforts.
- **Environmental Regulation Compliance.** The last few years has brought about a renewed awareness of the impact that industry has on the environment. The Clean Air Act of 1990 imposed large fines on producers of ozone-depleting substances and foul-smelling gases, and governments have introduced laws regarding recycling content in industrial materials. As a result, a supplier's ability to comply with environmental regulations is becoming an important criterion for supply chain alliances.
- **Longer-Term Relationship Potential.** In some cases, the buying firm may be looking to develop a long-term relationship with a potential supplier. Perhaps the supplier has a proprietary technology or foreign market presence that the sourcing firm wants to tap into.

Multicriteria decision models
Models that allow decision makers to evaluate various alternatives across multiple decision criteria.

Multicriteria decision models, as the name suggests, are models that allow decision makers to evaluate various alternatives across multiple decision criteria. Multicriteria decision models are especially helpful when there is a mix of quantitative and qualitative decision criteria, when there are numerous decision alternatives to be considered, and when there is no clear "best" choice. As such, they are well suited to supplier evaluation efforts. At their best, multicriteria decision models help formalize what would otherwise be an ill-structured, poorly understood decision.

Weighted-Point Evaluation System

A common multicriteria decision model is the weighted-point evaluation system. In this model, the user is asked upfront to assign weights to the performance measures (W_Y), and rate the performance of each supplier with regard to each dimension ($Performance_{XY}$). The total score for each supplier is then calculated as follows:

$$Score_X = \sum_{Y=1}^{n} Performance_{XY} \times W_Y \quad [10\text{-}1]$$

[6]R. Monczka, R. Trent, and R. Handfield, *Purchasing and Supply Chain Management*, 3rd ed. (Cincinnati: Southwestern College Publishing, 2004).

where:

X = Supplier X

Y = Performance Dimension Y

$Performance_{XY}$ = rated performance of Supplier X with regard to Performance Dimension Y

W_Y = assigned weight for Performance Dimension Y, where $\sum_{Y=1}^{n} W_Y = 1$

Example 10.2

Using the Weighted-Point Evaluation System to Support Supplier Evaluation at Electra Company

The Electra Company is looking to award a new contract for 500,000 integrated circuit boards (ICBs). In the past, the company has shared all business equally across three suppliers, and has amassed a significant amount of information on their performance history. Table 10.6 summarizes the performance of its three major suppliers with regard to price, quality, and delivery.

TABLE 10.6 Summary Data for Three Possible Suppliers

PERFORMANCE DIMENSION	AARDVARK ELECTRONICS	BEVERLY HILLS INC.	CONAN THE ELECTRICIAN
Price	$4/unit	$5/unit	$2/unit
Quality	5% defects	1% defects	10% defects
Delivery Reliability	95% on-time	80% on-time	60% on-time

The process begins by developing a weight for each of the criteria used. The sum of the weights must equal one. In this case, the sourcing team assigned to evaluating suppliers for the new contract has decided that quality is the most important criteria, followed closely followed by delivery and price. The resulting weights are:

$$
\begin{aligned}
W_{Price} &= 0.3 \\
W_{Quality} &= 0.4 \\
W_{Delivery\ Reliability} &= \underline{0.3} \\
\text{Total} &= 1.0
\end{aligned}
$$

Next, the sourcing team evaluates each supplier's performance on each of the criteria, using the scales in Table 10.7.

TABLE 10.7 Scoring Scheme for Weighted-Point Evaluation System

5 = *Excellent*
4 = *Good*
3 = *Average*
2 = *Fair*
1 = *Poor*

Based on the product design team's specifications, the Electra sourcing team has assigned performance scores for each criterion, as shown in Table 10.8.

TABLE 10.8 $Performance_{XY}$ Values for the Three Suppliers

PERFORMANCE DIMENSION	AARDVARK ELECTRONICS	BEVERLY HILLS INC.	CONAN THE ELECTRICIAN
Price	4	3	5
Quality	3	5	1
Delivery Reliability	4	2	1

The total score for each supplier is then calculated by multiplying the respective performance ratings by the weight assigned to each performance dimension, and summing the results across all dimensions. For Aardvark Electronics:

$$\begin{aligned} Score_{Aardvark} &= Performance_{Aardvark,Price} \times W_{Price} \\ &+ Performance_{Aardvark,Quality} \times W_{Quality} \\ &+ Performance_{Aardvark,Delivery\ Reliability} \times W_{Delivery\ Reliability} \\ &= 4 \times 0.3 + 3 \times 0.4 + 4 \times 0.3 = 3.6 \end{aligned}$$

The scores for Beverly Hills and Conan the Electrician are calculated in a similar manner, and are 3.5 and 2.2, respectively. Based on the results, the Electra team must now decide on which source to use. Conan the Electrician is clearly out of the running. Though this supplier has the lowest price by far, its delivery and quality record is abysmal. This leaves Aardvark and Beverly Hills. Aardvark has a lower price, but needs to improve its quality. Beverly Hills has excellent quality, but it has a problem delivering on time, and must also find a way to reduce its prices. Because the final scores for the two suppliers are so close, the result of this decision might be one of the following outcomes:

1. Award the contract to Aardvark after a detailed negotiation in which Aardvark is asked to provide details on how it will improve quality.
2. Award the contract to Beverly Hills after a detailed negotiation in which the company is asked to reduce its price and explain how it will improve delivery performance.
3. Award a dual source contract, in which the volumes are split between two suppliers. The contract might state that future volumes will be assigned according to which supplier improves their performance most quickly.

Clearly, supplier evaluation requires a significant amount of judgment in awarding points and assigning weights. However, the process of identifying key criteria and assigning numerical scores to performance allows users to be more objective and comprehensive in their decision making. Furthermore, conscientious managers will make every effort to back up their ratings with hard data.

10.4 TRENDS IN SUPPLY MANAGEMENT

Our chapter would not be complete without a look ahead to the trends affecting supply management. These trends are based on research performed by the Center for Advanced Purchasing Management (www.capsresearch.org/), which conducts research on current issues in supply management. As the findings suggest, the changes occurring within purchasing are as dramatic as those in any business area.

Sustainable Supply (green)

As sustainability becomes more important, companies will look for suppliers who can provide environmentally friendly products and services, such as the packaging for the soups pictured here.

As more companies become conscious of the importance of being environmentally friendly, one trend is that environmental performance is becoming an important supplier selection criterion. Companies want to ensure that suppliers are in compliance with environmental regulations, and that they are well positioned to deal with changes in the regulatory environment. Similarly, companies are looking for ways to reduce packaging, promote recycling, and other strategies designed to reduce cost while being good for the environment. The *Supply Chain Connections* feature shows how Wal-Mart is emphasizing sustainability in the "scorecards" it uses to evaluate potential suppliers.

Supply Base Reduction

In 1990, the average buyer in an organization was responsible for 126 suppliers. Ten years later, buyers regularly did business with about 46 suppliers, representing a decline of 63%. This trend is still continuing. Note that a reduction in the number of suppliers a firm maintains is often just a reduction in the total number of first-tier suppliers (see Chapter 1). A trend within the automotive industry, for example, has been to rely on larger suppliers to design and build entire subsystems, such as the automobile's electrical system. Instead of dozens of smaller suppliers providing components for the subsystem, the purchaser uses one major supplier, who then uses dozens of suppliers to help build the system.

Global Sourcing

Many companies have sought to lower the cost of sourced products and services by outsourcing to countries with lower labor costs, such as India, China, Indonesia, and Vietnam. Interestingly, as these lower-cost countries gain more experience, they are providing products and services that rival the quality and performance of more mature economies (see the *Supply Chain Connections* feature "China's Rise as Auto-Parts Power Reflects New Manufacturing Edge").

SUPPLY CHAIN CONNECTIONS

WAL-MART USES SUSTAINABILITY IN ITS SUPPLIER EVALUATION CRITERIA[7]

Wal-Mart recently announced the early results from its Packaging Scorecard for suppliers, which it said showed "active use of the scorecard and a strong interest from product suppliers to make their packaging more sustainable." The scorecard evaluates the "green quotient" of product packaging based on a number of attributes, such as:

- Greenhouse gas emissions related to production
- Materials used
- Product-to-packaging ratio
- Cube utilization
- Recycled content usage
- Innovation
- The amount of renewable energy used to manufacture the packaging
- The recovery value of the raw materials and emissions-related to transportation of the packaging materials

The scorecard provides both vendor-product specific information as well as comparisons between vendors in a category. In parallel, Wal-Mart also announced plans for a similar scorecard for electronics suppliers, to be launched in 2008. The big news is probably that Wal-Mart plans to provide scorecard information to consumers, which may influence purchase decisions. Criteria for the electronics scorecard will include:

- Energy efficiency
- Durability
- Upgradability
- End-of-life solutions
- Size of the package containing the product
- Ability to use innovative materials that reduce the amount of hazardous substances, such as lead and cadmium, contained in the product

SUPPLY CHAIN CONNECTIONS

CHINA'S RISE AS AUTO-PARTS POWER REFLECTS NEW MANUFACTURING EDGE[8]

Raising the bar for competitors around the world, China is shifting its manufacturing resources to increasingly sophisticated goods, as shown by its rapid emergence as a global powerhouse in the auto-parts industry. Just a few years ago, Chinese-made automotive components were plagued by a reputation for poor quality, and often cost more than U.S. or German parts. Detractors said the precision engineering required for the best parts was beyond the reach of inexperienced Chinese companies and their low-cost workers.

In 2005, however, China for the first time exported more parts than its fast-growing auto industry purchased from abroad. Quality has improved so much that major Western automakers like **Volkswagen** AG and **DaimlerChrysler** AG say they plan in coming years to buy billions of dollars of Chinese-made components—such as brakes, fuel pumps, wheels, and steering systems.

Those gains show how China continues to evolve as a manufacturer, posing new challenges for rivals in the United States, Europe, and Japan. After earning its stripes as a maker of simple consumer goods, such as furniture and textiles, China has branched out, quickly coming to dominate more labor-intensive parts of the consumer-electronics business, such as computer assembly, and moving into a broader range of industries.

The country's production of machinery and transportation equipment has surged, and export of those goods—which range from auto parts to forklifts to vacuum cleaners—totaled $352 billion in 2005, a fourfold increase from 2000.

---

[7]"The Green Supply Chain: Wal-Mart Releases Packaging Scorecard Data, Plans for Electronics Suppliers," *Supply Chain Digest*, March 14, 2007, **www.scdigest.com/assets/newsViews/07-03-14-3.cfm?cid=955&ctype=content**.

[8]A. Baston, "China's Rise as Auto-Parts Power Reflects New Manufacturing Edge," *The Wall Street Journal*, Eastern Edition (August 1, 2006): A1.

Supply Chain Disruptions

As supply chains become more extended and firms depend even more on outside companies to provide critical goods and services, many firms are feeling the sting of disruptions to the supply chain.

The cause of these disruptions can take many forms, from natural disasters to economic or even political events. Some recent examples illustrate this phenomenon. Boeing experienced supplier delivery failure of two critical parts with an estimated loss to the company of $2.6 billion. In 2002, striking dockworkers disrupted port operations on the U.S. West Coast. As a result, it took six months for some containers to be delivered and schedules to return to normal. And in 2005 Hurricane Katrina resulted in billions of dollars of lost revenue to major retailers such as British Petroleum, Shell, Conoco Phillips, and Lyondell, as well as gasoline shortages in many parts of the United States. Given this and other events, it is not surprising that supply chain disruptions have caught the attention of executives.

In a recent survey of senior executives at Global 1000 companies, the respondents identified supply chain disruptions as the single biggest threat to their companies' revenue streams. Although senior executives now recognize that supply chain disruptions can be devastating to an enterprise's bottom line, strategies to mitigate supply chain disruptions are typically not well developed or even initiated. A concerning statistic is that only between 5% and 25% of Fortune 500 companies are estimated to be prepared to handle a major supply chain crisis or disruption.

One factor that is increasing the risk of supply chain disruptions is the propensity of companies to outsource processes to global suppliers. The complexity associated with multiple links in the supply chain increases the probability of disruptions. For example, as the number of "hand-offs" required to ship products through multiple carriers, multiple ports, and multiple government checkpoints increases, so does the likelihood of poor communication, human error, and missed shipments. An electronics executive we interviewed noted: "We have successfully outsourced production of our products to China. Unfortunately, we now recognize that we do not have the processes in place to manage risk associated with this supply chain effectively." As firms grapple with the risks associated with supply chain disruptions, expect to see more of them utilize the tactics and actions associated with "bottleneck" and "critical" products in Figure 10.1, and to develop comprehensive risk management strategies.

CHAPTER SUMMARY

This chapter was the first of two on sourcing decisions and purchasing. We discussed the key issues surrounding the sourcing decision, and presented a framework for developing sourcing strategies based on the particular characteristics of the product or service being sourced. We also discussed supplier evaluation criteria, and described one multicriteria decision model that can be used to evaluate potential or current suppliers. We ended the chapter by examining some of the major trends affecting supply management.

KEY FORMULAS

Overall preference score, weighted-point evaluation system (page 327):

$$Score_X = \sum_{Y=1}^{n} Performance_{XY} \times W_Y \qquad [10\text{-}1]$$

where:

$$X = \text{Supplier X}$$

$$Y = \text{Performance Dimension Y}$$

$$Performance_{XY} = \text{rated performance of Supplier X with regard to Performance Dimension Y.}$$

$$W_Y = \text{assigned weight for Performance Dimension Y, where } \sum_{Y=1}^{n} W_Y = 1$$

KEY TERMS

Core competencies 319
Cross sourcing 325
Direct costs 321
Dual sourcing 326
Electronic data interchange (EDI) 325
Indirect costs 322
Insourcing 319
Make-or-buy decision 319
Multicriteria decision models 327
Multiple sourcing 325
Outsourcing 319
Preferred supplier 325
Single sourcing 325
Sourcing decisions 319
Total cost analysis 321

SOLVED PROBLEM

Problem

Montoya-Weiss Engineering (MWE) is a Dallas engineering firm that produces customized instrumentation for the aerospace industry. MWE is thinking about outsourcing the production of a particular component to a Fort Worth manufacturer. The Fort Worth manufacturer has offered to make the components for a price of $25 each, based on an annual volume of 32,000. However, additional costs are associated with maintaining this supplier relationship. MWE management has developed the following cost figures:

CURRENT MANUFACTURING OPERATIONS	FORT WORTH MANUFACTURER
Fixed Costs:	**Price per component:**
Plant and overhead, $800,000 per year	$25
Variable Costs:	**Other Costs:**
Labor, $8.50 per unit	Administrative costs, $50,000 per year
Materials, $5.00 per unit	Inspection costs, $65,000 per year
	Shipping cost, $1.50 per unit

In addition to cost, MWE management has identified two other dimensions to consider: quality (specifically, the percent of defect-free items) and on-time delivery. MWE management has established importance weights of 0.2, 0.5, and 0.3 for cost, quality, and on-time delivery, respectively. Finally, purchasing experts at MWE have rated the performance of the current assembly operation and the Fort Worth manufacturer with regard to these three dimensions. Their ratings (1 = "poor" to 5 = "excellent") are as follows:

	Performance Ratings	
PERFORMANCE DIMENSION	CURRENT MFG. OPERATIONS	FORT WORTH CONTRACT MANUFACTURER
Cost	3	5
Quality	5	4
On-time delivery	3	3

Calculate the total cost of each option, as well as the overall preference score.

Solution

Total costs for the current manufacturing operations:

$$\$800{,}000 + 32{,}000 \text{ units} \times (\$8.50 + \$5.00) = \$800{,}000 + \$432{,}000 = \$1{,}232{,}000$$

Total cost for the Fort Worth contract manufacturer:

$$\$50{,}000 + \$65{,}000 + 32{,}000 \text{ units} \times (\$25.00 + \$1.50) = \$115{,}000 + \$848{,}000 = \$963{,}000$$

The total cost analysis suggests that the Fort Worth manufacturer has a yearly cost advantage of (\$1,232,000 – \$963,000) = \$269,000. This result would seem to strongly favor the Fort Worth option. However, the overall preference scores suggest that the choice is not so clear:

$$\begin{aligned} Score_{Current} &= Performance_{Current,Cost} \times W_{Cost} \\ &\quad + Performance_{Current,Quality} \times W_{Quality} \\ &\quad + Performance_{Current,Delivery} \times W_{Delivery} \\ &= 3 \times 0.2 + 5 \times 0.5 + 3 \times 0.3 = 4 \end{aligned}$$

and:

$$\begin{aligned} Score_{FtWorth} &= Performance_{FtWorth,Cost} \times W_{Cost} \\ &\quad + Performance_{FtWorth,Quality} \times W_{Quality} \\ &\quad + Performance_{FtWorth,Delivery} \times W_{Delivery} \\ &= 5 \times 0.2 + 4 \times 0.5 + 3 \times 0.3 = 3.9 \end{aligned}$$

What accounts for the discrepancy? Quite simply, the overall preference scores take into consideration more than just cost. This, plus the fact that MWE management places higher importance on quality and on-time delivery, tilts the preference scores in favor of the current assembly operation. Given these results, MWE might decide to stick with its current manufacturing operations, or perhaps work with the Fort Worth contract manufacturer to improve its quality and delivery performance *prior* to outsourcing the business.

DISCUSSION QUESTIONS

1. What are some of the pros and cons of outsourcing? Why do you think many firms are experiencing an increase in their levels of outsourcing?
2. Describe the problems associated with the allocation of indirect costs to a product or service. How does this complicate total cost analyses?
3. What is a preferred supplier? What are the advantages and disadvantages of using preferred suppliers?
4. Consider the cafeteria services available at a university. In many cases, these services are outsourced to a private firm. Use Tables 10.1 and 10.2 as a guide to explain why this is the case. In what quadrant would such services be positioned when determining a sourcing strategy (Figure 10.1)?

PROBLEMS

Additional homework problems are available at www.prenhall.com/bozarth. These problems use Excel to generate customized problems for different class sections or even different students.

(* 5 easy; ** 5 moderate; *** 5 advanced)

1. (**) Looking back at Example 10.2, suppose Conan the Electrician has implemented a Six Sigma program (Chapters 3 and 4), and as a result has brought defect levels down to just 1%, the same as Beverly Hills Inc. Recalculate the weighted performance score for Conan the Electrician using the weights provided in the example. Should Electra change its preferred supplier, based on these results?

2. The ABC Company (Example 10.1) has identified another potential supplier for the molded plastic parts. The new supplier has bid \$0.08 per part, but also will impose a shipping and handling charge of \$0.015 per unit. Additional inventory handling charges should amount to \$0.007 per unit. Finally, purchasing costs are estimated at \$25 per month for the length of the 36-month contract.

a. (*) Calculate the total costs for the new supplier. Which is cheaper, insourcing or outsourcing with the new supplier?

b. (**) Suppose the three-year volume is expected to rise to 1.5 million, rather than 1 million, molded plastic parts. Recalculate the total costs associated with insourcing. What explains the difference?

c. (**) What other factors, besides costs, should ABC consider when deciding whether or not to make the molded parts in-house?

3. Granville Community College is considering outsourcing the maintenance of its buildings and other facilities to an outside firm for \$300,000 per year. The 2009 budget is as follows:

GRANVILLE MAINTENANCE BUDGET—2009

Direct expenses (per worker)

- Wages—\$2500 per worker, per month
- Benefits—35% of wages per worker, per month
- Maintenance, repair, and operating supplies—\$2000 per worker, per month

Indirect expenses

- Supervisor salary—\$3000 per month
- Benefits—40% of wages
- Other office expenses—\$500 per month

a. (*) Calculate the total costs of insourcing versus outsourcing maintenance.

b. (**) What other reasons, besides costs, might Granville look at when deciding whether or not to outsource maintenance activities?

4. Lincoln Lights is considering hiring one of three software firms to implement its electronic data interchange (EDI) system. Lincoln management has decided to evaluate the firms along three dimensions: reputation, skill level, and price. Weights for each dimension, as well as performance ratings for each of the firms (1 = poor to 5 = excellent) are as follows:

		Software Firms		
DIMENSION	WEIGHT	ALTREX	TGI LTD.	PC ASSOCIATES
Reputation	0.2	3	4	5
Skill level	0.4	5	4	4
Price	0.4	5	3	2

a. (*) Use the weighted-point evaluation system to calculate weighted performance scores for each of the software firms. Would the results change if each dimension had a weight of 1/3?

b. (**) In Chapter 2, we described order qualifiers as performance dimensions on which customers demand a *minimum* level of performance. Basically, if a supplier fails to meet the minimum requirements on any of the qualifiers, that supplier would be eliminated from contention. How would you incorporate the concept of order qualifiers into the weighted-point evaluation system?

5. Flynn Industries has outsourced the delivery of its products, and now wants to develop a tool to help it evaluate its transportation carriers. The first table on the next page shows the rating values associated with different levels of price, quality, and delivery performance, as well as criteria weights that reflect the relative importance of these dimensions. To illustrate how the ratings work, suppose a carrier has a damage level of 0.82%. This would fall between 0.75% and 1.0%, thereby garnering a rating of two. The second table (on next page) shows actual average performance levels for three carriers.

Rating Values					
(SUPPLIERS ARE RATED ON A SCALE OF 1 TO 5, DEPENDING ON THEIR SPECIFIC PERFORMANCE LEVELS)					
CRITERION (WEIGHT)	1	2	3	4	5
Price (0.20)	>$2.50/lb	$2.01–$2.50/lb	$1.51–$2.00/lb	$1.00–$1.50/lb	<$1.00/lb
Quality (0.20)	Damage >1%	Damage 0.75–1.0%	Damage 0.5–0.74%	Damage 0.25–0.49%	Damage <0.25%
Delivery (0.60)	<82% on-time	82–84% on-time	85–90% on-time	91–95% on-time	>95% on-time

	CARRIER A	CARRIER B	CARRIER C
Price	$1.98/lb	Price $2.02/lb	$98.00/100 lbs
Quality	0.35% damaged	Quality 0.26% damaged	0.86% damaged
Delivery	93% on-time	Delivery 98% on-time	83% on-time

a. (*) Use the weighted-point evaluation system to calculate the weighted average performance for each carrier. Who is "best"?

b. (**) How would the results change if the weights for price, quality, and delivery shifted to 0.6, 0.2, and 0.2, respectively?

c. (**) Based on the results, should Flynn Industries single source or not? What might stop Flynn from single sourcing?

6. (***) *(Microsoft Excel problem)*. The following worksheet uses a weighted-point evaluation system to calculate weighted performance scores along four dimensions for up to four potential sources. **Re-create this spreadsheet in Microsoft Excel.** Code your spreadsheet so that any change in the highlighted cells will result in recalculated performance scores. Your formatting does not have to be exactly the same, but your numbers should be. (*Hint:* Changing all the importance weights to 0.25 should result in scores of 2.25 and 3.5 for Sources X1 and X2, respectively.)

	A	B	C	D	E	F
1	**Weighted-Point Evaluation System**					
2						
3			Potential Sources			
4	Dimension	Importance	X1	X2	X3	X4
5	A	0.20	1	3	2	4
6	B	0.30	2	4	3	2
7	C	0.30	2	4	3	2
8	D	0.20	4	3	2	1
9	Total:	1.00				
10		**Scores:**	**2.2**	**3.6**	**2.6**	**2.2**

CASE STUDY

PAGODA.COM

Introduction

Pagoda.com is an Internet service provider (ISP) that caters to individual consumers and small businesses who require a high level of service and are willing to pay a premium for it. Specifically, Pagoda.com offers state-of-the-art e-mail applications and web-building software, as well as plenty of storage space and fast access via its high-speed servers. Marketing vice president Jerry Hunter puts it this way: "There are a lot of companies out there distributing free CDs and promising the cheapest Internet access. But what do you get for your money? Slow or no access, a mailbox full of spam, and an endless stream of system crashes. And I won't even mention the lack of support if you have a technical question! For a few dollars more a month, we give our customers the environment they need to be productive—without having to think about whether or not they can retrieve their e-mail, or whether their Web site has crashed. It's no surprise, then, that we have the highest customer satisfaction and retention rates in the industry."

The Online Help Desk

One of Pagoda's services is its online help desk. The online help desk works as follows: Customers who are experiencing technical problems, or who simply have questions about their account, enter a one-on-one "chat room" where they can "talk" directly with an expert. Problems are usually resolved within 10 minutes, and customers have listed it as one of the top three reasons why they stick with Pagoda.com. Presently, Pagoda has enough capacity to handle up to 900,000 requests per year, although management doesn't expect the number of requests to change much from the current level of 800,000 per year.

A firm located in New Delhi, India, has approached Pagoda about outsourcing the online help desk. The firm's offer is attractive. The New Delhi firm's own personnel would handle the help desk function. These personnel all speak English fluently, and have college degrees or appropriate technical backgrounds. And because they are located in India, labor costs would be a fraction of what they are in the United States—a savings that would be passed on, in part, to Pagoda. And since the help desk "chat room" exists on the Internet, Pagoda's customers would be unaware of the switch.

Pagoda management has put together the following figures outlining the yearly costs associated with the current system and the Indian proposal:

Current Online Help Desk

Personnel Costs:
40 full-time-equivalent (FTE) technical experts @ $40,000 per year (salary and benefits)
3 supervisors @ $70,000 each per year (salary and benefits)

Equipment Costs:
4 servers @ $2000 per year
20 PCs @ $1000 per year

Variable Costs:
$1.50 per request (office supplies, fax paper, etc.)

New Delhi Proposal

Fixed Cost: $1,500,000 per contract year (to cover administrative and IT costs)
Charge: $0.50 per request

QUESTIONS

1. Calculate the total cost of outsourcing the online help desk versus staying with the current solution. Which option is cheaper?
2. What other factors, besides costs, should Pagoda consider? How would you weight these factors? Given these options, how might you use a weighted-point evaluation system to evaluate the two options?
3. Should Pagoda.com outsource its online help desk? Why or why not? Be sure to consider Table 10.1 when framing your answer.
4. A statement of work typically specifies performance measurements that the buying firm can use to determine whether or not the service provider is meeting the terms of the contract. What performance measurements would you recommend be put in place? What should happen if the service provider fails to meet these requirements?

REFERENCES

Books and Articles

Baston, A. "China's Rise as Auto-Parts Power Reflects New Manufacturing Edge," *The Wall Street Journal*, Eastern Edition (August 1, 2006): A1.

Chozik, A. "Japan's Car Makers Stall After Quake Hits Supplier," *The Wall Street Journal* (July 19, 2007): A3.

Forbes, N. "Tuning out Supply Chain Risk," ZD Net Asia, October 28, 2006, **www.zdnetasia.com/blog/bcp/0,39056819,61963177,00.htm**

"The Green Supply Chain: Wal-Mart Releases Packaging Scorecard Data, Plans for Electronics Suppliers," *Supply Chain Digest*, March 14, 2007, **www.scdigest.com/assets/newsViews/07-03-14-3.cfm?cid=955&ctype=content.**

"The Internet Age," *Business Week* (October 4, 1999): 103–104.

Kapadia, R., "The Brown Revolution," *Smart Money Magazine*, December, 2005, **www.smartmoney.com/mag/ceo/index.cfm?story=december2005**.

Monczka, R., R. Trent, and R. Handfield. *Purchasing and Supply Chain Management*, 3rd ed. Cincinnati: South-western College Publishing, 2004.

CHAPTER 11

Purchasing

CHAPTER OUTLINE

Chapter Objectives

By the end of this chapter, you will be able to:

- Make a strong case for why purchasing is a critical part of a firm's supply chain strategy.
- Identify and describe the various steps of the purchasing process, and discuss how this process will vary according to the type of good or service being purchased.
- Explain why spend analysis is important and perform a simple spend analysis.

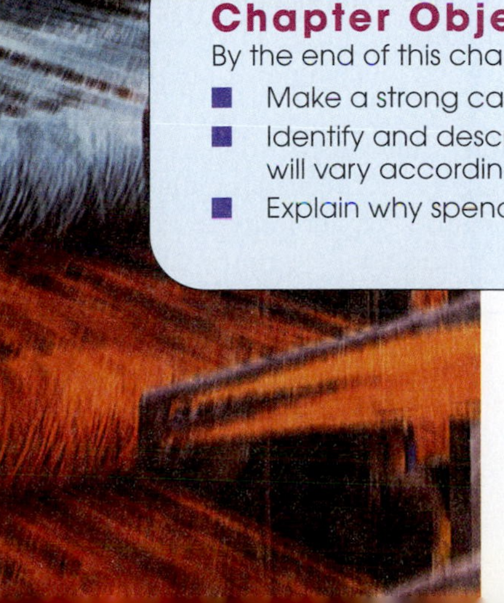

SciQuest

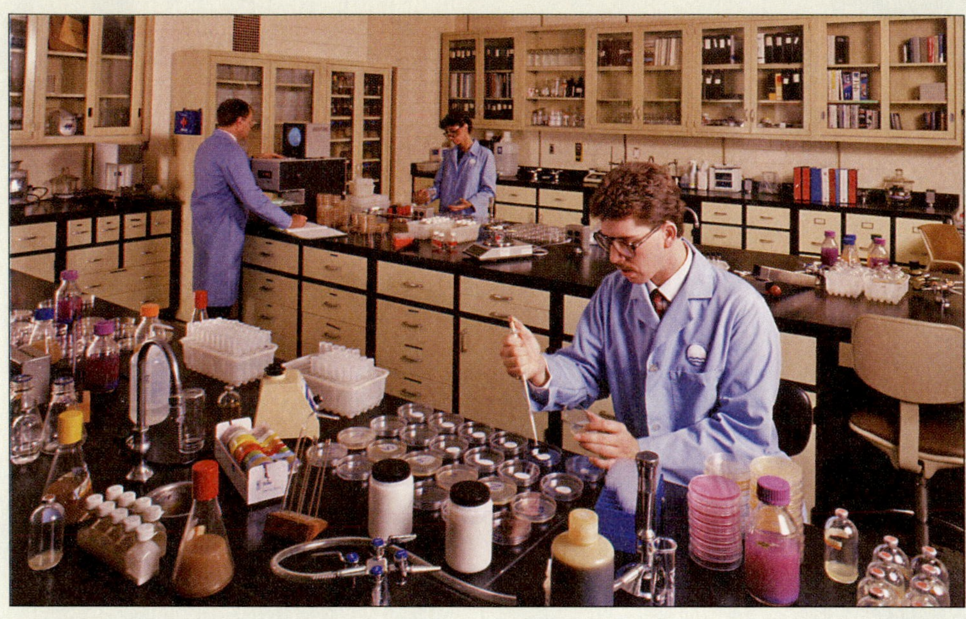

For an industry characterized by state-of-the-art research and technological breakthroughs, the purchasing process at many medical and scientific research companies has traditionally been decidedly *low* tech. In the typical research lab, someone—usually a lab technician not trained for the job—takes responsibility for ordering equipment and materials when they are needed. The lab technician hunts down one of the many paper catalogs provided by suppliers, searches through the catalog until he or she finds what is needed, and then fills out and mails or faxes in the order form. Besides the obvious slowness, the process is exposed to other problems, including errors in filling out the order forms and a general lack of control over which companies the various labs do business with and what they buy.

Enter SciQuest, a firm located in Cary, North Carolina (**www.sciquest.com**). SciQuest offers a set of software solutions that allow medical and research companies to automate many traditional purchasing activities. For example, SciQuest's applications allow individual buyers to search suppliers' catalogs and order items online. This paperless process saves both time and money. In addition, by having all purchasing activities go through SciQuest's applications, the buying organization can "see," and therefore manage, all of its purchasing activity. One result is that the buying organization can negotiate for volume discounts based on purchase quantities across all the individual buyers.

There are benefits to the suppliers as well. For one thing, SciQuest hosts virtual "catalogs" for the suppliers. These catalogs can be updated in real-time and even tailored to different buyers. This cuts down dramatically on the costs associated with getting product information in front of the potential buyers. Second, by automating the customer ordering process, suppliers experience fewer errors in the orders coming in to them. Some suppliers have even established direct information linkages between the buying organization's ordering process and the supplier's fulfillment systems, minimizing the chance of human error.

SciQuest's applications allow its customers to streamline the purchasing process, enabling these research and medical laboratories to put more resources into their core activities of research and development.

INTRODUCTION

Purchasing
The activities associated with identifying needs, locating and selecting suppliers, negotiating terms, and following up to ensure supplier performance.

Spend analysis
An activity, typically carried out by purchasing professionals, in which a firm examines spending patterns to identify irregularities or improvement opportunities.

In Chapter 10, we examined the strategic issues firms face when deciding whether to insource or outsource a product or service. If the decision is to outsource, then the firm must engage in purchasing. **Purchasing** includes all those activities associated with identifying needs, locating and selecting suppliers, negotiating terms, and following up to ensure supplier performance.

We start the chapter by making the case for why firms must carefully manage their purchasing efforts. We then describe the various steps that make up the purchasing process. But it doesn't end there—firms must regularly examine their spending patterns to identify irregularities or improvement opportunities. This activity, called **spend analysis**, is a key responsibility of the purchasing function. We finish the chapter with a discussion about the growing importance of the purchasing profession, and what this means for you.

11.1 WHY PURCHASING IS CRITICAL

Purchasing has always been an important, if underappreciated, function in many businesses. Several trends have worked together to push purchasing into the limelight. These include the changing global competitive landscape, the financial impact of purchasing, and its impact on such performance dimensions as quality, delivery, and technology utilization.

The Changing Global Competitive Landscape

Firms do not compete only against global competitors, but against their competitors' supply chains. Companies that were content to purchase services and goods from local suppliers are now seeking to build relationships with world-class suppliers, regardless of their location. Managers have come to realize that "to compete globally, you need to purchase globally."

To keep up with global competition and tap into the abilities of world-class suppliers, many companies are putting global purchasing systems in place. General Motors (GM) is a case in point. Every Friday morning at 6:30 A.M., the vice president in charge of worldwide purchasing presides over a global video conference in which dozens of purchasing executives share information and coordinate strategy. In addition, a few years back, a GM purchasing team completed a 12-day mission to Thailand, Taiwan, South Korea, and Japan. The primary purpose of the trip was to evaluate a dozen tool makers as potential sources of stamping dies, but GM also used the opportunity to develop valuable new sources.[1]

Advances in information systems have served as a catalyst for global purchasing efforts. SciQuest is just one example. Engineers and suppliers around the world can now share electronic "blueprints" instantaneously. An organization can maximize buying power by consolidating purchasing requirements for dozens of sites and suppliers around the world into one large order. Companies can share anticipated requirements with key suppliers around the clock, allowing suppliers to plan their activities accordingly.

[1]R. L. Simison, "Buyer's Market: General Motors Drives Some Hard Bargains with Asian Suppliers," *The Wall Street Journal*, Eastern Edition (April 2, 1999), A1.

TABLE 11.1
Material Cost Ratios for Different Industries

INDUSTRY	COST OF MATERIALS VALUE OF SHIPMENTS
Food	53.5%
Furniture and related products	45.8%
Chemicals	46.2%
Rubber and plastics	49.0%
Fabricated metal	45.3%
Computers and electronics	42.8%
Transportation equipment	60.5%
All manufacturers	***52.5%***

Source: General Summary: 1997 Economic Census, Manufacturing, U.S. Census Bureau, ECM315-GS, June 2001.

Financial Impact

If you were to look at the financial statements of an average organization, how much would you guess the company spends on purchased goods and services? In manufacturing, the figure is astonishingly high: For the average manufacturer, nearly 53% of the value of shipments comes from materials (Table 11.1). For some services, such as retailing or wholesaling, the figure can be even higher.

When much of the firm's revenue is spent on materials and services, purchasing represents a major opportunity to increase profitability through what's known as the *profit leverage effect* (Example 11.1). This effect has caught the eye of many Chief Financial Officers, as it means real money to the bottom line and improved shareholder performance. Let's explore this effect in more detail.

Example 11.1

Profit Leverage at Lowe's Company

The costs of purchased goods can have a critical impact on the profitability of retailers such as Lowe's.

Consider the following financial information for Lowe's, a service firm in the home improvements retailing sector. Table 11.2 shows earnings for the company for the fiscal year ending January 31, 2003, as well as key balance statement figures.

TABLE 11.2 Selected Financial Data for Lowe's Company (all figures in millions $)

EARNINGS AND EXPENSES (FISCAL YEAR ENDING 1/31/03)	
Sales	\$26,491
Cost of goods sold (COGS)	\$18,465
Pretax earnings	\$2359
SELECTED BALANCE SHEET ITEMS (AS OF 1/31/03)	
Merchandise inventory	\$3968
Total assets	\$16,109

Cost of goods sold (COGS)
The purchased cost of goods from outside suppliers.

Merchandise inventory
A balance sheet item that shows the amount a company paid for the inventory it has on hand at a particular point in time.

Profit margin
The ratio of earnings to sales for a given time period.

Return on assets (ROA)
A measure of financial performance, generally defined as Earnings/Total Assets. Higher ROA values are preferred, since it indicates that the firm is able to generate higher earnings from the same asset base.

Cost of goods sold (COGS) is the purchased cost of goods from outside suppliers. It tells us how much the company has paid for the goods that it sold to its customers. **Merchandise inventory** shows us how much the company paid for the inventory it had on hand at the time of the report.

With this financial data, we can calculate some basic financial performance measurements for Lowe's. **Profit margin** is defined as the ratio of earnings to sales for a given time period:

$$\text{Profit margin} = 100\% \times \frac{\text{Earnings}}{\text{Sales}} \qquad \textbf{[11-1]}$$

The pretax profit margin for the company is:

$$100\% \times \frac{\$2,359}{\$26,491} = 8.9\%$$

The pretax profit margin means that every dollar of sales generates about nine cents in pretax earnings. Another commonly used financial measure is **return on assets (ROA)**. ROA is a measure of financial performance, generally defined as Earnings/Total Assets. Higher ROA values are preferred because it indicates that the firm is able to generate higher earnings from the same asset base:

$$\text{Return on assets (ROA)} = 100\% \times \frac{\text{Earning}}{\text{Assets}} \qquad \textbf{[11-2]}$$

For this company, the pretax ROA for the fiscal year is:

$$100\% \frac{\$2,359}{\$16,109} = 14.6\%$$

So what can this company do to improve these figures? There are two things to note:

1. *Every dollar saved in purchasing lowers COGS by one dollar and increases pretax profit by one dollar.* In contrast, because the current pretax profit margin is 8.9%, Lowe's would have to generate:

$$\$1.00/8.9\% = \$11.24 \text{ in new sales}$$

Profit leverage effect A term used to describe the effect that a dollar in cost savings increases pretax profits by one dollar, while a dollar increase in sales only increases pretax profits by the dollar multiplied by the pretax profit margin.

to have the same impact. This is known as the profit leverage effect. The **profit leverage effect** holds that a dollar in cost savings increases pretax profits by one dollar, while a dollar increase in sales only increases pretax profits by the dollar multiplied by the pretax profit margin. This effect is particularly important for lower-margin businesses, such as retailing.

2. *Every dollar saved in purchasing also lowers the merchandise inventory figure—and as a result, total assets—by one dollar*. The result is a higher ROA for the same level of sales.

To illustrate these points, let's see what would happen if Lowe's was able to cut its COGS by just 3%. Notice that COGS and merchandise inventory each decrease by 3%:

$$\begin{aligned}
\text{New COGS} &= \text{Old COGS} \times (100\% - 3\%) \\
&= \$18{,}465 \times (.97) \\
&= \$17{,}911 \\
\text{Reduction in COGS} &= \text{Old COGS} - \text{New COGS} \\
&= \$18{,}465 - 17{,}911 \\
&= \$554 \\
\text{Reduction in merchandise inventory} &= \text{Old merchandise inventory} \times (3\%) \\
&= \$3{,}968 \times (.03) = \$119 \\
\text{New total assets} &= \text{Old total assets} - \text{Reduction in merchandise inventory} \\
&= \$3{,}968 - 119 = \$15{,}990
\end{aligned}$$

EARNINGS AND EXPENSES (FISCAL YEAR ENDING 1/31/03)	
Sales	$26,491
New cost of goods sold (COGS)	**$17,911**
Old pretax earnings	$2,359
+ 3% reduction in COGS:	+554
New pretax earnings	**$2,913**

SELECTED BALANCE SHEET ITEMS	
New merchandise inventory	**$3,849**
Old total assets	$16,109
−3% reduction in merchandise inv.	−$119
Net total assets	**$15,990**

The result is that pretax earnings increase by 23.5%, from $2,359 to $2,913. Under the *old* pretax profit margin, sales would have to increase by ($2,913 – $2,359)/(8.9%) = $6,225 [*million*] to have the same impact.

Finally, the *new* pretax profit margin and ROA values are:

$$\text{New pretax profit margin} = 100\% \times \frac{\$2{,}913}{\$26{,}491} = 11\%$$

$$\text{New ROA} = 100\% \times \frac{\$2{,}913}{\$15{,}990} = 18.2\%$$

Performance Impact

But cost is not the only consideration. Purchased goods and services can have a major effect on other performance dimensions as well, including such diverse areas as quality, delivery, and the ability of companies to exploit new technologies. The following example illustrates how delivery reliability can come into play.

Example 11.2

Purchasing Valves at Springfield Hospital

Springfield Hospital has two dialysis machines, each with a special valve that is normally replaced every two weeks when the machines are idle. As a result, Springfield uses about 50 valves per year. The hospital has two alternative sources for the valves. The cost, quality, and delivery lead times for these two suppliers are as follows:

	SUPPLIER A	SUPPLIER B
Cost per Valve	$10	$2
% Good	99.8%	95%
Delivery Lead Time	Overnight delivery	1 day to 3 weeks

Defective valves can cause an interruption in the treatment of patients, which can lead to rescheduling nightmares, a reduction in the effective capacity of the dialysis machines, and may even result in a medical emergency. The quality of the medical service will clearly fall if Springfield goes with Supplier B.

Now suppose that Springfield management has estimated that the cost of a failed valve is about $1000 per incident. Furthermore, if Springfield goes with Supplier A, then it will be able to get by with one valve as a "backup," since overnight delivery is guaranteed. But if Springfield uses Supplier B, it will need three "backup" valves (about three weeks worth) to protect itself against Supplier B's unreliable delivery patterns.

Even before we calculate all of the costs associated with each supplier, we can see that using Supplier B has the potential to seriously disrupt Springfield's operations. These concerns are reflected in the following cost estimates:

YEARLY COSTS	SUPPLIER A	SUPPLIER B
Valve Costs	50 × $10 = $500	50 × $2 = $100
Failure Costs	0.2% of all valves fail: 0.2% × 50 valves × $1000 = $100	5% of all valves fail: 5% × 50 valves × $1000 = $2500
Backup Inventory	1 valve × $10 = $10	3 valve × $2 = $6
Total Cost:	$610	$2606

Purchasing can also help an organization incorporate state-of-the-art technologies into its products and services. This is especially common in the electronics industry, where firms such as Hewlett Packard, Dell, Nortel Networks, and others have outsourced design and manufacturing to suppliers in places like Malaysia, China, and Eastern Europe. These suppliers are sometimes called original design manufacturers, original equipment manufacturers, or contract manufacturers.

11.2 THE PURCHASING PROCESS

Now that we understand why purchasing is critical to firm success, let's examine in detail the purchasing process, which includes all the steps that must be completed when someone requires a product or service from outside the organization. These steps are highlighted in Figure 11.1.

There are two things to keep in mind as we describe the purchasing process. First, how much effort a company spends on these activities will differ greatly from one situation to the next. The purchasing process for a $30 billion contract for military jets is much different from that for a routine purchase of office supplies! The portfolio matrix approach discussed in Chapter 10 is a good way to help identify how much effort should be spent on different types of purchases.

Second, as you look at the steps in the purchasing process, recognize that companies can often gain a competitive advantage by performing these activities *better* than their competitors do. Many organizations, for example, use information systems to automate routine purchase order preparation, while others even use Six Sigma teams (Chapter 3) to improve the outcome of supplier evaluation and selection efforts.

The eight steps of the purchasing process are:

1. Needs identification
2. Description
3. Supplier selection and contracting

FIGURE 11.1
The Generic Purchasing Process

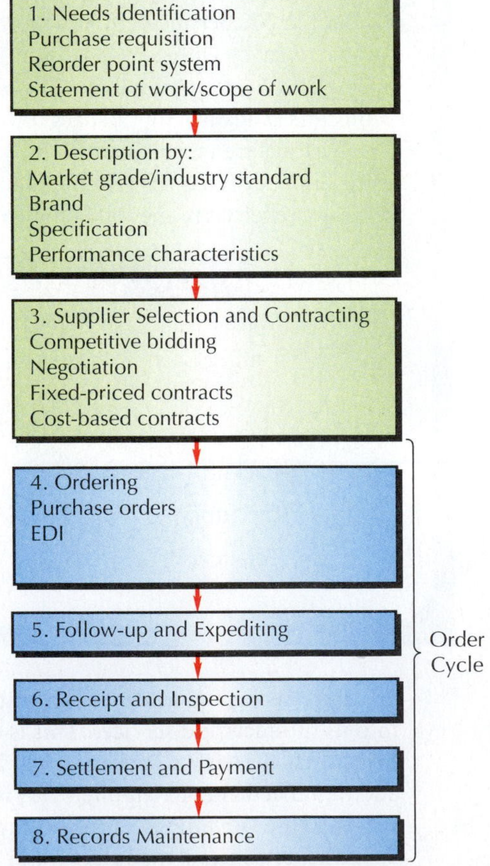

4. Ordering
5. Follow-up and expediting
6. Receipt and inspection
7. Settlement and payment
8. Records maintenance

Needs Identification

The purchasing process begins with the identification of a need (i.e., a requirement). This need may take the form of a component, a raw material, a subassembly, or even a completely finished item. In other cases, the need may be a service, such as consulting or building maintenance. Because purchasing is responsible for acquiring products and services for the entire organization, the information flows between the purchasing function and other areas of the organization can be extensive.

Internal customers communicate their needs to purchasing in a variety of ways. In some cases, it might take the form of a forecast for the upcoming quarter or year. For routine items and services, internal customers often use purchase requisitions or reorder point systems to communicate their needs to purchasing. A **purchase requisition** is an internal document that informs purchasing of a specific need. Although varieties of formats exist, at a minimum a purchase requisition should include a detailed description of the material or service, quantity, date required, estimated cost, and authorization.

Purchase requisition An internal document completed by a user that informs purchasing of a specific need.

A **reorder point system** is another method used to initiate the purchase of routine items. Each item in a typical reorder point system has a predetermined order point and order quantity. When inventory is depleted to a given level, the system signals the material control department (or the buyer in some organizations) to issue a request to the supplier. While requisition forms and reorder point systems have traditionally been paper-based, this is changing quickly as more firms switch to computer-based processing for routine items and services.

Reorder point system A method to initiate the purchase of routine items.

In services, communicating the "need" can be more complicated. Purchasing and the internal customer might work together to generate a **statement of work or scope of work (SOW)**, which documents specifically the type of service required; the qualifications of the individual(s) performing the work; the outcome or deliverables expected at the conclusion of the work; and any prescreening requirements, safety requirements, or the like. For example, a statement of work might state that a programmer qualified to work in Visual Basic is needed to work on a software project for six months.

Statement of work or scope of work (SOW) Terms and conditions for a purchased service that indicate, among other things, what services will be performed and how the service provider will be evaluated.

However the need is communicated, a requisition document will need to be completed by someone who is authorized by purchasing to complete the needs clarification process. In some cases, the internal customer might be given this authority. This occurs in situations where a supplier has already been identified, and the internal customer has the authority to order the product or service directly. This process is often used for relatively low-value products and services.

Description

Description The communication of a user's needs to potential suppliers in the most efficient and accurate way possible.

Whatever the good or service, purchasing must ensure that the user's needs get communicated to *potential suppliers* in the most efficient and accurate way possible. This process is known as **description.** How purchasing accomplishes this will differ dramatically from one situation to the next. Varieties of methods exist for communicating the user's requirements. **Description by market grade or industry standard** might be the best choice for standard items, where the requirements are well understood and there is common agreement between supply chain partners about what certain terms mean. For example, a 1/8″ hexnut

Description by market grade or industry standard A description method used when the requirements are well understood and there is common agreement between supply chain partners about what certain terms mean.

is a piece of hardware that is an industry standard, and can be used across multiple industry categories. **Description by brand** is used when a product or service is proprietary or when there is a perceived advantage to using a particular supplier's products or services. A builder of residential communities, for example, might tell his purchasing staff to purchase R21 insulation (an industry standard) for the walls, and finish-grade lumber (a market grade) for the trim and fireplace mantles. In addition, he might specify brands such as Georgia-Pacific's Catawba® hardboard siding, Kohler® faucets, and TruGreen-Chemlawn® lawn treatment for all the homes.

Description by brand
A description method used when a product or service is proprietary, or when there is a perceived advantage to using a particular supplier's products or services.

As you can see, the use of brand names, market grades, and industry standards provides purchasing with an effective and accurate "shortcut" for relaying the user's needs to potential suppliers.

More detailed and expensive methods of description will be needed when the items or services to be purchased are more complex, when "standards" do not exist, or when the user's needs are harder to communicate. Three common methods include description by specification, by performance characteristics, and by prototypes or samples.

In some cases, the buyer might need to provide very detailed descriptions of the characteristics of an item or service. We refer to such efforts as **description by specification**. Specifications can cover such characteristics as the materials used, the manufacturing or service steps required, or even the physical dimensions of the product. Consider one extreme example: the special heat shield tiles used on NASA's space shuttles. Each tile has a unique shape and location on the space shuttle. Furthermore, each shield must be able to protect the space shuttle from heat generated by reentry into the Earth's atmosphere. In providing a description of these tiles, NASA will almost certainly include specifications regarding the exact dimensions of the tiles and the composite materials to be used in making them. Such information might be relayed in the form of detailed blueprints and supporting documentation. Furthermore, NASA will probably specify the precise manufacturing steps and quality checks to be performed during the manufacture of the tiles.

Description by specification
A description method used when an organization needs to provide very detailed descriptions of the characteristics of an item or service.

In contrast, **description by performance characteristics** focuses attention on the *outcomes* the buyer wants, not on the precise configuration of the product or service. The assumption is that the supplier will know the best way to meet the buyer's needs. A company purchasing hundreds of PCs from Hewlett Packard might demand (1) 24-hour support available by computer or phone and (2) a 48-hour turnaround time on defective units. How HP chooses to meet these performance characteristics is its choice.

Description by performance characteristics
A description method that focuses attention on the *outcomes* the customer wants, not on the precise configuration of the product or service.

Firms often develop prototypes or samples to share with their suppliers. Prototypes can provide critical information on the look or feel of a product or service. Such information is often difficult to convey in drawings or written descriptions. Note that prototypes or samples are not limited to physical products. An excellent example is a prototype information system that a company might share with potential software vendors. The prototype may include sample output screens and reports. Through the prototype, the company can give its software vendors a clearer idea of how the company expects its users to interact with the system.

Supplier Selection and Contracting

Supplier Selection. Once the needs identification and description steps have been completed, one of two things can happen: (1) the need can be filled by an existing qualified supplier, or (2) purchasing will need to turn to a new supplier. The second case occurs when a suitable supplier has not yet been identified, or when the internal customer requests a specific new supplier that has not yet been approved. When internal customers purchase directly from nonqualified suppliers and bypass established purchasing procedures, this is known as **maverick spending**. Although some level of maverick spending is always going to

Maverick spending
Spending that occurs when internal customers purchase directly from nonqualified suppliers and bypass established purchasing procedures.

occur in organization (especially for low-value goods), significant risks can occur when it reaches high proportions.

Final supplier selection begins once the buying firm completes the activities required of its supplier evaluation process. As we discussed in Chapter 10, the criteria used to evaluate suppliers can include quantitative measures (such as costs, on-time delivery rates, etc.) and more qualitative factors, such as "management stability" or "trustworthiness."

Preferred supplier
A supplier that has demonstrated its performance capabilities through previous purchase contracts, and therefore receives preference during the supplier selection process.

Request for quotation (RFQ)
A formal request for the suppliers to prepare bids, based on the terms and conditions set by the buyer.

For some items, firms may maintain a list of preferred suppliers who receive the first opportunity for new business. A **preferred supplier** has demonstrated its performance capabilities through previous purchase contracts and therefore receives preference during the supplier selection process. By maintaining a preferred supplier list, purchasing personnel can quickly identify suppliers with proven performance capabilities. When there is not a preferred supplier, competitive bidding and negotiation are two methods commonly used to select a supplier.

Competitive bidding entails a request for bids from suppliers with whom the buyer is willing to do business. This process is typically initiated when the purchasing manager sends a **request for quotation (RFQ)** to qualified suppliers. The RFQ is a formal request for the suppliers to prepare bids based on the terms and conditions set by the buyer. Buyers often evaluate the resulting bids based on price. If the lowest bidder does not receive the purchase contract, the buyer has an obligation to inform that supplier why it did not receive the contract. Competitive bidding is most effective when:[2]

- The buying firm can provide qualified suppliers with clear descriptions of the items or services to be purchased.
- Volume is high enough to justify the cost and effort.
- The buying firm does not have a preferred supplier.

Buying firms use competitive bidding when price is a dominant criterion and the required items or services have straightforward specifications. In addition, government agencies often require competitive bidding. If major nonprice variables exist, then the buyer and seller usually enter into direct negotiation. Competitive bidding can also be used to identify a short list of suppliers with whom the firm will begin detailed purchase contract negotiation.

In recent years, firms have also begun to use an electronic competitive bidding tool called a *reverse auction* or an *e-auction*. These mechanisms work exactly like an auction, but in reverse—the buyer identifies potential qualified suppliers, the suppliers go to a specific Web site at a designated time, and the suppliers "bid" to get the business. In such cases, the lowest bid will often occur as suppliers see what other suppliers are bidding for the business, and in an effort to win the contract, submit lower bids.

Negotiation is a more costly, interactive approach to final supplier selection. Face-to-face negotiation is best when:

- The item may be a new and/or technically complex item with only vague specifications.
- The purchase requires agreement about a wide range of performance factors.
- The buyer requires the supplier to participate in the development effort.
- The supplier cannot determine risks and costs without additional input from the buyer.

[2]Monczka, R., R. Trent, and R. Handfield. *Purchasing and Supply Chain Management*, 3rd ed. (Cincinnati: Southwestern College Publishing, 2004).

One thing is certain—the process that buying firms use to select suppliers can vary widely depending on the required item and the relationship that a firm has with its suppliers. For some items, a buyer may know which supplier to use before the development of final specifications even occurs. For standard items, the competitive bid process will remain an efficient method to purchase relatively straightforward requirements. The bid process can also reduce the list of potential suppliers before a buyer begins time-consuming and costly negotiations.

Contracting. Often, a detailed purchasing contact is required to formalize the buyer–supplier relationship. A contract can be required if the size of the purchase exceeds a predetermined monetary value (e.g., $10,000), or if there are specific business requirements that need to be put in writing, such as quality levels or delivery lead times.

Because purchasing professionals buy products and services as a career, it is not surprising that they deal regularly with contracts. It is therefore critical for purchasing managers to understand the underlying legal aspects of business transactions and develop the skills to manage those contracts and agreements on a day-to-day basis. Once a contract has been negotiated and signed, the real work begins. From the moment of signing, it is the purchasing manager's responsibility to ensure that all of the terms and conditions of the agreement are fulfilled. If the terms and conditions of a contract are breached, purchasing is also responsible for resolving the conflict. Contracts are an important part of managing buyer–supplier relationships because they explicitly define the roles and responsibilities of both parties, as well as how conflicts will be resolved if they occur (which they almost always do!).

Purchasing contracts can be classified into different categories based on their characteristics and purpose. Almost all purchasing contracts are based on some form of pricing mechanism and can be categorized as a variation on two basic types: fixed-price and cost-based contracts.

Fixed-price contract
A type of purchasing contract in which the stated price does not change, regardless of fluctuations in general overall economic conditions, industry competition, levels of supply, market prices, or other environmental changes.

The most basic contract is a **fixed-price contract**. In this type of purchase contract, the stated price does not change, regardless of fluctuations in general overall economic conditions, industry competition, levels of supply, market prices, or other environmental changes.

If market prices for a purchased good or service rise above the stated contract price, the seller bears the brunt of the financial loss. However, if the market price falls below the stated contract price due to outside factors such as competition, changes in technology, or raw material prices, the buyer assumes the risk or financial loss. If there is a high level of uncertainty from the supplier's point of view regarding its ability to make a reasonable profit under competitive fixed-price conditions, then the supplier might add to its price to cover potential increases in component, raw materials, or labor prices. If the supplier increases its contract price in anticipation of rising costs, and the anticipated conditions do not occur, then the buyer has paid too high a price for the good or service. For this reason, it is very important for the buying firm to adequately understand existing market conditions prior to signing a fixed-price contract.

Cost-based contract
A type of purchasing contract in which the price of a good or service is tied to the cost of some key input(s) or other economic factors, such as interest rates.

In contrast, a **cost-based contract** ties the price of a good or service to the cost of some key input(s) or other economic factors, such as interest rates. Cost-based contracts are often used when the goods or services procured are expensive, complex, or when there is a high degree of uncertainty regarding labor and material costs. Cost-based contracts typically represent a lower risk level of economic loss for suppliers, but they can also result in lower overall costs to the buyer through careful contract management. It is important for the buyer to include contractual terms and conditions that require the supplier to carefully monitor and control costs. The two parties must also stipulate how costs are to be included in the calculation of the price of the goods or services procured.

Ordering

Once the buyer and supplier have agreed to enter into a relationship, the buyer must periodically signal to the supplier that delivery of the product or service is required. This begins what is known as the *order cycle* (Figure 11.1). The order cycle is completed once the goods or services have been received, the supplier has been paid, and the information has been recorded into the database.

Purchase order (PO)
A document that authorizes a supplier to deliver a product or service and often includes key terms and conditions such as price, delivery, and quality requirements.

Electronic data interchange (EDI)
An information technology that allows supply chain partners to transfer data electronically between their information systems.

The most common way ordering occurs is through the release of a purchase order. A **purchase order (PO)** is simply a document that authorizes a supplier to deliver a product or service, and often includes terms and conditions, such as price, delivery, and quality requirements. More and more often, POs are released through **electronic data interchange (EDI)**. EDI is an information technology that allows supply chain partners to transfer data electronically between their information systems. By eliminating the time associated with the flow of physical documents between supply chain partners, EDI can reduce the time it takes suppliers to respond to customers' needs. This, in turn, leads to shorter order lead times, lower inventory, and better coordination between the supply chain partners. Not surprisingly, the use of EDI has increased significantly over the last several years. The emergence of the Internet has only served to accelerate this process.

Follow-up and Expediting

Someone (typically purchasing or materials personnel) must monitor the status of open purchase orders. There may be times when the buying firm has to expedite an order or work with a supplier to avoid shipment delays. The buying firm can minimize order follow-up by selecting only the best suppliers and developing internally stable forecasting and ordering systems.

Receipt and Inspection

When the order for a physical good arrives at the buyer's location, it is received and inspected to ensure that the right quantity was shipped, and that it was not damaged in transit. Assuming that the product or service was provided on time, it will be entered into the company's purchasing transaction system. Physical products delivered by suppliers then become part of the company's working inventory.

In the case of services, the buyer must ensure that the service is being performed according to the terms and conditions stated in the purchase order. For services, the user will typically sign off on a supplier time sheet or other document to signal to purchasing that the service was delivered as promised, on time, and satisfied the conditions stated in the statement of work (SOW). Deviations from the statement of work must be noted and passed on to the supplier, which in some cases might require modifications to the original agreement.

Settlement and Payment

Electronic funds transfer (EFT)
The automatic transfer of payment from the buyer's bank account to the supplier's bank account.

Once the item or service is delivered, the buying firm will issue an authorization for payment to the supplier. Payment is then made through the firm's accounts payable department. As with ordering, this is increasingly being accomplished through electronic means. Suppliers are more often being paid through **electronic funds transfer (EFT)**, which is the automatic transfer of payment from the buyer's bank account to the supplier's bank account.

Records Maintenance

After the product or service has been delivered and the supplier paid, a record of critical events associated with the purchase is entered into a supplier performance database. The supplier performance database accumulates critical performance data over an extended period. These data are often used in future negotiations and dealings with the supplier in question. The data gathered here can also support spend analysis efforts, described in the next section.

11.3 SPEND ANALYSIS

As noted at the beginning of the chapter, there is more to purchasing than just having a well-honed purchasing process. On a regular basis, the purchasing team must carefully examine spending patterns to identify any irregularities or possible areas for cost savings. This activity is known as *spend analysis.*

Spend analysis is used to answer a wide variety of questions. For example, senior management might want to know:

- What categories of products or services make up the bulk of company spending? How do these figures compare to historical levels or to other firms in our industry?
- Are suppliers meeting our cost and performance criteria? Are some *categories* of goods or services better served than others? Are some *suppliers* performing better than others?
- Are there opportunities to improve the firm's purchasing performance? For instance, can we use **purchase consolidation** to lower costs by pooling purchasing requirements across multiple areas?

Purchase consolidation The pooling of purchasing requirements across multiple areas in an effort to lower costs.

Because the questions can vary so widely, there is no single "correct" approach to spend analysis. Rather, the approach used will depend on the questions at hand. This means that personnel responsible for spend analysis must have the flexibility and skills needed to analyze large quantities of data. The types of tools used can range from relatively sophisticated statistical techniques, such as regression analysis (Chapter 9) to simple graphing techniques, such as Pareto charts (Chapter 3). Furthermore, some organizations have sophisticated spend analysis applications that draw data from the company's financial and accounting applications, while others may depend on simpler Excel spreadsheets or Access databases.

In Example 11.3, we illustrate the power of spend analysis using some simple tools. Our intent here is not to cover every possible type of spend analysis, but to give you an appreciation of the insights that can be gained.

Example 11.3

Spend Analysis for Purchasing Categories

Susan Abraham has just been hired as a purchasing analyst for PH Industries. Susan's boss, Mark Pfaltzgraff, has asked Susan to use the company's purchasing database to answer the following questions:

- What are the top 10 commodities, by annual spend?
- Which commodities currently have the most suppliers?
- Which commodities currently have the *lowest* spend per supplier?

Figure 11.2 shows a small portion of the database (the entire database consists of an Excel spreadsheet with over 2500 lines of data). Each row contains information on how much was spent last year with a particular supplier on a specific commodity. Susan notes that each supplier can provide more than one commodity, and each commodity can have multiple suppliers.

Supplier	Commodity	Annual Spend
TRB PROMO SERVICES LTD	Rebate Fulfillment & Call Center	$329,873,663
SCHWORB FINANCIAL	Investments	$130,328,512
ADSUPRA	Advertising	$56,134,490
NATIONAL ELECTRONICS REPAIR CORP	Service Repairs	$49,339,218
INSIGHT INSURANCE CO	Benefits	$48,969,149
DELL	Hardware	$40,572,450
US PARTS INC	Service Parts	$39,910,372
VERIZON COMMUN	Telecommunications	$31,055,599
BOZARTH MERCHANDISING	Store Displays	$30,020,969
CHATAM CONSOLIDATED PAPER	Paper	$29,175,843
TEMPAMERICA	Contract Labor	$27,880,363
SKYLINE PAPER COMPANY	Paper	$23,844,707
EDWARDS CONSTRUCTION	General Contracting	$22,579,113
PULP WORLD	Paper	$22,257,690
CARY GRAPHICS	Graphic Design	$21,966,989
EXPENELL PAYMENT SERVICES	Business & Management Services	$20,380,275
JBO DELIVERY	Surface Freight	$19,369,010
NORWEGIAN WOOD & PAPER COMPANY	Paper	$15,603,682
SORBET CONSULTING	Service Plan	$15,478,827
RANDALL TECHNOLOGIES	Service Parts	$14,868,023
HOMESTEAD FINANCIAL	Consumer Financing	$14,833,333
TARHEEL INC	Energy	$14,087,177
ERP SYSTEMS INC	Software	$12,664,424

FIGURE 11.2 Sample Purchasing Data, PH Industries

To answer the first question—What are the top 10 commodities, by annual spend?—Susan sorts the database by commodity and calculates the total spend for each one. She then uses a Pareto chart to rank the top 10 commodities by annual spend. Figure 11.3 shows the resulting Pareto chart.

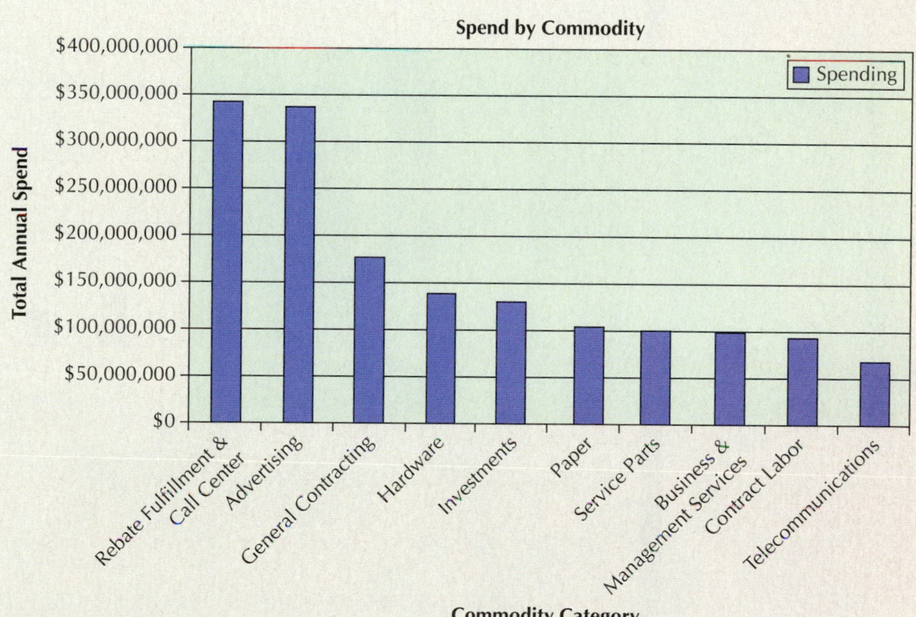

FIGURE 11.3 Pareto Chart Showing the Top 10 Commodities for PH Industries, by Total Annual Spend

Susan notices that the top 10 categories of spending include rebate fulfillment, advertising, general contracting, hardware, investments, paper, service parts, business and management services, contract labor, and telecommunications. These areas represent the highest level of spend, and therefore the greatest potential opportunity for cost savings or price reductions.

But Susan isn't done yet. Her boss still wants to understand which commodities are using the most suppliers. Susan uses the spreadsheet to calculate the number of suppliers by commodity. (*Hint:* The pivot table function in Excel can help here.) She then performs a descending sort based on number of suppliers by commodity, and creates a Pareto chart of the top 10 commodities by descending number of suppliers.

As Figure 11.4 shows, the advertising category has the highest number of suppliers, followed by small-dollar suppliers (a "catchall" category), energy, security, general contracting, and business and management services. At first blush, the figure for advertising seems high to Susan. However, business units will often use local suppliers, such as radio and newspapers, to provide advertising services.

Finally, Susan must determine which commodities currently have the *lowest* spend per supplier. A low spend figure here would suggest that there might be too many suppliers. After sorting by commodity, Susan calculates the average spend per supplier by commodity. She then creates an *ascending* sort of these values (smallest to highest).

The Pareto chart in Figure 11.5 shows the commodities with the lowest volume of spending per supplier. Susan also notes that none of these commodities show up in Figure 11.3 as major spend areas, suggesting a relatively low potential for savings.

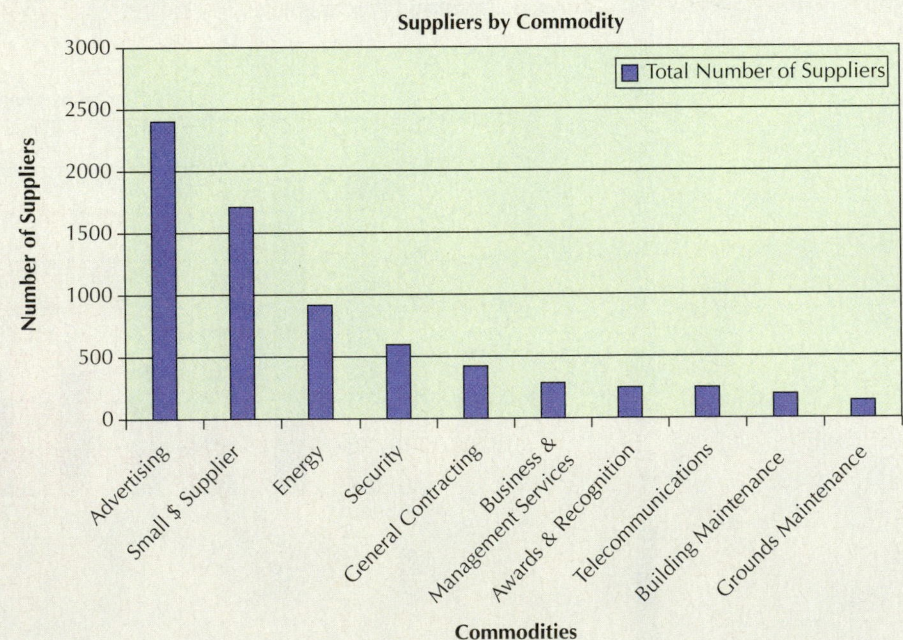

FIGURE 11.4 Pareto Chart Showing the Top 10 Commodities, by Total Number of Suppliers

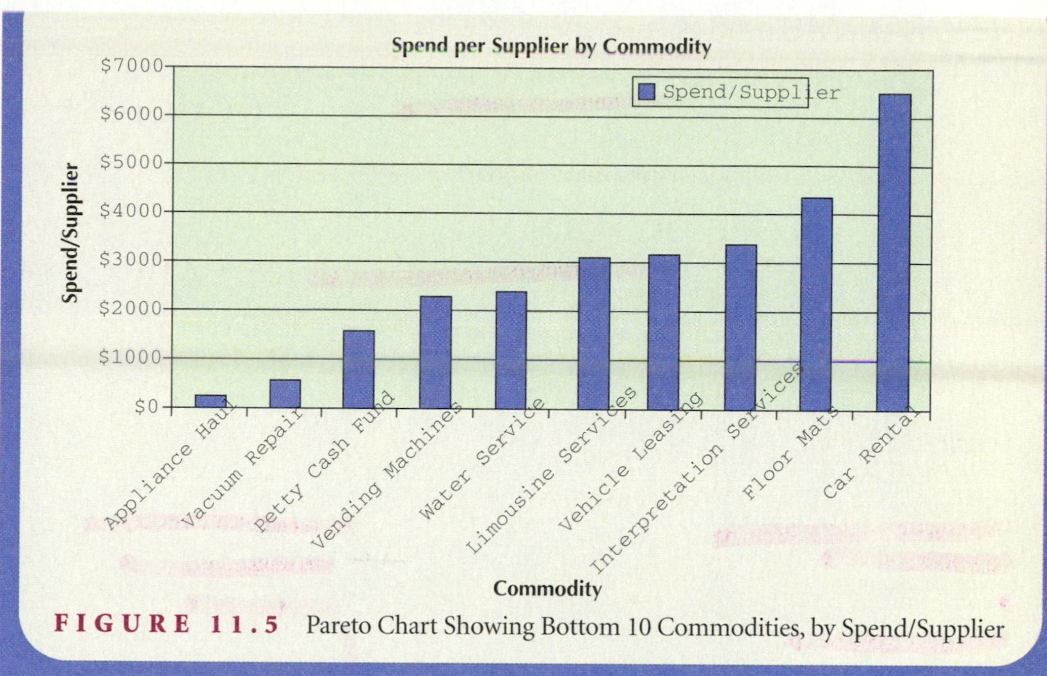

FIGURE 11.5 Pareto Chart Showing Bottom 10 Commodities, by Spend/Supplier

CHAPTER SUMMARY

This chapter served as the second of two chapters on sourcing decisions and purchasing. In this chapter, we talked in depth about the different steps of the purchasing process, and also illustrated how spend analysis can be used to proactively manage the spending activities at a firm.

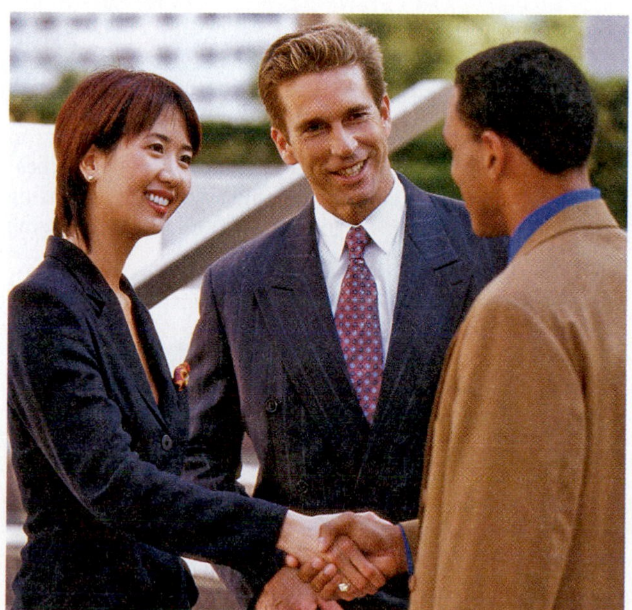

Purchasing professionals play a crucial role in identifying potential sources and managing supplier relationships.

We end this chapter with a brief discussion on the future of the purchasing profession. Every year purchasing professionals perform fewer day-to-day buying activities and spend more time on activities such as spend analysis, supplier evaluation and selection, new product development, and insourcing/outsourcing decisions. These activities require individuals with a solid mix of quantitative and interpersonal skills.

At the same time, information technology is reducing or even eliminating the clerical tasks that were traditionally carried out by purchasing professionals. By relying on information systems, end users can order directly what they require through their computer terminals. Also, production planning and control systems (Chapter 15) will generate orders automatically, based on production requirements. These systems will use EDI to forward component requirements immediately to suppliers, reducing the need for direct purchasing intervention.

Another development that will reduce the clerical work assumed by purchasing is the use of suppliers to manage inventory at the customer's site. This is a classic example of an outsourced activity that was previously performed by purchasing or materials management professionals.

Organizations such as the Institute for Supply Management (ISM) help serve the needs of professionals in the purchasing area. The organization's Web site, **www.ism.ws**, is an excellent place to learn about trends in purchasing and current research, as well as ISM's professional certification programs.

KEY FORMULAS

Profit margin (page 343):

$$\text{Profit margin} = 100\% \times \frac{\text{Earnings}}{\text{Sales}} \qquad [11\text{-}1]$$

Return on assets (ROA) (page 343):

$$\text{Return on assets (ROA)} = 100\% \times \frac{\text{Earnings}}{\text{Assets}} \qquad [11\text{-}2]$$

KEY TERMS

Cost of goods sold (COGS) 343
Cost-based contract 350
Description 347
Description by brand 348
Description by market grade or industry standard 347
Description by performance characteristics 348
Description by specification 348
Electronic data interchange (EDI) 351
Electronic funds transfer (EFT) 351
Fixed-price contract 350
Maverick spending 348
Merchandise inventory 343
Preferred supplier 349
Profit leverage effect 344
Profit margin 343
Purchase consolidation 352
Purchase order (PO) 351
Purchase requisition 347
Purchasing 341
Reorder point system 347
Request for quotation (RFQ) 349
Return on assets (ROA) 343
Spend analysis 341
Statement of work or scope of work (SOW) 347

DISCUSSION QUESTIONS

1. Someone says to you, "All purchasing does is place orders for goods. What's the big deal?" Is this true? What *is* the big deal?
2. What is a preferred supplier? What are the advantages and disadvantages of using preferred suppliers?
3. Under what conditions might a company prefer to negotiate rather than use competitive bidding to select a supplier?
4. When would it make sense to use a reverse auction? Is every type of purchase a candidate for a reverse auction? Why or why not?
5. In the chapter, we suggested that advanced information systems will automate some of the more routine purchasing activities. What are the implications for purchasing professionals? Is this a good time to join the purchasing profession? Explain.
6. In Chapter 3, we discussed the Six Sigma methodology for process improvement, including the DMAIC (Define-Measure-Analyze-Improve-Control) process. Give an example of how this process could be used to structure a spend analysis effort.

PROBLEMS

The spend analysis problems for this chapter require students to manipulate data contained in a large Excel file. This Excel file, problems, and instructions can be accessed by going to www.prenhall.com/bozarth and selecting Chapter 11 on the navigation bar.

The Web site also has other problems available that use Excel to generate customized problems for different class sections or even different students.

(* = easy; ** = moderate; *** = advanced)

Use the following information to solve Problems 1 through 3. Dulaney's Stores has posted the following yearly earnings and expenses:

EARNINGS AND EXPENSES (YEAR ENDING JANUARY 2008)	
Sales	$50,000,000
Cost of goods sold (COGS)	$30,000,000
Pretax earnings	5,000,000
SELECTED BALANCE SHEET ITEMS	
Merchandise inventory	$2,500,000
Total assets	$8,000,000

1. (*) What is Dulaney's current profit margin? What is its current yearly ROA?
2. (**) Suppose COGS and merchandise inventory were each cut by 10%. What would be the new pretax profit margin and ROA?
3. (**) Based on the *current* profit margin, how much additional sales would Dulaney have to generate in order to have the same effect on pretax earnings as a 10% decrease in merchandise costs?

CASE STUDY

THE ABCs OF SPEND ANALYSIS[3]

Spend analysis is one of the most important parts of strategic sourcing. Before you can source anything strategically, you have to know how much you're spending; whom you're; buying from; how much you are spending with each supplier; and what parts, materials; and other tools you're getting from each supplier. Theoretically, all that information should be easy to get. Realistically, it often isn't easy. The data can be spread around several departments within a company and can reside in several different databases that may not be compatible. In the following paragraphs, you'll read how different companies get around these and other problems—and actions they have taken after analyzing their spend.

(A)cquire the Data Skills

Data is only data until it's analyzed and acted upon—then it becomes information. And the procurement function is learning this lesson in increments—as more companies begin collecting data, they realize that the biggest resource they require next is the knowledge and brainpower to analyze that data and turn it into actionable information.

Of course, first you need to know how to collect and analyze data. According to a recent *Purchasing* survey, 91% of buyers say the profession is more reliant on data analysis skills than it was a mere five years ago. Despite that clear indication, only two-thirds of buyers polled say they have taken steps to improve their data analysis skills to meet today's requirements.

Sharon Flanagan, a procurement professional at Washington D.C.-based Pepco Holdings, took an internal training class called "Strategic Cost Management" that introduced her to the greater value that advanced data analysis skills can bring. "Strengthening your data analysis skills will benefit your company as well as your suppliers because you will be better able to assist your internal clients in planning spend strategies and also better understand your supplier's cost proposals," she says.

The line between data analysis skills and advanced knowledge of technology to help analyze data has blurred. Many buyers said the most important training they've received has been on database and spreadsheet tools like Microsoft Access and Excel. Many companies offer training internally or will pay for external training.

Jon Martin, a purchasing manager at Celerity in Milpitas, California, says buyers need to learn how to manipulate data out of large databases because, "Most canned reports do not give you the information that is needed in the daily purchasing, or planning activities. The data is in the systems but you need to be able to access the data and use commonplace tools to get what you need out of the data."

Don Moak, director of purchasing at Chattem in Chattanooga, Tennessee, adds, "Buyers must be able to select the important data from the large amount we are exposed to daily, rather than expect someone to hand us a list of numbers to stick into a spreadsheet. And once the data analysis is complete, we must understand what the output means and how to employ it in a real world application. Thinking is still the most critical skill we bring to the party."

(B)ring the Data Together

It's all well and good to try implementing a spend analysis program, but the very first steps—getting support, deciding

[3]Excerpted from D. Hannon, M. Varmazis, and P. Teague, "The ABCs of Spend Analysis," *Purchasing Magazine*, May 7, 2007, **www.purchasing.com/article/CA6436721.html**.

what data is needed, then finding that data—can be daunting. The process known as ETL—*extract, transform, and load*—means pulling every morsel of data together and cleaning it up before funneling it through a spend analysis program.

Purchasers can get overwhelmed by the amount of data they must sift through, with little direction on how to make sense of it, but there are several pointers to guide this step:

1. Before sorting one spreadsheet or pulling information from a database, sit down and plan concretely the data needed, at both the macro and micro levels. Companies about to undergo spend analysis often seek a complete and detailed understanding of their spend habits, while others have vendor consolidation more specifically in mind. On the micro level, specifically map what needs to be tracked in the final spend reports—which items, which categories, how much, where, and who.
2. Determine how often data will need to be pulled ("refreshed") from the company's information systems. Some companies prefer quarterly refreshes, while others employ monthly or weekly refreshes. Phil Mingin, director of materials management for the Memorial Sloan-Kettering Cancer Center in New York, says before the hospital revamped its spend management system, it took months just to get spend data from the previous year. "We had an ERP system where by the time we loaded everything and made sure it didn't include extra information, everything was a few months old," he says. Mingin's colleague Bill Abeltin, assistant director of corporate procurement, adds that the hospital's goal is to get to up-to-date monthly refreshes via SciQuest: "We want to be able to look at last year's data at the beginning of January to make strategic decisions, especially in contract negotiations."
3. Get finance on the team. A best practice that Arun Prakash, senior director of products at Santa Clara, California–based Ketera, recommends is to team up with finance and go through the accounts payable or invoice systems data. This spend information is usually the easiest to obtain, and by grabbing requisition, purchase order, invoice, or purchase card data, spend analysis teams can gain fast results to demonstrate the worth of the project. Having finance representatives on the team provides a big advantage. Finance can verify if the easy-target spend data is correct or pinpoint any other easy spend targets. Starting small with the finance data serves as a base for the rest of the data extraction process.

(C)hange the Way You Source

A company never knows what it might learn in a spend-analysis exercise—or what its suppliers might learn. But the lessons can prompt changes that improve supplier relations and supply chain management.

Motorola's director of global procurement, David Buck and his team follow a rigorous strategic sourcing process they call the Rapid Sourcing Initiative (RCI). Spend analysis is a critical part of the process and it has helped the company cut its supply base, develop successful enterprise-wide category-leverage programs, and save significant amounts of money. It has also uncovered ways for Motorola to work with suppliers to reduce lead times, which in turn has benefited Motorola via additional savings and stronger supplier partnerships.

Traditionally, purchasing staffs think of spend analysis as an opportunity for finding where to consolidate their own spend, and that is certainly important. It's the other benefits of spend analysis that many don't think about right away. Jeff Garg, director of new product introduction and supplier readiness within Motorola's ISC, has found many uses of spend analysis in his career. While analyzing spend at one company, he discovered that payments to suppliers varied quite a bit. So, he and his team used Orbian services for independent payment processing, which gave an incentive to suppliers to have 60-day payment terms. That resulted in better working capital and standard payment terms in contracts. In another case, after analyzing three years of spare-parts spending by one customer, the team helped the customer accurately project its needs for the next 12 months.

QUESTIONS

1. Why are data analysis skills and thinking so important to spend analysis? Can't software applications be used to generate the information needed automatically?
2. How might a structured process such as Six Sigma methodology (Chapter 3) be useful here?
3. Why is it important to get other functional areas, notably finance, involved in spend analysis efforts? Can you think of some other functional areas that should be involved?

REFERENCES

Books and Articles

General Summary: 1997 Economic Census, Manufacturing. U.S. Census Bureau, ECM315-GS, June 2001.

Hannon, D., M. Varmazis, and P. Teague. "The ABCs of Spend Analysis," *Purchasing Magazine*, May 7, 2007, **www.purchasing.com/article/CA6436721.html**

Monczka, R., R. Trent and R. Handfield. *Purchasing and Supply Chain Management*, 3rd ed. Cincinnati: Southwestern Publishing, 2004.

Simison, R. L. "Buyer's Market: General Motors Drives Some Hard Bargains with Asian Suppliers." *The Wall Street Journal*, Eastern Edition (April 2, 1999), A1.

Internet

Institute for Supply Management,**www.ism.ws**

CHAPTER 12

Logistics

CHAPTER OUTLINE

Chapter Objectives

By the end of this chapter, you will be able to:

- Describe why logistics is important and discuss the major decision areas that make up logistics.
- List the strengths and weaknesses of the various modes of transportation and discuss the role of multimodal solutions.
- Identify the major types of warehousing solutions and their benefits.
- Discuss the purpose of a logistics strategy and give examples of how logistics can support the overall business strategy.
- Calculate the percentage of perfect orders.
- Calculate landed costs.
- Explain what reverse logistics systems are, and some of the unique challenges they create for firms.
- Use the weighted center of gravity method to identify a potential location for a business.
- Develop and then solve, using Microsoft Excel's Solver function, an assignment problem.

KRAFT FOODS

In the 1990s, Kraft Foods set out to redesign the logistics system it used to deliver products to its various customers, such as major grocery chains and food distributors.[1] Kraft's efforts were centered on three major customer requirements:

1. Customers wanted to be able to order a wide variety of Kraft's products and receive the shipment the next day. This would give the customers greater flexibility and allow them to hold fewer inventories in their facilities.
2. Customers wanted the option of being able to place large orders directly with the plants in return for significant price discounts. Under Kraft's old logistics system, this was not always possible.
3. Customers wanted to "order from one price list and obtain volume discounts based on their entire network of business relationships with Kraft." In 1995, customers had to deal with three different divisions, each with its own pricing and logistics system.

In response to these needs, Kraft set up a new logistics system. Figure 12.1 shows how the new system works. First, plant-based warehouses allow customers to place orders for direct plant shipments (DPSs) with any of the plants. At the same time, regional mixing centers hold the entire line of Kraft products. These mixing centers are strategically located to provide overnight shipments to the maximum number of customers. Kraft also consolidated all of its pricing, ordering, and invoicing systems into one single system to ease the administrative burden placed on customers and to assure that customers received appropriate volume discounts. The ultimate result was that Kraft was able to meet its customers' key requirements, resulting in greater customer satisfaction and high profits for Kraft.

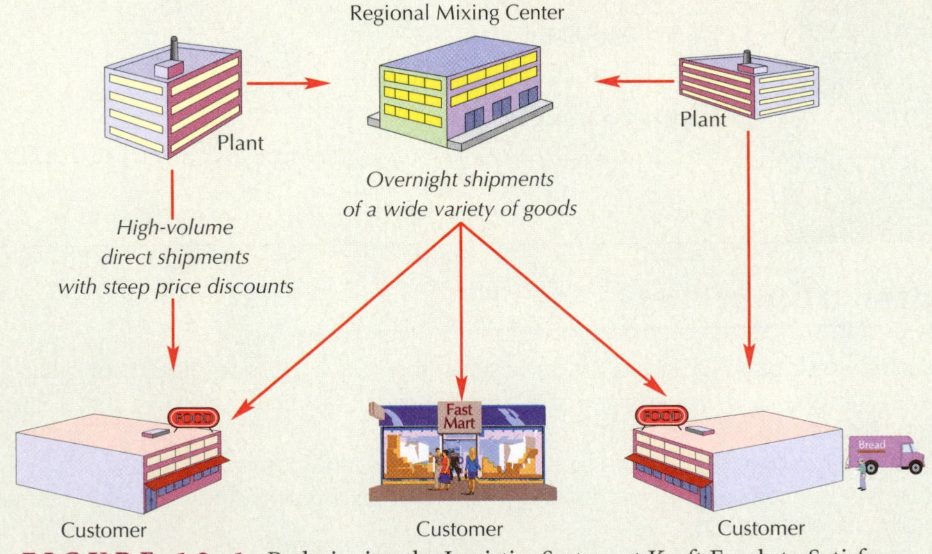

FIGURE 12.1 Redesigning the Logistics System at Kraft Foods to Satisfy Customer Needs

[1] S. Tibey, "How Kraft Built a 'One-Company' Supply Chain," *Supply Chain Management Review* 3, no. 3 (Fall 1999): 34–42.

INTRODUCTION

Logistics management "That part of supply chain management that plans, implements, and controls the efficient, effective forward and reverse flow and storage of goods, services, and related information between the point of origin and the point of consumption in order to meet customers' requirements."

Logistics management is "that part of supply chain management that plans, implements, and controls the efficient, effective forward and reverse flow and storage of goods, services and related information between the point of origin and the point of consumption in order to meet customers' requirements."[2] Companies depend on their logistics systems to move goods and materials among supply chain partners, and to manage the information flows necessary to carry out these tasks. Logistics covers a wide range of business activities, including:

- Transportation,
- Warehousing,
- Material handling,
- Packaging,
- Inventory management, and
- Logistics information systems.

As you can imagine, the interrelationships among these business activities are quite complex. At Kraft, inventory management tasks changed with the introduction of the mixing centers and direct plant shipments. Similarly, the decision to use a particular type of packaging can directly affect how transportation and material handling are carried out.

The purpose of this chapter is to introduce you to the field of logistics. After describing its strategic importance, we survey the major decision areas that make up logistics: the choice of transportation modes, warehousing, logistics information systems, and material handling and packaging systems. We also pay particular attention to the interrelationship between inventory management and the other logistics decision areas. Then we turn to the concept of a logistics strategy and examine two measures of logistics performance: the perfect order and landed costs. We also highlight reverse logistics systems, which are becoming a more important part of a firm's logistics strategy. We end the chapter with a detailed presentation of two commonly used logistics decision models, the weighted center of gravity method and the assignment problem.

12.1 LOGISTICS IN THE TWENTY-FIRST CENTURY

Prior to 1980, U.S. railroad, truck, and air transportation was tightly controlled by the government. Regulations dictated the rates a carrier could charge, the geographic area a carrier could serve, and even the number of competitors allowed in a particular area. If you wanted to ship a crate of oranges from Orlando to Detroit, the cost was set by the government and was non-negotiable. Furthermore, if you were unhappy with the performance of local trucking firms and wanted to deliver the oranges yourself, you could face additional governmental hurdles.

Beginning in 1980, this regulatory nightmare began to change. The federal government passed the Motor Carrier Regulatory Reform and Modernization Act (MCA–80) and the Staggers Rail Act, which marked the beginning of deregulation in the trucking and rail industries. Similar changes followed in the air carrier industry. At long last, logistics managers could negotiate costs and other performance dimensions (such as delivery speed, flexibility, and additional services) with carriers. Logistics quickly went from a clerical function to an area in which savvy firms could gain a strategic advantage over their competitors. The logistics renaissance was on.

---

[2]Council of Supply Chain Management Professionals (CSCMP), **http://cscmp.org/**.

12.2 WHY LOGISTICS IS CRITICAL

Beyond deregulation, businesses are beginning to recognize the impact of logistics on their cost, flexibility, and delivery performance. At the same time, information system advances and the globalization of markets are creating challenges and opportunities that did not exist just a few years ago. Logistics has evolved from a short-term, tactical concern into a long-term, strategic imperative for many firms.

The performance effects of logistics are numerous. Recent studies show that in the United States, logistics costs account for between 5% and 35% of total sales costs, depending on the business, geographic area, and type of product being sold. These costs are expected to grow as businesses and consumers move toward smaller, more frequent shipments of goods and materials, and more companies depend on foreign sources. For many firms, logistics expenses now are second only to material costs in terms of their impact on cost of goods sold.

As Table 12.1 shows, logistics expenditures continue to represent one of the largest costs in global commerce. According to estimates, in 2002 nearly 14% of the world's gross domestic product (GDP) was spent on logistics. Interestingly, between 1997 and 2002, all but one region—North America—experienced an increase in absolute logistics expenditures as well as logistics expenditures as a percentage of GDP. And these costs are certain to go up as the cost of fuel increases.

Logistics can also have a profound impact on other performance dimensions, such as delivery. Many companies have spent enormous amounts of money to decrease the lead times within their organizations, only to discover that their customers never saw much benefit due to long shipping times. These same companies are now concentrating intensively on the logistics systems that link them to their customers. Because logistics systems often interface directly with the customer, they can have a considerable impact on overall customer satisfaction.

Consider the experience of Ford Motor Company. Traditionally, once a vehicle left Ford's factory, a dealer didn't know where it was until it arrived at the lot. Many consumers, unwilling to wait to find out whether the car they wanted was on its way, simply went elsewhere for a car.[3] But in 2000, Ford struck a deal with UPS. Under the agreement, UPS used its advanced logistics capabilities to track Ford's vehicle shipments so that dealers could

TABLE 12.1 Comparative GDP and Logistics Expenditures (in billions of $)

	1997		*2000*		*2002*	
Region	EXPENDITURES ($ billions)	% GDP	EXPENDITURES ($ billions)	% GDP	EXPENDITURES ($ billions)	% GDP
Pacific Rim	$1459	14.5%	$1939	15.3%	$2127	15.7%
North America	$1035	11.0%	$1240	10.6%	$1203	9.9%
Europe	$884	12.2%	$1100	12.8%	$1229	13.3%
South America	$225	14.3%	$280	14.4%	$272	14.3%
Remaining other countries	$1492	15.4%	$1778	15.7%	$1902	16.0%
Total	**$5095**	**13.4%**	**$6,387**	**13.7%**	**$6,732**	**13.8%**

Source: A. M. Rodriguez, D. Bowersox, and R. Calatone, "Estimation of Global and National Logistics Expenditures: 2002 Data Update," *Journal of Business Logistics,* 26, no. 2 (2005): 1–15.

[3]F. Warner and R. Brooks, "Ford Is Hiring UPS to Track Vehicles as They Move from Factories to Dealers," *The Wall Street Journal*, February 2, 2000.

find the exact location of a particular vehicle by logging onto the UPS Web site. The system was a major improvement in the way Ford does business.

What drove Ford to make such a change? Quite simply, customer expectations exceeded the performance of Ford's old logistics system. As one Ford dealer pointed out, "Consumers are spoiled. . . . They can track a package on FedEx, but I can't tell them when a vehicle will be in my dealership."

12.3 LOGISTICS DECISION AREAS

As Ford's story illustrates, logistics includes not just physical flows, such as the delivery of new automobiles, but also informational flows. Transportation and warehousing systems define the physical network of a logistics system and play a major role in determining its overall cost, delivery, and flexibility performance. Logistics information systems create and manage the informational flows in the network. Order management systems, warehouse storage and retrieval systems, transportation scheduling and package routing systems, and even tracking systems like the one UPS uses to track Ford vehicles are all part of the logistics information system. Over the last five years, logistics information systems have seen explosive growth; in many supply chains, they represent the single greatest opportunity for improvement in supply chain performance. Typically, a firm's material handling and packaging systems are tightly intertwined with both its transportation and its information systems. While a full treatment of material handling and packaging is beyond the scope of this book, we will provide examples in this section to illustrate their importance.

Transportation

There are five widely recognized transportation modes: highway, water, air, rail, and pipeline.[4] Table 12.2 compares the total item value, tons, and ton-miles shipped via each mode in the United States.

HIGHWAY. Highway transportation, including parcel, postal, and courier services as well as trucking, dominates the U.S. logistics infrastructure. In 2002 alone, U.S. businesses and individuals moved over $8 *trillion* in goods via highway transportation, or 86% of the total

TABLE 12.2
Modal Shares of U.S. Domestic Freight for 2002

TRANSPORTATION MODE	VALUE (PERCENT)	TONS (PERCENT)	TON-MILES (PERCENT)
Highway (trucking, parcel, postal, courier)	86.0	67.4	28.7
Water	1.1	11.1	13.6
Rail	3.7	16.1	36.8
Air	3.2	0.0	0.4
Pipeline	1.8	5.9	20.5
Multimodal/unknown	5.6	5.5	6.8

Source: U.S. Department of Transportation, *National Transportation Statistics 2006* (Washington, DC: April 2006, Table 1-52).

[4]Unless otherwise stated, the figures given in this section are from U.S. Department of Transportation, *National Transportation Statistics 2006* (Washington, DC: April 2006).

value of goods moved. In the same year, highway transportation accounted for nearly 1.3 trillion ton-miles, or roughly 29% of the total ton-miles shipped. By whatever metric one uses (the value of goods shipped, tons moved, or ton-miles), highway transportation is dominant. Several factors account for this:

- **Geographic extension of supply chains.** As more companies developed supply chain relationships with nonlocal suppliers and customers, highway traffic increased.
- **Greater emphasis on delivery speed and flexibility.** Highway transportation has stolen market share from slower rail and water systems, which have experienced negative or stagnant growth in recent years. In a world that places great emphasis on delivery speed and flexibility, highway transportation has a clear advantage over both rail and water.
- **Changing supply chain linkages among manufacturers, wholesalers, and consumers.** The greatest growth in highway transportation has been in parcel, postal, and courier services. This substantial growth has been driven by consumers who are buying small, high-value items *directly* from manufacturers or wholesalers, skipping traditional "bricks and mortar" retailers.

Highway transport is a high-growth industry because it is one of the most flexible modes of transportation: If the source or destination point for goods can be reached by road, then the goods can be shipped by highway. In fact, very few goods are moved without highway transportation at some point in transit. Highway transport has also become more cost effective over time. Better scheduling and better use of vehicle capacity, more efficient and reliable vehicles, and increased cost competition due to deregulation have all contributed to this trend.

WATER. Water-based transport accounts for around 14% of all ton-miles shipped in the United States and is ideal for materials with a high weight-to-value ratio, especially if delivery speed is not critical. Examples of such materials include farm produce, timber, and petroleum-based products. Because of their relatively high weight-to-value ratio, shipping

A truck pulling two pup trailers.

can significantly add to the cost of these commodities. Water-based transportation, with one of the lowest ton-mile rates of any mode, helps to hold those costs down.

Air. At the opposite end of the scale, air transport is ideal for materials with a low weight-to-value ratio, especially if delivery speed or delivery reliability is critical. An example is a high-value electronic component, which might weigh only a few ounces yet be worth hundreds or even thousands of dollars. Spending $10 (or $2.50 per ounce) to guarantee next-day delivery of such a valuable product hardly seems outrageous.

Even though air transport is the least used mode in terms of tons and ton-miles, it grew explosively between 1993 and 2002 in terms of the value of goods shipped (90.5%). The reasons for this phenomenal growth are similar to those for the growth of highway transport: geographic extension of supply chains, greater emphasis on delivery speed and flexibility, and changes in the supply chain linkages between manufacturers and consumers.

Rail. Rail transport has cost characteristics similar to those of water transport, but it is somewhat more flexible. By 2002, rail's percentage of U.S. domestic ton-miles shipped had actually grown to 36.8%, up significantly from 1997s estimate of 26.7%. The rail carriers' tactics have included doubling the number of lines along busy corridors, changing the physical configuration of the trains themselves, and using multimodal solutions, which we describe in more detail in the following paragraphs.

Selecting a Transportation Mode

As Table 12.3 shows, the major transportation modes differ greatly in terms of their relative strengths and weaknesses. Firms must therefore carefully select a mode, based on their particular competitive or operational requirements. In some cases, companies are even redesigning their products to be able to reduce their size and facilitate transfer to different

TABLE 12.3
Strengths and Weaknesses of the Major Transportation Modes

TRANSPORTATION MODE	STRENGTHS	WEAKNESSES
Highway	Flexibility to deliver where and when needed.	Neither the fastest nor the cheapest option.
	Often the best balance among cost, flexibility, and reliability/speed of delivery.	
Water	Highly cost effective for bulky items.	Limited locations.
	Most effective when linked to a multimodal system.	Relatively poor delivery reliability/speed.
Rail	Highly cost effective for bulky items.	Limited locations, although less so than water.
	Can be most effective when linked to a multimodal system.	Better reliability/speed of delivery than water.
Air	Quickest mode of delivery. Flexible, especially when linked to the highway mode.	Often the most expensive mode on a per-pound basis.

types of transportation modes. One example is Lenovo, who manufactures the Thinkpad laptop. Lenovo recently made a decision to reduce the number of options and the size of its desktop computers to facilitate shipment of the product from China to the US via air instead of ocean, thereby reducing lead time, work in process inventory, and customer responsiveness.[5]

Example 12.1

Choosing a Transportation Mode at Seminole Glassworks[6]

Seminole Glassworks needs to ship 3,500 pounds of custom-built office windows from Miami, Florida, to Columbus, Ohio. Seminole has three transportation options:

MODE	DELIVERY SPEED	VEHICLES	EXTRA HANDLINGS	COST
Air	8.75 hours	3	2	$12,100
Direct truck	27.75 hours	1	0	$2,680
LTL truck	3 days	3	2	$445

With a **direct truck shipment**, Seminole would contract with a carrier to pick up the windows at its Miami plant and carry them *directly*—no stops, no changing of trucks or loading of additional cargo—to the customer's site in Columbus. With **LTL (less than truckload)** shipping, the carrier could combine Seminole's windows with other loads going to Columbus. Note that if LTL is used, Seminole's windows are likely to switch trucks at a centralized sorting hub, which would result in additional handlings and delays.

Which option should Seminole choose? The answer depends on the firm's business requirements. While LTL shipping has a clear cost advantage, direct trucking is quicker and requires fewer handlings. Air transportation would get the windows to the customer about 19 hours earlier. That advantage might be critical if the glass is needed to replace broken windows in an occupied building or if leaving a new building without windows for just a day can cause serious damage to the interior.

Direct truck shipment
A shipment made directly, with no additional stops, changing of trucks, or loading of additional cargo.

Less than truckload (LTL) shipment
A smaller shipment, often combined with other loads to reduce costs and improve truck efficiencies.

Multimodal Solutions

Few companies or supply chains use just one transportation mode, however. In fact, many depend on multimodal solutions to get goods from one end of the supply chain to the other. A garment manufacturer, for instance, might use ocean freight to move 40-foot containers from Taiwan to Long Beach, California; rail to move those same containers from Long Beach to Atlanta; and trucks to distribute the garments in the containers throughout the southeastern United States.

Multimodal solutions
Transportation solutions that seek to exploit the strengths of multiple transportation modes through physical, information, and monetary flows that are as seamless as possible.

Multimodal solutions, as the name implies, are transportation solutions that seek to exploit the strengths of multiple transportation modes through physical, information, and monetary flows that are as seamless as possible. For instance, today's rail carriers regularly use standardized containers that can be quickly moved from flatcar to truck with no unloading and reloading of material. The result is significant time and cost savings. Some

[5]Lenovo Selects D&H Distributing to Carry Its Desktop and Notebook Computers; The D&H/Lenovo Agreement Will Focus on Accelerating the Adoption of Lenovo Computing Products in the SMB Marketplace *Business Wire*, August 14, 2006.

[6]Adapted from J. Childs, "Transportation and Logistics: Your Competitive Advantage or Your Downfall?" *APICS—The Performance Advantage,* 6, no. 4 (April 1996): 44–48.

Roadrailers
Specialized rail cars the size of standard truck trailers that can be quickly switched from rail to ground transport by changing the wheels.

rail carriers even use **roadrailers**, which are cars the size of standard truck trailers that can be quickly switched from rail to ground transport by changing the wheels.

Airports and water ports are other major points of transfer from one mode to another. These ports, which serve as transfer points for global supply chains, have experienced significant growth over the past decade. For example, JFK International Airport in New York handled $89 billion worth of goods in 1997; by 2005, this figure had risen to $134.9 billion. The water port of Long Beach, California, saw a similar increase from $85 billion to $124.6 billion over the same period.

Just as important are recent improvements in information technology. Returning to the rail industry, the Union Pacific Railroad (**www.up.com**) has invested heavily in information technologies that allow it to plan and track customers' shipments across multiple transportation modes (rail, water, and highway), as well as multiple logistics firms. To its customers, Union Pacific offers one-stop logistics shopping.

As shipping containers have become more standardized across transportation modes and information systems for tracking shipments have become more accurate, multimodal transportation has grown in importance. In the United States alone, multimodal shipments of domestic freight increased from $662.6 billion to $1,079.2 billion between 1993 and 2002, a 63% increase. International freight saw similar rates of growth in multimodal shipments.

Warehousing

Warehousing
Any operation that stores, repackages, stages, sorts, or centralizes goods or materials. Organizations use warehousing to reduce transportation costs, improve operational flexibility, shorten customer lead times, and lower inventory costs.

Transportation systems represent just one part of the physical flow of goods and materials. The other part is warehousing. Since the 1980s, many companies have put an emphasis on minimizing inventory levels. As a result, many people now think of warehouses only as places where goods and materials sit idle, taking up space and tying up capital. This negative concept of warehousing is unwarranted, however.

In fact, warehousing plays a much broader role in a firm's operations and supply chain strategy. Formally defined, **warehousing** refers to any operation that stores, repackages, stages, sorts, or centralizes goods or materials. As we will see, warehousing can be used to reduce transportation costs, improve operational flexibility, shorten customer lead times, and lower inventory costs.

Consolidation warehousing
A form of warehousing that pulls together shipments from a number of sources (often plants) in the same geographical area and combines them into larger—and hence more economical—shipping loads.

Reducing Transportation Costs. Anyone who thinks warehouses do nothing but store goods should consider consolidation, cross-docking, and hub-and-spoke systems. These systems have little or no long-term storage. Rather, all three are designed primarily to exploit economies of scale in transportation.

Consolidation warehousing pulls together shipments from a number of sources (often plants) in the same geographical area and combines them into larger—and hence more economical—shipping loads. Figure 12.2 shows an example of this.

FIGURE 12.2
Consolidation Warehousing

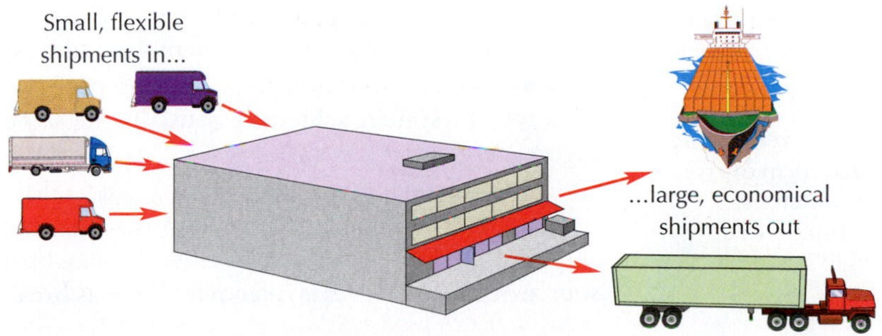

There are several variations of this type of system. A single manufacturer may use a consolidation warehouse to pull together the output from several plants, combining it when possible into a single large shipment to a major customer. In another variation, a contract carrier may use its own consolidation warehouse to combine shipments from several local businesses.

Example 12.2

Consolidation Warehousing at Bruin Logistics

Bruin Logistics handles hundreds of shipments from businesses in the Los Angeles area. At present, Bruin has three shipments to deliver to the Atlanta area:

CUSTOMER	SHIPMENT	WEIGHT
Venetian Artists Supply	100 boxes, drawing paper	3000 lbs.
Kaniko	100 PC printers	3000 lbs.
Ardent Furniture	10 dining room sets	4000 lbs.
	Total:	10,000 lbs.

The cost to Bruin of sending a truck from Los Angeles to Atlanta is $2000. The maximum load per truck is 20,000 lbs. If Bruin was to use a direct truck shipment for each customer, the shipping costs would be $2,000 per customer, or $6000 total. The weight utilization across all three trucks would be 10,000 lbs./60,000 lbs., or just 17%.

But suppose Bruin has a consolidation warehouse where loads from multiple customers can be combined. Of course, there are costs associated with consolidation. Assume that the cost of running the warehouse is approximately $90 per 1000 lbs., or in logistics lingo, $9 per hundred-weight. Furthermore, if Bruin decides to consolidate the three shipments, it must consider the additional cost of breaking them up for local delivery, which is not an issue in direct trucking. Suppose the cost of breaking up the shipments is $200 for each customer. Under these conditions, the costs of consolidating the three shipments to Atlanta would be

Warehousing costs:	$9(10,000 lbs./100 lbs.) =	$900
Cost of one truck to Atlanta:		$2,000
Delivery to final customer:	3 customers × $200 =	$600
	Total:	$3,500

Note that the cost of consolidating the shipments is just over half the cost of the direct truck shipments. Furthermore, weight utilization increases to 10,000 lbs./20,000 lbs., or 50%.

Cross-docking
A form of warehousing in which large incoming shipments are received and then broken down into smaller outgoing shipments to demand points in a geographic area. Cross-docking combines the economies of large incoming shipments with the flexibility of smaller local shipments.

Break-bulk warehousing
A specialized form of cross-docking in which the incoming shipments are from a single source or manufacturer.

In **cross-docking**, another system that reduces transportation costs, the approach used in consolidation warehousing—large shipments in; small shipments out—is reversed. This type of system achieves essentially the same benefits, however, as is illustrated in Figure 12.3.

Like consolidation, cross-docking can be done in several ways. A manufacturer may use a cross-docking warehouse to break up large rail or truck shipments into smaller shipments to local customers. A cross-docking operation that receives goods from a single source or manufacturer is often referred to as **break-bulk warehousing**.

FIGURE 12.3
Cross-docking

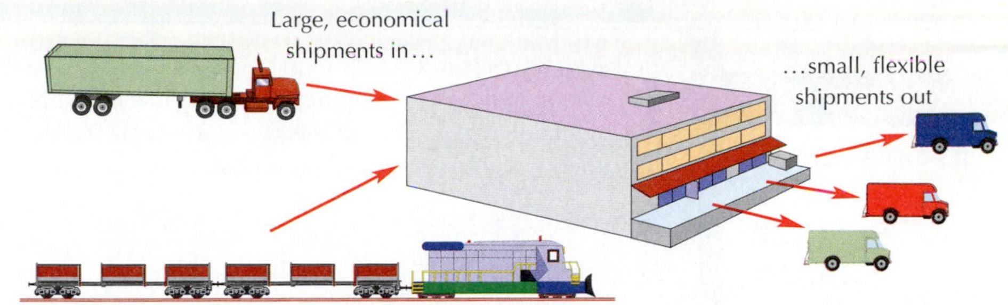

Retailers also use cross-docking to receive large shipments from multiple suppliers and re-sort the goods into customized shipments to individual stores. Recall the discussion of Lowe's regional distribution centers (DCs) at the end of Chapter 2. Lowe's DCs are classic examples of cross-docking warehouses (see Figure 12.4). They receive large truckload shipments from suppliers. Employees then remix the incoming goods and deliver them to individual stores, often multiple times per day. Computer-based information systems closely coordinate *incoming* shipments from suppliers with *outgoing* shipments to individual stores, so that more than half the goods that come off suppliers' trucks are immediately loaded onto trucks bound for individual stores. The result is that both the DCs and the retail stores hold minimal amounts of inventory, yet Lowe's receives the cost breaks associated with large shipments from suppliers.

Hub-and-spoke systems
A form of warehousing in which strategically placed "hubs" are used as sorting or transfer facilities. The hubs are typically located at convenient, high-traffic locations. The "spokes" refer to the routes serving the destinations associated with the hubs.

Hub-and-spoke systems combine the benefits of consolidation and cross-docking warehouses, but differ from them in two important ways. First, the warehouses, or "hubs," in these systems are purely sorting or transfer facilities. Hubs are designed to take advantage of transportation economies of scale; they do not hold inventory. Second, hubs are typically located at convenient, high-traffic locations, such as major airports, water ports, or the intersections of interstate highways. (Consolidation and cross-docking operations tend to be located close to the source of goods or to final customers.) One of the largest providers of transportation services in the United States, J. B. Hunt (**www.jbhunt.com**), has a comprehensive hub-and-spoke system consisting of 18 major hubs or terminals located throughout the United States, as well as 20 smaller satellite terminals.

FIGURE 12.4
Cross-docking at Lowe's

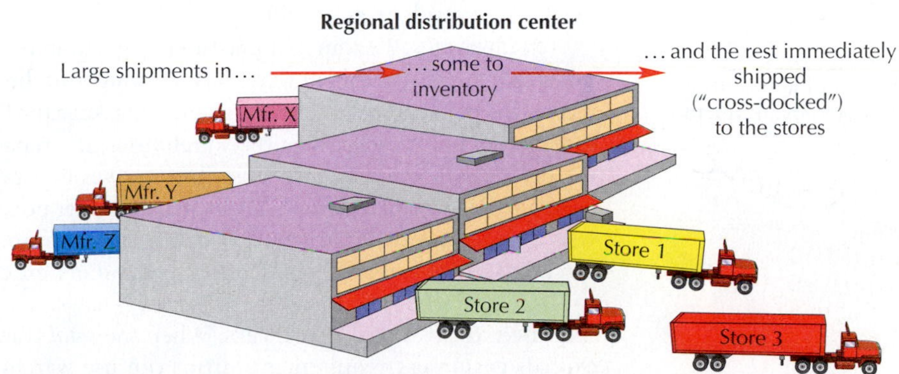

Example 12.3

Hub-and-Spoke System at Prakston Carriers

Prakston Carriers is a trucking firm with 15 hubs throughout the United States. Prakston has two customers with shipments coming out of the Northeast. Each shipment is packed in a **pup trailer**, which is half the size of a regular trailer. One is bound for Los Angeles and the other for El Paso, Texas (Figure 12.5).

Pup trailer
A type of truck trailer that is half the size of a regular truck trailer.

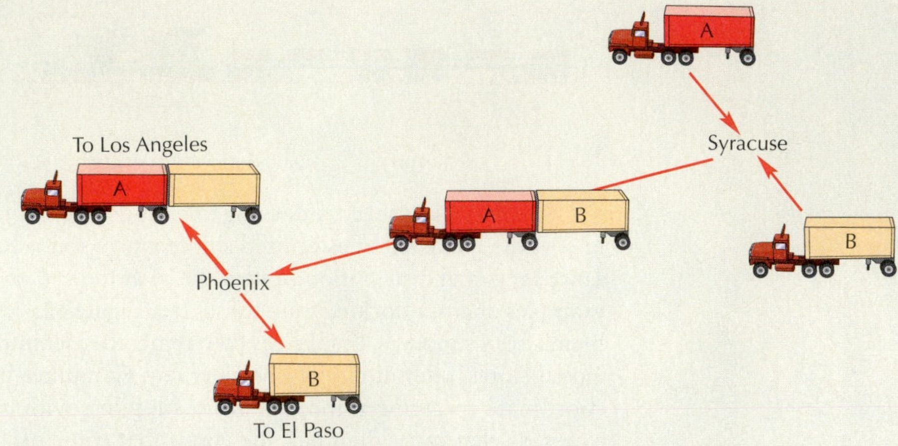

FIGURE 12.5 Hub-and-Spoke System at Prakston Carriers

Prakston might decide that the most economical way to ship the two pup trailers is to join them together at its hub in Syracuse, New York, and use a single truck to haul them to another hub in Phoenix, Arizona. In this case, Syracuse and Phoenix are the "hubs," while the routes to Los Angeles and El Paso are the "spokes." When the truck arrives in Phoenix, the two pup trailers will be separated and perhaps combined with different pup trailers for transport to their final destinations.

Improving Operational Flexibility

Warehouses not only help to lower transportation costs, but can actually improve operational flexibility as well. **Postponement warehousing** combines classic warehouse operations with light manufacturing and packaging duties to allow firms to put off final assembly or packaging of goods until the last possible moment. This strategy adds flexibility because goods and materials can be maintained in their most generic (and therefore flexible) form as long as possible.

Postponement warehousing
A form of warehousing that combines classic warehouse operations with light manufacturing and packaging duties to allow firms to put off final assembly or packaging of goods until the last possible moment.

ex. coke

To illustrate, a Korean manufacturer might ship reinforced pallets carrying 1440 light bulbs each to postponement warehouses throughout the world. At the warehouses, workers receive the pallets, break them down, and repackage the light bulbs in private-label boxes of three or six bulbs each. From the warehouses, the repackaged bulbs are shipped to local retailers. The manufacturer or distributor saves money on shipping costs (as reinforced pallets are less costly to ship than cartons of smaller boxes), but can still provide customers with a wide variety of packaging options. Furthermore, the manufacturer or distributor can hold off on final packaging until the customers' exact requirements are known.

SHORTENING CUSTOMER LEAD TIMES. When the *total* transportation time to the customers exceeds customers' requirements, firms can use warehousing to reduce the *realized* lead time to customers. They perform this service by breaking the total transportation time into two parts: (1) time to the warehouse and (2) time to the customer. In theory, goods arrive at the warehouse *prior* to the customer's order. As a result, transportation time to the warehouse is of no concern to the customer; it is "off-line." The only transportation time that is "on-line," or realized by the customer, is the time from the warehouse.

Assortment warehousing A form of warehousing in which a wide array of goods is held close to the source of demand in order to assure short customer lead times.

Spot stock warehousing A form of warehousing that attempts to position seasonal goods close to the marketplace. At the end of each season, the goods are either liquidated or moved back to a more centralized location.

Assortment and spot stock warehousing are the two major approaches used to shorten customer lead times. **Assortment warehouses** tend to carry a wider array of goods than spot stock warehouses, and carry them for a longer period. **Spot stock warehouses** focus more on the positioning of seasonal goods such as lawn care products, fashion goods, and recreational equipment. Both are attractive options when distances between the originating source and the customers are long and when customers emphasize high availability or quick delivery.

Lowering Inventory-Related Costs. Used wisely, warehouses can dramatically lower overall inventory levels and related costs throughout the supply chain. To those who associate warehousing with increased inventory levels, this idea may seem counterintuitive. But consider the case of *inventory pooling* at Boyers', a fictional retailer with eight stores in the Detroit area. For its best-selling goods, Boyers' would like to keep extra inventory, called *safety stock*, to meet unexpected spurts in customer demand. However, management doesn't want to keep this safety stock in the stores, where floor space is expensive. And it seems wasteful to keep extra inventory in each store, as it is unlikely that *all* the stores will experience unusually high demand levels at the same time. Instead, Boyers' might consolidate the safety stock for all eight stores into one centralized location, which can provide same-day service to all the stores. Not only would this free up retail floor space, but also, as we will show in Chapter 14, it would actually reduce the amount of inventory needed to protect the stores against demand surges.

Logistics Information Systems

Now that we have discussed the physical infrastructure of a logistics system, we will turn our attention to the information systems piece. In the simplest terms, logistics information systems fall into three major categories: decision support tools, planning systems, and execution systems.

Decision Support Tools. Logistics managers often use decision support tools to design and fine-tune their logistics systems. Such tools help managers choose locations for their warehouses, determine the number of containers or vessels they need, and estimate costs and travel times. Some decision support tools even have simulation and optimization capabilities. For example, a simulation model might be used to simulate actual traffic conditions in order to evaluate the impact of traffic on a proposed warehousing system. An optimization model might be used to identify the warehousing network with the lowest overall cost or shortest average travel time. In the last section of this chapter, we show how optimization modeling can support logistics decisions.

Planning Systems. Planning systems help managers with specific activities, such as selecting a carrier for an outgoing shipment or developing a weekly schedule of deliveries. Of course, such activities have been going on for a long time. But with the aid of computer-based planning systems, today's logistics managers can more quickly analyze a wider range of options and identify the delivery schedule or carrier that best suits their needs.

Execution Systems. Execution systems are the most detailed level of a logistics information system. As the name implies, execution systems take care of the hundreds of small details associated with logistics activities, ensuring that planned activities take place as expected. They oversee order and shipment management, shipper/receiver management, satellite and bar code tracking, and automated payment and billing systems.

Execution systems can also help managers monitor the logistics system and identify problems before they get out of hand. Consider the online tracking system used by FedEx. Every time FedEx handles a package (picking it up, sorting it at a major hub, loading it onto a plane), a bar code is read into its execution system. Authorized users can then go online to track the package's progress. But this same information can be used to identify potential problems automatically. Suppose the tracking system indicates that a package has not left the hub within a few hours, as expected. The tracking system may automatically generate an exception report, indicating that someone needs to check on the package's status.

A relatively new information technology that has garnered much attention recently is *radio-frequency identification, or RFID*. RFID systems use small electronic "tags" to track the position and movement of items. The *Supply Chain Connections* feature shows how one logistics company is using RFID to track the position and contents of thousands of containers.

SUPPLY CHAIN CONNECTIONS

USING RADIO-FREQUENCY IDENTIFICATION (RFID) TO TRACK SHIPPING CONTAINERS[7]

NYK Logistics, based in Secaucus, New Jersey, had a big parking problem. The company manages the shipment and distribution of a high volume of products, including garments and accessories, consumer and industrial goods, computer software, food and beverages, and natural resources, for Global 1000 companies. But NYK's yard-management system was no match for the more than 50,000 inbound ocean freight containers and 30,000 outbound trailers annually passing through the gates of its Long Beach, California, distribution center.

As this picture of a Hong Kong container port suggests, tracking the position and contents of shipping containers is no small task.

[7]Adapted from J. Maselli, "Logistics Gets Cheaper by the Yard," *RFID Journal*, October 20, 2003, **www.rfidjournal.com/article/articleprint/617/-1/1**.

Several months ago, the company implemented a **real-time locating system (RTLS)** at the Long Beach facility that uses battery-powered RFID tags to track the location of assets in the yard. Now NYK knows exactly where each trailer is parked and can locate containers to within 10 feet. The system has cut costs and increased operational efficiency in numerous ways, including slashing the average turn time—how long a trailer stays in its yard—by 20% to 40%.

The old yard-management system relied on people to track containers and trailers manually, and to coordinate the seven hostler tractors used to move containers around the 70-acre yard. But the manual system lent itself to a number of problems, and as volume in the yard grew, the problems were compounded. For example, NYK employees used to manually enter information about when a truck arrived at the yard, what it was carrying, and where it would drop its load. But once the driver left the main gate to drop his cargo off and pick up his next shipment, snafus were common. Often, the designated parking spot was filled, forcing the driver to park in a different spot. Employees at the main gate would have no way of knowing where the truck was. The problems rippled through the yard as subsequent drivers found their spots taken for the day.

That wasn't the only challenge. During peak seasons, NYK usually hires temporary yard hostlers to pull loaded trailers out of their parking spots and stage them in the yard for pickup. The hostlers also retrieve empty containers and move them to appropriate areas. But the temporary drivers had a hard time maneuvering through the yard. "We're a 24 × 7 operation, so the guy driving around trying to find a trailer at 3:30 in the morning when he doesn't know the yard that well can run into problems," says Rick Pople, NYK's general manager.

Pople began searching for an automated yard-management system that could eliminate these headaches and help NYK create a more organized yard. The company considered bar-code-based technology but decided against it, he says, because it had pitfalls that were similar to the existing manual system. "Although the bar code was associated with the unit, the unit still had to be associated with a location," says Pople. "So if a driver doesn't follow instructions to record that data, we'd be back to square one."

Pople decided to use an active-tag RFID system. Thirty-five tag readers were installed around the perimeter of the yard. They monitor 1100 parking spaces and 250 dock doors. When a truck arrives at NYK's entrance gate, its trailer is tagged with a RFID transmitter. The tag broadcasts its ID signal at three regular intervals as the container moves through the yard. Each signal is picked up by a different reader. Software uses those signals, along with a time stamp that indicates when the signal was transmitted, to calculate the exact location of the asset to within 10 feet.

All this happens in real time, which is critical, according to Pople, because the yard operates around the clock. NYK's three logistics partners bring in containers from 11 different steamship lines and as many as 15 different domestic carriers. "We couldn't have enough people with clipboards and bicycles to monitor all that," he says.

Now, NYK has implemented a dual-process system at the yard: When a driver enters the yard, a worker uses a handheld computer to enter information about the driver by scanning the magnetic stripe on the driver's license into the system. Then the worker attaches an RFID tag to the container or trailer. The tag is fastened using a clip mount on the container or trailer and removed before the container or trailer leaves the yard. The tag is scanned and the unit is associated with the driver. The system then prints a ticket for the driver that tells him where to park the unit he is delivering and where to find the unit he needs to pick up. This has cut check-in time at the gate in half.

NYK integrated the RFID system with another information system that contains a list of advance shipping notices, the contents of the shipment, and distributor information. That means that workers can later use a handheld RFID reader to scan the container's tag, find out its contents, and receive instructions on where to take the container. "Not only do we know the name and identity of the unit, we also know its DNA," says Pople. "We can see the yard and the containers."

Material Handling and Packaging

Material handling and packaging are important because of the impact they can have on transportation, warehousing, and logistics information systems. **Material handling systems** include the equipment and procedures needed to move goods *within* a facility, *between* a facility and a transportation mode, and *between* different transportation modes

Material handling systems The equipment and procedures needed to move goods *within* a facility, *between* a facility and a transportation mode, and *between* different transportation modes (e.g., ship-to-truck transfers).

Packaging From a logistics perspective, the way goods and materials are packed in order to facilitate physical, informational, and monetary flows through the supply chain.

(e.g., ship-to-truck transfers). Forklifts, cranes, conveyor belts, and computer-controlled automated storage and retrieval systems (ASRS) are just a few examples of material handling equipment. From a logistics perspective, **packaging** refers to the way goods and materials are packed in order to facilitate physical, informational, and monetary flows through the supply chain.

Following are two examples that illustrate how intertwined material handling and packaging are with other aspects of logistics. The first example, Lowe's stores, shows how material handling can be integrated with logistics information systems and how a firm's material handling system can affect the performance characteristics of the overall logistics system. The second example, wine packaging, illustrates how a simple packaging decision can affect transportation costs and operational flexibility.

MATERIAL HANDLING AT LOWE'S DCS. Recall the discussion of Lowe's cross-docking operation. In the DCs that perform the cross-docking, Lowe's uses a sophisticated conveyer system to move products to the trucks. Workers place the outgoing items into standardized trays, each of which bears a bar code indicating the items' final destination. The conveyor system "reads" these bar codes and automatically routes the trays to the appropriate trucks.

Lowe's conveyer system is fast and accurate and minimizes labor costs. For the vast majority of goods Lowe's sells, the system is an effective material handling solution. But it does have one major limitation: It can handle only those items that fit into the trays. Larger items, such as storage sheds, must be handled separately.

PACKAGING WINE. Many wine producers now ship wine in reinforced, vacuum-sealed plastic bags. Though one could argue about the aesthetic appeal of the bags, they make good sense from a logistics perspective. First, plastic bags cost less to ship and handle than glass bottles (because they are lighter and less fragile). Plastic bags also keep the wine fresher, an important consideration for seasonal wines. Finally, the bags give the wine producers greater product flexibility. At postponement warehouses, wine that has been packaged in plastic bags can quickly be repackaged into bottles, wine boxes, or psuedo-"casks," as demand dictates.

Inventory Management

Inventory is such a critical resource in many organizations that we have devoted a later chapter to examining the tools and techniques firms use to manage it. However, it is worth taking some time here to consider how inventory decisions are intertwined with the physical network (transportation and warehousing).

In general, using slower and cheaper transportation modes will cause inventory levels within the supply chain to rise, while using faster and more expensive modes will enable firms to lower inventory levels. For example, transportation modes such as water and rail are economical only for high-volume shipments; therefore, the amount of inventory in the physical network will tend to rise when these transportation modes are favored. In contrast, air and truck allow goods to be delivered in a speedy fashion, thereby enabling firms to get by with less inventory in the network. Of course, the lower inventory levels (and associated costs) are offset by higher transportation costs.

With regard to warehousing, the relationship is more complex, and inventory managers have to work closely with warehouse managers to achieve the desired business outcome. For example, spot stock and assortment warehouses need inventory to shorten delivery lead times and provide better customer service. But unilateral efforts on the part of the material managers to cut inventory levels might "starve" such warehouses, reducing their usefulness. On the other hand, to make cross-docking economical, firms must be able to match the large incoming shipments with the smaller outgoing ones. If this doesn't happen, inventory levels can rapidly spin out of control.

12.4 LOGISTICS STRATEGY

Logistics strategy
A functional strategy that ensures that an organization's logistics choices—transportation, warehousing, information systems, and even form of ownership—are consistent with its overall business strategy and support the performance dimensions that targeted customers most value.

Rail or air? Consolidation warehousing or direct shipment? A **logistics strategy** ensures that an organization's logistics choices—transportation, warehousing, information systems, and even form of ownership—are consistent with its overall business strategy and support the performance dimensions that targeted customers most value. Like sourcing, a firm's logistics strategy is an extension of its overall operations and supply chain strategy.

We saw in Chapter 2 that operations and supply chain strategies address four key performance dimensions: quality, time, flexibility, and cost. Time can be further divided into delivery reliability and delivery speed, and flexibility can be subdivided into mix flexibility, design flexibility, and volume flexibility. Table 12.4 shows the transportation and warehousing choices that are consistent with these performance dimensions.

As Table 12.4 implies, a firm cannot select its transportation and warehousing options without first considering their strategic implications. A firm that is interested in keeping costs to a minimum is likely to favor different transportation and warehousing options than companies that are interested in maximizing flexibility.

Owning versus Outsourcing

One topic we have not discussed, yet one that is critical to developing a firm's logistics strategy, is the question of ownership. Should the firm maintain its own trucks, warehouses, and information systems or outsource those services? As you might imagine, the best choice

TABLE 12.4
The Linkage between Key Performance Measures and Transportation and Warehousing Choices

PERFORMANCE DIMENSION	TRANSPORTATION MODE	WAREHOUSING SYSTEM
Delivery reliability Deliver on time consistently	Highway Air	None (direct ship) Assortment Spot stock
Delivery speed Minimal time from order to delivery	Air Highway	None (direct ship) Assortment Spot stock
Mix flexibility Support a wide range of different products/delivery needs	Highway Air Rail	Assortment Spot stock
Design flexibility Support design changes/unique customer needs	Highway Air	Postponement
Volume flexibility Provide products/delivery services in whatever volume the customer needs	Highway Air	None (direct ship) Assortment Spot stock
Cost Minimize the cost of transportation	Rail Water Pipeline Highway	Consolidation Cross-docking Hub and spoke

depends on many factors. Some of the major considerations are reflected in the following questions:

- **Does the firm have the volume needed to justify a private logistics system?** Firms with low volumes or sporadic shipping needs (such as the transport of seasonal produce) are probably better off contracting for those services.
- **Would owning the logistics system limit the firm's ability to respond to changes in the marketplace or supply chain?** Investing in a private fleet of trucks or network of warehouses ties up capital and commits a firm to managing those systems. While that may be fine for firms with stable supply chains, it can present a problem for firms whose markets or supply chain partners are changing rapidly. A manufacturer who wants the flexibility to quickly change from domestic to foreign suppliers probably should not own the trucks and warehouses it uses.
- **Is logistics a core competency for the firm?** In Chapter 2, core competencies were defined as organizational strengths or abilities, developed over a long period, that customers find valuable and competitors find difficult or impossible to copy. Many firms have decided that logistics is not one of their core competencies. These firms generally outsource the logistics function to **common carriers** (also known as public carriers), which handle shipments on a case-by-case basis, or to **contract carriers**, which enter into long-term agreements with firms. Another choice is **third-party logistics providers (3PLs)**, which are service firms that handle all of the logistics requirements for other companies. Using 3PLs allows companies to focus on their core competencies, yet still enjoy access to state-of-the-art logistics capabilities.

Common carriers
Also known as public carriers; transportation service providers who handle shipments on a case-by-case basis, without the need for long-term agreements or contracts.

Contract carriers
Transportation service providers who handle shipments for other firms based on long-term agreements or contracts.

Third-party logistics providers (3PLs)
Service firms that handle all of the logistics requirements for other companies.

The *Supply Chain Connections* feature highlights the logistics strategy employed by Kellogg Company. As you read through it, ask yourself the following questions:

- What product characteristics did managers consider in designing Kellogg's logistics system?
- What performance dimensions are most important to Kellogg?
- Who owns and manages Kellogg's transportation and warehousing systems? Why?
- What informational and physical flows must occur for an order to travel from Kellogg to a customer?

Measuring Logistics Performance

To better understand the real impact of their logistics choices, many companies evaluate their logistics performance in terms of two measures, the perfect order and landed costs. The perfect order measure indicates how *effectively* logistics serves the customer. The second measure, landed costs, indicates how *efficiently* logistics provides that service.

Perfect order
A term used to refer to the timely, error-free provision of a product or service in good condition.

THE PERFECT ORDER. In theory, the **perfect order** represents the timely, error-free provision of a product or service in good condition. For example, a company might define the perfect order as one that is:

- Delivered on time—according to the buyer's requested delivery date;
- Shipped complete;
- Invoiced correctly; and
- Undamaged in transit.

SUPPLY CHAIN CONNECTIONS

LOGISTICS STRATEGY AT THE KELLOGG COMPANY

The Kellogg Company of Battle Creek, Michigan, sells ready-to-eat cereal (RTEC), which accounts for 60% of the company's sales, as well as convenience foods, including Pop-tarts®, Nutri-Grain® Cereal Bars, Eggo® Waffles, and Rice Krispies Treats®. Kellogg's primary sales are made to grocery store chains in the United States. The company also has a manufacturing and distribution division in Canada (Kellogg's Canada) and another one in Europe. Competition in the food industry is fierce, and Kellogg is constantly under pressure to keep costs low.

For logistics purposes, Kellogg's products can be divided into two major types: frozen foods (bagels, waffles) and dry products (everything else). The two product types require different logistics solutions.

Dry Products. Kellogg produces dry products at 15 North American plants. To handle their distribution, the company depends on seven regional distribution centers (managed by outside firms) and multiple carriers. Managers recently went through a strategic sourcing exercise in which they attempted to lower warehousing and transportation costs. On the transportation side, they were able to reduce costs 15% by increasing the number of contract carriers from 25 to 30. But because the volume that the carriers handled decreased, Kellogg's business became less attractive to them. In the end, managers had to raise the prices paid to some key carriers.

Frozen Products. Kellogg's frozen products are more difficult to manage. To handle its frozen foods, Kellogg depends on 35 to 40 carriers with frozen-food capabilities. The company shares six distribution centers with other producers. Companies that specialize in frozen food operate these distribution centers for Kellogg and the other producers.

The Order Process. The order process begins when one of Kellogg's field representatives enters an order on behalf of the customer, typically a large grocery chain. Kellogg's customer service department receives the order and determines whether the quantity requested can be delivered by the desired delivery date. Customer service representatives may encourage customers to increase the size of their orders to take advantage of full-truckload shipment rates.

Once the order has been confirmed, the customer service department must decide how to fulfill it. The department follows these general guidelines:

- If an order is for a full truckload and the lead time is long enough, it will be filled and shipped directly from a plant. Kellogg personnel will take responsibility for arranging transportation.
- If an order is for a mix of products or if lead times are short, it will be filled from one of Kellogg's distribution centers. In that case, the outside firm responsible for managing the distribution center will arrange for transportation.

Under this concept, performance can be measured as the percentage of orders that meet these criteria. To find this percentage, managers must calculate the number of processed orders that did not meet all the company standards in a particular period:

$$\text{Percent perfect orders} = 100\%\left(\frac{\text{Total orders} - \text{Orders with} \geq 1 \text{ defect}}{\text{Total Orders}}\right) \qquad [12\text{-}1]$$

Example 12.4

Measuring Perfect Orders at Bartley Company

Last year Bartley Company experienced the following results:

- 5.4 million orders processed;
- 30,000 delivered late;
- 25,000 incomplete;
- 25,000 damaged; and
- 20,000 billed incorrectly.

Furthermore, these 100,000 failures were spread across 90,000 orders, which meant that some orders had more than one problem. The percentage of perfect orders is therefore

$$\text{Percent perfect orders} = 100\%\left(\frac{5,400,000 - 90,000}{5,400,000}\right) = 98.3$$

Landed Costs

Landed cost
The cost of a product plus all costs driven by logistics activities, such as transportation, warehousing, handling, customs fees, and the like.

Earlier we noted that U.S. logistics costs account for 5% to 35% of total sales costs. To make sure these costs aren't overlooked, particularly when making sourcing decisions, managers often estimate the landed cost of a product. **Landed cost** is the cost of a product plus all costs driven by logistics activities, such as transportation, warehousing, handling, customs fees, and the like.

Example 12.5

Analyzing Landed Costs at Redwing Automotive

Redwing Automotive has requested price quotations from two wiring harness manufacturers, Subassembly Builders Company (SBC) in Atlanta, Georgia, and Product Line Systems (PLS) of Nagoya, Japan. Redwing's estimated demand for the harnesses is 5000 units a month.

SBC's quote includes the following unit price, packing cost, and freight cost:

Unit price = \$25.00
Packing cost = \$0.75 per unit
Freight cost = \$0.73 per unit

PLS quotes a lower unit price of \$21.50. But each month PLS would also need to pack the harnesses in three containers, ship them overland to a Japanese port, transfer them to a container ship headed for Seattle, and then transport them overland again to Detroit. The costs associated with this movement—costs Redwing will have to pick up—are not reflected in PLS's unit price. The additional logistics-related costs Redwing would have to cover include:

- Packing cost = \$1.00 per unit
- Inland transportation cost to the port of export = \$200 per container (3 containers are needed per month)
- Freight forwarder's fee = \$100 per shipment (letter of credit, documentation for international shipments, etc.)
- Ocean transport cost = \$2067 per container
- Marine insurance = \$.50 per \$100 of shipment
- U.S. port handling charges = \$640 per container
- Customs duty = 5% of unit price
- Customs broker's fee = \$150 per year
- Transportation from Seattle to Detroit = \$1.86 per unit
- Additional paperwork = \$100 per year

Freight forwarder
An agent who serves as an intermediary between the organization shipping the product and the actual carrier, typically on international shipments.

Customs broker
An agent who handles customs requirements on behalf of another firm. In the United States, customs brokers must be licensed by the Customs Service.

A couple of these cost items deserve further explanation. A **freight forwarder** is an agent who serves as an intermediary between the organization shipping the product and the actual carrier, typically on international shipments. A **customs broker**, in contrast, is an agent who handles customs requirements on behalf of another firm. In the United States, customs brokers must be licensed by the Customs Service. To further complicate things, PLS has told Redwing that shipping lead times can be anywhere from six to eight weeks. To compensate for this uncertainty, Redwing would need to lease additional warehousing space to hold a safety stock of 1000 harnesses, at a cost of $3.00 per harness per month. Redwing's personnel would also need to spend more time handling international shipments. Finally, each monthly PLS shipment is estimated to require four hours of additional administrative time, at a cost of $25 per hour.

Table 12.5 shows how these costs can mount up. For SBC, logistics-related costs account for $1.48 per wiring harness, or approximately 5.6% ($1.48/$26.48) of the total cost of the wiring harnesses. For PLS, logistics-related costs amount to $6.4309, or 23% ($6.4309/$27.9309) of the total cost of the wiring harnesses. In fact, PLS's logistics costs are so high, they eat up any advantage PLS might have with regard to unit price. This example shows why all costs—including logistics—must be considered in a sourcing decision. As more and more firms develop global supply chains, logistics costs will command more attention from managers.

TABLE 12.5 Landed Costs Analysis at Redwing Automotive

SBC QUOTE	PER UNIT	PER MONTH	PER YEAR
Acquisition	$25.00	$125,000.00	$1,500,000
Packing	0.75	3750.00	45,000
Freight	0.73	3650.00	43,800
Landed cost:	$26.48	$132,400.00	$1,588,800

PLS QUOTE	PER UNIT	PER MONTH	PER YEAR
Acquisition	$21.50	$107,500.00	$1,290,000
Packing	1.00	5000.00	60,000
Inland transport	0.12	600.00	7200
Freight forwarder's fee	0.02	100.00	1200
Ocean transport	1.24	6201.00	74,412
Marine insurance	0.11	537.50	6450
U.S. port handling	0.38	1920.00	23,040
Customs duty	1.08	5375.00	64,500
Customs broker's fee	0.00	12.50	150
U.S. transport	1.86	9300.00	111,600
Warehousing	0.60	3000.00	36,000
Administrative time	0.02	100.00	1,200
Paperwork	0.00	8.33	100
Landed cost:	$27.93	$139,654.33	$1,675,852

Reverse logistics system A complete supply chain dedicated to the reverse flow of products and materials for the purpose of returns, repair, remanufacture, and/or recycling.

Reverse Logistics Systems

So far we have spent most of our time talking about how logistics systems move products *from* upstream suppliers *to* downstream customers. The last several years, however, have seen enormous interest placed on reverse logistics systems. A **reverse logistics system** is "a complete supply chain dedicated to the reverse flow of products and materials for the purpose of returns, repair, remanufacture, and/or recycling."[8] As the definition suggests, firms are interested in reverse logistics for a number of reasons. In the case of returns and repairs, reverse logistics can play a large role in determining overall customer satisfaction. In other cases, firms might find it more economical to harvest used products than to purchase new parts or materials. Third, many governments and consumer groups are starting to put pressure on firms to incorporate recycling into their operations, thereby reducing the amount of material that eventually gets thrown away.

When incorporating a reverse logistics system into the overall logistics strategy, firms can face a number of challenges. Some of the key issues include:

- In general, firms have less control over the timing, transportation modes used, and packaging for goods flowing back up the supply chain. This often means reverse logistics systems have to be designed to be more flexible and less cost efficient than forward-based systems.
- Goods can flow back up the supply chain for a variety of reasons. Some might do so for service and repair, others for remanufacturing or recycling, and others may simply represent excess goods that need to be deployed somewhere else. The reverse logistics system must be able to sort and handle these different flows.
- Forward logistics systems typically aren't set up to handle reverse logistics. For example, imagine a cross-docking facility, which usually deals with large inbound shipments, trying to incorporate low-volume return shipments into its operations. The information systems, material handling systems, and procedures simply aren't suited to the challenges of reverse logistics. In many cases, firms are better off setting up independent operations for their forward and reverse logistics.

12.5 LOGISTICS DECISION MODELS

Given the critical importance of logistics, it should be no surprise that experts have developed a wide range of tools to help them make better decisions in this area. In this section, we look at two common models to demonstrate how modeling techniques can be applied to logistics decisions.

The weighted center of gravity method looks at the strategic location decision. This can be especially important when a firm is developing its logistics network and must decide where to place plants or warehouses. The second model, the assignment problem, is a specialized type of optimization model and looks at the tactical problem of deciding how to serve multiple demand points from various supply points at the least possible cost.

Weighted Center of Gravity Method

Weighted center of gravity method
A logistics decision modeling technique that attempts to identify the "best" location for a single warehouse, store, or plant, given multiple demand points that differ in location and importance.

The **weighted center of gravity method** attempts to identify the "best" location for a single warehouse, store, or plant, given multiple demand points that differ in location and importance. Location is typically expressed in (X, Y) coordinate terms, where the X and Y values represent relative position on a map. Importance can be captured through weighting factors such as population, shipment quantities, sales dollars, or whatever best suits the

[8]J. F. Cox and J. H. Blackstone, eds., *APICS Dictionary*, 11th ed. (Falls Church, VA: APICS, 2004).

situation. The weighted center of gravity method works by calculating the weighted average (X, Y) values of the demand locations. Specifically:

$$\text{Weighted } X \text{ coordinate} = X^* = \frac{\sum_{i=1}^{I} W_i X_i}{\sum_{i=1}^{I} W_i} \quad [12\text{-}2]$$

$$\text{Weighted } Y \text{ coordinate} = Y^* = \frac{\sum_{i=1}^{I} W_i Y_i}{\sum_{i=1}^{I} W_i} \quad [12\text{-}3]$$

where:

(X_i, Y_i) = position of demand point i

W_i = weighting factor for demand point i

The resulting (X^*, Y^*) values represent the ideal location, given the relative weight (that is, *importance*) placed on each demand point.

Example 12.6

Warehouse Location Decision at CupAMoe's

Robbie Roberts, owner of CupAMoe's Coffee, is trying to determine where to locate his newest distribution warehouse. Figure 12.6 shows the location and population of the three major towns to be served by the warehouse.

Robbie would like to locate the warehouse to minimize transportation costs and provide the best overall delivery speed to his three markets. One way to do this is by using a weighted center of gravity method to identify a possible site.

FIGURE 12.6 Coordinate Map of Demand Locations, CupAMoe's Coffee

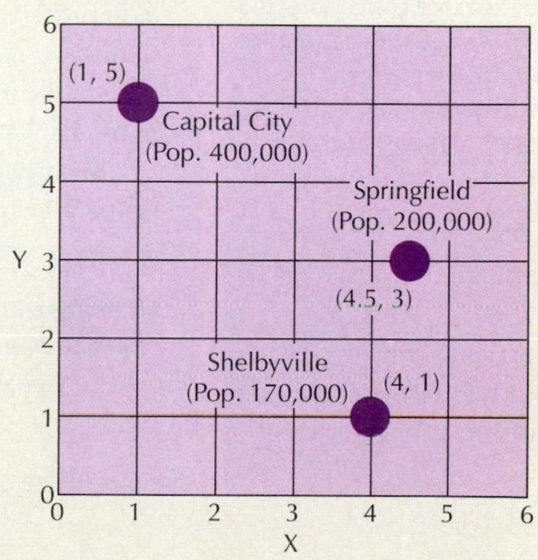

Using the populations as weight, the weighted X and Y coordinates are

$$X^* = (400{,}000 \times 1 + 200{,}000 \times 4.5 + 170{,}000 \times 4)/770{,}000$$
$$= 1{,}980{,}000/770{,}000 = 2.57$$
$$Y^* = (400{,}000 \times 5 + 200{,}000 \times 3 + 170{,}000 \times 1)/770{,}000$$
$$= 2{,}770{,}000/770{,}000 = 3.60$$

Figure 12.7 shows the suggested location of the new warehouse. Of course, a host of other factors such as available space, zoning considerations, and labor availability should be considered before Robbie makes a final decision. Nevertheless, the weighted center of gravity method provides a good first cut at the solution.

FIGURE 12.7 Suggested Warehouse Location for CupAMoe's Based on Weighted Center of Gravity Method

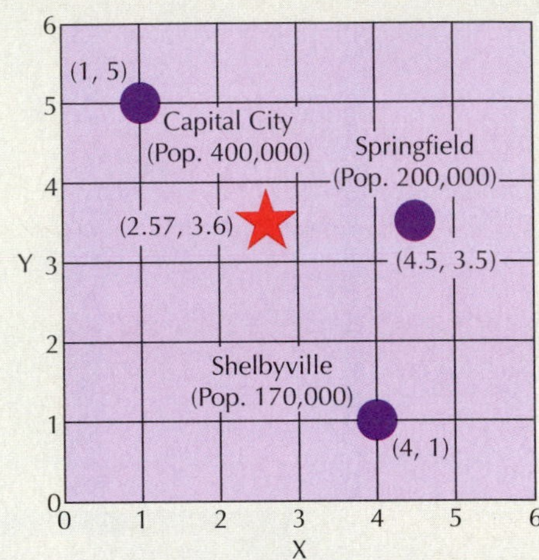

Optimization models
A class of mathematical models used when the user seeks to optimize some objective function subject to some constraints.

Objective function
A quantitative function that an optimization model seeks to optimize (maximize or minimize).

Constraints
Within the context of optimization modeling, quantifiable conditions that place limitations on the set of possible solutions. The solution to an optimization model is acceptable only if it does not break any of the constraints.

Optimization Models

Optimization models are a class of mathematical models used when the decision maker seeks to optimize some objective function subject to some constraints. An **objective function** is a quantitative function that we hope to optimize (maximize or minimize). **Constraints** are quantifiable conditions that place limitations on the set of possible solutions. A solution is acceptable only if it does not break any of the constraints. Some examples of business problems that can be addressed through optimization modeling are shown in Table 12.6.

In order for optimization modeling to work, the user must be able to state in mathematical terms both the objective function and the constraints, and the decision variables

TABLE 12.6 Business Problems That Can Be Addressed through Optimization Modeling

OBJECTIVE FUNCTION	CONSTRAINTS
Maximize profits	Limited demand, materials, and processing capabilities
Minimize delivery costs	Need to meet all demand and not exceed warehouse capacities
Minimize health care costs	Need to meet all patient demand

that will be manipulated to find the optimal solution. Once the user is able to do this, special modeling algorithms can be used to generate solutions.

The Assignment Problem

Assignment problem
A specialized form of optimization model that attempts to assign limited capacity to various demand points in a way that minimizes costs.

The **assignment problem** is a specialized form of an optimization model. Specifically, the assignment problem attempts to assign limited capacity (in this case, warehouse capacity) to various demand points in a way that minimizes costs. The generalized form of the assignment problem is as follows:

$$\text{Minimize} \sum_{i=1}^{I}\sum_{j=1}^{J} T_{ij} \times S_{ij} \qquad [12\text{-}4]$$

subject to the following constraints:

$$\sum_{j=1}^{J} S_{ij} \le C_i \qquad \text{for all warehouses } i \qquad [12\text{-}5]$$

$$\sum_{i=1}^{I} S_{ij} \ge D_j \qquad \text{for all demand points } j \qquad [12\text{-}6]$$

$$S_{ij} \ge 0 \qquad \text{for all combinations of shipments from warehouse } i \text{ to demand point } j \qquad [12\text{-}7]$$

where:

S_{ij} = number of units shipped from warehouse i to demand point j
T_{ij} = cost of shipping 1 unit from warehouse i to demand point j (these values are given)
C_i = capacity of warehouse i
D_j = demand at demand point j

Decision variables
Within the context of optimization modeling, those variables that will be manipulated to find the best solution.

The explanation behind these equations is actually quite simple. First, the only decision variables are the shipment quantities (S_{ij}). **Decision variables** are those variables that will be manipulated to find the best solution. Shipping costs (T_{ij}), warehouse capacity (C_i), and demand values (D_j), in contrast, are not decision variables, but known values.

The objective function (Equation 12-4) reflects the total shipment costs from I warehouses to J demand points. Note that at this point we don't know which shipping routes will actually be used. Therefore, we include all possible S_{ij} values multiplied by their associated per-unit shipping costs.

The constraints are found in Equations 12-5 through 12-7. Equation 12-5 requires that the total number of shipments out of a warehouse not exceed the warehouse's capacity. Similarly, Equation 12-6 requires that the total shipments into a demand point should at least cover the demand. Finally, Equation 12-7 assures that the modeling algorithm we use to solve the problem doesn't recommend negative shipments.

This last constraint may seem like an odd requirement, but if you look at Equations 12-5 and 12-6, in mathematical terms, negative shipments could be used to bring down shipping costs or to "add" capacity to the warehouses. Equation 12-7 prevents this from happening. In Example 12-7, we illustrate how the assignment problem can be set up and then solved using Microsoft Excel's Solver function.

Example 12.7

The Assignment Problem at Flynn Boot Company

The Flynn Boot Company imports boots from all over the world and ships them to major retail customers in the United States. Flynn currently has three assortment warehouses in the cities of Atlanta, Fort Worth, and Tucson. On the demand side, Flynn has four major customers: BillyBob, DudeWear, Slickers, and CJ's. The weekly capacities for the warehouses and weekly demands for the customers are shown in the Excel spreadsheet in Figure 12.8. The spreadsheet also shows the cost to ship a pair of boots from each warehouse to each customer.

	A	B	C	D	E	F	G
1	**The Assignment Problem: Flynn Boot Company**						
2							
3			Weekly			Weekly	
4			Capacity			Demand	
5		Warehouse	(Ci)		Customer	(Dj)	
6							
7		Atlanta	20,000		BillyBob	27,800	
8		Fort Worth	40,000		DudeWear	8000	
9		Tucson	30,000		Slickers	13,500	
10		TOTAL:	90,000		CJ's	33,000	
11					TOTAL:	82,300	
12							
13		Cost to ship one pair of boots from Warehouse i to Customer j (Tij)					
14							
15			BillyBob	DudeWear	Slickers	CJ's	
16		Atlanta	$2.00	$3.00	$3.50	$1.50	
17		Fort Worth	$5.00	$1.75	$2.25	$4.00	
18		Tucson	$1.00	$2.50	$1.00	$3.00	
19							

FIGURE 12.8 Spreadsheet for Flynn Boot Company

Total warehouse capacity (90,000 pairs per week) exceeds total demand (82,300), so Flynn has plenty of capacity. One question remains, however, given the different shipping costs: Which warehouse should serve which customer in order to minimize costs?

Following Equations 12-4 through 12-7 and using the first letter for each warehouse and customer as abbreviations, we can express the assignment problem as follows. Minimize total shipping costs (Equation 12-4):

$$\$2.00 \times S_{AB} + \$3.00 \times S_{AD} + \$3.50 \times S_{AS} + \$1.50 \times S_{AC}$$
$$+ \$5.00 \times S_{FB} + \$1.75 \times S_{FD} + \$2.25 \times S_{FS} + \$4.00 \times S_{FC}$$
$$+ \$1.00 \times S_{TB} + \$2.50 \times S_{TD} + \$1.00 \times S_{TS} + \$3.00 \times S_{TC}$$

subject to the following constraints:

Total shipments out of each warehouse must be less than its capacity (Equation 12-5):

$$S_{AB} + S_{AD} + S_{AS} + S_{AC} \leq 20{,}000$$
$$S_{FB} + S_{FD} + S_{FS} + S_{FC} \leq 40{,}000$$
$$S_{TB} + S_{TD} + S_{TS} + S_{TC} \leq 30{,}000$$

Total shipments to each customer must at least cover demand (Equation 12-6):

$$S_{AB} + S_{FB} + S_{TB} \geq 27{,}800$$
$$S_{AD} + S_{FD} + S_{TD} \geq 8{,}000$$
$$S_{AS} + S_{FS} + S_{TS} \geq 13{,}500$$
$$S_{AC} + S_{FC} + S_{TC} \geq 33{,}000$$

All shipment quantities must be nonnegative (Equation 12-7):

$$S_{AB}, S_{AD}, S_{AS}, S_{AC}, S_{FB}, S_{FD}, S_{FS}, S_{FC}, S_{TB}, S_{TD}, S_{TS}, S_{TC} \geq 0$$

So how do we solve this problem? Many software packages could be used to find the optimal answer. We use the Solver function of Microsoft Excel because it is readily available to most students. Solver is available as an add-on function for Excel. Once it has been installed, it can be accessed through the "Tools" drop-down menu.

The first step is to modify our spreadsheet so that we now have spaces to record the S_{ij} values and a cell that contains the formula for the objective function (in this case, total shipping costs). Figure 12.9 shows the expanded worksheet.

	A	B	C	D	E	F	G
1	**The Assignment Problem: Flynn Boot Company**						
2							
3			Weekly			Weekly	
4			Capacity			Demand	
5		Warehouse	(Ci)		Customer	(Dj)	
6							
7		Atlanta	20,000		BillyBob	27,800	
8		Fort Worth	40,000		DudeWear	8000	
9		Tucson	30,000		Slickers	13,500	
10		TOTAL:	90,000		CJ's	33,000	
11					TOTAL:	82,300	
12							
13		Cost to ship one pair of boots from Warehouse i to Customer j (Tij)					
14							
15			BillyBob	DudeWear	Slickers	CJ's	
16		Atlanta	$2.00	$3.00	$3.50	$1.50	
17		Fort Worth	$5.00	$1.75	$2.25	$4.00	
18		Tucson	$1.00	$2.50	$1.00	$3.00	
19							
20							
21		Number of pairs of boots shipped from Warehouse i to Customer j					
22							
23			BillyBob	DudeWear	Slickers	CJ's	TOTALS:
24		Atlanta	0	0	0	0	0
25		Fort Worth	0	0	0	0	0
26		Tucson	0	0	0	0	0
27		TOTALS:	0	0	0	0	
28							
29		**Objective Function: Minimum Total Shipping Costs:**					$0.00
30							

FIGURE 12.9 Expanded Spreadsheet for Flynn Boot Company

The S_{ij} values are shown in the highlighted cells. For example, Cell C24 contains the number of shipments from Atlanta to BillyBob's. These values are initially set to 0; we will let the Solver function determine the S_{ij} values that minimize total costs.

Some of the cells have formulas that calculate key values. In particular:

- Cells C27 through F27: Total shipments to each customer
- Cells G24 through G26: Total shipments out of each warehouse
- Cell G29: The objective function

To illustrate the formulas in these cells:

Formula in Cell C27 = ***SUM(C24:C26)*** = total shipment to BillyBob's
Formula in Cell G24 = ***SUM(C24:F24)*** = total shipments out of Atlanta
Formula for Cell G29 = ***SUMPRODUCT(C16:F18,C24:F26)*** = total shipping costs

With all the relevant information now in the spreadsheet, we next code the assignment problem (Equations 12-4 through 12-7) into Excel's Solver function. Figure 12.10 shows the Solver dialog box used to do this. The "Target Cell" is our objective function, Cell G29. Just below, we have clicked "Min" to indicate we want a solution that minimizes the value in Cell G29. Below that, there is a space labeled "By Changing Cells:". Here we tell Solver where our decision variables are located.

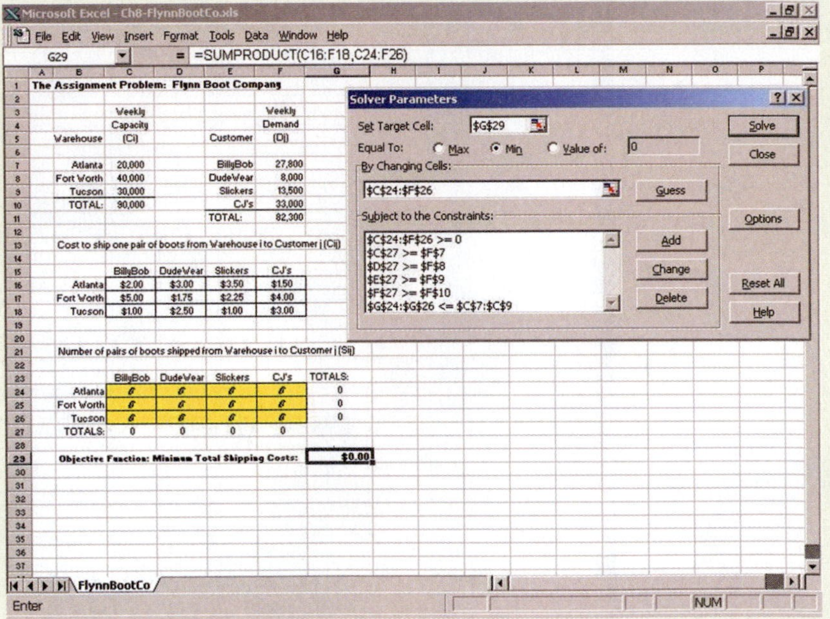

FIGURE 12.10 Solver Dialog Box for Flynn Boot Company Example

Below that is a list of all the constraints that must be met. The first constraint, ***$C$24:$F$26>=0***, ensures that none of our shipment quantities falls below zero (Equation 12-7). The next four constraints are the demand constraints; shipments to a customer must at least meet customer demand (Equation 12-6). Finally, ***$G$24:$G$26<=$C$7:$C$9=******$C$7:$C$9*** makes sure that total shipments from any warehouse do not exceed that warehouse's capacity (Equation 12-5).

Once we have finished defining the objective function, target cells, and constraints, we click the "Solve" button at the top right of the Solver dialog box. The resulting solution is shown in Figure 12.11.

	A	B	C	D	E	F	G
1	**The Assignment Problem: Flynn Boot Company**						
2							
3			Weekly			Weekly	
4			Capacity			Demand	
5		Warehouse	(Ci)		Customer	(Dj)	
6							
7		Atlanta	15,000		BillyBob	27,800	
8		Fort Worth	40,000		DudeWear	8000	
9		Tucson	30,000		Slickers	13,500	
10		TOTAL:	85,000		CJ's	33,000	
11					TOTAL:	82,300	
12							
13		Cost to ship one pair of boots from Warehouse i to Customer j (Tij)					
14							
15			BillyBob	DudeWear	Slickers	CJ's	
16		Atlanta	$2.00	$3.00	$3.50	$1.50	
17		Fort Worth	$5.00	$1.75	$2.25	$4.00	
18		Tucson	$1.00	$2.50	$1.00	$3.00	
19							
20							
21	Number of pair of boots shipped from Warehouse i to Customer j (Sij)						
22							
23			BillyBob	DudeWear	Slickers	CJ's	TOTALS:
24		Atlanta	0	0	0	20,000	20,000
25		Fort Worth	0	8000	11,300	13,000	32,300
26		Tucson	27,800	0	2,200	0	30,000
27		TOTALS:	27,800	8000	13,500	33,000	
28							
29		**Objective Function: Minimum Total Shipping Costs:**					**$151,425.00**

FIGURE 12.11 Lowest-Cost Solution for Flynn Boot Company

Does this answer make sense? First, none of the warehouse capacity limits is violated. Second, all the customer demand requirements are met. Two of the four customers (BillyBob and DudeWear) were completely served by the lowest cost option, while the remaining two had at least part of their shipment handled from the cheapest warehouse.

But what if conditions change? That is, what if demand levels shift or shipping costs change over time? In that case, we go into the spreadsheet, modify the relevant data, and *re-solve* the problem using Solver.

Suppose, for example, that part of the Atlanta warehouse has been shut down for repairs, cutting Atlanta's capacity to just 15,000. What should the new solution look like? Modifying the spreadsheet and using Solver to generate a new solution, we get the results shown in Figure 12.12.

	A	B	C	D	E	F	G
1	**The Assignment Problem: Flynn Boot Company**						
2							
3			Weekly			Weekly	
4			Capacity			Demand	
5		Warehouse	(Ci)		Customer	(Dj)	
6							
7		Atlanta	15,000		BillyBob	27,800	
8		Fort Worth	40,000		DudeWear	8000	
9		Tucson	30,000		Slickers	13,500	
10		TOTAL:	85,000		CJ's	33,000	
11					TOTAL:	82,300	
12							
13		Cost to ship one pair of boots from Warehouse i to Customer j (Tij)					
14							
15			BillyBob	DudeWear	Slickers	CJ's	
16		Atlanta	$2.00	$3.00	$3.50	$1.50	
17		Fort Worth	$5.00	$1.75	$2.25	$4.00	
18		Tucson	$1.00	$2.50	$1.00	$3.00	
19							
20							
21	Number of pair of boots shipped from Warehouse i to Customer j (Sij)						
22							
23			BillyBob	DudeWear	Slickers	CJ's	TOTALS:
24		Atlanta	0.00	0.00	0.00	15,000.00	15,000
25		Fort Worth	0.00	8000.00	11,300.00	18,000.00	37,300
26		Tucson	27,800.00	0.00	2,200.00	0.00	30,000
27		TOTALS:	27,800	8000	13,500	33,000	
28							
29		**Objective Function: Minimum Total Shipping Costs:**					**$163,925.00**

FIGURE 12.12 Lowest-Cost Solution for Flynn Boot Company, Atlanta Capacity Reduced to 15,000

With Atlanta's capacity reduced, Flynn is forced to ship 5000 more pairs of boots from Fort Worth to CJ's. The resulting change in costs is

$$5000(T_{FC} - T_{AC}) = 5000(\$4.00 - \$1.50) = \$12{,}500$$

which corresponds to the difference in total shipping costs between Figures 12.11 and 12.12.

$$\$163{,}925 - \$151{,}425 = \$12{,}500$$

CHAPTER SUMMARY

As critical as logistics is today, it will continue to grow in importance. In fact, several trends will keep logistics at the forefront of many firms' strategic efforts:

- Growth in the level of both domestic and international logistics;
- Shifts from slower to faster transportation modes; and
- Greater outsourcing opportunities.

The last two deserve special mention. As noted earlier, the value of air shipments in the United States grew by 90% between 1993 and 2002. One likely reason for this shift is the increased emphasis in many firms on lowering overall inventory levels. As we will see in Chapter 14, shorter transportation times often allow firms to lower their inventory levels. But whether the increase in transportation costs is more than offset by inventory cost savings remains to be seen.

Second, as logistics becomes more globalized and information-intensive, more firms are outsourcing the logistics function to specialists, most notably third-party logistics providers (3PLs). This trend is expected to continue. However, firms must carefully analyze the strategic benefits and risks of outsourcing. Firms must remember that outsourcing is *part* of a logistics strategy, not a substitute for one.

We started off this chapter by discussing why logistics is critical and by examining the major logistics decision areas, with particular emphasis on transportation modes and warehousing. We then discussed the concept of a logistics strategy and introduced some commonly used logistics decision models.

But we encourage you not to let your logistics education end here. The Council of Supply Chain Management Professionals or CSCMP (**www.cscmp.org**) is a valuable source of education materials, white papers on state-of-the-art research into logistics, and professional contacts.

KEY FORMULAS

Percent perfect orders (page 379):

$$\text{Percent perfect orders} = 100\%\left(\frac{\text{Total orders} - \text{Orders with} \geq 1 \text{ defect}}{\text{Total Orders}}\right) \qquad [12\text{-}1]$$

Weighted center of gravity method (page 383):

$$\text{Weighted } X \text{ coordinate} = X^* = \frac{\sum_{i=1}^{I} W_i X_i}{\sum_{i=1}^{I} W_i} \qquad [12\text{-}2]$$

$$\text{Weighted } Y \text{ coordinate} = Y^* = \frac{\sum_{i=1}^{I} W_i Y_i}{\sum_{i=1}^{I} W_i} \qquad [12\text{-}3]$$

where:

(X_i, Y_i) = position of demand point i

W_i = weighting factor for demand point i

Assignment problem (page 385):

$$\text{Minimize } \sum_{i=1}^{I}\sum_{j=1}^{J} T_{ij} \times S_{ij} \qquad [12\text{-}4]$$

subject to the following constraints:

$$\sum_{j=1}^{J} S_{ij} \leq C_i \qquad \text{for all warehouses } i \qquad [12\text{-}5]$$

$$\sum_{i=1}^{I} S_{ij} \geq D_j \quad \text{for all demand points } j \qquad [12\text{-}6]$$

$$S_{ij} \geq 0 \quad \text{for all combinations of shipments from warehouse } i \text{ to demand point } j \qquad [12\text{-}7]$$

where:

S_{ij} = number of units shipped from warehouse i to demand point j

T_{ij} = cost of shipping 1 unit from warehouse i to demand point j (these values are given)

C_i = capacity of warehouse i

D_j = demand at demand point j

KEY TERMS

Assignment problem 385
Assortment warehouses 373
Break-bulk warehousing 370
Common carriers 378
Consolidation warehousing 369
Constraints 384
Contract carriers 378
Cross-docking 370
Customs broker 380
Decision variables 385
Direct truck shipment 368
Freight forwarder 380
Hub-and-spoke systems 371
Landed cost 380
Less than truckload (LTL) shipment 368
Logistics management 363
Logistics strategy 377
Material handling systems 376
Multimodal solutions 368
Objective function 384
Optimization models 384
Packaging 376
Perfect order 378
Postponement warehousing 372
Pup trailer 372
Reverse logistics system 381
Roadrailers 369
Spot stock warehouses 373
Third-party logistics providers (3PLs) 378
Warehousing 369
Weighted center of gravity method 382

SOLVED PROBLEM

Problem

Candace Button has just taken a job with Vivette's Importers in New York. Vivette's makes daily shipments to customers in the Boston area. However, the number of customers, shipment sizes, and associated transportation and warehousing costs can vary considerably from one day to the next.

Candace would like to put together a spreadsheet that would allow her to quickly determine whether or not she should consolidate shipments, based on changing demand and cost information. To test the new spreadsheet, Candace has the following information for the next week:

Number of customers: 15
Average shipment size: 1400 pounds
Truck capacity: 20,000 pounds
Truck costs: $500 per truck going to Boston

For consolidated shipments:
Warehousing cost: $25 per hundred-weight
Delivery cost: $100 per customer

Solution

Figure 12.13 shows the resulting Microsoft Excel worksheet. The shaded cells represent the input variables; changes to these cells will result in changes to the number of trucks needed and the total costs of consolidation versus direct truck shipments.

	A	B	C	D
1	**Consolidation versus Direct Truck Shipments**			
2				
3	No. of customers:	15		
4	Ave. shipment size:	1400	pounds	
5	Truck capacity:	20,000	pounds	
6	Truck cost:	$500.00	per shipment	
7	Consolidation costs			
8	Warehousing cost:	$25.00	per hundred-weight	
9	Delivery cost:	$100	per customer	
10				
11	**SOLUTION**			
12		Consolidation	Direct ship	
13	No. of trucks needed:	2	15	
14	Warehousing costs:	$5250.00	$0.00	
15	Delivery cost:	$1500.00	$0.00	
16	Trucking costs:	$1000.00	$7500.00	
17	Total:	$7750.00	$7500.00	

FIGURE 12.13 Consolidation versus Direct Truck Shipment Spreadsheet

Three of the spreadsheet cells deserve special mention. Specifically:

$$\text{Cell B14} = \text{warehousing cost under consolidation}$$
$$= \frac{(\text{warehousing cost per hundred} - \text{weight}) \times (\text{number of customers}) \times (\text{average shipment size})}{100}$$
$$= \text{B8*B3*B4/100}$$

$$\text{Cell B13} = \text{number of trucks needed under consolidation}$$
$$= \text{rounded-up value of} \left[\frac{(\text{average shipment size})(\text{number of customers})}{\text{truck capacity}} \right]$$
$$= \text{ROUNDUP(B4*B3/B5,0)}$$

$$\text{Cell C13} = \text{number of trucks needed under direct shipment}$$
$$= (\text{number of customers}) \times \left(\text{rounded-up value of} \left[\frac{\text{average shipment size}}{\text{truck capacity}} \right] \right)$$
$$= \text{B3*ROUNDUP(B4/B5,0)}$$

The last two formulas make sure that the number of trucks is correct, even if the average shipment size is greater than the load capacity for a single truck.

An added advantage of this spreadsheet is that Candace can use it to understand how the various costs affect the final decision. For example, by playing around with the spreadsheet, Candace realizes that if she can lower the delivery cost to just $83 per customer, then the consolidation option looks cheaper (Figure 12.14).

	A	B	C	D
1	**Consolidation versus Direct Truck Shipments**			
2				
3	No. of customers:	15		
4	Ave. shipment size:	1400	pounds	
5	Truck capacity:	20,000	pounds	
6	Truck cost:	$500.00	per shipment	
7	Consolidation cost:			
8	Warehousing cost:	$25.00	per hundred-weight	
9	Delivery cost:	$83	per customer	
10				
11	**SOLUTION**			
12		Consolidation	Direct ship	
13	No. of trucks needed:	2	15	
14	Warehousing costs:	$5250.00	$0.00	
15	Delivery cost:	$1245.00	$0.00	
16	Trucking costs:	$1000.00	$7500.00	
17	Total:	$7495.00	$7500.00	

FIGURE 12.14 Impact of Lower Delivery Cost per Customer

DISCUSSION QUESTIONS

1. Someone tells you that logistics is really just trucking and warehousing. Explain why this view is inadequate.
2. A colleague tells you that warehousing is inconsistent with efforts to minimize inventory levels throughout the supply chain. Is this true or false? Explain.
3. Can a firm actually be part of the logistics industry without physically touching a product? Explain.
4. Why will landed costs become a more important consideration as firms participate in more international logistics arrangements?
5. Why is it important for firms to have a logistics strategy? What could happen if a firm did not logically link its logistics decisions to the needs of its customers?
6. Can logistics be an area of core competency for a company? Can you think of an example?

PROBLEMS

Additional homework problems are available at www.prenhall.com/bozarth. These problems use Excel to generate customized problems for different class sections or even different students.

(* = easy; ** = moderate; *** = advanced)

1. Consider the consolidation warehousing decision facing Bruin Logistics (Example 12.2). Recalculate the cost of the consolidation option if all costs remain the same *except*
   a. (*) The cost of running the warehouse doubles to $18 per hundred-weight.
   b. (*) Delivery costs to each customer fall to $150.
   c. (**) The cost of sending a truck from Los Angeles to Atlanta falls to $1800, but delivery costs rise to $250 per customer.
2. Every week BosssMustang of Oakland, California, receives shipments from 10 different suppliers in the

Los Angeles area. Each supplier's order weighs, on average, 500 lbs. A direct truck shipment from Los Angeles to Oakland costs $800.

A Los Angeles 3PL provider has offered to run a consolidation warehousing operation for BosssMustang. The 3PL provider would pick up the shipments from each supplier, process them, and put them on a single truck bound for Oakland. The pickup fee would be $100 per supplier, and the warehousing cost would be $55 per hundred-weight. The direct truck shipment cost would be the same as before, $800.

a. (*) How much would it cost BosssMustang per week to accept direct, single-order shipments from all of its suppliers? What would the utilization levels for the trucks look like, assuming each truck was capable of carrying 10,000 lbs.?
b. (**) How much would it cost BosssMustang per week to use the consolidation warehousing option? What would the utilization level for the truck look like?
c. (**) Suppose higher gasoline prices have caused the trucking cost to increase to $1200. Which option looks best now?

3. Astro Industries of Minneapolis, Minnesota, makes weekly shipments to 20 customers in the Dallas area. Each customer's order weighs, on average, 1500 lbs. A direct truck shipment from Minneapolis to Dallas costs $1800. The maximum load per truck is 40,000 lbs.
   a. (*) How much would it cost Astro to make direct, single-order shipments to all of its customers each week? What would the utilization levels for the trucks look like?
   b. (**) Suppose a Dallas-based warehousing firm has agreed to run a break-bulk warehousing operation for Astro at the cost of $75 per hundred-weight. Local deliveries to each customer would tack on another $100 per customer per week. How much money could Astro save by going with the break-bulk solution?
   c. (***) How high would the warehousing cost (currently $75 per hundred-weight) have to be before break-bulk warehousing is no more attractive than direct shipments? Round your answer to the nearest dollar.

4. Consider the perfect order calculation for Bartley Company (Example 12.4). Recalculate the percentage of perfect orders if all performance results remained the same *except*
   a. (*) 25,000 are delivered late, and total failures are now spread across 85,000 orders.
   b. (*) 25,000 are delivered late, but total failures are still spread across 90,000 orders.
   c. (**) According to the logic of the perfect order measure, does an incorrectly billed order have the same impact as a damaged order? Does this seem reasonable? What are the implications for interpreting this measure?

5. MountainMole Foods has decided to use the perfect order measurement approach to track its logistics performance. According to MountainMole, a perfect order is one that (1) is delivered on time, (2) arrives in one complete shipment, (3) arrives undamaged, and (4) is correctly billed. MountainMole has the following performance figures for the past four years:

YEAR	2000	2001	2002	2003
Total shipments	100,000	150,000	175,000	190,000
On-time shipments	95,000	145,000	170,000	180,000
Complete shipments	99,000	142,500	157,500	161,500
Undamaged shipments	98,000	147,500	173,000	189,000
Correctly billed shipments	55,000	97,500	132,000	161,500

   a. (**) Calculate performance for each of the four years. What is the overall trend in the performance, if any? What factors explain the results?
   b. (**) If you were looking to improve MountainMole's logistics performance, what areas might you concentrate on, based on these results?

6. Northcutt manufactures high-end racing bikes and is looking for a source of gear sprocket sets. Northcutt would need 1550 sets a month. Supplier A is a domestic firm, while Suppliers B and C are located overseas. Cost information for the suppliers is as follows:
   - **Supplier A**—Price of $100 per set, plus packing cost of $2 per set. Total inland freight costs for all 1550 units would be $800 per month.
   - **Supplier B**—Price of $96 per set, plus packing cost of $3.50 per set. International transportation costs would total $3500 per month, while total inland freight costs would be $800 per month.
   - **Supplier C**—Price of $93 per set, plus packing cost of $3.00 per set. International transportation costs would total $5000 per month, while total inland freight costs would be $1000 per month.

   a. (**) Calculate total landed costs per unit and per month for the three potential suppliers. Who is the cheapest? Who is the most expensive?
   b. (***) Suppose that international and inland freight costs are fixed for volumes up to 4000 units a month. Under this assumption, which supplier would have the lowest landed cost if demand was cut in half? If demand doubled? Whose landed cost is most sensitive to volume changes?
   c. (**) What factors other than landed costs might Northcutt consider when selecting the supplier?

(*Hint:* Incorporate what you learned in the chapters on quality, sourcing, and purchasing.)

7. Consider the Redwing Automotive total cost example summarized in Table 12.5.

a. (**) By how much would PLS have to cut its per-unit price in order to match SBC's landed costs? What percentage decrease does this translate into?

b. (**) If you were the president of PLS, where would you go about trying to lower your landed costs to better match those of SBC?

c. (**) What logistics performance dimensions other than landed costs might PLS emphasize in order to win Redwing's business?

8. Consider the warehouse location decision facing CupAMoe's (Example 12.6).

a. (**) Suppose Robbie has learned that Capital City's population is expected to grow by just 5% over the next five years, while Springfield's population is expected to increase by 50,000 over the same time period. Recalculate the *X* and *Y* coordinates using this new information.

b. (**) Now suppose Robbie has also learned that Capital City generates $800,000 in sales per year, while Springfield and Shelbyville both generate only $150,000 in sales each. Using sales dollars as the weights, recalculate the *X* and *Y* coordinates.

c. (**) Which do you think is a better weighting factor to consider, population or sales dollars? Explain.

9. The city of Green Valley, Arizona, is trying to determine where to locate a new fire station. The fire station is expected to serve four neighborhoods. The locations and number of homes in the neighborhoods are as follows:

NEIGHBORHOOD	*X* COORDINATE	*Y* COORDINATE	NUMBER OF HOMES
Birchwood	5	4	163
Cactus Circle	7	1	45
De La Urraca	2	2	205
Kingston	3.5	1.5	30

a. (**) Calculate the weighted center of gravity for the new fire station based on the given information.

b. (**) What other factors (for example, zoning laws, maximum response time) might come into play when making the final decision?

10. (***) (*Microsoft Excel problem*). The following figure shows an Excel spreadsheet that calculates weighted *X* and *Y* coordinates, based on values for up to five demand points. **Re-create this spreadsheet in Excel.** While your formatting does not have to be exactly the same, your answers should be. Your spreadsheet should recalculate results whenever any changes are made to the shaded cells. To test your logic, change the weight on demand point D to 300. Your new weighted *X* and *Y* coordinates should be 3.08 and 2.92, respectively.

Microsoft Excel Sheet for Problem 10

	A	B	C	D	E	F
1	**Weighted Center of Gravity Model for up to Five Demand Points**					
2						
3	Demand point	*X* coordinate	*Y* coordinate	Weighting factor		
4	A	1.00	5.00	300		
5	B	2.00	4.00	200		
6	C	3.00	3.00	100		
7	D	4.00	2.00	300		
8	E	5.00	1.00	300		
9						
10		Weighted *X* coordinate:		3.08		
11		Weighted *Y* coordinate:		2.92		

11. (***) (*Microsoft Excel problem*). Re-create the assignment problem spreadsheet for Flynn Boot Company, described in Figures 12.9. While your formatting does not have to be exactly the same, your spreadsheet should work the same. Specifically, the user should be able to change the weekly capacity (C_i), weekly demand (D_j), or shipping cost (T_{ij}) values and generate a new solution using Excel's Solver function. Test your spreadsheet by seeing whether you get a new solution when Atlanta's warehouse capacity changes from 20,000 to 15,000. Make sure your answers match those in Example 12.7.

12. (***) (*Microsoft Excel problem*). Consider the following information:

PLANT	CAPACITY	STORE	DEMAND
A	400	X	200
B	500	Y	250
C	100	Z	300
Total:	1000	Total:	750

Cost to shop from plant to store (per unit of demand)

	Store		
PLANT	X	Y	Z
A	$2.00	$2.00	$3.50
B	$4.00	$5.00	$4.50
C	$3.00	$3.00	$3.00

a. Write out the assignment problem by hand, using Equations 12-4 through 12-7 and Example 12-7 as a guide.

b. Develop an Excel spreadsheet that uses the Solver function to find the optimal shipping patterns between the plants and the stores. (*Hint:* The objective function for the optimal solution is $2200.) Interpret your answer. Is there any plant that is underutilized? If so, why do you think this is the case? How might you use this information in any future decision to expand plant capacities?

CASE STUDY

JUST-IN-TIME SHIPPING[9]

When Nintendo Co. shipped its new "Mario Kart: Double Dash" video game to stores in November 2003, most retailers agreed to pay a little extra to have the games sent directly to the stores within nine days. For about 60% of the stores, the games went from a packaging plant near Seattle straight to the retail-store shelves, no stops at warehouses or distribution centers, which can increase the time a product gets to the shelf to as long as six weeks.

As it turned out, speed was crucial. The game, which features characters racing go-carts while throwing things at each other, was out of stock by the first week of December, after sales of almost 500,000 games. Nintendo was able to restock shelves in time for the critical pre-Christmas rush—thanks to Atlanta-based United Parcel Service Inc.—and Nintendo sold more than 900,000 games in the U.S. by the end of the year.

The trend toward just-in-time retail shipments has been growing over the past decade. Nintendo began shipping videogames that way 10 years ago. But in 2003, with the economy sputtering, retailers strove to keep inventories low. So when an item like "Mario Kart" sold well, some retailers were in a bind, and relied on faster shipping of merchandise to stores to accommodate customers. "Really the biggest time of year for us is November and December," said George Harrison, senior vice president of marketing for Nintendo of America Inc., the U.S. unit of the Japanese company. "If it goes out of stock for a while, customers tend to lose interest in it."

UPS and FedEx have beefed up their services for retail shipments, not only delivering packages to stores on a tight schedule, but also handling customs or packing the goods exactly as the retailer wants. UPS goes so far as to inspect goods for retailers and to put clothes on hangers. Other transport companies are using their extensive delivery networks in new ways to handle direct-to-store shipments. Closely held truckload carrier Schneider National Inc., Green Bay, Wis., sees itself as a "rolling warehouse," delivering goods to retail stores as they are needed, said Tom Nightingale, vice president of marketing for the carrier. Schneider uses the same equipment to load goods on trucks or on trains, which has turned out to be one of the company's strengths as a retail-goods carrier. A shipment in the Schneider network can change its destination without having to be reloaded on different equipment, he said.

Working closely with retail stores to reduce inventory requires implementing expensive technology to track where products are selling the best. Transport companies must have the technology to track shipments and get them to the retailer at a specified time, and manufacturers must install their own tracking systems to match that of the retailers. Suppliers such as Scholastic and Nintendo tend to bear most of the costs of getting goods to the retailer, and in some cases that means paying to store inventory on behalf of the retailers.

As for Nintendo, a 10-year veteran of direct-to-store deliveries, the game maker has managed to pass along some of the shipping costs to retail customers. Marketing head Mr. Harrison said retailers that participate in the direct-to-store shipping program must pay extra, amounting to about 2% of total sales, allowing Nintendo and retailers to share the costs. "We try to show them the benefits" of cutting down on their own inventory and cycling fresh products on the shelves more quickly, he said.

QUESTIONS

1. From the retailer's perspective, what are the dangers of understocking a video game during the holiday season? What are the dangers of overstocking? How do direct shipments, like those described for Nintendo's products,

[9]E. Souder, "Retailers Rely More on Fast Deliveries," *The Wall Street Journal*, January 14, 2004.

help retailers deal with these dangers? Are the retailers simply trading inventory costs for transportation costs? Explain.

2. In addition to supporting tighter delivery schedules, how else are logistics service providers supporting their customers? In your opinion, is this "good" for the long-term competitive position of the logistics providers? Why?
3. What role will information systems play as retailers seek to reduce inventories by receiving smaller, yet more frequent and accurate shipments? What are the implications for the manufacturers and logistics providers who serve the retailers?
4. Currently, Nintendo is able to pass on some of the costs of the faster shipments to the retailers. In the long term, what do you think will happen?

REFERENCES

Books and Articles

Childs, J. "Transportation and Logistics: Your Competitive Advantage or Your Downfall?" *APICS—The Performance Advantage* 6, no. 4 (April 1996): 44–48.

Cox, J. F., and J. H. Blackstone, eds. *APICS Dictionary*, 11th ed. Falls Church, VA: APICS, 2004.

Lenovo Selects D&H Distributing to Carry Its Desktop and Notebook Computers; The D&H/Lenovo Agreement Will Focus on Accelerating the Adoption of Lenovo Computing Products in the SMB Marketplace. *Business Wire*, August 14, 2006.

Maselli, J. "Logistics Gets Cheaper by the Yard." *RFID Journal*, October 20, 2003, **www.rfidjournal.com/article/articleprint/617/-1/1**.

Rodriguez, A. M., D. Bowersox, and R. Calatone. "Estimation of Global and National Logistics Expenditures: 2002 Data Update." *Journal of Business Logistics* 26, no. 2 (2005): 1–15.

Souder, E. "Retailers Rely More on Fast Deliveries." *The Wall Street Journal*, January 14, 2004.

Tibey, S. "How Kraft Built a 'One-Company' Supply Chain." *Supply Chain Management Review* 3, no. 3 (Fall 1999): 34–42.

U.S. Department of Transportation. *National Transportation Statistics 2006*. Washington, DC: April 2006.

Warner, F., and R. Brooks. "Ford Is Hiring UPS to Track Vehicles as They Move from Factories to Dealers." *The Wall Street Journal*, February 2, 2000.

Internet

Council of Supply Chain Management Professionals, **http://cscmp.org/**

J.B. Hunt, **www.jbhunt.com**

Union Pacific Radio, **www.up.com**

PART IV PLANNING AND CONTROLLING OPERATIONS AND SUPPLY CHAINS

CHAPTER 13

Sales and Operations Planning (Aggregate Planning)

CHAPTER OUTLINE

Chapter Objectives

By the end of this chapter, you will be able to:

- Distinguish among strategic planning, tactical planning, and detailed planning and control.
- Describe why sales and operations planning (S&OP) is important to an organization and its supply chain partners.
- Generate multiple alternative sales and operations plans for a firm.
- Describe the differences between top-down and bottom-up S&OP and discuss the strengths and weaknesses of level, chase, and mixed production strategies.
- Discuss the organizational issues that arise when firms decide to incorporate S&OP into their efforts.
- Examine how S&OP can be used to coordinate activities up and down the supply chain.
- Apply optimization modeling techniques to the S&OP process.

COVOLO DIVING GEAR, PART 1

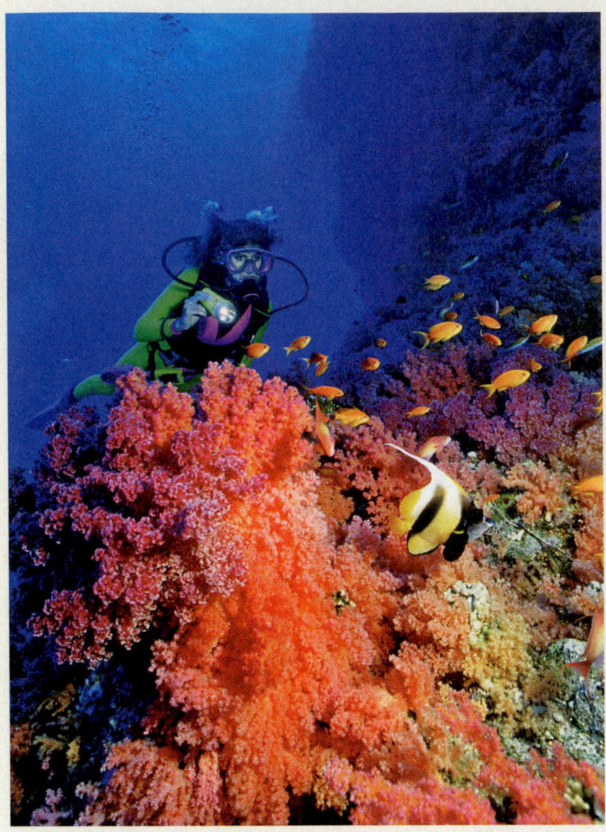

June 1, 2009.—The senior staff members for Covolo Diving Gear were sitting down for their semiannual planning meeting, and as it had been too often before, the mood was tense.

"This is nuts," complained David Griffin, the vice president of manufacturing. "Last January, marketing sat here and presented us with a sales forecast of 30,000 gauge sets each month, so that's what I planned on producing. But by March, they'd upped it to 33,000. How can I be expected to keep a smooth-running manufacturing organization under these conditions? I can't handle another six months like the last."

"We do the best we can, but it's hard to develop a dead-on forecast, especially for more than a few months in advance," countered Patricia Rodriguez, the vice president of marketing. "Besides, manufacturing was able to increase production to only 31,000, even though we both finally agreed on the higher number. Why is *that*?"

"I'll tell you why," said Jack Nelson, head of purchasing. "Each gauge set we make requires special parts that come from Germany, and our German suppliers just can't increase their shipments to us without *some* notice. Next time you guys plan on changing production levels, why don't you include me in on the conversation?"

At this point, Gina Covolo, the CEO, spoke up: "OK, folks, settle down. We work for the same company, remember? I've been reading up on something called sales and operations planning. If I understand it right, it will help us coordinate our efforts better than we have in the past. We will have to meet more often, probably monthly, but if we do it right, we will all be working from the same sales forecast, and we will know exactly what each of our areas has to do to execute the plan. I think that's a whole lot better than getting angry at one another." And to the accompanying groans of everyone in the room, Gina added: "Who knows, we might even be able to keep our heads above water."

INTRODUCTION

Sales and operations planning
A business process that helps firms plan and coordinate operations and supply chain decisions over a tactical time horizon (usually 4 to 12 months out).

Throughout this book, we have emphasized how critical it is to coordinate operations and supply chain decisions with other functional areas and the firm's supply chain partners. This theme appeared in our discussions of strategy, new product development, capacity planning, and process choice, to name a few. This chapter takes the concept of cross-functional and interfirm coordination a step further through a process known as **sales and operations planning** (also called **aggregate planning**). Oliver Wight Americas, Inc., a global management consulting and education firm with deep roots in the supply chain management area, describes it this way:

Aggregate planning
See sales and operations planning.

Sales & Operations Planning is a process led by senior management that, on a monthly basis, evaluates revised, time-phased projections for supply, demand, and the resulting financials. It's a decision-making process that ensures that tactical plans in all business functions are aligned and in support of the business plan. The objective of S&OP is to reach consensus on a single operating plan that allocates the critical resources of people, capacity, materials, time, and money to most effectively meet the marketplace in a profitable way.[1]

We start by describing how sales and operations planning, or S&OP for short, fits into an organization's planning scheme. We then present several methods for generating and selecting plans and for implementing the S&OP process in an organization.

13.1 S&OP IN THE PLANNING CYCLE

Strategic planning
Planning that takes place at the highest levels of the firm, addressing needs that might not arise for years into the future.

Tactical planning
Planning that covers a shorter period, usually four months to a year out, although the planning horizon may be longer in industries with very long lead times (such as engineer-to-order firms).

Detailed planning and control
Planning that covers time periods ranging from weeks, down to just a few hours out into the future.

In most organizations, planning really takes place at several levels, each covering a certain period of time into the future (Figure 13.1). **Strategic planning** takes place at the highest levels of the firm; it addresses needs that might not arise for years into the future. **Tactical planning** covers a shorter period, usually four months to a year out, although the planning horizon may be longer in industries with very long lead times (such as engineer-to-order firms). Tactical planning is typically more detailed, but is constrained by the longer-term strategic decisions. For example, managers responsible for tactical planning might be able to adjust overall inventory or workforce levels, but only within the constraints imposed by such strategic decisions as the size of the facilities and types of processes used.

Detailed planning and control covers time periods ranging from weeks to just a few hours into the future. Because the planning horizon is so short, managers who do detailed planning and control usually have few, if any, options for adjusting capacity levels. Rather, they must try to make the best use of available capacity in order to get as much work done as possible.

The three approaches differ in (1) the time frame covered, (2) the level of planning detail required, and (3) the degree of flexibility managers have to change capacity. See Figure 13.1. Strategic planning has the longest time horizon, has the least amount of specific information (after all, we are planning for years out), and affords managers the greatest degree of flexibility to change capacity. Detailed planning and control is just the opposite: Planning can cover daily or even hourly activity, and the relatively short time horizons leave managers with few, if any, options for changing capacity. Tactical planning fills the gap between these extremes.

Detailed planning and control	Tactical planning	Strategic planning
• Limited ability to adjust capacity • Detailed planning (day to day, hour to hour) • Lowest risk	• Workforce, inventory, subcontracting, and logistics decisions • Planning numbers somewhat "aggregated" (month by month) • Moderate risk	• "Bricks and mortar" and major process choice decisions • Planning done at a very high level (quarterly or yearly) • High risk
Now → *Days/weeks out*	*Months out*	*Years out*

FIGURE 13.1 Different Levels of Planning

[1]"S&OP Gives Caterpillar a Competitive Edge," Oliver Wight Case Study Series, **www.oliverwight.com/client/features/caterpillarna.pdf**.

Top-down planning
An approach to S&OP where a single, aggregated sales forecast drives the planning process. For top-down planning to work, the mix of products or services must be essentially the same from one time period to the next, *or* the products or services to be provided must have very similar resource requirements.

Bottom-up planning
An approach to S&OP that is used when the product/service mix is unstable and resource requirements vary greatly across the offerings. Under such conditions, managers will need to estimate the requirements for each set of products or services separately and then add them up to get an overall picture of the resource requirements.

S&OP is aimed squarely at helping businesses develop superior tactical plans. Specifically:

- **S&OP indicates how the organization will use its tactical capacity resources to meet expected customer demand.** Examples of tactical capacity resources include the size of the workforce, inventory, number of shifts, and even availability of subcontractors.
- **S&OP strikes a balance between the various needs and constraints of the supply chain partners.** For example, S&OP must consider not only customer demand, but also the capabilities of all suppliers, production facilities, and logistics service providers that work together to provide the product or service. The result is a plan that is not only feasible, but also balances costs, delivery, quality, and flexibility.
- **S&OP serves as a coordinating mechanism for the various supply chain partners.** At the end of the S&OP process, there should be common agreement about what each of the affected partners—sales, operations, and finance, as well as key suppliers and transportation providers—needs to do to make the plan a reality. Good S&OP makes it very clear what everyone should—and should not—do. This common agreement allows the different parties to make more detailed decisions with the confidence that their efforts will be consistent with those of other partners.
- **S&OP expresses the business's plans in terms that everyone can understand.** Finance personnel typically think of business activity in terms of cash flows, financial ratios, and other measures of profitability. Marketing managers concentrate on sales levels and market segments, while operations and supply chain managers tend to focus more on the activities associated with the particular products or services being produced. As we shall see, S&OP makes a deliberate effort to express the resulting plans in a format that is easy for all partners to understand and incorporate into their detailed planning efforts.

13.2 MAJOR APPROACHES TO S&OP

There are two major approaches to S&OP: top-down planning and bottom-up planning. Figure 13.2 summarizes the criteria organizations must consider when choosing between the two.

The simplest approach is **top-down planning**. Here a single, aggregated sales forecast drives the planning process. For top-down planning to work, the mix of products or services must be essentially the same from one time period to the next, *or* the products or services to be provided must have very similar resource requirements. The key assumption under top-down planning is that managers can make accurate tactical plans based on the overall forecast and then divide the resources across individual products or services later on, during the detailed planning and control stage.

Bottom-up planning is used when the product/service mix is unstable and resource requirements vary greatly across the offerings. Under such conditions, an *overall* sales forecast is not very helpful in determining resource requirements. Instead, managers will need to estimate the requirements for each set of products or services separately and then add them up to get an overall picture of the resource requirements.

Planning values
Values that decision makers use to translate the sales forecast into resource requirements and to determine the feasibility and costs of alternative sales and operations plans.

Regardless of the approach used, managers will need planning values to carry out the analysis. **Planning values** are values, based on analysis or historical data, that decision makers use to translate the sales forecast into resource requirements and to determine the feasibility and costs of alternative sales and operations plays. Example 13.1 shows one method of developing planning values when the product mix is stable.

FIGURE 13.2 Determining the Appropriate Approach to S&OP

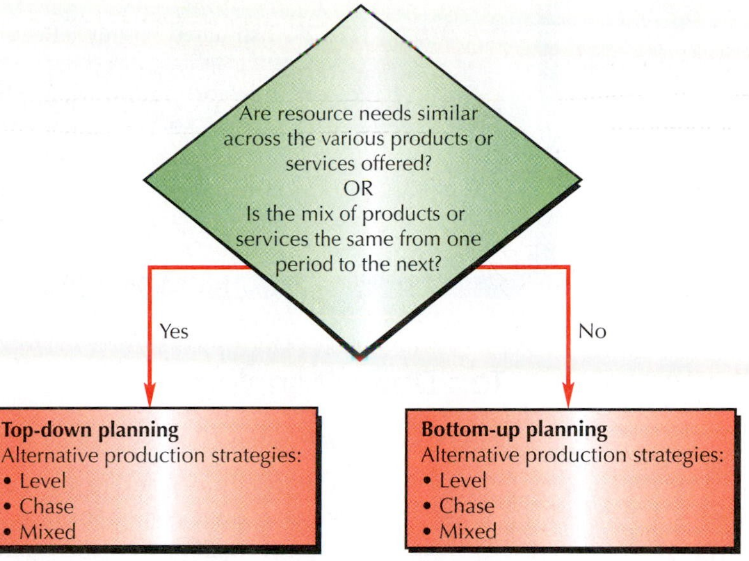

Example 13.1 Calculating Planning Values for Ernie's Electrical

Ernie's Electrical performs three services: cable TV installations, satellite TV installations, and digital subscriber line (DSL) installations. Table 13.1 shows Ernie's service mix, as well as the labor hours and supply costs associated with each type of installation.

TABLE 13.1 Service Mix at Ernie's Electrical

SERVICE DESCRIPTION	SERVICE MIX	LABOR HOURS PER INSTALLATION	SUPPLY COSTS PER INSTALLATION
Cable TV installation	40%	2	\$15
Satellite TV installation	40%	3	\$90
DSL installation	20%	4	\$155

Ernie's service mix is the same from one month to the next. As a result, the company can use a single set of planning values based on the weighted averages of labor hours and supply costs:

Estimated labor hours per installation:

$$40\% * 2 \text{ hours} + 40\% * 3 \text{ hours} + 20\% * 4 \text{ hours} = 2.8 \text{ hours}$$

Estimated supply costs per installation:

$$40\% * \$15 + 40\% * \$90 + 20\% * \$155 = \$73$$

Ernie expects total installations for the next three months to be 150, 175, and 200, respectively. With this sales forecast and the planning values just noted, Ernie can quickly estimate labor hours and supply costs for each month (Table 13.2).

TABLE 13.2 Estimated Resource Requirements at Ernie's Electrical

MONTH	SALES FORECAST (INSTALLATIONS)	LABOR HOURS (2.8 PER INSTALLATION)	SUPPLY COSTS ($73 PER INSTALLATION)
Month 1	150	420	$10,950
Month 2	175	490	$12,775
Month 3	200	560	$14,600

Top-Down Planning

The process for generating a top-down plan consists of three steps:

1. **Develop the aggregate sales forecast and planning values.** Top-down planning starts with the aggregate sales forecast. The planning values are used in the next two steps to help management translate the sales forecast into resource requirements and determine the feasibility and costs of alternative S&OP strategies.
2. **Translate the sales forecast into resource requirements.** The goal of this second step is to move the analysis from "sales" numbers to the "operations and supply chain" numbers needed for tactical planning. Some typical resources include labor hours, equipment hours, and material dollars, to name a few.
3. **Generate alternative production plans.** In this step, management determines the feasibility and costs for various production plans. We will describe three particular approaches—level production, chase production, and mixed production—in more detail later.

We illustrate top-down planning through a series of examples for a fictional manufacturer, Pennington Cabinets.

Example 13.2

Developing the Aggregate Sales Forecast and Planning Values for Pennington Cabinets

Pennington Cabinets is a manufacturer of several different lines of kitchen and bathroom cabinets that are sold through major home improvement retailers. Pennington's marketing vice president has come up with the following combined sales forecast for the next 12 months:

MONTH	SALES FORECAST (CABINET SETS)
January	750
February	760
March	800
April	800
May	820
June	840
July	910
August	910
September	910
October	880
November	860
December	840

Under top-down planning, managers base the planning process on *aggregated* sales figures such as those just shown. For example, January's forecast value of 750 reflects total expected demand across Pennington's *entire* line of cabinets. The primary advantage of top-down planning is that it allows managers to see the relationships among overall demand, production, and inventory levels. There will be plenty of time to do detailed planning and control later on.

In addition to the sales forecast, Pennington has also developed the planning values shown in Table 13.3.

TABLE 13.3 Planning Values for Pennington Cabinets

Cabinet Set Planning Values	
Regular production cost:	$2000 per cabinet set
Overtime production cost:	$2062 per cabinet set
Average monthly inventory holding cost:	$40 per cabinet set
Average labor hours per cabinet set:	20 hours
Production Planning Values	
Maximum regular production per month:	848 cabinet sets
Allowable overtime production per month:	1/10 of regular production
Workforce Planning Values	
Hours worked per month per employee:	160 hours
Estimated cost to hire a worker:	$1750
Estimated cost to lay off a worker:	$1500

Planning values such as these are often developed from company records, detailed analysis, and managerial experience. "Average labor hours per cabinet," for example, may be derived by looking at past production results, while "Maximum regular production per month" might be based on a detailed analysis of manufacturing capacity. In contrast, the human resources (HR) manager might use data on recruiting, interviewing, and training costs to develop estimates of hiring and layoff costs.

The sales forecast shows an expected peak from July through September. As stated in the planning values, Pennington can produce up to 848 cabinet sets a month using regular production time. Figure 13.3 graphs the expected sales level against maximum regular production per month.

FIGURE 13.3 Graphing Expected Sales Levels versus Capacity

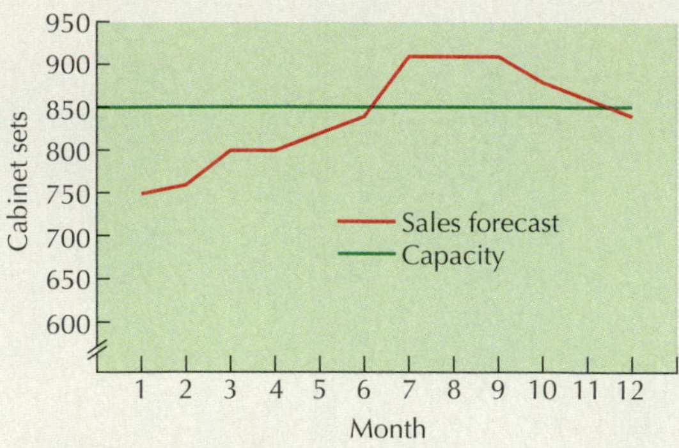

The implication of Figure 13.3 is clear: Pennington won't be able to meet expected demand in the peak months with just regular production.

Example 13.3

Translating the Sales Forecast into Resource Requirements at Pennington Cabinets

The next step for Pennington is to translate the sales forecast into resource requirements. The key resource Pennington is concerned about is labor, although other resources could be examined, depending on the needs of the firm. Translating sales into labor hours and, ultimately, workers needed allows Pennington to see how demand drives resource requirements. Table 13.4 shows the start of this process.

TABLE 13.4 Translating Sales Forecast into Resource Requirements, Pennington Cabinets

MONTH	SALES FORECAST	SALES (IN LABOR HOURS)	SALES (IN WORKERS)
January	750	15,000	93.75
February	760	15,200	95.00
March	800	16,000	100.00
April	800 →	16,000 →	100.00
May	820	16,400	102.50
June	840	16,800	105.00
July	910	18,200	113.75
August	910	18,200	113.75
September	910	18,200	113.75
October	880	17,600	110.00
November	860	17,200	107.50
December	840	16,800	105.00

To illustrate, April's demand represents (20 hours per cabinet)(800 cabinets) = 16,000 labor hours. If every worker works 160 hours a month, this is the equivalent of (16,000 labor hours)/(160 hours) = 100 workers.

Level, Chase, and Mixed Production Plans

Level production plan
A sales and operations plan in which production is held constant and inventory is used to absorb differences between production and the sales forecast.

Chase production plan
A sales and operations plan in which production is changed in each time period to match the sales forecast.

Mixed production plan
A sales and operations plan that varies both production and inventory levels in an effort to develop the most effective plan.

Once a firm has translated the sales forecast into resource requirements, generate alternative production plans. Three common approaches are the level pr chase production, and mixed production plans. The fundamental difference among the three is how production and inventory levels are allowed to vary.

Under a **level production plan**, production is held constant, and inventory is used to absorb differences between production and the sales forecast. This approach is best suited to an environment in which changing the production level is impossible or extremely costly (such as an oil refinery) and the cost of holding inventory is relatively low.

A **chase production plan** is just the opposite. Here production is changed in each time period to match the sales forecast in each time period. The result is that production "chases" demand. This approach is best suited to environments in which holding inventory is extremely expensive or impossible (as with services) or the costs of changing production levels are relatively low.

A mixed production plan falls between these two extremes. Specifically, a **mixed production plan** will vary both production and inventory levels in an effort to develop the most effective plan.

Example 13.4

Generating a Level Production Plan for Pennington Cabinets

After translating the sales forecast into resource requirements (Table 13.4), Pennington management decides to generate a level production plan. Pennington starts off January with 100 workers and 100 cabinet sets in inventory and wants to end the planning cycle with these numbers. Table 13.5 shows a completed level production plan for Pennington Cabinets. Following is a discussion of the highlights of this plan.

Actual Workers and Regular Production. Under the level production plan, the actual workforce is held constant at 105. Why 105? Because 105 represents the average workforce required over the 12-month planning horizon. By maintaining a workforce of 105 workers, Pennington produces:

$$105(160 \text{ hours per month}/20 \text{ hours per set}) = 840 \text{ sets per month}$$

or

$$(840 \text{ sets per month})(12 \text{ months}) = 10{,}080 \text{ cabinet sets for the year}$$

You may have noticed that this total matches sales for the entire year. The difference, of course, is in the *timing* of the production and the sales; inventory builds up when sales are less than the production level and drains down when sales outstrip production. Finally, with 105 workers, Pennington comes close to reaching the regular production maximum of 848 cabinet sets per month, but doesn't exceed it.

Hirings and Layoffs. Whenever the workforce level changes, Pennington must hire or release workers. This occurs at two different times in the level production plan. In January, Pennington hires 5 workers to bring the workforce up to 105 from the initial level of 100. To bring the workforce back down to its starting level, Pennington fires 5 workers at the end of December. While this may seem unrealistic, doing so (at least for calculation purposes) ensures Pennington that it will be able to compare alternative plans under the same beginning and ending conditions.

ABLE 13.5 Level Production Plan for Pennington Cabinets

MONTH	SALES FORECAST	SALES (IN LABOR HOURS)	SALES (IN WORKERS)	ACTUAL WORKERS	REGULAR PRODUCTION	ALLOWABLE OVERTIME PRODUCTION	OVERTIME PRODUCTION	HIRINGS	LAYOFFS	INVENTORY/ BACK ORDERS
				100.00						100.00
January	750	15,000	93.75	105.00	840.00	84.00	0	5.00	0.00	190.00
February	760	15,200	95.00	105.00	840.00	84.00	0	0.00	0.00	270.00
March	800	16,000	100.00	105.00	840.00	84.00	0	0.00	0.00	310.00
April	800	16,000	100.00	105.00	840.00	84.00	0	0.00	0.00	350.00
May	820	16,400	102.50	105.00	840.00	84.00	0	0.00	0.00	370.00
June	840	16,800	105.00	105.00	840.00	84.00	0	0.00	0.00	370.00
July	910	18,200	113.75	105.00	840.00	84.00	0	0.00	0.00	300.00
August	910	18,200	113.75	105.00	840.00	84.00	0	0.00	0.00	230.00
September	910	18,200	113.75	105.00	840.00	84.00	0	0.00	0.00	160.00
October	880	17,600	110.00	105.00	840.00	84.00	0	0.00	0.00	120.00
November	860	17,200	107.50	105.00	840.00	84.00	0	0.00	0.00	100.00
December	840	16,800	105.00	105.00	840.00	84.00	0	0.00	0.00	100.00
								0	5	
Totals:	10,080				10,080		0	5	5	2,870

INVENTORY LEVELS. The ending inventory level in any month is calculated as follows:

$$EI_t = EI_{t-1} + RP_t + OP_t - S_t \qquad [13\text{-}1]$$

where:

EI_t = ending inventory for time period t
RP_t = regular production in time period t
OP_t = overtime production in time period t
S_t = sales in time period t

For January

$$\begin{aligned} EI_{\text{January}} &= EI_{\text{December}} + RP_{\text{January}} + OP_{\text{January}} - S_{\text{January}} \\ &= 100 + 840 + 0 - 750 = 190 \text{ cabinet sets} \end{aligned}$$

Likewise, the ending inventory for February is:

$$\begin{aligned} EI_{\text{February}} &= EI_{\text{January}} + RP_{\text{February}} + OP_{\text{February}} - S_{\text{February}} \\ &= 190 + 840 + 0 - 760 = 270 \text{ cabinet sets} \end{aligned}$$

As expected, the level production plan builds up inventory from January through May (when production exceeds sales) and then drains it down during the peak months of July through December. But look at the ending inventory levels for each month: They are all greater than zero, suggesting that Pennington is holding more cabinet sets than it needs. This may seem wasteful at first glance. But remember that Pennington is developing a plan based on *forecasted* sales. The extra inventory protects the company if actual sales turn out to be higher than the forecast. Otherwise, Pennington might not be able to meet all the demand, resulting in back orders or even lost sales.

The Cost of the Plan. Of course, Pennington has no way of knowing at this point whether a level production plan is the best plan or not. To do so, management will need some way to compare competing plans. Management starts this process by calculating the costs of the level production plan, using the planning values in Table 13.3.

Regular Production Costs	
10,080 cabinet sets ($2000) =	$20,160,000
Hiring and Layoff Costs	
5 hirings($1750) + 5 layoffs ($1500) =	$16,250
Inventory Holding Costs	
2870 cabinet sets ($40) =	$114,800
Total:	$20,291,050

Example 13.5

Generating a Chase Production Plan for Pennington Cabinets

Table 13.6 shows a chase production plan for Pennington Cabinets. Notice that the first four columns are identical to those for the level production plan (Table 13.5). However, results for the remaining columns are quite different:

- Actual workforce production and overtime production vary so that total production essentially matches sales for each month. Because total production "chases" sales, inventory never builds up as it did under the level production plan. In fact, it never gets higher than 106 cabinet sets.
- From July through November, monthly sales are higher than the maximum regular production level of 848. Under the chase approach, Pennington will need to make up the difference through overtime production.
- While the chase production plan keeps inventory levels low, it results in more hirings and layoffs and in overtime production costs.
- Because Pennington can't hire fractional workers, the company can't always *exactly* match production to sales. In this example, Pennington ends up with slightly more cabinet sets in inventory at the end of the planning period (106 versus 100). Still, this is close enough to compare with other plans.

The cost calculations for the chase production plan follow. In this case, 9856 cabinet sets were produced through regular production, while the remaining 230 were produced using overtime.

TABLE 13.6 Chase Production Plan for Pennington Cabinets

MONTH	SALES FORECAST	SALES (IN LABOR HOURS)	SALES (IN WORKERS)	ACTUAL WORKERS	REGULAR PRODUCTION	ALLOWABLE OVERTIME PRODUCTION	OVERTIME PRODUCTION	HIRINGS	LAYOFFS	INVENTORY/ BACK ORDERS
				100.00						100.00
January	750	15,000	93.75	94.00	752.00	75.20	0	0.00	6.00	102.00
February	760	15,200	95.00	95.00	760.00	76.00	0	1.00	0.00	102.00
March	800	16,000	100.00	100.00	800.00	80.00	0	5.00	0.00	102.00
April	800	16,000	100.00	100.00	800.00	80.00	0	0.00	0.00	102.00
May	820	16,400	102.50	103.00	824.00	82.40	0	3.00	0.00	106.00
June	840	16,800	105.00	105.00	840.00	84.00	0	2.00	0.00	106.00
July	910	18,200	113.75	106.00	848.00	84.80	62	1.00	0.00	106.00
August	910	18,200	113.75	106.00	848.00	84.80	62	0.00	0.00	106.00
September	910	18,200	113.75	106.00	848.00	84.80	62	0.00	0.00	106.00
October	880	17,600	110.00	106.00	848.00	84.80	32	0.00	0.00	106.00
November	860	17,200	107.50	106.00	848.00	84.80	12	0.00	0.00	106.00
December	840	16,800	105.00	105.00	840.00	84.00	0	0.00	1.00	106.00
								0	5	
Totals:	10,080				9856		230	12	12	1256

Regular Production Costs	
9856 cabinet sets ($2000) =	$19,712,000
Overtime Production Costs	
230 cabinet sets ($2062) =	$474,260
Hiring and Layoff Costs	
12 hirings($1,750) + 12 layoffs ($1500) =	$39,000
Inventory Holding Costs	
1256 cabinet sets ($40) =	$50,240
Total:	$20,275,500

Example 13.6

Generating a Mixed Production Plan for Pennington Cabinets

In the real world, the best plan will probably be something other than a level or chase plan. A mixed production plan varies both production and inventory levels in an effort to develop the best plan. Because there are many different ways to do this, the number of potential mixed plans is essentially limitless.

Suppose Pennington's workers have strong reservations about working overtime during the summer months, a chief requirement under the chase plan. The mixed production plan shown in Table 13.7 limits overtime to just 12 cabinet sets per month in October and

TABLE 13.7 Mixed Production Plan for Pennington Cabinets

MONTH	SALES FORECAST	SALES (IN LABOR HOURS)	SALES (IN WORKERS)	ACTUAL WORKERS	REGULAR PRODUCTION	ALLOWABLE OVERTIME PRODUCTION	OVERTIME PRODUCTION	HIRINGS	LAYOFFS	INVENTORY/ BACK ORDERS
				100.00						100.00
January	750	15,000	93.75	100.00	800.00	80.00	0	0.00	0.00	150.00
February	760	15,200	95.00	100.00	800.00	80.00	0	0.00	0.00	190.00
March	800	16,000	100.00	103.00	824.00	82.40	0	3.00	0.00	214.00
April	800	16,000	100.00	106.00	848.00	84.80	0	3.00	0.00	262.00
May	820	16,400	102.50	106.00	848.00	84.80	0	0.00	0.00	290.00
June	840	16,800	105.00	106.00	848.00	84.80	0	0.00	0.00	298.00
July	910	18,200	113.75	106.00	848.00	84.80	0	0.00	0.00	236.00
August	910	18,200	113.75	106.00	848.00	84.80	0	0.00	0.00	174.00
September	910	18,200	113.75	106.00	848.00	84.80	0	0.00	0.00	112.00
October	880	17,600	110.00	106.00	848.00	84.80	12	0.00	0.00	92.00
November	860	17,200	107.50	106.00	848.00	84.80	12	0.00	0.00	92.00
December	840	16,800	105.00	106.00	848.00	84.80	0	0.00	0.00	100.00
								0	6	
Totals:	10,080				10,056		24	6	6	2,210.00

November. This is just one example of the type of qualitative issues any management team must consider when developing a sales and operations plan.

The cost of the mixed production strategy is

Regular Production Costs	
10,056 cabinet sets ($2000) =	$20,112,000
Overtime Production Costs	
24 cabinet sets ($2062) =	$49,488
Hiring and Layoff Costs	
6 hirings ($1750) + 6 layoffs ($1500) =	$19,500
Inventory Holding Costs	
2210 cabinet sets ($40) =	$88,400
Total:	$20,269,388

Bottom-Up Planning

Top-down planning works well in situations where planners can use a single set of planning values to estimate resource requirements and costs. But what happens when this is not the case? As noted earlier, bottom-up planning is used when the products or services have different resource requirements *and* the mix is unstable from one period to the next. The steps for generating a bottom-up plan are similar to those for creating a top-down plan. The main difference is that the resource requirements for each product or service must be evaluated individually and then added up across all products or services to get a picture of overall requirements.

Example 13.7

Philips Toys

Philips Toys produces a summer toy line and a winter toy line. Machine and labor requirements for each product line are given in Table 13.8.

TABLE 13.8 Machine and Labor Requirements for Philips Toys

PRODUCT LINE	MACHINE HOURS/UNIT	LABOR HOURS/UNIT
Summer toys	0.75	0.25
Winter toys	0.85	2.00

Both product lines have fairly similar machine hour requirements. However, they differ greatly with regard to labor requirements—products in the winter line need, on average, eight times as much labor.

The difference in labor requirements becomes important when the product mix changes. Look at the data in Table 13.9. Even though the *aggregate* forecast across both product lines is 700 units each month, the product mix changes as Philips moves into and then out of the summer season. The impact on resource requirements can be seen in the labor hours needed each month.

TABLE 13.9 Forecasted Demand and Resulting Resource Needs for Philips Toys

	Forecast				
MONTH	SUMMER LINE	WINTER LINE	AGGREGATE FORECAST	MACHINE HOURS	LABOR HOURS
January	0	700	700	595	1400
February	100	600	700	585	1225
March	500	200	700	545	525
April	700	0	700	525	175
May	700	0	700	525	175
June	700	0	700	525	175
July	700	0	700	525	175
August	500	200	700	545	525
September	400	300	700	555	700
October	200	500	700	575	1050
November	0	700	700	595	1400
December	0	700	700	595	1400

Load profile
A display of future capacity requirements based on released and/or planned orders over a given span of time.

Figure 13.4 graphs the projected machine hours and labor hours shown in Table 13.9. Such graphs are often referred to as load profiles. A **load profile** is a display of future capacity requirements based on released and/or planned orders over a given span of time.[2] As the load profiles suggest, machine hour requirements are fairly constant throughout the year. This is because both product lines have similar machine time requirements. In contrast,

[2] J. F. Cox and J. H. Blackstone, eds., *APICS Dictionary*, 10th ed. (Falls Church, VA: APICS, 2002).

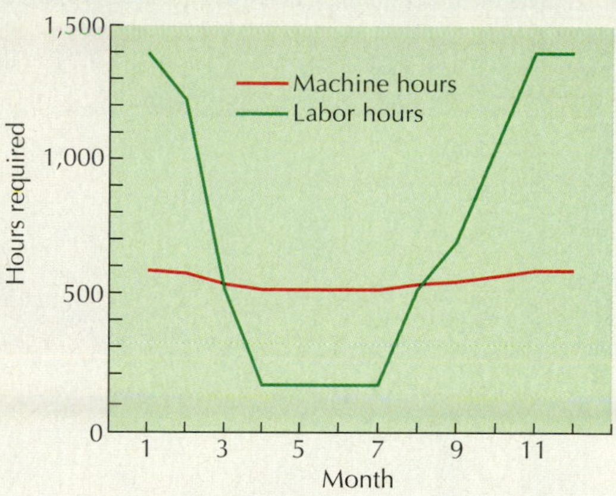

FIGURE 13.4 Load Profiles at Philips Toys

the load profile for labor dips dramatically in the summer months, reflecting the lower labor requirements associated with the summer product line.

To develop a sales and operations plan, Philips will need to maintain a separate set of planning values for each product line it produces and then total up the requirements. The rest of the planning process will be very similar to top-down planning. Philips will probably have to choose between adjusting the workforce to avoid excess labor costs in the summer months and finding some way to smooth the labor requirements, perhaps by making more winter toys in the summer months. This, however, will drive up inventory levels.

Cash Flow Analysis

Net cash flow
The net flow of dollars into or out of a business over some time period.

We stated earlier that one of the key benefits of S&OP is that it expresses the business plans in a common language that all partners can understand. Consider, for instance, the finance area. Among its many responsibilities, finance is charged with making sure that the business has the cash it needs to carry out the sales and operations plan and that any excess cash is put to good use. As such, finance personnel are very interested in assessing the net cash flow for any production plan. **Net cash flow** is defined as the net flow of dollars into or out of a business over some time period. In algebraic form:

$$\text{Net cash flow} = \text{cash inflows} - \text{cash outflows} \quad [13\text{-}2]$$

Example 13.8 Cash Flow Analysis at Pennington Cabinets

Pennington sells each cabinet set for $2800, on average. Management has already determined that the regular production cost for a cabinet set is $2000, the overtime production cost is $2062, and the monthly holding cost per cabinet set is $40 (Table 13.3).

Now suppose that Pennington incurs these revenues and expenses in the month they occur. That is, each sale of a cabinet set generates a cash inflow of $2800, while each cabinet set produced and each cabinet set held in inventory generates cash outflows of $2000 ($2062 if overtime is used) and $40, respectively. Table 13.10 shows a simplified cash flow analysis for the mixed production plan in Table 13.7.

TABLE 13.10 Cash Flow Analysis for Pennington Cabinets, Mixed Production Plan

MONTH	SALES FORECAST	REGULAR PRODUCTION	OVERTIME PRODUCTION	INVENTORY/ BACK ORDERS	CASH INFLOWS	CASH OUTFLOWS	NET FLOW	CUMULATIVE NET FLOW
January	750	800	0	150	2,100,000	1,606,000	494,000	494,000
February	760	800	0	190	2,128,000	1,607,600	520,400	1,014,400
March	800	824	0	214	2,240,000	1,656,560	583,440	1,597,840
April	800	848	0	262	2,240,000	1,706,480	533,520	2,131,360
May	820	848	0	290	2,296,000	1,707,600	588,400	2,719,760
June	840	848	0	298	2,352,000	1,707,920	644,080	3,363,840
July	910	848	0	236	2,548,000	1,705,440	842,560	4,206,400
August	910	848	0	174	2,548,000	1,702,960	845,040	5,051,440
September	910	848	0	112	2,548,000	1,700,480	847,520	5,898,960
October	880	848	12	92	2,464,000	1,724,424	739,576	6,638,536
November	860	848	12	92	2,408,000	1,724,424	683,576	7,322,112
December	840	848	0	100	2,352,000	1,700,000	652,000	7,974,112

To illustrate, the net cash flow calculation for January is

Net cash flow = cash inflows – cash outflows
= Sales revenues – regular production costs – overtime production costs – inventory holding costs
= \$2,800 (750 cabinet sets) – \$2,000 (800 cabinet sets) – \$2,062 (0 cabinet sets) – \$40 (150 cabinet sets)
= \$2,100,000 – \$1,600,000 – \$0 – \$6,000 = \$494,000

Applying the same logic, the net cash flow in February is \$520,400. Finally, Pennington can calculate the cumulative net cash flow through February as \$494,000 + \$520,400 = \$1,014,400. The cash flow analysis expresses the sales and operations plan in terms meaningful to financial managers. In this case, the cabinet set business is expected to generate anywhere from around \$500,000 to \$850,000 in positive cash flow each month and nearly \$8 million over the course of the year. These additional funds can be used to cover other expenses, retire debt, or perhaps support additional business investments.

Now let's consider an alternative scenario, shown in Table 13.11. Everything, including total sales for the 12-month planning period, is the same as before, except now the *timing* of the sales has changed. Specifically, sales in the first half of the year are much lower than previously, while sales increase dramatically in the last half.

The new sales pattern results in *negative* net cash flows for the first three months of the year and a cumulative negative net cash flow that does not disappear until May. In this case, finance will need to find the funds necessary to support this particular plan, or the company will need to go back and develop an alternative sales and operations plan that is not as burdensome. Finally, you may have noticed that the net cash flow at the end of the year is lower than before (\$7,766,512 versus \$7,974,112). The difference is due to the fact that the second plan results in higher inventory holding costs. Figure 13.5 compares the cash flow results for Tables 13.10 and 13.11.

TABLE 13.11 Cash Flow Analysis for Pennington Cabinets, *Different Sales Pattern*

MONTH	SALES FORECAST	REGULAR PRODUCTION	OVERTIME PRODUCTION	INVENTORY/ BACK ORDERS	CASH INFLOWS	CASH OUTFLOWS	NET FLOW	CUMULATIVE NET FLOW
January	*500*	800	0	400	1,400,000	1,616,000	(216,000)	(216,000)
February	*520*	800	0	680	1,456,000	1,627,200	(171,200)	(387,200)
March	*550*	824	0	954	1,540,000	1,686,160	(146,160)	(533,360)
April	*700*	848	0	1102	1,960,000	1,740,080	219,920	(313,440)
May	*880*	848	0	1070	2,464,000	1,738,800	725,200	411,760
June	*960*	848	0	958	2,688,000	1,734,320	953,680	1,365,440
July	*1040*	848	0	766	2,912,000	1,726,640	1,185,360	2,550,800
August	*1040*	848	0	574	2,912,000	1,718,960	1,193,040	3,743,840
September	*1040*	848	0	382	2,912,000	1,711,280	1,200,720	4,944,560
October	*980*	848	12	262	2,744,000	1,731,224	1,012,776	5,957,336
November	*970*	848	12	152	2,716,000	1,726,824	989,176	6,946,512
December	*900*	848	0	100	2,520,000	1,700,000	820,000	7,766,512

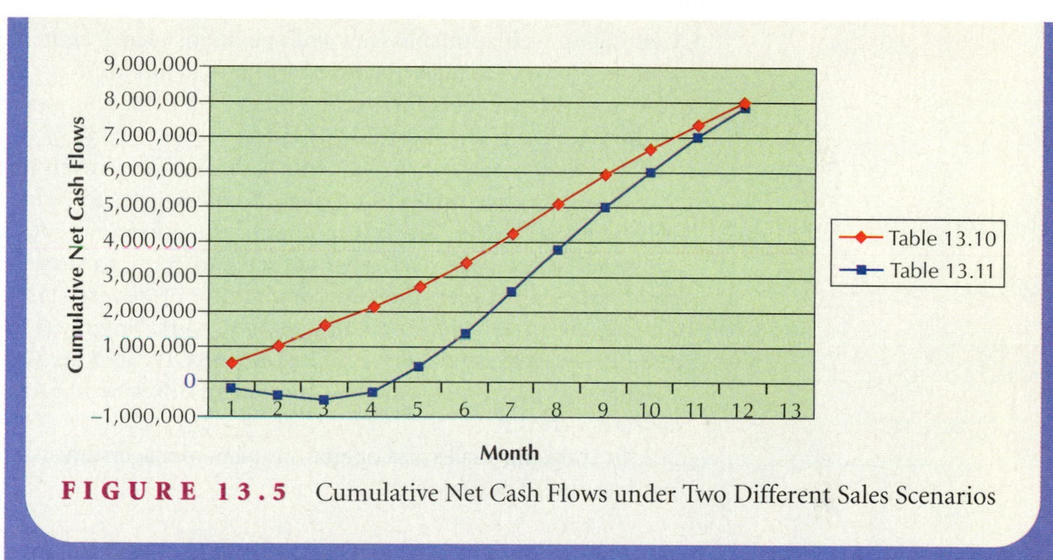

FIGURE 13.5 Cumulative Net Cash Flows under Two Different Sales Scenarios

13.3 ORGANIZING FOR AND IMPLEMENTING S&OP

We have spent a fair amount of time describing the basic calculations associated with S&OP. But S&OP is more than just "running the numbers." Richard Ling put it best when he stated, "S&OP is a people process supported by information."[3] In this section, we address some critical organizational questions associated with S&OP:

- How do we choose between alternative plans?
- How often should S&OP be done?
- How do we implement S&OP in our business environment?

[3]R. Ling, "For True Enterprise Integration, Turn First to SOP," *APICS—The Performance Advantage* 10, no. 3 (March 2000): 40–45.

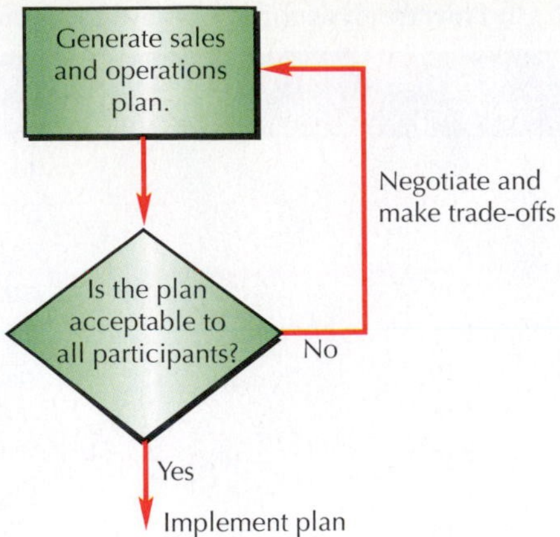

FIGURE 13.6
Fine-Tuning the Sales and Operations Plan

Choosing between Alternative Plans

Coming up with a suitable sales and operations plan is an iterative process. The organization may have to change a plan several times before coming up with a plan that is acceptable to all parties. This fine-tuning often means that decision makers will need to make trade-offs. Figure 13.6 illustrates this idea.

A classic example is the trade-off between inventory and customer service. Suppose that after reviewing a plan, finance wants to reduce inventory levels further to bring costs down. Marketing might raise concerns that this could potentially hurt customer service. All parties would have to come to some agreement concerning the right balance between the two competing objectives—cost and customer service. As another example, operations might want marketing to use pricing and promotion to smooth out peaks and valleys in demand. S&OP could be used to see if the cost of these pricing and promotion efforts is more than offset by improvements in production and inventory costs.

In choosing a sales and operations plan, managers must consider all aspects of a plan, not just costs. For example:

- What impact will the plan have on supply chain partners such as key suppliers and transportation providers? This could be particularly important if production levels vary considerably from one period to the next.
- What are cash flows like? Some plans may be profitable at the end of the planning cycle, but still include periods of time where cash expenses exceed revenues. We discussed earlier how cash flow analysis can be used to evaluate such plans.
- Do our supply chain partners and our own firm have the space needed to hold any planned inventories?
- Does the plan contain significant changes in the workforce? If so, what would be the impact on workforce satisfaction and productivity? Could the Human Resources department handle it?
- How flexible is the plan? That is, how easy or difficult would it be to modify the plan as conditions warrant?

This is just a small sample of the kinds of questions that need to be addressed, but it raises a key point: *Sales and operations plans help managers make a decision. They do not make the decisions for managers.*

Example 13.9

Selecting a Plan at Pennington Cabinets

Table 13.12 summarizes the costs, strengths, and weaknesses of the three alternative production strategies we developed for Pennington Cabinets (Examples 13.4 through 13.6). For all practical purposes, the costs are too close for us to say that one plan is clearly cheapest. After all, these are plans based on *forecasts* and planning values that represent, at best, rough estimates of resource requirements and costs. The point is, we can almost guarantee that actual results will be different.

TABLE 13.12 Summary of Alternative Plans at Pennington Cabinet

	LEVEL PLAN	CHASE PLAN	MIXED PLAN
Regular production costs	$20,160,000	$19,712,000	$20,112,000
Overtime production costs	0	$474,260	$49,488
Hiring and layoff costs	$16,250	$39,000	$19,500
Inventory costs	$114,800	$50,240	$88,400
Total costs	$20,291,050	$20,275,500	$20,269,388
Key factors	Flat production level. Inventory levels grow as high as 370 cabinet sets.	Minimal inventory. Significant overtime required in peak months.	Reasonably stable production. Inventory levels grow, but not as high as under pure level approach. Some overtime required.

To choose a plan, then, Pennington will need to consider other factors. The level plan has the advantage of consistency because the same amount is made each and every month. This eases production planning and allows for workforce stability for Pennington and its partners. Furthermore, it allows Pennington to avoid expensive overtime, but at the cost of holding additional inventory. The buildup of inventory under the level plan does pose a risk: What if actual demand takes a sharp downturn later in the year? If this happens, Pennington will have to cut production drastically or risk being stuck with expensive, unwanted inventory.

The chase plan is just the opposite. Inventory levels never rise much above 100 (the starting level), but production levels vary anywhere from 752 in January to 910 in each month of the third quarter. Such instability in production and workforce levels may have unanticipated consequences.

The mixed plan strikes a balance between these extremes. Inventory levels increase over the slower months, but not as drastically as under the level approach. Similarly, the mixed plan uses overtime production, but not to the same extent as the chase plan. Based on these results, Pennington management might select a plan, or even go back and develop another mixed plan in order to derive an even better solution.

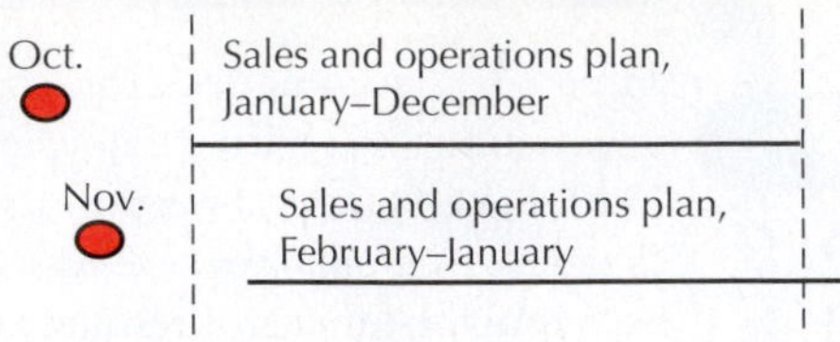

FIGURE 13.7
Updating the Sales and Operations Plan

Rolling Planning Horizons

Sales and operations plans *must* be updated on a regular basis to remain current. Most firms do this by establishing a **rolling planning horizon**, requiring them to update the sales and operations plan on a monthly or quarterly basis. For example, suppose it is now the beginning of October and Pennington has just completed the sales and operations plan for January through December of next year. (*Note*: October, November, and December are so close in time that they fall under detailed planning and control, discussed in Chapter 15). At the beginning of November, Pennington's planning team might come together and revisit the plan, rolling it forward one month and planning for February through January. Figure 13.7 illustrates the idea. By establishing a rolling planning horizon, firms can fine-tune the sales and operations plan as new information becomes available.

Implementing S&OP in the Organization

We have already discussed the steps involved in generating a sales and operations plan. But before these steps can even occur, managers have to commit themselves to the S&OP process. Furthermore, managers have to realize that excellent S&OP is an organizational skill that can take months, if not years, to develop. Ling describes the implementation of S&OP as a three-phase process:[4]

- Developing the foundation;
- Integrating and streamlining the process; and
- Gaining a competitive advantage.

Developing the Foundation. In the first phase, companies build the managerial support and infrastructure needed to make S&OP a success. Key steps include educating all participants about the benefits of S&OP, identifying the appropriate product or service families to plan around, and establishing the information systems needed to provide accurate planning values. Ling stresses the point that even though this phase typically takes six to nine months, many companies never progress further because "they expect the process to work immediately and don't establish the right quality and timing of information."[5]

Integrating and Streamlining the Process. In the second phase, S&OP becomes part of the organization's normal planning activities. Managers become accustomed to updating the plan on a regular basis and, more important, they use the planning results to guide key demand and resource decisions. The sales and operations plan becomes a focal point for cross-functional coordination. Managers also look for ways to improve the S&OP process

[4]Ibid.
[5]Ibid.

further. As Ling puts it, "[B]ecause implementing a process like this may not yield the right structure and organization on the first attempt, some restructuring and streamlining usually occurs at this point."

Gaining a Competitive Advantage. Finally, a few companies reach the point where their S&OP process actually becomes a source of competitive advantage—a core competency, if you will. Companies know they have reached this last phase when:[6]

- There is a well-integrated demand planning process, including the use of forecasting models;
- Continuous improvement is planned and monitored as an integral part of the S&OP process;
- Capital equipment planning can be triggered at any time; and
- "What if" analyses are a way of life and the S&OP database is networked to provide ready access to S&OP data.

The last two points deserve further discussion. Capital equipment decisions typically fall under the auspices of strategic planning. Yet S&OP can give managers an "early warning" when changes in long-term capacity are needed. Pennington's sales and operations plans (Examples 13.4 through 13.6) all show that demand is bumping up against the company's capacity limits. Top management can use this information to start planning for additional investments in manufacturing capacity.

Finally, most organizations that perform S&OP for any length of time end up developing relatively sophisticated databases and decision tools to support their efforts. These tools, in turn, often give managers greater power to perform "what if" analyses, in which the sales forecasts or even the planning values themselves can be varied in an effort to see how the plan reacts. The result is even more robust sales and operations plans.

13.4 SERVICES CONSIDERATIONS

In many ways, S&OP is even more critical in a service environment than it is in manufacturing. Services cannot be built ahead of time and stored in inventory. An empty airline seat or unused hour of a service technician's time is lost forever. For this reason, service capacity must be closely matched to demand in every period. The effect is to limit most services to following some form of a chase production plan.

Still, services do have many options for aligning resources with demand. These options fall into two camps:

- Making sales match capacity, and
- Making capacity (typically the workforce) match sales.

Making Sales Match Capacity

Yield management
An approach commonly used by services with highly perishable "products," in which prices are regularly adjusted to maximize total profit.

Firms have long used pricing and promotion to bring sales in line with production capacity. **Yield management** is an approach commonly used by services with *highly perishable* "products," such as airlines and hotels. These services have a real incentive to make sure every unit of capacity—whether it is an airline seat on the next flight or a hotel room for tonight—contributes to the firm's bottom line.

[6]Ibid.

Services with highly perishable "products," such as a ski resort, often vary the prices of their services to smooth out demand and maximize profits.

Put simply, the goal of yield management is to maximize total profit, where:

Total profit = (average profit per service unit sold)(number of service units sold)

Here's how it works. When demand levels are lower than expected, yield management systems boost demand by lowering the price, but *only if* the expected result is an increase in total profit. Conversely, when demand is higher than expected, prices are raised, but *only if* the expected result is higher total profit.

The idea seems pretty straightforward, but what makes yield management distinctive is the level of sophistication involved. The airline and hotel industries, in particular, have complex yield management systems that regularly and automatically adjust the price of their services for unbooked capacity in an effort to maximize total profit. If you have ever booked a hotel room or made a plane reservation, only to have the price for new reservations change two days later, you have seen yield management in action.

Tiered workforce
A strategy used to vary workforce levels, where additional full-time or part-time employees are hired during peak demand periods, while a smaller, permanent staff is maintained year-round.

Offloading
A strategy for reducing and smoothing out workforce requirements by having the customers perform part of the work themselves.

Making Capacity Match Sales

We have already seen how overtime can be used to vary capacity. Another method is to use a **tiered workforce**. For example, some service organizations hire additional full-time or part-time employees during peak demand periods, while maintaining a smaller, permanent staff year-round. This is common in the retailing, hospitality, and agricultural industries.

Other services use **offloading** to shift part of the work to the customer. Examples include companies that have customers deliver and assemble their own furniture (IKEA) and handle their own financial transactions over the Web (Fidelity Investments). Not only does this *reduce* overall workforce requirements for the service firm, but also it helps to *smooth out* workforce requirements. This is because the customer acts like a part-time employee, showing up just when the demand occurs.

By selling furniture unassembled, IKEA is able to offload part of the manufacturing task to the consumer, thereby holding costs down.

Example 13.10

Service Offloading at Adam's Carpet Cleaning Service

It takes Adam's Carpet Cleaning Service an average of four hours to clean the carpets in a home. This includes three hours of actual cleaning time plus one hour to move the furniture out of the way and then back into position. Adam's is considering modifying its service so that the customer takes responsibility for moving the furniture, in effect offloading 25% of the workload. The impact on Adam's labor hours can be seen in Table 13.13.

TABLE 13.13 Impact of Customer Offloading at Adam's Carpet Cleaning Service

		Labor Hours Needed	
MONTH	FORECAST	NO OFFLOAD TO CUSTOMER	25% OFFLOADED TO CUSTOMER
1	60	240	180
2	55	220	165
3	50	200	150
4	50	200	150
5	30	120	90
6	30	120	90
7	25	100	75
8	30	120	90
9	40	160	120
10	40	160	120
11	45	180	135
12	55	220	165

(Continued)

MONTH	FORECAST	Labor Hours Needed: NO OFFLOAD TO CUSTOMER	Labor Hours Needed: 25% OFFLOADED TO CUSTOMER
	Average:	170	127.5
	Lowest:	100	75
	Highest:	240	180
	Difference:	140	105

Not only do average monthly labor requirements drop by 25%, but also the absolute difference between the highest and lowest months drops by 25%. Of course, Adam's would need to balance the potential cost savings against the lowered revenues associated with the new service—after all, the customer can't be expected to work for free.

13.5 LINKING S&OP THROUGHOUT THE SUPPLY CHAIN

Earlier, we noted that the S&OP process should consider not only the impact on various parties *within* the firm, but also the impact on *outside* parties—the firm's supply chain partners. It makes little sense, for example, to try to implement a plan that cannot be supported by key suppliers or service providers who move or store the goods. This represents the potential downside of *not* considering supply chain partners when developing a plan.

But there is an upside to linking the S&OP process with supply chain partners. For one thing, coordinating plans across the supply chain can help firms do a better job of improving overall supply chain performance, particularly in the area of cost. Pennington, for example, might discover that suppliers are willing to give the company substantial price discounts if Pennington stabilizes its orders for materials—something easier to achieve under a level production plan.

Second, linking plans can help eliminate uncertainty, thereby improving synchronization between supply chain partners. For instance, once Pennington decides on a sales and operations plan, its supply chain partners can then use the information to precisely plan

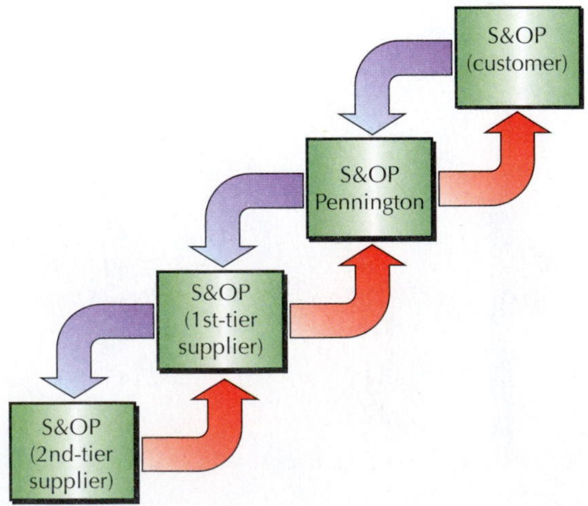

FIGURE 13.8
Linking S&OP up and down the Supply Chain

their own activities. By tying their plans to Pennington's, key suppliers can avoid "guessing" what demand will be. Even better, Pennington might try to establish linkages with its downstream partners—that is, its customers—in an effort to get even more accurate sales forecasts. This is exactly what Collaborative Planning, Forecasting, and Replenishment (CPFR), which we discussed in Chapter 9, hopes to accomplish.

Optimization models
A class of mathematical models used when the user seeks to optimize some objective function subject to some constraints.

Of course, the information can flow downstream as well as upstream. If, for example, a key supplier increases its capacity, such information would be useful for Pennington's S&OP effort. This linking of S&OP throughout the supply chain is shown in Figure 13.8. Sharing of plans already takes place in many industries, with the results being greater coordination, improved productivity, and fewer disruptions in the flow of goods and services through the supply chain.

13.6 APPLYING OPTIMIZATION MODELING TO S&OP

Objective function
A quantitative function that an optimization model seeks to optimize (maximize or minimize).

Constraints
Quantifiable conditions that place limitations on the set of possible solutions. The solution to an optimization model is acceptable only if it does not break any of the constraints.

In Chapter 12, we introduced optimization models. As you will recall, **optimization models** are a class of mathematical models used when the user seeks to optimize some objective function subject to some constraints. An **objective function** is a quantitative function that we hope to optimize (for example, we might want to maximize profits or minimize costs). **Constraints** are quantifiable conditions that place limitations on the set of possible solutions (demand that must be met, limits on materials or equipment, time, etc.). A solution is acceptable only if it does not break any of the constraints.

In order for optimization modeling to work, the user must be able to state in mathematical terms both the objective function and the constraints. Once the user is able to do this, special modeling algorithms can be used to generate solutions.

S&OP is ideally suited to such analyses. In particular, managers may be interested in understanding what pattern of resource decisions—labor, inventory, machine time, and so on—will result in the lowest total cost, while still meeting the sales forecast. In Example 13-11, we show how Microsoft Excel's Solver function can be used to apply optimization modeling to S&OP.

Example 13.11
S&OP Optimization Modeling at Bob Irons Industries

Bob Irons Industries manufactures and sells DNA testing equipment for use in cancer clinics around the globe. Bob, the owner and CEO, has developed a spreadsheet (Figure 13.9) to help him calculate the costs associated with various sales and operations plans.

It's worth taking a few minutes to see how Bob's spreadsheet works. First, the cells containing the planning values are highlighted, as well as the columns for the sales forecast, hirings, and layoffs, indicating that Bob can change these cells. The remaining numbers are all calculated values.

To illustrate, the calculations for January are as follows:

$$\text{Sales (in labor hours)} = \text{B15} * \text{D3} = 500 \text{ units} * 20 \text{ hours per unit} = 10{,}000 \text{ labor hours}$$

$$\text{Sales (in workers)} = \frac{\text{C15}}{\text{D4}} = \frac{10{,}000 \text{ labor hours}}{160 \text{ hours per worker}} = 62.5 \text{ workers}$$

$$\text{Actual workers} = \text{E14} + \text{G15} - \text{H15} = 100 \text{ beginning workers} + 25 \text{ hires} - 0 \text{ layoffs} = 125 \text{ workers}$$

$$\text{Actual production} = \frac{\text{E15} * \text{D4}}{\text{D3}} = \frac{125 \text{ workers} * 160 \text{ hours per month}}{20 \text{ hours per unit}} = 1{,}000 \text{ units}$$

$$\text{Ending inventory} = \text{I14} + \text{F15} - \text{B15} = 100 + 1{,}000 - 500 = 600 \text{ units}$$

	A	B	C	D	E	F	G	H	I
1	**S&OP Spreadsheet**								
2									
3			Labor hrs. per unit:	20					
4			Worker hrs. per month:	160					
5			Beginning & ending workforce:	100					
6			Beginning & ending inventory:	100					
7						Total plan cost			
8			Production cost per unit:	$550.00		$6,600,000			
9			Hiring cost:	$300.00		$7,500			
10			Layoff cost:	$200.00		$5,000			
11			Holding cost per unit per month:	$4.00		$54,800			
12						**$6,667,300**	**Grand total**		
13	Month	Sales Forecast	Sales (in labor hrs.)	Sales (in workers)	Actual Workers	Actual Production	Hirings	Layoffs	Ending Inventory/ Back Orders
14					100				100
15	January	500	10,000	62.5	125.00	1,000.00	25.00	0.00	600.00
16	February	600	12,000	75	125.00	1,000.00	0.00	0.00	1,000.00
17	March	700	14,000	87.5	125.00	1,000.00	0.00	0.00	1,300.00
18	April	800	16,000	100	125.00	1,000.00	0.00	0.00	1,500.00
19	May	900	18,000	112.5	125.00	1,000.00	0.00	0.00	1,600.00
20	June	1,000	20,000	125	125.00	1,000.00	0.00	0.00	1,600.00
21	July	1,000	20,000	125	125.00	1,000.00	0.00	0.00	1,600.00
22	August	1,100	22,000	137.5	125.00	1,000.00	0.00	0.00	1,500.00
23	September	1,200	24,000	150	125.00	1,000.00	0.00	0.00	1,300.00
24	October	1,300	26,000	162.5	125.00	1,000.00	0.00	0.00	1,000.00
25	November	1,400	28,000	175	125.00	1,000.00	0.00	0.00	600.00
26	December	1,500	30,000	187.5	125.00	1,000.00	0.00	0.00	100.00
27							0.00	25.00	
28	**Totals:**	**12,000**				**12,000.00**	**25.00**	**25.00**	**13,700.00**
29			**Average =**	**125**					

FIGURE 13.9 S&OP Spreadsheet for Bob Irons Industries (Level Plan)

The plan shown in Figure 13.9, is in fact, a level production plan with a total cost of $6,667,300. Looking at the plan, Bob wonders if he can do better. As an alternative, Bob updates the spreadsheet to show a chase plan. The results are shown in Figure 13.10.

The results surprise Bob—the total cost for the chase plan is exactly the same as that for the level plan. He wonders if there is a better solution that meets all of the constraints.

Bob decides to use the Solver function of Excel to find the lowest-cost solution. To start the process, Bob takes a few moments to identify the objective function, decision variables, and constraints for the optimization model and to match them up to his spreadsheet (Table 13.14).

As Table 13.14 indicates, Bob will need to set up the Solver function to minimize total costs (Cell F12) by changing the hiring and layoff values (Cells G15–H26). At the same time, the cells containing the ending inventory values must stay at or above zero for the first 11 months (Cells I15–I25), and at or above 100 in the last month (Cell I26).

Furthermore, Bob wants to make sure that none of the hiring or layoff numbers (Cells G15–H26) is negative. This may seem like a strange requirement, but unless Bob does this,

	A	B	C	D	E	F	G	H	I
1	**S&OP Spreadsheet**								
2									
3			Labor hrs. per unit:	20					
4			Worker hrs. per month:	160					
5			Beginning & ending workforce:	100					
6			Beginning & ending inventory:	100					
7						Total plan cost			
8			Production cost per unit:	$550.00		$6,600,000			
9			Hiring cost:	$300.00		$37,500			
10			Layoff cost:	$200.00		$25,000			
11			Holding cost per unit per month:	$4.00		$4,800			
12						**$6,667,300**	**Grand total**		
13	Month	Sales Forecast	Sales (in labor hrs.)	Sales (in workers)	Actual Workers	Actual Production	Hirings	Layoffs	Ending Inventory/ Back Orders
14					100				100
15	January	500	10,000	62.5	62.50	500.00	0.00	37.50	100.00
16	February	600	12,000	75	75.00	600.00	12.50	0.00	100.00
17	March	700	14,000	87.5	87.50	700.00	12.50	0.00	100.00
18	April	800	16,000	100	100.00	800.00	12.50	0.00	100.00
19	May	900	18,000	112.5	112.50	900.00	12.50	0.00	100.00
20	June	1,000	20,000	125	125.00	1,000.00	12.50	0.00	100.00
21	July	1,000	20,000	125	125.00	1,000.00	0.00	0.00	100.00
22	August	1,100	22,000	137.5	137.50	1,100.00	12.50	0.00	100.00
23	September	1,200	24,000	150	150.00	1,200.00	12.50	0.00	100.00
24	October	1,300	26,000	162.5	162.50	1,300.00	12.50	0.00	100.00
25	November	1,400	28,000	175	175.00	1,400.00	12.50	0.00	100.00
26	December	1,500	30,000	187.5	187.50	1,500.00	12.50	0.00	100.00
27							0.00	87.50	
28	**Totals:**	**12,000**				**12,000.00**	**125.00**	**125.00**	**1,200.00**
29			**Average =**	**125**					

FIGURE 13.10 S&OP Spreadsheet for Bob Irons Industries (Chase Plan)

TABLE 13.14 Description of the Optimization Problem for Bob Irons Industries

DESCRIPTION	CELL REFERENCE
Objective function:	
Minimize total production, hiring, layoff, and inventory costs	F12
By changing the following decision variables:	
Hiring and layoffs	G15:H26
Subject to the following constraints:	
Inventory in the last period must be at least 100 units	I26 ≥ 100
Inventory cannot go below zero (i.e., the sales forecast must be met)	I15:I25 ≥ 0
Hiring and layoff values cannot be negative	G15:H26 ≥ 0

the model will try to reduce costs forever by endlessly offsetting a negative hire with a negative layoff, each iteration of which would "save" \$300 + \$200 = \$500.

Figure 13.11 shows the lowest-cost solution, as identified by Solver. The open dialog box illustrates how the problem stated in Table 13.14 was encoded into Solver. The new plan is roughly \$18,000 cheaper than either the level or the chase approach. The suggested solution is to keep the workforce at around 92 workers for the first six months and then bump it up to around 158 workers for the last six months. Under this plan, the inventory level falls to zero only once (end of June).

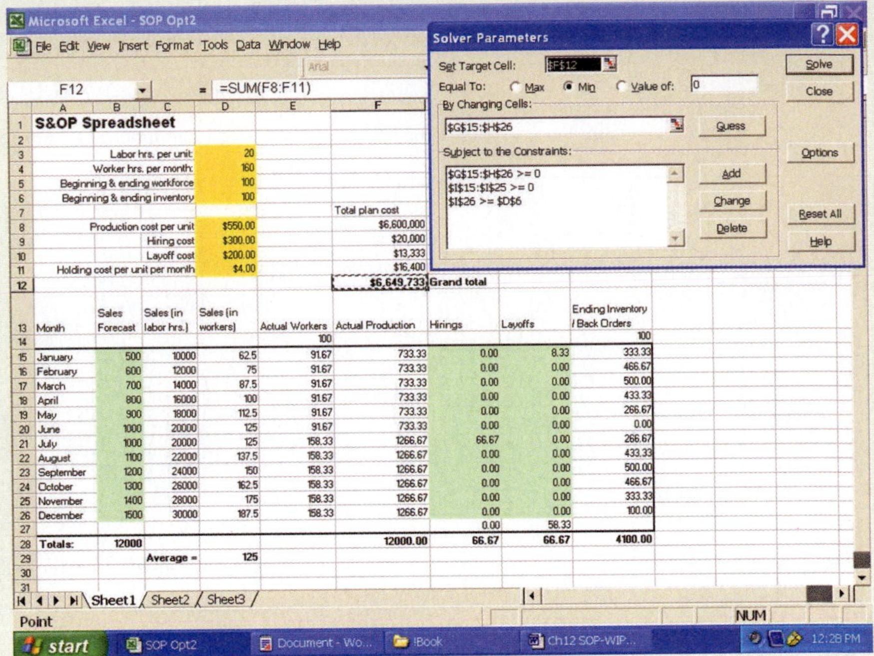

FIGURE 13.11 Solver-generated optimal solution for Bob Irons Industries

Before making a final decision, Bob has to consider other factors as well. The Solver solution contains fractional workers—will it still work for whole numbers? If so, will he be able to hire and train 67 workers in July? Does the company have enough space to store up to 500 units? Are the savings worth the added complexity? The point is that Solver can help Bob identify ways in which to lower costs, but the final decision is Bob's, not the spreadsheet's.

CHAPTER SUMMARY

S&OP fills the gap between long-term strategic planning and short-term planning and control. Through S&OP, firms can not only plan and coordinate efforts in their own functional areas—operations, marketing, finance, human resources, and so on—but also effectively communicate to other members of the supply chain what they expect to accomplish over the intermediate time horizon.

In this chapter, we described several approaches to S&OP and demonstrated the power of the technique. We discussed when and where top-down versus bottom-up planning could be used and showed three basic approaches to S&OP: level, chase, and mixed production.

We also touched on some of the more qualitative issues surrounding S&OP: How do we select a plan? How can we use

S&OP to foster agreement and cooperation among the various parties? How can we organize for S&OP?

We also argued for increased sharing of S&OP information across the supply chain. As information technologies become more sophisticated and organizations put more emphasis on the supply chain, expect to see more and more sharing of S&OP between supply chain partners. Last, we ended the chapter with a discussion of how optimization modeling techniques can be applied to the S&OP process.

KEY FORMULAS

Ending inventory level (page 408):

$$EI_t = EI_{t-1} + RP_t + OP_t - S_t \quad [13\text{-}1]$$

where:

EI_t = ending inventory for time period t

RP_t = regular production in time period t

OP_t = overtime production in time period t

S_t = sales in time period t

Net cash flow (page 413):

$$\text{Net cash flow} = \text{cash inflows} - \text{cash outflows} \quad [13\text{-}2]$$

KEY TERMS

Aggregate planning 401
Bottom-up planning 402
Chase production plan 407
Constraints 423
Detailed planning and control 401
Level production plan 407
Load profile 412
Mixed production plan 407
Net cash flow 413
Objective function 423
Offloading 420
Optimization models 423
Planning values 402
Rolling planning horizon 418
Sales and operations planning 400
Strategic planning 401
Tactical planning 401
Tiered workforce 420
Top-down planning 402
Yield management 419

SOLVED PROBLEM

Problem

Hua Ng Exporters makes commercial exercise equipment that is sold primarily in Europe and the United States. Hua Ng's two major product lines are stair steppers and treadmills. Resource requirements for both product lines, as well as six-month forecasts, are as follows:

PRODUCT LINE	LABOR HOURS PER UNIT	FABRICATION HOURS PER UNIT	ASSEMBLY LINE HOURS PER UNIT
Stair steppers	2.5	0.8	0.15
Treadmills	1.0	1.8	0.20

	Sales Forecast	
MONTH	STAIR STEPPERS	TREADMILLS
1	560	400
2	560	400
3	545	415
4	525	435
5	525	435
6	525	435

Assuming Hua Ng follows a chase production plan, develop load profiles for the next six months for labor, fabrication, and assembly line hours. Interpret the results.

Solution

The first step is to translate the sales forecasts for the two product lines into resource requirements. This will require us to calculate, and then combine, the resource needs for both product lines. Table 13.15 shows the results.

To illustrate how we arrived at these results, we calculated the total labor hours for month 1 as follows:

$$(560 \text{ stair steppers})(2.5 \text{ hours}) + (400 \text{ treadmills})(1 \text{ hour}) = 1400 + 400 = 1800 \text{ hours}$$

The remaining numbers are calculated in a similar fashion. Last, Figure 13.12 shows the load profiles for the three resources.

Total labor hours are expected to fall somewhat over time, while fabrication hours increase slightly. The reason is the change in the mix of products. Specifically, the forecast for stair steppers is falling, while the forecast for treadmills is rising.

TABLE 13.15 Resource Requirements at Hua Ng Exporters

	Sales Forecast				
MONTH	STAIR STEPPERS	TREADMILLS	TOTAL LABOR HOURS	TOTAL FABRICATION	TOTAL ASSEMBLY
1	560	400	1,800	1,168	164
2	560	400	1,800	1,168	164
3	545	415	1,777.5	1,183	164.75
4	525	435	1,747.5	1,203	165.75
5	525	435	1,747.5	1,203	165.75
6	525	435	1,747.5	1,203	165.75

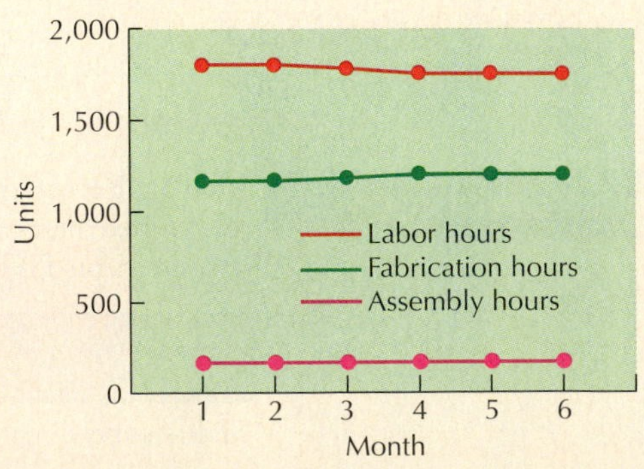

FIGURE 13.12 Load Profiles for Hua Ng Exporters

DISCUSSION QUESTIONS

1. Some people have argued that the process of developing the sales and operations plan is as important as the final numbers. How could this be?
2. How does S&OP differ from strategic capacity planning? From detailed planning and control? What role does S&OP play in the overall planning activities of an organization?
3. In general, under what conditions might a firm favor a level production plan over a chase plan? A chase production plan over a level plan?
4. Services, in general, cannot put "products" in inventory to be consumed at some later time. How does this limit service firms' S&OP alternatives?
5. Why is it important to update the sales and operations plan on a regular basis, using a rolling time horizon approach?
6. Ling suggests that superior S&OP planning can actually provide a firm with a competitive advantage. Do you agree? Can you think of any organizations that might benefit from better sales and operations planning?
7. What are the advantages to a firm of coordinating its S&OP process with key supply chain partners? What are the potential drawbacks?

PROBLEMS

Additional homework problems are available at www.prenhall.com/bozarth. These problems use Excel to generate customized problems for different class sections or even different students.

(* = easy; ** = moderate; *** = advanced)

1. Consider the following information for Sandy's Cleaning Service:

SERVICE	SERVICE MIX	LABOR HOURS PER JOB
Light cleaning	20%	0.20
Medium cleaning	60%	0.25
Deep cleaning	20%	0.35

   a. (*) Calculate the weighted planning value for labor hours per job.
   b. (**) Recalculate the weighted planning value based on a new service mix of 10%, 65%, and 25% for light, medium, and deep cleaning, respectively. What happened?

2. Consider the following information for Covolo Diving Gear:

GAUGE SET	PRODUCT MIX	MACHINE HOURS PER UNIT	LABOR HOURS PER UNIT
A20	60%	0.20	0.15
B30	15%	0.35	0.10
C40	25%	0.25	0.12

   a. (*) Calculate weighted planning values for machine hours and labor hours per gauge set. Interpret these planning values.
   b. (**) Recalculate the weighted planning values based on a new product mix of 45%, 30%, and 25% for the A20, B30, and C40 sets, respectively. What happened?

3. The typical monthly production mix at Bangor Industries is as follows:

Deluxe models	45%
Regular models	30%
Economy models	25%

   Each deluxe model typically requires 5 hours of labor and 10 hours of machine time. Each regular model takes 4 hours of labor and 8 hours of machine time. Finally, the economy model needs, on average, 3.5 hours of labor and 6 hours of machine time.
   a. (**) What should the weighted per-unit planning values be for labor? For machine time? What assumptions must be made in order to use these values?
   b. (**) Suppose for the next month the mix is expected to change to 30% deluxe, 30% regular, and 40% economy models. How would this affect the planning values?
   c. (**) When the product mix changes from month to month, should Bangor Industries use a top-down or a bottom-up approach to sales and operations planning? Explain.

4. (**) On average, each unit produced by the Kantor Company takes 0.90 worker hours and 0.02 hours of machine time. Furthermore, each worker and machine is available 160 hours a month. Use these planning values and the following sales forecast to estimate (1) the number of worker hours and machine hours needed each month, and (2) the number of workers and machines needed each month. Round your estimates of the number of workers and machines needed to the nearest whole number.

MONTH	SALES FORECAST
October	44,000
November	52,000
December	68,000
January	69,000
February	58,000
March	46,000

5. Consider the following sales forecasts for products A and B:

	Sales Forecasts	
MONTH	PRODUCT A	PRODUCT B
January	3500	700
February	3300	1000
March	3200	1200
April	3000	1500
May	2700	1900
June	2600	2100

Each unit of product A takes approximately 2.5 labor hours, while each unit of product B takes only 1.8 hours.

a. (**) What is the combined (aggregate) sales forecast for products A and B? If this was the *only* information you had, would you expect resource requirements to increase or decrease from January to June?

b. (**) Use the planning value information to calculate total labor hour requirements in each month. Compare your calculations to your answer to Part a. Interpret the results.

c. (**) Would top-down planning or bottom-up planning be better suited to S&OP in this situation? Explain.

6. (**) Complete the *level production plan* using the following information. The only costs you need to consider here are layoff, hiring, and inventory costs. If you complete the plan correctly, your hiring, layoff, and inventory costs should match those given.

	LAYOFF	HIRING	INVENTORY
Totals:	25	25	32,224
Costs:	$50,000	$75,000	$193,344
Cost of plan:		$318,344	
Planning values			
Starting inventory:			1000
Starting and ending workforce:			227
Hours worked per month per worker:			160
Hours per unit:			20
Hiring cost per worker:			$3000
Layoff cost per worker:			$2000
Monthly per-unit holding cost:			$6

Second Table for Problem 6

MONTH	FORECASTED SALES	SALES IN WORKER HOURS	WORKERS NEEDED TO MEET SALES AVERAGE = 252	ACTUAL WORKERS	ACTUAL PRODUCTION	LAYOFFS	HIRINGS	ENDING INVENTORY
March	1592							
April	1400							
May	1200							
June	1000							
July	1504							
August	1992							
September	2504							
October	2504							
November	3000							
December	3000							
January	2504							
February	1992							

7. (**) Complete the *chase production plan* using the following information. The only costs you need to consider here are layoff, hiring, and inventory costs. If you complete the plan correctly, your hiring, layoff, and inventory costs should match those given.

	LAYOFF	HIRING	INVENTORY
Totals:	250	250	12,000
Costs:	$500,000	$750,000	$72,000
Cost of plan:		$1,322,000	
Planning values			
Starting inventory:			1000
Starting and ending workforce:			227
Hours worked per month per worker:			160
Hours per unit:			20
Hiring cost per worker:			$3000
Layoff cost per worker:			$2000
Monthly per-unit holding cost:			$6

Second Table for Problem 7

MONTH	FORECASTED SALES	SALES IN WORKER HOURS	WORKERS NEEDED TO MEET SALES AVERAGE = 252	ACTUAL EMPLOYEES	ACTUAL PRODUCTION	LAYOFFS	HIRINGS	ENDING INVENTORY
March	1592							
April	1400							
May	1200							
June	1000							
July	1504							
August	1992							
September	2504							
October	2504							
November	3000							
December	3000							
January	2504							
February	1992							

8. (**) Consider the following partially completed sales and operations plan. Using the planning values and filled-in values as a guide, complete the plan and calculate the layoff, hiring, and inventory costs. Does this sales and operations plan reflect a chase, level, or mix strategy? Explain.

	LAYOFF	HIRING	INVENTORY
Totals:			
Costs:			
Cost of plan:			
Planning values			
Starting inventory:			500
Starting and ending workforce:			50
Hours worked per month per worker:			160
Hours per unit:			4
Hiring cost per worker:			$300
Layoff cost per worker:			$200
Monthly per-unit holding cost:			$4

Second Table for Problem 8

MONTH	FORECASTED SALES	SALES IN WORKER HOURS	WORKERS NEEDED TO MEET SALES AVERAGE = 252	ACTUAL WORKERS	ACTUAL PRODUCTION	LAYOFFS	HIRINGS	ENDING INVENTORY
March		8000				3	0	380
April		7680				0	0	
May		7360				0	0	
June	1800	7200				0	0	
July	1800					0	0	
August	1800					0	0	
September	1750					11	0	
October	1640					0	0	
				50		0	14	

9. (***) (*Microsoft Excel problem*) Note that Problems 6 through 8 all could be solved by a *single* spreadsheet that allows the user to change the planning, "Forecasted Sales," and "Actual Workers" values. **Create this spreadsheet.** Your spreadsheet should calculate new results any time the planning, "Forecasted Sales," or "Actual Workers" values change. Verify that your spreadsheet works by determining whether or not it generates the same costs for a level production plan and a chase production plan shown in Problems 6 and 7.

10. Castergourd Home Products makes two types of butcher-block tables: the Beefeater and the Deutschlander. The two tables are made in the same facility and use the same amount of labor and equipment. In addition, we know the following:

- Each table costs $300 to make, and each requires, on average, 3.2 hours of labor.
- Each employee works 160 hours per month, and there is no effective limit on the number of employees.
- The cost of hiring or laying off an employee is $300.
- The monthly holding cost for a table is $15.
- For planning purposes, Castergourd will begin and end with 20 employees and 0 tables in inventory.

Forecasted sales for the tables are as follows:

MONTH	BEEFEATER	DEUTSCHLANDER
November 2005	650	3048
December	676	2899
January 2006	624	3198
February	624	2671
March	696	2919
April	475	3102
May	566	2964
June	819	2409
July	754	3381
August	982	3965

a. (***) Develop a top-down *level production plan* for Castergourd for the 10-month planning period. Calculate the total production, hiring, layoff, and inventory costs for your plan.

b. (***) Repeat Part a, except in this case develop a *chase production plan*.

c. (**) Suppose hiring and layoff costs increase dramatically. In general, will this make a level plan look better or worse relative to a chase plan? Explain.

11. (**) Consider the level production plan for Pennington Cabinets shown in Table 13.5. Perform a cash flow analysis for this production plan, using the cash flow analysis in Example 13.8 as a guide. Assume that each cabinet set sold generates a cash inflow of $2800, while each unit produced using regular time generates a cash outflow of $2000 and each cabinet set held in inventory at the end of the month generates a cash outflow of $40. How does this cash flow compare with the one for the mixed strategy (Table 13.10)? Which plan do you think finance would prefer?

12. Consider the following information:

MONTH	FORECASTED SALES	REGULAR PRODUCTION	OVERTIME PRODUCTION	ENDING INVENTORY
January	800 units	1150 units	0 units	350 units
February	1000	1150	0	500
March	1200	1150	0	450
April	1400	1150	0	200
May	1600	1150	150	0
June	1500	1150	350	0

Each unit sells for $500. Regular production and overtime production costs are $350 and $450 per unit, respectively. The cost to hold a unit in inventory for one month is $10.

a. (**) Develop a cash flow analysis for this problem. Be sure to calculate net cash flow and cumulative net cash flow for each month.

b. (**) Why do the net cash flows for April and May look so much better than those for the other months? What are the implications for building up and draining down inventories under a level production plan?

13. (***) (*Microsoft Excel problem*) Recreate the S&OP spreadsheet used in Figures 13.10 and 13.11. (You do *not* have to build in the optimization model using the Solver function.) While your formatting may differ, your answers should be the same. Your spreadsheet should generate new results anytime any of the planning, sales forecast, or hiring/layoff values are changed. To test your spreadsheet, change the planning values to match the following:

	A	B	C	D
3			Labor hrs. per unit:	24
4			Worker hrs. per month:	150
5			Beginning & ending workforce:	100
6			Beginning & ending inventory:	100
7				
8			Prodction cost per unit:	$475.00
9			Hiring cost:	$400.00
10			Layoff cost:	$300.00
11			Holding cost per unit per month:	$3.00

If your spreadsheet works correctly, the new total cost for a *level production plan* should be $5,769,100, and for a *chase production plan*, it should be $5,755,600.

14. (***) (*Microsoft Excel problem*). Kumquats Unlimited makes large batches of kumquat paste for use in the food industry. These batches are made on automated production

lines. Kumquats Unlimited has the capability to start up or shut down lines at the beginning of each month, but at a cost. If a line is up, management has determined that it's best to keep the line busy, even if the resulting batches must be put in inventory.

Management has created the following Excel spreadsheet, which uses the Solver function to find the lowest-cost solution to the S&OP problem. **Re-create this spreadsheet, including the Solver optimization model** (use Example 13.11 as a guide). Your formatting does not have to be the same, but your answers should be. Your spreadsheet should allow the user to make changes *only* to the planning values, the sales forecast, and the number of production line start-ups and shutdowns. All other values should be calculated. Be sure that Solver does not let inventory drop below zero at the end of any month or end June with less inventory than was available at the beginning of January. To test your spreadsheet, modify the spreadsheet so that each batch requires 32 hours of production line time. The new optimal cost should be $16,215,000.

	A	B	C	D	E	F	G	H	I
1	Sales & Operations Planning Spreadsheet for Kumquats Unlimited								
2	(with Solver optimization)								
3									
4			Production cost per batch:	$ 2,400				Production costs:	$
5			Line hours per batch:	16				Line start-up costs:	$ 125,000
6			Production line hours per month:	$ 320	hours			Line shutdown costs:	$ 75,000
7			Cost to start up a line:	$ 25,000				Inventory holding costs:	$ 165,000
8			Cost to shut down a line:	$ 6,000					
9			Inventory holding cost:	$ 300	per batch, per month			Grand total:	$14,765,000
10			Beginning and ending lines:	55	production lines				
11			Beginning and ending inventory:	100	batches				
12									
13	Month	Sales Forecast	Sales (in line hours)	Sales (in production lines)	Actual Production Lines	Actual Production	Production Line Start-ups	Production Line Shutdowns	Ending Inventory
14					55				100
15	January	1,000	16,000	50	55.00	1,100	0	0	200
16	February	1,200	19,200	60	55.00	1,100	0	0	100
17	March	1,200	19,200	60	55.00	1,100	0	0	0
18	April	1,000	16,000	50	50.00	1,000	0	5	0
19	May	800	12,800	40	42.50	850	0	7	50
20	June	800	12,800	40	42.50	850	0	0	100
21					48		5	0	100
22	**Total =**	**6000**				**6,000**	5	**12.5**	**550**
23			**Average =**	**50**					

CASE STUDY

Covolo Diving Gear, Part 2

June 15, 2009.—It has been two weeks since their contentious semiannual planning meeting, and the senior staff members for Covolo Diving Gear are getting ready to start their first monthly S&OP meeting. Gina Covolo, CEO, gets the ball rolling:

> *I know it's been a busy two weeks for all of you, and I appreciate you working extra time to get ready for this meeting. Production is already set for the next two months, so we're going to start by planning for this September through the following August. I've had Patricia from marketing develop a sales forecast for these 12 months, and I've also had David from manufacturing estimate manufacturing costs and labor requirements, as well as capacity in the plant. Mary from HR was also good enough to come up with some estimates of how much it costs to hire and train new workers, as well as the cost of laying off folks. Finally, Jack from purchasing was able to get the accounting folks to estimate the cost of holding a gauge set in inventory for a month. So let's see what we've got.*

Mary passes out the following information to all of the attendees:

MONTH	SALES FORECAST
September 2006	30,000 gauge sets
October	31,500
November	35,000
December	37,000
January 2007	22,000
February	18,000
March	17,500
April	27,000
May	38,000
June	40,000
July	42,000
August	40,000

- Manufacturing cost per gauge set: $74.50
- Holding cost: $8 per gauge set per month
- Average labor hours required per gauge set: 0.25 hours
- Labor hours available per employee per month: 160
- Plant capacity: 35,000 gauge sets per month
- Cost to hire and train a new employee: $1250
- Cost to lay off an employee: $500
- Beginning and ending workforce is 50
- Beginning inventory is 10,000

QUESTIONS

1. Develop a *level production plan* for Covolo Diving Gear. What are the advantages and disadvantages of this plan? Could Covolo implement a pure chase plan, given the current capacity? Why? If sales continue to grow, what are the implications for production capacity at Covolo?
2. Patricia Rodriguez, vice president of marketing, states, "I've got to tell you all that I'm pretty comfortable with the forecasts for September through November, but after that, a lot could change. It's just very hard to forecast for four or more months out in this kind of market." How will a monthly S&OP update with rolling planning horizons help alleviate Patricia's concerns? Are there still advantages to S&OP, even though the forecasts may change?
3. After looking over the level production plan, David Griffin, vice president of manufacturing, speaks up: "This looks OK, but you know what bugs me about it? The assumption that if a worker is available, that worker *has* to be making gauge sets, even if we don't need any more. It might make sense in some cases to just have the worker *not* produce, rather than laying a worker off in one month and hiring someone else back the next." Do you agree? What are the holding costs associated with having an extra worker produce gauge sets for one month? How do these compare to the layoff and hiring costs? How might a strategy of keeping extra workers idle affect the estimated manufacturing costs for the gauge sets? (*Hint:* Labor costs have to be accounted for *somewhere.*)

REFERENCES

Books and Articles

Cox, J. F., and J. H. Blackstone, eds. *APICS Dictionary*. 10th ed. Falls Church, VA: APICS, 2002.

Ling, R. "For True Enterprise Integration, Turn First to SOP." *APICS—The Performance Advantage* 10 no. 3 (March 2000): 40–45.

Internet

"S&OP Gives Caterpillar a Competitive Edge," Oliver Wight Case Study Series, **www.oliverwight.com/client/features/caterpillarna.pdf**

CHAPTER 14

Managing Inventory throughout the Supply Chain

CHAPTER OUTLINE

Chapter Objectives

By the end of this chapter, you will be able to:

- Describe the various roles of inventory, including the different types of inventory and inventory drivers.
- Distinguish between independent demand and dependent demand inventory.
- Calculate the restocking level for a periodic review system.
- Calculate the economic order quantity (*EOQ*) and reorder point (*ROP*) for a continuous review system.
- Determine the best order quantity when volume discounts are available.
- Calculate the target service level and target stocking point for a single-period inventory system.
- Describe how inventory decisions affect other areas of the supply chain. In particular, you will be able to describe the bullwhip effect; inventory positioning issues, and the impact of transportation, packaging, and material handling considerations.

Inventory Management at Amazon.com

Employees pick books of the shelf at an Amazon.com warehouse

When they first started appearing in the late 1990s, Web-based "e-tailers" such as Amazon.com hoped to replace the "bricks" of traditional retailing with the "clicks" of online ordering via computer keyboards. Rather than opening dozens or even hundreds of stores filled with expensive inventory, an e-tailer runs a single virtual store that serves customers around the globe. The e-tailer business model suggested that inventory could be kept at a few key sites chosen to minimize costs and facilitate quick delivery to customers. In theory, e-tailers were highly "scalable" businesses that could add new customers with little or no additional investment in inventory or facilities. (Traditional retailers usually need to add stores to gain significant increases in their customer base.)

But how has this actually played out for Amazon.com? Table 14.1 contains sales and inventory figures for Amazon.com for the years 1997 through 2006. The first column reports net sales for each calendar year, while the second column contains the amount of inventory on hand at the end of the year. The third column shows inventory turns, which is calculated as (Net Sales/Ending Inventory). Retailers generally want higher inventory turns, indicating that they can support the same level of sales with less inventory.

Graphing these results provides some interesting insights. Consider Figure 14.1. In late 1999, Amazon.com learned that managing inventory can be a challenge even for e-tailers. That was the year the company expanded into new product lines, such as electronics and housewares, with which it had little experience. Amazon.com's purchasing managers were faced with the question of how many of these items to hold in inventory—too little, and they risked losing orders and alienating customers; too much, and they could lock up the company's resources in

TABLE 14.1 Amazon.com Financial Results, 1997–2006 (all figures in millions)

YEAR	NET SALES	INVENTORY (DEC. 31)	INVENTORY TURNS
1997	$148	$9	16.4
1998	$610	$30	20.3
1999	$1,640	$221	7.4
2000	$2,762	$175	15.8
2001	$3,122	$143	21.8
2002	$3,933	$202	19.5
2003	$5,264	$294	17.9
2004	$6,921	$480	14.4
2005	$8,490	$566	15.0
2006	$10,711	$877	12.2

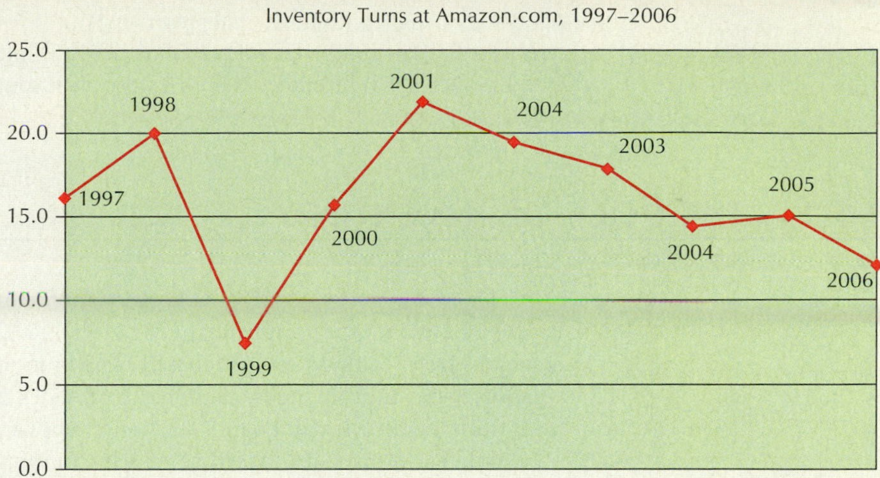

FIGURE 14.1
Inventory Turns at Amazon.com, 1997–2006

unsold products. Only later, when sales for the 1999 holiday season fell flat and Amazon.com's inventory levels skyrocketed, did they realize they had overstocked. In fact, as the figures show by the end of 1999, Amazon.com's inventory turnover ratio (Net Sales/Inventory) was 7.4—*worse* than that of the typical bricks-and-mortar retailer.

After 1999, Amazon seemed to learn its lesson. Inventory turns rose to nearly 22 in 2001, but have fallen steadily ever since, to 12.2 turns for 2006. Still, these results are better than the more typical bricks-and-mortar retailers. As a comparison, in 2006, Wal-Mart's consolidated operations generated just 9.7 inventory turns.

INTRODUCTION

Inventory
"[T]hose stocks or items used to support production (raw materials and work-in-process items), supporting activities (maintenance, repair, and operating supplies) and customer service (finished goods and spare parts)."

APICS defines **inventory** as "those stocks or items used to support production (raw materials and work-in-process items), supporting activities (maintenance, repair, and operating supplies) and customer service (finished goods and spare parts)."[1] In this chapter, we discuss the critical role of inventory—why it is necessary, what purposes it serves, and how it is controlled.

As Amazon's experience suggests, inventory management is still an important function, even in the Internet age. In fact, many managers seem to have a love-hate relationship with inventory. Michael Dell talks about inventory velocity—the speed at which components move through Dell Computer's operations—as a key measure of his company's performance.[2] In his mind, the less inventory the company has sitting in the warehouse, the better. Victor Fung of the Hong Kong–based trading firm Li & Fung goes so far as to say, "Inventory is the root of all evil."[3]

[1]J. F. Cox and J. H. Blackstone, eds., *APICS Dictionary*, 10th ed. (Falls Church, VA: APICS, 2002).

[2]J. Magretta, "The Power of Virtual Integration: An Interview with Dell Computer's Michael Dell," *Harvard Business Review* 76, no. 2 (March–April 1998): 72–84.

[3]J. Magretta, "Fast, Global, and Entrepreneurial: Supply Chain Management, Hong Kong Style," *Harvard Business Review* 76, no. 5 (September–October 1998): 102–109.

Yet look what happened to the price of gasoline in the United States during the spring of 2007. It skyrocketed, primarily because refineries were shut down for maintenance and suppliers were caught with inadequate reserves. And if you have ever visited a store only to find that your favorite product is sold out, you might think the *lack* of inventory is the root of all evil. The fact is that inventory is both a valuable resource and a potential source of waste.

14.1 THE ROLE OF INVENTORY

Consider WolfByte Computers, a fictional manufacturer of desktop computers and servers. Figure 14.2 shows the supply chain for WolfByte Computers. WolfByte assembles the machines from components purchased from companies throughout the world, three of which are shown in the figure. Supplier 1 provides the display unit, Supplier 2 manufactures the integrated circuit board (ICB), and Supplier 3 produces the mouse.

Looking downstream, WolfByte sells its computers through independent retail stores and through its own Web site. At retail stores, customers can buy a computer off the shelf, or they can order one to be customized and shipped directly to them. On average, WolfByte takes about a week to ship computers from its assembly plant to the retail stores or to customers. Both WolfByte and the retail stores keep spare parts on hand to handle customers' warranty claims and other service requirements.

With this background, let's discuss the basic types of inventory, and see how they fit into WolfByte's supply chain.

Inventory Types

Cycle stock
Components or products that are received in bulk by a downstream partner, gradually used up, and then replenished again in bulk by the upstream partner.

Two of the most common types of inventory are cycle stock and safety stock. **Cycle stock** refers to components or products that are received in bulk by a downstream partner, gradually used up, and then replenished again in bulk by the upstream partner. For example, suppose Supplier 3 ships 20,000 mice at a time to WolfByte. Of course, WolfByte can't use all those devices at once. More likely, workers pull them out of inventory as needed. Eventually, the inventory runs down, and WolfByte places another order for mice. When the new order arrives, the inventory level rises and the cycle is repeated. Figure 14.3 shows the classic sawtooth pattern associated with cycle stock inventories.

Cycle stock exists at other points in WolfByte's supply chain. Almost certainly, Suppliers 1 through 3 have cycle stocks of raw materials that they use to make components.

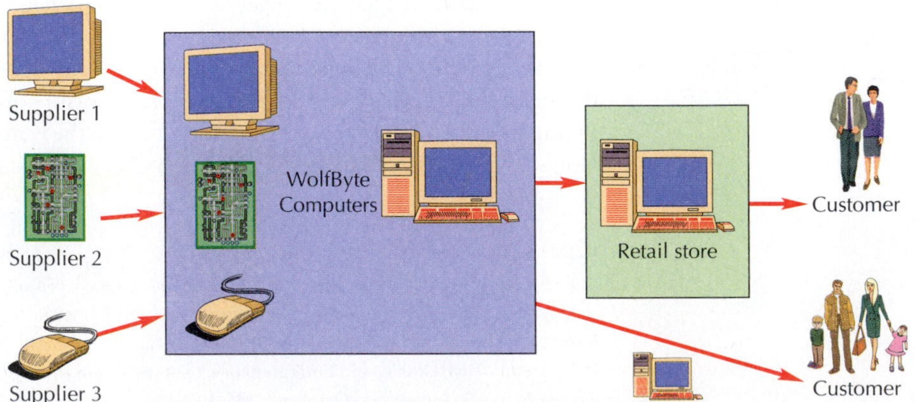

FIGURE 14.2 Supply Chain for WolfByte Computers

FIGURE 14.3
Cycle Stock at WolfByte Computers

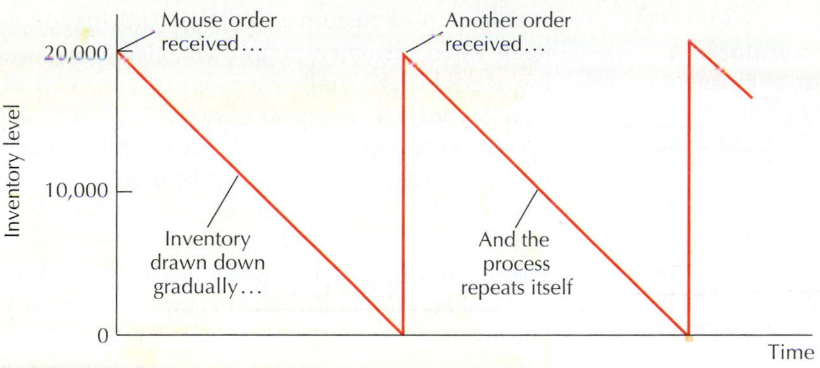

And retailers need to keep cycle stocks of both completed computers and spare parts in order to serve their customers.

Safety stock
Extra inventory that companies hold to protect themselves against uncertainties in either demand or replenishment time.

Cycle stock is often thought of as active inventory because companies are constantly using it up and their suppliers are constantly replenishing it. **Safety stock**, on the other hand, is extra inventory that companies hold to protect themselves against uncertainties in either demand or replenishment time. Companies do not plan on using their safety stock any more than you plan on using the spare tire in the trunk of your car; it is there *just in case*.

Let's return to the mouse example in Figure 14.3. WolfByte has timed its orders so that a new batch of mice comes in just as the old one is used up. But what if Supplier 3 is late in delivering the devices? What if demand is higher than expected? If either or both of these conditions occur, WolfByte could run out of mice before the next order arrives.

Imagine the resulting chaos: Assembly lines would have to shut down, customers' orders couldn't be filled, and WolfByte would have to notify customers, retailers, and shippers of the delays.

One solution is to hold some extra inventory, or safety stock, of mice to protect against fluctuations in demand or replenishment time. Figure 14.4 shows what WolfByte's inventory levels would look like if the company decided to hold safety stock of 1,000 mice. As you can see, safety stock provides valuable protection, but at the cost of higher inventory levels. Later in the chapter, we discuss ways of calculating appropriate safety stock levels.

Anticipation inventory
Inventory that is held in anticipation of customer demand.

There are four other common types of inventory: anticipation, hedge, transportation, and smoothing. **Anticipation inventory**, as the name implies, is inventory that is held in

FIGURE 14.4
Safety Stock at WolfByte Computers

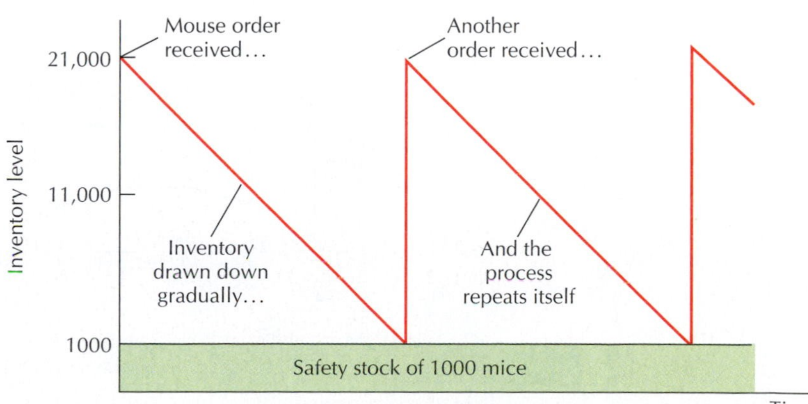

anticipation of customer demand. Anticipation inventory allows instant availability of items when customers want them. **Hedge inventory**, according to APICS, is "a form of inventory buildup to buffer against some event that may not happen. Hedge inventory planning involves speculation related to potential labor strikes, price increases, unsettled governments, and events that could severely impair the company's strategic initiatives."[4] In this sense, hedge inventories can be thought of as a special form of safety stock. WolfByte has stockpiled a hedge inventory of three months' worth of ICBs because managers have heard that Supplier 2 may experience a labor strike in the next few months. Ford followed a similar strategy when building up its inventory of palladium.

Hedge inventory
"[A] form of inventory buildup to buffer against some event that may not happen. Hedge inventory planning involves speculation related to potential labor strikes, price increases, unsettled governments, and events that could severely impair the company's strategic initiatives."

Transportation inventory represents inventory that is "in the pipeline," moving from one link in the supply chain to another. When the physical distance between supply chain partners is long, transportation inventory can represent a considerable investment. Suppose, for example, that Supplier 2 is located in South Korea, while WolfByte is located in Texas. ICBs may take several weeks to travel the entire distance between the two. As a result, multiple orders could be in the pipeline on any particular day. One shipment of ICBs might be sitting on the docks in Kimhau, South Korea; two others might be halfway across the Pacific; a fourth might be found on Route I-10, just outside Phoenix, Arizona. In fact, the transportation inventory of ICBs alone might dwarf the total cycle and safety stock inventories in the rest of the supply chain.

Transportation inventory
Inventory that is moving from one link in the supply chain to another.

Finally, **smoothing inventories** are used to smooth out differences between upstream production levels and downstream demand. Suppose management has determined that WolfByte's assembly plant is most productive when it produces 3000 computers a day (where productivity = output in dollars/input in dollars). Unfortunately, demand from retailers and customers will almost certainly vary from day to day. As a result, WolfByte's managers may decide to produce a constant 3000 computers per day, building up finished goods inventory during periods of slow demand and drawing it down during periods of high demand (Figure 14.5 illustrates this approach). Smoothing inventories allow individual links in the supply chain to stabilize their production at the most efficient level and to avoid the costs and headaches associated with constantly changing workforce levels and/or production rates. If you think you may have heard of this idea before, you have: It's part of the rationale for following a level production strategy in developing a sales and operations plan (see Chapter 13).

Smoothing inventories
Inventories used to smooth out differences between upstream production levels and downstream demand.

FIGURE 14.5
Smoothing Inventories at WolfByte Computers

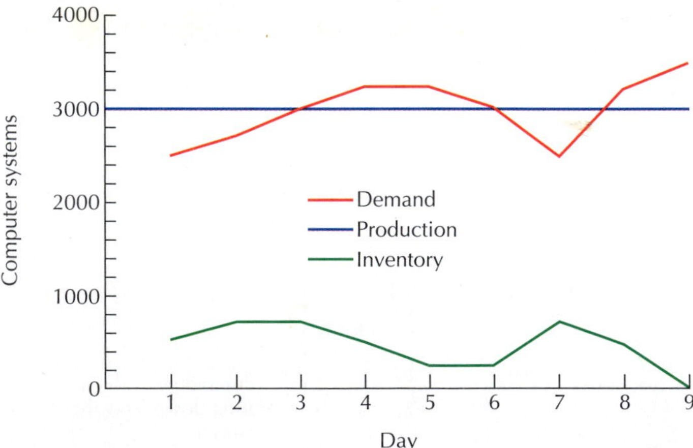

[4]Cox and Blackstone, *APICS Dictionary.*

Inventory Drivers

From this discussion, we can see that inventory is a useful resource. But at the same time, companies don't want to hold more inventory than necessary. First, inventory ties up space and capital: A dollar invested in inventory is a dollar that cannot be used somewhere else. Likewise, the space used to store inventory can often be put to more productive use. Inventory also poses a significant risk of obsolescence, particularly in supply chains with short product life cycles. Consider what happens when Intel announces the next generation of processor chips. Would *you* want to be stuck holding the old-generation chips when the new ones hit the market?

Finally, inventory is too often used to hide problems that management really should resolve. In this sense, inventory can serve as a kind of painkiller, treating the symptom without solving the underlying problem. Consider our discussion of safety stock. Suppose Wolf Byte's managers decide to hold additional safety stock of ICBs because of quality problems with units received from Supplier 2. While the safety stock may buffer Wolf Byte from these quality problems, it does so at a cost. A better solution might be to improve the quality of incoming ICBs, thereby reducing both quality-related costs and the need for additional safety stock.

Inventory drivers
Business conditions that force companies to hold inventory.

With these concerns in mind, let's turn our attention to **inventory drivers**—business conditions that force companies to hold inventory. Table 14.2 summarizes the ways in which various inventory drivers affect different types of inventory. To the extent that organizations can manage and control the drivers of inventories, they can reduce the supply chain's need for inventory.

Supply uncertainty
The risk of interruptions in the flow of components from upstream suppliers.

In managing inventory, organizations face uncertainty throughout the supply chain. On the upstream (supplier) end, they face **supply uncertainty**, or the risk of interruptions in the flow of components they need for their internal operations. In assessing supply uncertainty, managers need to ask themselves questions such as these:

- How consistent is the quality of the goods being purchased?
- How reliable are the supplier's delivery estimates?
- Are the goods subject to unexpected price increases or shortages?

Problems in any of these areas can drive up supply uncertainty, forcing organizations to hold safety stock or hedging inventories.

Demand uncertainty
The risk of significant and unpredictable fluctuations in downstream demand.

On the downstream (customer) side, organizations face **demand uncertainty**, or the risk of significant and unpredictable fluctuations in the demand for their products. For example, many suppliers of automobile components complain that the big automobile manufacturers' forecasts are unreliable and that order sizes are always changing, often at

TABLE 14.2
Inventory Drivers and Their Impact

INVENTORY DRIVER	IMPACT
Uncertainty in supply or demand	Safety stock Hedge inventory
Mismatch between downstream partner's demand and most efficient production or shipment volumes for upstream partner	Cycle stock
Mismatch between downstream demand levels and upstream production capacity	Smoothing inventory
Mismatch between timing of customer demand and supply chain lead times	Anticipation inventory Transportation inventory

the last minute. Under such conditions, suppliers are forced to hold extra safety stock to meet unexpected jumps in demand or changes in order size.

In dealing with uncertainty in supply and demand, the trick is to determine what types of uncertainty can be reduced and then to focus on reducing them. For example, poor quality is a source of supply uncertainty that can be substantially reduced or even eliminated through quality improvement programs, such as those we discussed in Chapters 3 and 4. On the other hand, forecasting may help to reduce demand uncertainty, but can never completely eliminate it. A change in forecasting methods, then, may not be helpful in reducing demand uncertainty.

Another common inventory driver is the mismatch between demand and the most efficient production or shipment volumes. Let's start with a simple example, facial tissue. When you blow your nose, how many tissues do you use? Most people would say 1, yet tissues typically come in boxes of 200 or more. Clearly a mismatch exists between the number you need at any one time and the number you need to purchase. The reason, of course, is that packaging, shipping, and selling facial tissues one at a time would be highly inefficient—especially because the cost of holding a cycle stock of facial tissues is trivial. On an organizational scale, mismatches between demand and efficient production or shipment volumes are the main drivers of cycle stocks. As we will see later in this chapter, managers can often alter their business processes to reduce production or shipment volumes, thereby reducing the mismatch with demand and the resulting need for cycle stocks.

Likewise, mismatches between overall demand levels and production capacity can force companies to hold smoothing inventories (Figure 14.5). Of course, managers can reduce smoothing inventories by varying their capacity to better match demand or by smoothing demand to better match capacity. As we saw in Chapter 13, either strategy has its pros and cons.

The last inventory driver we will discuss is a mismatch between the timing of the customer's demand and the supply chain's lead time. When you go to the grocery store, you expect to find fresh produce ready to bag and buy; your expected waiting time is zero. But produce can come from almost anywhere in the world, depending on the season. To make sure that bananas and lettuce will be ready and waiting for you at your local store, someone has to initiate their movement through the supply chain days or even weeks ahead of time and determine how much anticipation inventory to hold. Whenever the customer's maximum waiting time is shorter than the supply chain's lead time, companies must have transportation and anticipation inventories to ensure that the product will be available when the customer wants it. If there is no inventory, the company risks losing not only the current business, but future business as well.

How can businesses reduce the need to hold anticipation inventory? Often they do so both by shrinking their own lead time and by persuading customers to wait longer. For example, personal computers once took many weeks to work their way through the supply chain. As a result, manufacturers were forced to hold anticipation inventories to meet customer demand. Today some computer manufacturers will assemble and ship a *customized* PC directly to the customer's front door in just a few days. Customers get fast and convenient delivery of a product that meets their exact needs. At the same time, the manufacturer can greatly reduce or even eliminate anticipation inventory.

In the remainder of this chapter, we examine the systems that are used in managing various types of inventory. Before beginning a detailed discussion of these tools and techniques of inventory management, however, we need to distinguish between two basic inventory categories, independent demand and dependent demand inventory. The distinction between the two is crucial because the tools and techniques needed to manage each are *very* different.

Independent versus Dependent Demand Inventory

Independent demand inventory
Inventory items with demand levels that are beyond a company's complete control.

Dependent demand inventory
Inventory items whose demand levels are tied directly to the company's planned production of another item.

In general, **independent demand inventory** refers to inventory items with demand levels that are beyond a company's complete control. **Dependent demand inventory**, on the other hand, refers to inventory items whose demand levels are tied directly to the company's planned production of another item. Because the required quantities and timing of dependent demand inventory items can be predicted with great accuracy, they are under a company's *complete* control.

A simple example of an independent demand inventory item is a kitchen table. While a furniture manufacturer may use forecasting models to predict the demand for kitchen tables and may try to use pricing and promotions to manipulate demand, the actual demand for kitchen tables is unpredictable. The fact is, *customers* determine the demand for these items, so finished tables clearly fit the definition of independent demand inventory.

But what about the components that are used to make the tables, such as legs? Suppose for a moment that a manufacturer has decided to produce 500 tables five weeks from now. With this information, a manager can quickly calculate exactly how many legs will be needed:

$$500 \times 4 \text{ legs per table} = 2000 \text{ legs}$$

Furthermore, the manager can determine exactly when the legs will be needed, based on the company's production schedule. Because the timing and quantity of the demand for table legs are completely predictable and under the manager's total control, the legs fit the definition of dependent demand items. Dependent demand items require an entirely different approach to managing than do independent demand items. We discuss ways of managing dependent demand items in more depth in Chapter 15.

Three basic approaches are used to manage independent demand inventory items: periodic review systems, continuous review systems, and single-period inventory systems. We examine all three approaches in the following sections.

14.2 PERIODIC REVIEW SYSTEMS

Periodic review system
An inventory system used to manage independent demand inventory. The inventory level for an item is checked at regular intervals and restocked to some predetermined level.

One of the simplest approaches to managing independent demand inventory is based on a periodic review of inventory levels. In a **periodic review system**, companies check the inventory level of an item at regular intervals and restock to some predetermined level, R. The actual order quantity, Q, is the amount required to bring the inventory level back up to R. Stated more formally:

$$Q = R - I \qquad \textbf{[14-1]}$$

where:

Q = order quantity
R = restocking level
I = inventory level at the time of review

Figure 14.6 shows the fluctuations in the inventory levels of a single item under a two-week periodic review system. As the downward-sloping line shows, the inventory starts out full and then drains down as units are pulled from it. (Note that the line will be straight only if demand is constant.) After two weeks, the inventory is replenished, and the process begins again.

FIGURE 14.6
Periodic Review System

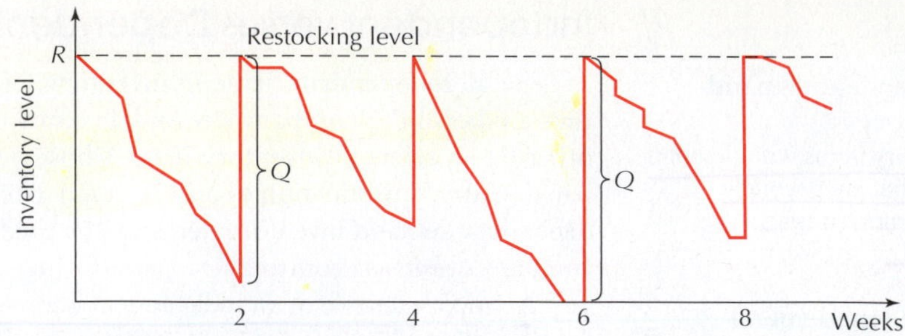

A periodic review system nicely illustrates the use of both cycle stock and safety stock. By replenishing inventory every two weeks, rather than daily or even hourly, the organization spreads the cyclical cost of restocking across more units. And the need to hold safety stock helps to determine the restocking level. Increasing the restocking level effectively increases safety stock: The higher the level is, the less likely the organization is to run out of inventory before the next replenishment period. On the flip side, because inventory is checked only at regular intervals, the company could run out of an item before the inventory is replenished. In fact, that is exactly what happens just before week 6 in Figure 14.6. If you have ever visited your favorite vending machine, only to find that the item you wanted has been sold out, you have been the victim of a periodic review system stockout.

As you might imagine, a periodic review system is best suited to items for which periodic restocking is economical and the cost of a high restocking level (and hence a large safety stock) is not prohibitive. A classic example is a snack food display at a grocery store. Constantly monitoring inventory levels for low-value items such as pretzels or potato chips makes no economic sense. Rather, a vendor will stop by a store regularly and top off the supply of all the items, usually with more than enough to meet demand until the next replenishment date.

Restocking Levels

The key question in setting up a periodic review system is determining the restocking level, *R*. In general, *R* should be high enough to meet all but the most extreme demand levels during the reorder period (*RP*) and the time it takes for the order to come in (*L*). Specifically:

$$R = \mu_{RP+L} + z\sigma_{RP+L} \qquad [14\text{-}2]$$

where:

μ_{RP+L} = average demand during the reorder period and the order lead time

σ_{RP+L} = standard deviation of demand during the reorder period and the order lead time

z = number of standard deviations above the average demand (higher z values increase the restocking level, thereby lowering the probability of a stockout)

Service level
A term used to indicate the percentage of time inventory levels will be high enough to meet demand during the reorder period.

Equation 14.2 assumes that the demand during the reorder period and the order lead time is normally distributed. By setting *R* a certain number of standard deviations above the average, firms can establish a **service level**, which indicates what percentage of the time inventory levels will be high enough to meet demand during the reorder period. For example, setting $z = 1.28$ would make *R* large enough to meet expected demand 90% of the time (i.e., provide a 90% service level), while setting $z = 2.33$ would provide a 99% service level. Different *z* values and the resulting service levels are listed in the following table. (More values can be derived from the normal curve area table in the appendices at the end of the book.)

z VALUE	RESULTING SERVICE LEVEL
1.28	90%
1.65	95
2.33	99
3.08	99.9

Example 14.1

Establishing a Periodic Review System for McCreery's Chips

McCreery's Chips sells large tins of potato chips at a grocery superstore. Every 10 days, McCreery's deliveryman stops by and checks the inventory level. He then places an order, which is delivered three days later. Average demand during the reorder period and order lead time (13 days total) is 240 tins. The standard deviation of demand during this same time period is 40 tins. The grocery superstore wants enough inventory on hand to meet demand 95% of the time. In other words, the store is willing to take a 5% chance that it will run out of tins before the next order arrives.

Using this information, McCreery's establishes the following restocking level:

$$R = \mu_{RP+L} + z\sigma_{RP+L}$$
$$= 240 \text{ tins} + 1.65 \times 40 \text{ tins} = 306 \text{ tins}$$

Suppose the next time the deliveryman stops by, he counts 45 tins. Based on this information, he will order $Q = 306 - 45 = 261$ tins, which will be delivered in three days.

14.3 CONTINUOUS REVIEW SYSTEMS

Continuous review system An inventory system used to manage independent demand inventory. The inventory level for an item is constantly monitored, and when the reorder point is reached, an order is released.

Though the periodic review system is straightforward, it is *not* well suited to managing critical and/or expensive inventory items. A more sophisticated approach is needed for these types of inventory. In a **continuous review system**, the inventory level for an item is constantly monitored, and when the reorder point is reached, an order is released.

A continuous review system has several key features:

1. Inventory levels are monitored constantly, and a replenishment order is issued only when a preestablished reorder point has been reached.
2. The size of a replenishment order is typically based on the trade-off between holding costs and ordering costs.
3. The reorder point is based on both demand and supply considerations, as well as on how much safety stock managers want to hold.

To simplify our discussion of continuous review systems, we will begin by assuming that the variables that underlie the system are constant. Specifically:

1. The inventory item we are interested in has a constant demand per period, d. That is, there is no variability in demand from one period to the next. Demand for the year is D.
2. L is the lead time, or number of periods that must pass before a replenishment order arrives. L is also constant.
3. H is the cost of holding a single unit in inventory for a year. It includes the cost of the space needed to store the unit, the cost of potential obsolescence, and the opportunity cost of tying up the organization's funds in inventory. H is known and fixed.

FIGURE 14.7
Continuous Review System (with Constant Demand Rate d)

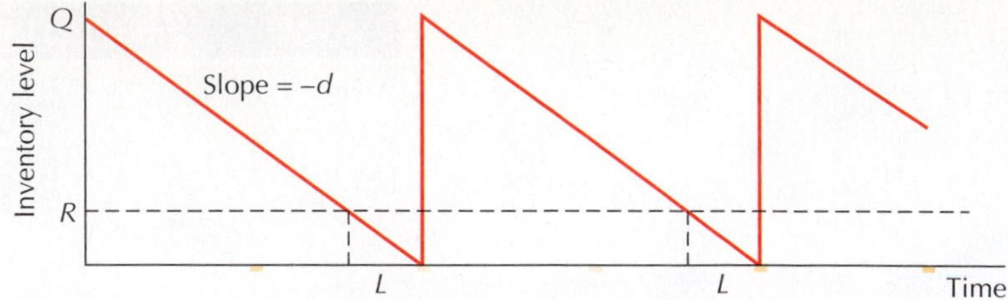

4. S is the cost of placing an order, regardless of the order quantity. For example, the cost to place an order might be \$100, whether the order is for 2 or 2000 units. S is also known and fixed.
5. P, the price of each unit, is fixed.

Under the assumptions just listed, the fluctuations in the inventory levels for an item will look like those in Figure 14.7. Inventory levels start out at Q, the order quantity, and decrease at a constant rate, d. Because this is a continuous review system, the next order is issued when the reorder point, labeled R, is reached. What should the reorder point be? In this simple model, in which the demand rate and lead time are constant, we should reorder when the inventory level reaches the point where there are just enough units left to meet requirements until the next order arrives:

$$R = dL \qquad \textbf{[14-3]}$$

For example, if the demand rate is 50 units a week and the lead time is three weeks, the manager should place an order when the inventory level drops to 150 units. If everything goes according to plan, the firm will run out of units just as the next order arrives. Finally, because the inventory level in this model goes from Q to 0 over and over again, the average inventory level is $Q/2$.

The Economic Order Quantity (*EOQ*)

How do managers of a continuous review system choose the order quantity (Q)? Is there a "best" order quantity, and if so, how do holding costs (H) and ordering costs (S) affect it? To understand the role of holding and ordering costs in a continuous review system, let's see what happens if the order quantity is sliced in half, to Q', as shown in Figure 14.8. The result: With quantity Q', the manager ends up ordering twice as often, which doubles the company's ordering costs. On the other hand, cutting the order quantity in half also halves the average inventory level, which lowers holding costs.

FIGURE 14.8
The Effect of Halving the Order Quantity

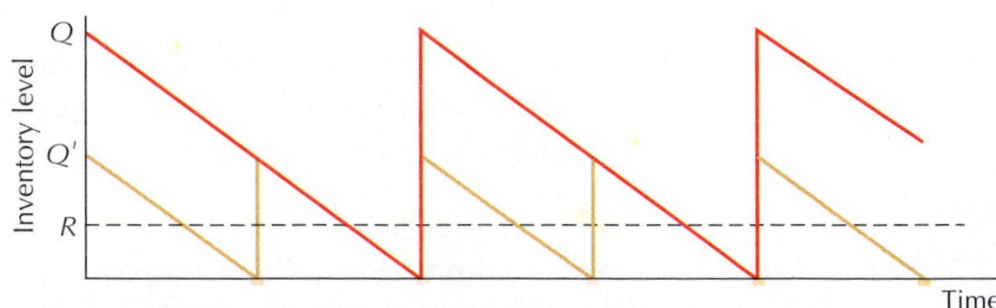

The relationship between holding costs and ordering costs can be seen in the following equation:

Total holding and ordering cost for the year = Total yearly holding costs + total yearly ordering costs

$$= \left(\frac{Q}{2}\right)H + \left(\frac{D}{Q}\right) \times S \qquad [14\text{-}4]$$

Yearly holding cost is calculated by taking the average inventory level ($Q/2$) and multiplying it by the per-unit holding cost. Yearly ordering cost is calculated by calculating the number of times we order per year (D/Q) and multiplying this by the fixed ordering cost.

As the equation suggests, there is a trade-off between yearly holding costs and ordering costs. Reducing the order quantity, Q, will decrease holding costs, but force the organization to order more often. Conversely, increasing Q will reduce the number of times an order must be placed, but result in higher average inventory levels.

Figure 14.9 shows graphically how yearly holding and ordering costs react as the order quantity, Q, varies. In addition to showing the cost curves for yearly holding costs and yearly ordering costs, Figure 14.9 includes a total cost curve that combines these two. If you look closely, you can see that the lowest point on the total cost curve also happens to be where yearly holding costs equal yearly ordering costs.

Economic order quantity (EOQ)
The order quantity that minimizes annual holding and ordering costs for an item.

Figure 14.9 illustrates the **economic order quantity (EOQ)**, the particular order quantity (Q) that minimizes holding costs and ordering costs for an item. This special order quantity is found by setting yearly holding costs equal to yearly ordering costs and solving for Q:

$$\left(\frac{Q}{2}\right)H = \left(\frac{D}{Q}\right)S$$

$$Q^2 = \frac{2DS}{H} \qquad [14\text{-}5]$$

$$Q = \sqrt{\frac{2DS}{H}} = EOQ$$

where:

Q = order quantity
H = annual holding cost per unit
D = annual demand
S = ordering cost

FIGURE 14.9
The Relationships among Yearly Holding Costs, Yearly Ordering Costs, and the Order Quantity, Q

As Figure 14.9 shows, order quantities that are higher than the *EOQ* will result in annual holding costs that are higher than ordering costs. Conversely, order quantities that are lower than the *EOQ* will result in annual ordering costs that are higher than holding costs.

Example 14.2

Calculating the *EOQ* at Boyer's Department Store

You are in charge of ordering items for Boyer's Department Store, located in Chicago. For one of the products Boyer's carries, the Hudson Valley Model Y ceiling fan, you have the following information:

$$\text{Annual demand } (D) = 4000 \text{ fans a year}$$
$$\text{Annual holding cost } (H) = \$15 \text{ per fan}$$
$$\text{Ordering cost } (S) = \$50 \text{ per order}$$

Your predecessor ordered fans four times a year, in quantities (Q) of 1000. The resulting annual holding and ordering costs were

$$\begin{aligned}&\text{Holding costs for the year} + \text{ordering costs for the year}\\&= (1{,}000/2)\$15 + (4{,}000/1{,}000)\$50\\&= \$7{,}500 + \$200 = \$7{,}700\end{aligned}$$

Because holding costs are much higher than ordering costs, we know that the *EOQ* must be much lower than 1000 fans. In fact:

$$EOQ = \sqrt{\frac{2 \times 4{,}000 \times \$50}{\$15}}, \text{ which rounds to 163 fans per order}$$

The number 163 seems odd, so let's check to see if it results in lower annual costs:

$$\begin{aligned}&\text{Holding costs} + \text{ordering costs}\\&= (163/2)\$15 + (4{,}000/163)\$50\\&= \$1{,}222.50 + \$1{,}226.99 = \$2{,}449.49\end{aligned}$$

Notice that holding costs and ordering costs are essentially equal, as we would expect. More important, *simply by ordering the right quantity*, we could reduce annual holding and ordering costs for this item by

$$\$7700 - \$2449 = \$5251$$

Now suppose Boyer's carries 250 other products with cost and demand structures similar to that of the Hudson Valley Model Y ceiling fan. In that case, we might be able to save $250 \times \$5251 = \$1{,}312{,}750$ per year just by ordering the right quantities!

Of course, the *EOQ* has some limitations. Holding costs (H) and ordering costs (S) cannot always be estimated precisely, so managers may not always be able to calculate the true *EOQ*. However, as Figure 14.9 suggests, total holding and ordering costs are relatively flat over a wide range around the *EOQ*. So order quantities can be off a little and still yield total costs that are close to the minimum.

A more valid criticism of the *EOQ* is that it does not take into account volume discounts, which can be particularly important if suppliers offer steep discounts to encourage customers to order in large quantities. Later in the chapter, we examine how volume discounts affect the order quantity decision.

Other factors that limit the application of the *EOQ* model include ordering costs that are not always fixed and demand rates that vary throughout the year. However, the *EOQ* is a good starting point for understanding the impact of order quantities on inventory-related costs.

Reorder Points and Safety Stock

The *EOQ* tells managers *how much* to order, but not *when* to order. We saw earlier that when the demand rate (d) and lead time (L) are constant, the reorder point is easily calculated as

$$ROP = dL \qquad [14\text{-}3]$$

But d and L are rarely fixed. Consider for a moment the data in Table 14.3, which lists 10 different combinations of demand rates and lead times. The average demand rate, $\bar{d}$, and average lead time, $\bar{L}$, are 50 units and three weeks, respectively. Our first inclination in this case might be to set the reorder point at $\bar{d}\bar{L} = 150$ units. Yet 5 out of 10 times, dL exceeds 150 units (see Table 14.3). A better solution—one that takes into account the variability in demand rate and lead time—is needed.

When either lead time or demand—or both—varies, a better solution is to set the reorder point higher than $ROP = dL$. Specifically:

$$ROP = \bar{d}\bar{L} + SS \qquad [14\text{-}6]$$

where:

SS = safety stock

Recall that WolfByte Computers carried a safety stock of 1000 mice (Figure 14.4). Again, safety stock (SS) is an extra amount beyond that needed to meet average demand during lead time. This is added to the reorder point to protect against variability in both demand and lead time. Safety stock raises the reorder point, forcing a company to reorder earlier than usual. In doing so, it helps to ensure that future orders will arrive before the existing inventory runs out.

TABLE 14.3 Sample Variations in Demand Rate and Lead Time

DEMAND RATE (d) IN UNITS PER WEEK	LEAD TIME (L) IN WEEKS	DEMAND DURING LEAD TIME (dL) IN UNITS
60	3	180*
40	4	160*
55	2	110
45	3	135
50	3	150
65	3	195*
35	3	105
55	3	165*
45	4	180*
50	2	100
Average = 50 units	Average = 3 weeks	Average = 148 units

*Demand greater than $\bar{d}\bar{L}$

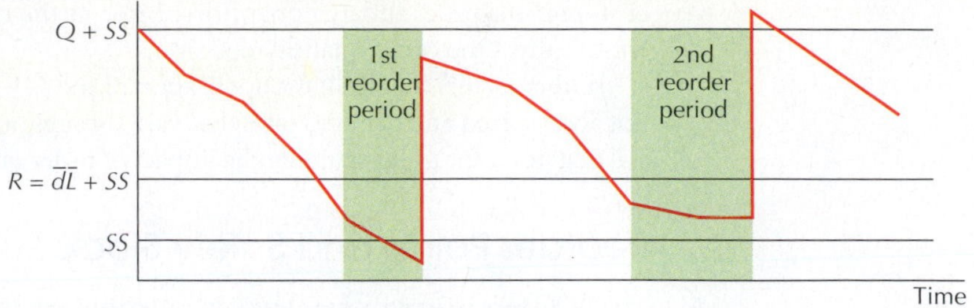

FIGURE 14.10
The Impact of Varying Demand Rates and Lead Times

Figure 14.10 shows how safety stock works when both the demand rate and the lead time vary. We start with an inventory level of Q plus the safety stock $(Q + SS)$. When we reach the new reorder point of $\bar{d}\bar{L} + SS$, an order is released. But look what happens during the first reorder period: Demand exceeds $\bar{d}\bar{L}$, forcing workers to dip into the safety stock. If the safety stock had not been there, the inventory would have run out. In the second reorder period, even though the lead time is longer than before, demand flattens out so much that workers do not need the safety stock.

In general, the decision of how much safety stock to hold depends on five factors:

1. The variability of demand;
2. The variability of lead time;
3. The average length of lead time; and
4. The desired service level.
5. The average demand

Let's talk about each of these. First, the more the demand level and the lead time vary, the more likely it is inventory will run out. Therefore, higher variability in demand and lead time will tend to force a company to hold more safety stock. Furthermore, a longer average lead time exposes a firm to this variability for a longer period. When lead times are extremely short, as they are in just-in-time (JIT) environments (see Chapter 16), safety stocks can be very small.

The service level is a managerial decision. Service levels are usually expressed in statistical terms, such as "During the reorder period, we should have stock available 90% of the time." Though the idea that management might agree to accept even a small percentage of stockouts may seem strange, in reality, whenever demand or lead time varies, the *possibility* exists that a firm will run out of an item, no matter how large the safety stock. The higher the desired service level is, the less willing management is to tolerate a stockout, and the more safety stock is needed.

Example 14.3

Calculating the Reorder Point and Safety Stock at Boyer's Department Store

Let's look at one approach to calculating the reorder point with safety stock, which, like others, is based on simple statistics. To demonstrate the math, we'll return to Boyer's Department Store and the Hudson Valley Model Y ceiling fan. Boyer's sells, on average, 16 Hudson Valley Model Y ceiling fans a day ($\bar{d} = 16$), with a standard deviation in daily demand of 3 ($\sigma_d = 3$). This demand information can be estimated easily from past sales history.

If the store reorders fans directly from the manufacturer, they will take, on average, nine days to arrive ($\bar{L} = 9$), with a standard deviation in lead time of 2 ($\sigma_L = 2$). The store manager has decided to maintain a 95% service level. In other words, the manager is willing to run out of fans only 5% of the time before the next order arrives.

From these numbers, we can see that

$$\text{Average demand during the reorder period} = \bar{d}\bar{L} = 144 \text{ fans}$$

Taking the analysis a step further, we can show using basic statistics that:

Standard deviation of demand during the reorder period

$$= \sigma_{dL}$$

$$= \sqrt{\bar{L}\sigma_d^2 + \bar{d}^2\sigma_L^2} = \sqrt{9 \times 9 + 256 \times 4} \qquad [14\text{-}7]$$

$$= 33.24$$

To ensure that Boyer's meets its desired service level, we need to set the reorder point high enough to meet demand during the reorder period 95% of the time. Put another way, the reorder point (*ROP*) should be set at the 95th percentile of demand during the reorder period. Because demand during the reorder period is often normally distributed, basic statistics tells us that:

Reorder point (*ROP*) = 95th percentile of demand during the reorder period

$$= \bar{d}\bar{L} + z\sigma_{dL}$$
$$= 144 + 1.65 \times 33.24$$
$$= 198.8, \text{ or } 199$$

In this equation, 1.65 represents the number of standard deviations (z) above the mean that corresponds to the 95th percentile of a normally distributed variable. (Other z values and their respective service levels are shown in Table 14.4.) The more general formula for calculating the reorder point is therefore:

$$ROP = \bar{d}\bar{L} + z\sqrt{\bar{L}\sigma_d^2 + \bar{d}^2\sigma_L^2} \qquad [14\text{-}8]$$

where:

$\bar{d}$ = average demand per time period

$\bar{L}$ = average lead time

σ_d^2 = variance of demand per time period

σ_L^2 = variance of lead time

z = number of standard deviations above the average demand during lead time (higher z values lower the probability of a stockout)

TABLE 14.4 z Values Used in Calculating Safety Stock

z VALUE	ASSOCIATED SERVICE LEVEL
0.84	80%
1.28	90
1.65	95
2.33	99

Notice that the first part of the equation, $\bar{d}\bar{L}$, covers only the average demand during the reorder period. The second part of the equation, $z\sqrt{\bar{L}\sigma_d^2 + \bar{d}^2\sigma_L^2}$, represents the safety stock. For Boyer's, then, the amount of safety stock needed is:

$$z\sqrt{\bar{L}\sigma_d^2 + \bar{d}^2\sigma_L^2} = 1.65 \times 33.24 = 54.88, \text{ or } 55 \text{ fans}$$

Of course, there are other methods for determining safety stock. Some managers consider variations in both the lead time and the demand rate; others use a definition of service level that includes the frequency of reordering. (Firms that reorder less often than others are less susceptible to stockouts.) In practice, many firms take an unscientific approach to safety stock, such as setting the reorder point equal to 150% of expected demand. Whatever the method used, however, these observations will still hold: The amount of safety stock needed will be affected by the variability of demand and lead time, the length of the average lead time, and the desired service level.

Quantity Discounts

In describing the economic order quantity, one of our assumptions was that the price per unit, P, was fixed. This was a convenient assumption because it allowed us to focus on minimizing just the total holding and ordering costs for the year (Equation 14-5). But what if a supplier offers us a price discount for ordering larger quantities? How will this affect the EOQ?

When quantity discounts are in effect, we must modify our analysis to look at total ordering, holding, *and item costs* for the year:

Total holding, ordering, and item costs for the year =

$$\left(\frac{Q}{2}\right)H+\left(\frac{D}{Q}\right)S+DP \qquad [14\text{-}9]$$

where:

Q = order quantity

H = holding cost per unit

D = annual demand

P = price per unit (which can now vary)

S = ordering cost

Because the EOQ formula (Equation 14-5) considers only holding and ordering costs, the EOQ may not result in lowest total costs when quantity discounts are in effect. To illustrate, suppose we have the following information:

D = 1,200 units per year

H = \$10 per unit per year

S = \$30 per order

P = \$35 per unit for orders less than 90; \$32.50 for orders of 90 or more

If we ignore the price discounts and calculate the EOQ, we get the following:

$$EOQ=\sqrt{\frac{2\times 1{,}200\times \$30}{\$10}}\text{, which rounds to 85 units}$$

Total annual holding, ordering, and item costs for an order quantity of 85 are:

$$\left(\frac{85}{2}\right)\$10+\left(\frac{1{,}200}{85}\right)\$30+\$35\times 1{,}200=\$425+\$423.53+\$42{,}000$$
$$=\$42{,}848.53$$

But note that if we increase the order size by just 5 units to 90, we can get a discount of \$35 − \$32.50 = \$2.50 per unit. Selecting an order quantity of 90 would give us the following annual holding, ordering, and item costs:

$$\left(\frac{90}{2}\right)\$10+\left(\frac{1{,}200}{90}\right)\$30+\$32.50\times 1{,}200=\$450+\$400+\$39{,}000$$
$$=\$39{,}850.00$$

When volume price discounts are in effect, we must follow a two-step process:

1. Calculate the *EOQ*. If the *EOQ* number represents a quantity that can be purchased for the lowest price, stop—you have found the lowest-cost order quantity. Otherwise, go to step 2.
2. Compare total holding, ordering, and item costs at the *EOQ* quantity with total costs at each price break *above* the *EOQ*. There is no reason to look at quantities below the *EOQ*, as these would result in higher holding and ordering costs, as well as higher item costs.

Example 14.4

Volume Discounts at Hal's Magic Shop

Hal's Magic Shop purchases masks from a Taiwanese manufacturer. The manufacturer has quoted the following price breaks to Hal:

ORDER QUANTITY	PRICE PER MASK
1–100	\$15
101–200	\$12.50
201 or more	\$10

Hal sells 1000 masks a year. The cost to place an order is \$20, and the holding cost per mask is about \$3 per year. How many masks should Hal order at a time?

Solving for the *EOQ*, Hal gets the following:

$$EOQ = \sqrt{\frac{2 \times 1{,}000 \times \$20}{\$3}} = 115 \text{ masks}$$

Unfortunately, Hal cannot order 115 masks and get the lowest price of \$10 per mask. Therefore, he compares total holding, ordering, and item costs at $Q = 115$ masks to those at the next highest price break, 201 masks:

Total annual holding, ordering, and item costs for an order quantity of 115 masks =

$$\left(\frac{115}{2}\right)\$3 + \left(\frac{1{,}000}{115}\right)\$20 + 12.50 \times 1{,}000 = \$172.50 + \$173.91 + \$12{,}500$$
$$= \$12{,}846.41$$

Total annual holding, ordering, and item costs for an order quantity of 201 masks =

$$\left(\frac{201}{2}\right)\$3 + \left(\frac{1{,}000}{201}\right)\$20 + \$10.00 \times 1{,}000 = \$301.50 + \$99.50 + \$10{,}000$$
$$= \$10{,}401.00$$

So even though an order quantity of 115 would minimize holding and ordering costs, the price discount associated with ordering 201 masks more than offsets this. Hal should use an order quantity of 201 masks.

14.4 SINGLE-PERIOD INVENTORY SYSTEMS

So far, our discussions have assumed that any excess inventory we order can be held for future use. But this is not always true. In some situations, excess inventory has a very limited life and must be discarded, sold at a loss, or even hauled away at additional cost if not sold in the period intended. Examples include fresh fish, magazines and newspapers, and Christmas trees. In other cases, inventory might have such a specialized purpose (such as some spare parts for a specialized machine) that any unused units cannot be used elsewhere.

When these conditions apply, companies must weigh the cost of being short against the cost of having excess units, where:

Single-period inventory system
A system used when demand occurs in only a single point in time.

$$\text{Shortage cost} = C_{\text{Shortage}} = \text{value of the item } \textit{if} \text{ demanded} - \text{item cost} \quad \textbf{[14-10]}$$

$$\text{Excess cost} = C_{\text{Excess}} = \text{item cost} + \text{disposal cost} - \text{salvage value} \quad \textbf{[14-11]}$$

Target service level
For a single-period inventory system, the service level at which the expected cost of a shortage equals the expected cost of having excess units.

For example, an item that sells for \$200 that costs \$50, but must be disposed of at a cost of \$5 if not used, has the following shortage and excess costs:

$$C_{\text{Shortage}} = \$200 - \$50 = \$150$$
$$C_{\text{Excess}} = \$50 + \$5 = \$55$$

Target stocking point
For a single-period inventory system, the stocking point at which the expected cost of a shortage equals the expected cost of having excess units.

The goal of a **single-period inventory system** is to establish a stocking level that strikes the *best balance* between expected shortage costs and expected excess costs. Developing a single-period system for an item is a two-step process:

1. Determine a **target service level** (SL_T) that strikes the best balance between shortage costs and excess costs.
2. Use the target service level to determine the **target stocking point** (TS) for the item.

We describe each of these steps in more detail in the following sections.

Target Service Level

For the single-period inventory system, service level is simply the probability that there are enough units to meet demand. Unlike a periodic and continuous review system, there is no reorder period to consider here—either there is enough inventory or there isn't. The target service level, then, is the service level at which the expected cost of a shortage equals the expected cost of having excess units:

$$\text{Expected shortage cost} = \text{expected excess cost}$$

or

$$(1 - p)C_{\text{Shortage}} = pC_{\text{Excess}} \tag{14-12}$$

where:

p = probability that there are enough units to meet demand
$(1 - p)$ = probability that there is a shortage
C_{Shortage} = shortage cost
C_{Excess} = excess cost

The target service level (SL_T) is the p value at which Equation 14-12 holds true:

$$(1 - SL_T)C_{\text{Shortage}} = SL_T C_{\text{Excess}}$$

$$SL_T = \frac{C_{\text{Shortage}}}{C_{\text{Shortage}} + C_{\text{Excess}}} \tag{14-13}$$

Let's use Equation 14-13 to test our intuition. Suppose the shortage cost and the excess cost for an item are both \$10. In this case, we would be indifferent to either outcome, and we would set the inventory level so that each outcome would be equally likely. Equation 14-13 confirms our logic:

$$SL_T = \frac{C_{\text{Shortage}}}{C_{\text{Shortage}} + C_{\text{Excess}}} = \frac{\$10}{\$10 + \$10} = 0.50, \text{ or } 50\%$$

But what if the cost associated with a shortage is much higher—say, \$90? In this case, we would want a much higher target service level because shortage costs are so much more severe than excess costs. Again, Equation 14-13 supports our reasoning:

$$\frac{C_{\text{Shortage}}}{C_{\text{Shortage}} + C_{\text{Excess}}} = \frac{\$90}{\$90 + \$10} = 0.9, \text{ or } 90\%$$

Example 14.5

Determining the Target Service Level at Don's Lemonade Stands

Don Washing is trying to determine how many gallons of lemonade to make each day. Don needs to consider a single-period system because whatever lemonade is left over at the end of the day must be thrown away due to health concerns. Every gallon he mixes costs him \$2.50, but will generate \$10 in revenue if sold.

In terms of the single-period inventory problem, Don's shortage and excess costs are defined as follows:

$$C_{\text{Shortage}} = \text{revenue per gallon} - \text{cost per gallon} = \$10.00 - \$2.50 = \$7.50$$
$$C_{\text{Excess}} = \text{cost per gallon} = \$2.50$$

From this information, Don can calculate his target service level:

$$SL_T = \frac{C_{\text{Shortage}}}{C_{\text{Shortage}} + C_{\text{Excess}}} = \frac{\$7.50}{\$7.50 + \$2.50} = 0.75, \text{ or } 75\%$$

Interpreting the results, Don should make enough lemonade to meet demand approximately 75% of the time.

Example 14.6

Determining the Target Service Level at Fran's Flowers

Every day, Fran Chapman of Fran's Flowers makes floral arrangements for sale at the local hospital. The arrangements cost her approximately \$12 to make, but sell for \$25. Any leftover arrangements can be sold at a heavily discounted price of \$5 the following day. Fran wants to know what her target service level should be.

Fran's shortage and excess costs are as follows:

$$C_{\text{Shortage}} = \text{revenue per arrangement} - \text{cost per arrangement} = \$25 - \$12 = \$13$$
$$C_{\text{Excess}} = \text{cost per arrangement} - \text{salvage value} = \$12 - \$5 = \$7$$

Fran's target service level is therefore

$$SL_T = \frac{C_{\text{Shortage}}}{C_{\text{Shortage}} + C_{\text{Excess}}} = \frac{\$13}{\$13 + \$7} = 0.65, \text{ or } 65\%$$

Fran should make enough arrangements to meet demand approximately 65% of the time.

Target Stocking Point

To complete the development of a single-period inventory system, we next have to translate the target service level (a probability) into a target stocking point. To do so, we have to know something about how demand is distributed. Depending on the situation, we can approximate the demand distribution from historical records, or we can use a theoretical distribution, such as the normal distribution or Poisson distribution. Furthermore, the distribution may be continuous (i.e., demand can take on fractional values) or discrete (i.e., demand can take on only integer values). Example 14.7 shows how the process works when we can model demand using the normal distribution, while Example 14.8 demonstrates the process for a historically based discrete distribution.

Example 14.7

Determining the Target Stocking Point at Don's Lemonade Stands

In Example 14.5, Don determined that the target service level for lemonade was

$$\frac{C_{\text{Shortage}}}{C_{\text{Shortage}} + C_{\text{Excess}}} = \frac{\$7.50}{\$7.50 + \$2.50} = 0.75, \text{ or } 75\%$$

Don knows from past experience that the daily demand follows a normal distribution. Therefore, Don wants to set a target stocking point (*TS*) that is higher than approximately 75% of the area under the normal curve. Figure 14.11 illustrates the idea.

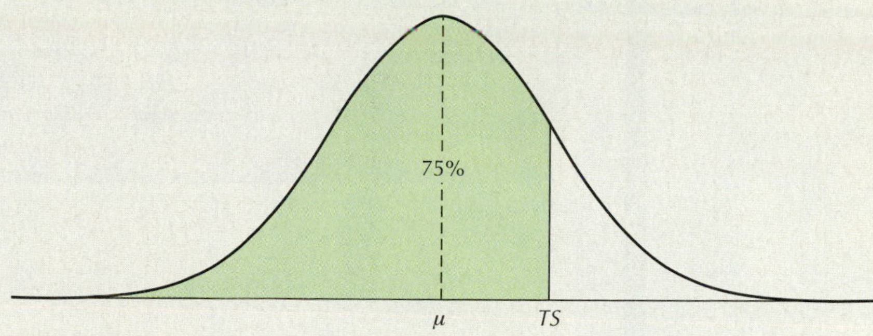

FIGURE 14.11 Target Stocking Point for Don's Lemonade Stands

Don also knows that even though the daily demand for lemonade is normally distributed, the mean values and standard deviations differ depending on the day of the week (Table 14.5). Therefore, he will have to calculate different target stocking points for Monday through Friday, Saturday, and Sunday.

TABLE 14.5 Demand Values for Don's Lemonade Stands

DAY OF THE WEEK	MEAN DEMAND, μ	STANDARD DEVIATION OF DEMAND, σ
Monday–Friday	422 gallons	67 gallons
Saturday	719 gallons	113 gallons
Sunday	528 gallons	85 gallons

Using a cumulative normal table (Appendix I), Don quickly determines that a service level of 75% would require the target stocking point to be approximately 0.68 standard deviations above the mean. Therefore, the target stocking points are as follows:

Monday–Friday:	$422 + 0.68 \times 67 = 467.56$ gallons
Saturday:	$719 + 0.68 \times 113 = 795.84$ gallons
Sunday:	$528 + 0.68 \times 85 = 585.8$ gallons

Example 14.8

Determining the Target Stocking Point at Fran's Flowers

In Example 14.6, Fran calculated her target service level for floral arrangements:

$$\frac{C_{\text{Shortage}}}{C_{\text{Shortage}} + C_{\text{Excess}}} = \frac{\$13}{\$13 + \$7} = 0.65, \text{ or } 65\%$$

Fran has kept track of arrangement sales for the past 34 days and has recorded the demand numbers shown in Table 14.6.

Looking at Table 14.6, Fran realizes that if she wants to meet her target service level of 65%, she will need to stock 15 arrangements each day. This is because 15 arrangements is the first stocking point at which the probability of meeting expected demand (73.5%) is greater than the target service level of 65%. Conversely, if Fran stocked just 14 arrangements, according to Table 14.6 she would meet demand only 52.9% of the time.

TABLE 14.6 Demand History for Fran's Flowers

DAILY DEMAND	NO. OF DAYS WITH THIS DEMAND LEVEL DURING THE PAST 34 DAYS	PERCENTAGE OF DAYS EXPERIENCING THIS DEMAND LEVEL	CUMULATIVE PERCENTAGE
10 or fewer	0	0/34 = 0%	0%
11	2	2/34 = 5.9%	5.9%
12	5	5/34 = 14.7%	20.6%
13	5	5/34 = 14.7%	35.3%
14	6	6/34 = 17.6%	52.9%
15	7	7/34 = 20.6%	73.5%
16	5	5/34 = 14.7%	88.2%
17	3	3/34 = 8.8%	97%
18	1	1/34 = 2.9%	100%
19 or more	0	0%	100%

14.5 INVENTORY IN THE SUPPLY CHAIN

So far, we have discussed the functions and drivers of inventory, and we have identified some basic techniques for managing independent demand inventory items. In this section, we broaden our scope to consider the ramifications of inventory decisions for the rest of the supply chain.

The Bullwhip Effect

Bullwhip effect
An extreme change in the supply position upstream in a supply chain generated by a small change in demand downstream in the supply chain.

A major limitation of the *EOQ* model is that it considers the impact on costs for only a single firm. No consideration is given to how order quantity decisions for one firm affect other members of the supply chain. Therefore, even though the *EOQ* minimizes costs for a particular firm, it can cause problems for other partners and may actually increase *overall* supply chain costs. An example of this is the bullwhip effect.[5] APICS defines the **bullwhip effect** as "an extreme change in the supply position upstream in a supply chain generated by a small change in demand downstream in the supply chain."[6] The bullwhip effect was first discovered and noted by an economist named Forrester, so it is also sometimes called the Forrester Effect. Forrester noted that when there were small perturbations in demand, parties in the supply chain held extra inventory as a precaution, and the further one went back in the chain, the higher the inventory buildup.

[5] Hau L. Lee, V. Padmanabhan, and S. Whang, "The Bullwhip Effect in Supply Chain," *Sloan Management Review* 38, no. 3 (Spring 1997): 70–77.

[6] Cox and Blackstone, *APICS Dictionary*.

FIGURE 14.12
Total Demand across the Six Distributors

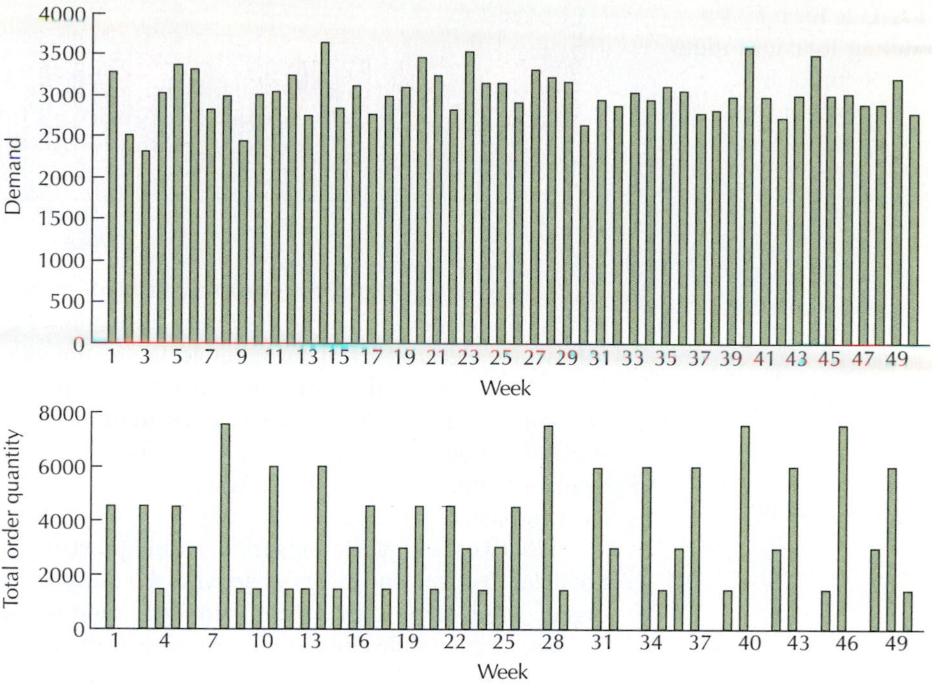

To illustrate, suppose the ABC plant makes pool cleaners that are sold through six distributors. The distributors have similar demand patterns and identical *EOQ* and *ROP* quantities:

Average weekly demand = 500 pool cleaners (standard deviation = 100)
Order quantity = 1500
Reorder point = 750

Figure 14.12 shows the results of a simulation covering 50 weeks of simulated demand across the six distributors. Even though total weekly demand across the six distributors ranged from 2331 to 3641, the quantities ordered from the plant ranged from 0 to 7,500.

What causes this? Quite simply, if a distributor reaches its reorder point, it places a large order. Otherwise, it does nothing. Therefore, a single unit change in demand may determine whether or not the distributor places an order. So even though the distributors may be following good inventory practice by ordering in quantities of 1500, the impact on the supply chain is to increase demand variability at the plant. Ultimately, this demand variability will drive up costs at the plant, which will then be forced to pass at least some of these costs on to the distributors.

In order to reduce the bullwhip effect, many supply chain partners are working together to reduce order quantities by removing volume discount incentives and reducing ordering costs. Figure 14.13 shows, for example, what the quantities ordered from the plant would look like if order quantities were cut in half to 750. Now the orders range from 750 to 4500—not perfect, but a big improvement over what they were before.

Inventory Positioning

Managers must also decide *where* in the supply chain to hold inventory. At the risk of oversimplifying, the decision as to where to position inventory is based on two general truths:

1. The cost and value of inventory increase as materials move down the supply chain.
2. The flexibility of inventory decreases as materials move down the supply chain.

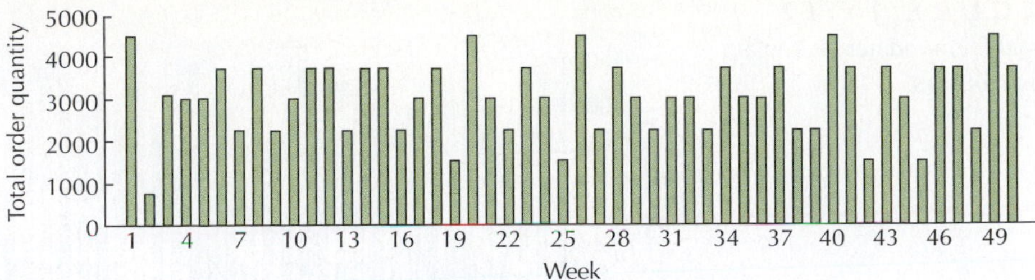

FIGURE 14.13 Resulting Total Quantities (Q=750 for Each Distributor) Ordered from the ABC Plant

That is, as materials work their way through the supply chain, they are transformed, packaged, and moved closer to their final destination. All these activities add both cost and value. Take breakfast cereal, for example. By the time it reaches the stores, cereal has gone through such a significant transformation and repackaging that it appears to have little in common with the basic materials that went into it. But the value added goes beyond transformation and packaging; it includes location as well. A product that is in stock and available immediately is always worth more to the customer than the same product available later.

What keeps organizations from pushing inventory as far down the supply chain as possible? Cost, for one thing. By delaying the transformation and movement of materials, organizations can postpone the related costs. Another reason for holding inventory back in the supply chain is flexibility. Once materials have been transformed, packaged, and transported down the chain, reversing the process becomes very difficult, if not impossible. Wheat that has been used to make a breakfast cereal cannot be changed into flour that is suitable for making a cake. Likewise, repackaging shampoo into a different-sized container is impractical once it has been bottled. The same goes for transportation: Repositioning goods from one location to the next can be quite expensive, especially compared to the cost of delaying their movement until demand has become more certain. This loss of flexibility is a major reason why materials are often held back in the supply chain. In short, supply chain managers are constantly trying to strike a balance between costs, on the one hand, and flexibility, on the other, in deciding where to position inventory.

Example 14.9

Pooling Safety Stock at Boyer's Department Store

An especially good case for holding inventory back can be made if an organization can hold all of its safety stock in a single central location. This is one example of **inventory pooling**, in which several locations share safety stock inventories in order to lower overall holding costs. Suppose, for instance, that Boyer's has eight stores in the Chicago area. Each store sells, on average, 16 ceiling fans a day. Suppose that the standard deviation of daily demand at each store is 3 ($\sigma_d = 3$) and the average lead time is nine days, with a standard deviation of two days. We showed in Example 14.3 that to maintain a 95% service level ($z = 1.65$), a store would need to maintain a safety stock of 55 fans. The total safety stock across all eight stores would therefore be $8 \times 55 = 440$ fans.

But what if Boyer's could pool the safety stock for all eight stores at a single store, which could provide same-day service to the other seven stores? Because a single location would have a demand variance equal to n times that of n individual stores:

$$\text{Standard deviation of demand during lead time across } n \text{ locations} = \sqrt{n} \times \sigma_{dL}$$

For Boyer's this calculates out to:

$$= \sqrt{8} \times \sqrt{\bar{L} \times \sigma_d^2 + \bar{d}^2 \times \sigma_L^2} = \sqrt{8} \times 33.24 = 94 \text{ fans}$$

Inventory pooling
The act of holding safety stock in a single location instead of multiple locations. Several locations then share safety stock inventories to lower overall holding costs by reducing overall safety stock levels.

And the pooled safety stock would be:

$$z \times 94 = 1.65 \times 94 = 155.1, \text{ or } 155 \text{ fans}$$

By pooling its safety stock, Boyer's could reduce the safety stock level by $(440 - 155) =$ 285 fans, or 65%. Considering the *thousands* of items stocked in Boyer's eight stores, centralizing Boyer's safety stock could produce significant savings.

SUPPLY CHAIN CONNECTIONS

INVENTORY MANAGEMENT AND POOLING GROUPS AT SATURN[7]

Automobile dealerships face a classic dilemma in deciding how to manage their inventories of service parts. On the one hand, customers expect their cars to be fixed promptly. On the other hand, dealerships typically do not have the space or financial resources to stock all the possible items a customer's car may need. If this wasn't difficult enough, most dealerships do not have the inventory expertise on site to deal with these issues.

To address these concerns, Saturn has developed a system in which the company makes inventory decisions for the dealerships, based on calculated reorder points. Of course, the dealerships may override Saturn's recommendations if they like. And if a part placed in the dealership under the recommendation of Saturn sits at the dealership for more than nine months, Saturn will buy it back.

Saturn has also helped the dealerships establish "pooling groups" made up of Saturn dealerships in the same geographic region. These dealerships agree to "share" safety stocks for expensive or slow-moving items. Saturn provides an information system that helps the dealerships divide the safety stocks of these items among themselves. If one dealership runs out of the part, it can instantly check on the part's availability within the pooling group (via the information system run by Saturn) and arrange to have the item picked up. The result is lower overall inventories and better parts availability for the customers.

[7]M. A. Cohen, C. Cull, H. L. Lee, and D. Willen, "Saturn's Supply-Chain Innovation: High-Value in After-Sales Service," *Sloan Management Review* 41, no. 4 (Summer 2000): 93–101.

Transportation, Packaging, and Material Handling Considerations

We will wrap up our discussion of inventory in the supply chain by considering how inventory decisions—most notably, order quantities—are intertwined with transportation, packaging, and material handling issues. The point of this discussion is to recognize that, in the real world, there is more to determining order quantities than just holding, ordering, and item costs.

Consider the following example. Borfax Industries buys specialized chemicals from a key supplier. These chemicals can be purchased in one of two forms:

FORM	QUANTITY	WEIGHT	DIMENSIONALITY (WIDTH/DEPTH/ HEIGHT)	PRICE PER BAG
Carton	144 bags	218 lbs.	2′ × 2′ × 1′	$25
Pallet	12 cartons; 1728 bags	2626 lbs.	4′ × 4′ × 3.5′	$18

First, notice that the chemicals can be purchased in multiples of 144 bags (cartons) or 1728 bags (pallets). It is highly unlikely that any *EOQ* value calculated by Borfax will fit perfectly into either of these packaging alternatives.

If Borfax purchases a full pallet, it can get a substantial price discount per bag. The supplier will also make a direct truck shipment if Borfax purchases five or more pallets at a time. This will reduce the lead time from 15 days to 5. However, pallets require material handling equipment capable of carrying nearly 3000 lbs., as well as suitable storage space. On the other hand, the cartons are less bulky but will still require some specialized handling due to their weight. In choosing the best order quantity, Borfax must not only look at the per-bag price, but must also consider its material handling capabilities, transportation costs, and inventory holding costs.

CHAPTER SUMMARY

Inventory is an important resource in supply chains, serving many functions and taking many forms. But like any resource, it must be managed well if an organization is to remain competitive. We started this chapter by examining the various types of inventory found in a simple supply chain. We also discussed what drives inventory. To the extent that organizations can leverage inventory drivers, they can bring down the amount of inventory they need to hold in order to run their supply chains smoothly.

In the second part of this chapter, we introduced some basic tools for managing independent demand inventory. These tools provide managers with simple models for determining how much to order and when to order. We then examined the relationship between inventory decisions and the bullwhip effect, the decision about where to position inventory in the supply chain, and how transportation, packaging, and material handling considerations might impact inventory decisions.

KEY FORMULAS

Restocking level under a periodic review system (page 444):

$$R = \mu_{RP+L} + z\sigma_{RP+L} \qquad [14\text{-}2]$$

where:

μ_{RP+L} = average demand during the reorder period and the order lead time

σ_{RP+L} = standard deviation of demand during the reorder period and the order lead time

z = number of standard deviations above the average demand (higher z values lower the probability of a stockout)

Total holding and ordering costs for the year (page 447):

$$\text{Total yearly holding costs} + \text{total yearly ordering costs} = \left(\frac{Q}{2}\right)H + \left(\frac{D}{Q}\right) \times S \qquad [14\text{-}4]$$

where:

Q = order quantity
H = annual holding cost per unit
D = annual demand
S = ordering cost

Economic order quantity (EOQ) (page 447):

$$EOQ = \sqrt{\frac{2DS}{H}} \qquad [14\text{-}5]$$

where:

H = annual holding cost per unit
D = annual demand
S = ordering cost

Reorder point under a continuous review system (page 451):

$$ROP = \bar{d}\bar{L} + z\sqrt{\bar{L}\sigma_d^2 + \bar{d}^2\sigma_L^2} \qquad [14\text{-}8]$$

where:

$\bar{d}$ = average demand per time period
$\bar{L}$ = average lead time
σ_d^2 = variance of demand per time period
σ_L^2 = variance of lead time
z = number of standard deviations above the average demand during lead time (higher z values lower the probability of a stockout)

Total holding, ordering, and item costs for the year (page 452):

$$\text{Total holding, ordering, and item costs for the year} = \left(\frac{Q}{2}\right)H + \left(\frac{D}{Q}\right)S + DP \qquad [14\text{-}9]$$

where:

Q = order quantity
H = holding cost per unit
D = annual demand
P = price per unit
S = ordering cost

Target service level under a single-period inventory system (page 455):

$$SL_T = \frac{C_{\text{Shortage}}}{C_{\text{Shortage}} + C_{\text{Excess}}} \quad [14\text{-}13]$$

where:

C_{Shortage} = shortage cost
C_{Excess} = excess cost

KEY TERMS

Anticipation inventory 439
Bullwhip effect 458
Continuous review system 445
Cycle stock 438
Demand uncertainty 441
Dependent demand inventory 443
Economic order quantity (EOQ) 447
Hedge inventory 440
Independent demand inventory 443
Inventory 437
Inventory drivers 441
Inventory pooling 460
Periodic review system 443
Safety stock 439
Service level 444
Single-period inventory system 454
Smoothing inventories 440
Supply uncertainty 441
Target service level 454
Target stocking point 454
Transportation inventory 440

USING EXCEL IN INVENTORY MANAGEMENT

Several of the models described in this chapter depend on estimates of average demand and average lead time and on associated measures of variance (σ^2) or standard deviation (σ). The spreadsheet model in Figure 14.14 shows how such values can be quickly estimated from historical data using Microsoft Excel's built-in functions. The spreadsheet contains historical demand data for 20 weeks, as well as lead time information for 15 prior orders. From this information, the spreadsheet calculates average values and variances and then uses these values to calculate average demand during lead time, safety stock, and the reorder point. The highlighted cells represent the input values. The calculated cells are as follows:

Cell C32 (average weekly demand):	= AVERAGE(C12:C31)
Cell C33 (variance of weekly demand):	= VAR(C12:C31)
Cell G27 (average order lead time):	= AVERAGE(G12:G26)
Cell G28 (variance of lead time):	= VAR(G12:G26)
Cell F5 (average demand during lead time):	= C32*G27
Cell F6 (safety stock):	= F3*SQRT(G27*C33+C32^2*G28)
Cell F7 (reorder point):	= F5+F6

	A	B	C	D	E	F	G	H	I
1	Calculating the Reorder Point from Demand and Order History								
2									
3		z value (for desired service level:)				1.65			
4									
5			Average demand during lead time:			280.72	units		
6					+ Safety stock:	125.47	units		
7					Reorder point:	406.19	units	(Equation 14-6)	
8									
9		*** Demand History ***				*** Order History ***			
10							Lead time		
11		Week	Demand			Order	(days)		
12		1	33			1	10		
13		2	14			2	6		
14		3	18			3	12		
15		4	37			4	9		
16		5	34			5	10		
17		6	53			6	8		
18		7	31			7	8		
19		8	21			8	8		
20		9	19			9	7		
21		10	44			10	3		
22		11	43			11	8		
23		12	37			12	9		
24		13	45			13	7		
25		14	43			14	8		
26		15	36			15	8		
27		16	40			Average:	8.07		
28		17	28			Variance:	4.07		
29		18	41						
30		19	36						
31		20	43						
32		Average:	34.80						
33		Variance:	106.27						

FIGURE 14.14 Excel Solution to Reorder Point Problem

SOLVED PROBLEMS

Problem 1

Jake Fleming sells distributor rebuild kits used on old Ford V-8 engines. Jake purchases these kits for $20 and sells about 250 kits a year. Each time Jake places an order, it costs him $25 to cover shipping and paperwork. Jake figures that the cost of holding a rebuild kit in inventory is about $3.50 per kit per year. What is the economic order quantity? How many times per year will Jake place an order? How much will it cost Jake to order and hold these kits each year?

Solution

The economic order quantity for the kits is:

$$\sqrt{\frac{2 \times 250 \times \$25}{\$3.50}} = 59.76, \text{ or } 60 \text{ kits}$$

The number of orders placed per year is:

$$\frac{250}{60} = 4.17 \text{ orders per year}$$

The total holding and ordering costs for the year (not counting any safety stock Jake might hold) are:

$$\frac{60}{2}\$3.50 + \frac{250}{60}\$25 = \$105 + \$104.17 = \$209.17$$

Problem 2

The manufacturer of the distributor rebuild kits has agreed to charge Jake just \$15 per kit if he orders 250 at a time. Should Jake take the manufacturer up on its offer?

Solution

For the *EOQ*, the total holding, ordering, and item costs for the year are:

$$\frac{60}{2}\$3.50 + \frac{250}{60}\$25 + 250 \times \$20 = \$105 + \$104.17 + \$5{,}000 = \$5{,}209.17$$

If Jake takes the volume discount, he will order 250 at a time (after all, ordering more than 250 would only move him further away from the *EOQ*, which minimizes holding and ordering costs):

$$\frac{250}{2}\$3.50 + \frac{250}{250}\$25 + 250 \times \$15 = \$437.50 + \$25 + \$3{,}750 = \$4{,}212.50$$

Therefore, Jake should take the volume discount and order just once a year.

DISCUSSION QUESTIONS

1. You hear someone comment that *any* inventory is a sign of waste. Do you agree or disagree? Can managers simultaneously justify holding inventories and still seek out ways to lower inventory levels?
2. In your own words, what is an inventory driver? What is the difference between a controllable and an uncontrollable inventory driver? Give examples.
3. Which of the following are independent demand inventory items? Dependent demand inventory items?
   a. Bicycles in a toy store
   b. Bicycle wheels in a bicycle factory
   c. Blood at a blood bank
   d. Hamburgers at a fast-food restaurant
   e. Hamburger buns at a plant producing frozen dinners
4. In a supply chain, what are the pros and cons of pushing inventory downstream, closer to the final customer? How might modular product designs (Chapter 6) make it more profitable for companies to postpone the movement of inventory down the supply chain?
5. (Use the *EOQ* and *ROP* formulas to answer this question.) Which variables could you change if you wanted to reduce inventory costs in your organization? Which ones would you prefer to change? Why?
6. The JIT movement has long argued that firms should
   a. Maximize their process flexibility so that ordering costs are minimal;
   b. Stabilize demand levels;
   c. Shrink lead times as much as possible; and
   d. Assign much higher holding costs to inventory than has traditionally been the case.

   Using the *EOQ* and *ROP* formulas, explain how such efforts would be consistent with JIT's push for lower inventory levels.

PROBLEMS

Additional homework problems are available at www.prenhall.com/bozarth. These problems use Excel to generate customized problems for different class sections or even different students.

(* = easy; ** = moderate; *** = advanced)

1. (*) Pam runs a mail-order business for gym equipment. Annual demand for the TricoFlexers is 16,000. The annual holding cost per unit is $2.50, and the cost to place an order is $50. What is the economic order quantity?

2. (**) Using the same holding and ordering costs as in Problem 1, suppose demand for TricoFlexers doubles to 32,000. Does the *EOQ* also double? Explain what happens.

3. (**) The manufacturer of TricoFlexers has agreed to offer Pam a price discount of $5 per unit ($45 rather than $50) if she buys 1,500. Assuming annual demand is still 16,000, how many units should Pam order at a time?

4. (*) Jimmy's Delicatessen sells large tins of Tom Tucker's Toffee. The deli uses a periodic review system, checking inventory levels every 10 days, at which time an order is placed for more tins. Order lead time is 3 days. Average daily demand is 7 tins, so average demand during the reorder period and order lead time (13 days) is 91 tins. The standard deviation of demand during this same 13-day period is 17 tins. Calculate the restocking level. Assume the desired service level is 90% percent.

5. (**) For Problem 4, suppose the standard deviation of demand during the 13-day period drops to just 4 tins. What happens to the restocking level? Explain why.

6. (***) For Tom Tucker's Toffee in Problem 4, draw a sawtooth diagram similar to the one in Figure 14.3. Assume that the beginning inventory level is equal to the restocking level and that the demand rate is a *constant* 7 tins per day. What is the safety stock level? (*Hint:* Look at the formula for calculating restocking level.) What is the average inventory level?

7. (*) KraftyCity is a large retailer that sells power tools and other hardware supplies. One of its products is the KraftyMan workbench. Information on the workbench is as follows:

   Annual demand = 1,200
   Holding cost = $15 per year
   Ordering cost = $200 per order

   What is the economic order quantity for the workbench?

8. (**) Suppose that KraftyCity has to pay $50 per workbench for orders under 200, but only $42 per workbench for orders of 201 or more. Using the information provided in Problem 7, what order quantity *should* KraftyCity use?

9. (*) The lead time for KraftyCity workbenches is 3 weeks, with a standard deviation of 1.2 weeks, and average weekly demand is 24, with a standard deviation of 8 workbenches. What should the reorder point be if KraftyCity wants to provide a 95% percent service level?

10. (**) Now suppose the supplier of workbenches guarantees KraftyCity that the lead time will be a constant 3 weeks, with no variability (i.e., standard deviation of lead time = 0). Recalculate the reorder point, using the demand and service level information in Problem 9. Is the reorder point higher or lower? Explain why.

11. (*) Refer to problem 11. Ollah's Organic Pet Shop sells about 4,000 bags of free-range dog biscuits every year. The fixed ordering cost is $15, and the cost of holding a bag in inventory for a year is $2. What is the economic order quantity for the biscuits?

12. (**) Refer to Problem 11. Suppose Ollah decides to order 200 bags at a time. What would the total ordering and holding costs for the year be? (For this problem, don't consider safety stock when calculating holding costs.)

13. (**) Refer to Problem 11. Average weekly demand for free-range dog biscuits is 80 bags per week, with a standard deviation of 16 bags. Ollah uses a continuous inventory review system to manage inventory of the biscuits. Ollah wants to set the reorder point high enough that there is only a 5% percent chance of running out before the next order comes in. Assuming the lead time is a constant 2 weeks, what should the reorder point be?

14. (**) Suppose Ollah decides to use a periodic review system to manage the free-range dog biscuits, with the vendor checking inventory levels every week. Under this scenario, what would the restocking level be, assuming the same demand and lead time characteristics listed in Problem 13 and the same 95% percent service level? (Note that because the standard deviation of weekly demand is 16, basic statistics tells us the standard deviation of demand over three weeks will be $\sqrt{3} \times 16 \cong 28$.)

15. Ollah's Organic Pet Shop also sells bags of cedar chips for pet bedding or snacking (buyer's choice). The supplier has offered Ollah the following terms:

    Order 1–100 bags, and the price is $6.00 a bag.
    Order 101 or more bags, and the price is $4.50 a bag.

Annual demand is 630, fixed ordering costs are \$9 per order, and the per-bag holding cost is estimated to be around \$2 per year.

a. (*) What is the economic order quantity for the bags?
b. (**) What order quantity *should* Ollah order, based on the volume discount? Is this different from the *EOQ*? If so, how could this be?
c. (**) Suppose the lead time for bags is a constant 2 weeks, and average weekly demand is 12.6 bags, with a standard deviation of 3.2 bags. If Ollah wants to maintain a 98% percent service level, what should her reorder point be?

16. (**) David Polston prints up T-shirts to be sold at local concerts. The T-shirts sell for \$20, but only cost David \$6.50. However, because the T-shirts have concert-specific information on them, David can sell leftover shirts for only \$3.00. Suppose the demand for shirts can be approximated with a normal distribution and the mean demand is 120 shirts with a standard deviation of 35. What is the target service level? How many shirts should David print up for a concert?

17. Sherry Clower is trying to figure out how many custom books to order for her class of 25 students. In the past, the number of students buying books has shown the following demand pattern:

NUMBER OF STUDENTS WHO BOUGHT A BOOK	PERCENTAGE OF OBSERVATIONS
16 or fewer	0%
17	4%
18	15%
19	17%
20	18%
21	26%
22	10%
23	6%
24	4%
25	0%

a. (**) Suppose each custom book costs Sherry \$12 to print and she sells them to the students for \$50. Excess books must be scrapped. What is the target service level? What is the target stocking point?
b. (**) Suppose printing costs increase to \$22. Recalculate the new target service level and target stocking point. What happened?

18. One of the products sold by OfficeMax is a Hewlett-Packard DeskJet 7000C printer. As purchasing manager, you have the following information for the printer:

Average weekly demand (52 weeks per year):	60 printers
Standard deviation of weekly demand:	12 printers
Order lead time:	3 weeks
Standard deviation of order lead time:	0 (lead times are constant)
Item cost:	\$120 per printer
Cost to place an order:	\$2
Yearly holding cost per printer:	\$48
Desired service level during reordering period:	99% ($z = 2.33$)

a. (*) What is the economic order quantity for the printer?
b. (**) Calculate annual ordering costs and holding costs (ignoring safety stock) for the *EOQ*. What do you notice about the two?
c. (**) Suppose OfficeMax currently orders 120 printers at a time. How much more or less would OfficeMax pay in holding and ordering costs per year if it ordered just 12 printers at a time? Show your work.
d. (**) What is the reorder point for the printer? How much of the reorder point consists of safety stock?

For Parts e and f, use the following formula to consider the impact of safety stock (*SS*) on average inventory levels and annual holding costs:

$$\left(\frac{Q}{2}+SS\right)H$$

e. (***) What is the annual cost of holding inventory, including the safety stock? How much of this cost is due to the safety stock?
f. (***) Suppose OfficeMax is able to cut the lead time to a constant one week. What would the new safety stock level be? How much would this reduce annual holding costs?

19. (***) OfficeMax is considering using the Internet to order printers from Hewlett-Packard. The change is expected to make the cost of placing orders drop to almost nothing, although the lead time will remain the same. What effect will this have on the order quantity? On the holding and ordering costs for the year? Explain, using any formulas/examples you find helpful.

20. Through its online accessory store, Gateway sells its own products, as well as ones made by other companies. One of these products is the Viewsonic VP150 LCD monitor:

Estimated *annual* demand:	15,376 monitors (50 weeks per year)
Cost:	$640 per monitor
Lead time:	2 weeks
Standard deviation of weekly demand:	16 monitors
Standard deviation of lead time:	0.3 weeks
Holding cost per unit per year:	40% of item cost
Ordering cost:	$25 per order
Desired service level:	95% ($z = 1.65$)

a. (*) What is the economic order quantity for the monitor? Calculate annual ordering costs and holding costs (ignoring safety stock) for the *EOQ*.
b. (**) What is the reorder point for the monitor? How much of the reorder point consists of safety stock?
c. (**) Suppose Gateway decides to order 64 monitors at a time. What would its yearly ordering and holding costs (ignoring safety stock) for the monitor be?
d. (**) Because computer technologies become obsolete so quickly, Gateway is thinking about raising holding costs from 40% of item cost to some higher percentage. What will be the impact on the economic order quantity for monitors? Explain why.

For Parts e and f, use the following formula to consider the impact of safety stock (*SS*) on average inventory levels and annual holding costs:

$$\left(\frac{Q}{2}+SS\right)H$$

e. (***) What is the annual cost of holding inventory, including the safety stock? How much of this cost is due to the safety stock?
f. (***) Suppose Gateway is able to cut the lead time to a constant one week. What would the new safety stock level be? How much would this reduce annual holding costs?

21. One of the products stocked by Sam's Club is *SamsCola*, which is sold in cases. The demand level for *SamsCola* is highly seasonal.

- During the *slow season*, the demand rate is approximately 650 cases a month, which is the same as a yearly demand rate of $650 \times 12 = 7800$ cases.
- During the *busy season*, the demand rate is approximately 1300 cases a month, or 15,600 cases a year.
- The cost to place an order is $5, and the yearly holding cost for a case of *SamsCola* is $12.

a. (**) According to the *EOQ* formula, how many cases of *SamsCola* should be ordered at a time during the *slow season*? How many cases of *SamsCola* should be ordered during the *busy season*?
b. (**) Suppose Sam's Club decides to use the same order quantity throughout the year, $Q = 150$. Calculate total holding and ordering costs for the year. Do not consider safety stock in your calculations. (Annual demand can be calculated as an average of the slow and busy rates just given.)

22. (**) During the busy season, the store manager has decided that 98% of the time he does not want to run out of *SamsCola* before the next order arrives. Use the following data to calculate the reorder point for *SamsCola*:

Weekly demand during the busy season:	325 cases per week
Lead time:	0.5 weeks
Standard deviation of weekly demand:	5.25
Standard deviation of lead time:	0 (lead time is constant)
Number of standard deviations above the mean needed to provide a 98% service level (z):	2.05

23. Mountain Mouse makes freeze-dried meals for hikers. One of Mountain Mouse's biggest customers is a sporting goods superstore. Every 5 days, Mountain Mouse checks the inventory level at the superstore and places an order to restock the meals. These meals are delivered by UPS in two days. Average demand during the reorder period and order lead time is 100 meals, while the standard deviation of demand during this same time period is about 20 meals.

a. (**) Calculate the restocking level for Mountain Mouse. Assume the superstore wants a 90% service level. What happens to the restocking level if the superstore wants a higher level of service—say, 95%?
b. (*) Suppose there are 20 meals in the superstore when Mountain Mouse checks inventory levels. How many meals should be ordered, assuming a 90% service level?

24. (**) Dave's Sporting Goods sells Mountain Mouse freeze-dried meals. Dave's uses a continuous review system to manage meal inventories. Suppose Mountain Mouse offers the following volume discounts to its customers:

1–500 meals: $7 per meal
501 or more meals: $6.50 per meal

Annual demand is 2000 meals, and the cost to place an order is $15. Suppose the holding cost is $2 per meal per year. How many meals should Dave's order at a time? What are the total holding, ordering, and item costs associated with this quantity?

25. (***) (*Microsoft Excel problem*). The following figure shows an Excel spreadsheet that compares total ordering and holding costs for some current order quantity to the same costs for the *EOQ* and calculates how much could be saved by switching to the *EOQ*. **Re-create this spreadsheet in Excel.** You should develop the spreadsheet so that the results will be recalculated if any of the values in the highlighted cells are changed. Your formatting does not have to be exactly the same, but the numbers should be. (As a test, see what happens if you just change the annual demand and cost per order to 5000 and $25, respectively. Your new *EOQ* should be 91.29, and the total savings under the *EOQ* should be $5011.39.)

	A	B	C	D	E	F
1	**Calculating Savings under EOQ**					
2						
3			Annual demand:	4000		
4			Annual holding cost, per unit:	$30.00		
5			Cost per order:	$30.00		
6						
7			Current order quantity:	500		
8			Current annual holding cost:	$7500.00		
9			Current annual ordering cost:	$240.00		
10			Total cost:	$7740.00		
11						
12			Economic order quantity:	89.44		
13			EOQ annual holding cost:	$1341.64		
14			EOQ annual ordering cost:	$1341.64		
15			Total cost:	$2683.28		
16						
17			**Total savings under EOQ:**	**$5056.72**		
18						

26. (***) (*Microsoft Excel Problem*). The following figure shows an Excel spreadsheet that calculates the benefit of pooling safety stock. Specifically, the sheet calculates how much could be saved in annual holding costs if the safety stocks for three locations were held in a single location. **Re-create this spreadsheet in Excel.** You should develop the spreadsheet so that the results will be recalculated if any of the values in the highlighted cells are changed. Your formatting does not have to be exactly the same, but the numbers should be. (As a test, see what happens if you change Location 1's average daily demand and variance of daily demand to 100 and 15, respectively. Your new pooled safety stock should be 30.34, and the total savings due to pooling safety stock should be $108.21.)

	A	B	C	D	E	F	G
1	**Calculating Savings Due to Pooling Safety Stock**						
2							
3	Annual holding cost per unit:			$5.00			
4	Lead time (fixed):			8	days		
5	z value (for desired service level):			2.33			
6							
7						Average demand	
8			Average	Variance of	Reorder	during	
9			daily demand	daily demand	point	lead time	Safety stock
10		Location 1	50	4.5	413.98	400.00	13.98
11		Location 2	40	6.2	336.41	320.00	16.41
12		Location 3	30	5	254.74	240.00	14.74
13						Total units:	45.13
14						**Total annual holding cost:**	**$225.63**
15							
16						Average demand	
17			Average	Variance of	Reorder	during	
18			daily demand	daily demand	point	lead time	Safety stock
19		**Pooled SS**	120	15.7	986.11	960.00	26.11
20						**Total annual holding cost:**	**$130.56**
21							
22						**Savings due to pooling safety stock:**	**$95.07**

CASE STUDY

NORTHCUTT BIKES: THE SERVICE DEPARTMENT

Introduction

Several years ago, Jan Northcutt, owner of Northcutt Bikes, recognized the need to organize a separate department to deal with service parts for the bikes her company made. Because the competitive strength of her company was developed around customer responsiveness and flexibility, she felt a separate department focused exclusively on aftermarket service was critical in meeting that mission.

When she established the department, she named Ann Hill, one of her best clerical workers at the time, to establish and manage the department. At first, it occupied only a corner of the production warehouse, but now it has grown to occupy its own 100,000-square-foot warehouse. The service business has also grown significantly, in that it now represents over 15% of the total revenue of Northcutt Bikes. The exclusive mission of the service department is to provide parts (tires, seats, chains, etc.) to the many retail businesses that sell and service Northcutt Bikes.

While Ann has turned out to be a very effective manager (and now has the title of Director of Aftermarket Service), she still lacks a basic understanding of materials management. To help her develop a more effective materials management program, she hired Mike Alexander, a recent graduate of an outstanding business management program at North Carolina State University, to fill the newly created position of Materials Manager of Aftermarket Service.

The Current Situation

During the interview process, Mike got the impression that there was a lot of opportunity for improvement. It was only after he selected his starting date and requested some information that he started to see the full extent of the challenges that lay ahead. His first day on the job really opened his eyes. One of the first items he had requested was a status report on inventory history and shipped orders. In response, the following note was on his desk the first day from the warehouse supervisor, Art Demming:

> *We could not compile the history you requested, as we keep no such records. There's just too much stuff in here to keep a close eye on it all. Rest assured, however, that we think the inventory positions on file are accurate, as we just completed our physical count of inventory last week. I was able to track down a demand history for a couple of our items, and that is attached to this memo. Welcome to the job!*

When Mike learned this, he decided to investigate further. Although the records were indeed difficult to track down and compile, by the end of his second week he had obtained a fairly good picture of the situation based on an investigation of 100 parts selected at random. He learned, for example, that although there was an average of over 70 days' worth of inventory (annual sales/average inventory), the fill rate for customer orders was less than 80%, meaning only 80% of the items requested were in inventory. The remaining orders were backordered. Unfortunately, many customers viewed many service parts as generic and would take their business elsewhere when parts were not available from Northcutt Bikes.

What really hurt was when those businesses sometimes canceled their entire order for parts and placed it with another parts supplier. The obvious conclusion was that while there was plenty of inventory overall, the timing and quantities were misplaced. Increasing the inventory did not appear to be the answer, not only because a large amount was already being held, but also because the warehouse space (built less than two years ago) had increased from being 45% utilized just after the company moved in to its present utilization of over 95%.

Mike decided to start his analysis and development of solutions on the two items for which Art had already provided a demand history. He felt that if he could analyze and correct any problems with those two parts, he could expand the analysis to most of the others. The two items on which he had history and concentrated his initial analysis were the FB378 Fender Bracket and the GS131 Gear Sprocket. The FB378 is purchased by Northcutt Bikes from a Brazilian source. The lead time has remained constant at three weeks, and the estimated cost of a purchase order for these parts is given at $35 per order. Currently Northcutt Bikes uses an order lot size of 120 for the FB378 and buys the items for $5.00 apiece.

The GS131 part, on the other hand, is a newer product only recently being offered. It is produced for Northcutt Bikes by a machine shop in Nashville, Tennessee, which gives Northcutt Bikes a fairly reliable six-week lead time. The cost of placing an order with the machine shop is only about $15, and currently Northcutt Bikes orders 850 at a time. Northcutt Bikes buys the item for $10.75.

Following is the demand information that Art had given to Mike on his first day for the FB378 and the GS131:

WEEK	FORECAST FB378	ACTUAL DEMAND, FB378	FORECAST, GS131	ACTUAL DEMAND, GS131
1	30	34		
2	32	44		
3	35	33		
4	34	39		
5	35	48		
6	38	30		
7	36	26		
8	33	45		
9	37	33		
10	37	30		
11	36	47	10	16
12	37	40	18	27
13	38	31	30	35
14	36	38	42	52
15	36	32	55	51
16	35	49	54	44
17	37	24	52	57
18	35	41	53	59
19	37	34	53	46
20	36	24	52	62
21	34	52	53	51
22	36	41	53	60
23	37	30	54	46
24	36	37	53	58
25	36	31	54	42
26	35	45	53	57
27	36		53	

Mike realized he also needed input from Ann as to her perspective on the business. She indicated that she felt strongly that with better management they should be able to use the existing warehouse for years to come, even with the anticipated growth in business. Currently, however, she views the situation as a crisis because "we're bursting at the seams with inventory. It's costing us a lot of profit, yet our service level is very poor at less than 80%. I'd like to see us maintain a 95% or better service level without backorders, yet we need to be able to do that with a net reduction in total inventory. What do you think, Mike—can we do better?"

QUESTIONS

1. Use the available data to develop inventory policies (order quantities and reorder points) for the FB378 and GS131. Assume holding cost is 20% of unit price.
2. Compare the inventory costs associated with your suggested order quantities with those of the current order quantities. What can you conclude?
3. Do you think the lost customer sales should be included as a cost of inventory? How would such an inclusion impact the ordering policies you established in Question 1?

REFERENCES

Books and Articles

Cohen, M. A., C. Cull, H. L. Lee, and D. Willen. "Saturn's Supply-Chain Innovation: High-Value in After-Sales Service." *Sloan Management Review* 41, no. 4 (Summer 2000): 93–101.

Cox, J. F., and J. H. Blackstone, eds. *APICS Dictionary,* 10th ed. Falls Church, VA: APICS, 2002.

Lee, Hau L., V. Padmanabhan, and S. Whang. "The Bullwhip Effect in Supply Chain." *Sloan Management Review* 38, no. 3 (Spring 1997): 70–77.

Magretta, J. "Fast, Global, and Entrepreneurial: Supply Chain Management, Hong Kong Style." *Harvard Business Review* 76, no. 5 (September–October 1998): 102–109.

Magretta, J. "The Power of Virtual Integration: An Interview with Dell Computer's Michael Dell." *Harvard Business Review* 76, no. 2 (March–April 1998): 72–84.

CHAPTER 15

Managing Production across the Supply Chain

CHAPTER OUTLINE

Chapter Objectives

By the end of this chapter, you will be able to:

- Explain the activities that make up planning and control in a typical manufacturing environment.
- Explain the linkage between sales and operations planning (S&OP) and master scheduling.
- Complete the calculations for the master schedule record and interpret the results.
- Explain the linkage between master scheduling and material requirements planning (MRP).
- Complete the calculations for the MRP record and interpret the results.
- Discuss the role of production activity control and vendor order management and how these functions differ from the higher-level planning activities.
- Explain how distribution requirements planning (DRP) helps synchronize the supply chain, and complete the calculations for a simple example.

HERMAN MILLER[1]

Ordering office furniture has long been a dreaded chore. The typical customer for office furniture is a facilities manager who is responsible for furnishing dozens or even hundreds of offices and cubicles. In the past, pricing and configuring office furniture solutions were complex processes that could take weeks and were fraught with errors in pricing and product specifications. Furthermore, once an order was placed, there was no guarantee that all the pieces would arrive together, on schedule. Someone (usually the furniture dealer) was forced to order far in advance and hold the inventory until it was needed.

But Herman Miller has transformed this frustrating process. Through state-of-the-art planning and control systems, this manufacturer of office furnishings has developed a set of core competencies that leverage advances in information technology, including proprietary software and applications. Here, in a nutshell, is how the system works. Using a laptop computer, a Herman Miller dealer can quickly develop some three-dimensional computer graphics of different furniture configurations, varying key features such as panel height and fabric. Every time the dealer changes the configuration, the computer updates all related component hardware, the price, and the graphics instantly. Once a customer decides to place an order, the dealer sends the information electronically to Herman Miller's factory, where it is translated into production jobs and material orders. Within hours, the customer knows the shipping date for the order.

Herman Miller's planning and control systems are so advanced they can schedule the dozens or even hundreds of small manufacturing jobs required to fill each customer's order to finish within hours of one another. Not only does this synchronization simplify the task of pulling together all the manufacturing jobs that make up a customer's order, but also it actually helps to improve delivery reliability. Even better, Herman Miller shares this information with suppliers, in real time, via a proprietary Web portal. As a result, suppliers know exactly what materials need to be delivered and when. The result is lower overall inventory levels and fewer interruptions in production.

How good is this system? Consider these facts:

- Herman Miller is committed to satisfying customers "this-day-only" delivery request 100% of the time and is virtually always successful.

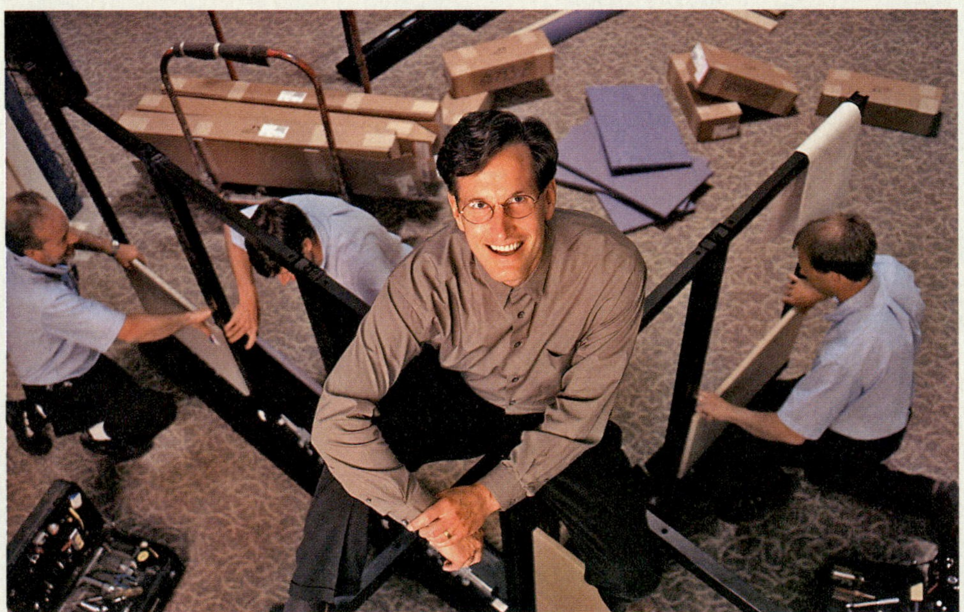

Herman Miller Chairman of the Board Michael Volkema

[1] W. Bundy, "Miller SQA: Leveraging Technology for Speed and Reliability," *Supply Chain Management Review* 3, no. 2 (Spring 1999): 62–69.

- An average of 99.9% of all orders ship on time, and 100% deliver on time.
- In fiscal year 2004, inventory turned 48 times across the corporation, versus 9 turns in fiscal year 1999. The inventory dollar value has dropped 50% in the same period. The company's goal is 100 inventory turns, and some manufacturing plants have already exceeded this goal.

Though the technical details behind these statistics can be complex, the basic premise behind Herman Miller's operations is not. Put simply, Herman Miller uses excellent planning and control both to provide customers with superior service and to improve performance throughout its supply chain.

INTRODUCTION

The purpose of this chapter is to introduce you to some of the tools manufacturers use to manage production and to coordinate these activities with their supply chain partners. While the focus here is on physical goods, bear in mind that many service firms also depend on the information generated by these efforts. For instance, furniture dealers, distributors, and transportation carriers all use output from Herman Miller's SQA system to plan their own activities.

Planning and control
A set of tactical- and execution-level business activities that includes master scheduling, material requirements planning, and some form of production activity control and vendor order management.

Planning and control can be best thought of as a set of tactical- and execution-level business activities that includes master scheduling, material requirements planning, and some form of production activity control and vendor order management. Planning and control begins where sales and operations planning (S&OP) ends, as Figure 15.1 shows. The first step in planning and control is master scheduling, in which the overall resource levels established by S&OP begin to be fleshed out with specifics. The master schedule states exactly when and in what quantities specific products will be made. It also links production with specific customer orders, allowing the firm to tell the customer exactly when

FIGURE 15.1
A Top-Down Model of Manufacturing Planning and Control Systems

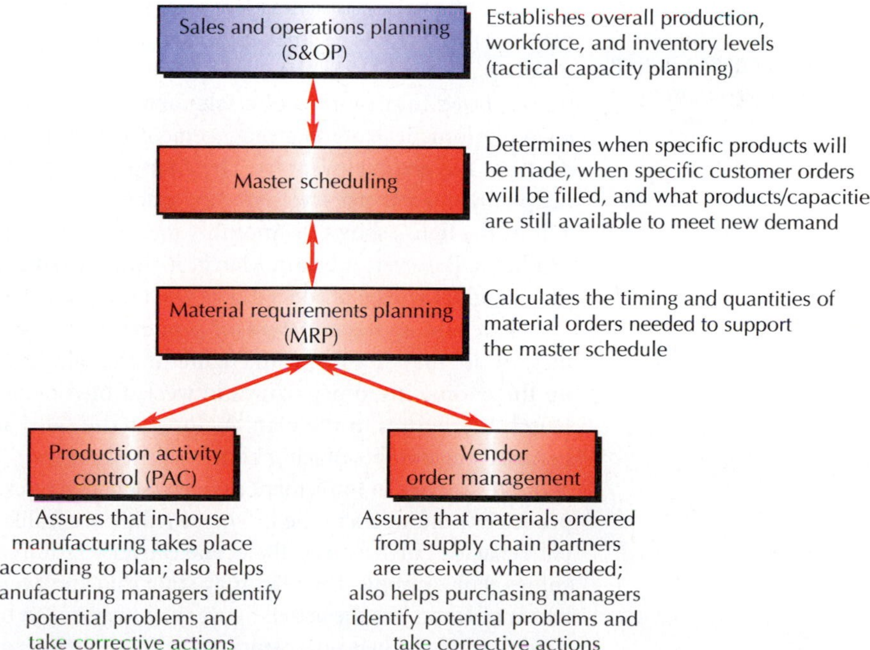
Sales and operations planning (S&OP)
Establishes overall production, workforce, and inventory levels (tactical capacity planning)
Master scheduling
Determines when specific products will be made, when specific customer orders will be filled, and what products/capacities are still available to meet new demand
Material requirements planning (MRP)
Calculates the timing and quantities of material orders needed to support the master schedule
Production activity control (PAC)
Assures that in-house manufacturing takes place according to plan; also helps manufacturing managers identify potential problems and take corrective actions
Vendor order management
Assures that materials ordered from supply chain partners are received when needed; also helps purchasing managers identify potential problems and take corrective actions

an order will be filled. Finally, master scheduling informs the operations manager what inventory or resources are still available to meet new demand. As we shall see, the concept of *available to promise* is an important function of master scheduling.

Material requirements planning (MRP) takes the process one step further: It translates the master schedule for final products into detailed material requirements. For example, if the master schedule indicates that 500 chairs will be finished and ready to sell in week 5, MRP determines when the individual pieces—seats, legs, back spindles, and so on—need to be made or purchased.

At the lowest level in the hierarchy are two systems, production activity control (PAC) and vendor order management. At this point, all the plans have been made; the only task remaining is to make sure they are executed properly. Because materials ultimately come either from in-house manufacturing or from outside suppliers, two distinct types of control systems have sprung up to handle those different environments.

Our description of planning and control seems to suggest a top-down process, with higher-level plans feeding into more detailed lower-level systems. Why, then, do the arrows in Figure 15.1 run in both directions? The reason is simple: Changes in the business environment or other conditions may become apparent at lower levels, requiring the organization to adjust its plans and actions in real time.

In the rest of this chapter, we describe planning and control tools in more detail, starting with master scheduling and ending with PAC and vendor order management systems. We also discuss one tool for synchronizing planning and control across the supply chain, distribution requirements planning (DRP). As thorough as this chapter is, it cannot begin to cover all the choices firms face in designing their planning and control systems. Our intent, rather, is to give you an appreciation of both the advantages and the effort needed to run these systems.

15.1 MASTER SCHEDULING

Master scheduling
A detailed planning process that tracks production output and matches this output to actual customer orders.

Master scheduling is a detailed planning process that tracks production output and matches this output to actual customer orders. We have already said that master scheduling picks up where S&OP leaves off. Figure 15.2 gives an example of this linkage. The top of the figure shows four months of a sales and operations plan for a fictional manufacturer of lawn equipment. Note that management has established *overall* targets for demand, production, and ending inventory. These targets will guide the firm's tactical decisions, including planned workforce levels, storage space requirements, and cash flow needs. The bottom half of the figure shows the monthly master schedules for the three products the company produces. For every week in March, it shows what the expected demand is, how many of each product will be produced, and what the projected ending inventory is.

If we add up the numbers for production and demand across the three master schedules, we see that they match the figures in the sales and operations plan. Similarly, if we add up the ending inventory figures in week 4 of the master schedules, we see that they, too, match the figures in the plan. As long as the sales and operations planning values (for instance, the number of labor hours required per unit) are correct, the company should have enough capacity to implement these master schedules. In reality, however, the demand and production numbers in the master schedule are unlikely to match the sales and operations plan exactly. Furthermore, the actual capacity requirements might not match the planning values. For example, the plan may state that the average product needs an estimated 4.5 hours of labor, but the actual figure may turn out to be 4.7 hours. In such cases, firms may need to dip into their safety stock, schedule overtime, or take other measures to make up the

FIGURE 15.2
The Link between the Sales and Operations Plan and the Master Schedule

Partial sales and operations plan

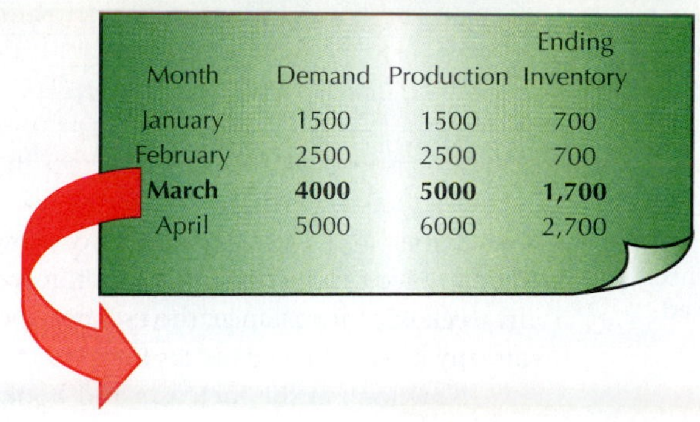

Month	Demand	Production	Ending Inventory
January	1500	1500	700
February	2500	2500	700
March	**4000**	**5000**	**1,700**
April	5000	6000	2,700

Master schedules March

			Week 1	Week 2	Week 3	Week 4
	Demand		200	250	300	350
Push mowers	Production		650	0	650	0
	Ending inventory	**200**	650	400	750	**400**
	Demand		400	500	600	700
Power mowers	Production		0	1,350	0	1350
	Ending inventory	**400**	0	850	250	**900**
	Demand		100	150	200	250
Lawn tractors	Production		250	250	250	250
	Ending inventory	**100**	250	350	400	**400**

Beginning inventory =	**700**
Total monthly production =	+5000
Total monthly demand =	−4000
Ending inventory =	**1700**

difference between the plan and reality. As long as the numbers in the sales and operations plan are *close* to those in the master schedule, firms will be able to manage the differences.

The Master Schedule Record

Now that we understand the linkage between the sales and operations plan and the master schedule, let's look at the master schedule record in more detail. Because firms tailor the master schedule record to their manufacturing environment and the characteristics of their product, generalizing about its precise form is difficult. Nevertheless, most master schedule records track several key pieces of information:

- Forecasted demand;
- Booked orders;
- Projected inventory levels;
- Production quantities; and
- Units still available to meet customer needs (*available to promise*).

To illustrate how the master schedule works, let's look at the master schedule record for Sandy-Built, a company that makes snow blowers (Figure 15.3).

Forecasted demand
In the context of master scheduling, the company's best estimate of the demand in any period.

Forecasted Demand versus Booked Orders. At the beginning of November (week 45), Sandy-Built's management is reviewing the master schedule for the company's newest model, the MeltoMatic. The master schedule record in Figure 15.3 shows the **forecasted demand**—the company's best estimate of the demand in any period—for the months of

FIGURE 15.3
Partial Master Schedule Record for the MeltoMatic Snowblower

MeltoMatic snowblower								
Month	************November************				************December************			
Week	45	46	47	48	49	50	51	52
Forecasted demand	150	150	150	150	175	175	175	175
Booked orders	170	165	140	120	85	42	20	0
Master production schedule	300	0	300	0	350	0	350	0

Booked orders
In the context of master scheduling, confirmed demand for products.

November and December. It also shows **booked orders**, which represent confirmed demand for products. At this point, forecasted demand is running behind booked orders. In week 45, for instance, the estimated demand for snowblowers is 150, yet Sandy-Built already has confirmed orders for 170.

Now look at the forecasts and booked orders for December. In that month, booked orders appear to be lagging forecasted demand. Perhaps more orders will materialize as December draws nearer. But if booked orders do not increase, managers may need to take action, either by cutting back production or by lowering the price of the MeltoMatic, to move more units. One of the benefits of master scheduling is that it allows managers to take corrective action when needed.

Master production schedule
The amount of product that will be finished and available for sale at the beginning of each week. The master production schedule drives more detailed planning activities, such as material requirements planning.

Another line on the master schedule record, called the **master production schedule**, shows how many products will be finished and available for sale at the beginning of each week. In our example, Sandy-Built seems to be producing enough snowblowers every other week to meet the forecasted demand.

ENDING INVENTORY. With these basic numbers, we can start to get a picture of what overall inventory levels should look like and, more important, how many more snow blowers we can sell. Figure 15.4 contains a new row called **projected ending inventory**, which is simply our best estimate of what inventory levels will look like at the end of each week, based on current information.

Projected ending inventory is calculated as follows:

$$EI_t = EI_{t-1} + MPS_t - \text{maximum}\ (F_t, OB_t) \qquad \textbf{[15-1]}$$

where:

EI_t = ending inventory in time period t

MPS_t = master production schedule quantity available in time period t

F_t = forecasted demand for time period t

OB_t = orders booked for time period t

Note that projected ending inventory is a *conservative* estimate of the inventory position at the end of each week. In our example, the inventory at the end of week 44 is 100. Therefore, the projected inventory at the end of week 45 is 100 + 300 − 170 = 230, and the same calculation for week 46 is 230 + 0 − 165 = 65. In each case, we use booked orders because this number is higher than the forecasted demand. This makes sense because using the lower forecasted demand numbers would overestimate inventory levels.

FIGURE 15.4
Partial Master Schedule Record for the MeltoMatic Snowblower

On-hand inventory at end of week 44	100							
MeltoMatic snowblower								
Month	************November************				************December************			
Week	45	46	47	48	49	50	51	52
Forecasted demand	150	150	150	150	175	175	175	175
Booked orders	170	165	140	120	85	42	20	0
Projected ending inventory	**230**	**65**	**215**	**65**	**240**	**65**	**240**	**65**
Master production schedule	300	0	300	0	350	0	350	0

FIGURE 15.5
Calculating Available to Promise (ATP) for Week 45

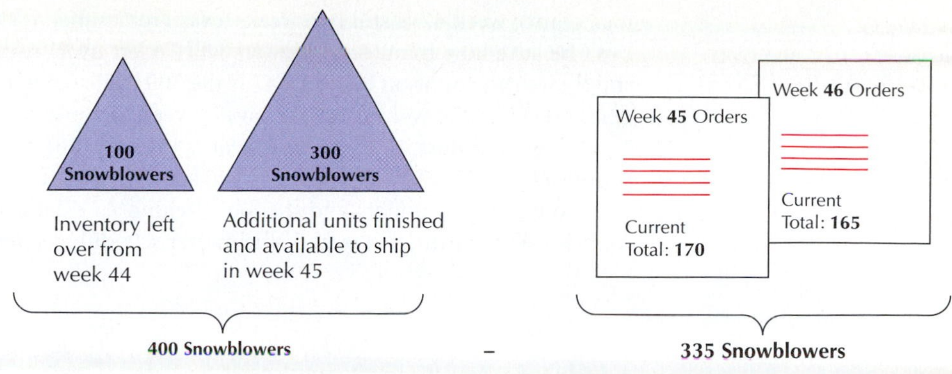

But what about other weeks, such as week 47, in which the forecasted demand is *higher* than booked orders? In this case, the assumption is that the booked orders (140) probably do not reflect all the demand that will eventually occur in that week (150). To be conservative, we subtract the higher number in calculating ending inventory: $65 + 300 - 150 = 215$.

AVAILABLE TO PROMISE. Now suppose you work for Sandy-Built's sales department and it is the beginning of week 45. You have the information shown in Figure 15.4 sitting in front of you. A customer calls up and asks how many snowblowers you can sell them at the beginning of week 45 and week 47. To answer this question, you need to know how many snowblowers are available to promise. **Available to promise (ATP)** indicates the number of units that are available for sale each week, given those that have already been promised to customers.

Available to promise (ATP) A field in the master schedule record that indicates the number of units that are available for sale each week, given those that have already been promised to customers.

To illustrate how ATP is calculated, consider Figure 15.5, which represents MeltoMatic's master schedule at the beginning of week 45. On the supply side, there are 100 snowblowers left over from the previous week. Three hundred more snow blowers are scheduled to be finished in week 45. As a result, there will be a total supply of 400 snowblowers. On the demand side, Sandy-Built has already booked orders for 170 and 165 snowblowers in weeks 45 and 46, respectively (we need to consider orders through week 46 because no new snowblowers are expected to be completed until week 47). When we take the difference between the supply (400) and the demand ($170 + 165 = 335$) shown in Figure 15.5, we get a value of 65. This figure represents the number of additional units we can sell—the available to promise—until the next MPS quantity comes in.

Figure 15.5 tells us the available-to-promise quantity for the next two weeks, but what about for week 47, which corresponds with the next MPS quantity? Figure 15.6 shows the

FIGURE 15.6
Calculating Available to Promise (ATP) for Week 47

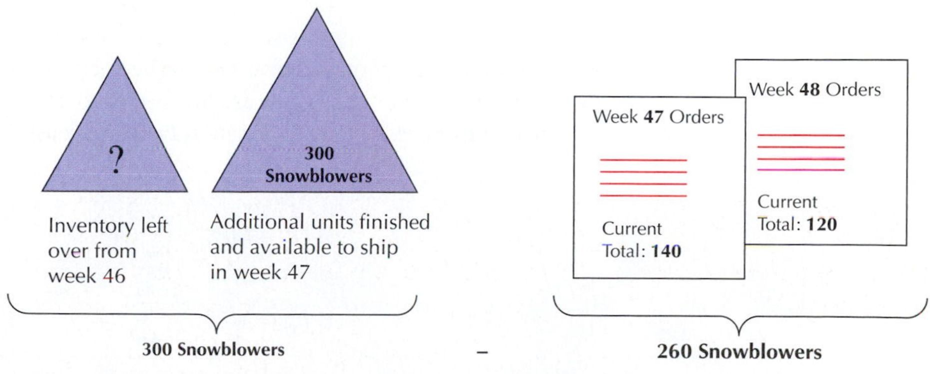

logic. Since week 47 is still two weeks away (remember, it's the beginning of week 45), we can't be sure how many snowblowers will be left over from week 46. Therefore, the only supply we can count on for week 47 is the 300 units being completed in that week. On the demand side, whatever supply we have in week 47 must carry us through weeks 47 and 48. Total booked orders for these weeks equal (140 + 120) = 260. Therefore, the available to promise for week 47 = (300 – 260) = 40 snowblowers.

Now that you understand the logic behind ATP, let's state it more formally. The formula for ATP for the *first week* of the master schedule record is

$$ATP_t = EI_{t-1} + MPS_t - \sum_{i=t}^{z-1} OB_i \qquad \textbf{[15-2]}$$

and for any subsequent week *in which* MPS > 0, it is

$$ATP_t = MPS_t - \sum_{i=t}^{z-1} OB_i \qquad \textbf{[15-3]}$$

where:

ATP_t = available to promise in week t

EI_{t-1} = ending inventory in week $t - 1$ = beginning inventory in week t

MPS_t = master production schedule quantity in week t

$\sum_{i=t}^{z-1} OB_i$ = sum of all orders booked from week t until week z (when the next positive MPS quantity is due)

Because week 45 is the first week of the master schedule record, we use Equation 15-2 to calculate the available-to-promise numbers:

$$ATP_t = EI_{t-1} + MPS_t - \sum_{i=t}^{z-1} OB_i$$

$$ATP_{45} = EI_{44} + MPS_{45} - \sum_{i=45}^{46} OB_i$$

$$= 100 + 300 - (170 + 165) = 65 \text{ snowblowers}$$

Note that an ATP number must *always* be calculated for the first week in the record, regardless of whether or not any units are finished that week. Look again at Figure 15.7. The ATP calculation for week 47 follows Equation 15-3, which assumes there is no holdover inventory:

$$ATP_t = MPS_t - \sum_{i=t}^{z-1} OB_i$$

$$ATP_{47} = MPS_{47} - \sum_{i=47}^{48} OB_i$$

$$= 300 - (140 + 120) = 40 \text{ snowblowers}$$

FIGURE 15.7
Complete Master Schedule Record for the MeltoMatic Snowblower

On-hand inventory at end of week 44	100							
MeltoMatic snowblower								
Month	***********November******				*************December******			
Week	45	46	47	48	49	50	51	52
Forecasted demand	150	150	150	150	175	175	175	175
Booked orders	170	165	140	120	85	42	20	0
Projected ending inventory	**230**	**65**	**215**	**65**	**240**	**65**	**240**	**65**
Master production schedule	300	0	300	0	350	0	350	0

Looking at it another way, total booked orders for November are 170 + 165 + 140 + 120 = 595 snowblowers, while the total units that we can sell are 100 + 300 + 300 = 700. The difference between these two totals is 700 − 595 = 105 snowblowers: 65 in the first two weeks of November and 40 in the last two weeks.

In sum, Equation 15-2 is used to calculate the ATP for the first week of the master schedule record; Equation 15-3 is used for subsequent periods in which the MPS is positive. In calculating the ATP, managers must look ahead to see how many periods will go by before the next batch of finished products is ready.

Example 15.1

Completing the Master Schedule Record for Karam's Alpine Hiking Gear

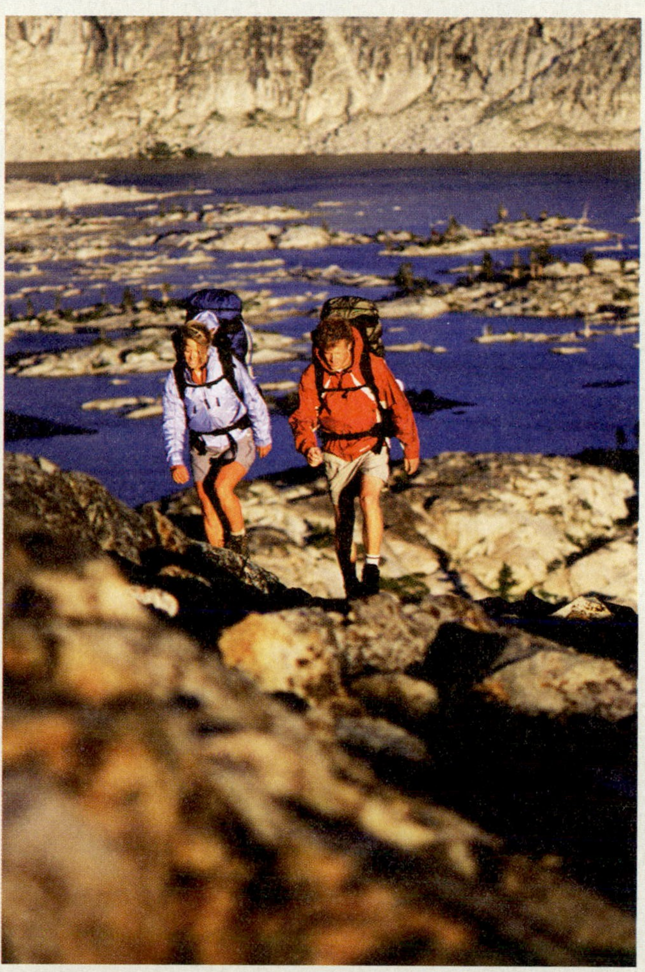

On-hand inventory at end of week 36	2000							
Eiger1 backpack								
Month	************September************				************October************			
Week	37	38	39	40	41	42	43	44
Forecasted demand	1500	1500	1500	1400	1400	1250	1250	1250
Booked orders	1422	1505	1471	1260	980	853	534	209
Projected ending inventory								
Master production schedule		4500			4000			3700
Available to promise								

FIGURE 15.8 Incomplete Master Production Schedule Record for Eiger1 Backpack

Lisa Karam is the owner of Karam's Alpine Hiking Gear. Lisa has set up the following master schedule record for one of her most popular products, the Eiger1 backpack. She needs to complete the projected ending inventory and available-to-promise calculations (Figure 15.8).

Using Equation 15-1, the projected ending inventory values for weeks 37 through 39 are calculated as follows:

$$EI_t = EI_{t-1} + MPS_t - \text{maximum}\ (F_t, OB_t)$$
$$EI_{37} = 2{,}000 + 0 - \text{maximum}\ (1500, 1422) = 500 \text{ backpacks}$$
$$EI_{38} = 500 + 4{,}500 - \text{maximum}\ (1500, 1505) = 3{,}495 \text{ backpacks}$$
$$EI_{39} = 3{,}495 + 0 - \text{maximum}\ (1500, 1471) = 1{,}995 \text{ backpacks}$$

The remaining projected ending inventory values are calculated in a similar fashion. The master schedule record will also have *four* ATP calculations: one for the first week (week 37) and one for each week in which the MPS is positive (weeks 38, 41, and 44):

$$ATP_{37} = 2{,}000 + 0 - 1{,}422 = 578 \text{ backpacks}$$
$$ATP_{38} = 4{,}500 - (1{,}505 + 1{,}471 + 1{,}260) = 264 \text{ backpacks}$$
$$ATP_{41} = 4{,}000 - (980 + 853 + 534) = 1{,}633 \text{ backpacks}$$
$$ATP_{44} = 3{,}700 - 209 = 3{,}491 \text{ backpacks}$$

The completed master schedule record is shown in Figure 15.9. Interpreting the results, Lisa would expect the inventory to drop no lower than about 500 backpacks (week 37). In addition, Lisa has 578 backpacks left to sell in the current week. If she enters week 38 with no inventory, she will have only an additional 264 backpacks to sell over the following three weeks. Because of this, Lisa might try to get customers who aren't in a hurry to book orders in October, where the ATP quantities are much higher.

On-hand inventory at end of week 36	2000							
Eiger1 backpack								
Month	************September************				************October************			
Week	37	38	39	40	41	42	43	44
Forecasted demand	1500	1500	1500	1400	1400	1250	1250	1250
Booked orders	1422	1505	1471	1260	980	853	534	209
Projected ending inventory	**500**	**3495**	**1995**	**595**	**3195**	**1945**	**695**	**3145**
Master production schedule		4500			4000			3700
Available to promise	**578**	**264**			**1633**			**3491**

FIGURE 15.9 Completed Master Production Schedule Record for Eiger1 Backpack

FIGURE 15.10
Updated Master Schedule Record for the MeltoMatic Snowblower

On-hand inventory at end of week 44	100							
MeltoMatic snowblower								
Month	************November************				************December************			
Week	45	46	47	48	49	50	51	52
Forecasted demand	150	150	150	150	175	175	175	175
Booked orders	**235**	165	**180**	120	**130**	42	20	0
Projected ending inventory	165	0	120	0	175	0	175	0
Master production schedule	300	0	300	0	350	0	350	0
Available to promise	**0**		**0**		**178**		**330**	

Planning horizon
The amount of time the master schedule record or MRP record extends into the future. In general, the longer the production and supplier lead times are, the longer the planning horizon must be.

THE PLANNING HORIZON. The master schedule records we have shown so far happen to extend eight weeks into the future. In reality, the appropriate **planning horizon** will depend on the lead time a firm needs to source parts and build a product. Products with very short lead times may have planning horizons that are just a few weeks long, but more complex products may need horizons of several months or more.

As the weeks go by, the firm will need to revise the numbers in the master schedule record, a task that is referred to as "rolling through" the planning horizon. For example, the current week in Figure 15.7 is week 45. At the end of week 45, the master schedule record will roll forward, and the new current week will be week 46.

Using the Master Schedule

We have shown how to calculate the master schedule numbers, but how do real firms use the results of these calculations? Look again at Figure 15.7. Imagine Sandy-Built receives a call from a large retail chain that the company has never dealt with before. The buyer needs 150 snowblowers "as soon as possible." Sandy-Built would like to do business with this customer, but management had not anticipated such a huge order. When can Sandy-Built ship the snowblowers, and what will be the impact on production?

With a formal master schedule, managers can quickly answer these questions. According to the ATP figures in Figure 15.7, Sandy-Built can ship 65 snowblowers now, 40 more in week 47, and the remaining 45 in week 49 ($65 + 40 + 45 = 150$). If Sandy-Built decides to accept this order, however, managers will need to recalculate the ending inventory and ATP numbers. Figure 15.10 shows the updated master schedule record.

Booked orders in weeks 45, 47, and 49 are now 235, 180, and 130. Because the order is so large, projected ending inventories drop dramatically. In fact, the calculations suggest that inventories will drop to zero on a regular basis *unless* management alters production levels to increase the safety stock. Finally, the retailer's large order will use up all the ATP for November. Unless another order is canceled, Sandy-Built cannot accept new orders until December—a change the sales force should be made aware of. In such cases, it is better to inform a customer that you will NOT be able to accept a new order, rather than promise something that cannot be completed in time.

Example 15.2
Booking More Orders at Karam's Alpine Hiking Gear

After completing the master schedule record in Figure 15.9, Lisa receives a call from a hiking outfitter in Montana. The customer would like Lisa to send 50 of the Eiger1 backpacks in the third week of September (week 39). Can Lisa do it? Lisa updates the master schedule record to reflect the change. The results are shown in Figure 15.11.

Comparing the updated master schedule record to the old one in Figure 15.9, booking the new order increases orders booked in week 39 by 50 backpacks and reduces the ATP for week 38 by 50. The projected ending inventory for week 39 also falls but not by 50 backpacks, as one might expect. Rather, it falls by just 21 backpacks—the difference between new orders booked and forecasted demand ($1521 - 1500$).

On-hand inventory at end of week 36	**2000**							
Eiger1 backpack								
Month	************September************				************October************			
Week	37	38	39	40	41	42	43	44
Forecasted demand	1500	1500	1500	1400	1400	1250	1250	1250
Booked orders	1422	1505	1521	1260	980	853	534	209
Projected ending inventory	500	3495	**1974**	**574**	**3174**	**1924**	**674**	**3124**
Master production schedule		4500			4000			3700
Available to promise	578	**214**			1633			3491

FIGURE 15.11 Updated Master Production Schedule Record for Eiger1 Backpack

The master schedule calculations might seem complicated at first, but imagine what could go wrong if a business did not have this information available. Salespeople wouldn't be sure if and when they could fill customer orders. Production managers might not become aware of the impact of new demand on inventory levels in time to do something about it. Worse still, salespeople might continue to promise products to customers, unaware that all output has already been spoken for. In short, chaos would result. When master scheduling works well, it allows organizations to avoid these problems by closely matching demand with supply, anticipating customers' needs, and adjusting the organization's plans accordingly.

15.2 MATERIAL REQUIREMENTS PLANNING

With strategic capacity planning (Chapter 8), S&OP (Chapter 13), and master scheduling, we have a comprehensive set of higher-level planning tools. Master scheduling, as we have seen, is particularly valuable because it allows managers to match production figures to actual customer demand. In addition, some firms use the master production schedule to monitor key resource requirements, an activity called **rough-cut capacity planning**. For instance, Sandy-Built's managers, seeing that 350 snowblowers are scheduled to be completed in week 49, might check to make sure the company has the capacity to meet that production goal. Rough-cut capacity planning verifies the feasibility of the master schedule.

Rough-cut capacity planning
A capacity planning technique that uses the master production schedule to monitor key resource requirements.

Material requirements planning, more commonly known as **MRP**, takes planning one step further by translating the master production schedule into planned orders for the actual parts and components needed to produce the master schedule items. The logic of the MRP approach to inventory management is *completely different* from the independent inventory approaches described in Chapter 14. That is because MRP is used to manage **dependent demand inventory**, or inventory items whose demand levels are tied directly to the production of another item. Suppose, for instance, that each MeltoMatic snowblower Sandy-Built produces requires three wheels. Once managers know how many snowblowers they are going to make, they can calculate exactly how many wheels will be needed. The demand for wheels is completely dependent on the number of snowblowers made. Unlike independent demand items, then, there is no mystery about how many dependent demand items a firm will need and when. MRP takes advantage of this fact to manage inventory quite differently—and more percisely—than an EOQ-based system.

Material requirements planning (MRP)
A planning process that translates the master production schedule into planned orders for the actual parts and components needed to produce the master schedule items.

Dependent demand inventory
Inventory items whose demand levels are tied directly to the production of another item.

MRP is based on three related concepts:

1. The bill of material, or BOM;
2. Backward scheduling; and
3. Explosion of the bill of material.

We will illustrate these concepts using a simple example, the assembly of a furniture piece called the King Philip chair.

Example 15.3

The Bill of Materials (BOM) for the King Philip Chair

Bill of material (BOM) "[A] listing of all the subassemblies, intermediates, parts, and raw materials that go into a parent assembly showing the quantity of each required to make an assembly."

Product structure tree A record or graphical rendering that shows how the components in the BOM are put together to make the Level 0 item.

Planning lead time Within the context of MRP, the time from when a component is ordered until it arrives and is ready to use.

The **bill of material (BOM)** is "a listing of all the subassemblies, intermediates, parts, and raw materials that go into a parent assembly, showing the quantity of each required to make an assembly."[2] The bill of material for the King Philip chair has 10 different components, shown in Figure 15.12.

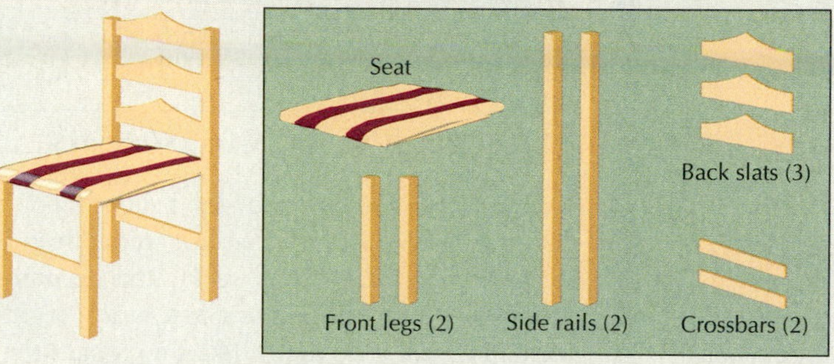

FIGURE 15.12 Bill of Material (BOM) for the King Philip Chair

The **product structure tree** in Figure 15.13 shows how the components in the BOM are put together to make the chair. The chair is assembled using a leg assembly, a back assembly, and a seat; the leg and back assemblies, in turn, are assembled from individual components such as legs, back slats, and crossbars. In MRP jargon, the complete chair is a Level 0 item; the leg assembly, back assembly, and seat are Level 1 items; and the remaining components are Level 2 items. In practice, product assemblies can be dozens of levels deep.

The product structure tree also shows the planning lead times for each component. The **planning lead time** is the time from when a component or material is ordered until it arrives and is ready to use. For instance, the finished chair has a planning lead time of one week, the amount of time workers need to assemble a typical batch of chairs using the Level 1 items. Seats have a planning lead time of two weeks, which may reflect the time an outside supplier takes to fill an order for seats. We will discuss planning lead times in more detail later in this chapter.

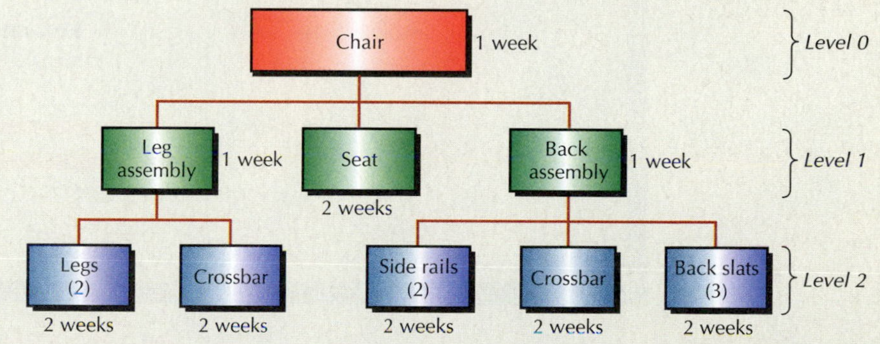

FIGURE 15.13 Product Structure Tree for the King Philip Chair

[2]J. F. Cox and J. H. Blackstone, eds., *APICS Dictionary*, 10th ed. (Falls Church, VA: APICS, 2002).

Example 15.4

Backward Scheduling (Exploding the BOM) for the King Philip Chair

We can now show how backward scheduling (exploding the BOM) is used in MRP. The master schedule record in Figure 15.14 shows that 500 finished chairs should be ready to sell at the beginning of week 5. How do managers ensure that this commitment is met?

On-hand inventory at end of December	600							
King Philip chair								
Month	************January************				************February************			
Week	1	2	3	4	5	6	7	8
Forecasted demand	100	100	100	100	100	100	100	100
Booked orders	100	90	85	80	70	85	80	90
Projected ending inventory	500	400	300	200	600	500	400	300
Master production schedule	0	0	0	0	500	0	0	0
Available to promise	245				175			

FIGURE 15.14 Master Schedule Record for the King Philip Chair

Exploding the BOM
The process by which one works backwards from the master production schedule for a Level 0 item to determine the quantity and timing of orders for the various subassemblies and components. Exploding the BOM is the underlying logic used by MRP.

To finish 500 chairs by the beginning of week 5, workers must start assembling the chairs at the beginning of week 4 (recall from Figure 15.13 that the planning lead time for the assembled chair is one week). This deadline can be met only if the back assemblies, leg assemblies, and seats are available at the beginning of week 4. Continuing to work backward in time, we see that workers must start the back and leg assemblies at the beginning of week 3 in order to have them ready by the beginning of week 4. Seats have a two-week lead time, so they must be ordered no later than the beginning of week 2. Back slats, crossbars, side rails, and legs must be ordered at the beginning of week 1—*right now!*—if managers want to have 500 chairs ready to go in week 5.

The timeline in Figure 15.15 shows the logic behind backward scheduling. From a single order for 500 chairs in week 5, we worked backward, first through the Level 1 items and then through the Level 2 items. This process is called **exploding the BOM.**

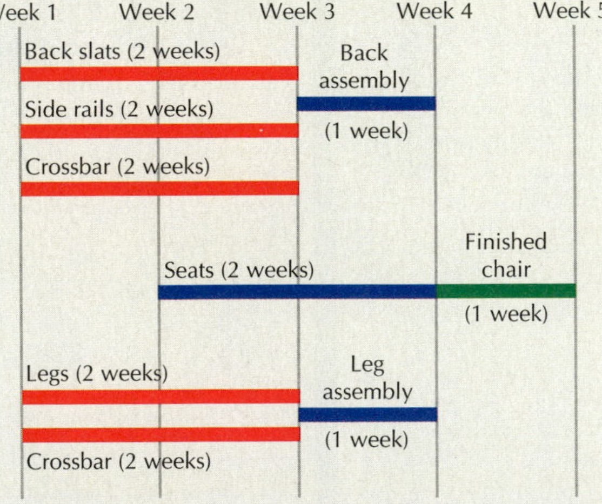

FIGURE 15.15 Exploding the BOM for the King Philip Chair

The MRP Record

The simple MRP record builds on the backward scheduling logic but provides some additional information. Like the master schedule record, the format of the MRP record may differ slightly from one firm to the next, but the basic principle—working backward from the planned completion date for the final item—is the same.

FIGURE 15.16
Calculating the MRP Record for Seats (King Philip Chair)

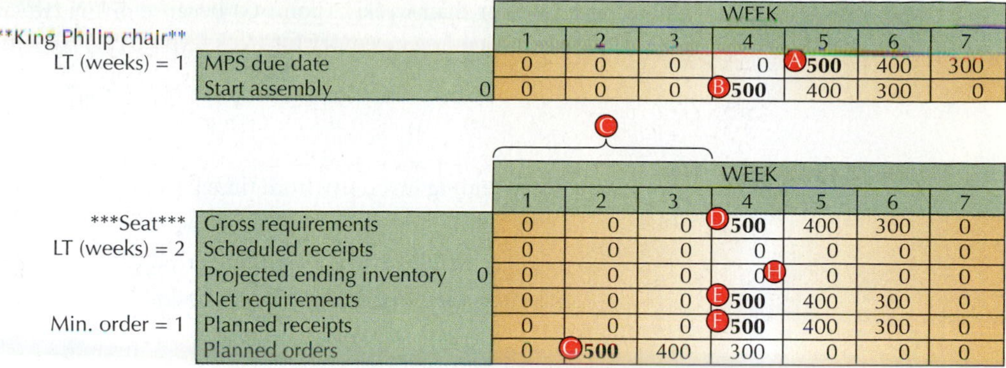

King Philip chair			WEEK 1	2	3	4	5	6	7
LT (weeks) = 1	MPS due date		0	0	0	0	(A) 500	400	300
	Start assembly	0	0	0	0	(B) 500	400	300	0

(C) (weeks 1–3)

Seat			WEEK 1	2	3	4	5	6	7
	Gross requirements		0	0	0	(D) 500	400	300	0
LT (weeks) = 2	Scheduled receipts		0	0	0	0	0	0	0
	Projected ending inventory	0	0	0	0	0 (H)	0	0	0
	Net requirements		0	0	0	(E) 500	400	300	0
Min. order = 1	Planned receipts		0	0	0	(F) 500	400	300	0
	Planned orders		0	(G) 500	400	300	0	0	0

Figure 15.16 shows an example of how the MRP record is calculated.

Looking at point A in the top row of Figure 15.16, we see that management has committed itself to having 500 chairs ready at the beginning of week 5. Given the planning lead time from Figure 15.13, workers need to start assembling the chairs in week 4 (point B). This assembly task triggers the need for Level 1 components such as seats.

The bottom half of Figure 15.16 shows the MRP record for the seat. The top row shows **gross requirements**—that is, how many seats are needed each week. Because no chairs are being assembled in weeks 1 through 3, the gross requirement for seats in those weeks is zero (point C). In week 4, the gross requirement for seats is 500 (point D). This number is drawn directly from the "Start assembly" quantity at point B.

Gross requirements can be met by drawing from three sources: inventory carried over from the previous week, or the projected ending inventory; units already on order, referred to as **scheduled receipts**; and new orders, termed **planned receipts**. To determine whether any new orders need to be placed, we must first calculate **net requirements**:

$$NR_t = \text{maximum } (0; GR_t - EI_{t-1} - SR_t) \quad \textbf{[15-4]}$$

where:

NR_t = net requirement in time period t
GR_t = gross requirement in time period t
EI_{t-1} = ending inventory from time period $t - 1$
SR_t = scheduled receipts in time period t

Put another way, if enough seats can be obtained from inventory and scheduled receipts to cover the gross requirements, then managers don't need to order any more seats (net requirement equals zero). Otherwise, they have a net requirement that must be met with new planned receipts.

In our chair example, the projected inventory at the end of week 3 is zero, and there are no scheduled receipts in week 4. Therefore, the net requirement for seats in week 4 is

$$NR_4 = \text{maximum } (0;\ GR_4 - EI_3 - SR_4)$$
$$= \text{maximum } (0;\ 500 - 0 - 0) = 500$$

This result is shown in Figure 15.16 as point E. If you look in the lower left-hand corner of Figure 15.16, you will see that the minimum order size for seats is one. In general, a business would not want to order more units than necessary, as doing so would increase inventory levels and costs. Therefore, managers should plan on ordering just enough seats to meet the net requirement (point F). If they plan to receive 500 seats in week 4, they must release the order no later than week 2 (point G) because of the two-week planning lead time for seats. Finally, the ending inventory for week 4 (point H) is calculated using Equation 15-5:

$$EI_t = EI_{t-1} + SR_t + PR_t - GR_t \qquad [15\text{-}5]$$

where:

EI_t = ending inventory from time period t
EI_{t-1} = ending inventory from time period $t - 1$
SR_t = scheduled receipts in time period t
PR_t = planned receipts in time period t
GR_t = gross requirements in time period t

$$EI_4 = EI_3 + SR_4 + PR_4 - GR_4 = 0 + 0 + 500 - 500 = 0 \text{ seats}$$

To test your understanding of the MRP record, try tracing the calculations through weeks 5 and 6. Figure 15.17 shows the complete MRP record for all the Level 1 items, including the leg assembly and the back assembly. The logic behind the calculations is the same, but a couple of things should be noted. First, the factory begins week 1 with 25 leg assemblies in inventory (point I). Because there are no gross requirements in the first three weeks, these assemblies gather dust until they are needed in week 4. Though the net requirement in week 4 is only 475, managers place an order for 1000 (point J) because that is the minimum order size. The result is excess inventory at the end of week 4.

In week 5, the factory has more than enough leg assemblies (525) in beginning inventory to meet the gross requirement (400). As a result, managers do not place any additional orders

FIGURE 15.17
MRP Records for the Level 1 Components

King Philip chair LT (weeks) = 1		WEEK 1	2	3	4	5	6	7
MPS due date		0	0	0	0	**500**	400	300
Start assembly	0	0	0	0	**500**	400	300	0

Seat LT (weeks) = 2, Min. order = 1		WEEK 1	2	3	4	5	6	7
Gross requirements		0	0	0	500	400	300	0
Scheduled receipts		0	0	0	0	0	0	0
Projected ending inventory	0	0	0	0	0	0	0	0
Net requirements		0	0	0	500	400	300	0
Planned receipts		0	0	0	500	400	300	0
Planned orders		0	500	400	300	0	0	0

Leg asm LT (weeks) = 1, Min. order = 1000		WEEK 1	2	3	4	5	6	7
Gross requirements		0	0	0	500	400	300	0
Scheduled receipts	(I)	0	0	0	0	0	0	0
Projected ending inventory	25	25	25	25	525	125	825	825
Net requirements		0	0	0	475	0	175	0
Planned receipts		0	0	0 (J)	1000 (K)	0	1000	0
Planned orders		0	0	1000	0	1000	0	0

Back asm LT (weeks) = 1, Min. order = 250		WEEK 1	2	3	4	5	6	7
Gross requirements		0	0	0	500	400	300	0
Scheduled receipts		0	(L) 250	0	0	0	0	0
Projected ending inventory	0	0	250	250	0	0	0	0
Net requirements		0	0	0	250	400	300	0
Planned receipts		0	0	0	250	400	300	0
Planned orders		0	0	250	400	300	0	0

(point K). Finally, for the back assemblies, the factory has a scheduled receipt of 250 units in week 2 (point L). These units will sit in inventory until week 4, when they are needed.

Just as the gross requirements for Level 1 items are determined by the number of finished chairs (Level 0) to be manufactured, the gross requirements for Level 2 items depend on the *planned orders* for Level 1 items.

Figure 15.18 shows the complete MRP calculations for all components in the King Philip chair. Notice that managers want to put together 1000 leg assemblies in week 3 (planned orders = 1000). Because each leg assembly requires two legs (Figure 15.13), the gross requirement for legs in week 3 is 2000 (point M). Similarly, each back assembly requires two side rails. Therefore, a planned order for 300 back assemblies in week 5 results in a gross requirement of 600 side rails in the same week (point N).

FIGURE 15.18
Complete MRP Records for the King Philip Chair

			WEEK						
			1	2	3	4	5	6	7
** Chair kit**	MPS due date						500	400	300
LT (weeks) = 1	Start assembly					500	400	300	
** Seat **	Gross requirements					500	400	300	
LT (weeks) = 2	Scheduled receipts								
	Projected ending inventory	0	0	0	0	0	0	0	0
	Net requirements					500	400	300	
Min. order = 1	Planned receipts					500	400	300	
	Planned orders			500	400	300			
** Leg asm **	Gross requirements					500	400	300	
LT (weeks) = 1	Scheduled receipts								
	Projected ending inventory	25	25	25	25	525	125	825	825
	Net requirements					475		175	
Min. order = 1000	Planned receipts					1000		1000	
	Planned orders				**1000**		**1000**		
** Back asm **	Gross requirements					500	400	300	
LT (weeks) = 1	Scheduled receipts			250					
	Projected ending inventory	0	0	250	250	0	0	0	0
	Net requirements		M			250	400	300	
Min. order = 250	Planned receipts					250	400	300	
	Planned orders				**250**	**400**	**300**		
** Legs **	Gross requirements				**2000**		**2000**		N
LT (weeks) = 2	Scheduled receipts								
	Projected ending inventory	25	25	25	0	0	0	0	0
	Net requirements				1975		2000		
Min. order = 1	Planned receipts				1975		2000		
	Planned orders		1975		2000				
** Side rails **	Gross requirements				**500**	**800**	**600**		
LT (weeks) = 2	Scheduled receipts		500						
	Projected ending inventory	100	600	600	100	0	0	0	0
	Net requirements					700	600		
Min. order = 500	Planned receipts					700	600		
	Planned orders			700	600				
** Back slats **	Gross requirements				750	1200	900		
LT (weeks) = 2	Scheduled receipts					75			
	Projected ending inventory	0	0	0	0	0	0	0	0
	Net requirements				750	1125	900		
Min. order = 1	Planned receipts				750	1125	900		
	Planned orders		750	1125	900				
** Crossbars **	Gross requirements				1250	400	1300		
LT (weeks) = 2	Scheduled receipts								
	Projected ending inventory	0	0	0	0	600	300	300	300
	Net requirements				1250	400	700		
Min. order = 1000	Planned receipts				1250	1000	1000		
	Planned orders		1250	1000	1000				

Now for a *real* test. Where do the crossbar's gross requirements in Figure 15.18 come from? Because the crossbar is used in two different Level 1 items, we must calculate gross requirements based on planned orders for *both* the leg assemblies and the back assemblies. Therefore:

Gross requirements for crossbars = Leg assembly planned orders + back assembly planned orders

Week 3: $1{,}000 + 250 = 1{,}250$

Week 4: $0 + 400 = 400$

Week 5: $1{,}000 + 300 = 1{,}300$

Once we have calculated the gross requirements, filling out the rest of the MRP records is a matter of following the rules outlined earlier.

Example 15.5

Using MRP at Karam's Alpine Hiking Gear

The BOM and associated planning lead times for the Eiger1 backpack are shown in Figure 15.19.

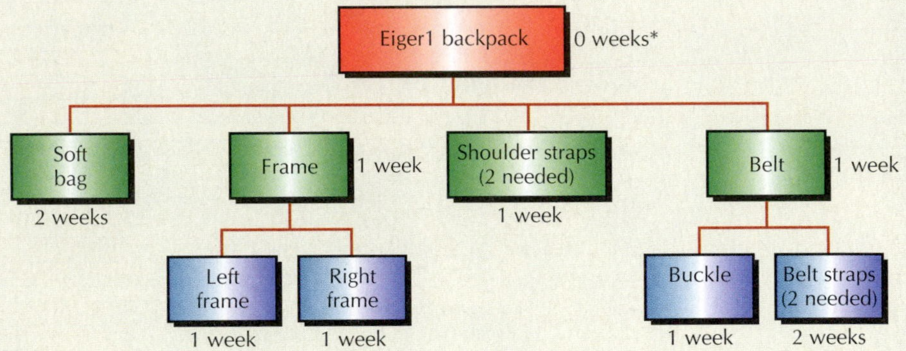

*To save on shipping and assembly costs, the Eiger1 backpack is sold unassembled. The dealer takes the Level 1 components and puts them together at the shop.

FIGURE 15.19 BOM for the Eiger1 Backpack

Lisa Karam has asked you to set up the MRP records for all the components for the next six weeks. Lisa also tells you the following:

- According to the master production schedule, Karam is planning on having 850 new backpacks ready to sell at the beginning of weeks 4, 5, and 6.
- Currently, there is no component inventory of any kind in the plant.
- The soft bag, shoulder straps, and belt straps all have minimum order quantities of 1500 units. All of the other components have no minimum order quantity.
- At present, the only scheduled receipt is for 50 left frames in week 1 (the result of an earlier partial shipment on the part of a vendor).

The completed MRP records are shown in Figure 15.20. There are a couple of interesting points to note:

1. In the current week, the *only* action that needs to be taken is to release an order for 1700 belt straps.
2. Because the Eiger1 backpacks do not have to be assembled, the final assembly planning lead time is zero.
3. The gross requirements for the shoulder straps are twice those of any other Level 1 item. This is because each backpack requires two shoulder straps.

4. The MRP record for the left frame is nearly identical to that for the right frame. The difference is due to the 50 "extra" left frames arriving in week 1. These extra left frames reduce the planned order release in week 2 by 50 units.

			WEEK					
			1	2	3	4	5	6
Eiger1 packs	MPS due date					850	850	850
LT (weeks) = 0	Start assembly					850	850	850
** Soft bag **	Gross requirements		0	0	0	850	850	850
LT (weeks) = 2	Scheduled receipts							
	Projected ending inventory	0	0	0	0	650	1300	450
	Net requirements					850	200	
Min. order = 1500	Planned receipts					1500	1500	
	Planned orders			1500	1500			
** Frame **	Gross requirements		0	0	0	850	850	850
LT (weeks) = 1	Scheduled receipts							
	Projected ending inventory	0	0	0	0	0	0	0
	Net requirements					850	850	850
Min. order = 1	Planned receipts					850	850	850
	Planned orders				850	850	850	
** Shoulder straps **	Gross requirements		0	0	0	1700	1700	1700
LT (weeks) = 1	Scheduled receipts							
	Projected ending inventory	0	0	0	0	0	0	0
	Net requirements					1700	1700	1700
Min. order = 1500	Planned receipts					1700	1700	1700
	Planned orders				1700	1700	1700	
** Belt **	Gross requirements		0	0	0	850	850	850
LT (weeks) = 1	Scheduled receipts							
	Projected ending inventory	0	0	0	0	0	0	0
	Net requirements					850	850	850
Min. order = 1	Planned receipts					850	850	850
	Planned orders				850	850	850	
** Left frame **	Gross requirements		0	0	850	850	850	0
LT (weeks) = 1	Scheduled receipts		50					
	Projected ending inventory	0	50	50	0	0	0	0
	Net requirements				800	850	850	
Min. order = 1	Planned receipts				800	850	850	
	Planned orders			800	850	850		
** Right frame **	Gross requirements		0	0	850	850	850	0
LT (weeks) = 1	Scheduled receipts							
	Projected ending inventory	0	0	0	0	0	0	0
	Net requirements				850	850	850	
Min. order = 1	Planned receipts				850	850	850	
	Planned orders			850	850	850		
** Buckle **	Gross requirements		0	0	850	850	850	0
LT (weeks) = 1	Scheduled receipts							
	Projected ending inventory	0	0	0	0	0	0	0
	Net requirements				850	850	850	
Min. order = 1	Planned receipts				850	850	850	
	Planned orders			850	850	850		
* Belt straps *	Gross requirements		0	0	1700	1700	1700	0
LT (weeks) = 2	Scheduled receipts							
	Projected ending inventory	0	0	0	0	0	0	0
	Net requirements				1700	1700	1700	
Min. order = 1500	Planned receipts				1700	1700	1700	
	Planned orders		1700	1700	1700			

FIGURE 15.20 MRP Records for the Eiger1 Backpack

The Advantages of MRP

Just as in master scheduling, getting lost in the calculations is easy to do with MRP. Figures 15.18 and 15.20 showed all the MRP records for two *very* simple products. Imagine what the MRP records must look like in a firm that produces hundreds of products, with dozens of BOM levels and thousands of components!

So now is a good time to pull back and consider just what the benefits of MRP are:

1. MRP is *directly tied* to the master production schedule and indicates the *exact* timing and quantity of orders for *all* components. By eliminating a lot of the guesswork associated with the management of dependent demand inventory, MRP simultaneously lowers inventory levels and helps firms meet their master schedule commitments.
2. MRP allows managers to trace every order for lower-level items through all the levels of the BOM, up to the master production schedule. This logical linkage between higher and lower levels in the BOM is sometimes called the **parent/child relationship**. If for some reason the supply of a lower-level item is interrupted, a manager can quickly check the BOM to see the impact of the shortage on production.
3. MRP tells the firm and its suppliers precisely what needs to be made when. This information can be invaluable in scheduling work or shipments, or even in planning budgets and cash flows. In fact, MRP logic is often called the "engine" of planning and control systems. MRP plays a big part in many enterprise resource planning (ERP) systems, described in this chapter's supplement.

Parent/child relationship
Refers to the logical linkage between higher- and lower-level items in the BOM.

Special Considerations in MRP

The complexity of MRP demands that these systems be computerized. But even with the help of computers, MRP requires *organizational discipline*. Like an electronic personal organizer, which provides incredible functionality if the owner takes the time to read the instructions and use the device properly, MRP provides little benefit to those who do not understand and exploit the system.

For an MRP system to work properly, it must have *accurate information*. Key data include the master production schedule, the BOM, inventory levels, and planning lead times. If any of this information is inaccurate, components will not be ordered at the right time or in the right quantity. In some cases, the correct components won't be ordered at all. As a result, most firms that want to implement MRP find that they must first ensure accurate planning information.

Yet MRP systems must also accommodate *uncertainty* about a host of factors, including the possibility of variable lead times, shipment quantities and quality levels, and even changes to the quantities in the master production schedule. In general, firms deal with this uncertainty by lengthening the planning lead times or by holding additional units as safety stock. Of course, such buffers increase the amount of inventory in the system. As a result, many firms make a conscious effort to *eliminate* uncertainty. They do so by choosing suppliers and processes that offer reliable lead times and high quality levels and by keeping the quantities on the master production schedule firm. Reducing uncertainty requires a high degree of organizational discipline, but the rewards can be pronounced.

A final consideration in implementing an MRP system is a phenomenon called **MRP nervousness**. Because higher-level items drive the requirements for lower-level items in an MRP system, any change, even a small one, in the requirements for upper-level items can have drastic effects on items listed further down the bill of material. Example 15.6 shows how such changes can affect the MRP records.

MRP nervousness
A term used to refer to the observation that any change, even a small one, in the requirements for items at the top of the bill of material can have drastic effects on items further down the bill of material.

Example 15.6

MRP Nervousness for the King Philip Chair

After completing the MRP records for the King Philip chair (Figure 15.18), management decides to change the number of chairs to be completed in week 7 from 300 to 125. Figure 15.21 shows the impact of this change on the MRP records. As you can see, no MRP record is left untouched.

Compared to Figure 15.18, the change eliminates the need for a second planned order of 1000 leg assemblies in week 5. That, in turn, affects the gross requirements for legs and crossbars. The change in planned production also spills over to the records for

			WEEK						
			1	2	3	4	5	6	7
** Chair kit**	MPS due date						500	400	**125**
LT (weeks) = 1	Start assembly					500	400	**125**	
** Seat **	Gross requirements					500	400	**125**	
LT (weeks) = 2	Scheduled receipts								
	Projected ending inventory	0	0	0	0	0	0	0	0
	Net requirements					500	400	**125**	
Min. order = 1	Planned receipts					500	400	**125**	
	Planned orders			500	400	**125**			
** Leg asm **	Gross requirements					500	400	**125**	
LT (weeks) = 1	Scheduled receipts								
	Projected ending inventory	25	25	25	25	525	**125**	0	0
	Net requirements					475			
Min. order = 1000	Planned receipts					1000			
	Planned orders				1000				
** Back asm **	Gross requirements					500	400	**125**	
LT (weeks) = 1	Scheduled receipts			250					
	Projected ending inventory	0	0	250	250	0	0	0	0
	Net requirements					250	400	**125**	
Min. order = 250	Planned receipts					250	400	**125**	
	Planned orders				250	400	**125**		
** Legs **	Gross requirements				**2000**				
LT (weeks) = 2	Scheduled receipts								
	Projected ending inventory	25	25	25	0	0	0	0	0
	Net requirements				1975				
Min. order = 1	Planned receipts				1975				
	Planned orders		1975						
** Side rails **	Gross requirements				500	800	**250**		
LT (weeks) = 2	Scheduled receipts		500						
	Projected ending inventory	100	600	600	100	0	**250**	**250**	**250**
	Net requirements					700	**250**		
Min. order = 500	Planned receipts					700	**500**		
	Planned orders			700	**500**				
** Back slats **	Gross requirements				750	1200	375		
LT (weeks) = 2	Scheduled receipts					75			
	Projected ending inventory	0	0	0	0	0	0	0	0
	Net requirements				750	1125	**375**		
Min. order = 1	Planned receipts				750	1125	**375**		
	Planned orders		750	1125	**375**				
** Crossbars **	Gross requirements				1250	400	125		
LT (weeks) = 2	Scheduled receipts								
	Projected ending inventory	0	0	0	0	600	**475**	**475**	**475**
	Net requirements				1250	400			
Min. order = 1000	Planned receipts				1250	1000			
	Planned orders		1250	1000					

FIGURE 15.21 MRP Nervousness for the King Philip Chair

seats, back assemblies, side rails, and back slats, although the impact is not quite as pronounced. The point is that a minor change at the top can cause huge changes at lower levels. Planners must take MRP nervousness into consideration when making changes, especially with higher-level items. They must also choose their minimum order quantities with care. Notice the impact of the minimum order, or **lot size**, for leg assemblies: The firm went from ordering 1,000 leg assemblies in week 5 to ordering none at all that week. Because large lot sizes make MRP systems more nervous, firms that take this approach to inventory management usually try to keep their minimum order quantities as small as possible, especially for higher-level items that have the potential to disrupt lower-level requirements.

15.3 PRODUCTION ACTIVITY CONTROL AND VENDOR ORDER MANAGEMENT SYSTEMS

To this point, we have been discussing planning tools: S&OP for planning overall resource levels, master scheduling for planning the production and shipment of end items, and MRP for planning orders for manufacturing components. With production activity control (PAC) and vendor order management systems, the emphasis shifts from planning to *execution*. Besides their many other capabilities, these systems can:

1. Route and prioritize jobs going through the supply chain;
2. Coordinate the flow of goods and materials between a facility and other supply chain partners; and
3. Provide supply chain partners with performance data on operations and supply chain activities.

Job Sequencing

Job sequencing rules Rules used to determine the order in which jobs should be processed when resources are limited and multiple jobs are waiting to be done.

The tools and techniques used to perform PAC and vendor order management are as varied as the operational environments in which they are used. They can be as simple as the rules for deciding which manufacturing job should be processed next or as complex as high-tech software or hardware solutions for tracking the flow of materials among supply chain partners. **Job sequencing rules** have been used for decades to determine the order in which jobs should be processed when resources are limited and multiple jobs are waiting to be done. And as Example 15.7 shows, job sequencing is just as valid in a services environment as it is in manufacturing.

Example 15.7

Job Sequencing at Carlos's Restoration Services

Carlos's Restoration Services restores antique paintings. The process consists of three steps. Each of these steps must be completed prior to moving on to the next step. Furthermore, Carlos's can work on only one job at a time at each step.

Carlos's has four jobs waiting to be started. Information on these jobs, shown in the order they arrived, is contained in Table 15.1.

Total task times range from 8 to 11 days. Chester College has requested that its job be completed in 10 days, while Uptown Gallery is willing to wait 21 days. One way to determine

TABLE 15.1 Job Requirements for Carlos's Restoration Services

JOB	*Estimated Days* STEP 1	STEP 2	STEP 3	TOTAL TASK TIME	DAYS UNTIL DUE	CRITICAL RATIO
Uptown Gallery	3	2	3.5	8.5	21	2.47
High Museum	5	2	1	8	20	2.50
Chester College	3	2	5	10	10	1.00
Smith	6	4	1	11	15	1.36

the order in which jobs should be sequenced is based on the critical ratio. The **critical ratio** is calculated as follows:

$$\text{Critical Ratio} = \frac{\text{Days until due}}{\text{Total task time remaining}} \qquad [15\text{-}6]$$

A critical ratio of 1 indicates that the amount of task time equals the amount of time left; hence, any time spent waiting will make the job late. A critical ratio of less than 1 indicates that the job is going to be late unless something changes. When the critical ratio is used to sequence work, the jobs with the lowest critical ratio are scheduled to go first. Carlos's decides to test three common job sequencing rules—first come, first served (FCFS), earliest due date (EDD), and the critical ratio—to see which one performs best. The results are shown in Table 15.2.

Processing the jobs on a first come, first served basis might seem the fairest, but in this case, the result is that two jobs are finished long before they're due, while two jobs are considerably late. Sequencing the jobs according to the earliest due date results in somewhat

TABLE 15.2 Testing Three Common Job Sequencing Rules at Carlos' Restoration Services

First come–first served	*Step 1*		*Step 2*		*Step 3*		
JOB	START	END	START	END	START	END	DAYS LATE
Uptown Gallery	0	3	3	5	5	8.5	0
High Museum	3	8	8	10	10	11	0
Chester College	8	11	11	13	13	18	8
Smith	11	17	17	21	21	22	7
					Average lateness:		**3.75** days

Earliest due date	*Step 1*		*Step 2*		*Step 3*		
JOB	START	END	START	END	START	END	DAYS LATE
Chester College	0	3	3	5	5	10	0
Smith	3	9	9	13	13	14	0
High Museum	9	14	14	16	16	17	0
Uptown Gallery	14	17	17	19	19	22.5	1.5
					Average lateness:		**0.375** days

Critical ratio	*Step 1*		*Step 2*		*Step 3*		
JOB	START	END	START	END	START	END	DAYS LATE
Chester College	0	3	3	5	5	10	0
Smith	3	9	9	13	13	14	0
Uptown Gallery	9	12	13	15	15	18.5	0
High Museum	12	17	17	19	19	20	0
					Average lateness:		**0** days

better results—only the Uptown Gallery job is late (1.5 days), for an average lateness of 0.375 days.

Carlos's then sequences the jobs from highest to lowest critical ratio value. In this case, all the jobs are completed prior to the due date. Based on these results, Carlos's decides to use the critical ratio to set the sequence.

Monitoring and Tracking Technologies

More recently, radio frequency identification (RFID), bar coding, and online order tracking systems have been developed to trace the movement and location of materials in the supply chain and report on the progress of specific jobs. Such systems depend on computer hardware and software that can interpret the information gathered by the system. Herman Miller, described at the beginning of this chapter, incorporates PAC and vendor order management tools. Besides helping the company to control its operations and supply chain activities, these systems also alert managers to potential problems. For example, computer terminals located throughout Herman Miller's plant provide users with real-time information about the status of manufacturing jobs and required materials. If a shortage of materials threatens to delay a job, the system flags the problem and indicates which jobs will be affected. Managers at Herman Miller or at supply chain partners' facilities can then take corrective action.

15.4 SYNCHRONIZING PLANNING AND CONTROL ACROSS THE SUPPLY CHAIN

Throughout this book, we have emphasized the need to synchronize decisions across the supply chain. That need is especially critical in planning and control activities. In this section, we introduce one technique for synchronizing planning and control decisions, distribution requirements planning (DRP). In Chapter 16, we will talk about another technique called "kanban." DRP helps to synchronize supply chain partners at the *master schedule level*, while kanban systems help to synchronize them at the PAC and vendor order management levels (Figure 15.22).

Distribution requirements planning (DRP)
A time-phased planning approach similar to MRP that uses planned orders at the point of demand (customer, warehouse, etc.) to determine forecasted demand at the source level (often a plant).

Distribution Requirements Planning

Distribution requirements planning (DRP) is a time-phased planning approach similar to MRP that uses planned orders at the point of demand (customer, warehouse, etc.) to determine forecasted demand at the source level (often a plant). DRP is one of many ways

FIGURE 15.22
Synchronized Planning and Control

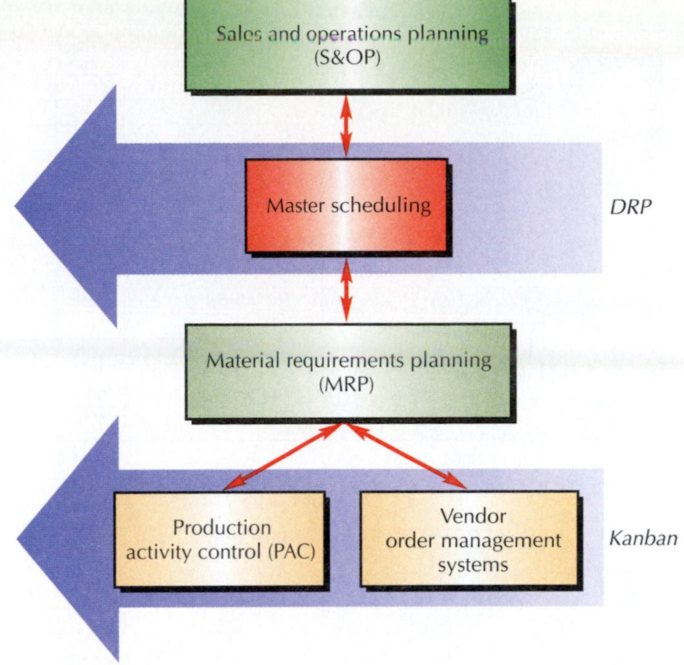

in which supply chain partners can synchronize their planning efforts at the master schedule level. These forecasted demand numbers then become input to the master scheduling process.

To illustrate how DRP works, let's return to the example of Sandy-Built's MeltoMatic snowblower. When you first looked at the master schedule record shown in Figure 15.7, you may have wondered where the forecasted demand numbers came from. After all, much of the value of master scheduling hinges on the accuracy of forecasts. Managers typically base their forecasts on past history or educated guesses, but DRP forecasts are calculated directly from downstream supply partners' requirements. That is, DRP uses MRP-style logic to feed accurate demand information into the master schedule.

Suppose the MeltoMatic is sold through two regional distribution centers, one in Minneapolis, Minnesota, and the other in Buffalo, New York. These distribution centers, in turn, sell directly to retailers. Figure 15.23 shows the structure of this downstream supply chain.

FIGURE 15.23
Downstream Supply Chain for MeltoMatic Snowblowers

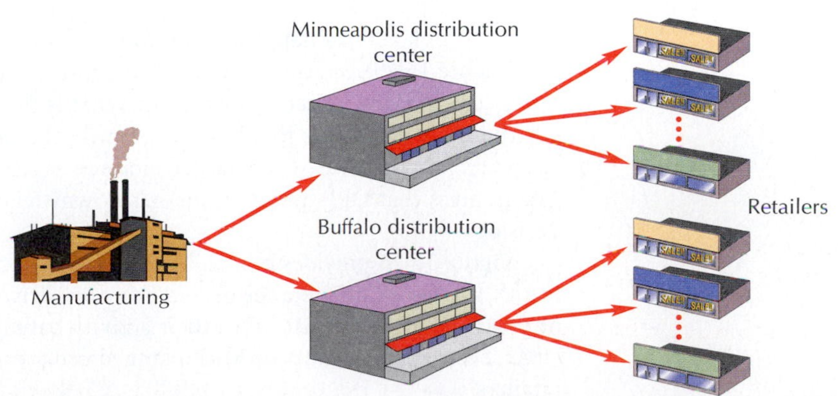

Minneapolis distribution center

		Month	********November********				********December********				********January********			
		Week	45	46	47	48	49	50	51	52	1	2	3	4
	Forecasted demand		60	60	60	60	75	75	75	75	90	90	120	120
LT (weeks) = 2	Scheduled receipts			120										
	Projected ending inventory	75	15	75	15	75	0	45	90	15	45	75	75	75
	Net requirements		0	0	0	45	0	75	30	0	75	45	45	45
Min. order = 120	Planned receipts		0	0	0	120	0	120	120	0	120	120	120	120
	Planned orders		0	120	0	120	120	0	120	120	120	120	0	0

Buffalo distribution center

		Month	********November********				********December********				********January********			
		Week	45	46	47	48	49	50	51	52	1	2	3	4
	Forecasted demand		80	80	85	85	90	90	95	95	100	100	105	105
LT (weeks) = 1	Scheduled receipts		100											
	Projected ending inventory	25	45	65	80	95	5	15	20	25	25	25	20	15
	Net requirements		0	35	20	5	0	85	80	75	75	75	80	85
Min. order = 100	Planned receipts		0	100	100	100	0	100	100	100	100	100	100	100
	Planned orders		100	100	100	0	100	100	100	100	100	100	100	0

Master schedule, MeltoMatic snow blowers

	Month	********November********				********December********			
	Week	45	46	47	48	49	50	51	52
Forecasted demand		**100**	**220**	**100**	**120**	**220**	**100**	**220**	**220**
Booked orders		100	0	0	0	0	0	0	0
Projected ending inventory	37	257	37	157	37	137	37	257	37
Master production schedule		320		220		320		440	0
Available to promise		257		220		320		440	

FIGURE 15.24 DRP Records for the MeltoMatic Snowblower

Each distribution center has its own weekly demand forecasts, inventory data, order lead times, and minimum order quantities. Both centers use this information to estimate when they will need to place orders with the main plant.

The two sections at the top of Figure 15.24 show the DRP records for the two distribution centers. Note that these records are almost identical to MRP records, with one exception: Instead of gross requirements, they show forecasted demand. Here the term *forecasted demand* refers to the number of snowblowers each center expects to ship to retail customers each week. By substituting forecasted demand for gross requirements, managers at the distribution centers can calculate net requirements, planned receipts, and planned orders. Finally, activities at these two distribution centers are synchronized when their total weekly planned orders become forecasted demand in the factory's master schedule (see the third section of Figure 15.24). Master scheduling occurs as usual, except that the forecasted demand is tied explicitly to planned orders at the distribution centers.

Now look at what happens when forecasted demand changes at the distribution centers (Figure 15.25). Starting in week 49, the forecasted demand at the Minneapolis distribution center has increased dramatically. What is the impact of this change on the master schedule? Logic suggests that in order to meet the increased demand, Sandy-Built's managers will need to increase the master production schedule to 440 snowblowers in week 49. The point is that DRP quickly translates downstream demand into upstream production decisions.

Figure 15.26 provides a final, high-level view of how DRP helps synchronize Sandy-Built's supply chain. Retailer orders not only drive Sandy-Built's plans, but also those of upstream suppliers who plan their activity based on Sandy-Built's material orders. In effect, every MPS quantity or MRP planned order can be traced back to demand from the retailers.

Minneapolis distribution center		Month	********November********				********December********				********January********			
		Week	45	46	47	48	49	50	51	52	1	2	3	4
	Forecasted demand		60	60	60	60	90	90	90	90	110	110	130	130
LT (weeks) = 2	Scheduled receipts			120			0							
	Projected ending inventory	75	15	75	15	75	105	15	45	75	85	95	85	75
	Net requirements		0	0	0	45	15	0	75	45	35	25	35	45
Min. order = 120	Planned receipts		0	0	0	120	120	0	120	120	120	120	120	120
	Planned orders		0	120	120	0	120	120	120	120	120	120	0	0

Buffalo distribution center		Month	********November********				********December********				********January********			
		Week	45	46	47	48	49	50	51	52	1	2	3	4
	Forecasted demand		80	80	85	85	90	90	95	95	100	100	105	105
LT (weeks) = 1	Scheduled receipts		100											
	Projected ending inventory	25	45	65	80	95	5	15	20	25	25	25	20	15
	Net requirements		0	35	20	5	0	85	80	75	75	75	80	85
Min. order = 100	Planned receipts		0	100	100	100	0	100	100	100	100	100	100	100
	Planned orders		100	100	100	0	100	100	100	100	100	100	100	0

Master schedule, MeltoMatic snow blowers		Month	********November********				********December********			
		Week	45	46	47	48	49	50	51	52
	Forecasted demand		100	220	220	0	220	220	220	220
	Booked orders		100	0	0	0	0	0	0	0
	Projected ending inventory	37	257	37	37	37	257	37	257	37
	Master production schedule		320		220		440		440	
	Available to promise		257		220		440		440	

FIGURE 15.25 The Impact of Forecast Changes on DRP Records

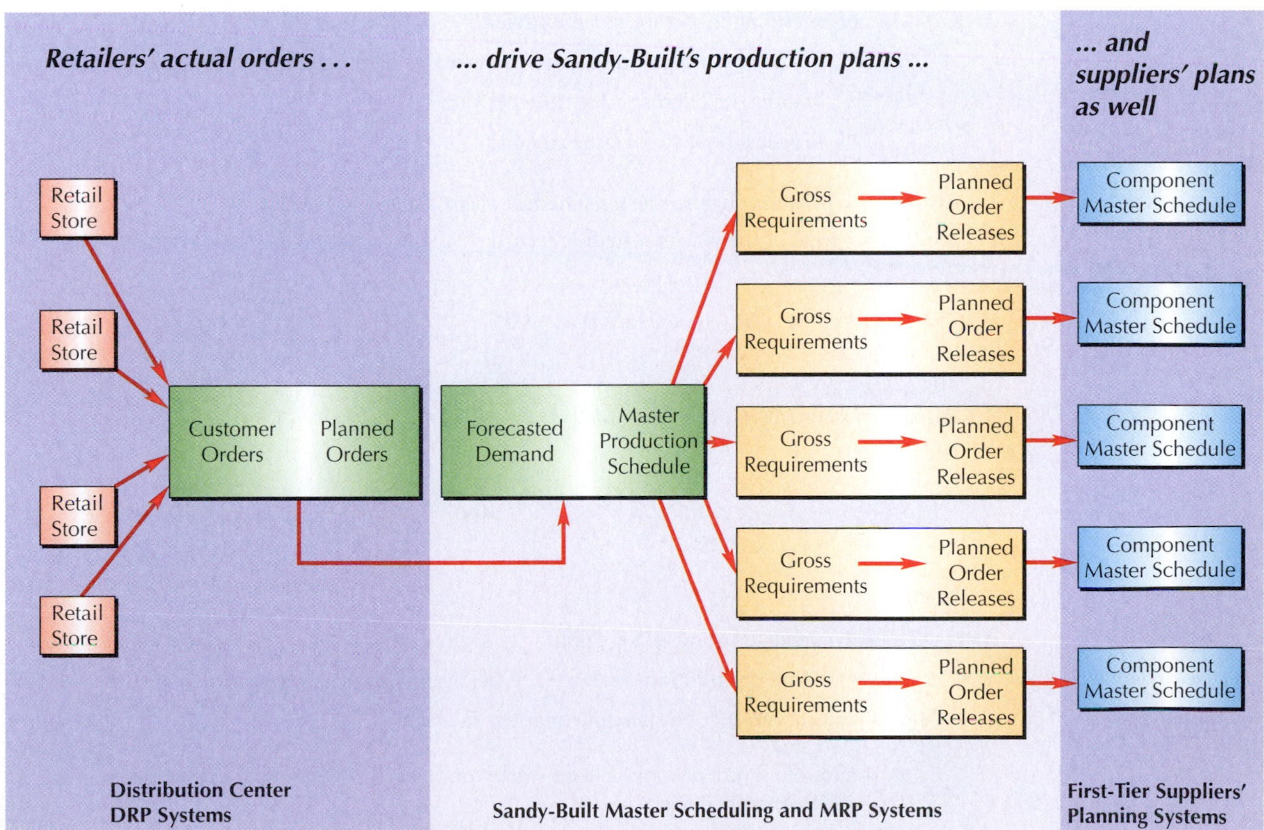

FIGURE 15.26 Synchronizing Plans across the Supply Chain

CHAPTER SUMMARY

This chapter has provided a comprehensive overview of the various tools companies use to manage production, starting with master scheduling, then MRP and job sequencing, and ending with DRP. Planning and control systems aid manufacturers and service firms alike by helping them to determine the quantities and timing of their activities. Put another way, production management should be of interest not only to manufacturing firms, but also to virtually all firms involved in the flow of physical products.

Today, advances in information technology are radically changing planning and control systems in two fundamental ways. First, faster computers and extensive communications networks are expanding the depth and breadth of planning and control activities. Firms can replan and share new information with their supply chain partners almost instantaneously. Second, planning and control software tools are becoming more sophisticated. Some firms even have advanced decision support tools that allow them to quickly evaluate multiple plans or even to generate an optimal plan.

That said, the usefulness of planning and control systems still depends on people who understand how they work and how to use them correctly. This fundamental requirement will never change.

KEY FORMULAS

Projected ending inventory for the master schedule record (page 480):

$$EI_t = EI_{t-1} + MPS_t - \text{maximum } (F_t, OB_t) \qquad [15\text{-}1]$$

where:

EI_t = ending inventory in time period t

MPS_t = master production schedule quantity available in time period t

F_t = forecasted demand for time period t

OB_t = orders booked for time period t

Available to promise for the master schedule record (page 481–182):

For the *first week* of the master schedule record:

$$ATP_t = EI_{t-1} + MPS_t - \sum_{i=t}^{z-1} OB_i \qquad [15\text{-}2]$$

For any subsequent week *in which* MPS > 0:

$$ATP_t = MPS_t - \sum_{i=t}^{z-1} OB_i \qquad [15\text{-}3]$$

where:

ATP_t = available to promise in week t

EI_{t-1} = ending inventory in week $t-1$ = beginning inventory in week t

MPS_t = master production schedule quantity in week t

$\sum_{i=t}^{z-1} OB_i$ = sum of all orders booked from week t until week z (when the next positive MPS quantity is due)

Net requirements for the MRP record (page 489):

$$NR_t = \text{maximum}(0; GR_t - EI_{t-1} - SR_t) \qquad [15\text{-}4]$$

where:

NR_t = net requirement in time period t

GR_t = gross requirement in time period t

EI_{t-1} = ending inventory from time period $t - 1$

SR_t = scheduled receipts in time period t

Projected ending inventory for the MRP record (page 490):

$$EI_t = EI_{t-1} + SR_t + PR_t - GR_t \qquad [15\text{-}5]$$

where:

EI_t = ending inventory from time period t

EI_{t-1} = ending inventory from time period $t - 1$

SR_t = scheduled receipts in time period t

PR_t = planned receipts in time period t

GR_t = gross requirements in time period t

Critical ratio (page 497):

$$\text{Critical Ratio} = \frac{\text{Days until due}}{\text{Total task time remaining}} \qquad [15\text{-}6]$$

KEY TERMS

Available to promise (ATP) 481
Bill of material (BOM) 487
Booked orders 480
Criticial ratio 497
Dependent demand inventory 486
Distribution requirements planning (DRP) 498
Exploding the BOM 488
Forecasted demand 479
Gross requirements 489
Job sequencing rules 496
Lot size 496
Master production schedule 480
Master scheduling 478
Material requirements planning (MRP) 486
MRP nervousness 494
Net requirements 489
Parent/child relationship 494
Planned receipts 489
Planning and control 477
Planning horizon 485
Planning lead time 487
Product structure tree 487
Projected ending inventory 480
Rough-cut capacity planning 486
Scheduled receipts 489

SOLVED PROBLEM

Problem

Complete the projected ending inventory and available-to-promise calculations for the following master schedule record. Interpret the results.

On-hand inventory at end of week 15		**222**						
Week	16	17	18	19	20	21	22	23
Forecasted demand	220	220	215	215	210	210	205	205
Booked orders	192	189	233	96	135	67	85	40
Projected ending inventory								
Master production schedule		450		430		415		400
Available to promise								

Solution

The projected ending inventory values can be found using Equation 15-1:

$$EI_t = EI_{t-1} + MPS_t - \text{maximum}\ (F_t, OB_t) \qquad \textbf{[15-1]}$$

For weeks 16 through 18, the projected ending inventories are

$$EI_{16} = 222 + 0 - \text{maximum}\ (220, 192) = 2$$
$$EI_{17} = 2 + 450 - \text{maximum}\ (220, 189) = 232$$
$$EI_{18} = 232 + 0 - \text{maximum}\ (215, 233) = -1$$

Weeks 19 through 23 are calculated in a similar manner. Interpreting the projected ending inventory in week 18, the negative value suggests that there is not enough inventory to meet the forecasted demand. But has the company overpromised yet? To see, we need to calculate the *ATP* numbers:

$$ATP_{16} = 222 + 0 - 192 = 30$$
$$ATP_{17} = 450 - (189 + 233) = 28$$
$$ATP_{19} = 430 - (96 + 135) = 199$$
$$ATP_{21} = 415 - (67 + 85) = 263$$
$$ATP_{23} = 400 - 40 = 360$$

The completed master schedule record is as follows:

On-hand inventory at end of week 15		**222**						
Week	16	17	18	19	20	21	22	23
Forecasted demand	220	220	215	215	210	210	205	205
Booked orders	192	189	233	96	135	67	85	40
Projected ending inventory	**2**	**232**	**–1**	**214**	**4**	**209**	**4**	**199**
Master production schedule		450		430		415		400
Available to promise	**30**	**28**		**199**		**263**		**360**

The master schedule record suggests that, as of right now, the company has not overpromised. However, if the company wants to meet all the forecasted demand (or keep some safety stock available just in case), it should consider taking steps to bump up its master production schedule quantities.

DISCUSSION QUESTIONS

1. Someone says to you, "If a company is already using sales and operations planning to coordinate marketing and operations, then it doesn't need master scheduling as well." Is this true? How are S&OP and master scheduling similar? How are they different? What information does master scheduling provide that S&OP does not? How difficult would it be to develop successful master schedules without doing S&OP first?

2. Can a company complete its material requirements plans before it does master scheduling? Explain.

3. Discuss the importance of accurate forecasting to planning and control systems. What happens if an organization's planning efforts are strong, except for forecasting?

4. What is MRP nervousness? Can this condition affect DRP systems as well?

5. Master scheduling, MRP, and DRP have been around for a long time, but too many companies still do an inadequate job of using these tools. How can this be? In particular, what role do you think organizational discipline plays in making these tools work?

6. What are the benefits of having a formal master scheduling process? What could happen to firms that don't follow some of the basic rules of master scheduling?

7. Explain in your own words how tools such as master scheduling, MRP, and DRP can be used to coordinate activity up and down a supply chain. For example, what information might we share with our customers? Our suppliers? What information might we want from them to do master scheduling, MRP, and DRP effectively?

PROBLEMS

Additional homework problems are available at www.prenhall.com/bozarth. These problems use Excel to generate customized problems for different class sections or even different students.

(* = easy; ** = moderate; *** = advanced)

1. (*) Complete the following master schedule record:

On-hand inventory at end of week 1		**65**						
Week	2	3	4	5	6	7	8	9
Forecasted demand	45	50	55	60	65	70	75	80
Booked orders	15	100	48	25	72	22	67	10
Projected ending inventory								
Master production schedule	150			200			150	
Available to promise							**73**	

2. (**) Consider the master schedule record shown in Problem 1. Suppose marketing books an order for an additional 10 units in week 4. Recalculate the projected ending inventory and available-to-promise numbers. How low does the projected ending inventory get? What actions might the company take as a result?

3. (**) Complete the following master schedule record:

On-hand inventory at end of week 1		**100**						
Week	2	3	4	5	6	7	8	9
Forecasted demand	250	250	300	300	350	350	250	250
Booked orders	265	255	270	245	260	235	180	100
Projected ending inventory								
Master production schedule	500		600		700		500	
Available to promise							**220**	

4. (**) Consider the master schedule record shown in Problem 3. Suppose the production manager calls up and says that only 600 units will be finished in week 6, not the 700 units originally called for. Recalculate the projected ending inventory and available-to-promise numbers. What does a negative projected ending inventory value mean? How does it differ from a negative available-to-promise number? As a manager, which would be easier to deal with—a negative projected ending inventory value or a negative ATP?

5. Consider the following partially completed master schedule record:

On-hand inventory at end of April 40								
Month	************May************				************June************			
Week	19	20	21	22	23	24	25	26
Forecasted demand	200	200	200	225	225	225	200	200
Booked orders	205	203	201	195	193	190	182	178
Projected ending inventory								
Master production schedule	600	0	0	675	0	0	600	0
Available to promise							**240**	

a. (*) Complete the projected ending inventory calculations and the available-to-promise calculations.

b. (**) Suppose that a customer calls and cancels an order for 50 units in week 25. Which of the following statements are *true*?
   - The ATP for week 25 will increase by 50 units.
   - The projected ending inventory for week 25 will increase by 50 units.
   - The ATP for weeks 19 and 22 will be unaffected.

6. (*) Complete the following MRP record. All gross requirements, beginning inventory levels, and scheduled receipts are shown.

WEEK		1	2	3	4	5	6
A2	Gross requirements	200	200	200	300	300	300
LT (weeks) = 2	Scheduled receipts		200				
	Projected ending inventory: 260						
	Net requirements						
Min. order = 1	Planned receipts						
Planned orders							

7. (**) Now suppose the lead time for item A2, shown in Problem 6, is three weeks, rather than two weeks. Based on this information, can the company support the current gross requirements for the A2? Why? What are the implications of having reliable supplier and manufacturing lead times in an MRP environment?

8. (**) Complete the following MRP record. Note that the minimum order quantity is 900. What is the average ending inventory over the six weeks?

WEEK		1	2	3	4	5	6
B3	Gross requirements	0	400	400	400	0	400
LT (weeks) = 1	Scheduled receipts						
	Projected ending inventory: 0						
	Net requirements						
Min. order = 900	Planned receipts						
	Planned orders						

9. (**) Now suppose the minimum order quantity for item B3 in Problem 8 is reduced to 300 units. Redo the MRP record. What is the new average ending inventory level over the six weeks? What are the implications for setting order quantities in an MRP environment?

10. (**) The following figure shows the bill of material (BOM) for the Acme PolyBob, a product that has proven unsuccessful in capturing roadrunners. Complete the MRP records. All the information you need is shown in the BOM and on the MRP records.

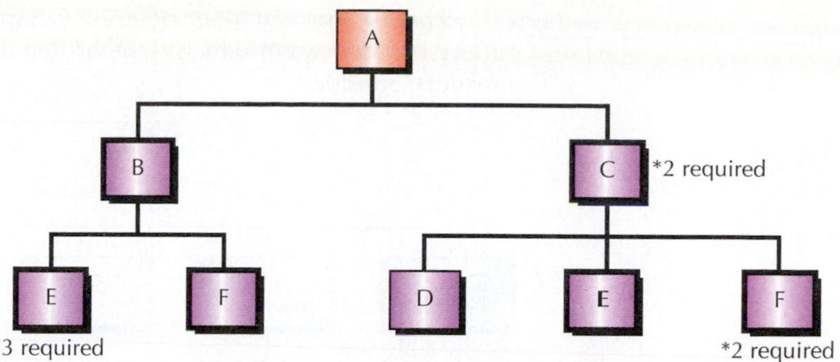

Item B: Lead time = 1 week; Minimum order quantity = 1

WEEK	1	2	3	4	5	6
Gross requirements		250	300	300	300	200
Scheduled receipts						
Projected ending inventory: 0						
Net requirements						
Planned receipts						
Planned orders						

Item C: Lead time = 3 weeks; Minimum order quantity = 500

WEEK	1	2	3	4	5	6
Gross requirements						
Scheduled receipts		500	600			
Projected ending inventory: 0						
Net requirements						
Planned receipts						
Planned orders						

Item E: Lead time = 4 weeks; Minimum order quantity = 5000

WEEK	1	2	3	4	5	6
Gross requirements						
Scheduled receipts						
Projected ending inventory: 5750						
Net requirements						
Planned receipts						
Planned orders						

Item F: Lead time = 5 weeks; Minimum order quantity = 750

WEEK	1	2	3	4	5	6
Gross requirements						
Scheduled receipts						
Projected ending inventory: 4750						
Net requirements						
Planned receipts						
Planned orders						

11. (**) Republic Tool and Manufacturing Company of Carlsbad, California, makes a wide variety of lawn care products. One of Republic's products is the Model Number 540 Broadcast Spreader.

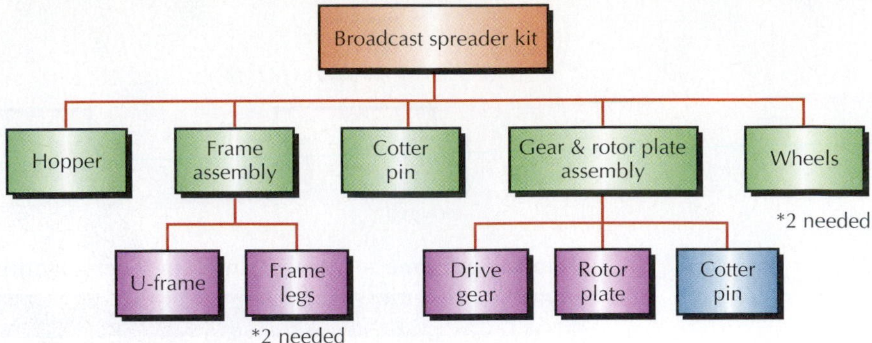

Complete the following MRP records. Note the following:

- Republic intends to start assembling 2000 broadcast spreader kits in weeks 2, 4, and 6.
- The gross requirements for the gear and rotor plate assembly have already been given to you. For the remaining items, you will need to figure out the gross requirements.
- All scheduled receipts, lead times, and beginning inventory levels are shown.
- Note that cotter pins appear *twice* in the bill of material.

Gear and rotor plate assembly: Lead time = 1 week; Minimum order quantity = 2500

WEEK	1	2	3	4	5	6
Gross requirements		2000		2000		2000
Scheduled receipts						
Projected ending inventory: 1000						
Net requirements						
Planned receipts						
Planned orders						

Wheels: Lead time = 1 week; Minimum order quantity = 1

WEEK	1	2	3	4	5	6
Gross requirements						
Scheduled receipts						
Projected ending inventory: 0						
Net requirements						
Planned receipts						
Planned orders						

Cotter Pins: Lead time = 3 weeks; Minimum order quantity = 15,000

WEEK	1	2	3	4	5	6
Gross requirements						
Scheduled receipts						
Projected ending inventory: 11,000						
Net requirements						
Planned receipts						
Planned orders						

12. (**) Each Triam Deluxe computer system consists of *two* speakers, a monitor, a system unit, a keyboard, and an installation kit. These pieces are packed together and shipped as a complete kit. In MRP terms, all of these items are Level 1 items that make the Level 0 kits. Complete the following MRP records, using this information.

- Production plans for complete kits are as follows:
  Start assembling 2500 kits in week 2
  Start assembling 3000 kits in weeks 3, 4, and 5
  Start assembling 2000 kits in week 6
- The gross requirements for the system unit have already been given to you. For the remaining items, you will need to figure out the gross requirements.
- All scheduled receipts, lead times, and beginning inventory levels are shown.

System unit: Lead time = 1 week; Minimum order quantity = 1

WEEK	1	2	3	4	5	6
Gross requirements		2500	3000	3000	3000	2000
Scheduled receipts						
Projected ending inventory: 0						
Net requirements						
Planned receipts						
Planned orders						

Speakers: Lead time = 1 week; Minimum order quantity = 5000

WEEK	1	2	3	4	5	6
Gross requirements						
Scheduled receipts	5000					
Projected ending inventory: 0						
Net requirements						
Planned receipts						
Planned orders						

CD–ROM drives: Lead time = 6 weeks; Minimum order quantity = 5000

WEEK	1	2	3	4	5	6
Gross requirements						
Scheduled receipts						
Projected ending inventory: 13,500						
Net requirements						
Planned receipts						
Planned orders						

Vaxidene (Problems 13 and 14)

After graduating from college, you take a job with Baxter Pharmaceuticals. Once there, you are made the product manager for Vaxidene, a new vaccine used to fight bacterial meningitis. The bill of material (BOM) for a *single 4-milligram dose* of Vaxidene follows.

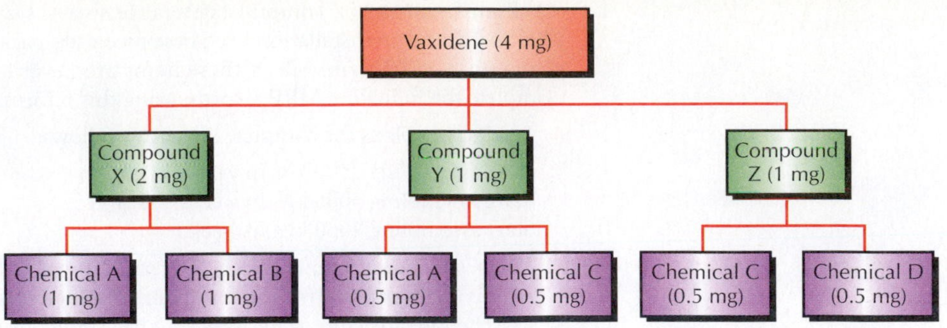

Each dose is actually a mixture of three proprietary compounds, called compounds X, Y, and Z. It takes one week to mix them together to make doses of Vaxidene. You also have the following information:

- Compound X is made up of two chemicals (A and B) and takes one week to synthesize (i.e., lead time = 1 week).
- Compound Y is made up of two chemicals (A and C) and takes one week to synthesize.
- Compound Z is made up of two chemicals (C and D) and takes one week to synthesize.
- The lead times for chemicals A through D are all one week.

13. Consider the following master schedule record for Vaxidene:
   a. (*) Complete the master schedule record.
   b. (**) Suppose a hospital in the Tucson area calls and says it is facing an epidemic of bacterial meningitis. It needs 2000 doses as soon as possible. Assuming Baxter can make no changes to the master production schedule quantities or orders booked, how quickly can it get the hospital the 2000 doses? Be specific with regard to what quantities Baxter can ship and when.
   c. (**) Suppose the hospital says it needs the doses now, not in three weeks. What steps could Baxter Pharmaceuticals take to deal with this emergency? Who would Baxter need to talk to? (*Hint:* Consider the current booked orders and their sources.)

14. (***) Complete the following MRP records for the Vaxidene drug. Note the following:

- Doses have been converted into milligrams to facilitate material planning (4250 doses = 17,000 milligrams).
- Make sure that you calculate the correct requirements for each compound and drug. For instance, each 4-milligram dose requires 2 milligrams of compound X (2 to 1). Therefore, to start mixing 17,000 milligrams of Vaxidene, Baxter Pharmaceuticals will need 8500 milligrams of compound X.

Vaxidene

		Week						
		1	2	3	4	5	6	7
LT (weeks) = 1	MPS due date		0	0	17,000	0	0	14,000
Start mixing				17,000			14,000	
Compound X	Gross requirements							
LT (weeks) =	Scheduled receipts							
	Projected ending inventory: 1500							
	Net requirements							
Minimum order (mgs) =	Planned receipts							
20,000	Planned orders							

******Compound Y******	Gross requirements							
LT (weeks) =	Scheduled receipts							
	Projected ending inventory: 1000							
	Net requirements							
Minimum order (mgs) =	Planned receipts							
5000	Planned orders							
*****Compound Z*****	Gross requirements							
LT (weeks) =	Scheduled receipts	200						
	Projected ending inventory: 0							
	Net requirements							
Minimum order (mgs) = 1	Planned receipts							
	Planned orders							
*****Chemical A*****	Gross requirements							
LT (weeks) =	Scheduled receipts							
	Projected ending inventory: 500							
	Net requirements							
Minimum order (mgs) =	Planned receipts							
9500	Planned orders							
*****Chemical B*****	Gross requirements							
LT (weeks) =	Scheduled receipts							
	Projected ending inventory: 0							
	Net requirements							
Minimum order (mgs) =	Planned receipts							
4000	Planned orders							
*****Chemical C*****	Gross requirements							
LT (weeks) =	Scheduled receipts							
	Projected ending inventory: 0							
	Net requirements							
Minimum order (mgs) =	Planned receipts							
2000	Planned orders							
*****Chemical D*****	Gross requirements							
LT (weeks) =	Scheduled receipts							
	Projected ending inventory: 3000							
	Net requirements							
Minimum order (mgs) = 1	Planned receipts							
	Planned orders							

15. (**) Consider the following job information. Each job must proceed sequentially through the different work areas, and each area can work on only one job at a time. Sequence the jobs according to the (1) first come, first served rule, (2) earliest due date, and (3) critical ratio. Calculate the average lateness under each rule. Which rule performs best? Are any of the results completely satisfactory? What are the implications?

	Estimated Days				
JOB	PAINTING	ASSEMBLY	PACKING	TOTAL TASK TIME	DAYS UNTIL DUE
A	1.5	2	0.5	4	15
B	4	3	1	8	16
C	3	2	0.5	5.5	8
D	6	4	1	11	20

16. (**) Recall Example 15.7, where Carlos's Restoration Services wanted to determine the best sequence for four jobs. According to Table 15.2, the critical ratio was the only rule tested that resulted in an estimated average lateness value of 0 days.

Now suppose a representative of Chester College calls up and says it won't need the restored art piece for 14 days. At the same time, the High Museum leaves a message saying it would really like its job completed in 15 days.

How would these requests change the suggested sequence, based on the critical ratio rule? If Carlos's uses the critical ratio rule to sequence the jobs, will they all be done on time?

17. (***) Due to unusual weather conditions in Minneapolis and Buffalo, Sandy-Built has changed the forecasted demand numbers for MeltoMatic snow blowers at its two distribution centers. Using Figures 15.24 and 15.25 as guides, complete the following DRP records and master schedule record.

Minneapolis Distribution Center

		Month	*November*				*December*				*January*			
		WEEK	45	46	47	48	49	50	51	52	1	2	3	4
	Forecasted demand		80	80	80	80	90	90	100	100	120	120	140	140
LT (weeks) = 2	Scheduled receipts													
	Projected ending inventory: 160													
	Net requirements													
Minimum order =	Planned receipts													
120	Planned orders													

Buffalo Distribution Center

		Month	*November*				*December*				*January*			
		WEEK	45	46	47	48	49	50	51	52	1	2	3	4
	Forecasted demand		60	60	70	70	80	80	80	80	90	90	95	95
LT (weeks) = 1	Scheduled receipts		100											
	Projected ending inventory: 25													
	Net requirements													
Minimum order =	Planned receipts													
100	Planned orders													

Master Schedule

Month	*November*				*December*			
WEEK	45	46	47	48	49	50	51	52
Total planned orders								
Booked orders	120	0	0	0	0	0	0	0
Projected ending inventory: 37								
Master production schedule	340		320		340		440	
Available to promise								

CASE STUDY

THE REALCO BREADMASTER

Two years ago, Johnny Chang's company, Realco, introduced a new breadmaker, which, due to its competitive pricing and features, was a big success across the United States. While delighted to have the business, Johnny felt uneasy about the lack of formal planning surrounding the product. He found himself constantly wondering, "Do we have enough to meet the orders we've already accepted? Even if we do, will we have enough to meet expected future demands? Should I be doing something *right now* to plan for all this?"

To get a handle on the situation, Johnny decided to talk to various folks in the organization. He started with his inventory manager and found out that inventory at the end of last week was 7000 units. Johnny thought this was awfully high.

Johnny also knew that production had been completing 40,000 breadmakers every other week for the last year. In fact, another batch was due this week. The production numbers were based on the assumption that demand was roughly 20,000 breadmakers a week. In over a year, no one had questioned whether the forecast or production levels should be readjusted.

Johnny then paid a visit to his marketing manager to see what current orders looked like. "No problem," said Jack Jones, "I have the numbers right here."

WEEK	PROMISED SHIPMENTS
1	23,500
2	23,000
3	21,500
4	15,050
5	13,600
6	11,500
7	5400
8	1800

Johnny looked at the numbers for a moment and then asked, "When a customer calls up, how do you know if you can meet his order?" "Easy," said Jack, "We've found from experience that nearly all orders can be filled within two weeks, so we promise them three weeks. That gives us a cushion, just in case. Now look at weeks 1 and 2. The numbers look a little high, but between inventory and the additional 40,000 coming in this week, there shouldn't be a problem."

QUESTIONS

1. Develop a master production schedule for the breadmaker. What do the projected ending inventory and available-to-promise numbers look like? Has Realco "overpromised"? In your view, should Realco update either the forecast or the production numbers?
2. Comment on Jack's approach to order promising. What are the advantages? The disadvantages? How would formal master scheduling improve this process? What organizational changes would be required?
3. Following up on Question 2, which do you think is worse, refusing a customer's order upfront because you don't have the units available or accepting the order and then failing to deliver? What are the implications for master scheduling?
4. Suppose Realco produces 20,000 breadmakers every week, rather than 40,000 every other week. According to the master schedule record, what impact would this have on average inventory levels?

REFERENCES

Books and Articles

Bundy, W. "Miller SQA: Leveraging Technology for Speed and Reliability." *Supply Chain Management Review* 3, no. 2 (Spring 1999): 62–69.

Cox, J. F., and J. H. Blackstone, eds. *APICS Dictionary*, 10th ed. Falls Church, VA: APICS, 2002.

CHAPTER **15** SUPPLEMENT

Supply Chain Information Systems

SUPPLEMENT OUTLINE

Supplement Objectives

By the end of this supplement, you will be able to:

- Explain why information flows are a necessary part of any supply chain.
- Describe in detail how supply chain information needs vary according to the organizational level and the direction of the linkages (upstream or downstream).
- Describe and differentiate among ERP, DSS, CRM, SRM, and logistics applications.

INTRODUCTION

Whether we are talking about purchasing or forecasting, master scheduling or project planning, information is an essential part of managing operations and supply chains. Imagine, for example, trying to decide how much capacity your organization needs or how much of a product to make if you don't have a clear idea of what the demand will be or what the relevant costs are.

The importance of information is reflected in the APICS definition of a supply chain: "The global network used to deliver products and services from raw materials to end customers through an engineered flow of information, physical distribution, and cash."[1] In fact, one could argue that neither physical nor monetary flows could take place without information flows.

Information system (IS) "[A] set of interrelated components that collect (or retrieve), process, store, and distribute information to support decision making, coordination, and control in an organization."

In this supplement, we look at supply chain information flows and the types of information systems firms use to carry them out. Laudon and Laudon define an **information system (IS)** as "a set of interrelated components that collect (or retrieve), process, store, and distribute information to support decision making, coordination, and control in an organization."[2] We should note that not all information systems are computer-based systems. Nevertheless, much of the growth and interest in supply chain information systems lies in computer-based applications.

This supplement is divided into two parts. In the first, we discuss the critical role information flows play in the supply chain. Our purpose here is to give you an understanding of the different ways in which information is used. The second section shifts the focus away from information *flows* to information *systems*. In particular, we discuss some of the major categories of supply chain information systems, including enterprise resource planning (ERP) systems.

15S.1 UNDERSTANDING SUPPLY CHAIN INFORMATION NEEDS

Companies use information to help them do everything from handling routine billing transactions to developing new business strategies. It makes sense, then, to start our discussion of supply chain information flows by describing the different ways in which information supports supply chain activities. Common sense tells us that if we understand what the information needs are, we will be in a better position to identify possible solutions later on.

Differences across Organizational Levels

Some of the supply chain activities we have described in this book are particularly information intensive. These include:

1. Execution and transaction processing (e.g., vendor order management systems);
2. Routine decision making (e.g., master scheduling and supplier evaluation systems);
3. Tactical planning (e.g., S&OP); and
4. Strategic decision making (e.g., location modeling, capacity decisions).

[1] J. F. Cox and J. H. Blackstone, eds., *APICS Dictionary*, 10th ed. (Falls Church, VA: APICS, 2002).

[2] K. Laudon and J. Laudon, *Essentials of Management Information Systems*, 5th ed. (Upper Saddle River, NJ: Prentice Hall, 2003), p. 7.

TABLE 15S.1 Supply Chain Information Needs

SUPPLY CHAIN ACTIVITY	PURPOSE	CHARACTERISTICS	KEY PERFORMANCE DIMENSIONS FOR INFORMATION FLOWS
Strategic decision making	Develop long-range strategic plans for meeting the organization's mission	• Focus is on long-term decisions, such as new products or markets and "bricks-and-mortar" capacity decisions • Least structured of all; information needs can change dramatically from one effort to the next • Greatest user discretion	• Flexibility
Tactical planning	Develop plans that coordinate the actions of key supply chain areas, customers, and suppliers across the tactical time horizon	• Focus is on tactical decisions, such as inventory or workforce levels • *Plans*, but does not carry out, physical flows • Greater user discretion	• Form • Flexibility
Routine decision making	Support rule-based decision making	• Fairly short time frames • User discretion	• Accuracy • Timeliness • Limited flexibility
Execution and transaction processing	Record and retrieve data and execute and control physical and monetary flows	• Very short time frames, very high volumes • Highly automated • Standardized business practices • Ideally no user intervention	• Accuracy • Timeliness

Table 15S.1 arranges these categories vertically, with longer-term strategic decision making at the top and day-to-day, routine activities at the bottom. By doing this, we can begin to see how supply chain information needs differ at various levels of the organization.

At the lowest levels, supply chain information flows record and retrieve necessary data and execute and control physical and monetary flows. This is referred to as execution and transaction processing. Information flows at this level tend to be highly automated, with a great deal of emphasis put on performing the activity the same way each time. The best execution and transaction processing flows require little or no user intervention and are very accurate and fast.

At a somewhat higher level, information flows are used to support routine decision making. Here users often must have some flexibility to handle exceptions. For example, a retailer might use an inventory management system to forecast, calculate order quantities, establish reorder points, and release orders for the vast majority of items. But the retailer may still want the ability to override the software when the situation warrants.

The next level up is tactical planning. Here managers are responsible for developing plans that coordinate the actions of key supply chain areas, customers, and suppliers across some tactical time horizon, usually a few months to a year out. Information requirements at this level differ from lower-level ones in a number of ways. First, the information must support *planning* activities, *not* actual execution. As such, the time frames are somewhat

FIGURE 15S.1 Supply Chain Information Flows

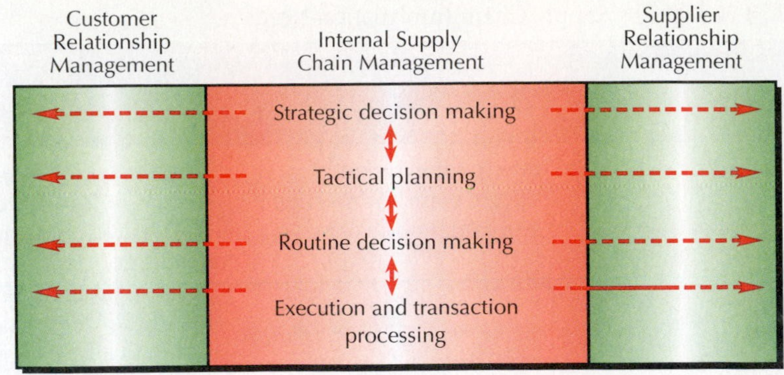

longer and accuracy is important, but not to the same degree as at lower levels. Second, the information must be widely available and in a form that can be interpreted, manipulated, and used by parties with very different perspectives. A classic example is sales and operations planning (S&OP), which we described in Chapter 13.

Finally, information is needed to support strategic decision making. Here sophisticated analytical tools are often used to search for patterns or relationships in data. Examples include customer segment analysis, product life cycle forecasting, and "what if" analyses regarding long-term product or capacity decisions. An excellent example of this is the simulation model we developed for Luc's Deluxe Car Wash in the Chapter 8 supplement. Information systems at the strategic level must be highly flexible in how they manipulate and present the data because the strategic question of interest may change from one situation to the next. Later in the chapter, we talk about decision support systems (DSS), which are specifically geared to support strategic decision making. Notice how the name emphasizes the fact that these systems *support*, but do not *make*, the decision for top managers.

Customer relationship management (CRM) A term that broadly refers to planning and control activities and information systems that link a firm with its downstream customers.

Supplier relationship management (SRM) A term that broadly refers to planning and control activities and information systems that link a firm with its upstream suppliers.

Internal supply chain management A term referring to the information flows between higher and lower levels of planning and control systems within an organization.

Direction of Linkages

In addition to the organizational level, we need to consider the direction of the linkages. For example, there are planning and control activities that link a firm with its downstream customers, broadly referred to as **customer relationship management (CRM)** activities, and those that link a firm with its upstream suppliers, known as **supplier relationship management (SRM)** activities (Figure 15S.1). There are also flows that link higher-level planning and decision making with lower-level activities *within* the firm (dubbed **internal supply chain management** by Chopra and Meindl[3]).

15S.2 SUPPLY CHAIN INFORMATION SYSTEMS

In this section, we shift our focus from a general discussion of supply chain information flows to a description of the different *solutions* currently being offered. The basis of our map was first laid out in 1999 by Steven Kahl,[4] then a software industry analyst at Piper

[3]S. Chopra and P. Meindl, *Supply Chain Management: Strategy, Planning and Operation* (Upper Saddle River, NJ: Prentice Hall, 2004).

[4]S. Kahl, "What's the 'Value' of Supply Chain Software?" *Supply Chain Management Review* 2, no. 4 (Winter 1999): 59–67.

FIGURE 15S.2
A Map of SCM Information Systems

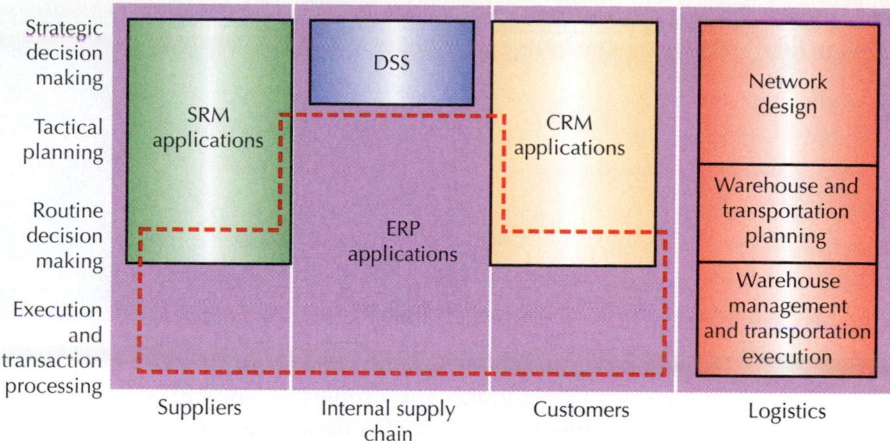

Jaffray. Kahl's map was later refined by Chopra and Meindl,[5] who applied the labels *customer relationship management (CRM)*, *supplier relationship management (SRM)*, and *internal supply chain management (ISCM)* to various areas of the map.

Our map (Figure 15S.2) parallels Figure 15S.1 in that it distinguishes the various applications by organizational level and the direction of linkages. Here we add an additional column labeled "Logistics." Logistics applications deal with facilities and transportation issues, such as determining facility locations, optimizing transportation systems, and controlling the movement of materials between supply chain partners.

Enterprise resource planning (ERP) systems Large, integrated, computer-based business transaction processing and reporting systems. ERP systems pull together all of the classic business functions such as accounting, finance, sales, and operations into a single, tightly integrated package that uses a common database.

Enterprise resource planning (ERP) systems are large, integrated, computer-based business transaction processing and reporting systems. The primary advantage of ERP systems is that they pull together all of the classic business functions, such as accounting, finance, sales, and operations, into a single, tightly integrated package that uses a common database (Figure 15S.3).

To understand why this is such a big deal, imagine what the information systems for a typical company looked like before ERP. First, every functional area had its own set of software applications, often running on completely different systems. Sharing information (such as forecasts or customer information) between systems was a nightmare. To make matters worse, the same information often had to be entered multiple times in different ways. ERP pulled all of these disparate systems into a single, integrated system. (One of the authors still remembers a company whose bills referred to him as "Cecil Bozarthiii," while all shipments were addressed to "Cecil Bozrat.")

FIGURE 15S.3
ERP Systems

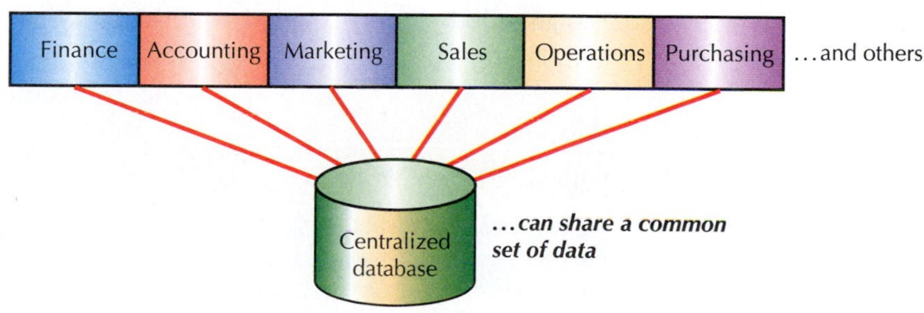

[5] Chopra and Meindl, *Supply Chain Management.*

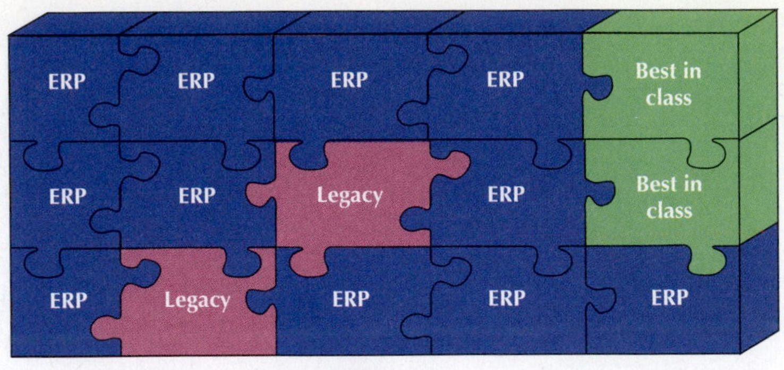

FIGURE 15S.4 Integrating ERP Systems with Legacy and Best-in-Class Applications

In practice, few companies use ERP systems to serve all of their information requirements. Rather, companies will use ERP systems to meet the bulk of their needs and "plug in" preexisting legacy systems and best-in-class applications to tailor the system to their exact needs.[6] Figure 15S.4 illustrates the idea. As you can imagine, integrating ERP systems with other applications presents a significant technological challenge.

ERP's traditional strengths lie in routine decision making and in execution and transaction processing. To the extent that ERP systems support higher-level planning and decision making, the focus is on the internal supply chain. ERP systems also capture much of the raw data needed to support higher-level decision support systems. **Decision support systems (DSSs)** are computer-based information systems that allow users to analyze, manipulate, and present data in a manner that aids higher-level decision making.

Decision support systems (DSSs) Computer-based information systems that allow users to analyze, manipulate, and present data in a manner that aids higher-level decision making.

Supplier relationship management (SRM) and customer relationship management (CRM) applications, in contrast, are computer-based information systems specifically designed to help plan and manage the firm's external linkages with its suppliers and customers, respectively. Table 15S.2 gives examples of the types of functionality provided by SRM and CRM applications.

Vendors specializing in CRM and SRM applications tend to provide greater functionality in their chosen areas than do ERP vendors. As a result, many firms choose a standard ERP package for routine decision making and for execution and transaction processing and use "best-in-class" CRM and SRM applications to manage external relationships. However, this situation is changing as the major ERP vendors, such as SAP and Oracle, look for ways to increase the CRM and SRM functionality of their own systems. Whether or not the specialized CRM and SRM vendors can maintain enough of a functionality lead to justify a separate system remains to be seen.

TABLE 15S.2 Examples of SRM and CRM Applications

SRM APPLICATIONS	CRM APPLICATIONS
Design collaboration	Market analysis
Sourcing decisions	Sell process
Negotiations	Order management
Buy process	Call/service center management
Supply collaboration	

Source: S. Chopra and P. Meindl, *Supply Chain Management: Strategic Planning and Operation* (Upper Saddle River, NJ: Prentice Hall, 2004), p. 522.

[6] V. Mabert, A. Soni, and M. Venkataramanan, "Enterprise Resource Planning Survey of US Manufacturing Firms," *Production and Inventory Management Journal* 41, no. 2 (Second Quarter 2000): 52–58.

The last set of supply chain IS applications we will discuss deals directly with logistics decisions. These applications can be divided into three main categories: network design applications, warehouse and transportation planning systems, and warehouse management and transportation execution systems. **Network design applications** address such long-term strategic questions as facility location and sizing, as well as transportation networks. These applications often make use of simulation and optimization modeling.

Network design applications
Logistics information systems that address such long-term strategic questions as facility location and sizing, as well as transportation networks. These applications often make use of simulation and optimization modeling.

Warehouse and transportation planning systems support tactical planning efforts by allocating "fixed" logistics capacity in the best possible way, given business requirements. These IS applications can also use optimization modeling and simulation. The warehouse assignment problem in Chapter 12, where we had to decide how many units to ship from each warehouse to each demand point, is a classic example of a warehouse and transportation planning system. To find the optimal answer, we built an optimization model that used data on fixed warehouse capacities, demand levels, and shipping costs to generate the lowest-cost solution.

Warehouse and transportation planning systems
Logistics information systems that support tactical planning efforts by allocating "fixed" logistics capacity in the best possible way, given business requirements.

Finally, **warehouse management and transportation execution systems** initiate and control the movement of materials between supply chain partners. Within a warehouse, for example, sophisticated execution systems tell workers where to store items, where to go to pick them up, and how many to pick. Similarly, bar code systems and global positioning systems (GPSs) have dramatically changed the ability of businesses to manage actual movements in the distribution system. Ten years ago, the only thing most transportation firms could tell you was that your shipment was "on the way" and "should be there in a day or two." Now carriers can tell their customers the exact location of a shipment and the arrival time within hours, if not minutes.

Warehouse management and transportation execution systems
Logistics information systems that initiate and control the movement of materials between supply chain partners.

As important as the logistics applications are, historically the level of integration between these applications and those in the other areas of the map has been weak. Increasing the level of integration between logistics and other SCM applications presents both technical and organizational hurdles to firms. On the technical side, efforts to integrate decisions across sales, operations, and distribution will increase the complexity of the optimization and simulation models currently used by logistics managers. On the organizational side, firms will have to get used to involving logistics personnel earlier in the decision-making process, rather than just calling on them when it's time to move goods through the supply chain.

SUPPLEMENT SUMMARY

In this supplement, we discussed the critical role information flows play in the supply chain, and laid out a map of supply chain information systems. To finish this discussion, we will consider the various ways in which information adds value and how breakthroughs in technology will affect this over time. In 1995, just as the Internet was becoming popular, Jeffrey Rayport and John Sviokla wrote an article in which they talked about three ways in which information adds value.[7] These were, in order of increasing value added:

1. Visibility;
2. Mirroring; and
3. Creation of new customer relationships.

Visibility represents the most basic function of information in the supply chain. Here information allows managers to "see" the physical and monetary flows in the supply chain and, as a result, to better manage them. Classic examples include forecasts and point-of-sales data, as well as information regarding inventory levels and the status of jobs in the production system.

Mirroring takes it a step further and seeks to *replace* certain physical processes with virtual ones. For example, Rayport and Sviokla describe Boeing's efforts to design new engine housings. In the past, Boeing had to create physical mock-ups of the housings and test them in a wind tunnel in order to evaluate their performance. This was a long and

[7]J. Rayport, and J. Sviokla, "Exploiting the Virtual Value Chain," *Harvard Business Review* 73, no. 6 (November–December 1995): 75–85.

expensive process. But with the advent of powerful computers, Boeing was able to replace this physical process altogether:

> *Boeing engineers developed the prototype as a virtual product that incorporated relevant laws of physical and material sciences and enabled the company to test an evolving computer-simulated model in a virtual wind tunnel. As a result, engineers could test many more designs at dramatically lower costs and with much greater speed.*[8]

The third stage, creation of new customer relationships, involves taking raw information and organizing, selecting, synthesizing, and distributing it in a manner that creates whole new sources of value. Creating virtual, customized textbooks with hotlinks to Web sites and spreadsheets is one example. Other examples include taking raw supply chain data and turning them into graphical executive "dashboards" that allow managers to see, at a glance, how the overall business is performing.

So what are the implications for the future? Visibility systems will continue to improve and provide more real-time data. As this occurs, managers will find themselves making decisions more often to take advantage of this. Second, more mirroring will occur as many physical flows are replaced with virtual ones. Of course, replacement will be limited to those physical flows whose mission is to create or disseminate information (such as letters). It is highly unlikely that physical goods will be transformed and moved over the electronic superhighway anytime soon!

Finally, expect to see to more information-based products aimed at the creation of new customer relationships. Because raw data can be used repeatedly and the variable costs of rearranging and organizing information is so low, this area is really limited only by the imagination and needs of businesses.

KEY TERMS

Customer relationship management (CRM) 518
Decision support systems (DSSs) 520
Enterprise resource planning (ERP) **systems** 519
Information system (IS) 516
Internal supply chain management 518
Network design applications 521
Supplier relationship management (SRM) 518
Warehouse and transportation planning systems 521
Warehouse management and transportation execution systems 521

DISCUSSION QUESTIONS

1. What is the difference between an information *flow* and an information *system*? Do information systems always have to be computerized? Why?
2. Consider Figure 15S.1. Some people have argued that companies need to put in place information systems that address routine decision making and transactional requirements *prior* to tackling higher-level planning and decision making. Others strongly disagree, pointing out that the higher-level functions are a prerequisite to good tactical planning and execution. What do you think?
3. Back in the early 1980s, dozens of software vendors offered word-processing and spreadsheet applications for PCs. Considering what happened to the PC market, what do you think will happen to the market for SCM IS applications? Are these markets comparable? Why?
4. SAP is the world leader in ERP systems software, and has developed tailored ERP systems for different industries. Go to **www.sap.com/industries/index.epx** and examine the solutions for (1) a service industry and (2) a manufacturing industry of your choice. How are they similar? How are they different?

[8]Ibid., p. 79.

REFERENCES

Books and Articles

Chopra, S., and P. Meindl. *Supply Chain Management: Strategy, Planning and Operation.* Upper Saddle River, NJ: Prentice Hall, 2004.

Cox, J. F., and J. H. Blackstone, eds. *APICS Dictionary*, 10th ed. Falls Church, VA: APICS, 2002.

Kahl, S. "What's the 'Value' of Supply Chain Software?" *Supply Chain Management Review* 2, no. 4 (Winter 1999): 59–67.

Laudon, K., and J. Laudon. *Essentials of Management Information Systems,* 5th ed. Upper Saddle River, NJ: Prentice Hall, 2003.

Mabert, V., A. Soni, and M. Venkataramanan. "Enterprise Resource Planning Survey of US Manufacturing Firms." *Production and Inventory Management Journal* 41, no. 2 (Second Quarter 2000): 52–58.

Rayport, J., and J. Sviokla. "Exploiting the Virtual Value Chain." *Harvard Business Review* 73, no. 6 (November–December 1995): 75–85.

Internet

SAP, AG, **www.sap.com/industries/index.epx**

SAS, **www.sas.com**

Seibel Systems, **www.seibel.com**

CHAPTER 16

JIT/Lean Production

CHAPTER OUTLINE

Chapter Objectives

By the end of this chapter, you will be able to:

- Describe what JIT/Lean is and differentiate between the Lean philosophy and kanban systems.
- Discuss the Lean perspective on waste and describe the eight major forms of waste, or *muda*, in an organization.
- Discuss the Lean perspective on inventory and describe how a kanban system helps control inventory levels and synchronize the flow of goods and materials across a supply chain.
- Describe how the concepts of the Lean supply chain and Lean Six Sigma represent natural extensions of the Lean philosophy.
- Explain how a two-card kanban system works.
- Calculate the number of kanban cards needed in a simple production environment.
- Show how MRP and kanban can be linked together and illustrate the process using a numerical example.

Toyota Motor Company[1]

No one knows what sparked the fire that roared through Aisin Seiki Co.'s Factory No. 1 before dawn on Saturday, February 1, 1997, leveling the huge auto-parts plant. But one thing is clear: The crisis-control efforts that followed it dramatically illustrate one reason Toyota Motor Corp. is among the world's most admired and feared manufacturers. The fire incinerated the main source of a crucial brake valve that Toyota buys from Aisin and uses in most of its cars. Most Toyota plants kept only a four-hour supply of the $5 valve; without it, Toyota had to shut down its 20 auto plants in Japan, which build 14,000 cars a day. Some experts thought Toyota couldn't recover for weeks.

But five days after the fire, its car factories started up again. The secret lay in Toyota's close-knit family of parts suppliers. In the corporate equivalent of an Amish barn raising, suppliers and local companies rushed to the rescue. Within hours, they had begun taking blueprints for the valve, improvising tooling systems, and setting up makeshift production lines. By the following Thursday, the 36 suppliers, aided by more than 150 other subcontractors, had nearly 50 separate lines producing small batches of the brake valve. In one case, a sewing-machine maker that had never made car parts spent about 500 man-hours refitting a milling machine to make just 40 valves a day. "Toyota's quick recovery," says Yoshio Yunokawa, general manager of Toyoda Machine Works Ltd., a Toyota-group maker of machine tools and steering systems, "is attributable to the power of the group, which handled it without thinking about money or business contracts."

The fire and its aftermath have left Toyota executives convinced that they have the right balance of efficiency and risk. "Many people say you might need to scatter production to different suppliers and plants, but then you have to think of the costs" of setting up expensive milling machines at each site, Mr. Ikebuchi says. "We re-learned that our system works."

On February 1, 1997, Aisen Seiki Factory 1 burned down, causing an immediate shortage of critical components at the Toyota assembly plants.

A few days after the fire, the site had been cleared and other Toyota suppliers had already started to produce the needed components.

[1]V. Reitman, "To the Rescue: Toyota's Fast Rebound after Fire at Supplier Shows Why It Is Tough," *The Wall Street Journal*, May 8, 1997.

INTRODUCTION

Just-in-time (JIT)
A philosophy of manufacturing based on planned elimination of all waste and on continuous improvement of productivity. In the broad sense, it applies to all forms of manufacturing and to many service industries as well. Used synonymously with Lean.

Lean
A philosophy of production that emphasizes the minimization of the amount of all the resources (including time) used in the various activities of the enterprise. It involves identifying and eliminating non-value-adding activities in design, production, supply chain management, and dealing with the customers. Used synonymously with JIT.

In Chapter 15, we presented a top-down model of production planning and control and offered detailed discussions of several of the more common techniques, including master scheduling, MRP, and DRP. The focus of this chapter is the **just-in-time (JIT)** or **Lean** philosophy and, in particular, kanban production techniques.

As the following APICS definition suggests, Lean touches on many of the areas we have dealt with throughout this book:

> *Lean is a philosophy of production that emphasizes the minimization of the amount of all the resources (including time) used in the various activities of the enterprise. It involves identifying and eliminating non-value-adding activities in design, production, supply chain management, and dealing with the customers. Lean producers employ teams of multiskilled workers at all levels of the organization and use highly flexible, increasingly automated machines to produce volumes of products in potentially enormous variety. It contains a set of principles and practices to reduce cost through the relentless removal of waste and through the simplification of all manufacturing and support processes.*[2]

In the case of the Toyota's supply chain in the opening case study, "waste" included excess inventory. To make the supply chain work, Toyota needed a supply base capable of responding rapidly to an interruption in the flow of material.

The Lean philosophy has extended beyond just manufacturing to include services and essentially all aspects of supply chain management. Firms following a Lean philosophy often experience remarkable improvements in their productivity (outputs/inputs), inventory levels, and quality.

To understand why Lean has made such an impact, consider some eye-opening statistics from 1986, which compared performance at Toyota's Takaoka facility with that at GM's Framingham plant (Table 16.1). Numbers such as these kicked off what was then called the JIT/Lean production revolution in the American automotive industry during the late 1980s and early 1990s.

Notice how the Toyota plant needed fewer hours and much less inventory to do its job. This ability to do more with less is what first led people to refer to JIT as Lean production. Similarly, the phrase "just-in-time" reflected the idea that the timing and level of inventory and production activities are closely matched to demand. With average inventory levels of only two hours, the Toyota plant was clearly receiving parts and materials "just" before they were needed.

Even though we cover Lean production and kanban in a separate chapter from the other production planning techniques, it would be erroneous to assume that companies using traditional planning and control techniques can't adopt a Lean philosophy. For one

TABLE 16.1
The Performance Advantage of a JIT Plant, Circa 1986

	GM FRAMINGHAM	TOYOTA TAKAOKA
Assembly hours per vehicle	40.7 hours	16 hours
Defects per 100 vehicles	130 defects	45 defects
Average inventory levels	2 weeks	2 hours

Source: J. Womack, D. Jones, and D. Daniel Roos, *The Machine That Changed the World: The Story of Lean Production* (New York: HarperCollins, 1991).

[2]J. F. Cox and J. H. Blackstone, eds., *APICS Dictionary*, 11th ed. (Falls Church, VA: APICS, 2004).

thing, the underlying emphasis of Lean—to eliminate all forms of waste—is relevant to all organizations, regardless of the specific planning and control tools that are used. Second, even though some techniques such as kanban are not suitable in certain production and service environments, it is entirely possible that an organization can follow the Lean philosophy. To summarize:

Lean Six Sigma
A methodology that combines the organizational elements and tools of Six Sigma with Lean's focus on waste reduction.

Lean supply chain management
An extension of the Lean philosophy to supply chain efforts beyond production. Lean supply chain management seeks to minimize the level of reources required to carry out *all* supply chain activities.

- The Lean philosophy can be applied to a wide range of production and service environments. In fact, one could easily argue that there is no environment that wouldn't benefit from adopting its core principles.
- Companies following the Lean philosophy can and do use a wide range of planning and control techniques, not just kanban.
- The Lean philosophy is entirely consistent with business process improvement (Chapter 3), quality improvement (Chapter 4), and supplier management initiatives (as we saw in the opening case). It's no surprise, then, that the business world has seen the advent of such approaches as **Lean Six Sigma** and **Lean supply chain management**, which we describe in Section 16.3.

With this background, let's look at the historical roots of JIT/Lean, the various forms of waste and uncertainty, the special role of inventory in a Lean environment, and kanban systems in particular.

16.1 THE LEAN PERSPECTIVE ON WASTE

Waste
According to the JIT/Lean perspective, "any activity that does not add value to the good or service in the eyes of the consumer."

Muda
A Japanese term meaning waste.

A key component of the Lean philosophy is a never-ending effort to eliminate **waste**, which is defined as "any activity that does not add value to the good or service in the eyes of the consumer."[3] Starting with Taiichi Ohno, a Toyota engineer, experts have sought to identify the major sources of waste (or **muda** in Japanese). Following are eight commonly recognized ones:[4]

1. **Overproduction**—caused by inflexible or unreliable processes that cause organizations to produce goods before they are required.
2. **Waiting**—caused by inefficient layouts or an inability to match demand with output levels.
3. **Unnecessary transportation**—transporting goods always increases costs and the risk of damage, but it does not necessarily provide value to the final customer.
4. **Inappropriate process**—using overly complex processes when simpler, more efficient ones would do.
5. **Unnecessary inventory**—caused by uncertainty with regard to quality levels, delivery lead times, and the like.
6. **Unnecessary/excess motion**—caused by poorly designed processes.
7. **Defects**—not only do defects create uncertainty in the process, they rob production capacity by creating products or services that require rework or must be scrapped.
8. **Underutilization of employees**—the newest form of waste added to the list, which recognizes that too often companies do not fully utilize the skills and decision-making capabilities of their employees.

---

[3]Cox and Blackstone, *APICS Dictionary*.

[4]J. Womack and D. Jones, *Lean Thinking: Banish Waste and Create Wealth in Your Corporation, Revised and Updated* (New York: Free Press, 2003).

To put these forms of waste in context, suppose it takes an inspector at a manufacturing plant 15 minutes to inspect an incoming batch of material. The pre-Lean perspective would be that inspections like these are a necessary and prudent business expense. But according to Lean, this is a waste of *both* time and manpower caused by defects. Services examples abound as well. If you have to wait even *five minutes* at the doctor's office before being seen, then waste has occurred.

If this definition seems harsh, it is meant to be. The point is to get organizations thinking critically about the business processes they use to provide products and services, as well as the outcomes of these processes. As far as Lean is concerned, if there is any waste at all, there is room for improvement.

Example 16.1

Unnecessary Inventory Caused by Supplier Problems at Riggsbee Boating Supply

For several years now, Riggsbee Boating Supply has purchased life vests from the same U.S. supplier. Jermaine Riggsbee, owner of the company, has collected the following information on the life vests:

Weekly demand	50 vests, with a variance of 9.5 vests
Supplier lead time	6 weeks, with a variance of 3.2 weeks

Using Equation 14-8 from Chapter 14, Jermaine calculates the reorder point for the life vests based on a 90% service level ($z = 1.28$):

$$\begin{aligned} ROP_{\text{Taiwan}} &= \bar{d}\bar{L} + z\sqrt{\bar{L}\sigma_d^2 + \bar{d}^2\sigma_L^2} \\ &= 50\times 6 + 1.28\sqrt{6\times 9.5 + 2{,}500\times 3.2} \\ &= 300 + 114.9 \\ &= 414.9\text{, or } 415 \text{ life vests} \end{aligned}$$

Looking at the results, Jermaine realizes that the second half of the equation, or about 115 vests, represents safety stock, or extra inventory *he* has to hold (and pay for!).

Jermaine had already been considering switching to a Mexican supplier with similar quality levels and prices but a *constant* lead time of two weeks. Plugging the new numbers into the equation, Jermaine generates the following results:

$$\begin{aligned} ROP_{\text{Mexico}} &= \bar{d}\bar{L} + z\sqrt{\bar{L}\sigma_d^2 + \bar{d}^2\sigma_L^2} \\ &= 50\times 2 + 1.28\sqrt{2\times 9.5 + 2{,}500\times 0} \\ &= 100 + 5.6 \\ &= 105.6\text{, or } 106 \text{ life vests} \end{aligned}$$

With the Mexican supplier, the reorder point drops to about 106 vests. More important, the safety stock level falls to just 5.6 or 6 vests. Put another way, supplier problems were causing Jermaine to hold a safety stock of $(115 - 6) = 109$ more vests than he needed, a clear example of unnecessary inventory.

16.2 THE LEAN PERSPECTIVE ON INVENTORY

One hallmark of a Lean environment is the strong emphasis placed on reducing raw material, work-in-process, and finished goods inventories throughout the system. This is not only because inventory is seen as a form of waste in and of itself, but also because inventory can *cover up* wasteful business practices. Under the Lean philosophy, lowering inventory levels *forces* firms to address these poor practices.

To illustrate how inventory can hide problems, consider a simple facility consisting of three work centers (A, B, and C), shown in Figure 16.1.

The triangles in the diagram represent inventory. In addition, between each work center is plenty of room for inventory. Take one of the work centers—say, center B—and consider what happens if it has an equipment breakdown that reduces its output. The answer is that, *in the short run*, only center B is affected. Because there is plenty of space for inventory between centers A and B, center A can continue to work. And because inventory exists between centers B and C, center C can continue to work as long as the inventory lasts. Most important, the customer can continue to be served. The same result occurs regardless of the reason for any disruption in center B, including worker absenteeism, poor quality levels, and so forth. Whatever the problem, inventory hides it (but at a cost).

Now let's take the same facility after a successful Lean program has been put in place. The work centers have been moved closer together, eliminating wasted movement and space where inventory could pile up. Setup times have also been reduced, allowing the work centers to make only what is needed when it is needed. If we assume the program has been in place for a while, we can also assume that the inventory levels have been reduced dramatically, giving us a revised picture of the facility (Figure 16.2).

FIGURE 16.1
Inventory Positioned throughout a Supply Chain

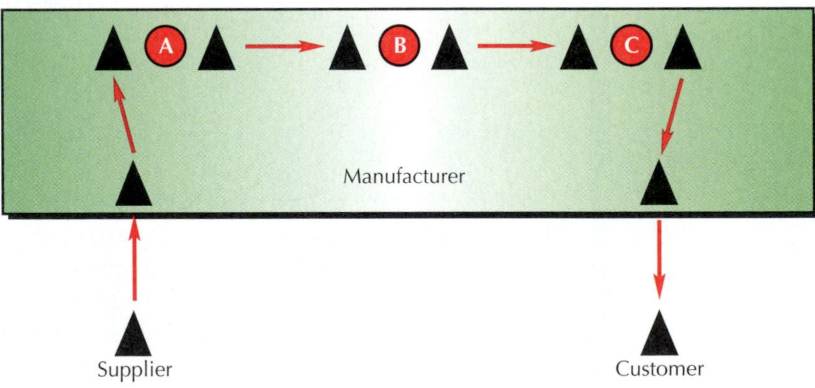

FIGURE 16.2
Supply Chain after the Elimination of Excess Inventories

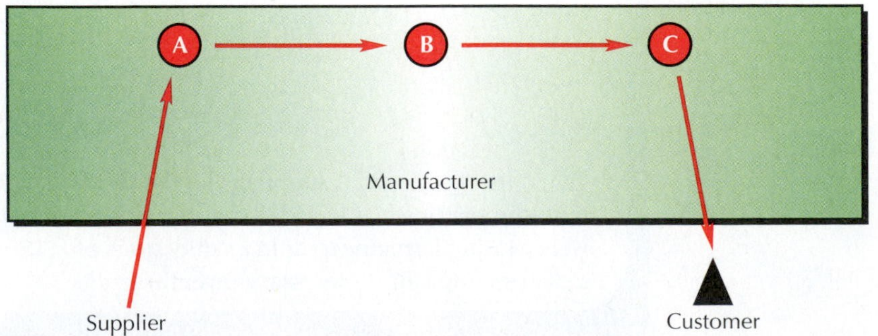

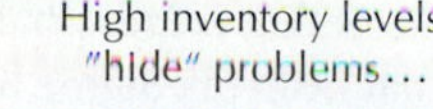

FIGURE 16.3 How Inventory Hides Problems

Now inventory has been reduced to the point where it shows up only in the customer facility. Under these conditions, what happens in the short run if the equipment at center B breaks down? The answer this time is that *everything stops*, including shipments to the customer. Center A has to stop because there is no spot for it to put inventory and no demand for it. Center C has to stop because there is no inventory on which to work.

Inventory in the supply chain is often compared to water in a river. If the "water" is high enough, it will cover all the "rocks" (quality problems, absenteeism, equipment breakdowns, etc.), and everything will appear to be running smoothly.

Under Lean, the approach is to gradually remove the "water" until the first "rock" is exposed, thereby establishing a priority as to the most important obstacle to work on. After resolving this problem, inventory levels are reduced further until another problem (and opportunity to eliminate waste) appears. This process continues indefinitely, or until all forms of waste and uncertainty have been eliminated (Figure 16.3).

This is not an easy approach to implement. The implication is that every time a process is working smoothly, there may be too much inventory and more should be removed until the organization hits another "rock." That is certainly not a natural action for most people, and the performance evaluation system needs to be altered to reflect this type of activity. Very often firms will employ Six Sigma methods to identify the root cause of the waste, and will apply problem-solving and resolution methods to drive excessive inventory out of the system. Such approaches fall under the concept of Lean Six Sigma, which we describe in the next section.

16.3 RECENT DEVELOPMENTS IN LEAN THINKING

It shouldn't be surprising that businesses have looked for ways to combine the Lean philosophy with other management efforts. One such hybrid is Lean Six Sigma. In Chapter 3, we defined the Six Sigma methodology as "a business improvement methodology that focuses an organization on understanding and managing customer requirements, aligning key business processes to achieve those requirements, utilizing rigorous data analysis to understand and ultimately minimize variation in those processes, and driving rapid and sustainable improvement to business processes."[5]

Lean Six Sigma combines the organizational elements and tools of Six Sigma with Lean's focus on waste reduction. As Paul Mullenhour and Jamie Flinchbaugh put it, "Lean encourages action along a broad front by empowering people at all levels to contribute. This allows organizations to welcome challenges and implement improvement initiatives. Six Sigma brings the discipline of define, measure, analyze, improve and control, as well as the rigor of statistical analysis, to identify a root cause, sustain improvement and provide

[5]Motorola University, **www.motorola.com/motorolauniversity.jsp.**

the solid measurements that create a balanced scorecard."[6] A 2006 presentation by a Nortel executive suggests that Lean Six Sigma has found an audience: 100 of the Fortune 500 companies were using Lean Six Sigma. Furthermore, these companies had experienced on average a return of $8 for every dollar invested in these efforts.[7]

The *Supply Chain Connections* feature contains an extended example of how Lean Six Sigma was applied in a hospital setting. Notice how this example combines all the elements of the Six Sigma methodology—black belts and green belts, process mapping, careful use of statistics, and the DMAIC cycle—with Lean's focus on waste reduction; in this case, waste-reduction efforts focus on patient waiting time and unused beds.

SUPPLY CHAIN CONNECTIONS

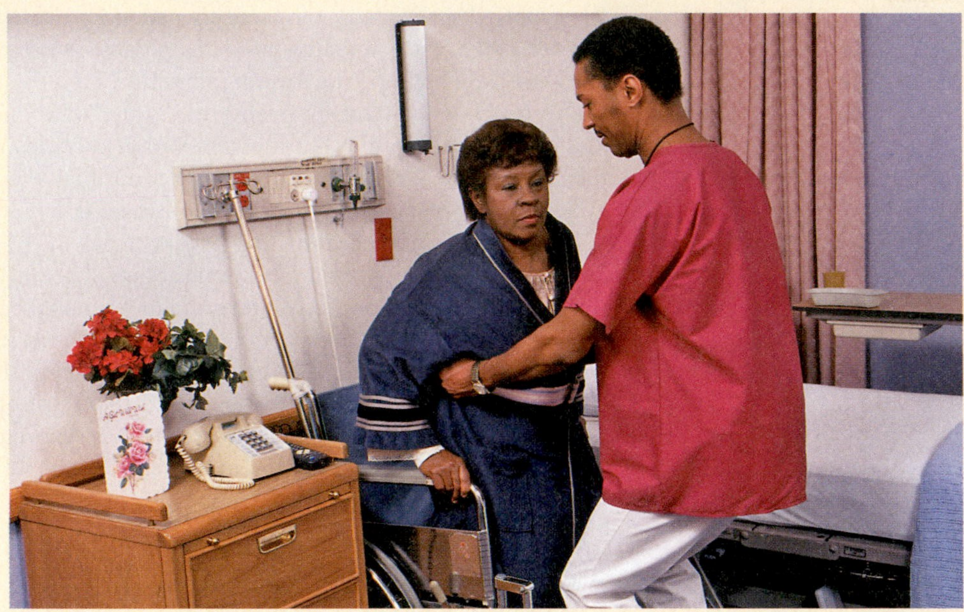

CREATING A LEAN SIX SIGMA HOSPITAL DISCHARGE PROCESS[8]

A lengthy, inefficient process for discharging in-patients is a common concern of hospitals. It not only causes frustration for patients and family members, but also leads to delays for incoming patients from Admitting, the Post-Anesthesia Care Unit, and the Emergency Department.

When Valley Baptist Medical Center in Harlingen, Texas, faced this issue, it decided to apply Lean Six Sigma and change management techniques within one pilot unit. A multidisciplinary project team led by a black belt included nursing staff, case managers, an information

[6]P. Mullenhour and J. Flinchbaugh, "Bring Lean Systems Thinking to Six Sigma," *Quality Digest*, March 2005, **www.qualitydigest.com/mar05/articles/05_article.shtml.**

[7]E. Bovarnick, "The Power of Lean Six Sigma: The Nortel Journey," November 16, 2006, **www.nortel.com/corporate/investor/events/investorconf/collateral/breakout_leansixsigma_nov16.pdf.**

[8]C. Debusk and A. Rangel, "Creating a Lean Six Sigma Hospital Discharge Process," iSixSigma.com, September 15, 2004, **http://healthcare.isixsigma.com/library/content/c040915a.asp.**

technology green belt, and the chief medical officer, also a green belt.

The project was to reduce the time between when a discharge order for a patient was entered into the computer and when the room was ready for the next patient. During the initial scoping of this project, the team divided the process into four components:

1. From discharge order entry to discharge instructions signed
2. From discharge instructions signed to patient leaving
3. From patient leaving to room cleaned
4. From room cleaned to discharge entered in the computer (thus indicating the bed was ready for another patient)

Because of the hospital's commitment to customer service, the team was asked to concentrate on the first two components. The goal was for this first subprocess to be completed in less than 45 minutes. To minimize the time a bed was empty, the team realized it also would need to address the time between when a patient's room was cleaned and the time a discharge was entered into the computer, or the second subprocess. This would address the problem that arises when Admitting does not have the necessary information to assign a new patient to a clean and empty bed.

Mapping the Process

The team began with a process map to visually understand how the process was currently working. When several nurses were asked to help develop a detailed process map on the discharge process, they initially could not reach consensus, since they each followed their own methods for discharging the patient. This lack of standard operating procedures had led to widespread process variation.

The team developed a representative process map, printed a large copy, and placed it in the nurses' lounge. Each staff member was encouraged to review the map and add comments on the flow. After a week, the team retrieved the inputs and revised the "as-is" process map accordingly. Elements of Lean thinking were combined with this map to help identify *muda* (a Lean term, Japanese for waste). To understand which steps were not contributing to timely discharge, aspects of the existing process were categorized as value-added, non-value-added, and value-enablers.

Baseline data revealed the "from-discharge-order-entry-to-patient-leaving" subprocess required 184 minutes with a standard deviation of 128 minutes. The second subprocess of "patient leaving-to-discharge-in-computer" had an average of 36 minutes with a standard deviation of 36 minutes. When compared against an upper specification limit of 45 minutes, the first subprocess had a yield of 7% (i.e., 7% of the patients were able to leave in 45 minutes or less) while the second subprocess did better, with a yield of 25% compared to its upper specification of 5 minutes.

Behind the Waste and Variation

The most important tool for determining the critical drivers of waste and variation was the Lean process map. The staff segmented the process into key steps and used the value-added and non-valued-added times to understand the delays and rework involved.
The segments of the process were:

- Secretary processes discharge order entry
- Discharge order processed to nurse begins (delay)
- Nurse begins computer entry (to create discharge instructions)
- Computer entry to patient signature

The team found that three factors were critical drivers of waste and variation.

1. **Clarification:** In 21% of the cases, clarification from the physician was needed before the nurse could enter the information in the computer. The team confirmed that clarification processes added a significant amount of time. The median of the process increased from 12 minutes to 45 minutes when clarification was required.
2. **Handoff:** The current process required a handoff as the charge nurse placed vital signs and other relevant information in the computer system, printed out the discharge instructions, and then placed them in a bin for the primary nurse to pick up. In many cases, the primary nurse would then review the information with the patient and obtain the patient's signature. In

a small number of cases, however, the primary nurse completed all tasks without any handoff. The median time increased from 9 minutes when one nurse completed all tasks to 73 minutes when a handoff between nurses was required. Without a signal for the handoff, the patient's paperwork often waited up to an hour before it was acted upon.

3. **Aftercare:** Finally, the team tested the hypothesis that when aftercare was required (the social services department, ordering equipment, etc.), there was an increase in median cycle time from 121 minutes in the current process to 160 minutes when aftercare was required.

Improving the Process

Since variations in the "as is" process were contributing greatly to long cycle times and delays, a new standard operating procedure (SOP) was developed containing six steps:

- Unit secretary enters discharge order.
- Unit secretary tells primary nurse via spectra link phone that he/she is next in the process.
- Primary nurse verifies order and provides the assessment.
- Primary nurse enters information into computer system.
- Primary nurse prints instructions and information.
- Primary nurse reviews instructions and obtains patient signature.

Having the primary nurse complete all discharge tasks eliminated the bottlenecks created by time-consuming handoffs, the need for signaling those handoffs, and the fact that the charge nurse, who has many responsibilities, was not always readily available.

With the first subprocess of their deliverable improved—from discharge order entry to patient leaving—the team focused on getting information into the computer so the bed could be filled. A session was conducted with transporters and unit secretaries to determine the best way to improve the computer entry process. It was immediately clear that the current process was not working. Unit secretaries were not always aware when a patient was transferred from the unit. No signal was provided when a transporter moved a patient. Since the secretaries performed numerous activities (not always at the nurses' station), they could easily forget a patient had been discharged.

A small discharge slip was developed containing the patient name, room number, and time of call. The transporter would pick up the patient and then go to the nurses' station and ask the secretary to provide the time on the computer. The transporter would write the time and hand the slip to the secretary. This served as a trigger and transferred the process from the transporter to the secretary.

Maintaining Improvement

Two tactics employed simultaneously helped to sustain the improvements. The first was the use of a change acceleration process (CAP) and the second was an ongoing tracking system. Four CAP sessions were guided by the black belt and process owner, increasing understanding as to why the initiative was undertaken, providing baseline data, and establishing the rationale for improvements.

Each session also included an exercise to help participants better appreciate Lean and Six Sigma, with a catapult exercise as a learning tool. Participants split into groups and worked to meet customer needs. They then reviewed the process, made adjustments, and developed standard operating procedures. Upon execution, the new plan showed improved performance.

A tracking system included three components:

1. A daily report of the prior day's discharges, including discharge times, primary nurse, and unit secretary responsible for discharging the patient from the computer.
2. A performance tracker to ensure individual accountability for primary nurses and unit secretaries in terms of mean, standard deviation, and yield.
3. A control chart that tracked the means and standard deviations.

Summary: Process in Control

With the process now in control, the components were remeasured (Table 16.2). The from-discharge-order-entry-to-patient-leaving subprocess showed a mean improvement of 74%, with a 70% decrease in the standard deviation. The second subprocess, from patient leaving to discharge in computer, showed an improvement of 90% in the mean and 58% in the standard deviation. (See accompanying tables.) With success in this unit, a translation

TABLE 16.2
Results of Lean Six Sigma Effort at Valley Baptist Medical Center

	From Discharge Order Entry to Patient Leaving Upper Specification Limit: 45 Minutes		*From Patient Leaving to Discharge in Computer Upper Specification Limit: 5 Minutes*	
	BASELINE	CURRENT	BASELINE	CURRENT
Mean	184.8	47.8	36.6	3.47
St.Dev.	128.7	37.2	36.1	16.9
Yield	6.9%	61.7%	24.6%	95.4%

effort would be undertaken for the entire hospital. This will be an ongoing effort requiring change management for the entire hospital and training sessions on the new standard operating procedures.

Some practitioners and researchers have moved beyond Lean production to what can be called *Lean supply chain management*. In a nutshell, Lean supply chain management seeks to minimize the level of resources required to carry out *all* supply chain activities. Lean principles are applied to eliminate waste in a firm's sourcing and logistics activities, as well as within the firm's internal operations. But it doesn't end there. The Lean philosophy is applied to all relevant flows—physical, informational, and monetary—and, where possible, to supply chain partners. This means that firms might need to work closely with key partners to eliminate waste within *their* operations. Lean supply chain management is certainly consistent with what we have emphasized throughout this book; namely, it is not enough for a firm to manage the activities that occur within its four walls.

16.4 KANBAN SYSTEMS

The first part of this chapter dealt with the philosophical underpinnings of the Lean philosophy. In this section, we take a decidely more *tactical* view, focusing on one particular approach to production control in a Lean environment, known as kanban. But even as you are working through the logic of kanban systems, keep in mind that the focus is still on reducing waste.

Kanban system
A production control approach that uses containers, cards, or visual cues to control the production and movement of goods through the supply chain.

A **kanban system** is a production control approach that uses containers, cards, or visual cues to control the production and movement of goods through the supply chain. These systems have several key characteristics:

1. Kanban systems use simple signaling mechanisms, such as a card or even an empty space or container, to indicate when specific items should be produced or moved. Most kanban systems, in fact, do not require computerization.
2. Kanban systems can be used to synchronize activities either within a plant or between different supply chain partners. As such, a kanban system can be an important part of both PAC and vendor order management systems (Chapter 15).
3. Kanban systems are *not* planning tools. Rather, they are control mechanisms that are designed to pull parts or goods through the supply chain based on downstream demand. As a result, many firms use techniques such as MRP (Chapter 15) to *anticipate* requirements but depend on their kanban systems to control the actual execution of production and movement activities.

FIGURE 16.4
Kanban System for Two Work Centers

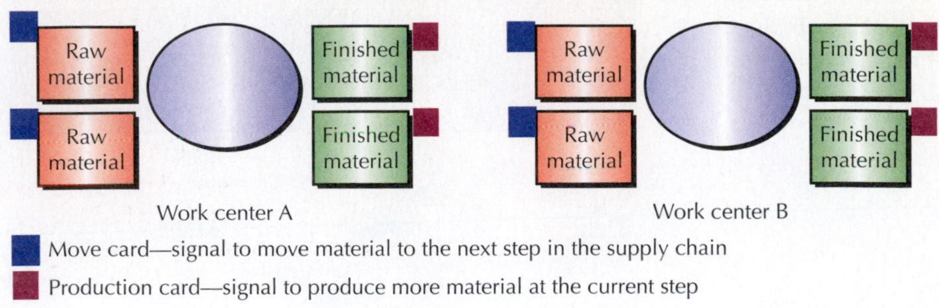

Two-card kanban system
A special form of the kanban system that uses one card to control production and another card to control movement of materials.

Move card
A kanban card that is used to indicate when a container of parts should be moved to the next process step.

Production card
A kanban card that is used to indicate when another container of parts should be produced.

To illustrate how a kanban system works, we will describe a **two-card kanban system** that links the production and movement of units at two work centers. Figure 16.4 shows a diagram of the system, in which output from work center A flows into work center B.

Note that each work center has boxes of raw material and finished material. Under kanban system rules, each box of raw material must have a **move card**, while each box of finished goods must have a **production card**. These cards are used to precisely control the amount and movement of material in the supply chain. We will see in a moment how the system works.

Now suppose that the next station in the supply chain (work center C or perhaps a customer) pulls a box of finished material out of work center B. Immediately, the production card is removed from the box and placed in a conspicuous location in work center B. The card signals to personnel in work center B that they need to produce more parts (Figure 16.5).

To produce more parts, employees in work center B must pull a box of raw materials into the production process. As they do so, they remove the move card from the box and replace it with the production card that was freed up in the previous step. The newly freed-up move card then signals to employees that they need to move, or "pull," more materials out of work center A (Figure 16.6). Note that B's "raw" material is A's "finished" material.

When the freed-up move card arrives at work center A, it takes the place of a production card on a box of finished materials, and that box is transferred to work center B (Figure 16.7). The freed-up production card then signals employees in work center A to produce more parts.

FIGURE 16.5
Release of Finished Materials from Work Center B

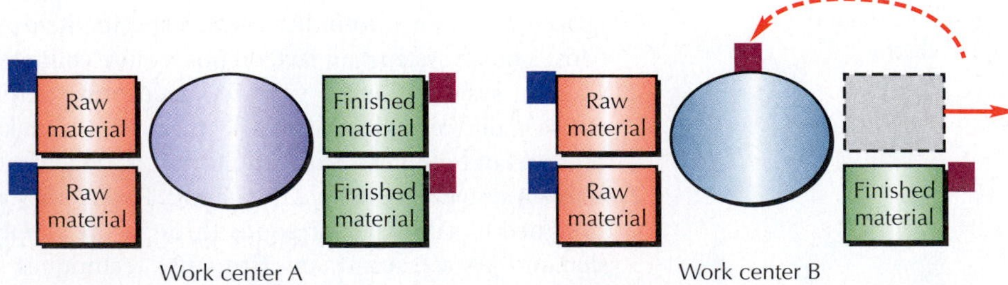

FIGURE 16.6
Pulling of Raw Materials into Production at Work Center B

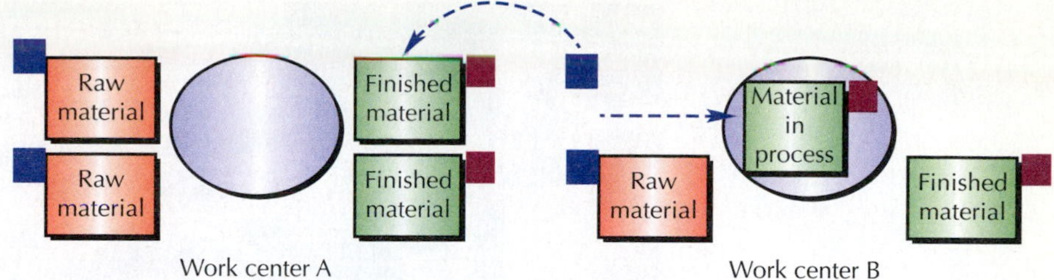
Raw material
Raw material
Finished material
Finished material
Work center A
Material in process
Raw material
Finished material
Work center B
• Box of raw material is "pulled" into production at work center B
• Freed-up move card is signal to move material from work center A

FIGURE 16.7
Removal of Finished Materials from Work Center A

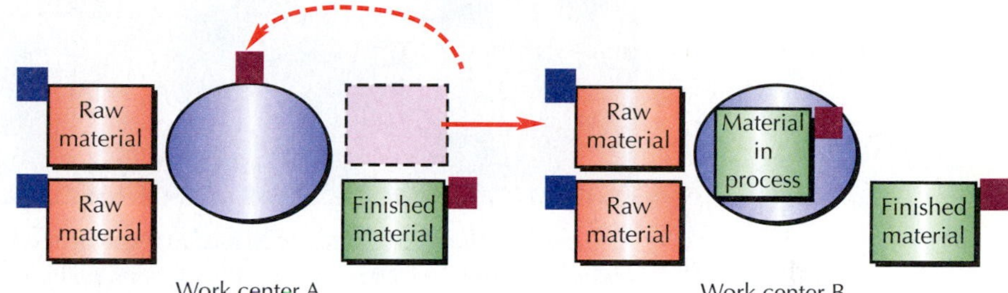
Raw material
Raw material
Finished material
Work center A
Raw material
Raw material
Material in process
Finished material
Work center B
• Box of finished material from work center A is "pulled" into raw material at work center B
• Freed-up production card is signal to produce more at work center A
• And the cycle continues with work center A . . .

To summarize this system:

- A downstream station pulls finished material out of work center B (Figure 16.5).
- Work center B pulls raw material into production (Figure 16.6).
- Demand for more raw material in work center B pulls finished material out of work center A (Figure 16.7).

The beauty of this system is that all production and movement of materials is controlled by a set of cards. If workers see a freed-up production card, they produce more units; if they don't, they stop producing units. Likewise, if they see a move card, they move materials; if not, they leave materials where they are. You can see now why a kanban system is also called a **pull system**—actual downstream demand sets off a chain of events that pulls materials through the various process steps.

Pull system
A production system in which actual downstream demand sets off a chain of events that pulls materials through the various process steps.

As we noted before, cards aren't the only signaling method used in a kanban system. Some other methods include:

- Single-card systems, where the single card is the production card and the empty container serves as the move signal;
- Color coding of containers;
- Designated storage spaces; and
- Computerized bar-coding systems.

An example of how floor space can be used to implement a kanban system. As the sign indicates, since the green line on the floor is covered with tote pans, no more parts should be produced.

Controlling Inventory Levels Using Kanbans

It is a simple fact that by controlling the number of production kanbans—whether they be cards, containers, or some other signaling mechanism—organizations can control the amount of inventory in the system. Consider our previous example. Work center A could not produce unless it had a freed-up production card. As a result, the number of production cards set precise limits on the amount of inventory between work centers A and B.

While reading the last section, you may have wondered how organizations determine the number of kanbans needed to link two process steps together. The answer depends on several factors, including the lead time between the two steps being linked, the size of the containers that hold the parts, the demand level, and the stability of demand. A general formula for calculating the number of kanbans is:

$$y = \frac{DT(1+x)}{C} \qquad [16\text{-}1]$$

where:

y = number of kanbans (cards, containers, etc.)

D = demand per unit of time (from the downstream process)

T = time it takes to produce and move a container of parts to the downstream demand point

x = a safety factor, expressed as a decimal (for example, 0.20 represents a 20% safety factor)

C = container size (the number of parts it will hold)

Example 16.2

Determining the Number of Kanbans at Marsica Industries, Part 1

At Marsica Industries, workcell H provides subassemblies directly to final assembly. The production manager for workcell H, Ann, is trying to determine how many production cards she needs. Ann has gathered the following information:

D	Final assembly's demand for subassemblies from workcell H	300 assemblies per hour, on average
T	Time it takes to fill and move a container of subassemblies from workcell H to final assembly	2.6 hours, on average
x	Safety factor to account for variations in D or T	15%
C	Container size	45 subassemblies

Using Equation 16-1, the number of production cards needed is:

$$y = \frac{DT(1+x)}{C}$$

$$= \frac{300 \times 2.6(1+0.15)}{45} = 17.59, \text{ or } 18 \text{ production cards}$$

Ann rounds up her answer because there is no such thing as a fractional production card. Evaluating the results, she notes that 18 production cards is the equivalent of 18 containers of subassemblies, or:

$$(18 \text{ containers})(45 \text{ subassemblies per container}) = 810 \text{ subassemblies}$$

And in hourly terms, 810 subassemblies equals

$$\frac{810 \text{ subassemblies}}{300 \text{ units of demand each hour}} = 2.7 \text{ hours worth of subassemblies}$$

The fact that there are slightly more subassemblies than needed is due to the safety factor and the rounding up of the number of production cards.

While Equation 16-1 is useful as a starting point, another approach used by many companies is to start with more than enough kanbans. The organization then slowly removes kanbans in an attempt to uncover the "rocks," or problems (similar to Figure 16.3). At the same time, the organization will try to shorten lead times and stabilize demand levels as much as possible, thereby further reducing the need for inventory.

Example 16.3

Recalculating the Number of Kanbans at Marsica Industries, Part 2

After nearly a year of continuous improvement efforts in workcell H, Ann feels it is time to reevaluate the number of production cards, and hence inventory in the workcell. In particular, Ann has made the following changes:

- Production lead time has been cut from 2.6 hours to a constant 1.6 hours.
- Demand from final assembly has been stabilized at 300 subassemblies per hour.
- Smaller, standardized containers that hold just 25 subassemblies are now being used.

Because production lead time (T) and demand rate (D) have been stabilized, Ann feels she can reduce the safety factor to just 4%. Recalculating the number of kanban cards to reflect all of these changes:

$$y = \frac{DT(1+x)}{C}$$

$$= \frac{300 \times 1.6(1+0.04)}{25} = 19.97, \text{ or } 20 \text{ production cards}$$

Ann is not concerned that the number of cards has increased. In fact, 20 production cards is now the equivalent of:

$$(20 \text{ containers})(25 \text{ subassemblies per container}) = 500 \text{ subassemblies}$$

and

$$\frac{500 \text{ subassemblies}}{300 \text{ units of demand each hour}} = 1.67 \text{ hours worth of subassemblies}$$

Either way she looks at it, by improving the process, Ann has been able to cut inventory by approximately 38%.

Synchronizing the Supply Chain Using Kanbans

In Chapter 15, we alluded to the idea that kanban systems can be used to synchronize the supply chain at the production activity control (PAC) and vendor order management levels. Put another way, kanban can be used to link supply chain partners, as well as the work centers in a factory. Suppose, for instance, that work center B in our earlier examples was located in a facility 200 miles from work center A. In this case, fax or computer requests for more materials would be substituted for the factory's move cards.

Figure 16.8 shows how kanban can be used to synchronize the production and movement of goods among multiple supply chain partners. You might even think of customer demand as a pull on a rope (the kanban system) that ties all members of the supply chain together. One pull at the end of the supply chain triggers movement and production down the chain.

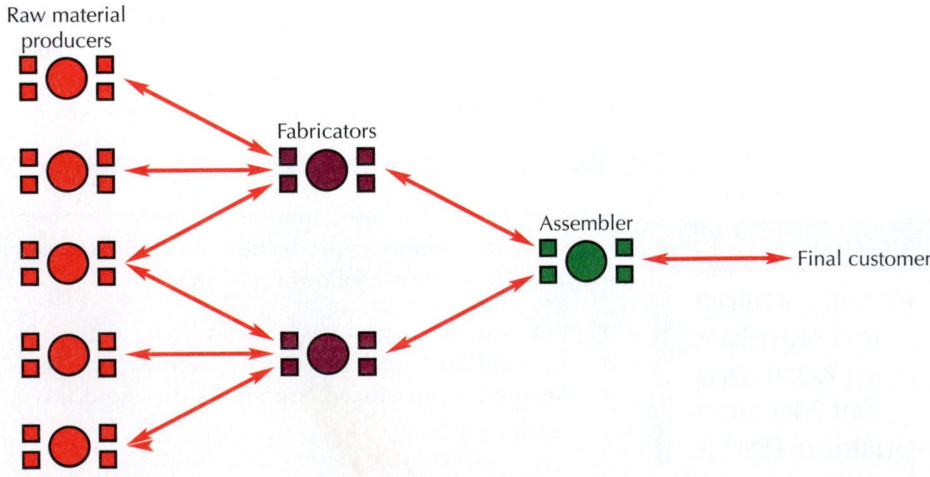

FIGURE 16.8 Using Kanban to Synchronize the Supply Chain

FIGURE 16.9
Work Centers A and B as Part of a Larger Supply Chain

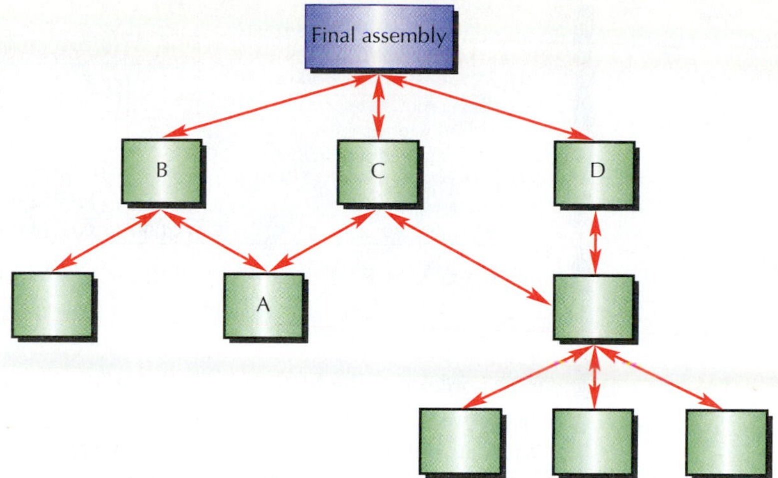

For a kanban system to work properly, however, there must be a *smooth, consistent* pull of material through the links. Consider the supply chain shown in Figure 16.9. As we have seen, the number of kanbans linking work centers A and B is based on an understanding of the demand rate coming from B.

But what happens if the demand rate changes or there is an interruption in the flow of goods? If final assembly demand doubles, work center B may quickly use up all the material linking it with A, and subsequent shipments from B to final assembly may be slowed down as a result.

If there is an *interruption* in the flow of goods—say, within work center B—the result could be even worse: Final assembly may have to stop production, thereby stopping the pull of goods from work centers C and D as well and shutting down the entire supply chain. This is not as far-fetched as it seems; in fact, it is exactly what happened to Toyota in the opening case study.

The point is this: For a kanban system to work properly, demand rates must be relatively stable, and interruptions must be minimized.

Using MRP and Kanban Together

Some companies have actually found it beneficial to combine the *planning* capabilities of MRP with the *control* capabilities of kanban. In particular, MRP can be used to anticipate changes in planned order quantities over the planning horizon. This information is then used to recalculate the number of production kanbans (containers or cards) needed. Example 16.4 illustrates how the concept works.

Example 16.4

Using MRP and Kanban Together at Marsica Industries, Part 3

The last six months have been tumultuous ones for Marsica Industries; demand levels have varied dramatically from one week to the next as the company has taken on seasonal customers and marketing has used pricing changes to either boost or limit demand. The result for Ann, production manager for workcell H, has been that the D values underlying her kanban calculations have been all over the place, undercutting the effectiveness of the kanban system. Ann knows that she needs some way to anticipate these changes and adjust the number of kanban production cards accordingly.

Ann knows that Marsica uses MRP to estimate planned orders for components, including the subassemblies coming out of workcell H. She finds the MRP record for the subassembly shown in Figure 16.10.

** Subassembly, workcell H **		WEEK							
		1	2	3	4	5	6	7	8
Gross requirements		12,000	12,000	14,000	14,000	14,000	16,000	16,000	16,000
Scheduled receipts									
Projected ending inventory	0	0	0	0	0	0	0	0	0
Net requirements		12,000	12,000	14,000	14,000	14,000	16,000	16,000	16,000
Planned receipts		12,000	12,000	14,000	14,000	14,000	16,000	16,000	16,000
Planned orders		**12,000**	**12,000**	**14,000**	**14,000**	**14,000**	**16,000**	**16,000**	**16,000**

FIGURE 16.10 MRP Record for Workcell H's Subassembly

Looking at the MRP record, Ann notices a couple of interesting points. First, there is no projected ending inventory. This is consistent with the Lean philosophy of having no more inventory in the system than is needed. Second, the planned orders all occur *in the same week* as the planned receipts. This is because the planning lead time for subassemblies is just 1.6 hours (Example 16.3); therefore, any orders released in a week should be completed in that week.

But the most interesting line for Ann is the planned order quantities. These tell her the total weekly demand for the subassemblies. Assuming this demand is spread evenly across a 40-hour work week, Ann can use the planned orders to calculate the D values for the various weeks:

$$D_{\text{weeks } 1-2} = \frac{12{,}000}{40 \text{ hours per week}} = 300 \text{ subassemblies per hour}$$

$$D_{\text{weeks } 3-5} = \frac{14{,}000}{40 \text{ hours per week}} = 350 \text{ subassemblies per hour}$$

$$D_{\text{weeks } 6-8} = \frac{16{,}000}{40 \text{ hours per week}} = 400 \text{ subassemblies per hour}$$

Finally, Ann can use the different demand rates and the other values from Example 16.3 to determine the number of production cards needed each week:

$$y_{\text{weeks } 1-2} = \frac{300 \times 1.6(1+0.04)}{25} = 19.97, \text{or } 20 \text{ production cards}$$

$$y_{\text{weeks } 3-5} = \frac{350 \times 1.6(1+0.04)}{25} = 23.29, \text{or } 24 \text{ production cards}$$

$$y_{\text{weeks } 6-8} = \frac{400 \times 1.6(1+0.04)}{25} = 26.62, \text{or } 27 \text{ production cards}$$

In practice, Ann will adjust the number of production cards by adding new cards in when she anticipates that demand will go up and "retiring" freed-up production cards when she anticipates that demand will go down. But the key insight is this: Ann can use the MRP records to help her anticipate needs and control production at the workcell level.

CHAPTER SUMMARY

JIT/Lean is both a business philosophy for reducing waste and a specific approach to production control. In this chapter, we reviewed the philosophical elements behind Lean and discussed how these elements fit in with many of the other topics covered throughout this book, including quality management and supplier development. Even though it started out in manufacturing, the Lean philosophy has a lot to say to any organization wishing to eliminate waste.

We paid particular attention to the role of inventory in Lean environments and showed how kanban systems can be used to control the flow of materials in a Lean environment and across the supply chain. We also demonstrated why kanban systems may not be appropriate in all environments (particularly ones in which demand "pull" varies greatly) and illustrated how the planning capabilities of MRP can be combined with the control strengths of kanban.

KEY FORMULA

Number of production kanbans required (page 538):

$$y = \frac{DT(1+x)}{C} \qquad \textbf{[16-1]}$$

where:

y = number of kanbans (cards, containers, etc.)

D = demand per unit of time (from the downstream process)

T = time it takes to produce and move a container of parts to the downstream demand point

x = a safety factor, expressed as a decimal (for example, 0.20 represents a 20% safety factor)

C = container size (the number of parts it will hold)

KEY TERMS

Just-in-time (JIT) 527
Kanban system 535
Lean 527
Lean Six Sigma 528
Lean supply chain management 528
Move card 536
Muda 528
Production card 536
Pull system 537
Two-card kanban system 536
Waste 528

SOLVED PROBLEMS

Problem

Because of her success in setting up a kanban system in workcell H, Ann has been brought over to help to fix the kanban system at workcell K. According to workcell K's current production manager, Tom Tucker, "We're swimming in inventory here. I thought I calculated the right number of production cards, but something must have changed."

Tom provides Ann with the information he used to determine the number of production cards:

Assumed demand rate, $D = 260$ units per hour
Lead time, $T = 2$ hours
Container size = 50 units
Safety factor, $x = 5\%$

Tom notes, "Of course, there have been a few changes, but they're really no big deal. Demand is off slightly, down to 220 units an hour, and we've increased the container size to 100 units. But I can't see that making much of a difference."

Questions

1. Calculate the number of production cards needed, based on the original set of values given by Tom. According to the results, how many hours' worth of inventory would there be, given the original set of assumptions?
2. Now consider the changes to demand and container sizes noted by Tom. If Tom uses the *old* number of production cards, how many hours' worth of inventory would there be in the system?
3. Recalculate what the *new* number of production cards should be, and estimate how many hours' worth of inventory this would equal.

Solution

1. Based on the old values, the number of production cards needed is

$$y = \frac{DT(1+x)}{C}$$

$$= \frac{260 \times 2(1+0.05)}{50} = 10.92, \text{ or 11 production cards}$$

which is the equivalent of

$$(11 \text{ containers})(50 \text{ units per container}) = 550 \text{ units}$$

or

$$\frac{550 \text{ units}}{260 \text{ units of demand each hour}} = 2.12 \text{ hours' worth of units}$$

2. The problem, however, is that the values behind the production card calculation have changed. With a new container size of 100 units and a new demand rate of 220 units per hour, 11 production cards translates into

$$(11 \text{ containers})(100 \text{ units per container}) = 1100 \text{ units}$$

or

$$\frac{1{,}100 \text{ units}}{220 \text{ units of demand each hour}} = 5 \text{ hours' worth of units}$$

3. Which is clearly too much inventory. After showing Tom the error of his ways, Ann helps him recalculate the new kanban level

$$\frac{220 \times 2(1+0.05)}{100} = 4.62, \text{or 5 production cards}$$

which is the equivalent of

$$(5 \text{ containers})(100 \text{ units per container}) = 500 \text{ units}$$

or

$$\frac{500 \text{ units}}{220 \text{ units of demand each hour}} = 2.27 \text{ hours' worth of units}$$

DISCUSSION QUESTIONS

1. Transportation can create value, as when an ambulance takes a patient to the hospital or a truck delivers fruits and vegetables to the grocery store. How would you differentiate between "necessary" and "unnecessary" transportation?
2. Even though waiting is a form of waste, when might it make sense to allow waiting lines?
3. Comment on the relationship between quality management (Chapter 4) and Lean. Are they the same thing, or are there some differences?
4. We noted in the chapter that kanban is not a planning tool but a control mechanism. What did we mean by that? How does the MRP-kanban example in Example 16.4 illustrate the point?
5. In what ways might a firm's suppliers improve or undermine the firm's Lean efforts? Can you think of any examples from the chapter that illustrate this idea?

PROBLEMS

Additional homework problems are available at www.prenhall.com/bozarth. These problems use Excel to generate customized problems for different class sections or even different students.
(* = easy; ** = moderate; *** = advanced)

1. (*) Suppose you have the following information:

   Demand rate (D) = 750 units per hour
   Lead time (T) = 40 hours
   Container capacity (C) = 1000 units
   Safety factor (x) = 10%

   The number of kanban cards required is
   a. 59
   b. 28
   c. 30
   d. 33

2. Consider the following information:

   Demand rate (D) = 200 units per hour
   Lead time (T) = 12 hours
   Container capacity (C) = 144 units
   Safety factor (x) = 15%

   a. (*) How many kanban production cards are needed?
   b. (**) How many hours' worth of demand will these cards represent?
   c. (**) Suppose the container size is cut in half. Will this make any difference in the inventory levels? Show your work.

3. Consider the following information:

   Demand rate (D) = 300 units per hour
   Lead time (T) = 4 hours
   Container capacity (C) = 40 units
   Safety factor (x) = 10%

   a. (*) How many kanban production cards are needed?
   b. (**) How many hours' worth of demand will these cards represent?
   c. (**) Suppose the lead time is reduced to three hours. Will this make any difference in the inventory levels? Show your work.

4. Consider the following information:

   Demand rate (D) = 1000 units per hour
   Lead time (T) = 2 hours
   Container capacity (C) = 250 units
   Safety factor (x) = 15%

   a. (*) How many kanban production cards are needed?
   b. (**) How many hours' worth of demand will these cards represent?
   c. (**) Suppose the safety factor is eliminated. Will this make any difference in the inventory levels? Would this be a wise thing to do? Show your work.

5. Consider the following information:

   Demand rate (D) = 60 units per hour
   Lead time (T) = 40 hours
   Container capacity (C) = 20 units
   Safety factor (x) = 10%

   a. (*) How many kanban production cards are needed?
   b. (**) How many hours' worth of demand will these cards represent?
   c. (**) Suppose the demand rate is doubled but the lead time is cut in half. Will this make any difference in the inventory levels? Show your work.

6. (***) (*Microsoft Excel problem*). The following figure shows a Microsoft Excel spreadsheet that calculates the number of kanban production cards needed, based on the MRP planned orders. **Re-create this spreadsheet in**

Excel. Your spreadsheet should calculate new results any time a change is made to any of the highlighted cells. Your formatting does not need to be the same, but your answers should be. To test your spreadsheet, change the production lead time to 2.5 hours and the container size to 144. The number of production cards (not rounded up) for week 1 should be 6.84, and there should be 2.69 hours' worth of inventory. *Note:* To round up the kanban card calculation, use Excel's =*ROUNDUP* function.

	A	B	C	D	E	F	G	H	I	J	K	L
1	**Using MRP Planned Orders to Determine the Number of Kanban Production Cards Needed**											
2												
3			Hours per week:	40								
4			Production lead time (T):	3	hours							
5			Container size (C):	5.0%								
6			Safety factor (x):	300								
7												
8							WEEK					
9				1	2	3	4	5	6	7		
10			Planned orders (from MRP):	15,000	16,000	15,000	15,000	14,500	14,000	13,000		
11												
12												
13			Hourly demand (D):	375	400	375	375	362.5	350	325		
14												
15			# of production cards (not rounded)	3.94	4.20	3.94	3.94	3.81	3.68	3.41		
16			# of production cards (rounded up)	4	5	4	4	4	4	4		
17												
18			Hours' worth of inventory	3.20	3.75	3.20	3.20	3.31	3.43	3.69		

CASE STUDY

A Bumpy Road for Toyota[9]

By many measures, Toyota is still barreling along. The company's net income of $10.49 billion in yen in the year ended March 31 [2004] not only exceeded those of rivals General Motors Corp. and Ford Motor Co. combined, but set a record for any Japanese company. Toyota's next big goal is to expand its share of the global market to 15% over the next decade, from 10% now. That would make Toyota roughly the same size No. 1 auto maker GM is today.

But there are signs that the company's ambitious growth agenda is straining human and technical resources and undercutting quality, one of Toyota's most critical strategic advantages. It is the kind of paradox many highly successful companies face: Getting bigger doesn't always mean getting better.

Toyota still tends to outscore most rivals, including Detroit's Big Three auto makers and European brands, on industry surveys of quality and reliability. But Toyota's lead has narrowed and in certain key segments disappeared. "Toyota quality isn't improving as fast as it should," Toyota's president, Fujio Cho, concedes in an interview. To stop the quality slide, Mr. Cho says Toyota has launched multiple "special task forces" at trouble spots in places such as North America and China to overhaul shop-floor management. Toyota also has established a Global Production center in Toyota City to train midlevel factory managers so they can more effectively run plants outside Japan. Toyota now is re-evaluating some of its most fundamental operating strategies. "We are getting back to basics," says Gary Convis, a Toyota managing officer, who is also president of the Georgetown plant.

An important part of that effort focuses not on machines or high-speed information technology, but on replicating a special class of people who were instrumental in making Toyota a manufacturing powerhouse during the past 25 years. When Toyota first began opening factories in the U.S. in the mid-1980s, kicking off its dramatic global expansion, some of the most important people in the new plants weren't top executives, but midlevel Japanese managers commonly known as coordinators. These coordinators were experts in Toyota's Lean-manufacturing techniques and philosophies, commonly known as the Toyota Production System, or TPS. These coordinators, usually with 20 or more years of experience, generally shunned classrooms. Instead

[9]N. Shirouzu and S. Moffett, "As Toyota Closes in on GM, Quality Concerns also Grow," *The Wall Street Journal*, August 4, 2004.

they trained American shop-floor managers and hourly associates by attacking issues directly on the assembly line.

The principles behind Lean production took shape over five decades, starting with efforts in the 1930s by one of the company's founding fathers, Kiichiro Toyoda. The Toyota system took its current form during the 1950s with the leadership of Taiichi Ohno, a legendary Toyota engineer who drew inspiration from a trip to the U.S. during which he watched how a supermarket stocked its shelves using a just-in-time delivery of goods.

Mr. Ohno preached there are seven forms of muda, or waste, in any process. When Mr. Ohno trained recruits to Toyota's elite Operations Management Consulting Division, he drew a chalk circle on the floor in front of a process on the assembly line and told the trainee to watch that job until he could identify how it could be improved. A trainee could stand for nearly a day before he was able to satisfy Mr. Ohno with his answer.

When Mr. Ohno began applying his production approach full-scale, Toyota factories achieved huge gains in productivity and efficiency. The marriage of efficient production to an obsessive concern for quality helped Toyota establish a reputation for bullet-proof reliability that remains a huge competitive advantage. By the late 1980s, Lean production was a deeply entrenched way of life at Toyota, governing just about every aspect of its corporate activities. Hajime Oba, a retired TPS guru who still works for the company in North America on a project-by-project basis, likens the system to a form of religion. Managers at Detroit's Big Three auto makers, he says, use Lean techniques simply as a way to slash inventory. "What [they] are doing is creating a Buddha image and forgetting to inject soul in it," Mr. Oba says.

But as years went by, Toyota discovered that its corporate faith was getting watered down as the company spread its operations world-wide and hired generations of employees ever more distant from Mr. Ohno. A case in point is Toyota's massive factory in Georgetown, Ky., the first plant the auto maker built in the U.S. from the ground up. Georgetown began production in 1986, and throughout the 1990s the plant routinely claimed the top spots in J.D. Power & Associates' widely watched initial quality survey for cars sold in the U.S.

But after being named North America's second-best plant in 2001 behind Toyota's Canadian plant in Cambridge, Ontario, Georgetown has slumped. This year, it ranked No. 14, after placing No. 15 in 2003 and No. 26 in 2002. Two GM plants in Michigan, the Lansing Grand River Cadillac factory and a large car plant in Hamtramck, and Ford's luxury-car factory in Wixom, Mich., were North America's top three plants this year.

One big problem that Georgetown faced all along has been language. Most of the Toyota-production-system masters speak fluently only in Japanese. Most of their American employees speak only English. The linguistic and cultural barriers make deep discussions on Lean production almost impossible and can cause other problems.

Another issue is time—or the lack of it. As sales of Toyota vehicles in the North American market took off, Toyota factories had to ramp up quickly to keep up with demand. That meant a plant like Georgetown had to rapidly promote American shop-floor managers and hourly associates, instead of nurturing them gradually in the Toyota manufacturing way and deepening their skills and knowledge.

But by far the biggest headache at Georgetown now stems from a scarcity of TPS coordinators from Japan. As the auto maker stepped up the pace of factory openings globally, those expansion plans meant fewer coordinators for older, more established plants like Georgetown.

At Georgetown, one glaring symptom of trouble, its top executives say, is that some hourly assemblers began ignoring standardized work processes—considered one of the biggest sins inside Toyota plants because of the impact on the consistency and accuracy of manufacturing. Georgetown also lost some Lean-production masters to age and competitors. Kazumi Nakada, a TPS master, worked in tandem with Mr. Cho, the then-Georgetown president, to launch Georgetown in the mid-1980s. But Mr. Nakada left Toyota in 1995 to join GM, which was intensifying its efforts to catch up with Toyota in vehicle quality by copying its manufacturing methods.

To shore up Georgetown's mastery of Lean production to a level where it could function without relying so much on Japanese TPS coordinators, the plant's top management circle launched an emergency 18-month project in 2000 in order to gradually build back up the core of its front-line managers. The effort has since continued as a more formalized Organization Development Group.

Mr. Convis recruited Mr. Oba, the TPS guru, to help implement the Georgetown project. Among other issues, Mr. Oba found many shop-floor leaders would spend too much time in their offices, instead of prowling the factory floor coaching and leading kaizen projects with assembly workers. To shake things up, Mr. Convis and Mr. Oba dragged about 70 midlevel managers through projects at various Toyota parts suppliers for "real life" kaizen. The goal was in part to "embarrass the hell out of them" in front of suppliers whom they had been used to bossing around, says Mr. Oba, to highlight the need for them to learn more about TPS.

Still, in 2002, Georgetown suffered one of the biggest blows to its track record for quality. The plant began pumping out the new Camry sedan in the fall of 2001, and soon buyers began griping about the car's spongy brakes and cup holders that interfered with the shift lever when a tall travel mug was placed in them. Long skinny plastic strips, called "Mohican molding," that covered up weld marks on the car's roof also sometimes peeled off, in part because of lack of testing.

Those problems helped to send the number of customer complaints about the quality of the new Camry soaring in the annual initial quality survey by J.D. Power. In 2002, the car had 117 problems per 100 vehicles and was the sixth-best vehicle in the survey's "premium midsize car" category. Just two years earlier, in 2000, the Camry was America's best vehicle in that segment.

The Camry's initial quality ranking continued to decline to No. 7 in 2003 and No. 8 in 2004 despite the fact that the number of customer complaints declined, placing the car well behind rivals such as the Buick Century and the Chevy Monte Carlo. Now, with some rivals closing the gap in efficiency and quality, Toyota is scrambling to take Lean production to a new level—one that is simple enough to function without the constant help of Japanese coordinators with 20 years of experience or more in Lean production.

Epilogue

In June 2007, J.D. Power released its newest initial quality ratings.[10] The good news for Toyota was that for the entire brand, defects only averaged 112 per 100 vehicles. The bad news was that this tied Toyota with Jaguar for *sixth* place. The top five were Porsche (91 problems per 100 vehicles), Lexus (94), Lincoln (100), Honda (108) and Mercedes Benz (111).

QUESTIONS

1. Is Toyota's focus on quality consistent with the Lean philosophy? Can a firm actually follow the Lean philosophy without having a strong quality focus? Explain.
2. Who are the "coordinators" referred to in the article? What role have they played in educating Toyota's workforce in promoting the TPS (Toyota Production System) philosophy? Why are they so hard to replicate?
3. According to Hajime Oba, what is wrong with Detroit's approach to Lean? Based on your understanding of American auto manufacturers, do you agree or disagree?
4. There is an old saying, "Haste makes waste." How does this apply to what is happening in the Georgetown plant? What is Toyota doing about it?

REFERENCES

Books and Articles

Cox, J. F., and J. H. Blackstone, eds. *APICS Dictionary,* 11th ed. Falls Church, VA: APICS, 2004.

Mullenhour, P, and J. Flinchbaugh. "Bring Lean Systems Thinking to Six Sigma." *Quality Digest* (March 2005), www.qualitydigest.com/mar05/articles/05_article.shtml

Reitman, V. "To the Rescue: Toyota's Fast Rebound after Fire at Supplier Shows Why It Is Tough." *The Wall Street Journal*, May 8, 1997. p?

Shirouzu, N., and S. Moffett. "As Toyota Closes in on GM, Quality Concerns also Grow." *The Wall Street Journal*, August 4, 2004. p?

Womack, J., and D. Jones. *Lean Thinking: Banish Waste and Create Wealth in Your Corporation, Revised and Updated.* New York: Free Press 2003.

Womack, J., D. Jones, and D. Roos. *The Machine That Changed the World: The Story of Lean Production.* New York: HarperCollins, 1991.

Internet

Bovarnick, E. "The Power of Lean Six Sigma: The Nortel Journey." www.nortel.com/corporate/investor/events/investorconf/collateral/breakout_leansixsigma_nov16.pdf

Debusk, C and A. Rangel. "Creating a Lean Six Sigma Hospital Discharge Process." isixsigma.com, Sept. 15, 2004 http://healthcare.isixsigma.com/library/content/c040915a.asp www.jdpower.com/autos/quality_rating

Motorola University, www.motorola.com/motorolauniversity.jsp

[10]From **www.jdpower.com/autos/quality-ratings.**

Appendices

Appendix I Normal Curve Areas
Appendix II Poisson Distribution Values
Appendix III Values of $e^{-\lambda}$ for Use in the Poisson Distribution
Appendix IV Table of Random Numbers

APPENDIX I NORMAL CURVE AREAS

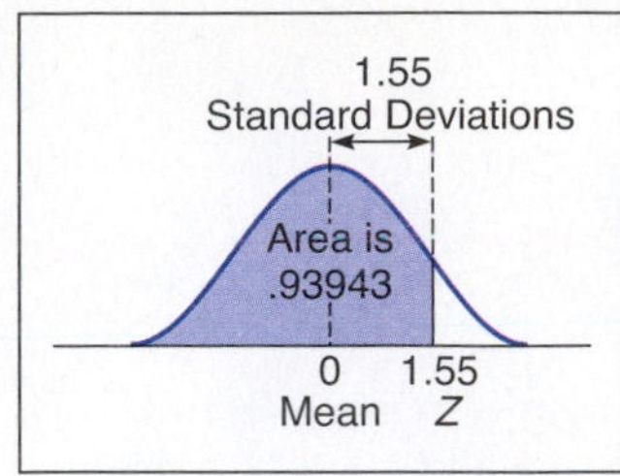

To find the area under the normal curve, you can apply either Table I.1 or Table I.2. In Table I.1, you must know how many standard deviations that point is to the right of the mean. Then, the area under the normal curve can be read directly from the normal table. For example, the total area under the normal curve for a point that is 1.55 standard deviations to the right of the mean is .93943.

TABLE I.1

	.00	.01	.02	.03	.04	.05	.06	.07	.08	.09
.0	.50000	.50399	.50798	.51197	.51595	.51994	.52392	.52790	.53188	.53586
.1	.53983	.54380	.54776	.55172	.55567	.55962	.56356	.56749	.57142	.57535
.2	.57926	.58317	.58706	.59095	.59483	.59871	.60257	.60642	.61026	.61409
.3	.61791	.62172	.62552	.62930	.63307	.63683	.64058	.64431	.64803	.65173
.4	.65542	.65910	.66276	.66640	.67003	.67364	.67724	.68082	.68439	.68793
.5	.69146	.69497	.69847	.70194	.70540	.70884	.71226	.71566	.71904	.72240
.6	.72575	.72907	.73237	.73536	.73891	.74215	.74537	.74857	.75175	.75490
.7	.75804	.76115	.76424	.76730	.77035	.77337	.77637	.77935	.78230	.78524
.8	.78814	.79103	.79389	.79673	.79955	.80234	.80511	.80785	.81057	.81327
.9	.81594	.81859	.82121	.82381	.82639	.82894	.83147	.83398	.83646	.83891
1.0	.84134	.84375	.84614	.84849	.85083	.85314	.85543	.85769	.85993	.86214
1.1	.86433	.86650	.86864	.87076	.87286	.87493	.87698	.87900	.88100	.88298
1.2	.88493	.88686	.88877	.89065	.89251	.89435	.89617	.89796	.89973	.90147
1.3	.90320	.90490	.90658	.90824	.90988	.91149	.91309	.91466	.91621	.91774
1.4	.91924	.92073	.92220	.92364	.92507	.92647	.92785	.92922	.93056	.93189
1.5	.93319	.93448	.93574	.93699	.93822	.93943	.94062	.94179	.94295	.94408
1.6	.94520	.94630	.94738	.94845	.94950	.95053	.95154	.95254	.95352	.95449
1.7	.95543	.95637	.95728	.95818	.95907	.95994	.96080	.96164	.96246	.96327
1.8	.96407	.96485	.96562	.96638	.96712	.96784	.96856	.96926	.96995	.97062
1.9	.97128	.97193	.97257	.97320	.97381	.97441	.97500	.97558	.97615	.97670
2.0	.97725	.97784	.97831	.97882	.97932	.97982	.98030	.98077	.98124	.98169
2.1	.98214	.98257	.98300	.98341	.98382	.98422	.98461	.98500	.98537	.98574
2.2	.98610	.98645	.98679	.98713	.98745	.98778	.98809	.98840	.98870	.98899
2.3	.98928	.98956	.98983	.99010	.99036	.99061	.99086	.99111	.99134	.99158
2.4	.99180	.99202	.99224	.99245	.99266	.99286	.99305	.99324	.99343	.99361
2.5	.99379	.99396	.99413	.99430	.99446	.99461	.99477	.99492	.99506	.99520
2.6	.99534	.99547	.99560	.99573	.99585	.99598	.99609	.99621	.99632	.99643
2.7	.99653	.99664	.99674	.99683	.99693	.99702	.99711	.99720	.99728	.99736
2.8	.99744	.99752	.99760	.99767	.99774	.99781	.99788	.99795	.99801	.99807
2.9	.99813	.99819	.99825	.99831	.99836	.99841	.99846	.99851	.99856	.99861
3.0	.99865	.99869	.99874	.99878	.99882	.99886	.99899	.99893	.99896	.99900
3.1	.99903	.99906	.99910	.99913	.99916	.99918	.99921	.99924	.99926	.99929
3.2	.99931	.99934	.99936	.99938	.99940	.99942	.99944	.99946	.99948	.99950
3.3	.99952	.99953	.99955	.99957	.99958	.99960	.99961	.99962	.99964	.99965
3.4	.99966	.99968	.99969	.99970	.99971	.99972	.99973	.99974	.99975	.99976
3.5	.99977	.99978	.99978	.99979	.99980	.99981	.99981	.99982	.99983	.99983
3.6	.99984	.99985	.99985	.99986	.99986	.99987	.99987	.99988	.99988	.99989
3.7	.99989	.99990	.99990	.99990	.99991	.99991	.99992	.99992	.99992	.99992
3.8	.99993	.99993	.99993	.99994	.99994	.99994	.99994	.99995	.99995	.99995
3.9	.99995	.99995	.99996	.99996	.99996	.99996	.99996	.99996	.99997	.99997

Source: From Richard I. Levin and Charles A. Kirkpatrick, *Quantitative Approaches to Management*, 4th ed. Copyright © 1978, 1975, 1971, 1965 by McGraw-Hill, Inc. Used with permission of McGraw-Hill Book Company.

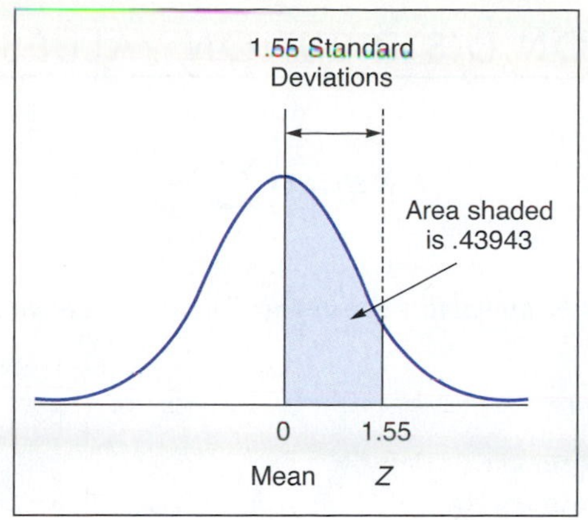

As an alternative to Table I.1, the numbers in Table I.2 represent the proportion of the total area away from the mean, μ, to one side. For example, the area between the mean and a point that is 1.55 standard deviations to its right is .43943.

TABLE I.2

Z	.00	.01	.02	.03	.04	.05	.06	.07	.08	.09
0.0	.00000	.00399	.00798	.01197	.01595	.01994	.02392	.02790	.03188	.03586
0.1	.03983	.04380	.04776	.05172	.05567	.05962	.06356	.06749	.07142	.07535
0.2	.07926	.08317	.08706	.09095	.09483	.09871	.10257	.10642	.11026	.11409
0.3	.11791	.12172	.12552	.12930	.13307	.13683	.14058	.14431	.14803	.15173
0.4	.15542	.15910	.16276	.16640	.17003	.17364	.17724	.18082	.18439	.18793
0.5	.19146	.19497	.19847	.20194	.20540	.20884	.21226	.21566	.21904	.22240
0.6	.22575	.22907	.23237	.23565	.23891	.24215	.24537	.24857	.25175	.25490
0.7	.25804	.26115	.26424	.26730	.27035	.27337	.27637	.27935	.28230	.28524
0.8	.28814	.29103	.29389	.29673	.29955	.30234	.30511	.30785	.31057	.31327
0.9	.31594	.31859	.32121	.32381	.32639	.32894	.33147	.33398	.33646	.33891
1.0	.34134	.34375	.34614	.34850	.35083	.35314	.35543	.35769	.35993	.36214
1.1	.36433	.36650	.36864	.37076	.37286	.37493	.37698	.37900	.38100	.38298
1.2	.38493	.38686	.38877	.39065	.39251	.39435	.39617	.39796	.39973	.40147
1.3	.40320	.40490	.40658	.40824	.40988	.41149	.41309	.41466	.41621	.41174
1.4	.41924	.42073	.42220	.42364	.42507	.42647	.42786	.42922	.43056	.43189
1.5	.43319	.43448	.43574	.43699	.43822	.43943	.44062	.44179	.44295	.44408
1.6	.44520	.44630	.44738	.44845	.44950	.45053	.45154	.45254	.45352	.45449
1.7	.45543	.45637	.45728	.45818	.45907	.45994	.46080	.46164	.46246	.46327
1.8	.46407	.46485	.46562	.46638	.46712	.46784	.46856	.46926	.46995	.47062
1.9	.47128	.47193	.47257	.47320	.47381	.47441	.47500	.47558	.47615	.47670
2.0	.47725	.47778	.47831	.47882	.47932	.47982	.48030	.48077	.48124	.48169
2.1	.48214	.48257	.48300	.48341	.48382	.48422	.48461	.48500	.48537	.48574
2.2	.48610	.48645	.48679	.48713	.48745	.48778	.48809	.48840	.48870	.48899
2.3	.48928	.48956	.48983	.49010	.49036	.49061	.49086	.49111	.49134	.49158
2.4	.49180	.49202	.49224	.49245	.49266	.49286	.49305	.49324	.49343	.49361
2.5	.49379	.49396	.49413	.49430	.49446	.49461	.49477	.49492	.49506	.49520
2.6	.49534	.49547	.49560	.49573	.49585	.49598	.49609	.49621	.49632	.49643
2.7	.49653	.49664	.49674	.49683	.49693	.49702	.49711	.49720	.49728	.49736
2.8	.49744	.49752	.49760	.49767	.49774	.49781	.49788	.49795	.49801	.49807
2.9	.49813	.49819	.49825	.49831	.49836	.49841	.49846	.49851	.49856	.49861
3.0	.49865	.49869	.49874	.49878	.49882	.49886	.49889	.49893	.49897	.49900
3.1	.49903	.49906	.49910	.49913	.49916	.49918	.49921	.49924	.49926	.49929

APPENDIX II POISSON DISTRIBUTION VALUES

$$P(X \le c;\lambda) = \sum_{0}^{c} \frac{\lambda^x e^{-\lambda}}{x!}$$

The following table shows 1,000 times the probability of c *or fewer occurrences of an event that has an average number of occurrences of* λ.

Values of c											
λ	0	1	2	3	4	5	6	7	8	9	10
.02	980	1000									
.04	961	999	1000								
.06	942	998	1000								
.08	923	997	1000								
.10	905	995	1000								
.15	861	990	999	1000							
.20	819	982	999	1000							
.25	779	974	998	1000							
.30	741	963	996	1000							
.35	705	951	994	1000							
.40	670	938	992	999	1000						
.45	638	925	989	999	1000						
.50	607	910	986	998	1000						
.55	577	894	982	998	1000						
.60	549	878	977	997	1000						
.65	522	861	972	996	999	1000					
.70	497	844	966	994	999	1000					
.75	472	827	959	993	999	1000					
.80	449	809	953	991	999	1000					
.85	427	791	945	989	998	1000					
.90	407	772	937	987	998	1000					
.95	387	754	929	984	997	1000					
1.00	368	736	920	981	996	999	1000				
1.1	333	699	900	974	995	999	1000				
1.2	301	663	879	966	992	998	1000				
1.3	273	627	857	957	989	998	1000				
1.4	247	592	833	946	986	997	999	1000			
1.5	223	558	809	934	981	996	999	1000			
1.6	202	525	783	921	976	994	999	1000			
1.7	183	493	757	907	970	992	998	1000			
1.8	165	463	731	891	964	990	997	999	1000		
1.9	150	434	704	875	956	987	997	999	1000		
2.0	135	406	677	857	947	983	995	999	1000		

Source: Adapted from E. L. Grant, *Statistical Quality Control*, McGraw-Hill Book Company, New York (1964). Reproduced by permission of the publisher.

Values of c																							
λ	0	1	2	3	4	5	6	7	8	9	10	11	12	13	14	15	16	17	18	19	20	21	22
2.2	111	359	623	819	928	975	993	998	1000														
2.4	091	308	570	779	904	964	988	997	999	1000													
2.6	074	267	518	736	877	951	983	995	999	1000													
2.8	061	231	469	692	848	935	976	992	998	999	1000												
3.0	050	199	423	647	815	916	966	988	996	999	1000												
3.2	041	171	380	603	781	895	955	983	994	998	1000												
3.4	033	147	340	558	744	871	942	977	992	997	999	1000											
3.6	027	126	303	515	706	844	927	969	988	996	999	1000											
3.8	022	107	269	473	668	816	909	960	984	994	998	999	1000										
4.0	018	092	238	433	629	785	889	949	979	992	997	999	1000										
4.2	015	078	210	395	590	753	867	936	972	989	996	999	1000										
4.4	012	066	185	359	551	720	844	921	964	985	994	998	999	1000									
4.6	010	056	163	326	513	686	818	905	955	980	992	997	999	1000									
4.8	008	048	143	294	476	651	791	887	944	975	990	996	999	1000									
5.0	007	040	125	265	440	616	762	867	932	968	986	995	998	999	1000								
5.2	006	034	109	238	406	581	732	845	918	960	982	993	997	999	1000								
5.4	005	029	095	213	373	546	702	822	903	951	977	990	996	999	1000								
5.6	004	024	082	191	342	512	670	797	886	941	972	988	995	998	999	1000							
5.8	003	021	072	170	313	478	638	771	867	929	965	984	993	997	999	1000							
6.0	002	017	062	151	285	446	606	744	847	916	957	980	991	996	999	999	1000						
6.2	002	015	054	134	259	414	574	716	826	902	949	975	989	995	998	999	1000						
6.4	002	012	046	119	235	384	542	687	803	886	939	969	986	994	997	999	1000						
6.6	001	010	040	105	213	355	511	658	780	869	927	963	982	992	997	999	999	1000					
6.8	001	009	034	093	192	327	480	628	755	850	915	955	978	990	996	998	999	1000					
7.0	001	007	030	082	173	301	450	599	729	830	901	947	973	987	994	998	999	1000					
7.2	001	006	025	072	156	276	420	569	703	810	887	937	967	984	993	997	999	999	1000				
7.4	001	005	022	063	140	253	392	539	676	788	871	926	961	980	991	996	998	999	1000				
7.6	001	004	019	055	125	231	365	510	648	765	854	915	954	976	989	995	998	999	1000				
7.8	000	004	016	048	112	210	338	481	620	741	835	902	945	971	986	993	997	999	1000				
8.0	000	003	014	042	100	191	313	453	593	717	816	888	936	966	983	992	996	998	999	1000			
8.5	000	002	009	030	074	150	256	386	523	653	763	849	909	949	973	986	993	997	999	999	1000		
9.0	000	001	006	021	055	116	207	324	456	587	706	803	876	926	959	978	989	995	998	999	1000		
9.5	000	001	004	015	040	089	165	269	392	522	645	752	836	898	940	967	982	991	996	998	999	1000	
10.0	000	000	003	010	029	067	130	220	333	458	583	697	792	864	917	951	973	986	993	997	998	999	1000

APPENDIX III VALUES OF $e^{-\lambda}$ FOR USE IN THE POISSON DISTRIBUTION

Values of $e^{-\lambda}$

λ	$e^{-\lambda}$	λ	$e^{-\lambda}$	λ	$e^{-\lambda}$	λ	$e^{-\lambda}$
.0	1.0000	1.6	.2019	3.1	.0450	4.6	.0101
.1	.9048	1.7	.1827	3.2	.0408	4.7	.0091
.2	.8187	1.8	.1653	3.3	.0369	4.8	.0082
.3	.7408	1.9	.1496	3.4	.0334	4.9	.0074
.4	.6703	2.0	.1353	3.5	.0302	5.0	.0067
.5	.6065	2.1	.1225	3.6	.0273	5.1	.0061
.6	.5488	2.2	.1108	3.7	.0247	5.2	.0055
.7	.4966	2.3	.1003	3.8	.0224	5.3	.0050
.8	.4493	2.4	.0907	3.9	.0202	5.4	.0045
.9	.4066	2.5	.0821	4.0	.0183	5.5	.0041
1.0	.3679	2.6	.0743	4.1	.0166	5.6	.0037
1.1	.3329	2.7	.0672	4.2	.0150	5.7	.0033
1.2	.3012	2.8	.0608	4.3	.0136	5.8	.0030
1.3	.2725	2.9	.0550	4.4	.0123	5.9	.0027
1.4	.2466	3.0	.0498	4.5	.0111	6.0	.0025
1.5	.2231						

APPENDIX IV TABLE OF RANDOM NUMBERS

52	06	50	88	53	30	10	47	99	37	66	91	35	32	00	84	57	07
37	63	28	02	74	35	24	03	29	60	74	85	90	73	59	55	17	60
82	57	68	28	05	94	03	11	27	79	90	87	92	41	09	25	36	77
69	02	36	49	71	99	32	10	75	21	95	90	94	38	97	71	72	49
98	94	90	36	06	78	23	67	89	85	29	21	25	73	69	34	85	76
96	52	62	87	49	56	59	23	78	71	72	90	57	01	98	57	31	95
33	69	27	21	11	60	95	89	68	48	17	89	34	09	93	50	44	51
50	33	50	95	13	44	34	62	64	39	55	29	30	64	49	44	30	16
88	32	18	50	62	57	34	56	62	31	15	40	90	34	51	95	26	14
90	30	36	24	69	82	51	74	30	35	36	85	01	55	92	64	09	85
50	48	61	18	85	23	08	54	17	12	80	69	24	84	92	16	49	59
27	88	21	62	69	64	48	31	12	73	02	68	00	16	16	46	13	85
45	14	46	32	13	49	66	62	74	41	86	98	92	98	84	54	33	40
81	02	01	78	82	74	97	37	45	31	94	99	42	49	27	64	89	42
66	83	14	74	27	76	03	33	11	97	59	81	72	00	64	61	13	52
74	05	81	82	93	09	96	33	52	78	13	06	28	30	94	23	37	39
30	34	87	01	74	11	46	82	59	94	25	34	32	23	17	01	58	73
59	55	72	33	62	13	74	68	22	44	42	09	32	46	71	79	45	89
67	09	80	98	99	25	77	50	03	32	36	63	65	75	94	19	95	88
60	77	46	63	71	69	44	22	03	85	14	48	69	13	30	50	33	24
60	08	19	29	36	72	30	27	50	64	85	72	75	29	87	05	75	01
80	45	86	99	02	34	87	08	86	84	49	76	24	08	01	86	29	11
53	84	49	63	26	65	72	84	85	63	26	02	75	26	92	62	40	67
69	84	12	94	51	36	17	02	15	29	16	52	56	43	26	22	08	62
37	77	13	10	02	18	31	19	32	85	31	94	81	43	31	58	33	51

Source: Excerpted from *A Million Random Digits with 100,000 Normal Deviates*, The Free Press (1955): 7. With permission of the Rand Corporation.

GLOSSARY

Acceptable quality level (AQL) A term used in acceptance sampling. A cut-off value, representing the maximum defect level at which a consumer would always accept a lot.

Acceptance sampling The process of sampling a portion of goods for inspection rather than examining the entire lot.

Activity on node (AON) diagram A network diagram in which each activity is represented by a node, or box, and the precedence relationships between various activities are represented with arrows.

Adjusted exponential smoothing model An expanded version of the exponential smoothing model that includes a trend adjustment factor.

Aggregate Planning *See* sales and operations planning.

Anticipation inventory Inventory that is held in anticipation of customer demand.

Appraisal costs Costs a company incurs to assess its quality levels.

Assemble- or finish-to-order (ATO) products Products that are customized only at the very end of the manufacturing process.

Assignment problem A specialized form of an optimization model that attempts to assign limited capacity to various demand points in a way that minimizes costs.

Assortment warehousing A form of warehousing in which a wide array of goods is held close to the source of demand in order to assure short customer lead times.

Attribute A characteristic of an outcome or item that is accounted for by its presence of absence, such as "defective" versus "good" or "late" versus "on-time."

Available to promise (ATP) A field in the master schedule record that indicates the number of units that are available for sale each week, given those that have already been promised to customers.

Back room The part of a service operation that is completed without direct customer contact.

Backward pass The determination of the latest finish and start times for each project activity.

Bar graph A graphical representation of data that places observations into specific categories.

Batch manufacturing A type of manufacturing process where items are moved through the different manufacturing steps in groups, or "batches."

Benchmarking The process of identifying, understanding, and adapting outstanding practices from within the same organization or from other businesses to help improve performance.

Bill of material (BOM) A listing of all the subassemblies, intermediates, parts, and raw materials that go into a parent assembly showing the quantity of each required to make an assembly.

Black belts "Fully-trained Six Sigma experts with up to 160 hours of training who perform much of the technical analyses required of Six Sigma projects, ususally on a full-time basis."

Black box design Used to describe a situation in which suppliers are provided with general requirements and are asked to fill in the technical specifications.

Booked orders In the context of master scheduling, confirmed demand for products.

Bottom-up planning An approach to S&OP that is used when the product/service mix is unstable and resource requirements vary greatly across the offerings. Under such conditions, managers will need to estimate the requirements for each set of products or services separately and then add them up to get an overall picture of the resource requirements.

Break-bulk warehousing A specialized form of cross-docking in which the incoming shipments are from a single source or manufacturer.

Break-even point The volume level for a business at which total revenues cover total costs.

Build-up forecasts A qualitative forecasting technique in which individuals familiar with specific market segments estimate the demand within these segments. These individual forecasts are then added up to get the overall forecast.

Bullwhip effect An extreme change in the supply position upstream in a supply chain generated by a small change in demand downstream in the supply chain.

Business process reengineering (BPR) A procedure that involves the fundamental rethinking and radical redesign of business processes to achieve dramatic organizational improvements in such critical measures of performance as cost, quality, service, and speed.

Business strategy The strategy that identifies the firm's targeted customers and sets time frames and performance objectives for the business.

Business-to-business exchanges (B2Bs) Online trading communities that put potential buyers and suppliers in touch with one another and automate the flow of information between the trading parties; can be public or private.

Capacity The capability of a worker, machine, work center, plant, or organization to produce output per time period.

Causal forecasting models A class of quantitative forecasting models in which the forecast is modeled as a function of something other than time.

Cause-and-effect diagram A graphical tool used to categorize the possible causes for a particular result.

Cellular layout A type of layout typically used in group technology settings; resources are physically arranged according to the dominant flow of activities for the product family.

Champions Senior-level executives who "own" Six Sigma projects and have the authority and resources needed to carry them out.

Changeover flexibility The ability to provide a new product with minimal delay.

Chase production plan A sales and operations plan in which production is changed in each time period to match the sales forecast.

Check sheet A sheet used to record how frequently a certain event occurs.

Closed phase The third and final phase of root cause analysis, where participants validate the suspected root cause(s) through the analysis of available data.

Collaborative planning, forecasting, and replenishment (CPFR) A set of business processes, backed up by information technology, in which members agree to mutual business objectives and measures, develop joint sales and operational plans, and collaborate electronically to generate and update sales forecasts and replenishment plans.

Commercial preparation phase The fourth phase of a product development effort. This phase is characterized by a "ramping up" of activities associated with the introduction of a new product or service. At this stage, firms start to invest heavily in the operations and supply chain resources needed to support the new product or service.

Common carriers Also known as public carriers; transportation service providers who handle shipments on a case-by-case basis, without the need for long-term agreements or contracts.

Competitive benchmarking The comparison of an organization's processes with those of competing organizations.

Computer-aided design (CAD) systems Information systems that allow engineers to develop, modify, share, and even test designs in a virtual world. CAD systems help organizations avoid the time and expense of paper-based drawings and physical prototypes.

Computer-aided design/computer-aided manufacturing (CAD/CAM) systems An extension of CAD. CAD-based designs are translated into machine instructions, which are then fed automatically into computer-controlled manufacturing equipment.

Concept development phase The first phase of a product development effort. Here a company identifies ideas for new or revised products and services.

Concept phase The first of five phases of a project. Here, project planners develop a broad definition of what the project is and what its scope will be.

Concurrent engineering An alternative to sequential development in which activities in different development stages are allowed to overlap with one another, thereby shortening the total development time.

Conformance perspective A quality perspective that focuses on whether or not a product was made or a service was performed as intended.

Conformance quality A subdimension of quality addressing whether the product was made or the service performed to specifications.

Consolidation warehousing A form of warehousing that pulls together shipments from a number of sources (often plants) in the same geographical area and combines them into larger—and hence more economical—shipping loads.

Constraint The process step (or steps) that limits throughput for an entire process chain.

Constraints Within the context of optimization modeling, quantifiable conditions that place limitations on the set of possible solutions. The solution to an optimization model is acceptable only if it does not break any of the constraints.

Consumer's risk A term used in acceptance sampling. Represents the probability of accepting a lot with quality worse than the LTPD level.

Continuous flow process A type of manufacturing process that closely resembles a production line process. The main difference is the form of the product, which usually cannot be broken into discrete units. Examples include yarns and fabric, food products, and chemical products such as oil or gas.

Continuous improvement A principle of TQM that assumes there will always be room for improvement, no matter how well an organization is doing.

Continuous review system An inventory system used to manage independent demand inventory. The inventory level for an item is constantly monitored, and when the reorder point is reached, an order is released.

Continuous variable A variable that can be measured along a continuous scale, such as weight, length, height, and temperature.

Contract carriers Transportation service providers who handle shipments for other firms based on long-term agreements or contracts.

Control chart A specialized run chart that helps an organization track changes in key measures over time.

Control limits The upper and lower limits of a control chart. They are calculated so that if a sample falls inside the control limits, the process is considered under control.

Core competencies Organizational strengths or abilities, developed over a long period, that customers find valuable and competitors find difficult or even impossible to copy.

Cost-based contract A type of purchasing contract in which the price of a good or service is tied to the cost of some key input(s) or other economic factors, such as interest rates.

Cost of goods sold (COGS) The cost of goods purchased from outside suppliers.

Crashing Shortening the overall duration of a project by reducing the time it takes to perform certain activities.

Critical activities Project activities for which the earliest start time and latest start time are equal. Critical activities cannot be delayed without lengthening the overall project duration.

Critical path The longest path in the network (or tied for longest path).

Critical path method (CPM) A network-based technique in which there is a single time estimate for each activity. An alternative approach is PERT, which has multiple time estimates for each activity.

Cross sourcing A sourcing strategy in which the company uses a single supplier for a certain part or service in one part of the business and another supplier with the same capabilities for a similar part in another area of the business. Each supplier is then awarded new business based on its performance, creating an incentive for both to improve.

Cross-docking A form of warehousing in which large incoming shipments are received and then broken down into smaller outgoing shipments to demand points in a geographic area. Cross-docking combines the economies of large incoming shipments with the flexibility of smaller local shipments.

Customer relationship management (CRM) A term that broadly refers to planning and control activities and information systems that link a firm with its downstream customers.

Customs broker An agent who handles customs requirements on behalf of another firm. In the United States, customs brokers must be licensed by the U.S. Customs Service.

Cycle stock Components or products that are received in bulk by a downstream partner, gradually used up, and then replenished again in bulk by the upstream partner.

Cycle time (a) For a line process, the actual time between completions of successive units on a production line. (b) The total elapsed time needed to complete a business process. Also called throughput time.

DMADV (Define-Measure-Analyze-Design-Verify) A Six Sigma process that outlines the steps needed to create *completely new* business processes or products.

Decision support systems (DSSs) Computer-based information systems that allow users to analyze, manipulate, and present data in a manner that aids higher-level decision making.

Decision tree A visual tool that decision makers use to evaluate capacity decisions. The main advantage of a decision tree is that the users can see the interrelationships between decisions and possible outcomes.

Decision variables Within the context of optimization modeling, those variables that will be manipulated to find the best solution.

Delivery reliability A performance dimension that refers to the ability to deliver products or services when promised.

Delivery speed A performance dimension that refers to how quickly the operations or supply chain function can fulfill a need, once it has been identified.

Delivery window The acceptable time range in which deliveries can be made.

Delphi method A qualitative forecasting technique that has experts work individually to develop forecasts. The individual forecasts are then shared among the group, after which each participant is allowed to modify his or her forecast based on information from the other experts. This process is repeated until a consensus is reached.

Demand uncertainty The risk of significant and uncertain fluctuations in the demand for their products.

Dependent demand inventory Inventory items whose demand levels are tied directly to the production of another item.

Description The communication of a user's needs to potential suppliers in the most efficient and accurate way possible.

Description by brand A description method; used when a product or service is proprietary or when there is a perceived advantage to using a particular supplier's products or services.

Description by market grade/industry standard A description method; used when the requirements are well understood and there is common agreement between supply chain partners about what certain terms mean.

Description by performance characteristics A description method; focuses attention on the outcomes the customer wants, not on the precise configuration of the product or service.

Description by specification A description method; used when an organization needs to provide very detailed descriptions of the characteristics of an item or service.

Design and development phase The third phase of a product development effort. Here the company starts to invest heavily in the development effort and builds and evaluates prototypes.

Design for maintainability (DFMt) The systematic consideration of maintainability issues over the product's projected life cycle in the design and development process.

Design for manufacturability (DFM) The systematic consideration of manufacturing issues in the design and development process, facilitating the fabrication of the product's components and their assembly into the overall product.

Design for Six Sigma (DFSS) An approach to product and process design that seeks to ensure the organization is capable of providing products or services that meet Six Sigma quality levels—in general, no more than 3.4 defects per million opportunities.

Design for the environment (DFE) An approach to new product design that addresses environmental, safety, and health issues over the product's projected life cycle in the design and development process.

Design to cost See **Target costing.**

Detailed planning and control Within the context of the planning cycle, planning that covers time periods ranging from weeks down to just a few hours out.

Development process A process that seeks to improve the performance of primary and support processes.

Direct costs Costs that are tied directly to the level of operations or supply chain activities, such as the production of a good or service, or transportation.

Direct truck shipment A shipment made directly, with no additional stops, changing of trucks, or loading of additional cargo.

Distribution requirements planning (DRP) A time-phased planning approach similar to MRP that uses planned orders at the point of demand (customer, warehouse, etc.) to determine forecasted demand at the source level (often a plant).

Downstream A term used to describe activities or firms that are positioned later in the supply chain relative to some other activity or firm of interest. For example, sewing a shirt takes place downstream of weaving the fabric, while weaving the fabric takes place downstream of harvesting the cotton.

Downstream activities In the context of manufacturing customization, activities that occur at or after the point of customization.

Dual sourcing A sourcing strategy in which two suppliers are used for the same purchased product or service.

Earliest finish time (EF) The earliest an activity can be finished, calculated by adding the activity's duration to its earliest start time.

Earliest start time (ES) The earliest an activity can be started, as determined by the earliest finish time for all immediate predecessors.

Economic order quantity (EOQ) The order quantity that minimizes annual holding and ordering costs for an item.

Efficiency A measure of process performance; the ratio of actual outputs to standard outputs. Usually expressed in percentage terms.

Electronic commerce Also called e-commerce. The use of information technology (IT) solutions to automate business transactions. Electronic commerce promises to improve the speed, quality, and cost of business communication.

Electronic data interchange (EDI) An information technology that allows supply chain partners to transfer data electronically between their information systems.

Electronic funds transfer (EFT) The automatic transfer of payment from the buyer's bank account to the supplier's bank account.

Employee empowerment Giving employees the responsibility, authority, training, and tools necessary to manage quality.

Engineering change A revision to a drawing or design released by engineering to modify or correct a part.

Engineer-to-order (ETO) products Products that are designed and produced from the start to meet unusual customer needs or requirements. They represent the highest level of customization.

Enterprise resource planning (ERP) systems Large, integrated, computer-based business transaction processing and reporting systems. ERP systems pull together all of the classic business functions such as accounting, finance, sales, and operations into a single, tightly integrated package that uses a common database.

Expected value A calculation that summarizes the expected costs, revenues, or profits of a capacity alternative based on several demand levels, each of which has a different probability.

Exploding the BOM The process by which one works backwards from the master production schedule for a Level 0 item to determine the quantity and timing of orders for the various subassemblies and components. Exploding the BOM is the underlying logic used by materials requirements planning (MRP).

Exponential smoothing model A special form of the moving average model in which the forecast for the next period is calculated as the weighted average of the current period's actual value and forecast.

External failure costs Costs incurred by defects that are not detected until a product or service reaches the customer.

First-tier supplier A supplier that provides products or services directly to a particular firm.

Five M's The five main branches of a typical cause-and-effect diagram: Manpower, Methods, Materials, Machines, and Measurement.

Five Why's An approach used during the narrow phase of root cause analysis, in which teams brainstorm successive answers to the question, "Why is this a cause of the original problem?" The name comes from the general observation that the questioning process can require up to five rounds.

Fixed costs The expenses an organization incurs regardless of the level of business activity.

Fixed-position layout A type of manufacturing process in which the position of the product is fixed. Materials, equipment, and workers are transported to and from the product.

Fixed-price contract A type of purchasing contract in which the stated price does not change, regardless of fluctuations in general overall economic conditions, industry competition, levels of supply, market prices, or other environmental changes.

Flexibility A performance dimension that considers how quickly operations and supply chains can respond to the unique needs of customers.

Flexible manufacturing systems (FMSs) Highly automated batch processes that can reduce the cost of making groups of similar products.

Forecast An estimate of the future level of some variable. Common variables that are forecasted include demand levels, supply levels, and prices.

Forecasted demand In the context of master scheduling, the company's best estimate of the demand in any period.

Forward pass The determination of the earliest start and finish times for each project activity.

Freight forwarder An agent who serves as an intermediary between the organization shipping the product and the actual carrier, typically on international shipments.

Front room The physical or virtual point where the customer interfaces directly with the service organization.

Functional layout A type of layout where resources are physically grouped by function.

Functional strategy Translates a business strategy into specific actions for the functional areas such as marketing, human resources, and finance. Functional strategies should align with the overall business strategy and with each other.

Gantt chart A graphical tool used to show expected start and end times for project activities, and to track actual progress against these time targets.

Gray box design Used to describe a situation in which the supplier works with the customer to jointly design the product.

Group technology A type of manufacturing process that seeks to achieve the efficiencies of a line process in a batch environment by dedicating equipment and personnel to the manufacture of products with similar manufacturing characteristics.

Hedge inventory A form of inventory buildup to buffer against some event that may not happen. Hedge inventory planning involves speculation related to potential labor strikes, price increases, unsettled governments, and events that could severely impair the company's strategic initiatives.

Histogram A special form of bar chart that tracks the number of observations that fall within a certain interval.

Hub-and-spoke systems A form of warehousing in which strategically placed "hubs" are used as sorting or transfer facilities. The hubs are typically located at convenient, high-traffic locations. The "spokes" refer to the routes serving the destinations associated with the hubs.

Hybrid manufacturing processes A general term referring to manufacturing processes that seek to combine the characteristics, and hence advantages, of more than one of the classic processes. Examples include flexible manufacturing systems, machining centers, and group technology.

Independent demand inventory Inventory items with demand levels that are beyond an organization's complete control.

Indifference point The output level at which two capacity alternatives generate equal costs.

Indirect costs Costs that are not tied directly to the level of operations or supply chain activity.

Information flow profile A tool that decision makers use to graph the relative performance of an information flow along a set of performance dimensions.

Information system (IS) A set of interrelated components that collect (or retrieve), process, store, and distribute information to support decision making, coordination, and control in an organization.

Infrastructural elements One of two major decision categories addressed by a strategy. Includes the policies, people, decision rules, and organizational structure choices made by a firm.

Insourcing The use of resources within the firm to provide products or services.

Internal failure costs Costs caused by defects that occur prior to delivery to the customer, including money spent on repairing or reworking defective products, as well as time wasted on these activities.

Internal supply chain management A term referring to the information flows between higher and lower levels of planning and control systems within an organization.

Inventory Those stocks or items used to support production (raw materials and work-in-process items), supporting activities (maintenance, repair, and operating supplies) and customer service (finished goods and spare parts).

Inventory drivers Business conditions that force companies to hold inventory.

Inventory policy A policy that indicates how much and when to order for an independent demand item.

Inventory pooling The act of holding safety stock in a single location instead of multiple locations. Several locations then share safety stock inventories to lower overall holding costs by reducing overall safety stock levels.

ISO 9000 A family of standards, supported by the International Organization for Standardization, representing an international consensus on good quality management practices. ISO 9000 addresses business processes rather than specific outcomes.

Job sequencing rules Rules used to determine the order in which jobs should be processed when resources are limited and multiple jobs are waiting to be done.

Job shop A type of manufacturing process used to make a wide variety of highly customized products in quantities as small as one. Job shops are characterized by general-purpose equipment and workers who are broadly skilled.

Just-in-time (JIT) A philosophy of manufacturing based on planned elimination of all waste and on continuous improvement of productivity. In the broad sense, it applies to all forms of manufacturing and to many service industries as well.

Kanban system A production control approach that uses containers, cards, or visual cues to control the production and movement of goods through the supply chain.

Lag capacity strategy A capacity strategy in which capacity is added only after demand has materialized.

Landed cost The cost of a product plus all costs driven by logistics activities, such as transportation, warehousing, handling, customs fees, and the like.

Latest finish time (LF) The latest an activity can be finished and still finish the project on time, as determined by the latest start time for all immediate successors.

Latest start time (LS) The latest an activity can be started and still finish the project on time, calculated by subtracting the activity's duration from its latest finish time.

Launch phase The final phase of a product development effort. For physical products, this usually means "filling up" the supply chain with products. For services, it can mean making the service broadly available to the target marketplace.

Law of variability The greater the random variability either demanded of the process or inherent in the process itself or in the items processed, the less productive the process is. This law is relevant to customization because completing upstream activities off-line helps isolate these activities from the variability caused by either the timing or the unique requirements of individual customers.

Lead capacity strategy A capacity strategy in which capacity is added in anticipation of demand.

Lean production A term commonly used to refer to just-in-time production.

Learning curve theory A body of theory based on applied statistics that suggests that productivity levels can improve at a predictable rate as people and even systems "learn" to do tasks more efficiently. In formal terms, learning curve theory states that for every doubling of cumulative output, there is a set percentage reduction in the amount of inputs required.

Less than truckload (LTL) shipment A smaller shipment, often combined with other loads to reduce costs and improve truck efficiencies. On the other hand, LTL shipments are more likely to experience multiple handlings, truck changes, and delays due to additional stops.

Level production plan A sales and operations plan in which production is held constant and inventory is used to absorb differences between production and the sales forecast.

Life cycle analogy method A qualitative forecasting technique that attempts to identify the time frames and demand levels for the introduction, growth, maturity, and decline life cycle stages of a new product or service. Often done by basing the forecast for the new product or service on the actual history of a similar product or service.

Linear regression A statistical technique that expresses the forecast variable as a linear function of some independent variable. Linear regression can be used to develop both time series and causal forecasting models.

Load profile A display of future capacity requirements based on released and/or planned orders over a given span of time.

Logistics That part of the supply chain process that plans, implements, and controls the efficient, effective flow and storage of goods, services, and related information from the point of origin to the point of consumption in order to meet customers' requirements.

Logistics management That part of supply chain management that plans, implements, and controls the efficient, effective forward and reverse flow and storage of goods, services, and related information between the point of origin and the point of consumption in order to meet customers' requirements.

Logistics strategy A functional strategy that ensures that an organization's logistics choices—transportation, warehousing, information systems, and even form of ownership—are consistent with its overall business strategy and support the performance dimensions that targeted customers most value.

Lot size Order size.

Lot tolerance percent defective (LTPD) A term used in acceptance sampling. Represents the highest defect level a consumer is willing to "tolerate."

Lower tolerance limit (LTL) The lowest acceptable value for some measure of interest.

Machining center A type of manufacturing process that completes several manufacturing steps without removing an item from the process.

Make-or-buy decision See **sourcing decision**.

Make-to-order (MTO) products Products that use standard components, but the final configuration of those components is customer-specific.

Make-to-stock (MTS) products Products that require no customization. They are typically generic products and are produced in large enough volumes to justify keeping a finished goods inventory.

Mapping The process of developing graphic representations of the organizational relationships and/or activities that make up a business process.

Market surveys Structured questionnaires submitted to potential customers, often to gauge potential demand.

Master black belts "Fulltime Six Sigma experts who are responsible for Six Sigma strategy, training, mentory, deployment and results."

Master production schedule The amount of product that will be finished and available for sale at the beginning of each week. The master production schedule drives more detailed planning activities, such as material requirements planning.

Master scheduling A detailed planning process that tracks production output and matches this output to actual customer orders.

Match capacity strategy A capacity strategy that strikes a balance between the lead and lag capacity strategies by avoiding periods of high under- or overutilization.

Material handling systems The equipment and procedures needed to move goods within a facility, between a facility and a transportation mode, and between different transportation modes (e.g., ship-to-truck transfers).

Material requirements planning (MRP) A planning process that translates the master production schedule into planned orders for the actual parts and components needed to produce the master schedule items.

Maverick spending Spending that occurs when internal customers purchase directly from nonqualified suppliers and bypass established purchasing procedures.

Merchandise inventory A balance sheet item that shows the amount a company paid for the inventory it has on-hand at a particular point in time.

Milestone A performance or time target for each major group of activities in a project.

Mission statement A statement that explains why an organization exists. It describes what is important to the organization, called its core values, and identifies the organization's domain.

Mix flexibility The ability to produce a wide range of products or services.

Mixed production plan A sales and operations plan that varies both production and inventory levels in an effort to develop the most effective plan.

Modular architecture A product architecture in which each functional element maps into its own physical chunk. Different chunks perform different functions; the interactions between the chunks are minimal, and they are generally well defined.

Move card A kanban card that is used to indicate when a container of parts should be moved to the next process step.

Moving average model A time series forecasting model that derives a forecast by taking an average of recent demand values.

MRP nervousness A term used to refer to the observation that any change, even a small one, in the requirements for items at the top of the bill of material can have drastic effects on items further down the bill of material.

Muda A Japanese term meaning "waste."

Multicriteria decision models Models that allow decision makers to evaluate various alternatives across multiple decision criteria.

Multifactor productivity A productivity score that measures output levels relative to more than one input.

Multimodal solutions Transportation solutions that seek to exploit the strengths of multiple transportation modes through physical, information, and monetary flows that are as seamless as possible.

Multiple regression A generalized form of linear regression that allows for more than one independent variable.

Multiple sourcing A sourcing strategy in which the buying firm shares its business across multiple suppliers.

Narrow phase The second phase of root cause analysis, during which the participants pare down the list of possible causes to a manageable number.

Net cash flow The net flow of dollars into or out of a business over some time period.

Network design applications Logistics information systems that address such long-term strategic questions as facility location and sizing, as well as transportation networks. These applications often make use of simulation and optimization modeling.

Network diagram A graphical tool that shows the logical linkages between activities in a project.

Network path A logically linked sequence of activities in the network diagram.

Objective function A quantitative function that an optimization model seeks to optimize (maximize or minimize).

Offloading A strategy for reducing and smoothing out workforce requirements by having the customers perform part of the work themselves.

Open phase The first phase of root cause analysis, devoted to brainstorming.

Operating characteristics (OC) curve Used in acceptance sampling. Shows the probability of accepting a lot, given the actual fraction defective in the entire lot and the sampling plan being used. Different sampling plans will result in difference OC curves.

Operations and supply chain strategy A functional strategy that indicates how structural and infrastructural elements within the operations and supply chain areas will be acquired and developed to support the overall business strategy.

Operations function Also called operations. The collection of people, technology, and systems within an organization that has primary responsibility for providing the organization's products or services.

Operations management The planning, scheduling, and control of the activities that transform inputs into finished goods and services.

Optimization models A class of mathematical models used when the user seeks to optimize some objective function subject to some constraints.

Order qualifiers Performance dimensions on which customers expect a minimum level of performance. Superior performance on an order qualifier will not, by itself, give a company a competitive advantage.

Order winners Performance dimensions that differentiate a company's products and services from its competitors'. Firms win the customer's business by providing superior levels of performance on order winners.

Outsourcing The use of supply chain partners to provide products or services.

***p* chart** A specific type of control chart for attributes, used to track sample proportions.

Packaging From a logistics perspective, the way goods and materials are packed in order to facilitate physical, informational, and monetary flows through the supply chain.

Panel consensus forecasting A qualitative forecasting technique that brings experts together to jointly discuss and develop a forecast.

Parent/child relationship Refers to the logical linkage between higher- and lowerlevel items in the BOM.

Pareto chart A special form of bar chart that shows frequency counts from highest to lowest.

Parts standardization The planned elimination of superficial, accidental, and deliberate differences between similar parts in the interest of reducing part and supplier proliferation.

Percent value-added time A measure of process performance; the percentage of total cycle time that is spent on activities that actually provide value.

Perfect order A term used to refer to the timely, error-free provision of a product or service in good condition.

Performance phase The fourth of five phases of a project. In this phase, the organization actually starts to execute on the project plan.

Performance quality A subdimension of quality, addressing the basic operating characteristics of the product or service.

Periodic review system An inventory system used to manage independent demand inventory. The inventory level for an item is checked at regular intervals and restocked to some predetermined level.

Planning and control A set of tactical and execution-level business activities that include master scheduling, material requirements planning, and some form of production activity control and vendor order management.

Planning and control systems Those systems that release, schedule, and control the flow of work in an organization.

Planning horizon The amount of time the master schedule record or MRP record extends into the future. In general, the longer the production and supplier lead times are, the longer the planning horizon must be.

Planning lead time Within the context of MRP, the time from when a component is ordered until it arrives and is ready to use.

Planning phase Where the company begins to address the feasibility of a product or service.

Planning values Values that decision makers use to translate the sales forecast into resource requirements and to determine the feasibility and costs of alternative sales and operations plans.

Postcompletion phase The fifth of five phases of a project. This is the phase in which the project manager or team confirms the final outcome, conducts a postimplementation meeting to critique the project and personnel, and reassigns project personnel.

Postponement warehousing A form of warehousing that combines classic warehouse operations with light manufacturing and packaging duties to allow firms to put off final assembly or packaging of goods until the last possible moment.

Preferred supplier A supplier that has demonstrated its performance capabilities through previous purchase contracts and therefore receives preference during the supplier selection process.

Presourcing The process of preapproving suppliers for specific commodities or parts.

Prevention costs The costs an organization incurs to actually prevent defects from occurring to begin with.

Primary process A process that addresses the main value-added activities of an organization.

Priority rules Rules for determining which customer, job, or product is processed next in a waiting line environment.

Process A set of logically related tasks or activities performed to achieve a defined business outcome.

Process benchmarking The comparison of an organization's processes with those of noncompetitors that have been identified as superior processes.

Process capability index (C_{pk}) A mathematical determination of a process's capability of meeting certain tolerance limits.

Process capability ratio (C_p) A mathematical determination of a process's capability to meet certain quality standards. A $C_p \geq 1$ means the process is capable of meeting the standard being measured.

Process map A detailed map that identifies the specific activities that make up the informational, physical, and/or monetary flow of a process.

Process mapping An activity that uses graphical symbols to document the physical and information flows of a process.

Process owner A team or individual who has the authority and responsibility for improving the organization's business processes and who is rewarded accordingly.

Producer's risk A term used in acceptance sampling. Represents the probability of rejecting a lot with quality better than the AQL level.

Product design The characteristics or features of a product or service that determine its ability to meet the needs of the user.

Product development process The overall process of strategy, organization, concept generation, product and marketing plan creation and evaluation, and commercialization of a new product.

Product family In group technology, a set of products with very similar manufacturing requirements.

Product structure tree A record or graphical rendering that shows how the components in the BOM are put together to make the Level 0 item.

Product-based layout A type of layout where resources are arranged sequentially according to the steps required to make a product.

Production card A kanban card that is used to indicate when another container of parts should be produced.

Production line A type of manufacturing process used to produce a narrow range of standard items with identical or highly similar designs.

Productivity A measure of process performance; the ratio of outputs to inputs.

Profit leverage effect A term used to describe the following effect: A dollar in cost savings increases pretax profits by one dollar, while a dollar increase in sales increases pretax profits only by the dollar multiplied by the pretax profit margin.

Profit margin The ratio of earnings to sales for a given time period.

Program evaluation and review technique (PERT) A network-based technique in which there are multiple time estimates for each activity. An alternative approach is CPM, which has a single time estimate for each activity.

Project A one-time undertaking designed to achieve a particular organizational goal, such as the development of a new product, construction of a new building, or implementation of a software system. Unlike more typical business activities, projects have clear starting and ending points, after which the people and resources dedicated to the project are reassigned.

Project definition phase The second of five phases in a project. Here, project planners identify how to accomplish the work, how to organize for the project, the key personnel and resources required to support the project, tentative schedules, and tentative budget requirements.

Proportion A measure that refers to the presence or absence of a particular characteristic.

Pull system A production system in which actual downstream demand sets off a chain of events that pull material through the various process steps.

Pup trailer A type of truck trailer that is half the size of a regular truck trailer.

Purchase consolidation The pooling of purchasing requirements by multiple areas in a company, or even across companies.

Purchase order (PO) A document that authorizes a supplier to deliver a product or service and that often includes key terms and conditions, such as price, delivery, and quality requirements.

Purchase requisition An internal document completed by a user that informs purchasing of a specific need.

Purchasing The activities associated with identifying needs, locating and selecting suppliers, negotiating terms, and following up to ensure supplier performance.

Qualitative forecasting techniques Forecasting techniques based on intuition or informed opinion. These techniques are used when data are scarce, not available, or irrelevant.

Quality (a) The characteristics of a product or service that bear on its ability to satisfy stated or implied needs. (b) A product or service free of deficiencies.

Quality assurance The specific actions firms take to ensure that their products, services, and processes meet the quality requirements of their customers.

Quality function deployment (QFD) A graphical tool used to help organizations move from vague notions of what customers want to specific engineering and operational requirements. Also called the "house of quality."

Quality function development (QFD) A technique used to translate customer requirements into technical requirements for each stage of product development and production.

Quantitative forecasting models Forecasting models that use measurable, historical data to generate forecasts. Quantitative forecasting models can be divided into two major types: time series models and causal models.

***R* chart** A specific type of control chart for a continuous variable, used to track how much the individual observations within each sample vary.

Randomness Within the context of forecasting, unpredictable movement from one time period to the next.

Range (*R*) A key measure that represents the variation of a specific sample group, used in conjunction with sample average ($\overline{X}$).

Rated capacity The long-term, expected output capability of a resource or system.

Relationship map A high-level map that shows the major organizational entities involved in a business process and how they are connected to one another via physical, informational, and/or monetary flows.

Reliability quality A subdimension of quality addressing whether a product will work for a long time without failing or requiring maintenance.

Reorder point system A method used to initiate the purchase of routine items.

Request for quotation (RFQ) A formal request for suppliers to prepare bids based on the terms and conditions set by the buyer.

Return on assets (ROA) A measure of financial performance, generally defined as earnings/total assets. Higher ROA values are preferred, as they indicate that the firm is able to generate higher earnings from the same asset base.

Reverse logistics system A complete supply chain dedicated to the reverse flow of products and materials for the purpose of returns, repair, remanufacture, and/or recycling.

Roadrailers Specialized rail cars the size of standard truck trailers that can be quickly switched from rail to ground transport by changing the wheels.

Robust design The design of products to be less sensitive to variations, including manufacturing variation and misuse, increasing the probability that they will perform as intended.

Rolling planning horizon Requires updates to sales and operations plan on a monthly or quarterly basis.

Root cause analysis A process by which organizations brainstorm about possible causes of problems (referred to as "effects") and then, through structured analyses and data-gathering efforts, gradually narrow the focus to a few root causes.

Rough-cut capacity planning A capacity planning technique that uses the master production schedule to monitor key resource requirements.

Run chart A graphical representation that tracks changes in a key measure over time.

Running sum of forecast errors The most recent sum of forecast errors is often called the running sum of forecast errors to emphasize the fact that it is updated each period.

Safety stock Extra inventory that companies hold to protect themselves against uncertainties in either demand or replenishment time.

Sales and operations planning A business process that helps firms plan and coordinate operations and supply chain decisions over a tactical time horizon (usually 4 to 12 months out).

Sample average A key measure that represents the central tendency of a group of samples used in conjunction with range (R).

Scatter plot A graphical representation of the relationship between two variables.

SCOR model Supply-Chain Operations Reference model. A comprehensive model of the core management processes and individual process types that together define the domain of supply chain management.

Seasonality A repeated pattern of spikes or drops in a time series associated with certain times of the year.

Second-tier supplier A supplier that provides products or services to a firm's first-tier supplier.

Sequential development process A process in which the product or service idea must clear specific hurdles before it can go on to the next development phase.

Service blueprinting A specialized form of business process mapping that allows the user to better visualize the degree of customer contact. The service blueprint lays out the service process from the viewpoint of the customer. It parses out the organization's service actions based on (1) the extent to which an action involves direct interaction with the customer, and (2) whether or not an action takes place as a direct response to a customer's needs.

Service level A term used to indicate the amount of demand to be met under conditions of demand and supply uncertainty.

Service package Includes all the value-added physical and intangible activities that a service organization provides to the customer.

Serviceability The ease with which parts can be replaced, serviced, or evaluated.

Single period inventory system A system used when demand occurs in only a single point in time.

Single sourcing A sourcing strategy in which the buying firm depends on a single company for all or nearly all of a particular item or service.

Single-factor productivity A productivity score that measures output levels relative to a single input.

Six-Sigma quality Used generally to indicate that a process is well controlled, that is, tolerance limits are ±6 sigma from the centerline in a control chart. The term is usually associated with Motorola, which named one of its key operational initiatives "Six Sigma Quality."

Slack time The difference between an activity's latest start time (LS) and earliest start time (ES). Slack time indicates the amount of allowable delay. Critical activities have a slack time of 0.

Smoothing inventories Inventories used to smooth out differences between upstream production levels and downstream demand.

Smoothing models Another name for moving average models. The name refers to the fact that using averages to generate forecasts results in forecasts that are less susceptible to random fluctuations in demand.

Sourcing decisions High-level, often strategic decisions regarding which products or services will be provided internally and which will be provided by external supply chain partners.

Spend analysis An activity, typically carried out by purchasing professionals, in which a firm examines spending patterns to identify irregularities or improvement opportunities.

Spot stock warehousing A form of warehousing that attempts to position seasonal goods close to the marketplace. At the end of each season, the goods are either liquidated or moved back to a more centralized location.

Standard output An estimate of what should be produced, given a certain level of resources.

Statement of work Terms and conditions for a purchased service that indicate, among other things, what services will be performed and how the service provider will be evaluated.

Statistical quality control The application of statistical techniques to quality control.

Strategic planning Within the context of the planning cycle, planning that takes place at the highest levels of the firm, addressing needs that might not arise for years into the future.

Strategic quality plan An organizational plan that provides the vision, guidance, and measurements to drive the quality effort forward and shift the organization's course when necessary.

Strategies The mechanisms by which businesses coordinate their decisions regarding structural and infrastructural elements.

Structural elements One of two major decision categories addressed by a strategy. Includes tangible resources, such as buildings, equipment, and computer systems.

Supplier relationship management (SRM) A term that broadly refers to planning and control activities and information systems that link a firm with its upstream suppliers.

Supply chain A network of manufacturers and service providers that work together to convert and move goods from the raw materials stage through to the end user. These manufacturers and service providers are linked together through physical flows, information flows, and monetary flows.

Supply chain design The process of designing the flow of goods and materials between multiple locations.

Supply chain management The active management of supply chain activities and relationships in order to maximize customer value and achieve a sustainable competitive advantage. It represents a conscious effort by a firm or group of firms to develop and run supply chains in the most effective and efficient ways possible.

Supply uncertainty The risk of interruptions in the flow of components from upstream suppliers.

Support process A process that performs necessary, albeit not value-added, activities.

Swim lane process map A process map that graphically arranges the process steps so that the user can see who is responsible for each step.

Tactical planning Within the context of the planning cycle, planning that covers a shorter period, usually four months to a year out, although the planning horizon may be longer in industries with very long lead times (such as engineer-to-order firms).

Takt time In a production line setting, the available production time divided by the required output rate. Takt time sets the maximum allowable cycle time for a line.

Target costing The process of designing a product to meet a specific cost objective. Target costing involves setting the planned selling price and subtracting the desired profit, as well as marketing and distribution costs, thus leaving the required target cost.

Target service level For a single period inventory system, the service level at which the expected cost of a shortage equals the expected cost of having excess units.

Target stocking point For a single period inventory system, the stocking point at which the expected cost of a shortage equals the expected cost of having excess units.

Team members Individuals who are not trained in Six Sigma, but are included on a Six Sigma project team due to their knowledge or direct interest in a process.

Testability The ease with which critical components or functions can be tested during production.

Theoretical capacity The maximum output capability, allowing for no adjustments for preventive maintenance, unplanned downtime, or the like.

Theory of Contraints (TOC) An approach to visualizing and managing capacity that recognizes that nearly all products and services are created through a series of linked processes, and in every case, there is at least one process step that limits throughput for the entire chain.

Third-party logistics providers (3PLs) Service firms that handle all of the logistics requirements for other companies.

Tiered workforce A strategy used to vary workforce levels, where additional full-time or part-time employees are hired during peak demand periods, while a smaller, permanent staff is maintained year-round.

Time series A series of observations arranged in chronological order.

Time series forecasting models Quantitative forecasting models that use time series to develop forecasts. With a time series model, the chronology of the observations, as well as their values, is important in developing forecasts.

Top-down planning An approach to S&OP where a single, aggregated sales forecast drives the planning process. For top-down planning to work, the mix of products or services must be essentially the same from one time period to the next, or the products or services to be provided must have very similar resource requirements.

Total cost analysis A process by which a firm seeks to identify and quantify all of the major costs associated with various sourcing options.

Total cost of quality curve A curve that suggests there is some optimal quality level, Q^*. The curve is calculated by adding costs of internal and external failures, prevention costs, and appraisal costs.

Total quality management (TQM) A managerial approach in which the entire organization is managed so that it excels in all quality dimensions that are important to customers.

Trade-off The decision by a firm to emphasize one performance dimension over another, based on the recognition that excellence on some dimensions may conflict with excellence on others.

Transportation inventory Inventory that is moving from one link in the supply chain to another.

Trend Long-term movement up or down in a time series.

Two-card kanban system A special form of the kanban system that uses one card to control production and another card to control movement of materials.

Upper tolerance limit (UTL) The highest acceptable value for some measure of interest.

Upstream A term used to describe activities or firms that are positioned earlier in the supply chain relative to some other activity or firm of interest. For example, corn harvesting takes place upstream of cereal processing, while cereal processing takes place upstream of cereal packaging.

Upstream activities In the context of manufacturing customization, activities that occur prior to the point of customization.

Value analysis (VA) A process that involves examining all elements of a component, assembly, end product, or service to make sure it fulfills its intended function at the lowest total cost.

Value index A measure that uses the performance and importance scores for various dimensions of performance for an item or service to calculate a score that indicates the overall value of an item or service to a customer.

Value perspective A quality perspective that holds that quality must be judged, in part, by how well the characteristics of a particular product or service align with the needs of a specific user.

Variable costs Expenses directly tied to the level of business activity.

Virtual supply chain A collection of firms that typically exists for only a short period. Virtual supply chains are more flexible than traditional supply chains, but less efficient.

Volume flexibility The ability to produce whatever volume the customer needs.

Waiting line theory A body of theory based on applied statistics that helps managers evaluate the relationship between capacity decisions and such importance performance issues as waiting times and line lengths.

Warehouse and transportation planning systems Logistics information systems that support tactical planning efforts by allocating "fixed" logistics capacity in the best possible way, given business requirements.

Warehouse management and transportation execution systems Logistics information systems that initiate and control the movement of materials between supply chain partners.

Warehousing Any operation that stores, repackages, stages, sorts, or centralizes goods or materials. Organizations use warehousing to reduce transportation costs, improve operational flexibility, shorten customer lead times, and lower inventory costs.

Waste according to the JIT perspective Any activity that does not add value to the good or service in the eyes of the consumer.

Weighted center of gravity method A logistics decision modeling technique that attempts to identify the best location for a single warehouse, store, or plant, given multiple demand points that differ in location and importance.

Weighted moving average model A form of the moving average model that allows the actual weights applied to past observations to differ.

$\bar{X}$ chart A specific type of control chart for a continuous variable, used to track the average value for future samples.

Yield management An approach commonly used by services with highly perishable products, in which prices are regularly adjusted to maximize total profit.

INDEX